SHAPING INTERIOR SPACE

INTERIOR

Presley Cortez

SHAPING INTERIOR SPACE

INTERIOR

THIRD EDITION

Roberto J. Rengel

University of Wisconsin—Madison

Fairchild Books
An imprint of Bloomsbury Publishing Inc.

BLOOMSBURY
NEW YORK • LONDON • NEW DELHI • SYDNEY

Fairchild Books

An imprint of Bloomsbury Publishing Inc.

1385 Broadway
New York
NY 10018
USA

50 Bedford Square
London
WC1B 3DP
UK

www.bloomsbury.com

This edition published 2014

Second edition published 2007

First edition published 2003

Library of Congress Cataloging-in-Publication Data

A catalog record for this book is available from the Library of Congress

Rengel, Roberto J.

Shaping interior space / Roberto J. Rengel, University of Wisconsin--Madison. -- Third edition.

pages cm

Includes bibliographical references and index.

ISBN 978-1-60901-896-2 (paperback)

1. Interior decoration. 2. Interior architecture. 3. Space (Architecture) I. Title.

NK2113.R45 2014

729--dc23

2014006889

ISBN: PB: 978-1-60901-896-2

Typeset by Precision Graphics

Cover Design by Simon Levy

Printed and bound in the United States of America

CONTENTS

EXTENDED CONTENTS

PREFACE

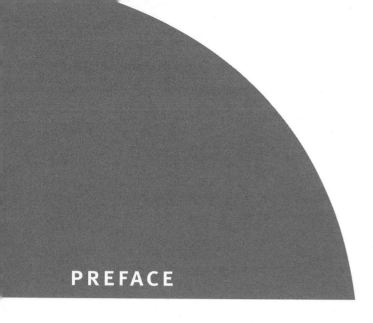

It continues to be gratifying to hear from the many users of *Shaping Interior Space*. I appreciate the good comments and many suggestions offered over the years. Writing the original version and the two updated editions continues to be a source of personal amazement, as I wrestle with my mind to come up with the best thing to say and the best way to say it.

In this third edition we have continued our efforts to improve the visual presentation of the book. Some figures have been replaced and others added where necessary. I have also sought ways to improve clarity, simplify the language, and reduce superfluous material. Some material has been reshuffled, and there is also new material, including all new case studies.

The structure of the book has been modified. The new structure features three parts, instead of four, and the order in which the chapters are presented has been modified. **Part One**, now called **General Principles**, remains essentially the same, but we have added a new fifth chapter, **Balance and Unity**. One may ask why a chapter on balance and unity and not one on all the basic design principles. One reason is my assumption that, by the time students use this book, they have had a course in basic design principles. The other reason is that, in the hierarchy of design principles, I consider balance and unity the most important.

The three main experiential goals that form the backbone of the book, order, enrichment, and expression, are now grouped in **Part Two** under the heading **Experiential Aims of Design**. One could argue that there are more experiential categories but, to me, these three serve as good overall umbrellas that capture the many dimensions of one's experience of the built environment.

Part Three is devoted to **Design Process**. The previous chapters on understanding and ideation have been moved to this section and a new chapter titled "Development" has been added as the final chapter. This chapter contains reorganized material from former Chapters 10 and 11 plus new material that elaborates the process of design beyond the plan. Included now are sections on the development of vertical surfaces, the spatial envelope, the ceiling plane, details, furniture, artwork, and accessories. The former Chapter 11, "Modifiers of Interior Space," has been eliminated. I came to the realization that attempting to meaningfully address complex topics such as lighting, acoustics, and color in one chapter is practically impossible. These subjects are best addressed in books entirely dedicated to them.

Another meaningful change has been the adoption of **new case studies**. The ones in the second edition have been replaced by six new case studies coming from Gensler, Flad, Sasaki Associates, and ASD.

ACKNOWLEDGMENTS

Once again, the production of this edition has been a team effort. I am indebted to the entire staff at Fairchild Books for their continued support and expertise. Very special thanks go to Olga Kontzias, Joe Miranda, and Priscilla McGeehon for their leadership, Susan Hobbs for her copyediting, and Edie Weinberg for the significant graphic enhancements of this edition. As before, my gratitude also goes to the professionals and reviewers who provided valuable feedback about the direction of the new edition, including Maruja Torres, University of Florida; David Lieb, New England Institute of Art; Paula J. Smith, IADT–Nashville; Beth Stokes, The Art Institute of Portland; Sheila S. Flener, Western Kentucky University; Christy Somerville, University of New Haven; Denese Menard, Art Institute of California–Orange County; Kerrie L. Kelly, Art Institute of California–Sacramento; Linda J. Cofiniotis, IADT–Orlando; and Herb Fremin, Wentworth Institute of Technology; and to the many students and educators who have used the previous editions and have approached me with useful comments and recommendations.

Roberto Rengel

February, 2014

PART ONE GENERAL PRINCIPLES

CHAPTER 1
SHAPING INTERIOR SPACE

INSTRUCTIONAL OBJECTIVES

- Explain the crucial role of the design studio in design education.
- Present several important sources of design knowledge.
- Explain the role of intentions and strategies in design.
- Introduce the concept of total design.
- Describe the evolving role of interior designers as shapers of space.
- Introduce the ten design principles that guide this book.

You employ stone, wood, and concrete, and with those materials you build houses and palaces. That is construction. Ingenuity is at work...

But suppose that walls rise towards heaven in such a way that I am moved. I perceive your intentions. Your mood has been gentle, brutal, charming, or noble. The stones you have erected tell me so. You fix me to the place and my eyes regard it. They behold something that expresses a thought. A thought that reveals itself without word or sound, but solely by means of shapes which stand in a certain relationship to one another. These shapes are such that they are clearly revealed in light. The relationships between them have not necessarily any reference to what is practical or descriptive. They are a mathematical creation of your mind. They are the language of Architecture. By the use of raw materials and starting from conditions more or less utilitarian, you have established certain relationships which have aroused my emotions.

—*Le Corbusier,* Towards a New Architecture

INTERIOR DESIGNERS LEARN EARLY on that the most important aspect of their designs is their responsiveness to a set of functional requirements needed for users of the environments to do their thing, whether it is working, selling, dining, or learning. Designers also learn that good environments have additional qualities that make them special, such as innovative aesthetic qualities that please and inspire. In fact, many students choose to become designers because they enjoy being creative and because of the prospect that their creations will arouse the emotions of those who come in contact with them. While engineers use their knowledge and training to provide practical and efficient solutions based on the physical laws of nature and builders use their knowledge to construct projects that are structurally sound and well crafted, interior designers use their knowledge to create designs that are functional and also touch the human heart in ways that neither the engineer's design nor the builder's construction usually does. A good interior design reflects a design solution conceived by and for human beings. It holds in high regard not only users' physical well-being but their emotional and spiritual well-being as well.

When clients hire interior designers, they know they are getting more than just a practical design solution; they are also buying style and substance. Although practically all interior designers are sincerely interested in creating special living environments, some do a better job at it than others. Many skilled and motivated designers fall short of designing great project not because they lack competence but because they lack awareness of the many possible ways to arouse human emotions. At a minimum designers have the obligation to create functional and aesthetically pleasing environments; however, it is when design intentions reach beyond these two basic necessities that designers truly engage in total design.

THE DIFFICULTY OF DESIGN

Designing good interior environments is difficult. The number of design problems and their complexity can be staggering. Designers are required to make sense of the realities and needs of a given client; translate them into collections of spaces subdivided in special ways in response to their functions; shape and select materials for the enclosing surfaces of those spaces; select or design suitable furnishings, accessories, and fixtures; and make it all work together and look good. Ultimately, full **synthesis** is the goal of every project. All the parts and pieces need to work together, but still be flexible to accommodate change over time.

One of the aspects of design that makes it so challenging is the fact that all the parts of a project have particular relationships with other parts. Designing interiors is like solving a giant table puzzle. What makes the interior design puzzle harder to solve than table puzzles is that the pieces can be placed in not just one but many locations, and they can interlock in a variety of ways. To make matters even more challenging, sometimes resolving one section of the design puzzle creates unintended problems for another section of the project.

Total design requires the resolution of a multitude of problems, involving issues of functional relationships, privacy, connections, enclosure, views, details, furnishings, lighting, and so on. On any given job, the designer needs to manipulate, control, and, ultimately, resolve how spaces are positioned and combined, pushing, pulling, and twisting as necessary to achieve a successful whole.

Whereas many of the practical tasks of design involve rational decision making, much about design relies on intuition and good design sense. Stanley Abercrombie has referred to the discipline of interiors as being "so subjective and so intimate, so immune to the calculations of science, so special to a singular circumstance and therefore so often ephemeral."[1] The elusive qualities of design make the application of exact rules and formulas unrealistic. Nevertheless, this book will offer some considerations related to both design content and process for interior projects.

Becoming a Designer

At its most general level, design requires two things to be successful: a fitting response to the design problem and its skillful execution (Figure 1.1). Proper response requires that the design problem (and subproblems) are understood correctly and that an appropriate design strategy is formulated to solve them. Choices have to be made about how to distribute space, assemble spatial sequences, determine levels of enclosure and articulation, and so on.

When a proper response is established, designers need to be able to execute the design with skill. This means developing the design ideas in detail and, ultimately, resolving all aspects of the design including the selection of compatible furnishings and miscellaneous nonpermanent pieces.

The Importance of the Design Studio

Learning how to design starts in school, specifically in the design studio where students learn to design hypothetical projects, similar to the ones encountered later in real practice.

The best way to learn design is by doing. Design is not learned by memorization or the application of formulas. Students learn design by solving design problems in the studio where they externalize their design solutions explicitly, thus revealing the virtues and shortcomings of the solution.

Students have to focus and limit their choices from the many possibilities available, resolving each part as best as possible within tight time constraints.

The process of review and critique is just as critical as the *doing* part of design. It is necessary to get beyond the fear of criticism and seek design feedback from peers, design instructors, and, most importantly, from yourself. What is right or wrong about this design approach? Is the overall approach appropriate? Is anything not working? Are there any good ideas not resolved properly? Are there any bad ideas resolved brilliantly? What needs further development? These are the important questions you need to ask constantly.

Only through this kind of ongoing questioning are students able to develop the kind of refinement process that produces good design. Developing a habit of critical questioning will develop your mental agility to solve problems. The more you do this in school, and beyond, the better.

In addition to good reasoning skills, proper response in design requires proper perspective. Novice designers lack perspective. Proper perspective is developed over time. It is, therefore, important to start acquiring a personal sense of what design ideas work well and are most appropriate. A good way to start is by learning from other designers. By asking questions and studying how other designers

DESIGN = PROPER UNDERSTANDING + PROPER RESPONSE + PROPER EXECUTION

Figure 1.1: Good design requires proper understanding, proper response, and proper execution. Proper understanding ensures you are solving the correct set of problems; proper response ensures you take that insightful understanding of the design problem and develop a responsive design solution for it. Proper execution requires that you take your good design ideas through a proper stage of development and end with a thoroughly resolved conclusion.

have responded to real design problems, you start to acquire a sense of effective ways to solve design problems. Developing an alert set of eyes and a good design memory that recalls characteristics of environments is invaluable. After you gain some experience, you'll start developing and trusting your own personal sense of design propriety.

Sources of Design Knowledge

There are many sources of useful information that help inform design. These include design journals, historical precedents, design theories, and personal observations made while traveling to new environments. Studying design history is an excellent way to gain design perspective. When studying design history, strive to understand the conditions that were present during specific times and to evaluate the kinds of design solutions conceived within the context of those conditions. Understanding what made certain design approaches fit a specific set of circumstances in the past helps you develop a better sense of judgment about design responses to specific needs.

Design students also need to become avid followers of current design trends by consulting design trade journals and books. By following the work being done by today's designers, you can get a sense of the breadth of recent trends and start developing your own opinions about what is good design.

Another important source of information for designers is the rapidly growing body of interior design research. Research studies provide valuable insights about the effects of certain types of environments or their environmental attributes on users. Although many areas of design have not been researched, others enjoy a good amount of published material. At present, there are countless educators worldwide engaged in research that continues to expand the available knowledge base of the field. Although it is normally not possible to utilize research findings directly in the form of rules and formulas, research findings establish a sound point of departure.

Remember that in design, however, every case is new and needs to be looked at with fresh eyes. You can think of and use research findings in the same way you think of and use advice from people possessing expertise and wisdom; what they have to say may be perceptive and truthful, but how you decide to use the information is up to you given the circumstances. The information may help to establish a general approach. Giving it specific form for the application at hand is your responsibility.

One last source of design knowledge is travel. Whether abroad, to a neighboring town or city, or to a local tavern, travel can provide invaluable insights to designers. Keeping a notebook of observations or taking pictures is also helpful. When you travel, things are fresh and you notice them more. There are design lessons everywhere. Whether you visit places known for their design quality or just ordinary places, you will notice many examples of elements or combinations that offer design insights. You will also notice examples of things you had never thought about or things you didn't think possible.

Intentions and Strategies

There are many important design considerations related to the design of interior environments. These occur at different hierarchical levels, from those addressing broad design goals to narrow considerations about how to treat a niche on a wall. It is important to expand your own personal range of design possibilities. The more possibilities and variations you have in your personal repertoire, the more intentionality you can bring to your projects. Having deliberate intentions is crucial to making projects come alive. The greater your awareness of design possibilities, the broader and deeper your intentions will be—and the resulting designs will acquire new layers of meaning.

Design problems, design intentions, and design strategies are part of one common string of thought that progresses sequentially from the identification of a problem to the implementation of a solution. **Design problems** involve specific needs and circumstances requiring a design solution. An example is the need for, say, a friendly and inviting reception area. This design problem already comes with the requirement that the space be friendly and inviting. Two general intentions have been declared from the outset. **Design intentions** are precise goals related to a design problem. They can be concerned with practical or experiential aspects of design. Design intentions for the design problem above (more specific than just "friendly and inviting") could include a bright, cheerful room with a clear, prominent reception desk, a cozy waiting area with a focal wall, and a good exterior view. These more specific ideas start to introduce potential design strategies.

Design strategies are specific means of implementing design intentions by using particular physical materials, compositions, finishes, and so forth. For our example, determining design strategies would require devising specific means to achieve a bright and cheerful room, a clear and emphasized reception desk, and so on. These might include using contrasting levels of light, varying the height of ceilings, using a reception desk with an unusual shape, adding a colorful focal wall, or framing a desirable exterior view. Remember that problems, intentions, and strategies progress in their level of specificity, getting more and more detailed as you move from problems to strategies.

Every intention in design needs to be followed by a corresponding strategy. You don't need to have an exact mental picture of the way it is going to look when it's done, but it helps to have a general strategy at the start. You can draw mental pictures from something you saw while traveling, or from a magazine, or even from an idea you doodled on a napkin one day. Ideas in your collection of personal strategies can also come from your own designs and those of your peers. The more of these you have stored in your internal design library, the faster your own ideas will pop up when thinking about design strategies.

Make a point of always looking around actively when you go places. When you see a good idea, make a mental or written note of the particulars and perhaps a note about the kind of application for which it may be appropriate.

Getting good at design requires conscious effort, resolve, and hard work. Competence comes with exposure and experience, but excellence requires more. It is quite common for designers to become adequate and coast through their careers producing acceptable, ordinary design. If you truly want to become good, you need to develop a commitment to design. If it is not ingrained in you during the early years, it is easily lost. The real practice of design is full of mundane requirements that will consume much of your effort, making it very tempting to aim for ordinary, acceptable design and never progress from there. If you choose to aim for excellence, you need to start now.

AIMS OF THIS BOOK

The goal of this book is to help make you a better designer. We assume that you have some design studio experience under your belt, have been exposed to the basics, and are ready to move into more advanced levels of design nuance and sophistication necessary for total design.

We present important aspects of both the design process and design content. Related to the design process, we particularly stress the important tasks of understanding, ideation, and development. Related to content, we touch on many aspects of interior design, with a special focus on design strategies that make for significant and experientially rich environments.

There is a fine line between architecture and interior design in this book. Both these disciplines come together in the creation of interior environments. The lessons of this book can be equally helpful to architecture students interested in interiors and to interior design students interested in spatial design. There are still a few basic and important differences between the realities encountered by architects and designers when they face the design of interior space. The most crucial one is that architects, for the most part, shape interior space in the process of designing an overall new building, and interior designers almost always design projects in existing interior spaces, usually starting from either empty building shells without internal construction or existing spaces to be altered or completely redesigned and rebuilt. The examples in the book are aimed at the interior designers who encounter existing shells as their points of departure.

Above all, this book aims to encourage a way of thinking about design that fosters the pursuit of design goals concerned with the experience of building users and to present specific design strategies and concepts that you may find useful. Judging whether the way you apply a certain strategy is appropriate for the circumstances or whether the execution is successful is beyond what the book can offer. That's where the design studio, peers, and instructors come in. The appropriateness of design is a subjective matter governed by the individual peculiarities of each situation, and constant evaluation and critique pertaining to the specific application at hand is necessary to ascertain the merits of any design attempt.

This book, then, is like a bridge between you and the design studio. It presents you with new information to consider and use, but you will have to try it within the context of the studio and learn by doing. Whether the design problem interpretation is sound, whether the strategies are appropriate and fitting, and whether the execution of the design ideas is carried out skillfully needs to be evaluated by you and your peers on a case-by-case basis.

TEN DESIGN PRINCIPLES

The contents of this book are based on ten principles about interior design. These are:

General Principles

1. Buildings are for people.
2. Place is the basic unit of interior design.
3. Place consists of space, enclosing surfaces, furnishings, and other important components.
4. Designers have the obligation to balance and unify all the physical components used in a project.

Principles Related to Design Strategies

5. A good design produces order.
6. To satisfy, projects need to have enriching qualities.
7. To have deeper meaning, projects need to incorporate a fitting expression.

Principles Related to Design Process

8. A good design solution requires a good understanding of the problem.
9. A good design starts with one or more overall concepts that give it a definite direction.
10. A good design develops the concept fully in order to arrive at the total environment.

General Principles

The first four principles lay the basic ground for the view of interior design advocated throughout. They reflect a basic attitude about the interior environment and its purpose.

1. Buildings are for people.

The fundamental purpose of all interior environments is to support people and their activities (Figure 1.2). Some buildings and individual spaces may command

Figure 1.2: Even when burdened by the many physical details and problems of a project, designers need to remember that buildings are for people. Every design effort should have as its goal the utility, convenience, comfort, safety, or delight it produces for people.

considerable attention due to their grandness or beauty, but their most basic function is to support the functions and dreams of those who use them.

Designers need to understand the needs of people in general and the needs of a project's users in particular and cultivate an appreciation of the types of rituals and events associated with life inside buildings. By listening, observing, and, most of all, experiencing directly the realities of those who use specific project types, designers can acquire the insights and sensibilities necessary to inform their designs.

The many activities associated with the use of buildings need to be understood. These are the subplots of the total building experience. The experiences of people approaching, arriving, moving around, interacting, performing tasks, and leaving a building environment are all important events with design implications. The rituals performed routinely in buildings, the specific occasions that vary from time to time, the people involved, and the effect of the surroundings all affect the total experience people have. Although the physical setting is only one of the components, it affects and is affected by the other factors present at the scene.

An important consideration is the fact that different users of a project have different perceptions of a situation depending on their role in it, their level of affinity with the situation, their familiarity with the place and the occasion, how challenging their involvement is, and how much control they have over what is going on. Designers have to be sensitive to all these considerations, for they affect the experience of the different users of a given facility.

2. Place is the basic unit of interior design.

Interior design is a unique discipline. The basic units of interior design are not points, lines, shapes, planes, or even space. Of course, these all are useful concepts that touch on specific aspects of design. However, none of them captures the essence of lived-in environments. The basic unit of interior design is place (Figure 1.3). Designers should learn to think about environment in terms of place, with each place having a unique character of its own and serving as coherent locations where life happens. They are holistic entities composed of many parts that work together as a functional and experiential total environment.

Figure 1.3: The basic unit of interiors is place. Interior environments need to be looked at holistically as assemblies of places for people. These range in size, character, and function but are always distinguishable as discrete locations where specific activities take place. Often there are places within places within single overall environments.

There are not too many different generic types of interior places. In most interior projects there are identifiable locations, such as rooms and circulation paths to get around. Some locations, because of their function or location, are more important. Some of these are arrival spaces or the strategic locations where main paths converge. Based on these differences, each place is assigned its appropriate location, degree of enclosure, connection to other parts, and arrangement so that people can sit, stand, and move as needed.

Designers have to spend considerable time orchestrating the individual components that make up place in order to arrive at the best possible arrangements.

3. Place consists of space, enclosing surfaces, furnishings, and other important components.

A solid understanding of architectural space, the manipulation of enclosing surfaces, and the furnishings and other objects that populate places is essential for designers of interior places (Figure 1.4). Most of us have spent considerable time during our formative years in enclosed rooms, either at home or school. Consequently, there is a natural tendency to equate architectural space with rooms. While in many cases space is defined as a room, in other cases it is not. Designers need to understand the many variations and subtleties of space beyond the single room.

Figure 1.4: The manipulation of interior space, including its distribution, composition, and sculpting, is one of the most basic and important requirements of design.

Space can be explicit (like a room with four walls, a floor, and a ceiling) or it can be implied. The level of enclosure is a crucial variable, because space can be defined with different degrees of enclosure from totally encapsulated to totally free of enclosing walls.

Space, although most often composed of regular, simple volumes, can be irregular. It comes in all sizes and shapes. Depending on its proportions, it suggests stability or induces movement. Many manipulations can be performed when designing spaces. Individual basic forms can be added to, divided, and distorted. Walls and other physical elements in space can be arranged to reveal or conceal views ahead, to control movement or to free it.

Equally as important as creating good individual spaces is composing the sequences of spaces that shape the entire project. Decisions have to be made about how all the spaces work as a system, with choices ranging from simple utilitarian compositions to more formal, classical ones, or organic, free-form ones.

4. Designers have the obligation to balance and unify all the physical components used in a project.

One of the fundamental tasks of interior design is the arrangement of parts and wholes into harmonious structures. Design elements need to be sized and balanced to look right. Their relative size in relation to humans and to other parts needs to be addressed and resolved. The proportions of parts and sections in relation to other parts and to the compositions they are a part of also must be resolved (Figure 1.5). Parts seen together or experienced sequentially have to be balanced for proper equilibrium. Additionally, despite the inherent or intentional variety of a project, ultimately it has to read as a unified totality, so it needs to have a degree of regularity and repetition.

Figure 1.5: The design task requires resolving all physical aspects of the project. The display shelves, graphics, lighting, accents, and products in this store have been carefully orchestrated and harmoniously resolved.

Principles Related to Design Strategies

The next three principles address strategies to enhance design solutions. They deal with the important goals of order, enrichment, and expression in design.

5. A good design produces order.

The need for order is one of the most basic human needs. A sense of correctness and confidence comes with order. Proper order provides points of reference to help people feel oriented and have a sense of where they are. It operates at many levels. Order is produced by strong and clear organization. A sense of order is also perceived when things appear to be where they belong, producing a tidy environment. Visual harmony produces a sense of order, too.

A sense of order in a project is perceived when the project's physical organization is understood. Projects with clear organizational structures, readable links between parts, and memorable spaces or elements are easier to understand. People seem to have a sense of where they are in relationship to the whole. Logical, well-structured sequences, clear intersections and groupings, distinctive parts, and the use of a hierarchical design approach are the kinds of attributes that contribute to a project's sense of order.

Designers need to learn to provide the optimal level of order for the project and for the different kinds of users of a project. Sometimes providing a clear, straightforward environment for the visitor and an interesting environment for the regular user present a unique design challenge.

6. To satisfy, projects need to have enriching qualities.

While the main functions of a project are to support and enhance the activities that take place in it, projects have a significant physical presence that strongly impacts the well-being of its users. Beyond the provision

Figure 1.6: Rich physical qualities bring projects to life. The shapes, patterns, textures, rhythms, and details of this bar contribute to its playfulness and richness.

Figure 1.7: A project needs to express qualities that its users will relate to and support. These become the project's personality. Many businesses, like this coffee store, make conscious efforts to portray very specific personalities targeted to their audiences.

of functional spaces, projects have the capacity to delight humans by providing enriching physical qualities and experiences (Figure 1.6).

Not all enriching experiences need to provide stimulus with the intent to excite and motivate. Enriching experiences can also be the kind that helps users relax and restores their emotional equilibrium. Variety and intricacy can be used to stimulate and create interest. Novelty and picturesqueness can provide momentary vacations and relax the busy mind.

Circulation areas present special opportunities for enrichment. They can be dramatic and full of pleasant surprises. Sequences can be made interesting; events can take place along the way; surfaces can incorporate engaging details, colors, and textures; and views can provide pleasant distractions and interesting information. Spaces for tasks involving mental concentration benefit from environmental qualities that promote a sense of stability. Establishing meaningful visual connections with the surroundings and providing views for relief and distraction also enrich the experience of a busy person.

7. In order to have deeper meaning, projects need to incorporate a fitting expression.

The spaces, surfaces, finishes, and other contents of a project carry with them inherent expressions and meanings. Designers need to give projects the right expression. The way of allocating and dividing space, the shapes of the architectural and decorative documents used, and the colors, furnishings, and accessories incorporated in a project all carry connotations of particular attitudes and stylistic tendencies (Figure 1.7). Care has to be exercised by the designer so that the chosen expressions are the appropriate ones.

The way design elements are arranged and shaped, and the characteristics of the products selected for a project can be expressive of universal human manifestations, such as constraint or freedom. They can also express significant historical or cultural associations, or important programmatic requirements, such as connection or segregation. Furthermore, and quite important, design can express dominant traits about the personality of the client. Manifestations of qualities related to status, control, hierarchy, and overall demeanor are all possible through design.

The expressions manifested in a project can also speak to the designer's own stylistic inclinations and personal preferences, as well as reflect the particular design tendencies of a specific location at a particular time in history.

Principles Related to Design Process

The final three principles address the design process in a general way, breaking it into the tasks of understanding, ideation, and development.

8. A good design solution requires a good understanding of the problem.

Good design is responsive to particular user needs, is appropriate to the specific circumstances at a particular time, and fits within its physical context. To achieve this kind of congruence between needs and solutions, it is important for designers to understand the requirements of a project in detail. Aspects include, but go beyond, the basic programmatic requirements of the project (Figure 1.8).

There are often significant contexts encompassing historical, cultural, and regional realities to consider and address. The local neighborhood, with its physical and environmental features and movement patterns, represents an immediate and important context. The building in which the project is housed also constitutes an important context. It comes with a set of suggestive attributes and patterns of use that you need to understand and respond to.

Usually, the most direct needs of a project are associated with the requirements outlined in the design program, which outlines the specific requirements to be addressed. Functions, as well as their space requirements and relationships, are included. Although most of the project's functional requirements are likely to be included in the program, some important considerations are sometimes omitted and require some perceptive questioning by the designer in order to come to the surface.

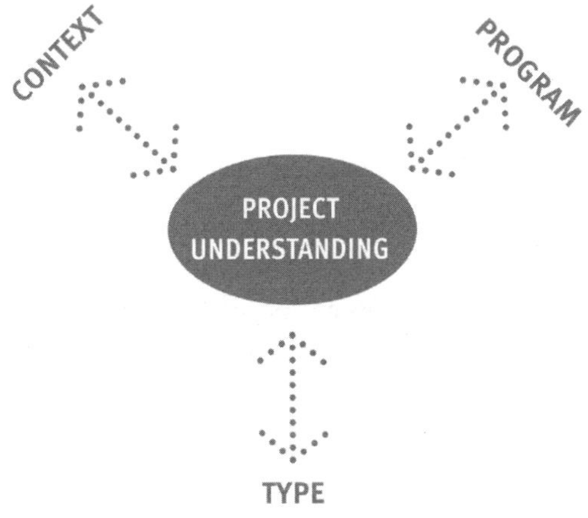

Figure 1.8: To respond appropriately to the particular realities of a project, the designer needs to understand its context, program, and type.

Designers need to fully understand the inherent requirements associated with specific types of projects. Projects are examples of a particular setting type having specific characteristics and needs based on its function. Whether it is a restaurant, store, or office, most projects have unique requirements characteristic of their type. Some of these will not be reflected in the program and will surface only if the designer is familiar with the specific nuances of the project type through study, observation, or experience.

Potential levels of understanding vary widely. You may feel you understand how a place functions, but if you have not spent time in a similar place before, your understanding is superficial. The people who really know how a place functions, at least in their corner of the world, are its users. For complex projects, designers need to make every effort possible to get to the users if they sincerely hope to understand how the facility is supposed to work.

To gain competence at understanding projects, designers need to develop the habits of proper questioning and good listening. Additionally, they need to develop effective and useful ways of recording the information collected. These efforts should not be limited to the beginning of a project. Although most information is collected at the beginning of a project, this information evolves, is expanded, and changes during the life of a project. Having defined processes to solicit and record this information throughout the life of a project will facilitate an evolving definition of the project's requirements.

9. A good design starts with one or more overall concepts that give it a definite direction.

When the requirements of a project are understood, what follows is a search for an appropriate direction in terms of both organization and character. After the designer has a good grasp of the basic essence of the project, he or she can devise a general organizational scheme. At first

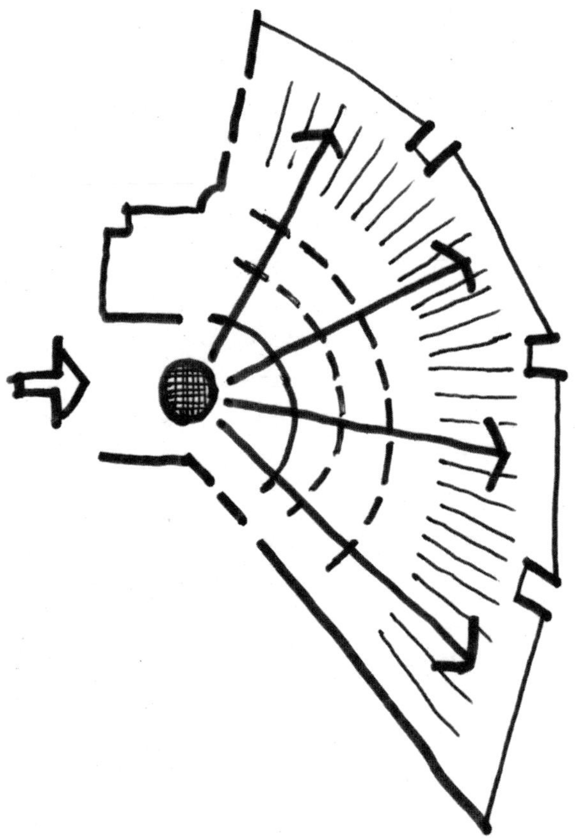

Figure 1.9: A project requires a proper response to its most fundamental design problem. It is embodied in a clear and powerful organizational idea, such as the one shown for a library building.

this is done quite generally with as little detail as possible. A certain project's realities may suggest a large central space. Another project's realities may suggest many small sequential units. After you have this understanding, you are prepared to make your first design move, like the painter's first stroke on a blank canvas. See Figure 1.9.

The success of a project's organizational idea depends on its appropriateness—how well it responds to the basic design problem. The idea may be bold or jazzy, but can also be understated and plain. The main goal is to establish an overall organizational system that addresses the project's fundamental essence and gives coherence and clarity.

In addition to the main organizational idea, designers also seek an overall approach that determines the project's character or personality and informs visual and thematic decisions.

10. A good design develops the concepts fully in order to arrive at the total environment.

Thomas Edison used to say that genius consisted of one percent inspiration and 99 percent perspiration, meaning that after you have that great idea it takes a great deal of work to make it happen. So it is with design. After you have a clear direction in terms of organization and character, you have to devote the majority of your design hours to develop and resolve all parts of the project. The detailed floor plan has to be produced and developed; the spatial envelope has to be determined; elevations addressing the vertical surfaces of the project have to be designed; and finishes and furnishings have to be selected in order to achieve full synthesis. Then the stage is set and the *actors* can literally step in and begin the *play* (Figure 1.10). There are so many physical parts and pieces in a typical interior project that solving the functional puzzle alone is quite a challenging task. The process of total resolution of the many components into a single unified entity is one of the greatest challenges and joys of design.

BEGINNING THE JOURNEY

The following chapters of this book are organized in the same order as the ten principles just introduced. Chapter 2 addresses what users do in buildings. The important role of place and its elements is explained in Chapter 3. Chapter 4 is a review of the many aspects of architectural space: how it is defined, enclosed, shaped, manipulated, combined, and composed into entire projects. Chapter 5 reviews design basics concerning the goals of balancing and unifying the physical parts of a project.

The fundamental ideas of order, enrichment, and expression are covered in Chapters 6, 7, and 8, respectively. Finally, Chapters 9, 10, and 11 cover, respectively, the design process tasks of understanding, ideation, and development.

We are ready to begin our journey. Open your mind and experiment with some of the ideas to infuse your projects with strong experiential qualities. Good luck.

Figure 1.10: Finally, the stage is set, and the environment is ready to receive its actors and the props they'll need to enact the play.

REVIEW

Summary

Good interior design projects provide safe and functional spaces. Additionally, interior environments have the capacity to delight and inspire. The process of design requires, at the most fundamental level, a proper understanding of the project, proper response to the specific problems of the project, and skillful execution of the response.

The design studio is the most important component of a design education, for it is there that students perform the act of designing. Also important is the practice of reviewing and critiquing design solutions. It is through proper questioning that students develop the reasoning skills necessary to become good design thinkers. It is also important for the young designer to expand his or her range of design ideas and strategies over time, expanding the designer's collection of potential design solutions.

Today's designers are responsible for the distribution of functions and the shaping of the interior spaces they design. It is, therefore, crucial that they become adept at working with interior space and be able to conceive, establish, develop, and complete space and its many components.

This book is organized around ten design principles. These address concepts students need to know regarding the realities of interior space and its design as well as specific design issues concerned with the tasks of establishing, developing, and completing design solutions.

1. Abercrombie, S. (1990). *A philosophy of interior design.* New York: Harper and Row.

Chapter 2
People in Buildings

Instructional Objectives

- Describe typical events during building visits.
- Highlight the importance of events preceding the main activity in buildings.
- Highlight the importance of secondary events in buildings.
- Highlight the distinction between stationary and transitory activities.
- Explain how situational factors affect users' experiences in buildings.
- Explain the ways certain variables affect how users react to situational factors.
- Explain how the various events people go through when visiting buildings add up to the total experience of the visit.

Architecture is more to do with making frames than painting pictures; more a matter of providing an accompaniment to life than the dance itself.

—*Simon Unwin,* Analysing Architecture

OUR EXPERIENCE IS MADE up largely of the activities we do to satisfy our human needs and the societal rituals we perform daily. These include learning, working, playing, and connecting with others. Although some of these take place outside, it seems like most of what we do, we do inside. We seem to spend most of our time either inside a building or in transit between buildings.

As the quote at the start of this chapter suggests, architecture is an accompaniment to the dance of life. Our conscious awareness, however, is usually more preoccupied with the dance of life itself than the surroundings in which the dance takes place. As we move from activity to activity and from goal to goal, our mind is focused on the meeting, the purchase, the meal, or the dance. People, goods, food, and dancing partners are our primary objectives. Yet, despite its seemingly secondary status in our lives, architecture is a crucial ingredient in the mix. Buildings provide the settings in which the various dances of life take place, and, as such, they play a vital supporting role. Buildings supply not only shelter, warmth, and safety but also favorable conditions for an effective meeting, a smooth sale, an unforgettable meal, or a flowing dance. Surely, the other meeting members, the merchandiser, the salesperson, the cook, the waiter, and the dance partner all have to do their share for our daily rituals to be successful and meaningful, but buildings and, specifically, their interior spaces carry their share of responsibilities. Human experience is a seamless phenomenon, involving not only people and their rituals but also the settings in which they occur.

Total design requires knowing the rituals people perform inside buildings and the distinct activities that go with them. Understanding the activities and the role that interior spaces we design play in the whole picture will allow you to respond with fitting solutions that facilitate and enhance the building experience.

There are countless activities that people perform in buildings; however, despite that fact, there are several sequential and predictable events that occur in most visits to building interiors. In this chapter, we present these events so that you can learn to design with an experiential focus in mind. Additionally, this chapter covers some of the main components involved in the mix of human activity and suggests how people's experiences in buildings vary depending on these components.

BASIC EVENTS OF THE BUILDING EXPERIENCE

The basic events that take place during building visits seem to be consistent and repetitive. Many of these events take place before or after the main activity associated with the visit. Take, for example, a scenario of a person's trip to the theater to see a live play, taken from Martin Bloom's book *Accommodating the Lively Arts.* In one of the chapters Bloom describes, in detail, the requirements of the spaces and places of a theater. The following is a description of one patron's experiences and observations as he visits the kind of theater described by Bloom, from the exterior approach toward the building to the moment preceding the start of the show.

> A patron approaches the theater on foot. The approach sets the tone for the experience. The ambience surrounding the theater is festive, creating a mood of anticipation of the event to come. The marquee projects, protects, and announces the current show. It welcomes, lures, and dazzles with light. The entranceways beneath the marquee welcome him to the attraction and feature promotional signs, posters, and photos on either side. Just beyond the entranceways, the box office allows sufficient space so that the long lines of ticket buyers do not impede the flow of patrons already ticketed and entering the theater. A staff member goes back to the administration area through a door accessible from the outer lobby, but located inconspicuously. The ample space in the outer lobby allows for discrete circulation, avoiding congestion from the crowd. Patrons not yet ready to enter the theater wait in allotted spaces away from the main paths of circulation.
>
> Although businesslike and efficient, the lobby space serves as a prelude to the performance, enhancing the anticipation

for the event to come. As the patron approaches the entrance to the inner lobby and passes through the control point, he surrenders his tickets and receives a stub indicating his seat assignment. At this point he begins to sense his relationship to the theater as a whole. The locations of checking facilities, restrooms, and public telephones become quickly apparent, and the pathway to the particular portion of the theater where he will eventually be seated is clearly disclosed.

Having unburdened himself of coats and parcels, he moves freely into the highly structured environment that begins to prepare him for the coming event. Having some time to wander, he contemplates images of past events in the theater, as well as historic artifacts related to the building. The main lobby is spacious, enabling the large audience to circulate freely and facilitating social interaction. The main lobby also provides glimpses of the immediate surroundings through window openings and through doors leading onto terraces, contributing a dynamic quality and aesthetic amenity. The grand stairway to the mezzanine contributes to the overall character of the lobby, providing viewing positions from the upper level that overlook the lobby below. The overall height and breadth of the space is monumental.

The lobby has established the patron's mindset for the ensuing event, transforming him into a participant in the event about to take place in the theater. Meanwhile, the patron becomes an actor in a secondary act, the drama created by the spectators in the lobby. As the patron approaches the entrance of the auditorium, he proceeds through a transitional zone in which the lighting and sound levels of the lobby are gradually diminished. Once inside, he takes measure of the totality of the space, gaining a sense of his relationship to it.

Understanding his position in relationship to the whole gives him a sense of security within the environment. After being conducted to his assigned row, he negotiates the space between the rows and gets to his seat. The seat, clearly identified by letter and number, is comfortable, with enough height, width, and elbow room to accommodate a wide range of physical types.

There is enough ambient light to allow him to grasp the size, shape, and appearance of the room. The colors and textures of the walls and ceilings relate harmoniously to the seating areas and tie the whole composition of the room into a cohesive whole. Narrowly focused downlights complement the ambient lighting, facilitate the reading of the programs, and provide adequate lighting levels for aisles and exits.

The focus of the auditorium lies within the performance space and the seating arrangement reinforces that focus. It provides good sight lines and acoustics so that the audience is able to see and hear the performance with ease. As the time for the event nears, individual members of the audience settle in their separate locations, begin to focus their attention on the performance space and, as they do, become a coherent and attentive body, ready to react to the stimuli of the production. As the house lights dim, the environment of the audience space gradually loses its identity and begins to yield to the reality of the stage. In it, shortly, the audience will witness a presentation of a heightened reality, one more focused and more persuasive than anything that can be experienced outside the theater.[1]

This description provides a rich account of the many events that take place even before the start of the big event, the theatrical production itself. In the case of a theater show, the production is the main activity. Actors act on stage, and the audience looks on attentively from their seats. Behind the scenes, countless workers perform their roles with scenery, costumes, lights, and other crucial backstage activities to make the production smooth and flawless. During intermission, our sample patron may take a trip to the restroom and then proceed to the lobby for a beverage and, perhaps, conversation with friends about the first half of the show and what may be in store for the second. At the end of the production, the entrance sequence is reversed. The patron proceeds from the auditorium to the cloakroom to the various lobbies and, finally, exits the building. This may be done in ceremonious fashion, as when arriving, although exiting often tends to be a bit more chaotic because of the large number of people leaving simultaneously.

A trip to the theater is representative of all the generic events a person is likely to go through in a building: from the building approach, to the arrival at the destination place, and, finally, the departure sequence. Although the specific nature of these experiences will vary from occasion to occasion, and from building type to building type, they are, essentially, the rituals people do in buildings. The following sections examine these rituals more closely.

Approach

Our journey to a building begins the moment we decide to go there. In most cases, we simply make a decision to engage in a certain activity, be it eating out, shopping, going to work, or meeting with friends.

Even before we can see the building, we may start thinking about it: where we will park the car, which entrance we'll use, and so on. Eventually, we see the building. It ceases to be a memory and becomes real. We start approaching it and recognize it as our destination (Figure 2.1). Depending on our familiarity with the building, the eventual entrance sequence will have different degrees of challenge depending on our individual level of familiarity.

The building surroundings and general conditions will have an effect on the experience of entering. If it is a beautiful day, we may delay the arrival; if it is cold and windy, we will welcome the building's warmth. The building may be handsome, ordinary, or ugly. Depending on how apparent these qualities are and our state of mind, we may or may not pay attention to them.

Overall Arrival 1

At some point we reach the building's front door, open it, and step inside—a significant event. The act of entering is usually straightforward and performed automatically. Few people stop and think: Wow, what an entrance! Most people's minds are engaged in wayfinding tasks so design attributes such as legibility and good circulation become important. Still, beyond helping with the wayfinding experience, a good first impression will have an effect on users' overall experience in a building (Figure 2.2).

If users are familiar with the building, they may proceed automatically toward their goal. For visitors it may take a few moments to get oriented and figure out where to go next while getting their first impression of the building's interior.

Users' ultimate destination in the building may be a short distance away, far in the back, or on a different floor. If they take the stairs or elevators to go to a different floor, they go through a similar arrival experience at the new level once they arrive.

There are opportunities to make the arrival memorable, to reveal the whole cohesively, and to make the path clear for all the building's users.

Overall Arrival 2

The experience of arriving at the destination space may be nonchalant, full of excitement, or filled with apprehension depending on the circumstances. For visitors like us, there will be first impressions of the new space, although the mind is preoccupied with the goal of finding the way to the ultimate destination.

Figure 2.1: The front of an academic building strongly announces its presence. Its solidity and elevated position make it stand out as an important destination.

Figure 2.2: A common arrival space in buildings is a public lobby. This figure shows a rich lobby for an academic building.

(a)

(b)

Figure 2.3: In buildings containing more than one facility, a second arrival takes place when one transitions into the specific place being visited. Here, we present the first views seen upon entering a dental clinic (a) and an office suite (b).

Depending on the type of space, there may or may not be someone to greet us. An office, a clinic, and a restaurant are likely to have a person greeting visitors; a store may not. Here, similar to the arrival at the destination floor, we may take a moment to glance around and get oriented. If we are familiar with the space, we simply proceed ahead.

This arrival, more than the others, is likely to give us a sense of accomplishment and relief because we are now in the exact place we came to visit. Design goals include providing features that help make a good first impression and determining how the space beyond is revealed. Figure 2.3 shows the arrival spaces of a dental clinic and an office suite.

Waiting

In many facilities, such as offices, clinics, and restaurants, visitors have to wait their turn. A waiting room or area is provided for that purpose. Waiting is one of those rare instances when we are neither engaged in the target activity nor traveling to it. We are at the general destination but must now wait before engaging in the main activity. Any potential anxiety related to finding the right place or getting there on time has likely subsided considerably. We now have some time on our hands.

Depending on the length of the wait and our disposable time, waiting may or may not be a relaxed experience. There may be other people waiting, too—strangers in close proximity. This could be pleasurable for the person who likes to make new friends but stressful for the person who feels uncomfortable among strangers. Looking at magazines in the clinic or menus at the restaurant may provide relief and comfort. If you bring company, this could become a welcome opportunity to talk.

Eventually, the person you are there to meet, or the waiter, or the nurse, arrives and calls your name. You are getting closer to the real purpose of your visit.

A couple of exceptions to the experience described here occur in some restaurants and most stores. Some restaurants have a bar and encourage patrons to wait there. The resulting waiting experience is different. In this case, you may start to consume a beverage and engage in conversation without having to whisper. Stores are still different. Stores, except by-appointment specialty stores, require no waiting; you proceed right in and start looking around. Many stores, however, notably grocery stores and convenience stores, have some waiting at the end, this time at the checkout counter. Retailers make attempts to make this idle time productive by placing small merchandise close to the registers for last-minute impulse purchases. Some include magazines and miscellaneous tabloids for our browsing pleasure and potential purchase. This kind of waiting occurs at the end of the sequence and represents the consummation of the shopping activity, rather than the waiting-at-the-gate kind of experience at the restaurant, office, or clinic.

A different kind of waiting occurs at the theater. There, you can wait in the lobby where you are free to move about at will, a much more active waiting experience. Part of what makes the typical waiting room experience uncomfortable for many is the lack of control and freedom of movement. There is usually nowhere to go, plus the close proximity to strangers is uncomfortable for many.

Waiting experiences are full of anticipation and expectation. They are instances of suspended attention, sort of a limbo between one place and another. People are not burdened with the logistics and challenges of finding the place and are not yet engaged with, maybe not even thinking about, the upcoming activity. This is an excellent opportunity for the designer to make an impression, perhaps by incorporating meaningful details. Figure 2.4 shows waiting areas for a doctor's office and an academic building.

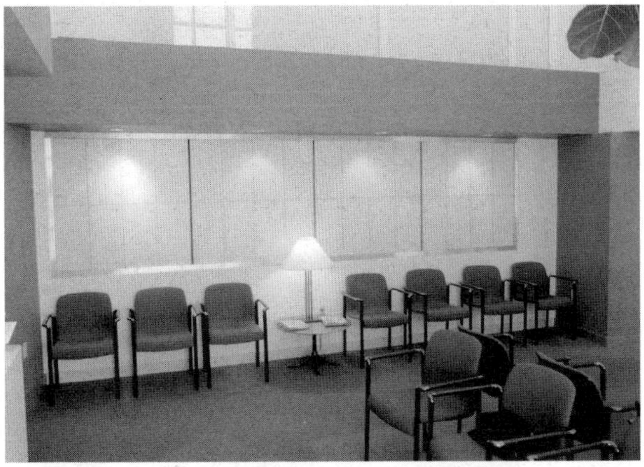

(a)

(b)

Figure 2.4: Waiting is an unavoidable reality for visitors of many facility types. Here, we present the waiting area in a doctor's office (a) and an academic building (b).

Moving to the Destination

The route taken and the experience of moving toward a principal destination is different for first-timers, frequent visitors, and day-to-day users of a given facility. Insiders will proceed ahead and often use the back way in. Visitors, whether alone or escorted, will be limited to the public corridors intended for them.

The walk to the destination can be straightforward and utilitarian, or it can be involved and eventful. While in transit, users get a chance to look around and get a better sense of the overall environment, even if they don't get to see it all. They form impressions based on what is revealed in the corridor and the views from it to the spaces beyond. Insiders know the environment well and are not as likely to focus consciously on it.

Moving to the destination is often the most revealing experience visitors have in a visit to a facility. The opportunities to make an impression and provide enriching experiences are plentiful. The circulation system can be experientially stimulating at different levels. At the most basic level, it can be clear and assist in orienting users.

(a)

(b)

Figure 2.5: The road to our destination can be an eventful and expressive journey in itself. The main paths to a dental clinic's main examination area (a) and a restaurant's dining room (b) start to reveal features of the spaces beyond.

At another level, it may provide a more subtle interest, the kind you notice after repeated exposures, such as intricate details about the carpet or fabric pattern or a distant view seen through a window on the way to the final destination. Figure 2.5 shows routes to the destinations of clinic and restaurant projects.

Arrival at the Target Destination

The experience of arriving at the activity destination varies depending on the role of the person getting there. In a restaurant, the cook will arrive in the kitchen, the food server will move around her area, the cashier will arrive at the front cashier station, and the customer will arrive at the table. Depending on the facility type and the target activity, the destination place may be a desk, a conference room, a doctor's examination room, a dentist's chair, or a dining table, among others. There are also more dynamic activities requiring movement.

The common denominator of all these cases is a sense of arrival at the precise place for the activity. It will be here that users, in their specific roles, will engage in the activities they came to perform.

The experience of customers in stores, however, is usually different because it involves moving about as one looks at the merchandise. The experience there is one of constant movement from one place to the next with no specific place of arrival as described earlier. Museums and galleries offer a similar kind of experience, featuring a progression from space to space rather than an experience involving one stationary activity place. Figure 2.6a–d shows views of the final destination places for a student going to class, a visitor attending a meeting at an office facility, a customer in a restaurant, and a patient at a dental office.

Engaging in the Target Activity

When we arrive at the target destination, we engage in the target activity. The nature of the activity will vary widely depending on facility type and our role in the activity. The visitor's activity may be dining at a table, meeting in a conference room, shopping somewhere in a store, being examined in an examination room, or watching a show in a theater. The host's activity may be serving the customer at the previously mentioned dining table, selling merchandise at the store, examining the patient in the examination room, or being the lead actor of the theatrical production in the theater. Additionally, there are usually back-of-the-house activities in places such as the kitchen and the loading dock.

Many activities are done while stationary, either standing or sitting, although some, like shopping, involve locomotion and exploration. Target activities are the functional activities of the facility. They require many functional provisions as well as ambient ones. Designs should take all aspects of the function into consideration and respond in ways that facilitate smooth and pleasant

(a)

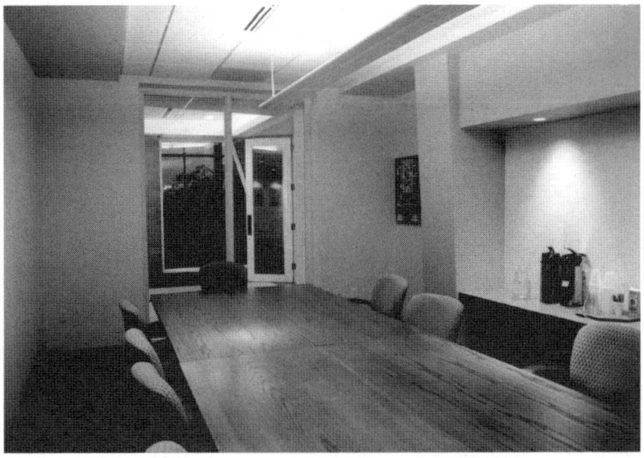

(b)

(c)

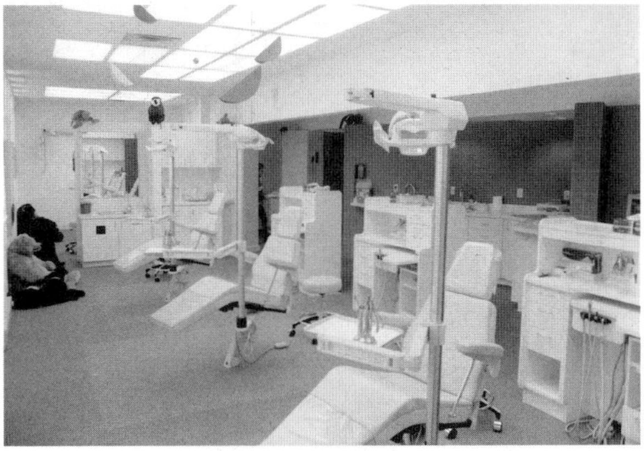

(d)

Figure 2.6: The heart of any facility is the place where the principal activity is conducted. Examples of these are the seats in a classroom (a), the conference table in the meeting room (b), the dining table in the restaurant (c), and the dental chair in the dentist's office (d).

exchanges and transactions. Figure 2.7a–c shows people performing their target activities in various settings.

Side Trips and Secondary Activities

Side trips are short-term visits to other spaces in the facility for personal or other reasons. These trips are not necessarily an essential component of the target activity, per se. The best known is the trip to the restroom. Whether at work, at a restaurant, or at the theater, there comes a time when users pay a visit to the restroom. This, in itself, becomes a mini-experience requiring them to leave the target destination and travel to the restroom. In too many facilities, unfortunately, the spaces leading to and from the restrooms are not given proper design attention and do not make a favorable impression. Figure 2.8 shows the unexpected and eclectic approach used for the vanity mirrors to enliven the restroom experience.

Another well-known side-trip destination is the concession stand in theaters and stadiums. Designers should think of the circulation leading to side-trip destinations and the destinations themselves as worthwhile secondary experiences deserving proper design attention.

In addition to side trips, some experiences require additional meaningful events as part of the total experience. A day at the office may involve a principal meeting in the boardroom, another meeting with staff, and a training session. In addition, there will usually be a time for lunch, whether taken in the lunchroom or outside the office. A visit to a clinic may involve important stops at the lab and the X-ray room. A trip to a museum may involve attending a talk before the exhibit opens and the usual stop at the gift shop on the way out. These are all examples of secondary activities, instances when functions related to the main activity take visitors temporarily

(a)

(b)

(c)

Figure 2.7: When stationed in the right place, facility users can engage in whatever their target activity is. Shoppers are an exception. They seldom settle down or linger much because shopping at a store involves exploration and movement (a). Others, like restaurant kitchen personnel (b) and restaurant attendants and visitors (c), usually conduct their business within the specific settings designated for their activities.

away from the main destination place and into another space for a related activity.

Settings housing secondary activities, obviously, deserve as much design attention as the main target destinations in a facility. Figure 2.9 shows a specialized examination room in a dental clinic, an example of the kind

Figure 2.8: The places we go during side trips don't always receive the attention they deserve. These places can be designed to entertain and provoke curiosity as evident in this restroom facility in a public building.

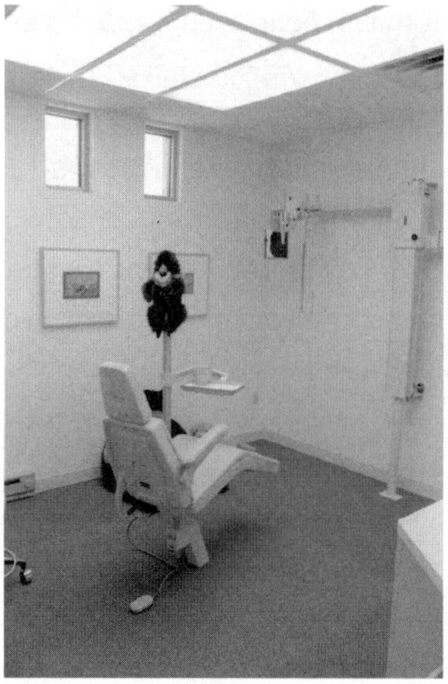

Figure 2.9: Secondary activities require us to leave the principal setting to visit a related setting. An example of this is an individual examination and X-ray room in a dental facility.

of secondary activity place a patient may need to visit in addition to the principal treatment room.

Departing the Destination and Moving Toward the Exit

At some point it is time to leave. The activity may have been completed (dinner is finished) or it is closing time. We start gathering our belongings to head out. At this point we may be preoccupied with activities such as paying the bill, gathering our possessions, and we may begin to anticipate and prepare for the next activities (getting to the car, making it to the movies on time, and so on).

After getting up and gathering our possessions we proceed toward the exit. The walk toward the exit may be hurried or relaxed, and we may have different degrees of awareness of the surroundings depending on the level of rush, mental preoccupation, or engagement with others. Nevertheless, it is a time of movement through the premises and has the potential, once again, for meaningful engagement with the surroundings. Therefore, serious consideration should be given to the experience offered as visitors travel back from the destination space. It may be the same route taken to the target destination or, perhaps, a different one. Figure 2.10a–c shows views of the exiting sequence from the dental clinic seen in some of the earlier figures.

Final Departure

Eventually we leave the last space behind and finally exit the facility. In some cases, the last space and the last wall may attempt to make one final impression on us. The collection of impressions has been made and is recorded in our minds. We can then start planning our next building experience, perhaps minutes away and substantially different.

These generic rituals we perform in buildings occur time and time again in different settings and in slightly different ways. They provide the designer an experiential, event-based framework useful for design. Designers should become more mindful of these events, consider inherent design opportunities, and act on them whenever possible to make the building experience a better one.

USERS' RESPONSE TO INTERIOR SPACES

In addition to becoming familiar with the rituals described in this chapter, designers must become aware of the situational factors that affect users' experiences in buildings and some important factors that influence how people react to their settings. We start with the situational factors.

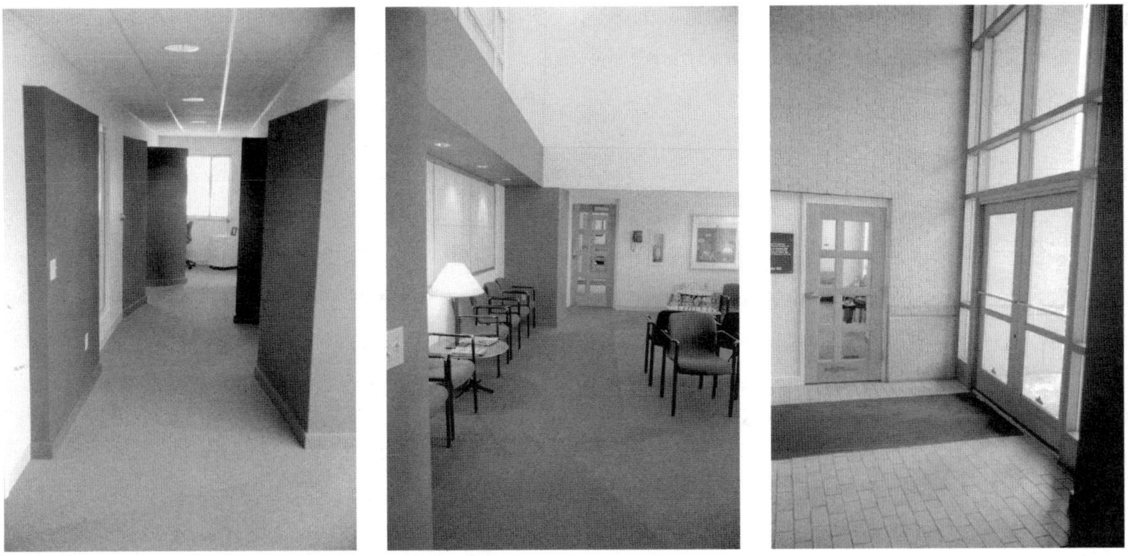

(a) (b) (c)

Figure 2.10: Leaving a facility usually involves a sequence similar to the arriving sequence, except in reverse. The three views seen here show the experience of leaving a dental clinic: the corridor leaving the examination area (a), the path through the waiting area leading to the exit door (b), and the exit doors from the building's public lobby (c).

Situational Factors Affecting Users' Experiences in Buildings

The experience of life is complex, consisting of many variables that interact in intricate and changing ways. The goal of this section is to increase your awareness about the situational factors that affect experiences in general and the role physical settings play in the overall experience. As stated in the opening quotation to this chapter, architecture is "more a matter of providing an accompaniment to life than the dance itself." Here we take a look at some of the important aspects of "the dance itself."

The things people do in life ("the dance") can be said to consist of specific occasions that take place in specific places, where people play specific roles, utilize available resources, and are surrounded by specific people, objects, and building features. All these combine in complex and intricate combinations to become unique contexts for our activities. To think of ways design can contribute to the enrichment of our experiences in them, we need to have an understanding of how these factors typically interact. These situational factors consist of occasions, players, resources, and surroundings, the latter consisting of architectural features, people, and objects.

Occasion

An occasion is a very particular kind of activity, such as, say, a formal dinner for the members of upper management of a given corporation. Here, the generic activity is dinner. However, it is a specific kind of dinner with specific connotations and requiring particular behaviors.

Players

The people involved in the occasion are the players. These can be locals (insiders) or visitors. Both the mix of players and the characteristics of individual ones will have an effect on the occasion. Are they lively or subdued? Formal or casual? Important or ordinary? Some of the key players in our example are the members of upper management attending the dinner, but also the waitstaff servicing the group.

Resources

Resources include the physical, such as space, equipment, and the like, plus important intangible ones, such as time and money. Our dinner example, for instance, may be taking place in a comfortable banquet room with ample space and tables. Let's suppose that this particular corporation is going through difficult economic times, and its members are holding a retreat the following day starting early in the morning. As a result, the budget for the dinner this year may be low, and the participants may not be able to stay as late as they did in past years because of the activity the next morning. Let's also pretend that this year's dinner is somewhat rushed because the room was not ready on time and they had to start late. This year's dinner, in all likelihood, will not be as pleasant as those of other years because of the effect of a number of negative situational factors.

Surroundings

The interior physical environment, of course, is more than just a resource. It also has a presence of its own as an entity, as do the other people and objects in the room. We refer to these here as the *surroundings*. In this group we can distinguish between surroundings directly related to the occasion and those peripheral ones in close enough proximity to be perceived, even though they play no direct role in the immediate occasion. Examples of the first group would be the activity room and its features, plus all the other furnishings, objects, utensils, and the like. Examples of the second group would be the people having a dinner next door and all the sights, sounds, and smells emanating from them and their activities.

The evening's experience will be a combination of complex dynamics involving all these factors and is likely to be different for the various attendees. Some factors will be experienced in approximately the same way by all, such as consistent, prompt, and courteous service and a fantastic view. The experience of other factors may vary from person to person, depending on considerations such as seating assignments and the quality of the meal ordered. In some cases, the same factor might be experienced differently by different people, such as one person liking and another disliking the same dish, or someone being more annoyed than others about the rushed nature of this year's dinner.

Factors Affecting Users' Reactions to Situational Factors

Human beings, despite their similarities, are different because of their personalities and backgrounds.

Some people like quiet environments; others like loud ones. Some like public over private places. Some people like old styles over contemporary ones. Some people like involvement; others are more restrained. Additionally, everyone brings with them the context of the recent past. A modest-sized room may seem splendid to someone moving in from tiny quarters, whereas it may seem insufficient for someone accustomed to large spaces. At an entirely different level, someone may have heard some good news and be in a happy mood, but the person next door may have just been laid off and is experiencing tremendous emotional pain.

In addition to personal traits and the recent events, a few other factors affect the way people react to events. These include their role in the occasion and their degrees of affinity, familiarity, demand, and control with the situational factors.

If you are part of the occasion, you have a role in it. You may be one of the people attending the dinner, or you may be one of the people servicing those having dinner. Among members of upper management you may be an old member or a new member; you may be the CEO or a treasurer. Furthermore, you may be the member who helped coordinate the event and might be quite busy attending to all kinds of details during the evening.

Another factor is related to people's preferences. Individuals have unique personal affinities. Not everyone likes the same settings, people, and so on. A member of the dinner example may not like going to formal dinners; another may like them but dislike her role as the event coordinator. Another person may like both the formal dinners and her role, but have a real problem with rushed dinners. Still another person may find everything else agreeable except the style of the furniture and paintings in the room and the person he has to sit next to, whom everyone else likes.

Familiarity is another factor. People may be more or less familiar with the particular event and the players, resources, and surroundings associated with it. In our management dinner example, some members may be familiar with the ritual of the yearly dinner, their role in it, the usual setting for the event, and even the occasional shortage of money and time. Newcomers may be unfamiliar with some or all of these factors. They may have a harder time making sense of the evening. On the other hand, the event may seem fresher to them than to the bored-with-it old-timers. The level of familiarity, then, is one of the variables that influences factors like the stress level and the sense of novelty associated with a particular occasion.

Different situations pose different degrees of demand on their participants. The demand of a situation is the degree of difficulty or effort associated with it. A casual family dinner is likely to be considerably less demanding than the formal business-type dinner in our example. Some roles will be more demanding and require more concentration than others. The management member in charge of coordinating the event will have a more demanding evening than the others. This, in turn, may be nothing compared to the demands of the cook in the kitchen. Inadequate resources will usually increase the level of demand of any task. People and environments come with their own degree of demand.

Finally, people have different degrees of control over certain aspects of the event, and this can also color one's experience. In our example, most of the participants had no control over the occurrence of the event. It was going to happen, and they were expected to attend. When there, they had to play their roles. For some it was playing the corporate persona many executives play in order to be like the rest of the crowd. They had no control over the time and budget limitations. Some may have had some creative ideas on how to deal with these problems but may have been reluctant to bring them up thinking it was inappropriate. Additionally, they certainly had no control over the setting, the group next door, and maybe even the choice of dish (these may have been predetermined). Compare this with the control you have over a casual, relaxed lunch with your best friend.

PEOPLE IN BUILDINGS AND DESIGN

As we have just seen, there are many aspects that contribute to lived experience. Although the physical setting is an important component of any experience, much of our satisfaction or dissatisfaction at home, work, or play is the result of factors unrelated to setting. The dance of life is intricate. Still, designers need to learn about the particular situational factors related to their projects in order to design responsive environments.

CAPSULE | People and the Environment

Have you ever wondered how a person will react to a particular environment? Or what type of environment is most suitable for a particular person? To be able to make these predictions, we need a workable model that links specific emotional reactions to the load (complexity, intensity) of a given environment. Fortunately, Albert Mehrabian and James Russell have devised a practical framework we can use to make reasonable predictions to these challenging questions. Their research has led them to conclude that people's reactions to environments are based on just a few emotional dimensions, which in turn can produce many different behaviors. The basic chain of events consists of a given environment experienced by a person, the person's processing of the conditions presented by the place and situation, and the person's behavioral reaction, be it jumping with excitement or running in disgust.

Three basic emotional dimensions determine how a person reacts to a situation in the environment. They are the level of arousal, the level of pleasure, and the level of dominance experienced by the person in relation to the conditions presented. Keep in mind that although our focus here is man's reaction to the built environment, there are, as we have seen, other factors at play, such as the influence of other people, the specific occasion, and so on. Arousal refers to the overall level of stimulation experienced. The qualities of an environment may excite you and increase your blood pressure and heart rate. A different environment may have the opposite effect and may cause you to feel relaxed, or even sluggish and sleepy.

The second emotional dimension is pleasure. It refers, as the word suggests, to the amount of pleasure derived from a particular environment. Some environments may cause contentment and an overall good feeling, while others annoy or depress. The third dimension, dominance, refers to the degree of control or influence one feels in relation to a specific situation. This depends on both the setting and the event. For example, working at home may be more relaxing than working at the office. The familiarity of home and the fact that you don't need to be on your best behavior give you greater control over the situation. You could be wearing your cutoff jeans and singing loudly and no one will complain. Even within the office, though, different events will produce different levels of dominance. If you are, say, a midlevel manager, you will feel more in control in a meeting with the people you supervise than in a meeting with the top executives from upper management.

According to Mehrabian and Russell, just these three dimensions of emotional reaction, in different combinations, produce all possible feelings. For example, high displeasure, high arousal, and high dominance equate to anger. Anxiety, on the other hand, involves high displeasure and high arousal but low dominance. Every feeling known, from joy to anguish, may be described as some combination of the three basic emotional dimensions.

Our emotional reaction to any given environment, then, can be measured as a certain combination of arousal, pleasure, and dominance. Depending on our particular reaction we will be more or less inclined to approach, or avoid, the environment. The graph in Figure C2.1 shows the approach/avoidance behaviors produced by different combinations of arousal and pleasure. In general, conditions of neutral pleasantness will be avoided at low and high levels of arousal and approached at some level of moderate arousal. Pleasant situations and environments will generally be

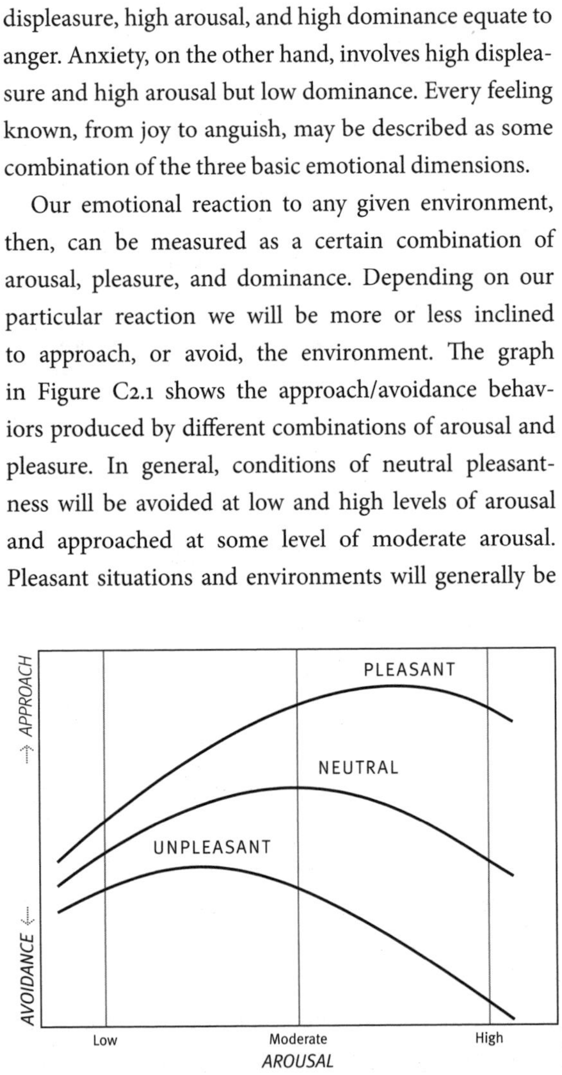

Figure C2.1: Approach/avoidance behaviors for different combinations of pleasantness and arousal.

Source: From *Public Places and Private Spaces: The Psychology of Work, Play, and Living Environment, by Albert Mehrabian.* Copyright © 1976 by Basic Books, Inc. Reprinted by permission of Basic Books, a member of Perseus Books, L.L.C.

approached increasingly as arousal increases up to some level of very high arousal, which will begin a downward trend in the degree of approach. Unpleasant situations and environments will be increasingly avoided as arousal levels increase. It is no surprise that an ugly but mild room is less offensive than an ugly and intense one.

The third dimension, dominance, also plays an important role in the overall effect produced by an environment. For example, an environment that produces low arousal, mild pleasure, and some dominance will be cozy and enjoyable and produce a relaxed and comfortable overall effect. Conversely, an environment that produces low arousal, mild displeasure, and low dominance (submissiveness) will cause boredom and avoidance.

Having established the basics, we can now address the important consideration of differences among people. The authors propose that the same three basic emotional dimensions be used to describe the particular emotional traits and temperaments of people. Thus, we have people of generally pleasant or unpleasant dispositions, people whose personality and/or role make them more or less dominant or submissive, and people who innately tolerate more or less arousal. This last one is the trickiest of the three dimensions.

It works like this: People, according to personality and temperament, screen out more or less of the stimuli presented by the environment in order to reduce the actual environmental load perceived. Some people screen a lot of the stimuli (screeners) and others don't (nonscreeners). Nonscreeners tend to pay attention to most of what the environment offers without attempting to discard nonessentials. As a result, they experience environments as being higher in arousal levels. Screeners, on the other hand, are selective in what they pay attention to. By subconsciously prioritizing the components of a complex situation and attending only to the relevant ones, they effectively reduce the total environmental load perceived. Therefore, the same amount of environmental stimulus will cause greater amounts of and longer-lasting arousal for nonscreeners than for screeners. That is why some people feel right at home in the loud, colorful, and blinking discotheque and others feel more at home sipping decaf tea at the muffled café in the bookstore.

If arousal serves as a magnet in neutral and pleasant environments and situations, at least up to a certain point, then the nonscreener, who is more susceptible to environmental stimulus, will feel attracted to a scene with progressively ascending arousal sooner than the screener. We have said, however, that all people tend to avoid situations when the load level gets too high. Predictably, the nonscreener will reach the point of avoidance earlier than the screener. As Mehrabian explains, the higher susceptibility of the nonscreener to become "more aroused in high-load settings causes them to exhibit more polarized approach-avoidance behaviors to pleasant and unpleasant situations: compared to screeners they have a stronger approach to high-load and pleasant places, and a stronger avoidance of high-load and unpleasant ones."[1]

While designers may be able to create a good match between the personality of a single client and the qualities produced for, say, an apartment designed for that specific person, most projects are designed for multiple, in some cases hundreds of, people. In those cases, obviously, it is impossible to please everyone. Nevertheless, what is possible, and makes this type of information highly useful, is to determine the collective ideal levels of the three variables that a certain environment should stimulate or offer. A good office setting would likely stimulate a low to moderate level of arousal (at least in areas requiring high concentration) and offer a pleasant environment that allows a moderate amount of control. An ideal store may strive to stimulate a moderate to high level of arousal (depending on the store) and offer high pleasantness and at least moderate levels of control and freedom (except for the full-service store). A fancy, intimate restaurant may want to stimulate a low to moderate level of arousal and offer high pleasantness (all restaurants want to be pleasant) and low to moderate control. A tavern, by contrast, wants to stimulate high arousal and offer a high level of freedom and control.

We know you like pleasant environments. How about the other two variables? Are you either dominant or submissive by nature? Are you a screener or a nonscreener? How does your personality match the types of places and situations you typically approach and avoid?

1. Mehrabian, A. (1976). *Public spaces and private places: The psychology of work, play, and living environment*. New York: Basic Books.

As a designer, you have no control over most of the factors that influence experience, nor should you try to take responsibility for them. It would be impossible to predict the infinite number of possible combinations of personalities, preferences, and chance occurrences that take place in particular settings; however, it is possible to get an understanding of the general factors present in a particular application of a project through familiarity with the building type, the typical roles associated with it, and some of the idiosyncrasies the current user group may share with you. Then you are equipped to use the environment as a balancing and enhancing force to do its share in the complex mix of activity components. Depending on the project and the particular setting within it, you may decide to reinforce some physical characteristics and downplay others in order to enhance the experience of as many users as possible. Better yet, you may provide a flexible environment that users can adapt as needed.

Although designers may have little control over who is and isn't familiar with the interior environment of a facility, they can make adequate provisions for the satisfaction of the greatest number. Similarly, knowing the various roles involved in a particular type of event, you may make special efforts to create enriching and satisfying environments for all, regardless of role. For instance, you may attempt to provide meaningful events not only for the customer in the restaurant dining room but also for the food preparation staff in the kitchen. Of course, the magnitude of these will be different, but so will the expectations. In other words, a small gesture that may go unnoticed in the main room may elicit cheers from the kitchen staff.

If the customary activities of a given environment are intense and demanding, you may want to compensate and seek a balance by providing a soothing environment. On the other hand, if it is a nightclub, you may want to actually magnify the experience by providing a charged physical environment. If the tasks performed are routine and monotonous, you may want to compensate by providing a lively environment that balances the experience.

In terms of control, if the atmosphere at a particular enterprise, such as an office, is very hierarchical and employees feel powerless, you could compensate by providing environments that offer choices and some control, thus empowering them to some extent. If, on the contrary, the atmosphere is excessively loose and unstructured, a healthy supply of formal structure may be desirable.

These are just some examples to illustrate the kind of thinking involved in using the environment as a balancing force in interior environments. Obviously, the correct response will depend on the exact circumstances of the project and the goals of both the people controlling the project and the eventual users.

It is up to individual designers to decide the level to which they will take their designs. We challenge you to become aware of the full possibilities and seek meaningful, deliberate design interventions aimed at enriching people's experiences in buildings.

If we compare the game of life to a dance or a series of dances, then it is your responsibility as an individual designer to know the stages of the dances, the people involved in them, and the particularities of each dance. Only then will you be able to design appropriate accompaniments.

REVIEW

Summary

Knowing the basic rituals people perform in buildings gives the designer valuable information that can be used to provide engaging experiences at every step of the process. These activities can be categorized into generic activities people perform in buildings. These start with their approach to and arrival at a building. Next comes the process of moving toward and arriving at the target destination, including any necessary waiting periods. Target destinations include primary and secondary ones. Additionally, users may need to make side trips to the restroom or other similar destinations. When finished, they begin a departure sequence that eventually leads to the exit from the building.

In addition to these rituals, this chapter explained that the spaces we design are one of many factors affecting people's experiences in buildings. These spaces are part of the surroundings and provide the setting for life's activities. Also affecting the experience will be the type of occasion, the other players associated with it, and the resources at their disposal. How people react to a particular experience depends on their relationship to the mix just described. Most notable are the role one plays in the occasion, the degrees of affinity and familiarity toward the other factors, the level of demand imposed by the circumstances, and the degree of control one has over them.

Although designers have little or no control over many of the nondesign factors that make up experience, they do control one of the most important ones—the setting in which the dance of life unfolds. The environments we design can often act as a balancing force, providing the right kinds and amounts of order, enrichment, and expression to optimize the conditions around the rituals of life enacted in them.

1. Bloom, M. (1997). *Accommodating the lively arts: An architect's view.* Lyme, NH: Smith and Kraus.

Chapter Questions

1. Name and describe the basic building events that involve arrival.
2. Name and describe the basic building events that involve movement from one place to another.
3. Name and describe the basic building events performed while stationary.
4. As a visitor to an office on the tenth floor, how many total transitions would you go through if you went there for a meeting and also made one trip to the restroom and one trip to the break room? Count from the moment you approach the building on foot to the moment you leave the building.
5. What makes a visit to the grocery store or to a museum different from visits to other building types in terms of the basic events described in this chapter?
6. What four factors that affect our experiences in buildings were discussed in this chapter? Explain your understanding of them.
7. What five variables affect the way you react to the four factors of Question 6? Explain how they affect your reactions.

Exercises

1. Increasing your awareness of the way the basic events occur in different building types requires consciously thinking about them and analyzing how the built environment contributes to each experience. To get some practice, try dissecting the visits to the following settings in terms of the 11 events discussed in this chapter. You may respond to Exercises 1–3 in either outline or essay format. Check with your instructor for the preferred format.
   A nightclub
   The movies
   The design studio
   The library
   A coffee shop
   The bookstore
2. For the settings mentioned in Exercise 1, analyze potential scenarios related to the occasion, the players, the resources, and the surroundings.
3. For each of the scenarios proposed, analyze possible reactions by you and some of the other players depending on role, affinity, familiarity, demand, and control.

Chapter 3 Interior Place and Its Components

Instructional Objectives

- Understand the concepts of function, space, and place.
- Present and describe the basic components of place.
- Explain the different prominence levels of domains.
- Describe the components of circulation systems: arrival spaces, paths, and nodes.
- Explain the hierarchical nature of paths.
- Explain the role and importance of nodes in interior circulation systems.
- Show and describe various levels of openness of barriers.
- Explain the various levels of invitation provided by different types of connectors.
- Explain the role of project ends in providing a connection to the rest of the world outside the project.
- Explain the role of furnishings as spatial modifiers in interior environments.
- Explain the role of interior landmarks in interior environments.

In the immensity and confusion of the environment, certain portions of space assume the value of place. They are identifiable, can be pointed out by others, and suggest ways of behavior. Some places are intended for our movements and exchanges, others encourage withdrawal and isolation. The place always suggests an action or a pause, even if only mental. Its forms are associated with events which it accommodates or which it has once accommodated, and with other similar places and events.

—*Pierre von Meiss,* Elements of Architecture: From Form to Place

IN CHAPTER 2 WE reviewed the basic events of people's experiences inside buildings and other considerations that affect the building experience. In this chapter we begin to focus on place as the basic unit of interior design. More specifically, we explain the components of projects in terms of place. You will see that there are not too many types of places in buildings when we generalize them into our basic categories.

We first explain the concept of place. Buildings are collections of places, not of functions. The basic components of place are explained as a system we can use to conceptualize projects.

FUNCTION, SPACE, AND PLACE

In design we commonly use the terms *function*, *space*, and *place*. It is important to understand the differences among these three concepts and how they are related. You are most likely familiar with the idea of **function** as used in the environmental design disciplines. It refers to the things people (or animals, plants, or machines) do in a specific environment. These translate to specific arrangements of spaces, furnishings, and equipment, as well as the people within the required spaces. To use an analogy from theater, function involves the actors (users), on a stage (space), using props (furnishings and equipment) to perform certain roles.

Space is all around us. When we design and build projects, we claim space and subdivide it in particular ways to suit the needs of the project. The spaces so defined have specific boundaries, shapes, and dimensions. This act of definition and shaping transforms generic space into the kind of space designers work with: **architectural space**. But designers do more than just define space. These defined spaces are given particular characteristics to suit those specific functions and to reflect the general character of the project. Openings are placed strategically, surfaces are articulated, and sub-areas defined during this process. The resulting environment ceases to be merely architectural space (although it can still be described in terms of boundaries, shapes, dimensions, and so on) and becomes a habitable place.

Of all the space in the theater, the space occupied by the stage has been claimed for the functions performed by the actors. It has some recognizable limits, and the actions of the actors occur on this stage. During a play, the stage scenery portrays distinct places that often change from scene to scene, each having unique physical qualities and related activities. In the interior projects we design, the settings within a particular space generally don't change as much, and defined places tend to have consistent qualities and functions. Thus, the bar in a restaurant or the waiting room in a dental clinic remains distinguishable as a specific and unique place from day to day and from week to week.

Places are recognizable as discrete entities having an identifiable purpose and a particular character. They become recognizable as having limits within which specific events or functions take place. Although the terms *space* and *place* can sometimes be used interchangeably, place tends to describe habitable space more holistically. A place can be composed of several sub-spaces as long as it hangs together as a whole (Figure 3.1).

A project having multiple functions can be shaped in many ways and consist of a collection of places. As a designer, you have a choice of how to break the functions into discrete compartments and how to combine these compartments. Delimitation and differentiation become powerful tools to do so. When these places are

Figure 3.1: A place, like this eating establishment, is a complete existential setting that includes the particular space contained, specific physical qualities, furnishings, actors, and rituals that make it a unique phenomenological entity.

well conceived, clear, and well placed, they create memorable projects.

In this chapter we are not concerned with properties of space such as size, proportion, and geometry. Our intent here is to discuss the generic types of places that occur in interior projects.

BASIC COMPONENTS OF THE ENVIRONMENT (PLACE ELEMENTS)

At the most basic level, interior environments can be reduced to places we visit to do something (destination places) and places that help us get there (circulation systems). The spatial characteristics of these two types of places are defined by their boundaries and the furnishings and other objects within these places. These four components (destination places, circulation systems, boundaries, and furnishings) plus a few others help us establish a useful conceptual framework for designers of interior space.

The group is a combination of Kevin Lynch's five elements of urban imageability,[1] Christian Norberg-Schulz's elements of existential space,[2] and some minor additions that address aspects specific to interiors. Lynch's studies revealed that people make sense of urban surroundings by making mental maps that consistently feature five kinds of elements: districts, paths, nodes, edges, and landmarks. They are defined in the following sections, where they occur. Norberg-Schulz's model of existential space features three core elements: centers, paths, and domains. For an explanation of these, see the capsule on page 43.

Destination Places

Destination places can be categorized as domains or centers, depending on their degree of prominence.

Domains

Domains are recognizable regions or areas. They are analogous to what Lynch called *districts*. Lynch defines districts as "medium to large sections of the city, conceived of as having two-dimensional extent, which the observer mentally enters inside of, and which are recognizable as having some common identifiable character."[3] Norberg-Schulz's concept of domain is better suited for interior spaces because domains don't carry the large area connotations of Lynch's districts. A district is usually some neighborhood (residential or otherwise) with recognizable boundaries and a particular character based on the kind of people who inhabit it and the things they do. You may not be familiar with the neighborhood, but you are likely to have at least some idea about its general extent. In some cases there may be multiple adjacent neighborhoods, and, even if you are not familiar with these neighborhoods, you may have a general idea of where one ends and the next one begins.

The concept is the same for interior projects, although the scale is smaller. The departments in an office or retail store, the units in a healthcare clinic, and the different dining rooms in a large restaurant are all examples of domains in interiors. Domains are the basic destinations in a facility. They usually are the places people go to perform whatever activities they came to do, be it work, shop, or eat.

Centers

Centers are special destination places. The term comes from Norberg-Schulz. Centers are well-known places where particularly meaningful activities and social interactions take place.

Of all the places people visit inside buildings, these are the most special. In public projects, they are usually the places where important group activities happen. Examples of centers include the principal conference room in an office, the main dining hall in a restaurant, and the main lounge of a hotel. These important locations require clear and direct access; in some cases, they even require a ceremonial approach.

Centers are important during planning because they require strategic placement. You should consider their locations before those of other, less important, places. In many projects, users will orient themselves in relation to these centers. Whether they become the great big space at the entrance, the sacred space in the middle, or the prestigious (or mysterious) destination at the end of an important path, centers always demand prominent placement.

Figure 3.2: This room is a center. It is one of the most prestigious spaces of this particular building and is used exclusively for very special events.

Not all projects need centers. It is quite common to find restaurants where all dining areas are of similar importance and retail stores with no dominant departments. It is the relative importance of a domain that makes it a center. Figure 3.2 shows a large and prestigious special events facility that leaves little doubt that it is, indeed, one of the truly special destinations within the building.

Circulation Systems

Circulation systems determine the way you move around a facility. To a great extent, your impressions of a particular interior environment will depend on your experience while moving from place to place through the circulation system. Here we distinguish among three basic components of these systems: arrival space, the paths, and nodes.

Arrival Space

At the city scale there are usually many access points, but in buildings and their interiors, there is usually only one main entrance. This makes it much easier to control the first impression of visitors.

The **arrival space** serves to make an initial overall impression on the visitor and also serves as a departure point to the rest of the facility. It is often the place where visitors stop and get directions on how to reach their

CAPSULE | Place Elements Help Conceptualize the Renovation of a Cultural Center

The *place elements* can be powerful tools to organize space and generate design strategies. They give us a basis for making decisions about the distribution of space and the nature of the separations and connections between them. The following is an example of how a student utilized them throughout the design process to develop a design for a cultural center project.

The initial analysis (Figure C3.1) of the place elements presented observations such as no sense of arrival, no landmarks or nodes, and destination spaces need to be defined.

Next, the designer developed a proposal that clearly defined the destination spaces and paths, and called them *destination spaces* and *paths* (although other common terms can also be used). Furthermore, she developed thoughtful nodes, focal points, and carefully located a few special objects that display jewelry (Figure C3.2).

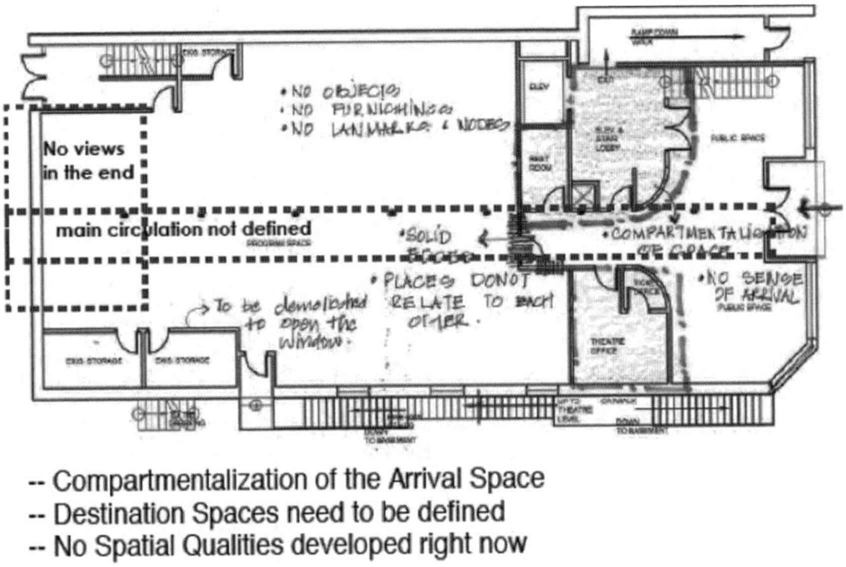

Figure C3.1: Site analysis diagram

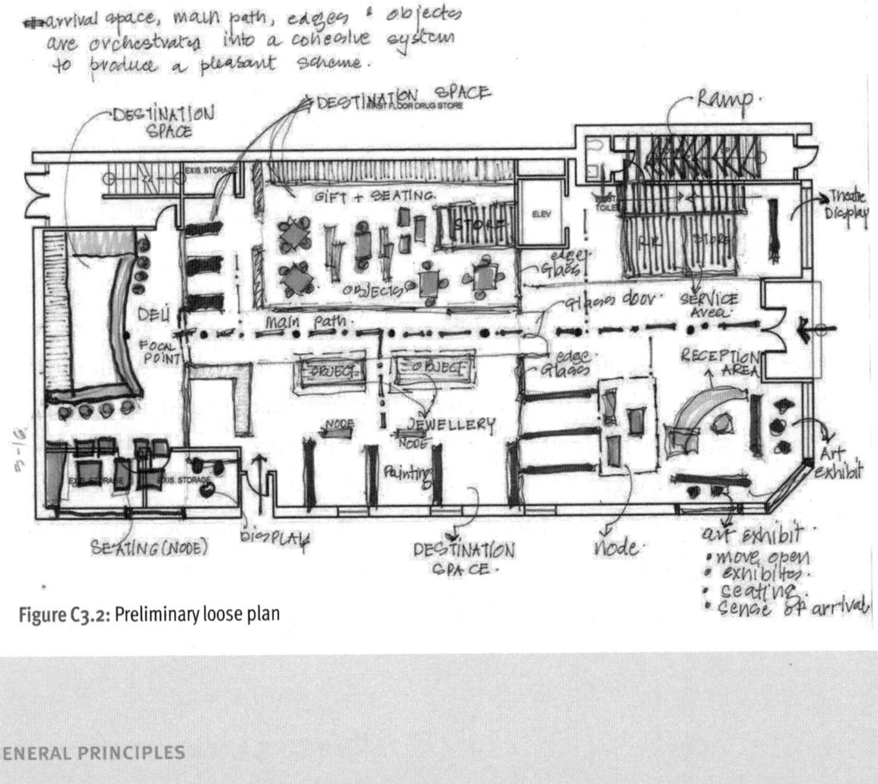

Figure C3.2: Preliminary loose plan

The final plan was then fully developed while maintaining the place elements as conceptual organizers. In the final presentation, the designer highlights the main path, the various destination places, nodes, and the main boundaries (Figure C3.3). Figures C3.4 and C3.5 show two elevations illustrating the final design.

The designer of this project, Tina Patel, was able to leverage the place elements as a useful collection of conceptual elements that help designers make decisions about placement, space definition, strategic positioning, and other functional and experiential factors.

(Courtesy of Tina Patel)

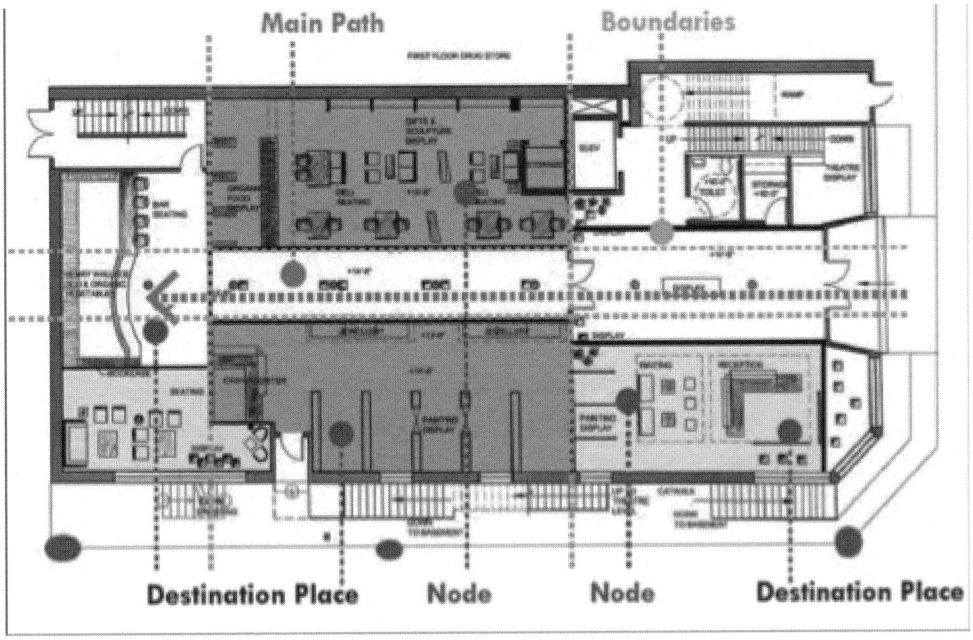

Figure C3.3: Final space plan

Figure C3.4: Elevation of retail area

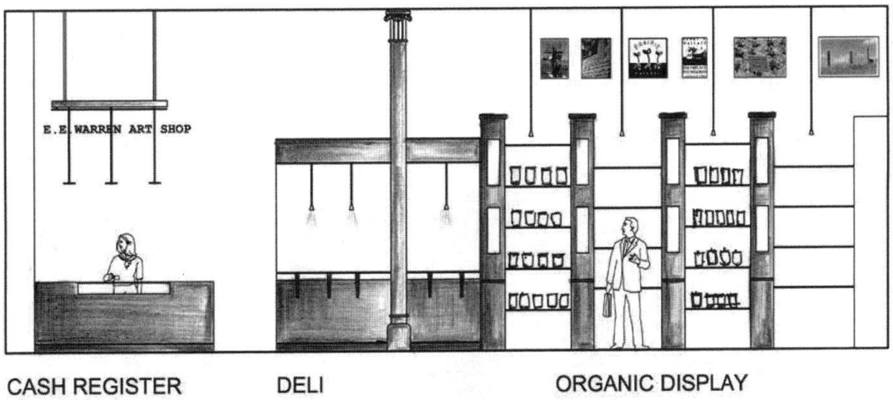

Figure C3.5: Elevation of art shop

Figure 3.3: This reception area is the arrival space of an office facility. It serves as a transition between the outside and what lies beyond within the facility.

destination within the building or project. Its importance and potential are enormous. Figure 3.3 shows the reception area of an office facility, very often the arrival space to such office suites. Figure 3.4 shows the arrival space to an academic building, although in this case there is no control function like the reception desk in Figure 3.3.

Arrivals represent transitions between the inside and outside of the project. There are circulation decisions to make regarding these locations, which often produce a state of heightened awareness.

Paths

Paths are the channels of movement that we use to get around. Lynch defines them as the "channels along which the observer customarily, occasionally, or potentially moves."[4] Paths connect spaces, allowing users to get from one to another. They can be autonomous paths occurring outside the areas they serve or integrated paths occurring within the spaces they serve. Figure 3.5a–c shows examples of different paths.

Figure 3.4: Some arrival spaces, such as this one, are relatively informal, without checkpoints. Notice, however, how the special decorative treatments at the ceiling help to define this as a location of above-average importance.

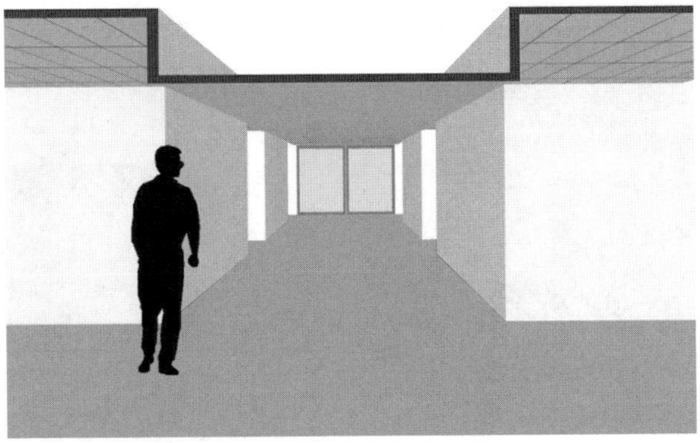

(a)

(b)

(c)

Figure 3.5: The degree of explicitness of a path can vary. It can be very explicit (a), clear but unaccented (b), or rather loose and ambiguous (c).

Not only do paths allow us to move to our destination, but they are also the vantage points from which we perceive the totality of a project, its spaces, and their sequences. So important was this secondary perceptual function for Swiss architect Le Corbusier that he developed the notion of **promenade architecturale**,[5] a carefully orchestrated route that revealed a building's spaces and their overall organization.

Paths are the heart of the circulation system. Although the circulation system refers to the total system of movement within a building or project, a path refers to a specific segment having specific characteristics.

Paths are hierarchical. Not all paths move as many people or share the same degree of importance. Just as with the circulation systems in the city where there are avenues, streets, and alleys, there are also different levels of circulation in interiors.

Main Paths Main paths define the main overall circulation system and get us to prominent destinations. They, like avenues, tend to be the most public thoroughfares for movement, the channels through which visitors move. As such, they not only get people to their destinations but also provide visual and other types of sensory experiences that make important impressions on users. Figure 3.6 shows an example of a main path in a prominent public area of an academic building.

Figure 3.6: This segment of a main path in an academic building is given prominence by its generous volume, articulated forms, crafted details, and elegant materials.

Main paths are important contributors to the perceptions people form of built environments. It is while moving through and looking from them that visitors collect impressions of facilities and their people. A main path's shape, proportion, degree of openness, level of detail, and number of events will communicate in important ways with users and visitors alike. Figure 3.7 shows a main path in a conferencing facility.

Figure 3.7: This is a main path in an institutional building. Carefully detailed, what sets it apart from other paths in the building is its generous and inviting width.

Secondary Paths Secondary paths are equivalent to the streets and alleys of our cities. In interiors, they are often narrower and less formal than the main paths. They tend to be more utilitarian, although there is no reason they cannot be experientially rewarding routes.

Distinguishing between main and secondary paths and designing spaces that physically show the difference between the two will produce clearer, easier-to-navigate projects.

Figure 3.8: Accessible seating nooks like this one provide a place to step off the main path and have a place to do some work or simply chat with coworkers.

Figure 3.9: Paths converging in a powerful and expanded center create a major node in this educational building.

Paths can be straight, curved, segmented, undulating, or any combination of these. Paths can also be combined in many ways. They can join as well as intersect.

A special component of a path is the occasional nook or zone off to the side or at the end of the corridor where users are encouraged to step aside to converse with others informally or get away temporarily (Figure 3.8).

Nodes

Nodes are areas of heightened activity along a circulation route. Nodes are not the paths themselves but, rather, special places along the paths. Lynch explains that they can be junctions, like a convergence of paths, or concentrations, like an enclosed square. Nodes can occur at significant intersections, off to one side along the route, or at end points. Space usually expands at these locations, and, often, one or more people-gathering places help to activate the area. In an urban neighborhood it may be an intersection with a coffee shop, a bakery, a convenience store, and a post office. In an office it may be a junction where conference rooms, a break room, and the mailroom converge, thus attracting people and fostering vitality.

The distinction between nodes and centers is helpful for design purposes. Centers are the principal domains. Nodes are in-between places where paths and strategic magnet destinations converge. A node may also be created by a combination of an intersection where space expands and well-integrated places to sit surrounding the intersection, such as the one shown in Figure 3.9, where horizontal and vertical circulation converge and expand to create a powerful node in a public circulation area.

Nodes provide relief, encourage social contact, accentuate transitions and entrances, and create memorable spaces along the way. Like paths, they are important components that contribute to order, enrichment, and expression. The architectural program given during the early stages of a project is not likely to ask for any nodes. Nodes happen because designers make them happen. They are strategically conceived and placed to create vital spaces which afford human connections and interaction (Figure 3.10).

A well-orchestrated mix of domains and paths, nooks and pockets along the paths, and well-placed nodes enhances the clarity and experiential appeal of interior projects. An interior space system consisting of just domains and undifferentiated paths lacks those qualities. Figure 3.11a shows a diagram of a hypothetical project expressed in terms of undifferentiated domains and paths. Figure 3.11b shows the same space, but this time centers, main circulation segments, and nodes are included. Notice how the clarity and general appeal of the project, even as seen as a plan diagram, are enhanced by the addition of hierarchy.

Figure 3.10: Nodes often happen at intersections and have magnet services, such as the mailboxes in this example, and other amenities to bring people together and encourage them to say for a while.

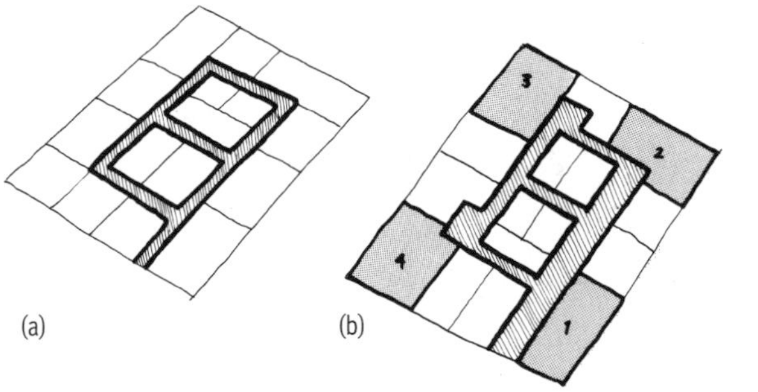

Figure 3.11: Projects without differentiation (a) are confusing and seldom memorable. The differentiation between domains and centers and between main and secondary paths, together with the addition of alcoves and nodes along the circulation route (b) greatly enhance the clarity and memorability of a project.

Boundaries

Boundaries serve as architectural elements that help determine how places are connected or segregated from one another. We present three elements related to boundaries: edges, connectors, and ends. Although edges are the only one of these addressed by either Lynch or Norberg-Schulz, connectors and ends are important basic elements and deserve special attention.

Edges

Edges, according to Lynch, are boundaries between two places. They can be more or less penetrable barriers, closing off one region from another, or seams, relating and joining two regions.[6]

After a decision has been made to have two places adjacent to each other, one has to think about the desired degree of physical separation between them (i.e., the nature of the barrier). The same is true between paths and adjacent spaces. We rely on barriers to separate adjacent spaces. Between the extremes of a full barrier or no barrier are other levels of potential separation. We could conveniently categorize the possibilities into four levels of barriers: solid, mostly solid, mostly open, and open. Totally solid and totally open boundaries are straightforward and easy to visualize. The in-between categories are varied and full of possibilities.

Mostly solid barriers have some openings that provide visual, auditory, haptic, and physical connection between one space and the next, but the solid portion dominates. Examples include a full-length partial-height wall; a partial-length full-height wall; and a full-length

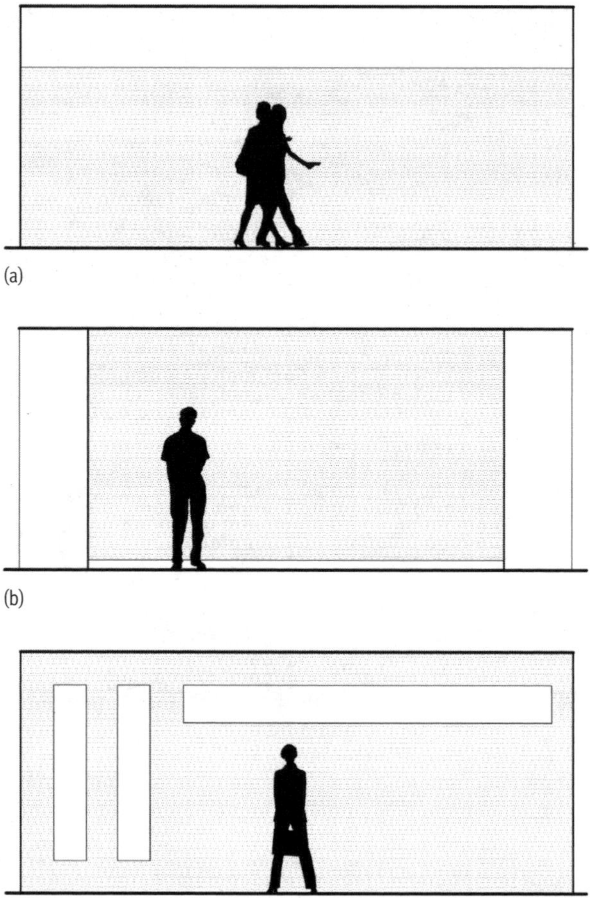

(a)

(b)

(c)

Figure 3.12: Mostly solid barriers come in many configurations. In these three examples, note that the solid area (shaded) is greater than the open area.

full-height wall with a few punched openings. Figure 3.12 shows elevation views of these examples.

With mostly open barriers the ratios are inverted and the open portions dominate. Examples include anything from a colonnade to examples similar to the ones in Figure 3.12, but with larger open areas. Figure 3.13 shows some examples.

Glass is a unique material that is hard to classify. Although it is a solid material it allows light to penetrate from one space to the next, and clear glass allows one to see through from one space to the next. There are many types of glass products available with various degrees of opacity allowing designers to create the desired level of transparency to fit the occasion.

Depending on their number, size, and configuration, barriers can have immense effects on how much of the visual field is disclosed at one time, thus influencing our sense of order and orientation. They can also enrich projects by contributing to the sense of drama as one moves about the project. A special kind of edge occurs at the limits of a project's allotted space. These are the boundaries within which you design a given office, store, or restaurant. Ends along the perimeter of a project are significant because they dictate the limits of your space and the type of relationship with adjacent spaces. In an office building, the outside walls are ends that relate to the exterior

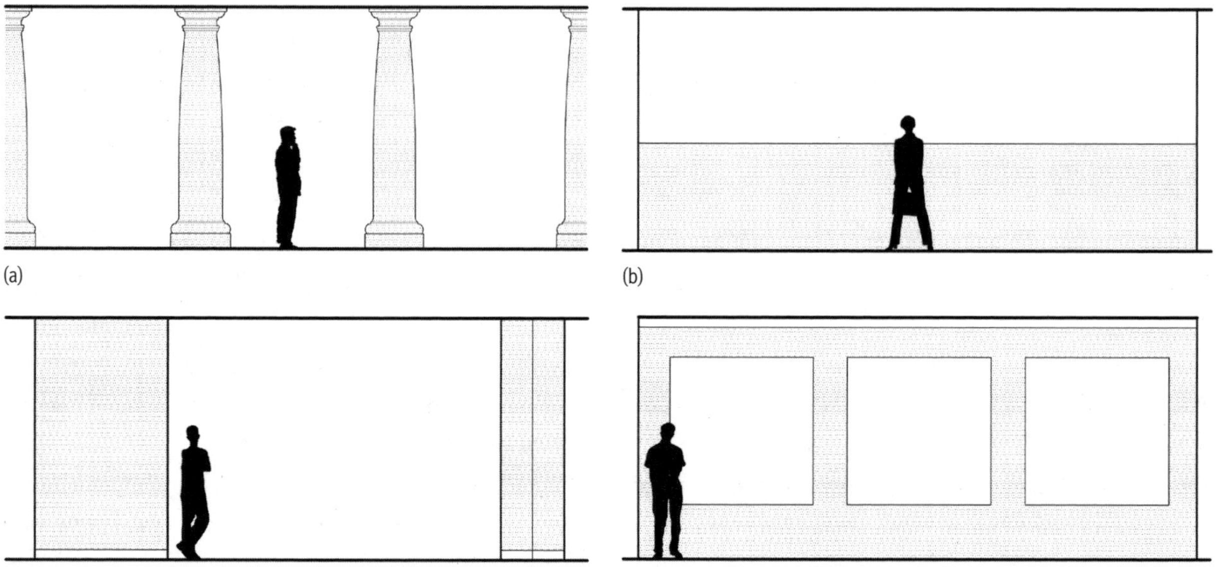

(a)

(b)

(c)

(d)

Figure 3.13: Mostly open barriers also come in many configurations. In these four examples, the amount of openness and connection to adjacent spaces is more than half of the barrier's area.

Figure 3.14: Ends can become special, as shown in this example of an informal and bright sitting area with views to the exterior.

context and are thus important. Exposure to views, the sun path, or important visual or symbolic elements outside rely on the proper placement of spaces in relation to these edges. Figure 3.14 shows an exterior edge made usable with seating and pleasant views to the outdoors. Similarly, whereas the exterior edge of an intimate—and therefore introverted—restaurant may not be that important, the opposite is true at a sidewalk cafe, where an important goal is to connect with street activity. For a retail store, for instance, it is important to use the main front edge, such as the storefront in Figure 3.15, to entice potential buyers to come inside.

Boundary edges facing the outdoors are important in providing a sense of orientation. They also provide daylight and views, important stimulators and enhancers.

Connectors

Contrary to the idea of barrier is that of access. The points of connection between adjacent spaces are important

Figure 3.15: An important end boundary of a retail store is its front. A generous and inviting gateway and a mostly transparent front dissolve the barrier, revealing the merchandise to lure shoppers inside.

determinants of the character and flow of those spaces. Options range from the well-known (and often overused) doorway to full-width openings between spaces. Here, we distinguish between formal openings and less formal passages, each with a multitude of variations. Formal openings read as formal access points and invite movement between spaces, while passageways allow movement between spaces in looser, less formal ways.

Gateway formal opening is a clearly defined point of entry. The most common one is the doorway. A formal opening can be a grand entryway but it can also be an ordinary point of access.

Ordinary entryways have single or double doors or cased openings of comparable size that invite us to enter. We are all familiar with these. Grand entryways are more formal and monumental. They are unmistakable and draw you in and are usually reserved for prominent destinations. The size of the door and frame as well as the size of the surrounding casing and the depth of the passage all contribute to their grandiosity. In interiors, grand entryways often consist of a specially detailed door or opening, usually oversized, and often placed in an extra-deep cavity. Figure 3.16 shows two examples of grand entryways in interiors.

Informal passageways are not framed openings like the ones just discussed. They can be either tunnel-like adjoining passages between spaces or merely openings in the wall that allow movement between spaces. In the first case, they invite movement; in the second, they allow

(a)

(b)

Figure 3.16: The generous arched entryway (a) is an example of an inviting grand gateway. Retail stores usually feature inviting grand gateways (b) to lure outsiders in.

it. Many modern interiors rely on wide passageways as a way to move between spaces. Openings allow movement between spaces, but the user relies on other directional cues from the furnishings or other objects to know which way to go. Figure 3.17 shows an example: Notice how it connects and invites in a casual way without doors or cased openings.

Connectors contribute much to a project's sense of order, enrichment, and expression. Their placement controls patterns of movement and the exact points of entry to the different parts of a project, affecting both our senses of orientation and stimulation. Their placement and detail also communicate certain types of expression and can contribute enriching qualities.

Furnishings

We will now inspect the role of furnishings and other objects in the orchestration of place. Under the general term **furnishings** we refer to fixtures, furniture pieces, and equipment of sufficient size to influence the experience of space. Designers of interiors often rely heavily on these to choreograph the interior experience; therefore, they represent an important category among our place element groups.

Examples of influential furnishings are freestanding fixtures or display cases in stores, tables in restaurants, and systems furniture in open office spaces. These types

Figure 3.17: Passageways informally allow users to go through to the space beyond, without formal doors or framed gateways.

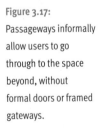

CAPSULE | A Phenomenological View of Place and Dwelling

Scholars in the design disciplines have pursued diverse avenues in search of a better understanding of the built environment. One notable scholar who has contributed much to our understanding of the significance of the man-made environment is Christian Norberg-Schulz. His primary aim, he explains, has been "to investigate the psychic implications of architecture rather than its practical side."[1] Norberg-Schulz has pursued architectural insights from every angle possible. After initial attempts to analyze art and architecture scientifically, he turned to other methods. Although a believer in the contributions of scientific methods, he found them limiting, noting that "when we treat architecture analytically, we miss the concrete environmental character, that is, the very quality that is the object of man's identification."[2] His diverse explorations into the minds of artists, philosophers, historians, and psychologists led him to phenomenology as a vehicle for architectural inquiry. It provided a mode of inquiry compatible with his desire to study architecture as a concrete phenomenon.

Phenomenology is an approach within the field of philosophy initiated by Edmund Husserl as a reaction to what he perceived as modern science's incapacity to help us understand the concrete "life-world." As Norberg-Schulz puts it, "the life-world does not consist of sensations, but is immediately given as a world of characteristic, meaningful things, which do not have to be 'constructed' through individual experience."[3] He further explains: "Phenomenology was conceived as a 'return to things,' as opposed to abstractions and mental constructions."[4] Encouraged by the potential contributions of phenomenology to architectural thinking, he embarked on the mission of developing a phenomenology of architecture.

Much of Norberg-Schulz's efforts have focused on the topics of place and dwelling. In the text that follows, we summarize some of his thinking on these topics to give you a sample of his views.

Place

> The place is the concrete manifestation of man's dwelling, and his identity depends on his belonging to places . . . [by place] we mean something more than abstract location. We mean a totality made up of concrete things having material substance, shape, texture and colour. Together these things determine an "environmental character," which is the essence of place. . . . A place is therefore a qualitative, "total" phenomenon, which we cannot reduce to any of its properties, such as spatial relationships, without losing its concrete nature out of sight.[5]

Because of their qualitative nature and levels of complexity, Norberg-Schulz believes places cannot be properly described by methods that rely on abstractions of concrete phenomena to arrive at neutral, objective knowledge. Lost by such approaches "is the everyday life-world, which ought to be the real concern of man in general, and planners and architects in particular."[6]

Places have a specific concrete presence. They can be either natural or man-made and are experienced as environments having a particular set of qualities, that is, particular characters. Concentration and enclosure are the properties of man-made places, be they cities, towns, or individual buildings. At any of their scales, man-made places are collections of things grouped together and somehow bound. Norberg-Schulz analyzes them in terms of "space" and "character." Space refers to the three-dimensional organization of the elements that make up place. He looks at space not as a mathematical concept but as an existential dimension. Character refers to the general atmosphere of a place. While spatial organizations may have different characters, space and character operate as a unit, and specific spatial organizations limit the possible characterizations within them.

The elements of existential place are center, path, and domain. At the heart of the notion of place is the center. The ultimate environmental center is the home, the center of each individual's personal world. Centers are known places where meaningful activities and social interactions take place. They are both the goals toward which people move and the points of departure from which they orient themselves in relation to the rest of the environment.

Beyond the home, other places become centers in our lives. Friends' houses and the meaningful public buildings

continued

of our lives, such as school, community center, and church, become centers. At different scales, certain specific rooms and spots within those buildings also become centers. Regardless of scale, a center, because it is a place, has recognizable limits. There is a definite sense of inside and outside defined by a physical or symbolic boundary between here and there.

The next basic property of human existence is the path. Any center, or place, exists within a context, never in isolation. As such, a place is physically related to the rest of the world around it. Thus, starting from the very center of a place, we can identify directions such as up and down and left and right. As Norberg-Schulz explains, "the simplest model of man's existential space is, therefore, a horizontal plane pierced by a vertical axis. But on the plane man chooses and creates paths which give his existential space a more particular structure."[7] The path connects the known with the unknown, and its presence sets in motion a cycle of departure and return. Contrary to the center, which is static and contained, the path is continuous and dynamic. Paths represent a direction to follow toward a goal, but, as Norberg-Schulz explains, "during the journey events happen and the path is also experienced as having a character of its own. What happens along the way, thus, is added to the tension created by the goal to be reached and the point of departure left behind."[8]

The last basic property of existential space is the domain. As we travel regularly along the same path toward a meaningful destination, the areas we pass on either side become somewhat well known, even if we don't enter them directly. Norberg-Schulz calls these areas domains and distinguishes them from the areas beyond them, the real unknown. Domains are not just the "everything else," but are distinct from one another and identifiable because of their boundaries or some other unifying characteristic, such as grouping of parts or common visual characteristics. The difference between domains and centers is that each person belongs in certain centers, and, therefore, these become his or her particular, personal goals. Despite the cohesiveness they may enjoy, domains are not destinations or goals, although they might very well be for someone else. For us, domains are "relatively unstructured 'ground' on which places and paths appear as more pronounced 'figures.'"[9]

Places, paths, and domains form the basic schemata for man's orientation and, thus, according to Norberg-Schulz's view, constitute the elements of existential space. Depending on where we find ourselves, a certain environment may be dominated by one or another of these three properties. The experience of driving toward a familiar destination may be dominated by paths and domains. Then, all of a sudden, we enter familiar and meaningful territory, and the experience gets transformed into a progression of centers at different scales, starting with the entrance into the familiar neighborhood and culminating with the final arrival at the dinner table.

The elements of existential space exist at different levels. The first and smallest level is determined by the hand and what it can grasp. It is the level of small things and objects. The next level is determined by the body. It is the level of the furniture on which we can sit, recline, or lie down. The third level is the house, or individual building, which allows movement and comprises defined territories. Beyond these, and less useful for the purposes of people concerned with interiors, are the urban, landscape, and regional levels.

The levels of house (meaning also familiar individual buildings) and things are the most relevant to the designer of interiors. The house represents the very center of human existence. It gives man a place to be, a place in which to stay and spend time in safety and comfort. Within it, of course, there are also rooms, each a place having a unique character. As we get into the smaller objects of life, the furnishings and other items of our lives, we get into objects of very precise forms that we come to know intimately. These are the objects with which our hands and bodies come into the most intimate contact. The fireplace, the dinner table, the bed, and even the chest of drawers become true foci in our lives and are known in the most direct ways. In fact, it is the progressively smaller levels of the hierarchy that give the larger ones their character. Thus, the character of the neighborhood is determined largely by its buildings, the character of the buildings by their details and objects, and so on.

Dwelling

By tracing its linguistic evolution, Heidegger uncovered the meanings associated with the word *dwell*. Combining these meanings, he defined dwelling as "to be at peace in a protected place."[10] To this, Norberg-Schulz adds some linguistic derivations of his own and adds that through dwelling, the life-world becomes habitual and "known." He goes on to distinguish among four modes of dwelling related to their scale, level of development, and how collective or individual the interactions occurring within are. The four modes are natural dwelling, collective dwelling, public dwelling, and private dwelling. For our purposes, the last two are the most significant. Public dwelling occurs within a community with shared common values and beliefs, such as the employees of a given company. In fact, it usually takes place in a public building. Private dwelling refers to the private and personal kind of dwelling required to develop one's individual identity. It finds its most pure expression in the home.

True dwelling requires a meaningful relationship between a person and a given environment. In other words, one has to establish a meaningful relationship with both the space and the character aspects of the given place. Where a person is and how he or she is in a given place have to be understood. Norberg-Schulz labels these two required psychological functions orientation and identification. "To gain an existential foothold," he explains, "man needs to orientate himself . . . he also has to identify himself with the environment."[11] Orientation is concerned with the spatial relationship of things, while identification is concerned with the qualities of places. The two are always present, although they don't necessarily have to correspond. In other words, it is possible to feel oriented in a place and not identify with it, and vice versa.

Orientation ties directly to our previous discussion of the three properties or elements of existential space: centers, paths, and domains. The designer's task becomes to translate these into physical form in a way that produces a good environmental image likely to facilitate the process of feeling oriented. For this, Norberg-Schulz uses Kevin Lynch's influential ideas on environmental imaging and his concepts of districts, paths, nodes, edges, and landmarks, which work nicely with the existential space concepts of center, path, and domain. The place elements introduced in this chapter, in fact, are a combination of the concepts from both Lynch and Norberg-Schulz.

Perhaps more important than orientation is the function of identification with a given environment. Identification means to relate meaningfully, to truly belong. It requires proper correspondence between the interior and exterior worlds of the individual, where the environment embodies aspects of existence meaningful to the person. This is the aspect that Norberg-Schulz feels has not been given proper attention in modern society, where "attention has almost exclusively been concentrated on the 'practical' function of orientation, whereas identification has been left to chance."[12] Proper dwelling requires the proper alignment of interior self, body, and exterior world. The interaction between internal and external things can be tricky to decipher. Norberg-Schulz believes that the identities of man and environment feed off each other. He explains: "Identity . . . consists in an interiorization of understood things, and . . . growing up therefore depends on being open to what surrounds us. Although the world is immediately given, it has to be interpreted and understood, and although man is part of the world, he has to concretize his belonging to feel at home."[13]

1. Norberg-Schulz, C. (1980). *Genius loci: Towards a phenomenology of architecture.* New York: Rizzoli.
2. Ibid.
3. Norberg-Schulz, C. (1985). *The concept of dwelling.* New York: Rizzoli.
4. Norberg-Schulz, 1980, p. 8.
5. Ibid.
6. Ibid.
7. Norberg-Schulz, C. (1971). *Existence, space, and architecture.* New York: Praeger.
8. Ibid.
9. Ibid.
10. Norberg-Schulz, 1980, p. 22.
11. Ibid.
12. Ibid.
13. Ibid.

of furnishings tend to work more as space modifiers than space creators except in cases where they are tall enough to provide a real sense of enclosure. In these cases they have an effect on the visual lines of a space and become important screening devices; their placement becomes critical, and a tug-of-war between placement for function and placement for effect is common.

Other than their important functional contributions for seating, working, and storage, one of the main attributes of furnishings in interior environments is how their placement affects the use of space and controls movement. The placement of furnishings dictates which areas of the floor remain open for human occupation and circulation. Figure 3.18 shows six different furniture arrangements in a simple waiting space and the resulting use patterns.

The way furnishings are grouped can also contribute to the definition of place. A group of furnishings can help define regions and, when used repetitively, can contribute a sense of continuity and rhythm (Figure 3.19). Furnishings can also have a strong effect on the general density of a space. Depending on their size, number, and spacing, they can produce various effects, from spare to crowded. In Figure 3.20, the furnishings have a major impact on the use and overall density of the respective spaces. The tall office cubicle panels in Figure 3.21 act as walls, defining the corridor strongly and reducing the sense of clutter, since the desks on the other side are hidden.

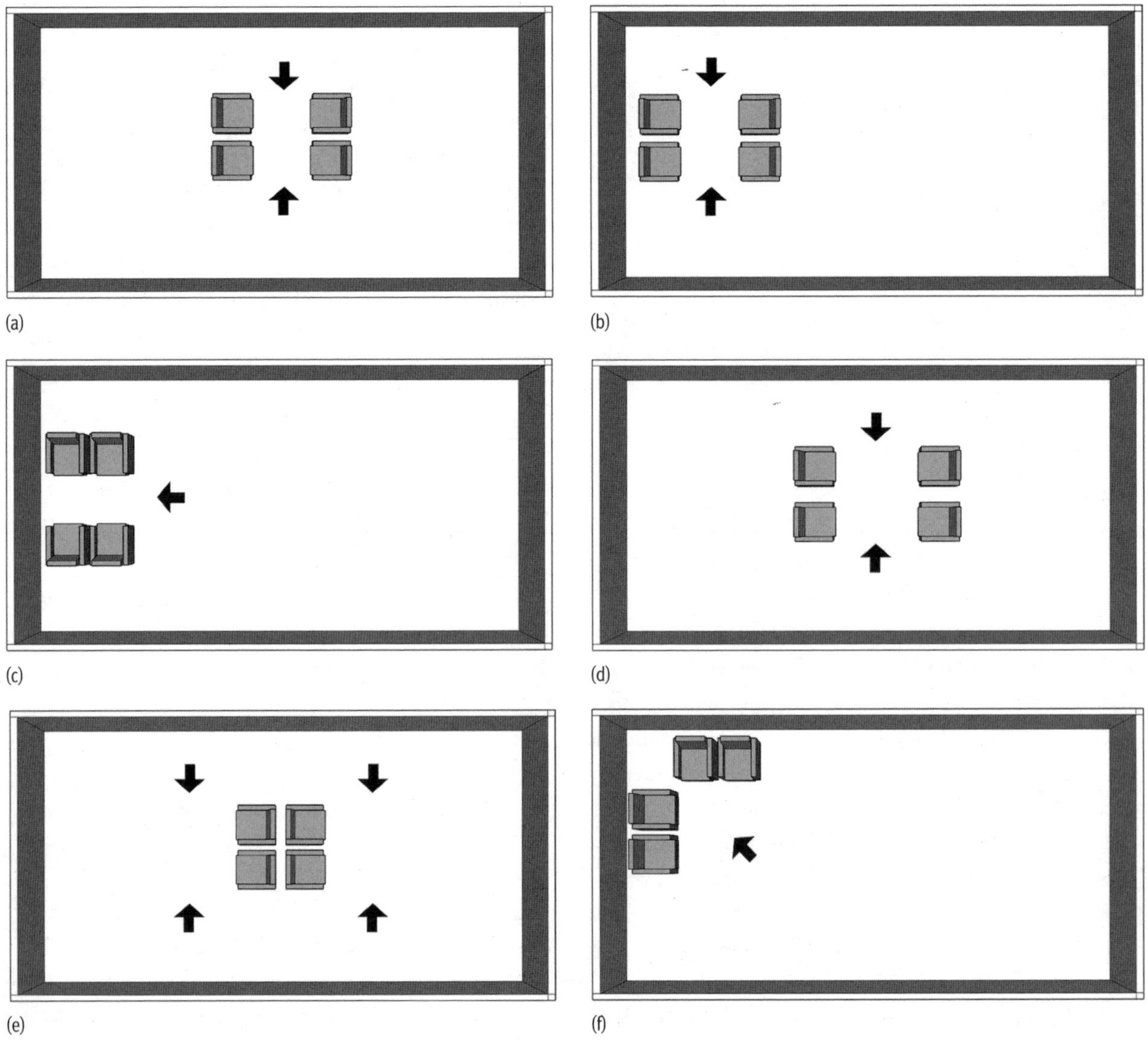

Figure 3.18: The number, placement, and arrangement of furnishings have important effects on the resulting use patterns of a space, as illustrated by these six simple scenarios.

Figure 3.19: This furniture arrangement complements the overall effect of the waiting area, defining two very distinct seating areas that become focal points in the space.

Figure 3.20: The high density of the workstations and medium-height panels are two of the principal factors that give this work area its spatial character.

Figure 3.21: The high furniture panels act like walls in this tall space, hiding the work areas behind them.

In addition to their specific functions, furnishings also contribute to order, enhanced experience, and expression. The paths dictated by their arrangement affect our experiences as we move around them. The degrees of balance and harmony in their layout greatly influence the project's sense of order. Their style helps define the project's expression.

Landmarks

Lynch defines **landmarks** as "simply defined physical object[s]. Their use involves the singling out of one element from a host of possibilities."[7] Their key physical characteristic is singularity, some aspect that is unique or memorable. Landmarks are more clearly identifiable if they have a clear form, if they stand out against their background, and if there is some prominence of location and/or scale. An example in an urban setting would be a statue or sculptural water feature at the center of a plaza. At the scale of interior space we rarely encounter the plazas with memorable monuments or the distinctive high-rise buildings that frequently become the landmarks at the city scale. The designer of interiors relies on other, less grandiose, types of landmarks. Possibilities include special features such as accent walls, art pieces, and special displays. Although typically more modest than their urban counterparts, interior landmarks stand out and are remembered. Like landmarks in cities, they are the kind of prominent and recognizable features you are likely to use as reference when you tell a friend to meet you by the sculpture, or by the pink wall, or by the information kiosk.

Landmarks are dominant focal points, and they give people points of reference around which to get oriented and contribute to both the experience and sense of expression of a space. Landmarks can be especially effective if they can be seen from multiple locations and if they occur at key intersections of a project. Figure 3.22a–b shows two examples of interior landmarks: a prominent statue in a lobby area and a magnificent stained-glass window in a library.

Landmarks, like nodes, mark important locations of projects. As such, they contribute much to order and orientation. Whether seen from a distance as goals to move toward, or discovered unexpectedly as surprises, they can serve to enhance users' experiences. Furthermore, their specific character and form contribute to the expressive qualities of a project.

(a)

(b)

Figure 3.22: Statues and prominent sculptures, so effective as outdoor landmarks, are also highly effective inside (a). Two-dimensional artwork, in this case an oversized stained-glass window that takes the entire wall, can also be memorable and, thus, effective as a landmark (b).

REVIEW

Summary

More than a collection of spaces, the interior environments you design are collections of places. Although the parts and elements of a project are always numerous, there are only a few basic components of place. Being aware of these will help you conceptualize settings more effectively.

The main activity of interior environments usually occurs in their destination places. Most of these are what we call domains. Centers are domains of special importance by virtue of their functional or symbolic prominence. Circulation systems provide networks of movement to get to the destination places. These include the project's arrival space, the network of paths to move around the facility (main paths and secondary paths), and nodes. Nodes are special locations along paths or at their intersections that incorporate magnets to attract people and increase vitality.

Projects, their places, and paths are confined and defined by boundaries. These include edges, barriers, and connectors between spaces. Barriers provide separation, connectors yield passage between areas. These can be formal and strongly defined gateways or informal and less defined passageways.

Interior places contain objects of different kinds. Furnishings are important functionally and spatially. The number, size, and placement of large pieces of furniture, fixtures, and equipment have a major impact on interior space and how it is perceived. Landmarks are prominent objects that usually occur in special locations of a project. These can be pieces of artwork or prominent building elements or fixtures. Their main attribute is singularity. They stand out and are remembered.

1. Lynch, K. (1960). *The image of the city*. Cambridge, MA: MIT Press.
2. Norberg-Schulz, C. (1971). *Existence, space and architecture*. New York: Praeger.
3. Lynch, 1960, p. 47.
4. Ibid.
5. Leupen, B., Grafe, C., Köining, N., Lampe, M., & de Zeeuw, P. (1997). *Design and analysis*. New York: Van Nostrand Reinhold.
6. Lynch, 1960, p. 47.
7. Ibid.

Chapter Questions

1. Think of important buildings in your life, past and present. What special domains can you recall? Can you recall special nodes along the circulation system? Describe them.
2. How would you introduce nodes in an office project? How about in an educational setting or clinic?
3. Try to recall some prominent, main interior paths. Were they appropriate for the occasion? Describe them.
4. What memorable arrival spaces have you experienced? What made them good or memorable?
5. How would you make a secondary path experientially rich? Could you do it without spending too much money?
6. Can you recall successful partially open barriers? Describe them.
7. Where would you use a partially solid barrier?
8. Where would you use a partially open barrier?
9. Recall and describe grand gateways you have experienced.
10. Can you describe effective passageways that invited passage without demanding it?
11. Can you describe effective passageways that didn't necessarily invite passage but allowed it?
12. Recall and describe successful transparent project edges you have seen.
13. Can you recall projects with tall furnishings that created a corridor-like effect as you moved between them? Describe them.
14. Can you recall instances where the furnishings enhanced or disturbed order due to their level of density or the level of order or disorder of the smaller objects placed on them? Describe them.
15. Describe interior landmarks you have seen. How are they effective? How are they memorable?
16. In what ways, which have not already been mentioned, would you create interior landmarks?
17. Diagram your current academic building in terms of the place components covered in this chapter.

CHAPTER 4
THE BASICS OF SPACE

INSTRUCTIONAL OBJECTIVES

- Explain different ways to define space.
- Present how spaces can occur in hierarchical fashion.
- Introduce the concepts of containment and encapsulation.
- Explain the effect of openings and edges on enclosure.
- Explain the role of edges on the definition of positive and negative space.
- Present four room-size scales useful for interior design.
- Describe five basic geometric forms used in interior spaces.
- Present different approaches to manipulate spatial form.
- Explain the concept of disclosure in design.
- Describe basic approaches to the design of circulation systems.
- Present basic types of path-to-space and space-to-space relationships.
- Present basic organization systems for interior projects.
- Present four basic spatial approaches commonly used in interior projects.

Everyone who has thought even casually about the subject knows that the specific property of architecture—the feature distinguishing it from all other forms of art—consists in its working with a three-dimensional vocabulary which includes man. Painting functions in two dimensions, even if it can suggest three or four. Sculpture works in three dimensions, but man remains apart, looking on from the outside. Architecture, however, is like a great hollowed-out sculpture which man enters and apprehends by moving about within it.

—*Bruno Zevi,* Architecture as Space: How to Look at Architecture

CHAPTER 3 WAS DEVOTED to the idea of environments as collections of places. We addressed the relationships among the concepts of function, space, and place and introduced the elements of place. These elements were discussed in terms of their role and significance, without elaborating on specifics concerning the treatment and manipulation of spaces. This chapter focuses on fundamental aspects of space. The aim is to learn to define and manipulate both individual spaces and systems of spaces.

A key to the success of a project is the proper arrangement of its parts according to function and hierarchy. It is also necessary to properly manipulate individual spaces to make them come alive and have engaging effects. The manipulation of a space involves the control of its shape, size, degree of enclosure, and relationship to other spaces. Possibilities increase with the designer's level of knowledge and skill. The more you know about the properties of spaces and ways to manipulate these properties to create specific effects, the better equipped you'll be to enrich the experience of users in your projects.

The spatial response to interior design projects varies widely. Decisions about the subdivision, placement, and composition of spaces respond primarily to the basic functional requirements of the project. A customer service office facility intended for the handling of telephone inquiries will require different spaces than, say, an accounting firm. The customer service facility will require large open spaces furnished with clusters of small cubicles where workers can receive calls from customers. The accounting firm, in turn, will need many private offices where accountants can work privately with a high degree of concentration.

In the two previous examples, the ratio of enclosed space to open space will be very different, the accounting office having a far greater area of enclosed space. Suppose the accounting firm has a floor devoted to training consisting of several large training rooms. This would also result in a high enclosed-to-open-space ratio. Yet, even if the total ratio of enclosed to open space was similar, the nature of their arrangement would be different. The training floor would consist of a few large rooms with easy public access, while the typical office floor would consist of many small private rooms.

Whether a project is more or less open, more or less rigid, or more or less innovative will depend greatly on its own set of circumstances. It is up to the designer to understand these and determine what type of arrangement is most responsive to the particular set of requirements at hand. In all these cases, it is the project that suggests the appropriate organization and treatment of spaces. A designer must be able to interpret the needs of the project and know how to shape and manipulate space.

In this chapter, we look at individual spaces and their spatial properties first. Then we look at some basic relationships between adjacent spaces and, finally, spatial organizations for entire projects. For much of the information contained here we are indebted to the contributions of previous authors who have tackled the subject of architectural space, particularly Francis Ching,[1] whose work has clarified its many manifestations.

PROPERTIES OF INDIVIDUAL SPACES

We will devote the first parts of this chapter to the examination of the issues of spatial definition, enclosure, size, form, permeability, and mobility in individual spaces.

Spatial Definition

Space, whether claimed (as a spot claimed with a blanket for a picnic in the park) or allocated (as the kind of space distribution designers perform), is usually marked or defined in some way. In the picnic example, you lay a large blanket over the desired spot, add the picnic basket and perhaps a few other personal items, and the space in the park becomes yours for the afternoon. In interiors, spaces are also demarcated in order to differentiate them from neighboring spaces and create different territories. A variety of architectural and interior design elements are used to define space. Depending on the choice of elements and their composition, space can be explicitly defined or simply suggested. Also, it is possible for various layers of a spatial hierarchy to operate simultaneously, creating multilayered arrangements. We look at space-defining elements first.

Space-Defining Elements

Space is defined by the marking of its boundaries. This is done by establishing and marking the lines that represent the limits between inside and outside. Designers use various devices to define space, the most recognizable being a vertical plane (usually a wall) placed along the boundary. This can be a solid wall or some sort of permeable screen. It can be full in height or a partial wall. Another way to define space is to just mark its corners with an object such as a column (or any other device), and, thus, define four (or more) corners that establish a particular space. Furthermore, one can define a space by differentiating its floor and/or ceiling plane from its surroundings through changes of level and/or material between adjacent areas. Figure 4.1a–f shows examples of these basic space-defining methods.

Space can be defined two- or three-dimensionally. *Two-dimensional definition* is achieved by claiming an area through the marking of its limits on a two-dimensional plane, usually the floor or the overhead plane. The extent of space demarcated is mentally completed by projecting upward or downward (depending on the case), and the implied volume of space is understood. In the earlier picnic example, the blanket demarcates an area using the floor plane. Note that you can demarcate territory two-dimensionally by marking the limits of the boundary only (fully or partially), or by changing the entire surface treatment of the floor or ceiling plane inside the territory through variations of material, color, texture, or pattern.

Three-dimensional definition is more explicit about the vertical extent of the defined volume. It not only defines the territory claimed but also indicates its vertical dimension. A minimal way to achieve this in a

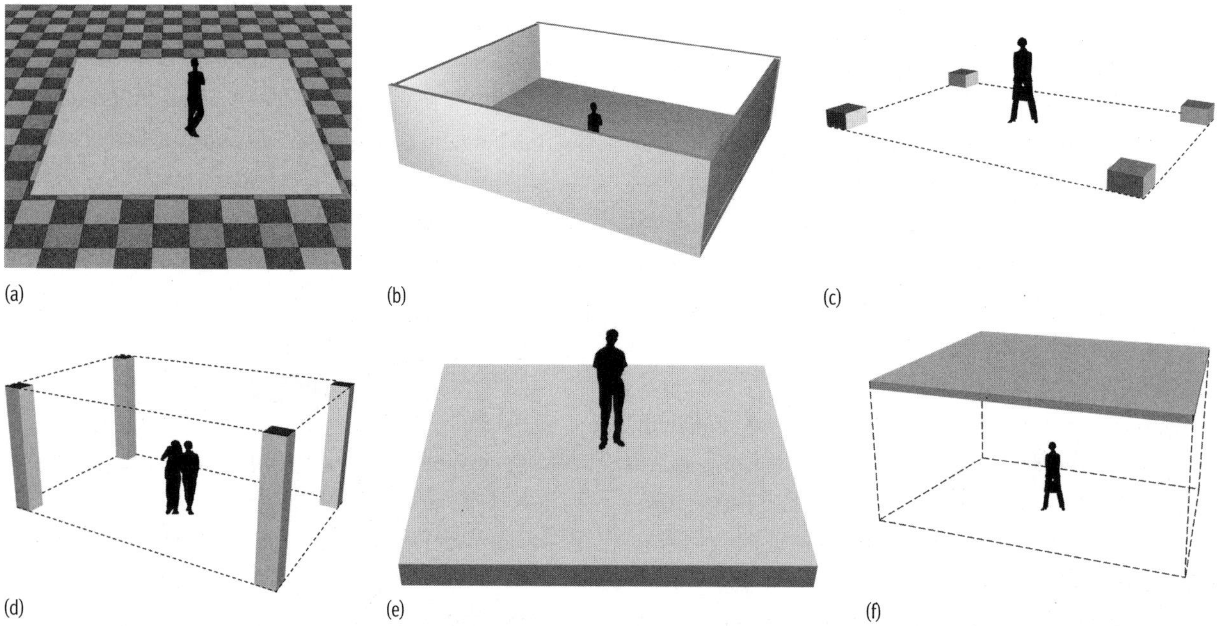

(a) (b) (c) (d) (e) (f)

Figure 4.1: Space can be defined by marking the boundary on the floor (a), erecting walls at the edges (b), marking strategic points along the edges with objects or columns (c and d), raising the floor area inside the boundary (e), and dropping the ceiling plane over the space (f).

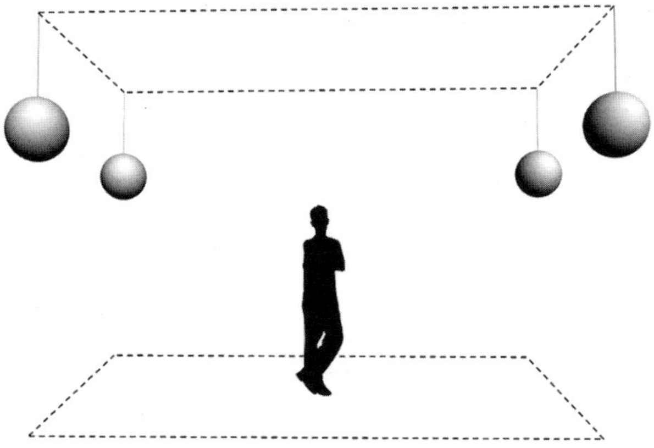

Figure 4.2: The suspended spheres at the corners help to complete the volume suggested here by defining its height.

square space would be to place four objects (such as suspended spheres) on the four corners at the desired height (Figure 4.2). This would complete the "box," suggesting the full extent of the space defined.

The issues of height and mass are important in establishing the precise character of a boundary. Points at corners and markers along a boundary line on the floor merely establish the boundary. If the line is solid and has some height, it becomes a partial wall and partial separation is created. If the line extends to the ceiling above, complete separation is accomplished.

So far we have suggested that you can demarcate space using points, lines, and planes. In interior projects, three types of space-defining elements can be placed strategically on these locations: objects (furnishings, columns, accessories), permeable barriers (colonnade, glass, partial walls), and full barriers (solid walls). In practice, these can be combined to create different configurations having strong spatial definition. Figure 4.3 shows two examples.

Literal and Implied Space

Space definition can be literal or suggested. The explicitness of definition varies, depending on the defining elements used and their placement. Solid, full-height walls at the boundaries define the edge assertively with a physical barrier that provides separation from one space to the next. When space is implied by objects at the corners or overhead planes, the resulting definition is not as strong, although it is still effective and even preferable when openness is desired. A wide range of possibilities exists

(a)

(b)

Figure 4.3: A simple system of posts and beams, as the one shown from Steelcase, can create a strong sense of space without walls (a). Similarly, ceiling elements, such as the floating curved ceiling (b), can define space strongly.

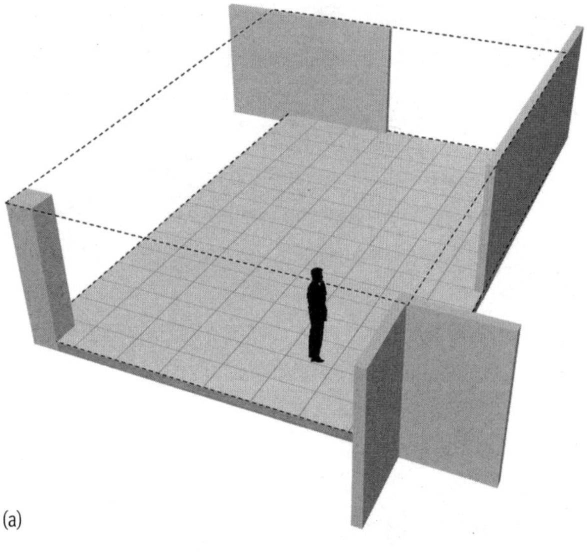

(a)

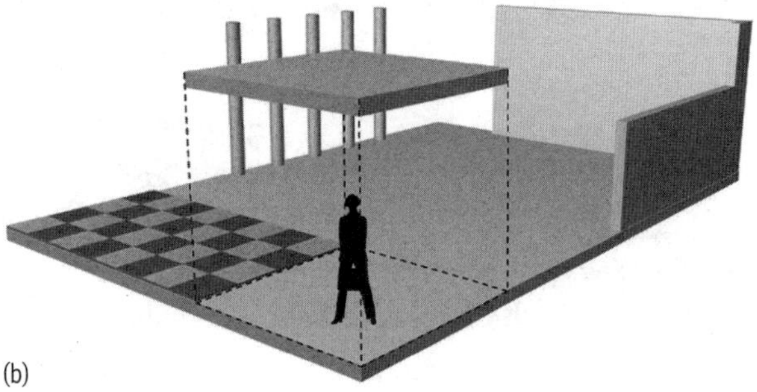

(b)

Figure 4.4: In (a), even though all the walls continue beyond the limits of the defined rectangular space, their placement on the boundary lines, together with the strong corner demarcation achieved by the two foreground elements, help to define the rectangular area shown. The space in (b) is defined by a combination of full and partial walls, a row of columns, a partial ceiling plane, and two types of contrasting floor patterns.

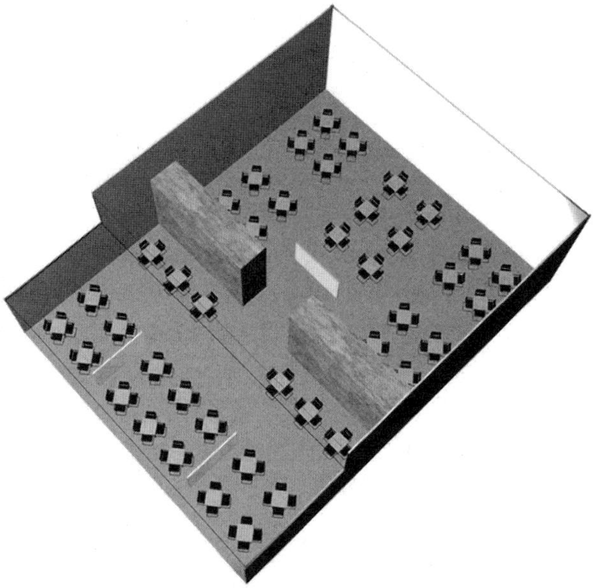

Figure 4.5: Spaces such as this hypothetical restaurant often have many levels of spatial definition defined by grouping or common enclosure.

between the two extremes. Figure 4.4 shows two examples of implied space: In Figure 4.4a, a rectangular area is defined by partial planes and a corner column. In Figure 4.4b, several spaces are defined within a larger rectangular area through the use of vertical planes, ceiling planes, and floor treatments.

Hierarchy of Space Definition

Space definition can occur at different levels simultaneously in such a way that an element can be a part of a whole which, in turn, is a part of a bigger whole and so on. Inside a building, say, a restaurant, you may be sitting at a table (space 1), which is part of a well-defined group of tables (space 2). The group of tables may be part of several groups of tables under a section defined by a lowered ceiling (space 3). This lower area, in turn, may be open to and part of a larger overall dining area in the restaurant (space 4), which may represent one-half of the total dining area (space 5). See Figure 4.5.

In this example, differentiation is achieved as follows:

Unit 1: Object – A single recognizable object, the table
Unit 2: Group – A group of closely spaced tables reading as a discrete region
Unit 3: Section – A collection of several groups of tables under a space defined by a lowered ceiling
Unit 4: Volume – Two sections within the same overall volumetric space
Unit 5: Overall project – Two sides of a restaurant, each with its own volume but linked as one overall project

An advantage of multilevel space definition is that it gives a sense of being part of various "spatial groups" simultaneously and, thus, helps to maintain a sense of place at the various levels of the hierarchy.

Enclosure

Closely related to levels of spatial definition are levels of enclosure. As we saw earlier in this chapter, a space can be defined strongly without having to be enclosed. Some spaces, of course, need to be fully enclosed for functional or practical reasons. Those spaces require not only definition but also a sense of separation and containment. Private offices, conference rooms, changing rooms, and restrooms all demand enclosure, some more than others. Other spaces, like open retail or office areas, do not require enclosure and can remain open within themselves and in relation to adjacent spaces.

There are many levels of definition between the two extremes of full enclosure and full openness. The choices made by designers regarding the openness or enclosure of spaces greatly determine the spatial character of a project. In this section we will examine various levels of enclosure, the characteristics of their space-defining edges, and the effect of different kinds of wall openings. We will begin with containment and encapsulation, two important concepts related to enclosure.

Containment

Some spaces are not only recognizable as well-defined areas but actually provide a strong sense of **containment**. Containment is a concept that refers to a space's ability to gather people and/or objects. You can test the containment capabilities of any given space by thinking of it as a container with more or less ability to hold its contents without spilling them. The three spaces shown in Figure 4.6a–c provide some degree of containment. The example with the L-shaped corner walls provides the strongest containment because of the sealed corner it offers. If you were to pour "contents" into these three shapes, the L-shaped configuration would best be able to contain them without spilling.

This concept is important in living environments because it translates into a sense of grounding and protection. The potential of the L-shaped configuration in Figure 4.6 to give us both a sense of protection and visibility appeals to our innate need for security. The configuration provides protection from two sides. Only the front sides are open, but they are visible straight ahead when looking diagonally from the sheltering corner. There are also configurations that provide stronger containment than the L-shape. Examples include U-shaped configurations and completely "boxed" rooms.

Encapsulation

Encapsulation is another term related to enclosure. It refers to the degree to which the enclosure of a space creates a complete seal at the boundaries. A fully encapsulated space is a fully sealed room with full walls on all sides, a floor, a ceiling, and no openings. Until the early 20th century, the norm in spatial design was to subdivide an overall space into many smaller encapsulated rooms. You always knew when you were entering a new room. In some cases, you walked through the actual rooms to go from one to another. The location of the doors established the path. Later on, corridors were added and one could move between spaces without passing through them. Still, the actual habitable spaces remained encapsulated, autonomous rooms separated from one another.

With the modern movement came more open configurations. Space was not to be encapsulated as in the past. Instead, space was thought of as a continuum of infinite space that could be defined minimally in order to distinguish one area from the next while maintaining flow and continuity. Edges were ambiguous and loosely defined by the strategic placement of a few non-aligning walls. Encapsulation was avoided except when absolutely necessary for privacy. Some of the work by Mies van der Rohe

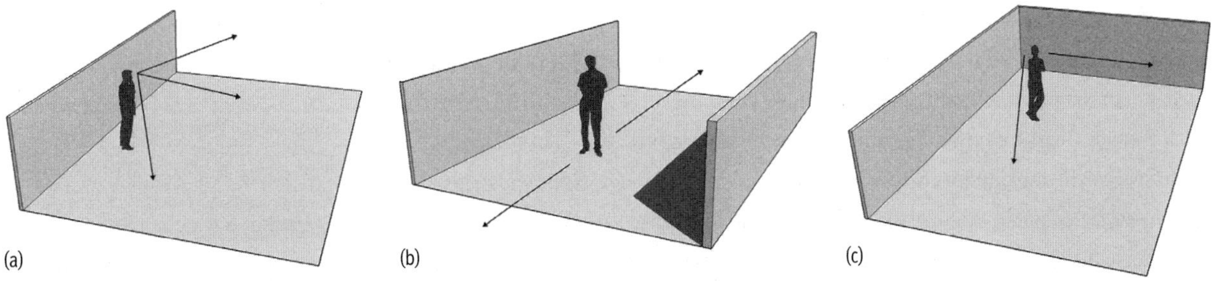

Figure 4.6: Containment is related to the perceived sense of shelter. You can think of containment as gathering without spilling. In examples a–c, example c shows the best ability to "contain without spilling."

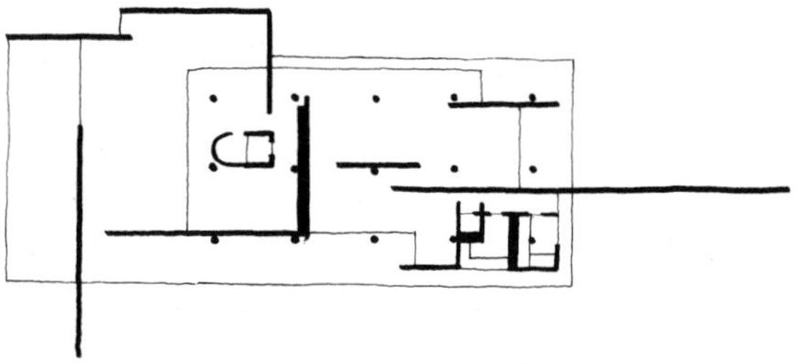

Figure 4.7: This house by Ludwig Mies van der Rohe represents the opposite of encapsulation. Spaces are free and flowing and not sealed in boxes.

and Frank Lloyd Wright represent the best examples of this approach to space planning. See Figure 4.7 and the capsule "Destruction of the Box."

Today, architects and designers employ many different levels of spatial definition. These range from the fully encapsulated to the barely differentiated. Although no strict categorization of the levels of enclosure exists, we may distinguish among four general levels to get an idea of the range.

Loosely defined space is implied or suggested space. No visual, acoustic, or haptic separation is required between it and the adjacent spaces. It relies on providing enough spatial clues to make the space readable. Strategies may include definition of corners and providing planar definition from above or below through floor or ceiling changes to demarcate limits.

In *moderately defined space* edges are explicit in at least two, sometimes three, sides. Space starts having a moderate degree of containment. Some visual separation may be desirable depending on the application, although it is possible to achieve strong definition with partial-height elements that allow strong visual connection between spaces.

Contained space has variable containment capacity, which is maximized by having walls on all sides. It provides visual separation when the walls are above eye level but no acoustic or haptic separation is necessary. Therefore, it can have some openings that achieve containment with partial height elements that do not provide a complete seal at the corners or overhead.

Encapsulated space not only has walls on all sides, but the overhead and floor planes are connected to create a sealed space, a totally enclosed room. Visual, acoustical, and haptic separations are required. Figure 4.8 shows

(a)

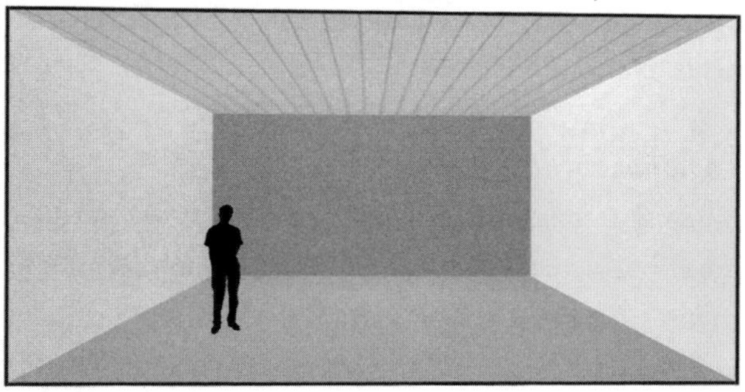

(b)

Figure 4.8: Contained space has surrounding walls but is not sealed (a). Encapsulated space is sealed on all sides (b).

examples of a contained space and an encapsulated space with the front walls removed.

Openings

The size and location of openings have a strong impact on the sense of containment of a space. Figure 4.9 shows the impact different opening configurations have on the perceived level of enclosure in a simple square room.

The location of openings in relation to one's approach also affects the first impression of a room's degree of enclosure. In general, spaces with an opening straight ahead will not have as strong a sense of enclosure as spaces with a solid barrier straight ahead as you enter (Figure 4.10).

Spatial Edges

We have seen how important spatial edges are in determining the degree of enclosure. We have also seen how edges can be, but don't need to be, defined by physical barriers. Alternatively, they can be defined by changes in

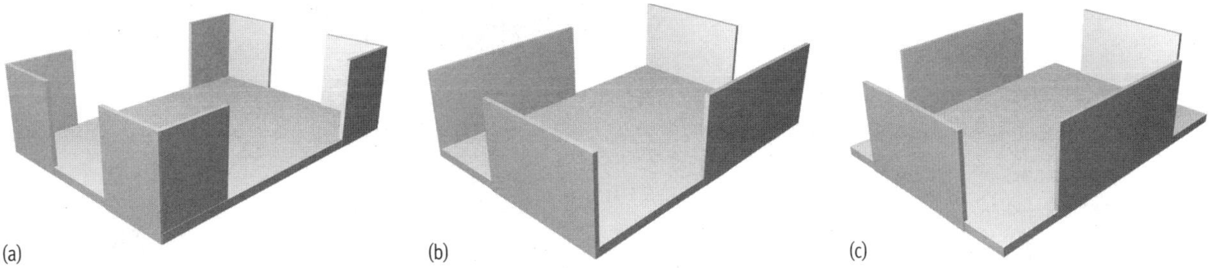

(a) (b) (c)

Figure 4.9: Closed corners facilitate the readability and increase the sense of containment of a room (a). Partially open corners (b) and fully open corners (c) can define and contain a space but with some degree of ambiguity.

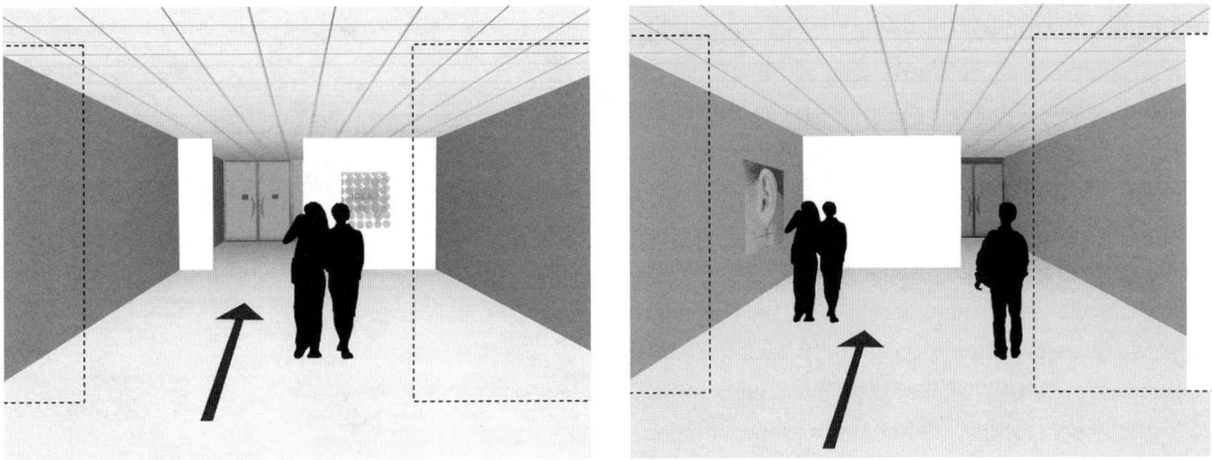

(a) (b)

Figure 4.10: An opening straight ahead produces a sense of openness (a). A wall straight ahead as you enter a room, on the other hand, will have the tendency of containing the space (b).

the materials or levels of ceilings or floors, by the strategic placement of freestanding objects, and by strategic alignment with adjacent elements. In considering spatial edges, next we explore the physical barriers that define and shape space. They tend to be of three kinds: vertical walls or screens around the sides, the horizontal base plane on which we stand (the floor), and a horizontal (although sometimes sloped) plane overhead (the ceiling).

Vertical Edges Walls or screens of various heights and thicknesses, whether freestanding or part of an adjoining room, are the most common vertical edges. Important design considerations include the relative degree of openness or closeness achieved by them, as well as their figural and textural character. The degree of openness is affected by the horizontal continuity of the barrier (it may be continuous or have gaps), the number and size of openings, and the barrier's height. We focus here on the issue of heights. Continuity and openings will be discussed later.

A vertical solid barrier can range from a low, bench-height partition to a full-height partition reaching the ceiling plane above,and the different heights will produce distinct effects.

Edges that are below eye level include low partitions, furnishings, and fixtures. These provide physical separation, but visual, auditory, and haptic connections are maintained. They are useful in instances where both definition and a strong sense of connection are desired.

Edges can also be above eye level but of partial height. These include partitions, furnishings, and fixtures. They provide not only physical but visual separation while maintaining auditory and haptic connections. You can still hear sounds from the adjacent space and feel the same air and temperature. These edges are useful when both visual privacy and a sense of connection are desirable.

Edges that are full height are most often walls and other kinds of partitions. They provide physical, visual (in most cases), auditory, and haptic separation between spaces and are commonly used where a full separation is desired. Figure 4.11 shows examples of these three types of vertical edges.

Figure 4.11: Below eye level, above eye level, and full height enclosing planes produce dramatically different perceptual effects when seen in space.

Horizontal Edges Base planes (floors) and overhead planes (ceilings) are the two types of horizontal edges that help to complete the spatial definition of enclosed space. Ceilings are not always horizontal but are included under horizontal edges for convenience, since they are commonly horizontal in interior spaces.

Floors are limited in their capacity to enclose and define space. They are always level (except at ramps) and for commercial applications require minimal changes in height because of issues of accessibility. Material, color, texture, and pattern variations are the most common ways of treating floors for space definition and differentiation.

Although floors are limited in their ability to differentiate space, ceilings offer many opportunities to do so. They offer two advantages. First, there is no issue of accessibility with ceilings since we don't walk on them. Second, being overhead, they are highly visible and have a strong effect on our perception of space. Figure 4.12a and b shows examples of how ceiling height changes can be used for spatial definition.

In addition to elevation changes at the ceiling, changes of ceiling material, color, texture, and pattern can also be used to distinguish between adjacent areas. The range of surface manipulations is not as wide as it is with floors, given the fairly neutral treatment normally provided for ceilings. Nevertheless, transitioning from a monolithic, smooth ceiling system to a grid and tile system at the same elevation, for instance, is often enough to achieve a subtle separation between areas. See Figure 4.12c.

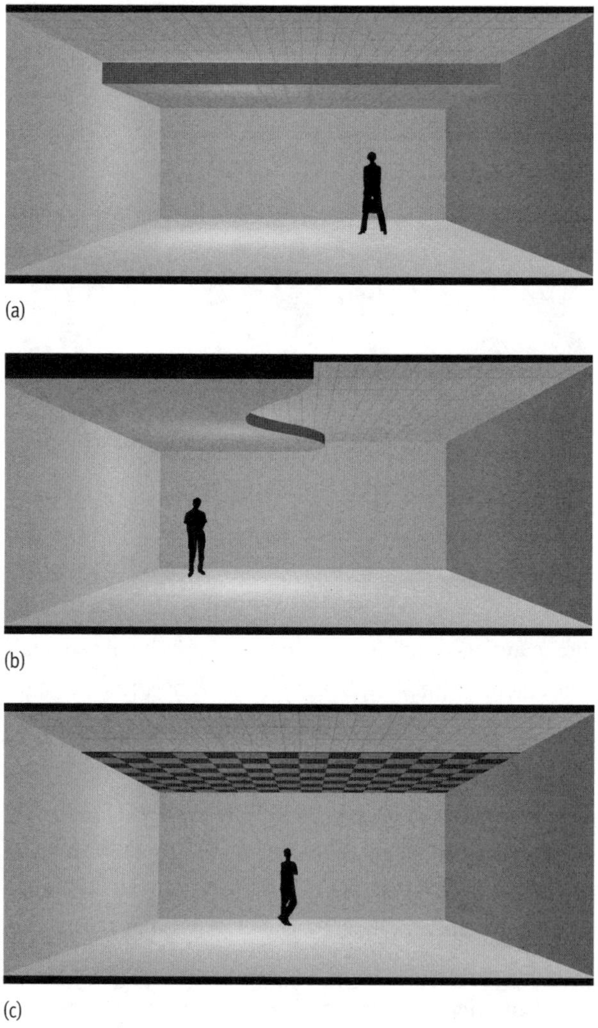

(a) (b) (c)

Figure 4.12: Ceilings are very effective in differentiating adjacent areas. Ceiling height changes (a), ceiling shape variations (b), and material changes (c) can all be effective to define edges.

Textural and Figural Aspects of Edges

In addition to their role of separating and containing spaces, edges contribute to the textural qualities of the space. We normally think of texture in relation to surfaces. Yet space can also be thought of as having texture. It is called **spatial texture**. *Random House College Dictionary* defines *texture* as "the characteristic physical structure given to a material (or space) by the size, shape, density, arrangement, and proportions of its elementary

CAPSULE | Destruction of the Box

Scientific developments in the early 20th century revolutionized the way people thought about the universe. It was seen as having four dimensions, time being the fourth dimension. Space and time became part of a relational continuum, with space changing as one moved in time. Artists, writers, and filmmakers started to adopt this new way of thinking about space, a radical departure from the perspectivism of the Renaissance, which perceived space from a single fixed point. This new idea soon influenced architects and designers. After all, of all the arts, it had the potential to affect architecture and interior design the most.

In addition to the new thinking, the development of new construction techniques utilizing steel and concrete made it possible to use slender skeletal support structures, thus providing the freedom necessary to revolutionize interior layouts. Perhaps the most significant design-related outcome resulting from these changes was the destruction of the box. Until then, interior environments consisted of collections of contained spaces arranged in various configurations. All of a sudden, corners opened up, walls disappeared, dividers and partial walls were introduced, and a freer way to design came about. Although the use of open flowing space has been prominent for many years, many design students still tend to design in boxes.

Frank Lloyd Wright was one of the most important catalysts for the destruction of the box, something that consciously preoccupied him as early as 1904, while designing the Larkin Building; however, it wasn't until later that this idea started to flourish. "Unity Temple is where I thought I had it, this idea that the reality of a building no longer consisted in the walls and roof," Wright explained. "In Unity Temple you will find the walls actually disappearing; you will find the interior space opening to the outside and see the outside coming in. You will see assembled about this interior space various free, related features screening it instead of enclosing walls. See, you now can make features of many types for enclosure and group the features about interior space with no sense of boxing it."[1]

Wright's destruction of the box entailed the opening of the corners, the use of walls as independent screens, and the detachment of the wall-to-roof connection. He explained: "I knew enough engineering to know that the outer angles of a box were not where its most economical support would be, if you made a building of it. No, a certain distance in each way from the corner is where the economic support of a box-building is invariably to be found. . . . Now, when you put support at these points you have created a short cantileverage to the corners that lessens actual spans and sets the corner free or open for whatever distance you choose. The corners disappear altogether if you choose to let space come in there, or let it go out."[2] In this way the corner was opened up: lesson number one.

The next task was to manipulate walls to open up space. "These unattached side walls," Wright said, "become something independent, no longer enclosing walls. They're separate supporting screens, any one of which may be shortened, or extended, or perforated, or occasionally eliminated."[3] So, walls started to acquire a new meaning. They were no longer continuous, uninterrupted enclosures placed exactly at the boundary of each room and sealed hermetically at the corners. They were now screens full of possibilities. Not only was it possible to free up the corner but now, by moving and shortening walls, it was possible to really open up a space and make the inside and outside continuous: lesson number two.

Next, Wright continued the liberation by transforming the connection between the horizontal plane and the vertical plane: "No one has looked through the box at the sky up there at the upper angle, have they? Why not? Because the box always had a cornice at the top. It was added to the sides in order that the box might not look so much like a box, but more classic."[4] According to Wright, it was possible to do more than just free up the four, or however many, corners of a room and move the walls within the room. By shortening the top of a wall along its length and using a transparent material such as glass to join the wall and roof so it appeared to float, it was possible to fully liberate space and do away with

continued

the box: lesson number three. Figure C4.1 shows representative sketches of the evolution from box to free plan.

Not only did it become important to break the box between interior and exterior but also the boxes within buildings in order to create more flowing arrangements symbolic of the times. Wright was not the only one concerned with the destruction of the box and the general opening up of interior space. Other well-known architects followed suit and experimented with various approaches to the same problem. The de Stijl movement in the Netherlands offered its own antibox theories involving dismembering via the disjointment of planes and their strategic positioning. Some of the best examples of such an approach can be found in the work of the German-born architect Mies van der Rohe. Some of his early designs employed a minimal number of strategically placed wall planes to achieve openness, flow, and connection to the exterior. A great example of this approach is his German Pavilion for the 1929 International Exposition in Barcelona, Spain (Figure C4.2). Mies, whose slogan was "less is more," succeeded in giving us one of the purer examples of free-flowing space unimpeded by structural walls and also provided one of the earliest examples of unadorned richness. His design relied on the purity, beauty, and texture of the chosen materials. Another notable example from Mies was the Tugendhat House in Czechoslovakia (1930) shown in Figure C4.3. This house employs an approach similar to that of the German Pavilion (lightweight skeletal structure and independent screens) to maintain a similar sense of openness and sparseness, despite the more demanding programmatic requirements of a real house.

In a similar vein as these two designs by Mies is Philip Johnson's well-known Glass House in New Canaan, Connecticut (1949) shown in Figure C4.4. It features an all-glass envelope and three masses, two linear masses providing storage, and one cylindrical mass containing the bathroom and a fireplace. These serve to subdivide the open space into three areas: a large living and dining area and two smaller areas, the bedroom and the

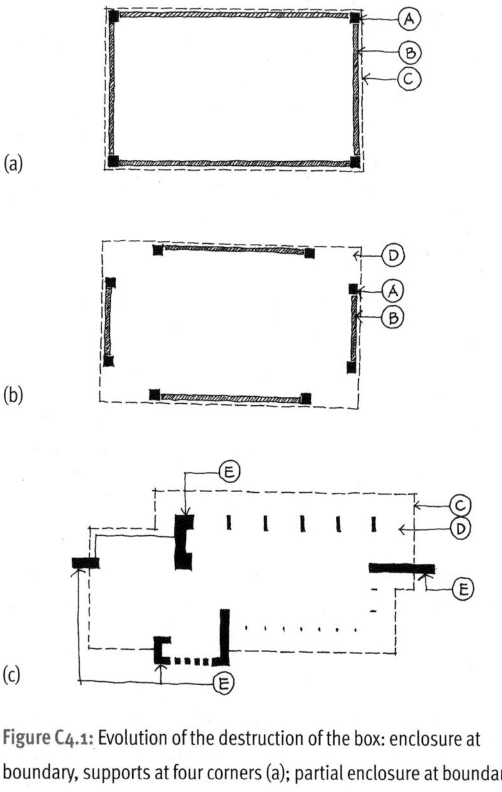

Figure C4.1: Evolution of the destruction of the box: enclosure at boundary, supports at four corners (a); partial enclosure at boundaries, supports "in" from corners (b); minimal enclosure, strategically located "free" walls act as supports (c).

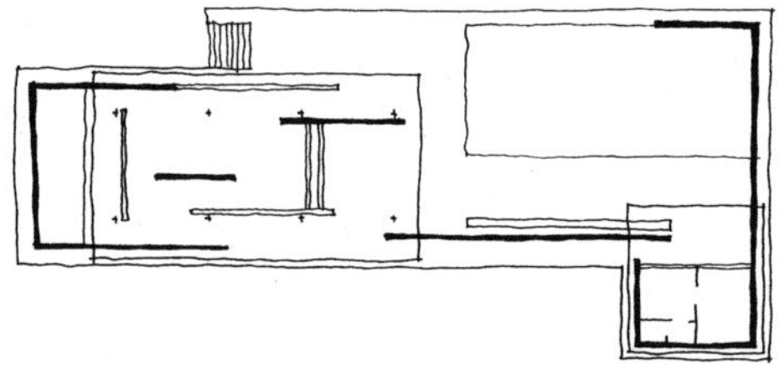

Figure C4.2: Floor plan of Mies's German Pavilion.

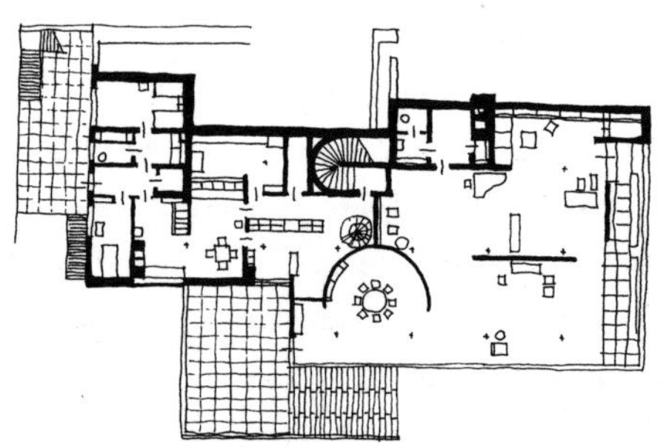

Figure C4.3: Floor plan of Mies's Tugendhat House.

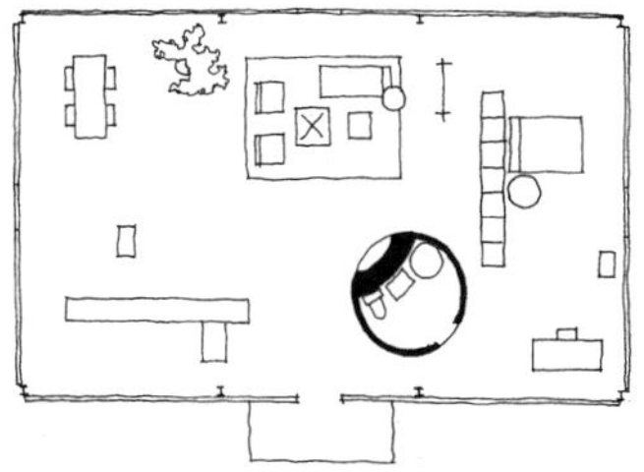

Figure C4.4: Floor plan of Johnson's Glass House.

kitchen. In this example, it is not thin screens but functional masses that serve as screens and perform the dividing task.

Other good examples of functional masses serving as screens can be found in Mies's Farnsworth House in Plano, Illinois (1950), and Wright's Robie (1909) and Zimmerman (1950) houses (Figure C4.5 a–c). These offer illuminating examples to the designer of interior space about how a single interior mass, strategically placed and carefully articulated, can screen, house, and divide while helping to keep the rest of the space free and open.

By using these simple approaches, designers can produce simple and flowing designs. Most interior design projects occur in empty open shells where the structural systems are already in place. The designer is given a clean space on which to plan the new project. Partitions and masses don't have to support any loads. They are free. They can be thin, curved, or movable. Spaces can overlap with and flow into one another. Imagine the possibilities!

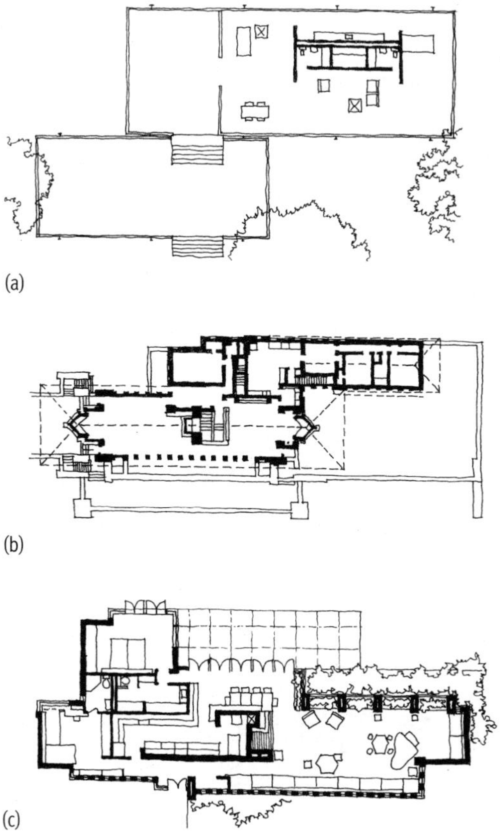

(a) (b) (c)

Figure C4.5: Floor plan of Mies's Farnsworth House (a), Wright's Robie House (b), and Wright's Zimmerman House (c).

Suggested Exercises

1. Pretend you are Wright. Start with a boxlike floor plan and destroy the box. Concern yourself only with the relation of the room to its exterior. Open up the room to achieve inside-outside continuity, by moving or shortening walls, freeing up corners, and any other devices you can think of.
2. Put on Mies van der Rohe's cap for a while. Using grid paper, take a rectangular area and subdivide it into sub-areas using thin planes, as Mies did with the German Pavilion. Try at least two versions.
3. Similar to the examples shown in Figure C4.5, in an otherwise open rectangular room, design a single mass that incorporates some function and, because of its strategic location and shape, helps to divide the room into various zones.
4. Pretend you are given a hypothetical store space to design. Without getting into design specifics, use one or more masses and one or more screens to define and subdivide several spaces in the store. Pretend the footprint of the space is approximately 40 by 120 feet.

---

1. Kaufmann, E., & Raeburn, B. (Eds.). (1960). *Frank Lloyd Wright: Writings and buildings*. New York: Meridian.
2. Ibid.
3. Ibid.
4. Ibid.

parts."[2] Whereas spatial texture is often determined by the objects (furnishings, suspended lights, and so on) in the space, the defining surfaces can also play an important part in supplying texture.

Enclosing walls can be smooth and plain, but they can also be highly articulated, thus adding textural qualities to the space. Ceilings and floors also offer opportunities to add spatial texture. For instance, ceilings can be subdivided into modules, rhythmic bands can be used, and so forth. Figure 4.13 shows a space with a textured side wall and ceiling.

Positive/Negative Spaces and Masses

An important contribution of defining edges is their role in defining the shape of space, both positive and negative. In **positive space**, space is the figure (recognized shape) and the surface is the background (leftover space). In **negative space**, space is the background and the surface is the figure. You cannot give geometric figural shape to a space without the contribution of the surrounding edges. A round room needs concave walls, an octagonal room needs eight wall segments, a domed space needs a domed ceiling plane. We rely on the shapes we give these edges to give the space its shape.

It is the enclosing surfaces of rooms that define their shape. In general, at any one time, either the enclosing plane or the shape of the space it defines has a more recognizable regular shape. In some cases, a certain wall may fluctuate back and forth, alternating between being the recognizable shape and being the background, thus letting the space have the recognizable shape. Figure 4.14a–b show an example of a curved wall seen from the outside and then from the inside, thus defining the shape of the surrounding space differently.

Figure 4.13: Articulation of walls and ceilings helps to produce spatial texture at a much different scale than the smaller surface texture, like that of a rough wall.

Size

It may seem as if designers have relatively little influence on the size of spaces. Most project programs prescribe the floor areas required by the different project functions, leaving little flexibility in the matter. Yet, while designers are often given specific size requirements for the spaces needed, they do have opportunities to influence the perceptual size of spaces.

Designers influence the size of the spaces they design to accentuate or downplay the perceptual size of the space. This is done by manipulating a room's horizontal

(a)

(b)

Figure 4.14: The enclosing planes here go back and forth between being a mold that shapes space and being a shape itself. Where the wall projects out (a), it becomes a cylindrical object that defines the exterior of a circle. On the inside the wall recedes in (b), acting as a mold that gives shape to the circular space experienced.

and height dimensions. Such manipulations can enhance qualities related to size, such as grandeur or intimacy.

When we say room scale we mean the overall relative size of the space or room (usually in relation to humans). For our purposes, it may be useful to think of spatial size in terms of four broad categories: monumental scale, generous scale, functional scale, and intimate scale.

There are no specific guidelines that prescribe specific dimensions for these various room scales since they depend on the specifics of the situation and are therefore relative. More important than thinking in terms of specific dimensions is understanding the traits of these different scales, the appropriate time to use them, and the experience they produce.

Monumental scale is the scale of grand cathedrals and palaces. It is usually conceived of as part of the architecture, used on very special buildings and very infrequently. Its key traits are verticality and spaciousness on a grand scale. It is always easily recognized.

Achieving monumental scale in interior projects is sometimes impossible due to the limited size of most existing interior building sites. Yet multifloor lobbies in some new office buildings and spaces in older buildings with large volumes sometimes present opportunities to achieve monumental space. This grand scale often presents design compositional challenges related to the large amounts of empty space overhead and the usually expansive surrounding surfaces high up. Decisions about the modulation and general treatment of these surfaces and spaces must be considered carefully to achieve satisfying and balanced results (Figure 4.15a).

Generous scale is the scale of very comfortable office and hotel lobbies, spacious dining areas in restaurants, and generous shopping areas in stores. It is more easily achievable than monumental scale, as it doesn't require as much volume. It is often up to the designer to push the limits of space and make otherwise ordinary spaces more generous. As with monumental scale, the feeling of spatial generosity relies heavily on the extension of the vertical dimension. Change an 8-foot-high, 5-foot-wide corridor to 10 feet high, and you will create a generously scaled corridor. Give a low lobby space a 14-foot-high ceiling, and you will have a generous lobby. Generous scale is important in design and is often achievable. All that's required is the awareness to recognize potential opportunities for it, the willingness to make it happen, and the ability to justify it. Figure 4.15b shows an example of a generously scaled room.

Functional scale provides an adequate amount of space to fulfill the basic requirements of a room or space. All of us see it every day and know it well. It ranges from sizes that are minimally acceptable to sizes that are slightly more comfortable but not generous. An example of the minimal approach is a project designed to meet the minimum requirements stated in the building codes. This is often the direction followed for projects requiring maximum economy. In these cases, room sizes and corridor widths are minimal. In multilevel buildings, the floor-to-ceiling heights are kept as low as possible to permit the stacking of as many floors as possible. The functional scale need not

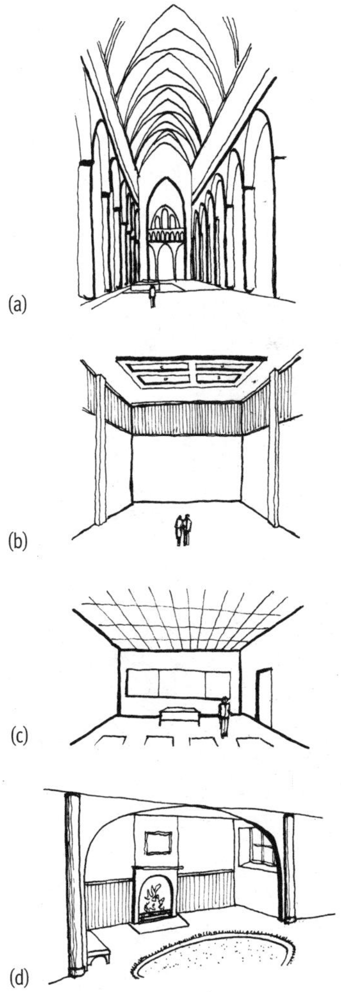

Figure 4.15: Space comes in many sizes. Depicted here are representations of four basic scales: monumental (a), generous (b), functional (c), and intimate (d).

be dictated by the minimum dimensions in reference and code books. It can certainly be more comfortable.

The functional scale will often do the job but will rarely motivate or inspire. However, this is the scale of everyday normal design and cannot be totally avoided. A good strategy to follow is to learn to use functional scale selectively and to balance it when possible with strategically placed generous scale spaces that provide relief and comfort (Figure 4.15c) as well as spaces of intimate scale.

Intimate scale is the scale of small spaces for one or a few occupants. Tighter spaces and lower ceilings are not only allowed but desirable. This is the scale of niches, alcoves, and inglenooks. The difference between spaces of intimate scale and spaces on the minimal end of the functional scale is that intimately scaled spaces are used when intimacy is appropriate. When designing intimately scaled spaces, care is taken to avoid an oppressive feeling.

You should not limit your idea of good spaces to comfortable, generous, and grand spaces. Learn how to create purposely cozy spaces and use them where appropriate. The library study carrel, the small break room in an office, and the dining table in an intimate restaurant become better spaces when endowed with the coziness of intimate scale (Figure 4.15d). Figure 4.16a–c shows three actual environments ranging in scale from intimate to grand.

Form

Another important property of space is its **form**. For our purposes, in this section the definition of form is limited to the basic geometric configuration of space, such as rectangular, circular, and so on; in other words, its shape.

The form of space has important implications concerning the dynamics of the space and its centers of energy. In general, spaces either have shapes that are narrow or linear, inducing movement, or have shapes with boundaries that are approximately equidistant from the center, such as squares and circles, which tend to be more static and promote habitation. The following discussion focuses on rooms and spaces belonging to the second category. We also focus on rooms having regular geometric shapes.

Square Space

Square spaces are pure, formal, and static. They are spaces to be occupied and normally do house a function.

(a) (b) (c)

Figure 4.16: Shown here are three examples of actual environments of different scales, ranging from intimate (a), to comfortable (b), and grand (c).

Figure 4.17: The extent and shape of the vertical dimension can produce dramatically different spaces given the same floor area. Here you see how they affect three square rooms of equal size.

Square spaces have a strong sense of definition because of their strongly defined and uniform corners. They also provide a strong sense of enclosure because of their four prominent walls. Furthermore, a square space possesses a strong sense of centrality. Although the only plan variation possible for square spaces is their size, square spaces can acquire different characteristics depending on the treatment of the third dimension. Different heights and ceiling shapes will give similarly sized rooms a substantially different feel (Figure 4.17).

Circular Space

The circle, like the square, is pure, formal, and static. The circle, however, more than the square, is a highly memorable shape. Circles can be places for habitation as well as circulation spaces. Unlike the square, the circle has no corners; however, it does possess a strong center and a very readable surrounding envelope that, like the square, provides a strong sense of containment and enclosure.

Rectangular Space

Rectangular spaces have different properties depending on their size and proportions. For that reason it is useful to divide them into two categories: short and long rectangles. The short rectangle is any rectangle whose length to width ratio does not exceed two to one. The proportions of the short rectangle produce spaces with a strong sense of place. Depending on their intended use and their size, these spaces can be left as one space with one center or subdivided into two or more zones, each having its own center.

In a long rectangular space, the length exceeds its width by a ratio greater than two to one. The long rectangle is very dynamic. It suggests movement along the long axis. Very long rectangular spaces sometimes become perceptually uncomfortable unless they are subdivided into smaller units. When they get very long and narrow, they start to acquire the qualities of a corridor. Subdivision can be accomplished by the articulation of the enclosing surfaces to suggest subcompartments, by the addition of physical edges between sections, or by the arrangement of the contents into subgroups (Figure 4.18a–b).

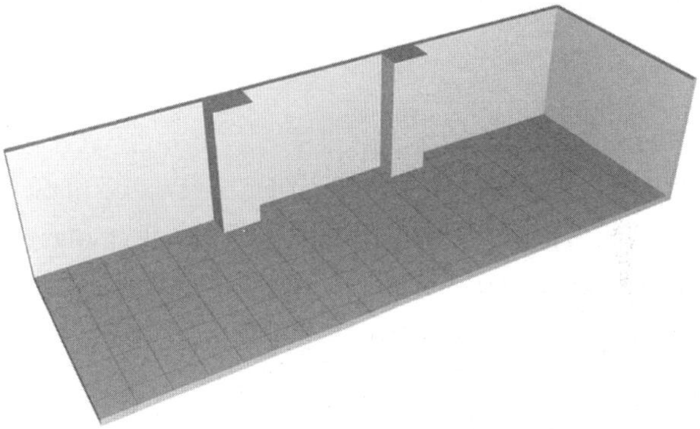

(a)

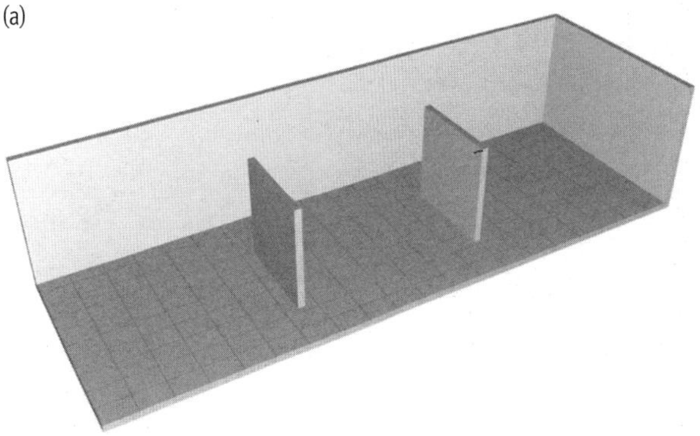

(b)

Figure 4.18: Long rectangular rooms are often more comfortable when subdivided. These illustrations show divisions created by articulations on the side walls (a), and actual dividing screens (b).

Triangular Space

The triangle, such as the equilateral triangle, is generally considered a problematic shape for interior spaces because of its functionally problematic acute angles. Nevertheless, it can sometimes be used successfully. In fact, one type of triangular shape can be used successfully in interiors to create dynamic areas while maintaining adequate functionality: the right triangle.

The right triangle is a dynamic shape because of its long diagonal side and the tension created between the right-angle sides and the diagonal side. All objects within the space can be placed either parallel or perpendicular to the two sides forming the right angle (Figure 4.19a), or placed diagonally in relation to the diagonal side (Figure 4.19b). Circulation can follow either the diagonal or the two sides of the right angle. In most cases, however, it will be more efficient to have circulation moving along the diagonal.

In general, triangular spaces can be used selectively for impact. Like the circle, the triangle is very memorable when kept pure. It is possible to truncate the sharp corners for increased functionality or to avoid configurations with acute angles, as shown in the two examples in Figure 4.19.

Manipulation of Form

All the basic shapes described earlier can be used in pure form or manipulated a number of ways for effect. Manipulation techniques include aggregation, fragmentation, segmentation, and distortion. These are derived from Rob Krier's studies of form manipulation.[3]

Aggregation consists of the addition of smaller, ancillary spaces to larger spaces, such as the pure shapes previously described. The art of creating the side niche or alcove is something every designer should learn and practice. In the case of aggregation, the main form remains dominant and recognizable and the ancillary spaces read clearly as additions (Figure 4.20a–c).

Fragmentation occurs when a pure shape is broken up into smaller fragments in such a way that, by virtue of their proximity and configuration, the overall shape remains recognizable (Figure 4.20d–f). It is also possible to achieve fragmentation by modulating a given spatial envelope into smaller compartments, as long as the overall shape is maintained. This is similar to aggregation, but in the case of fragmentation the total shape defined by the sub-spaces is the basic form without any protrusions.

Segmentation occurs when incomplete shapes (segments of a known shape) are complete enough that the shape is recognizable. The level of definition of the segment needs to have enough resolution to make the form readable. If this is done appropriately, the mind will complete closure of the shape suggested (Figure 4.20g–i).

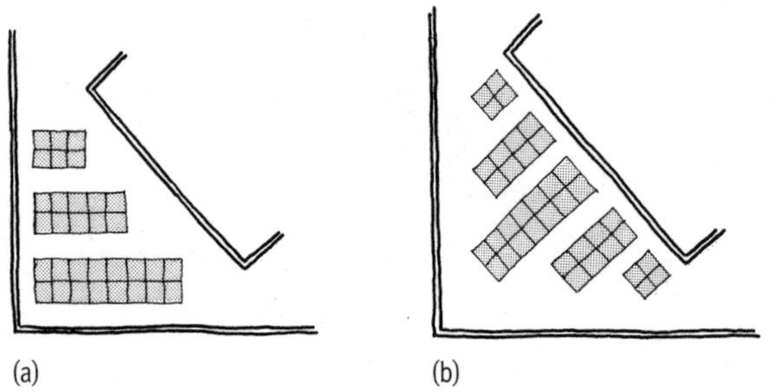

Figure 4.19: The right triangle is the most functional triangle for design. Notice the two basic variations possible for the placement of furniture. In these examples, the problem of acute angles at the ends is avoided because the angled walls stop and the ends are left open.

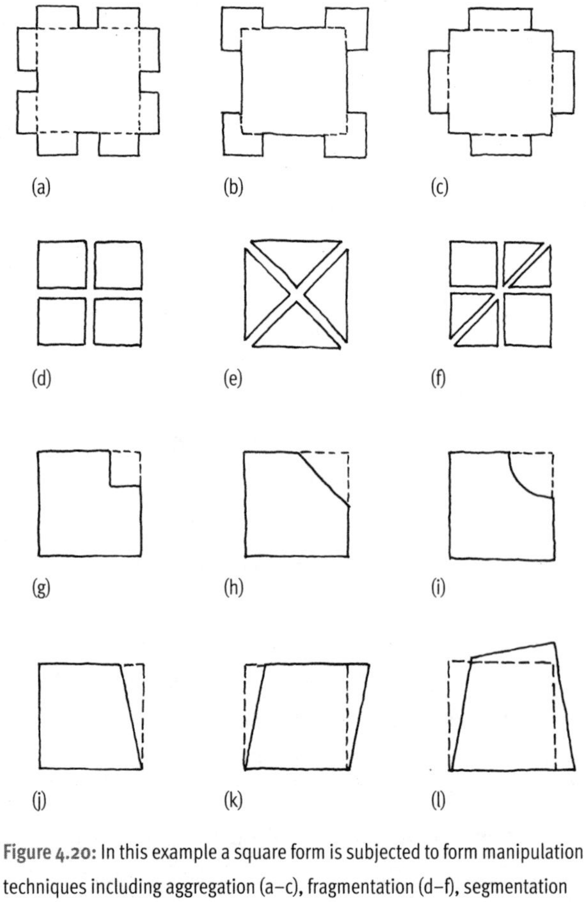

Figure 4.20: In this example a square form is subjected to form manipulation techniques including aggregation (a–c), fragmentation (d–f), segmentation (g–i), and distortion (j–l).

Distortion is achieved by inflecting the edges of a known form in order to alter it while keeping it somewhat recognizable. This is normally done for effect, based on specific design intentions such as the addition of texture or the creation of a more dynamic composition. The level of distortion is up to the designer and the circumstances. The key is for the basic shape to remain readable; otherwise, the shape gets transformed into an entirely different shape (Figure 4.20j–l).

Permeability

Interior spaces can be mostly sealed or they can also be permeable. **Permeability** in interiors refers to the extent to which air, smells, views, and paths are open from one space to the next. Designers have control over these variables and create different perceptual conditions based on how they manipulate them.

In this section we concentrate on two aspects of permeability: disclosure and mobility. **Disclosure** refers to how much of a space, and the other spaces beyond, is revealed as you walk around. **Mobility** refers to the relative degree of restraint or freedom a particular spatial arrangement affords those who move in it.

Disclosure

Imagine that on a given day you visit two offices for business meetings. You arrive at the first one (Figure 4.21), open the door, and find yourself in the reception area. From it, you can see a good portion of the facility. To the right are clusters of systems furniture with low dividing panels that let you see all the way to the end of the space. To the left are more low work-stations. If you move to the side, you can see all the way to the back of the room where a group of private offices is located against the end wall of the space. Straight ahead is the reception desk with a partial-height dividing wall behind it. Behind the wall is the route leading to a particular room with a central formal entrance: the conference room, your destination.

The second office space is quite different (Figure 4.22). Upon entering, you arrive at an enclosed reception area with high walls on all sides except for an opening to the left. From that room you get a glimpse beyond, but can't really see what's going on. To get to the conference room, you go through the opening on the left and enter an enclosed corridor. You cannot see much except for what's straight ahead. At one point, the corridor opens up into a large square area, an intersection. From there, you get a quick glimpse to either side, barely making out what lies beyond. You continue straight and arrive at a small anteroom, walk through it, and arrive, finally, at the conference room.

It is evident that the level of visual disclosure is remarkably different between these spaces. The first space is very open; the second is enclosed and quite controlled.

The first case is an example of projects that features large open spaces, which can be apprehended as a whole, with their parts and subdivisions acting as freestanding

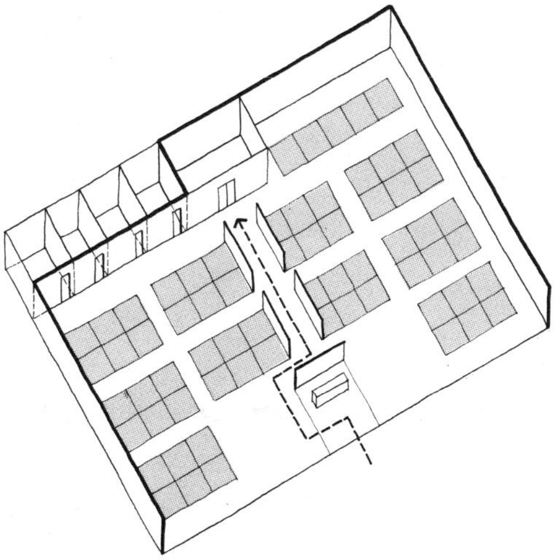

Figure 4.21: There is full visual disclosure in this example of a trip to a conference room in an office. The visitor sees most of the office upon entering as well as on the way to the conference room.

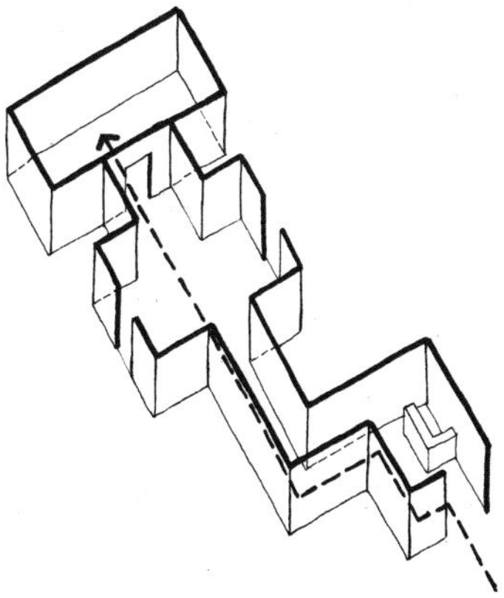

Figure 4.22: There is very little visual disclosure in this version of a trip to a conference room. The high degree of compartmentalization prevents the visitor from seeing beyond the high walls.

objects. The amount of visual disclosure in these projects is substantial. The second is an example of projects that are subdivided into compartments that are experienced sequentially, one at a time. Visual disclosure in these projects is very restrained.

Levels of visual disclosure are determined by the number, type, and placement of view-obstructing elements, whether they are walls, furnishings, equipment, or even plants. Their heights dictate whether uninterrupted views of the space or just an occasional glimpse are permitted. Views will range from panoramic views to glimpses and focused vistas.

Most spaces will have combinations of architectural elements, furnishings, and other objects of various heights positioned at various depths in space and producing numerous combinations of disclosure, depending on their height and placement (Figure 4.23). Additionally, these barriers can have different degrees of transparency and translucency.

The amount of disclosure can be manipulated within a single space and also from one space to the next. It is affected by the objects, furnishings, masses, and architectural visible in the scene. Disclosure, whether within the space or beyond it, should serve three important functions: provide orientation, focus attention, and provide relief.

Orientation The extent to which and the rate at which spatial information is revealed creates unique and specific experiences regarding orientation. If you allow visibility, you will make the process of understanding a particular space easy. Large or complex spaces will demand more clarity whereas smaller, simpler spaces may welcome some intentional complexity, as long as an acceptable degree of clarity is maintained.

Small rooms are easy to grasp all at once. Larger spaces, especially those with tall elements within, have the potential of being either interesting and engaging or confusing and discouraging. This depends on the composition of view-obstructing elements within them.

Internal disclosure beyond the immediate space provides important internal orientation that helps users get a clear mental picture of where they are in relation to the overall footprint of the facility. In general, the orientation provided by a clear view of what lies beyond is helpful in promoting a sense of order. The appropriate rate of disclosure depends on the circumstances and can be judged only on a case-by-case basis.

You can reveal everything at once, gradually, or piece by piece, to elicit some specific desired response, be it suspense or surprise. Access to the exterior is also desirable and, among other things helps our general sense of orientation. Seeing outside gives us a sense of the approximate time of the day, the weather conditions, and what side of the building we are on.

The degree of control you have over disclosure of the exterior varies depending on the circumstances. How we arrange the masses of enclosed spaces inside can produce different experiences in relation to external disclosure. It is usually how we treat the foreground that will determine how much of the outside we can see at any given point in a place.

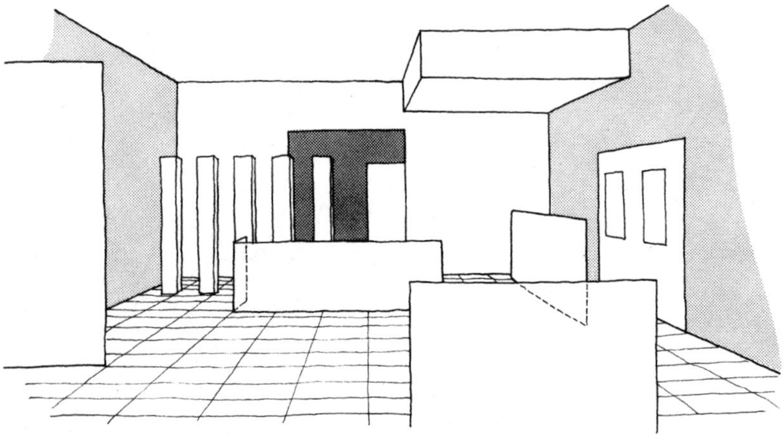

Figure 4.23: Planes, objects, and screens layered in space control what you see within a space as well as beyond the immediate space.

Focus Most spaces have one or several foci. In most teaching classrooms, for instance, there is one main focus: the front of the room, where the lecturer stands. A restaurant, in contrast, may not have a single communal focal point and instead may be designed to highlight each seating section so that each becomes an individual focus. An office space may have both individual foci at the workstations and a central team-oriented area. It is part of the designer's responsibilities to emphasize some views and deemphasize others in order to focus attention where it's needed. Guiding the eye toward focal areas can be done in subtle ways with elements such as lines, or more boldly, through room shapes and other techniques.

Focus between spaces calls attention to important features or destinations on the other side. You can highlight a nice feature of the next space to provide a pleasurable experience or you can reveal a key destination ahead to give people the proper direction in which to move. A proper orchestration of spaces and a helpful level of disclosure from one space to the next can provide the rewarding experience of moving from one goal to the next.

Relief Focus points can also provide welcomed relief. While a functional focus tends to be task oriented, relief is usually distraction oriented. You can think of relief as intentional distraction for the purpose of restoring tired or bored minds. Few designers may think consciously about providing relief to space users; however, many interior places can benefit from foci created for the purpose of relief, like the kind one gets from looking at the changing floor numbers displayed in a crowded elevator. The number display provides not only helpful information (letting you know how close you are to your destination floor) but also an acceptable area you can direct your attention to for distraction and relief.

Similarly, you may find opportunities to provide relief in settings like waiting rooms, office work areas, restaurants, and clinics. This type of internal relief usually translates into some sort of focal area, focal surface, or focal object. These, when supplied, are the areas where we direct our attention to get a momentary mental vacation. A focal area may be as simple as an open space amid an otherwise enclosed area. A focal surface can either provide information or something pleasant or stimulating to look at. A focal object can be an enclosed room strategically located amid an otherwise open area or a memorable freestanding object like a nice kiosk, a display, or a piece of sculpture.

As with disclosure within the space, you can also provide relief, and brief mental breaks, with views to other interior spaces or to the outside. Techniques for providing relief through other adjacent interior spaces include using contrast (open versus closed) or focusing on special objects or surfaces. Relief is also achieved by exposure to and disclosure of the exterior. Here, relief is associated with the feeling of spatial expansion one has when looking at the open space beyond as well as the picturesque qualities of certain views.

As important as the decision to reveal the exterior of a space is the decision on how to achieve it. How do you reveal, for instance, a particular side of a building that has a magnificent view? Can the view be seen as you approach that side of the building, thus generating a sense of anticipation? Do you reveal a glimpse, arouse the user's curiosity, then hide it momentarily before finally revealing it in full? Do you reveal it in chunks? Or, do you keep it hidden until the last possible moment and then, all of a sudden, surprise the user with the magnificent view?

Mobility

One of the ways building interiors affect our experience is by controlling the freedom we have to move about. When we start to think about circulation as more than a utilitarian commodity and consider its role in creating experience, we quickly become aware of the kind of control designers have over the experiential qualities related to movement. A project may have strongly prescribed paths or a somewhat freer circulation system. The goal of the thoughtful designer is to reach a compromise between the need for economy and clarity, on the one hand, and manipulations for particular experiential effects, on the other.

As a designer, you control whether or not people will have access to move in certain directions, and when they do have access, the level of relative constraint and freedom inherent in the route to get there. A place may have only one route that leads to it, and it may be a direct and clear route. Another place may have three alternative routes leading to it, and they may be indirect and meandering. In the following sections, we discuss three common ways of designing a path for movement.

Controlled Mobility: Only One Way to Go Controlled mobility occurs when there is a well-defined route (usually some sort of corridor) that everyone must follow to move around a given space. You move only within this corridor and there is little or no chance to improvise. In the case of a single route you have only one way to move

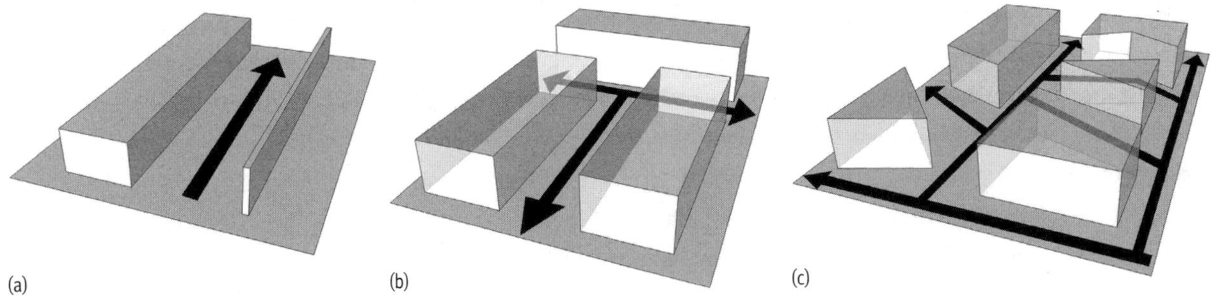

Figure 4.24: Movement in space can be controlled and unidirectional (a), controlled and multidirectional (b), or free (c).

back and forth between any two points (Figure 4.24a). The center aisle in an airport terminal is a perfect example of this scenario. This linear aisle represents the only way of moving back and forth between the spaces in the terminal.

Controlled Mobility: Multiple Direction This type of route features controlled movement, but, in this case, offers a network with more than one single way to move around and get to a destination. The paths may be tight and controlled, but at least you have more than one to take (Figure 4.24b). Having choices is not necessarily better. In some instances, you will want to provide multiple routes; other cases will be better served by having only one.

Free Mobility Free mobility occurs when routes are not explicitly differentiated by hard elements and simply become (or at least they seem to be) the leftover "space between things" (Figure 4.24c). There is usually some sort of implied route preconceived by the designer, but its definition is left loose and often somewhat ambiguous. Usually, you want enough differentiation so the user feels that it's okay to go down a suggested path. In areas that serve locals only, you can have a higher degree of intentional ambiguity. The users will be familiar with the space and will know it is okay to move in the suggested circulation spaces.

COMPOSING MULTIPLE SPACES

So far we have focused on characteristics of single spaces, such as ways to define space, different levels of enclosure, levels of visual disclosure, and patterns of movement within single spaces. Now we turn our attention to groups of spaces, starting with basic relationships between spaces and paths, and concluding with ways of organizing entire projects.

Space/Path Relationship and Level of Autonomy

Depending on the relationship between a space and the path providing access to it, different levels of spatial autonomy can be attained. By autonomy we mean the extent to which the room is differentiated and apart from the path. Figure 4.25 shows a range of possibilities. Figure 4.25a represents high autonomy. Despite the space's adjacency to the path, one enters it on the side opposite the path, therefore providing no easy linkage. Figure 4.25b shows another autonomous space. In this case access is straight from the main path, but it is through a transitional route, thus affording separation between the path and the space. Figure 4.25c and 4.25d show spaces right off the path, the only difference being the added wall in 4.25c, which provides increased separation and

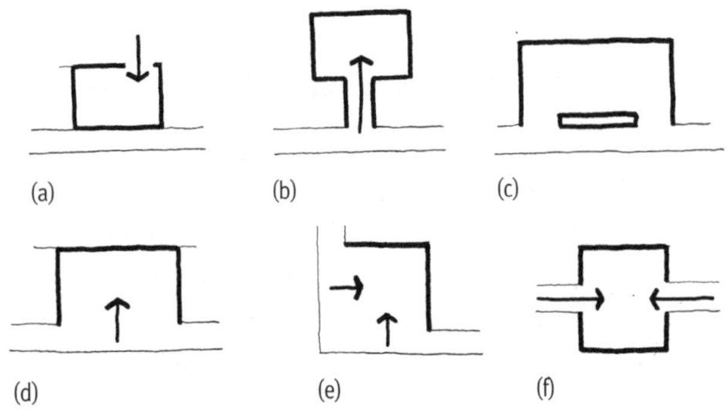

Figure 4.25: Space/path relationships involve issues of proximity and access. A path may be adjacent to a space but access may not be direct (a). Conversely, a space may be somewhat offset from the path but may enjoy direct access through a secondary space (b). The designed relationship may also combine both proximity and convenient direct access (c, d, and e), and, in some cases, the path may go right through the space (f).

some autonomy. Figure 4.25e is similar to 4.25d, both being very integrated with the path, but the corner location at the intersection between the space and the paths creates greater integration. Finally, Figure 4.25f shows a totally integrated configuration in which the path goes right through the space with no separation.

In cases where paths are kept physically detached from and outside the spaces they serve, the spaces remain autonomous and experience less intrusion from users going to other destinations. The optimal arrangement in any case depends on the desired level of privacy.

In the case of paths that pass through the served spaces, there is a planned, intentional integration. In these cases you, as the designer, have determined that the resulting integration between the path and the served space or spaces is desirable. In most of these instances the path blends spatially and decoratively with the served space or spaces.

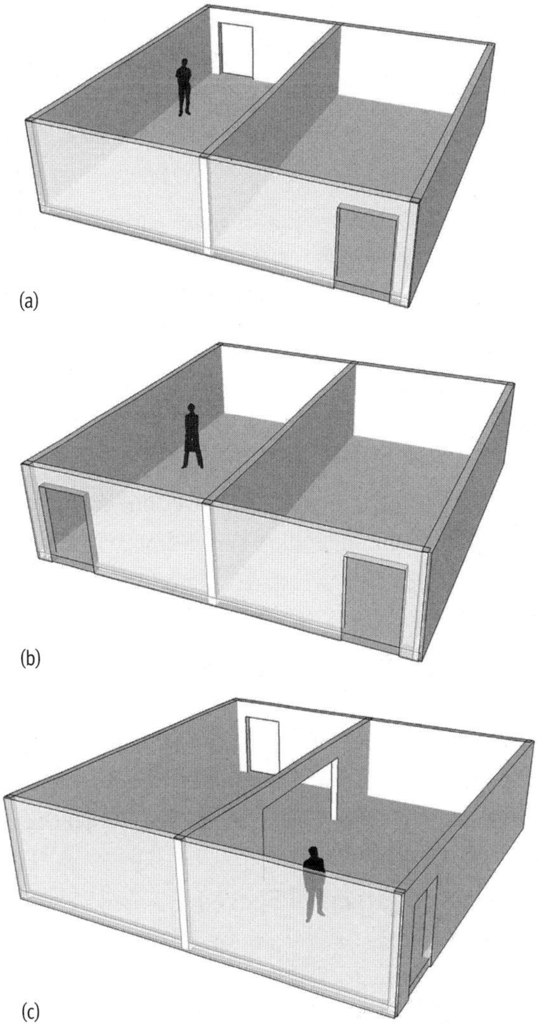

Figure 4.26: Space to space relationships involve issues of both proximity and access. Two adjoining rooms do not necessarily need direct access between them (a and b), but they may have an opening between them for better accessibility (c).

Connecting Adjacent Spaces

There are only a few ways to join adjacent spaces. We will point out six types of relationships between adjacent spaces. These vary in their relative degree of connection and integration.

Adjoining Spaces with No Physical Connection

In these cases, two spaces are attached as shown in Figure 4.26a but have no direct connection between them. In fact, the points of access are on opposite ends. Although they are close in proximity, the spaces are far apart in mutual accessibility.

Adjoining Spaces with an Off-Side Connection

Here spaces are attached and, as previously mentioned, lack a direct connection. In this case, however, both spaces are open to the same circulation spine, making it relatively easy to move from one to the other (Figure 4.26b).

Adjoining Spaces with a Direct Connection

In these cases, spaces are attached and also have a direct connection through the common wall providing direct passage between them. This connection may range from a standard door to a wide and generous opening (Figure 4.26c).

Proximate Spaces with an In-Between Space as Connection

Here spaces are adjacent, although not quite attached. They are connected by a third, smaller space providing direct linkage between them. This arrangement is useful when a strong and somewhat formal sense of transition is desired (Figure 4.27a).

Interpenetrated Spaces

With **interpenetrated spaces**, both spaces overlap partially, sharing a common area of ambiguous ownership. With this type of arrangement access is direct and flows from one space to the next, especially as one approaches the territory in the ambiguous common area (Figure 4.27b).

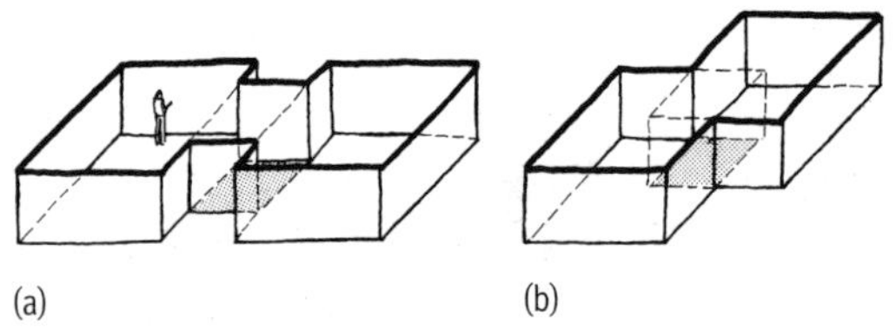

Figure 4.27: Adjacent spaces may be joined by an intermediate, in-between space that provides access between them (a) or, in the case of interpenetrated spaces, by the common space they share, in which case one can be in both simultaneously (b).

Superimposed Spaces

In the case of **superimposed spaces**, two (or more) spaces are literally superimposed over one another, creating a new spatial definition and geometry. Depending on the treatment of the surfaces and ceiling planes, both spaces can have equal dominance or one can dominate the other. Figure 4.28a–c shows some examples of superimposed spaces. The relationships between the spaces can be orthogonal, symmetrical, rotated, and so on. Also, it is possible to superimpose multiple shapes on top of each other, creating increasing degrees of complexity.

Composing Systems of Spaces

Most projects consist of many spaces, organized within some kind of cohesive structure. The relationships between project parts have to be resolved and unified through an overall organization scheme. The ways of combining these elements for a specific project may seem endless, yet the realities of the project and the specifics of context help to narrow down the possibilities.

Here, we will look at some of the basic choices you have as a designer to address the overall organization of the project. We will discuss several ways to arrange a project based on the circulation system and suggest four distinct spatial approaches you can adopt as the compositional rules for a given project. We will start with arrangement alternatives based on circulation, an approach suggested by Stanley Abercrombie, who analyzed plan types based on their circulation.[4]

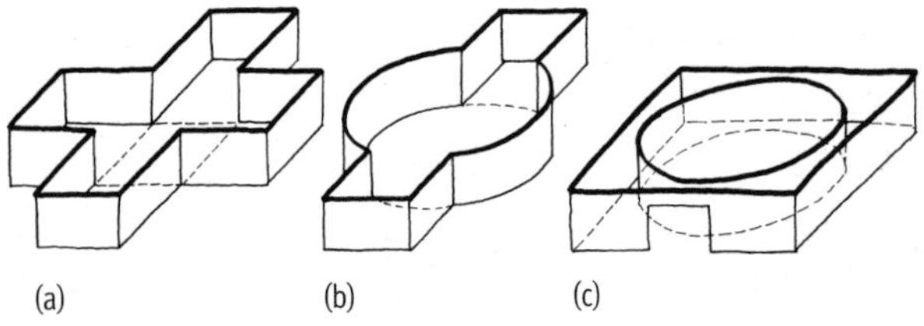

Figure 4.28: Superimposed spaces go beyond interpenetration. They actually coexist and share a major portion of their space. These examples show superimposition of two linear spaces (a), one linear and one circular space (b), and one square and one circular space (c). Notice that in all these cases the shared space is in the center.

To devise organization systems for entire projects, it is possible, theoretically, to begin with the circulation system as an organizing force and then plug in the spaces where appropriate. In reality, both the spaces and the routes feeding them are part of an inseparable system and need to be considered together. Yet, thinking of project organization in terms of its circulation system makes a lot of sense as we will see.

In the following sections, we present six movement-based models you can use to organize projects. Each is illustrated with examples of different geometries that work within that particular system.

Linear Systems

You may choose to use a **linear system** consisting of linear circulation with spaces on one or both sides. If there are spaces on both sides, you can balance them equally or make one of the two sides wider than the other. The circulation spine of linear systems can also go through the spaces it feeds, becoming part of those spaces (Figure 4.29a–c). There may be special goals (destinations) at the two ends of linear systems. Additionally, special spaces can occur near the center or even at more than one point along the route if the path is long enough.

Linear organizations may undulate and the linear paths may twist and turn. As long as the general character remains linear, we can still call them linear. Whether L-shaped, U-shaped, or linear segments at random angles, the system is still linear if its character remains linear. Where you have corners in L- and U-shaped configurations, these become potentially important junctions reserved for special destinations. Figure 4.29d–f shows additional variations of linear organizations.

Loop Systems

When a linear system closes itself up, forming a loop, it takes on a different character both geometrically and functionally and becomes a **loop system**. A loop can also be circular, segmented, or free-form. Its distinguishing attribute is that it is a closed system with no loose ends. A loop can be single- or double-loaded. An inner loop feeding outward and an outer loop feeding inward are both examples of single-loaded loop systems (Figure 4.29g–h). Double-loaded loop systems feed both an interior zone (inward) and an exterior zone (outward), as shown in Figure 4.29i. A double-loaded loop system requires many decisions regarding the placement of spaces. The central inner zone, for instance, can be either a space of great importance, or a utilitarian space. As with linear systems, the corners in loop systems have the potential of being special strategic destinations. Loop systems can have diverse geometries. Figure 4.29j–l shows some examples of alternative geometries.

Axial Systems

Axial systems consist of routes arranged around an axis; typically, these routes intersect at right angles. They often feature a main linear axis intersected by a secondary one. These configurations tend to be formal because of the linearity of the routes and their often perfect intersection at or near the center of the space. Oftentimes this center coincides with an important central space. The ends in both directions are all potential strategic locations, as are the four corners defined by the right-angle intersections.

While the traditional use of axial circulation systems tends to be formal and symmetrical, it is entirely possible to use this approach with asymmetrical compositions or even nonorthogonal configurations. These, of course, would instantly transform the formality usually associated with axial arrangements. Figure 4.30a–c shows some examples.

Radial Systems

Radial systems are characterized by linear routes that emanate radially from a common center. The common center can be a major place or an important node. It does not need to be at the geometric center of the project, although it often is. Other potential locations for the central space are edges and corners, whether inside or outside (Figure 4.30d–f). One drawback of this type of arrangement is the difficulty of using the wedge-shaped areas between the circulation spines efficiently.

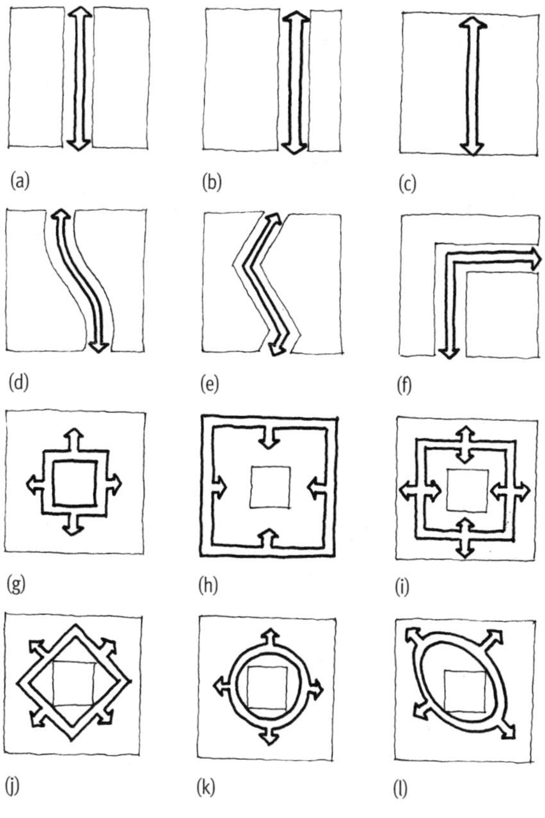

Figure 4.29: Linear and loop organizations have many possible variations, as these diagrams illustrate.

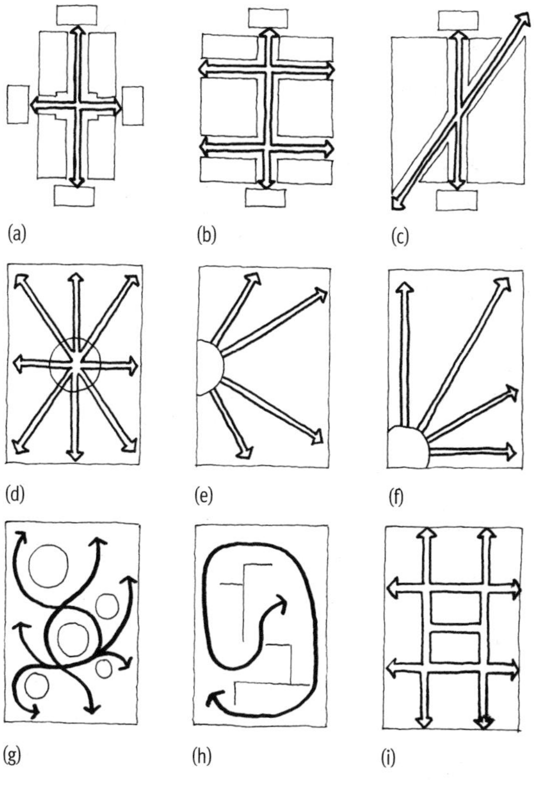

Figure 4.30: Variations of axial (a–c) and radial organizations (d–f) are shown, as well as two examples of free organizations (g and h) and one example of a network (i).

Free Movement Systems

Free movement systems are characterized by a free flow and at times an apparent lack of coherent geometry. Their success relies on the compositional balance achieved by the placement of project elements around which one circulates. These can be linear elements, like the walls of Mies van der Rohe's houses, or free-floating masses acting as islands. Given the many free-form configurations possible, it is difficult to generalize about specific attributes of these configurations. Free movement systems are viable and appropriate organizations used in many interior settings that do not require the strict geometry or formality of the other systems described here (Figure 4.30g–h).

Network Systems

Network systems are characterized by fairly complex circulation systems that are interconnected and form a network. They usually occur in large complex projects. For large projects with many circulation segments, maintaining a sense of hierarchy among the parts will help to ensure a sense of legibility and order. In contrast, in many retail settings, the segments are undifferentiated to achieve intentional disorientation. Figure 4.30i shows an example of a fairly straightforward network system.

Spatial Approaches

Project particularities such as size, complexity, client type, and site configuration will suggest some of the previously mentioned organizations more than others. We just described six basic types of spatial organization based on patterns of movement. You also need a clear direction about the general compositional approach to be used for the project. This requires not only route configuration but decisions about the character of spaces and the type of spatial model dominating the approach. Earlier we talked about different approaches to space definition, enclosure, and disclosure. When you consider all the variables, the number of possible compositional combinations can seem staggering.

Although the many ways of combining circulation systems and spatial approaches yield a great number of different solutions, we suggest four basic approaches to the orchestration of space: the functional approach, the classical approach, the modern approach, and the loose approach. Using these four approaches as a point of departure may facilitate your efforts to arrive at a model suitable for your project; however, do remember that these are only points of departure, and variations and combinations are often desirable. Descriptions of each follow. Figure 4.31 shows representative simple diagrams for each approach.

Functional Approach

The **functional approach** is, perhaps, the most common. This model uses an efficient, engineered approach that frequently features a highly efficient loop or network type of circulation system with spaces efficiently organized on both sides of the circulation.

You will have to adopt the functional approach for many projects during your career. It may seem boring, although there is no reason why it has to be so. As long as you are aware that the functional approach is what a particular project requires, you can avoid wasting time with other unrealistic approaches and focus on making the best of the project. You may be able to compensate for the strict circulation system by developing other aspects of the project.

Classical Approach

The **classical approach** is formal and likely to be symmetrical and ceremonial. Possible circulation organizations are linear, axial, and radial. Formal offices, restaurants, hotels, and retail stores can use this approach. With the

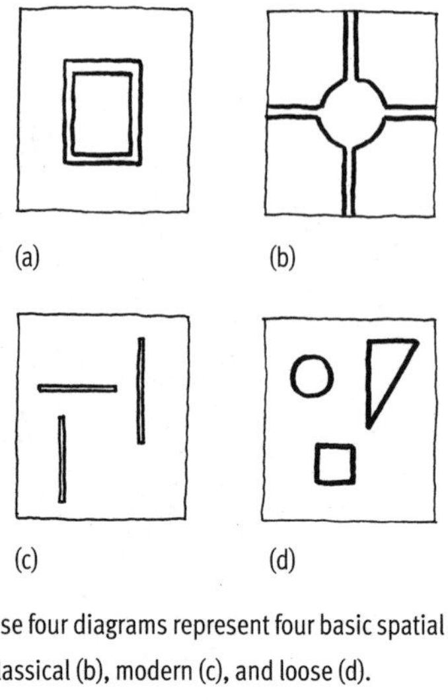

Figure 4.31: These four diagrams represent four basic spatial approaches: functional (a), classical (b), modern (c), and loose (d).

proper accompanying finishes it can convey class and sophistication.

Modern Approach

The **modern approach** is based on the clean modern compositional principles of certain modern designers such as Frank Lloyd Wright and Mies van der Rohe. It features simplicity and clean lines. General spaces are often loosely defined, not encapsulated. Movement tends to flow from space to space. Open spaces, even if not enclosed, are well defined and shaped geometrically so that they become positive spaces. Arrangements tend to be asymmetrical but balanced.

Loose Approach

In the **loose approach**, solids float in space in well-balanced arrangements. These solids tend to stand out as figures. The leftover space around them is often irregularly shaped and includes circulation and other adjoining open spaces. These spaces tend to be casual and are often playful as well.

REVIEW

Summary

The definition and manipulation of space is essential to the production of designs that are functional and provide order, enrichment, and expression. This chapter reviewed some basic considerations necessary for the composition of single spaces and systems of spaces.

Important spatial properties of individual spaces include their level of definition, the type of enclosure they provide, their size, shape, and form, and the degree of disclosure and movement they afford. Space can be articulated in many different ways, some literal and others implied. It can be highly contained and even totally encapsulated. The perceived degree of enclosure varies with the position of openings such as doorways and windows in the space. Walls sometimes act as backgrounds to the shape of space and at other times become the shapes themselves.

Spaces come in different sizes and shapes. Designers have considerable control over these variables. Spaces also have specific enclosure characteristics, and their form can be manipulated by techniques such as aggregation, fragmentation, segmentation, and distortion.

Levels and patterns of disclosure can be manipulated to create specific effects. Disclosure, whether within a space or beyond, affects a user's sense of orientation; it also contributes a sense of focus and relief.

When designing adjoining spaces, whether a space-to-path or a space-to-space relationship, issues of proximity and connection come into play. Spaces can be proximate without being directly accessible. They can have moderate or high levels of accessibility between them, depending on the location of openings and the geometry of the spaces. Some spaces are literally superimposed onto one another.

As one moves from designing a couple of spaces to the design of the entire project, certain organizational systems appear more appropriate than others. Based on movement patterns, potential systems include linear, loop, axial, radial, free, and network organizations. You may stick to one approach for a project or use a combination of two or more.

Finally, to help you think of approaches to the organization and spatial character of interior spaces it is useful to think in terms of four basic models that represent four different stylistic directions. These are the functional approach, the classical approach, the modern approach, and the loose approach.

1. Ching, F. D. K. (1979). *Form, space and order*. New York: Van Nostrand Reinhold.
2. Texture. (1987). In *Random house college dictionary* (The Random House Dictionary of the English Language, 2nd Edition, Unabridged).
3. Krier, R. (1992). *Elements of architecture*. London: Academy Editions.
4. Abercrombie, S. (1990). *A philosophy of interior design*. New York: Harper and Row.

In the course of designing interior space, designers always have to deal with walls, ceilings, and columns. Floors are another enclosing surface, although floors have limited opportunities for articulation. They simply need to be flat and, even so, everyone, regardless of physical ability, can move unimpeded from place to place. Walls, ceilings, and columns, on the other hand, present opportunities for articulation.

It is common for the novice designer to think of walls as something that happen when you need a room, of ceilings as something you need in order to hide ugly mechanical ductwork and suspend lights, and of columns as things that are just there and about which you can do nothing. There is much more to these important spatial elements.

Walls do more than just enclose rooms. They contain, define, separate, decorate, and can actually do work for you (Figure C4.6). Most individual walls are experienced as at least two, frequently more, realities. The darkened wall in Figure C4.7 is experienced as four different realities, three individual ones from inside the three rooms, and one from the other side of the offices. In other words, that particular wall could have four totally different expressions. Because walls have not one but two sides, proper consideration must be given to the appearance and effect of each side. Although walls normally conform to the thickness produced by the particular combination of the materials used and their widths and thicknesses, not all walls need to be of uniform depth. Either one or both sides of the wall can take off and expand to meet your design intentions (Figure C4.8).

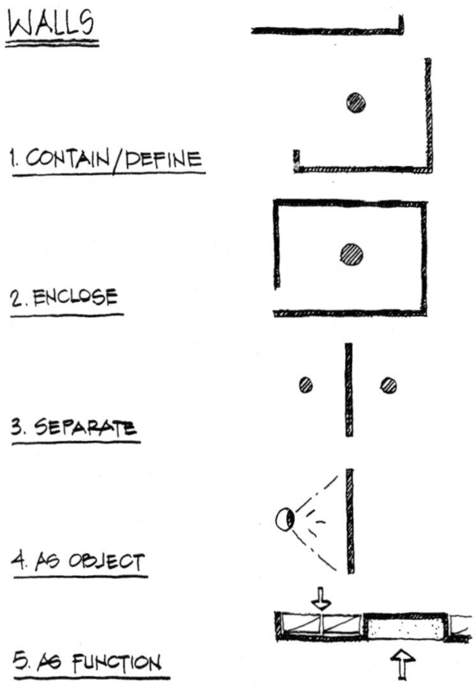

Figure C4.6: The many functions of walls: contain (1), enclose (2), separate (3), as object (4), as function (5).

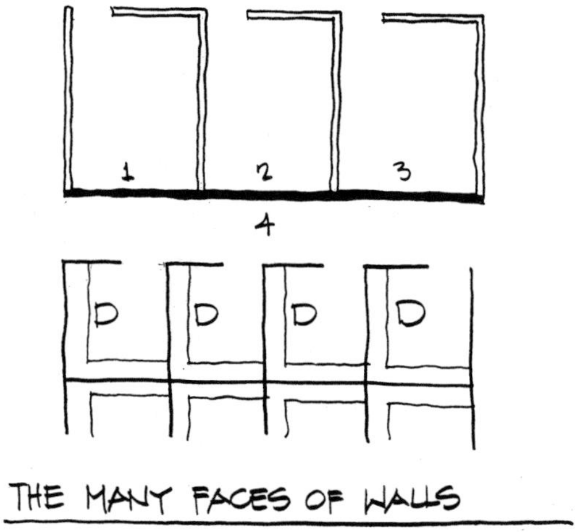

Figure C4.7: Walls have many sides. The dark wall shown is seen independently from three offices and from the open area outside the offices.

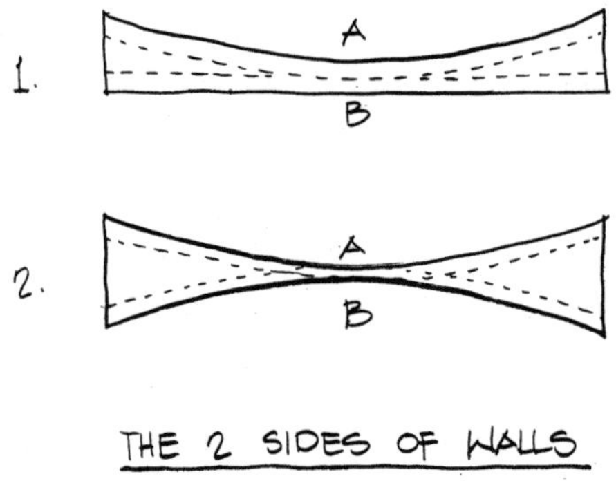

Figure C4.8: Walls have two sides. They may be straight, angled, curved, wide, or narrow.

Walls embody different personalities according to the roles they assume (Figure C4.9) and the treatment given them by the designer (Figure C4.10). They certainly do not have an obligation to extend to the ceiling (at least the nonstructural walls normally used in interiors). So, they can be of any height and shape you want. Different heights create different conditions (Figure C4.11), as do different shapes (Figure C4.12). You can even put a wall to work for you. Figure C4.13 suggests just a few of the many possibilities.

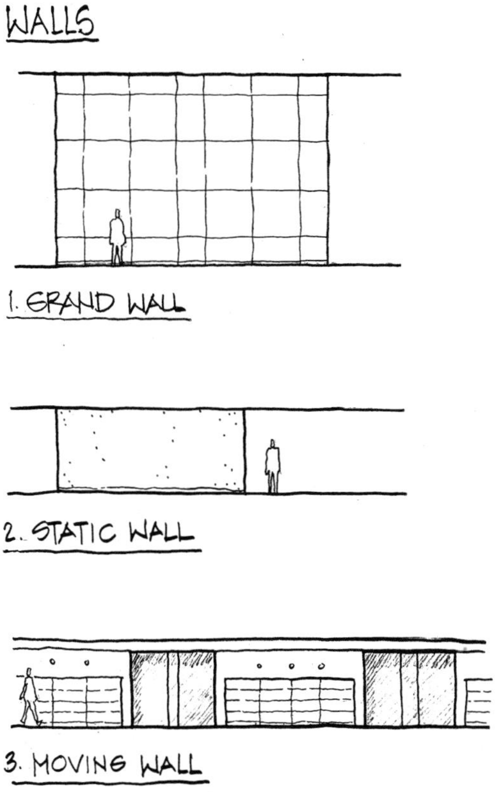

Figure C4.9: Some of the many types of walls: the grand wall (1), the static wall (2), the moving wall (3).

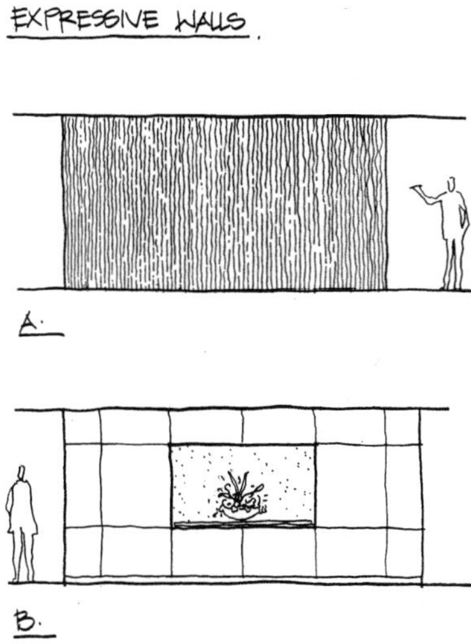

Figure C4.10: Walls can be expressive through surface treatment (a), or articulation and content (b).

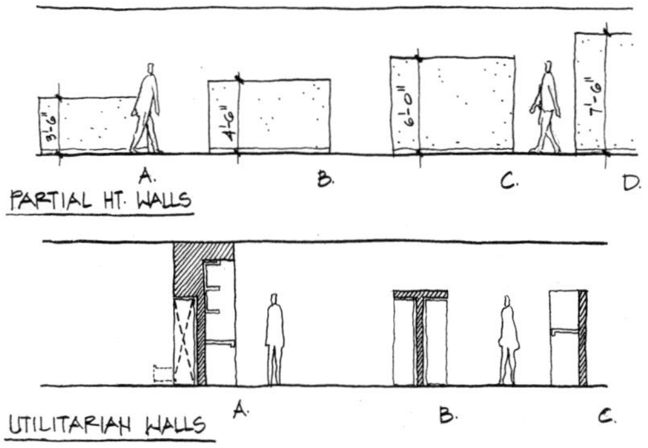

Figure C4.11: Walls are not always full height. Partial-height walls, however, come in many heights.

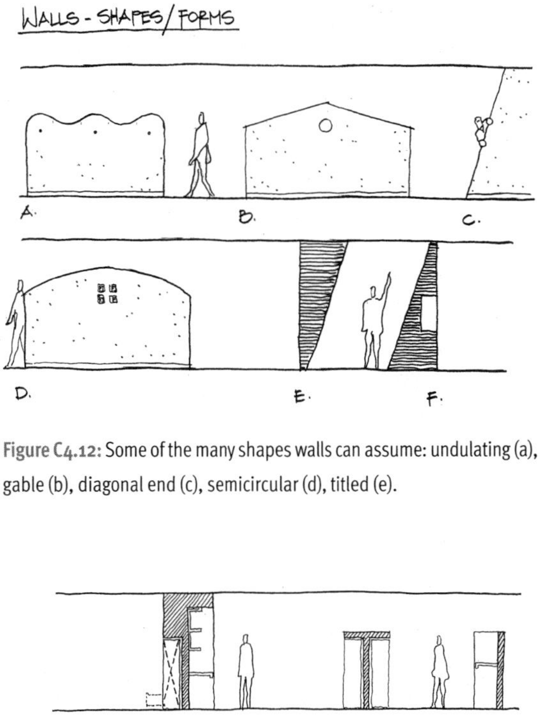

Figure C4.12: Some of the many shapes walls can assume: undulating (a), gable (b), diagonal end (c), semicircular (d), titled (e).

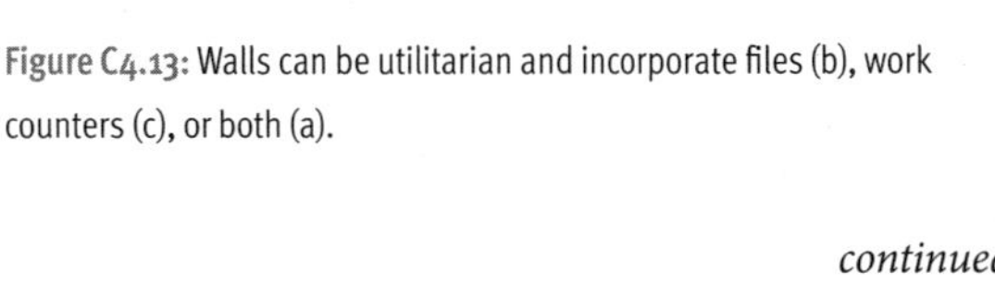

Figure C4.13: Walls can be utilitarian and incorporate files (b), work counters (c), or both (a).

continued

Some walls do have to extend all the way to the ceiling (or beyond) to meet particular enclosure and privacy requirements. Even in many of those cases, however, it is possible to maintain some visual continuity and light penetration through the use of glass. Even when privacy is required, a modest amount of glass can be used to achieve continuity between sides (Figure C4.14). Glass can also cover large areas to produce major connections between sides. The detailing of how this happens, by the way, presents opportunities for many different design expressions. The way glass panels are subdivided creates different looks with their own personalities (Figure C4.15), as do the weight and material of the trim used (Figure C4.16).

Ceilings can also perform expressive functions. In addition to the many effects that can be produced

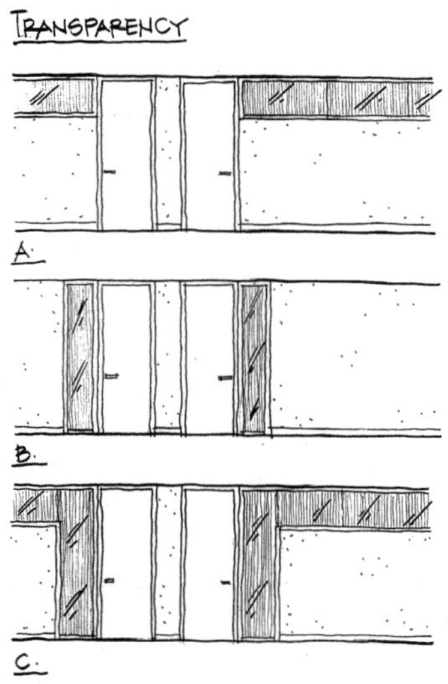

Figure C4.14: Walls can let light from the perimeter in through clerestory glass bands (a), sidelights (b), or both (c).

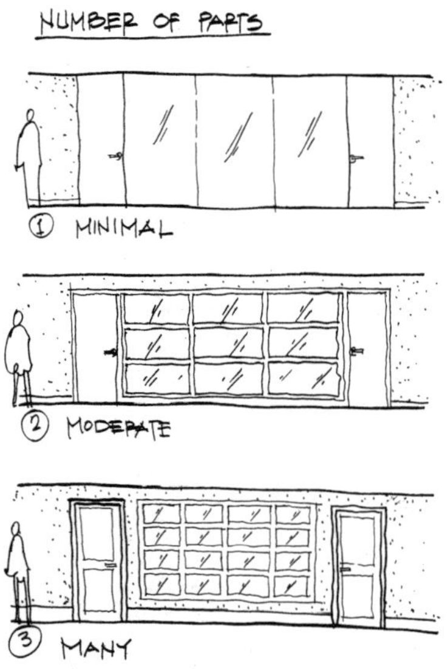

Figure C4.15: Large areas of glass can be subdivided minimally (1), moderately (2), or extensively (3).

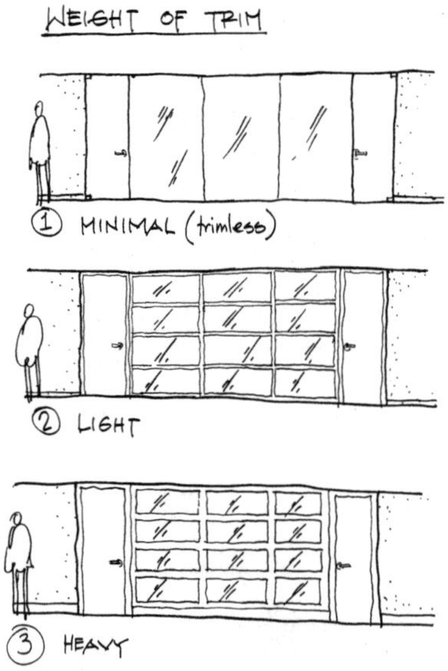

Figure C4.16: The weight of the trim framing window walls can be minimal (1), light (2), or heavy (3).

by ceiling height variations (Figure C4.17), the shape of ceilings can also be expressive. As Figure C4.18 shows, undulating ceilings, shallow gables, and vaults (half and full) are some of the possibilities.

Finally, structural columns, while impractical to remove, offer opportunities for expression. Depending on how you cover them (shapes and materials used), different effects can be produced. Figure C4.19 shows different approaches in plan, while Figure C4.20 displays different shapes in section. The fact that other effects are possible through detailing and articulation is suggested by the telescoping column shown in Figure C4.21.

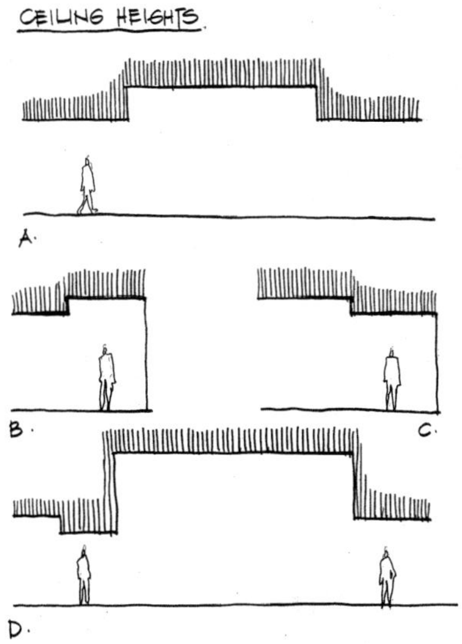

Figure C4.17: Ceiling height variations can produce many different effects.

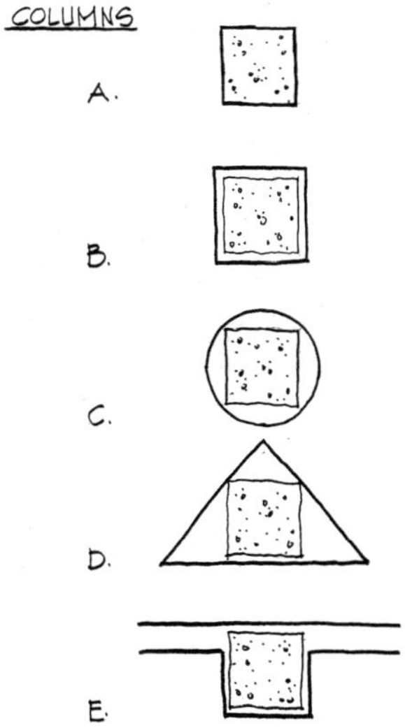

Figure C4.19: Columns can be given different shapes depending on how you cover them. They can be left rough (a), covered with a rectangular shape (b), a round shape (c), a triangular shape (d), or made to disappear on one side (e).

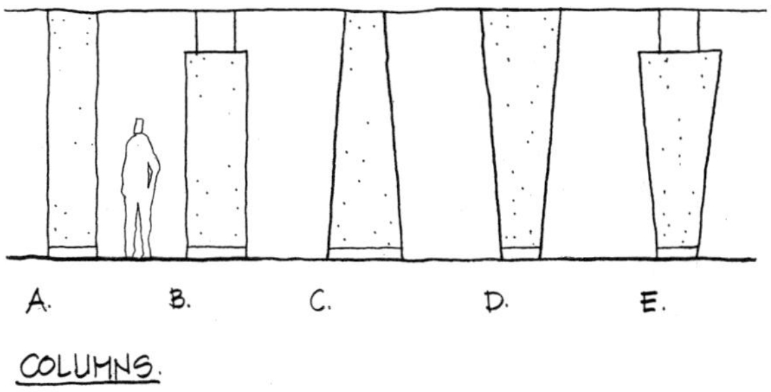

Figure C4.20: The shape of covered columns can assume many shapes: fully covered and full height (a), partial height (b), leaning (c and d), or spreading and partial height (e).

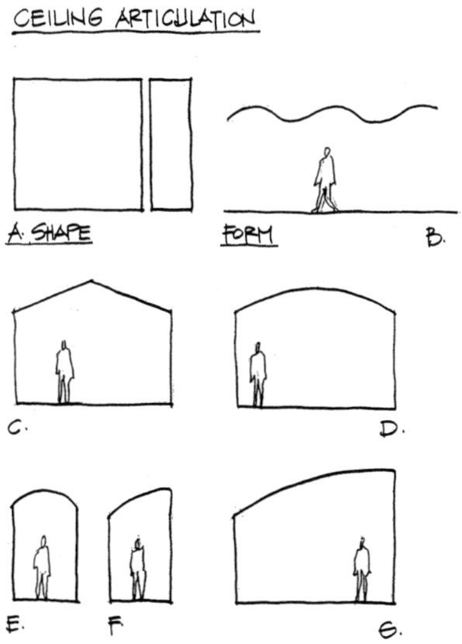

Figure C4.18: The articulation of the ceiling is one of the designer's main tools. Ceilings can be subdivided to define areas (a), undulated (b), gabled (c), or vaulted (d and e). Shapes don't always have to be completed symmetrically. It is possible to have, for instance, partial vaults (f and g).

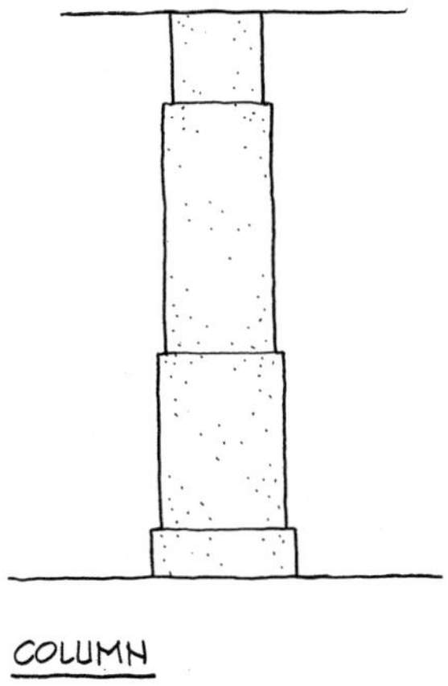

Figure C4.21: Columns can be articulated by varying the widths of their different sections. There are, of course, many other ways of articulating columns.

Chapter Questions

1. Explain the related concepts of space definition, containment, and encapsulation. When does a space go from definition to containment or encapsulation?
2. Recall monumental spaces you have visited. What were they like? How did it feel like to be inside them?
3. Can you recall a corridor, room, or open space you have experienced that had a very generous scale?
4. Recall intimate-scale spaces you have experienced. How did you feel in them?
5. As a designer, you will often be faced with decisions about whether to make a certain space a little more generous or more intimate. Depending on the space, its setting, and use, you may favor one approach over the other. What kinds of spaces would you make more generous? Which ones would you make more intimate?
6. Think of at least two instances where you would use each of the following:
   a) An off-the-path room with a short direct path to it.
   b) A corner space completely open to both side paths. Would you differentiate the path from the space or have it blend with the space?
   c) A path running through the heart of a space.
7. Sketch and briefly describe at least two instances where you would use each of the following:
   a) Two adjoining spaces with a prominent opening on the common side
   b) Two adjacent spaces with an intervening connecting space
   c) Two interpenetrated spaces
   d) Two superimposed spaces
8. In what types of projects would you consider the following systems?
   a) A linear system
   b) An axial system
   c) A radial system
   d) A free system
9. Describe two ideal types of projects for each of the following approaches:
   a) The functional approach
   b) The classical approach
   c) The modern approach
   d) The loose approach

Exercises

The recommended type of drawing for these exercises is a three-dimensional drawing, such as an axonometric or a perspective. In some cases, however, a floor plan will work. Check with your instructor to determine the type of drawings you should use.

1. Draw two minimally defined rectangular spaces, one straightforward and literal, the other implied.
2. Draw three rectangular rooms enclosed by walls. Add openings (number, size, and placement are up to you) to achieve the following:
   a) A very open space with minimal enclosure
   b) A space with an open feel but a moderate sense of containment
   c) A strongly contained space with as much openness as possible
3. Draw at least two similarly sized spaces with enclosing edges of different heights and different levels of transparency (using screens) to produce two very different effects.
4. Draw one space in which you use the ceiling to define:
   a) A sub-space in the center
   b) A path along one side
5. Draw a large space using the floor plane to define a sub-area near the center.
6. Draw two square, two circular, and two short rectangular spaces in which you use the placement of doors to achieve different circulation patterns. These will be rooms that users must go through, so the rooms will all need at least two doors—an inlet and an outlet.
7. Draw two long rectangular spaces and subdivide each into three compartments by using a combination of different techniques, such as wall articulations, dividing planes, furniture arrangements, or placement of doors.
8. Draw three rooms using one of the basic geometric forms you studied and manipulate their form by using:
   a) aggregation
   b) segmentation
   c) distortion
9. Using the concept of disclosure, draw a large space where the view within the space provides a general sense of orientation. This can be achieved by providing a constant (or periodic) view of a central prominent element, by providing a view of a set of regular elements that indicate a route, by providing an extensive disclosure that allows you to see the whole, and by other techniques.
10. Draw a portion of a retail space where the disclosure provided helps to focus attention on one particular display area.
11. Draw either an office or restaurant space where disclosure is planned in such a way that users get at least one instance of internal relief from their work station or dining table.

Chapter 5
Balance and Unity

Instructional Objectives

- Show several ways to manipulate scale for effect.
- Explain important peculiarities about the use of symmetrical compositions.
- Discuss ways of achieving balance with asymmetrical compositions.
- Explain how to use continuity to achieve unity.
- Explain how to use repetition to achieve unity.
- Explain how to use gradation and dispersion as vehicles for unity.

The reasoned relationship of parts to parts, of parts to wholes, of buildings to places, the power of repetition and modularity, the perception of complete units, the expression of construction realities, and the signification of inherent meaning—all are born only of order, not of chance.

Stanley Abercrombie, Architecture as Art

Interior design, being concerned with the composition of parts to assemble a whole, shares many characteristics with the other visual arts. They require the proper placement of, and equilibrium among, different components to achieve an agreeable, aesthetic effect. The aesthetic effect we refer to is not concerned with issues of style, but, rather, with the perceptual correctness of the composition of parts in the visual field. Relevant here are architectural issues such as the proper use of scale, the correct handling of proportions, and the proper balancing of project parts to achieve a harmonious state of balance and equilibrium. These concerns have been articulated from ancient times, beginning with the first treatise on architecture by Vitruvius and remaining relevant today. The sense of resolution and correctness that derives from the proper composition of architectural components gives environments a sense of equilibrium and stability.

This chapter is about the process of working out design ideas to achieve visual harmony and produce a unified creation. We will review some design principles that help designers produce environments that are perceptually harmonious and unified.

SIZING AND BALANCING PROJECT PARTS

Proper composition of parts is an obligation of design. It is one of the many things interior designers are trained to do. This involves tasks such as the proper placement of elements in a composition, the proper size of parts related to other elements, and the proper spacing between them. The craft of design involves the creation and disposition of so many physical parts and the resulting environments have a significant visual impact. When you design, you determine the look of the environment, and that is no small responsibility.

Aesthetic and stylistic approaches vary widely. A design may have more or less aesthetic merit, but regardless of the stylistic direction you choose for a project and the amount of art you inject into it, you have an obligation to produce good compositions. This is where the basic principles of design you learn in your design fundamentals classes come in handy.

It is assumed that you have been exposed to the basic elements and principles of design in previous courses. Here, we will elaborate on the principles that are the most crucial to the resolution and refinement of form. Three aspects deserve special attention: scale, proportion, and balance as their proper handling produces harmonious environments, ones where the elements will be in accord with each other, fit together, look right, and form a cohesive unit.

So basic are these concerns to design that they have been featured prominently in all the treatises on architecture and design, going as far back as Vitruvius's *Ten Books on Architecture.* In addressing the fundamental principles of architecture he refers to the "order which gives due measure to the members of a work considered separately, and symmetrical agreement to the proportions of the whole."[1] He goes on to discuss three essential concepts to good composition: arrangement, eurythmy, and symmetry.

Arrangement includes "the putting together of things in their proper places and the elegance of effect which is due to adjustments appropriate to the character of the work."[2] It is concerned with the project's agreeable composition at the overall scale. Vitrivius notes that it requires both reflection and invention.

Reflection is careful and laborious thought, and watchful attention directed to the agreeable effect of one's plan. Invention, on the other hand, is the solving of intricate problems and the discovery of new principles by means of brilliancy and versatility.

Eurythmy is beauty and fitness in the adjustment of the members, and refers to the agreeable scale and proportion of units in and of themselves. This is found when the members of a work are of a height suited to their breadth, of a breadth suited to their length, and in a word, when they all correspond symmetrically.[3] **Symmetry** is a proper agreement among the members of the work itself and relation among the different parts and the whole general scheme, in accordance with a certain part selected as standard.[4]

Note that Vitruvius's concept of symmetry refers to the agreeable relationships among the units or parts that form a composition and not to the use of symmetrical compositions.

These three aspects of design are related and part of a logical continuum that works at different scales, starting with one part and its relation to itself and the human body, then the combination of that part with others to create a group or sub-assembly, followed by the combination of sub-assemblies to produce, say, one level of an elevation, then the combination of levels to produce the entire elevation (Figure 5.1).

Translating Vitruvius's concerns into more familiar terms, we can then discuss the three design principles previously mentioned: scale, proportion, and balance.

Scale

Scale in design refers to the relative size of a space, object, or element in relation to some other part. That other part can be adjacent spaces, the immediate space where the element is housed, the human person, or other objects and elements in the space. The kind of scale we are talking about, although related to size, does not refer to the actual size of things, such as when we talk about a large-scaled complex, we mean a large project, referring to relative size.

Scale is influenced by use and custom. Thus, its appropriateness is also judged relative to the kind of space being evaluated and the type of activities that occur in it. Our judgments are also influenced by the preconceived ideas we have of similar elements based on what we have experienced in the past. If we are talking about a church and ask a group of people from diverse backgrounds just how grand the church should be, their answers will tend to vary depending on whether they are used to grand cathedrals or small parish churches. Which one is more appropriate for the occasion will require the judgment of the designer and the users associated with the project.

To become competent using scale, you need to understand how scale can be manipulated. You need to learn to design straightforward projects that handle scale in a customary and agreeable way. Additionally, you want to learn how to manipulate scale for effect. We will start with a presentation of the basic relationships affecting scale in interior environments.

The Size of Things in Relation to Humans

Of all the relationships concerning scale in interiors, none is more important than the relationship of space and its components to the human figure. This is especially true for the profession of interior design, a profession that specializes in the interaction of humans and environment at the proxemic scale. Height and depth dimensions of interior components, for instance, are governed by the size and reach of the persons using them. Scale decisions in relation to the human body affect the design of wall openings, privacy panels, cabinetry, furnishings, control devices, and so on. Proper dimensions for many different applications are usually well documented in reference books. However, keep in mind that when you design for special groups, such as young children, the elderly, and the physically disabled, there are likely to be unique needs that vary from the basic standards.

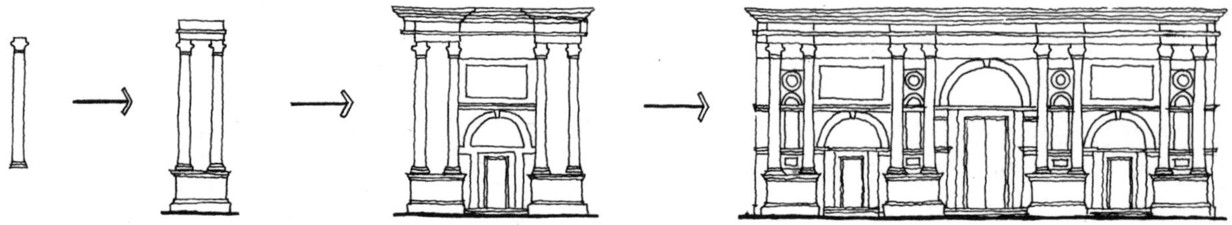

Figure 5.1: Resolution requires the proper disposition of parts, sub-wholes, and wholes. In this example the single column is an element complete in itself. Paired with another column, and with the addition of a pedestal below and entablature above, another whole unit is formed. The addition of a symmetrical entryway, flanked by two of the previous units, forms yet another whole unit. Finally, two of these latter units, with the addition of a central grand entrance, form the lower portion of a complete facade. All of these sub-parts need to be resolved individually and also as components of the entire totality.

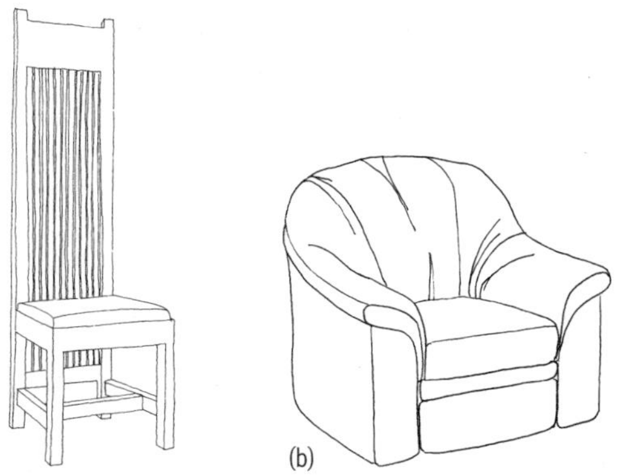

(a) (b)

Figure 5.2: The chair (a) designed by Frank Lloyd Wright is intentionally much taller than is needed. A lounge chair (b) is quite different. It is meant to embrace and comfort.

The sizes of objects can vary from the customary sizes people are used to. In some cases they can be manipulated in relation to the human body for effect. The size of a chair, for instance, can be exaggerated to increase definition, as the extra-tall chair in Figure 5.2a shows, or to create a feeling of comfort, as shown in Figure 5.2b. Door hardware can be oversized to accentuate the physicality of turning the handle to open the door and gain access. It can also be minimized, to create a more delicate and refined experience. Do keep in mind that, in spite of the desired effect, the scale manipulation has to satisfy the basic function it addresses, be it seating or opening, as in the previous examples.

There are other kinds of design elements that can be sized in different ways. A door, for example, as long as it meets building codes and provides proper clearance for normal individuals, can be relatively short. It can also be much taller than it needs to be. Figure 5.3a–c shows a range of heights.

Many elements used in interiors, from doors to furnishings, relate very closely to the human body. Although they all have optimal sizes, dimensions can be somewhat adjusted for effect as long as the resulting size is within the functional range.

Relation to Application

Also important is the size of things in relation to their application. Depending on the type of activity a space is designed for, its scale may need to be grand, normal, or intimate. Although the scale of palaces, churches, and prominent civic buildings may be monumental, the scale for certain areas in exclusive candlelit restaurants or the seating areas off a main corridor (Figure 5.4) will often want to be small and intimate.

Relation to Element Type

Objects, such as building elements, furnishings, and accessories, belong to their respective typological families. Windows, doors, tables, chairs, artwork, and plants are familiar objects for which we have preconceived mental images based on our previous encounters with them. Although the exact stylistic image that comes to mind when we think of any of these items will vary slightly from person to person based on background, the essence of the mental picture will be quite similar. Part of the preconceived image relates to the size we associate with that object and its parts. These establish a point of reference and any variation toward a larger or smaller version will constitute a change of scale.

Fortunately, most design-related elements are available in a range of sizes. Commercial-grade doors, for instance,

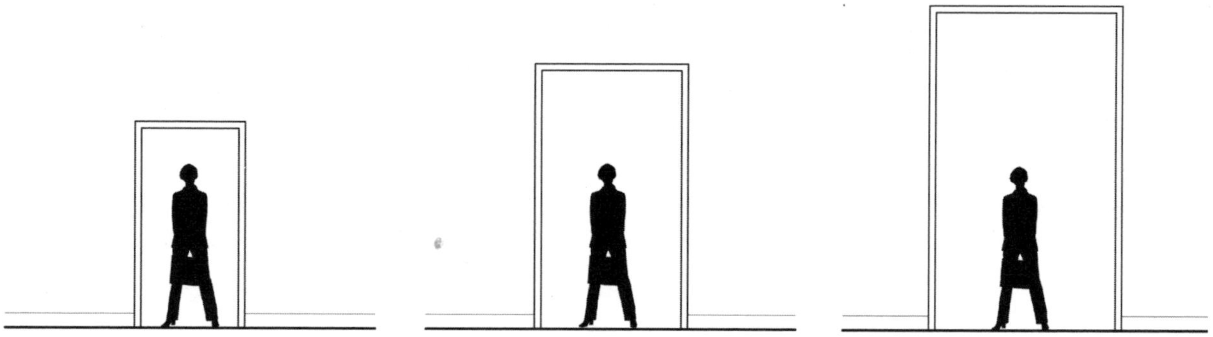

(a) (b) (c)

Figure 5.3: The three openings here show three distinct scales: minimal (a), comfortable (b), and grand (c). Each relates to the size of the human figure differently. Opening (a) is oppressive and uncomfortable, while (c) is generous to the point of excess.

Figure 5.4: The scale of this seating area off a main circulation space has been intentionally reduced to make it more intimate and inviting.

Figure 5.5: In addition to judging interior elements in relation to the size of the human body, we also make judgments in relation to the customary size of the components. This door is tall compared to most other doors we encounter.

although they tend to be of relatively uniform width, come in many heights. The relatively low 6-foot-8-inch doors used in residential construction are rarely used in commercial projects, where taller doors are usually preferred. Thus, one can choose to specify very tall doors for a project, like the one shown in Figure 5.5. Tables, although their height does not change much, come in a variety of widths, lengths, and shapes. Other items, such as art objects and plants, come in many sizes, and designers can choose among them to suit the scale needs of the project. Judgments related to scale will be made using the customary size of the object as a reference, so that one is likely to say, "That chair seems really small."

Relation of Space to Entire Project

The spaces of a project can also vary widely in their shape, size, and character. Within a single project, the predominant spaces may set an overall scale constituting a point of reference. Consequently, if their scale is generally consistent, any major scale deviations will be noticeable. "Aha," someone might say upon seeing a room with a more generous scale than the rest, "This must be an important space."

Relation of Contents to Space

When inside a specific space, the objects in it will have an important relationship to the overall space and its architectural features (doors, windows, columns, and so on). Among the important components are the furnishings, equipment, and accessories of the space. The correspondence between these objects and the space can be complementary or discordant. For instance, you may use oversized furnishings, fixtures, plants, and artwork to fill the volume of a large space and have good scale correspondence between the room and its contents

Figure 5.6: There is an important scale correspondence between a room and the objects in it. Rooms with a large volume often require large-scaled furnishings and accessories (as shown) to look right.

Figure 5.7: In contrast to large rooms, small rooms almost demand small-scaled furniture and accessories. Otherwise, the largeness of these objects can dwarf the room and make it perceptually uncomfortable.

(Figure 5.6). Conversely, you may use small furniture, fixtures, and artwork in a small space to make it congruous with the reduced size of the space and thus achieve a comfortable correspondence (Figure 5.7).

One final example of the relationship of the scale of objects to that of the space involves the number of pieces used and their sizes. That way, one can control the size of the components in a composition to emphasize a desired scale. This can be illustrated by the effects produced by different arrangements of artwork on a wall. The wall can be equally filled (proportionately) using different combinations of artwork of different number and size, thus producing different effects. Figure 5.8 shows three wall segments in a corridor, one of them having one large painting filling the wall, one having three medium pieces, and one having many smaller pieces covering approximately as much wall space as the large paintings. Notice how the feel of the applications is quite different, all due to the size and number of pieces used.

Relation of Contents to Other Contents

The last scale relationship we will discuss is that of the objects in relation to other objects in a space. Among these objects are the ones we previously referred to (furnishings, plants, and artwork) as well as fixtures, doors, cabinetry, and hardware. In general, the relative size of all these elements needs to be complementary so that everything works together. It is possible, though, to

Figure 5.8: The scale of a space can be affected by the size of the objects in it. In this example, the artwork on the three segments of wall shown varies. The effect produced by one large painting (a) is different from the effect produced by a series of smaller works (b and c).

(a)

(b)

(c)

purposefully work with more than one scale for effect and exaggerate the scale of, say, the artwork on the walls, for effect.

One final observation related to architectural scale is worth mentioning: the complementary nature of various scales within a space. Spaces that have a variety of scales from the architectural elements, the furnishings, the fixtures, and the accessories feel rich and satisfying. Figure 5.9 shows an example where we can distinguish among the variety of scales, ranging from the largest (the spatial volume) to the smallest (the salt and pepper shakers on the table).

Figure 5.9: Real environments, especially complex ones, are often composed of many scales working together and complementing each other. A good space will normally progress harmoniously from the largeness of the overall space to the in-between scale of objects in it, and the smallness of accessories and utensils around, as shown in this view.

Approaches to Scale

Resolving scale is a part of all interior projects. The approach taken may be straightforward or involve manipulation for effect. The criteria for judging the success of any attempt consist of two basic questions: Was the approach used appropriate? Was its execution done well?

The straightforward approach to scale, although apparently simple, requires good aesthetic sense. The goal is to size everything in the space to be in scale. With this approach, all layers of space and objects are treated in a complementary fashion and the approach kept consistent throughout.

The approach involving manipulation has many possible applications but can be harder to pull off successfully. In general, you manipulate scale to create a focus, establish dominance, define space, or produce tension. You create a focus by making the size of the desired element different (usually larger) so it stands out by contrast. Similarly, you can increase the size of any one type of item, be it the furniture or the artwork, in order to establish dominance or help define space. Figure 5.10 shows a design by Frank Lloyd Wright for a dining table setup in which he increased the height of the chairs surrounding the table to contain the area and make it more intimate. In this example he also used four special light fixtures at the corners to help define the area further.

Proportion

Proportion is also concerned with the size of architectural and decorative elements and the size of the leftover spaces between them. With proportion we look at elements in relation to the composition of which they are a part. Of concern is whether the dimensions of the individual pieces and the spaces in between are appropriate, given the dimensions of the overall composition. During the Renaissance the size and spacing of columns were considered at length and developed mathematically in order to produce agreeable compositions for temples,

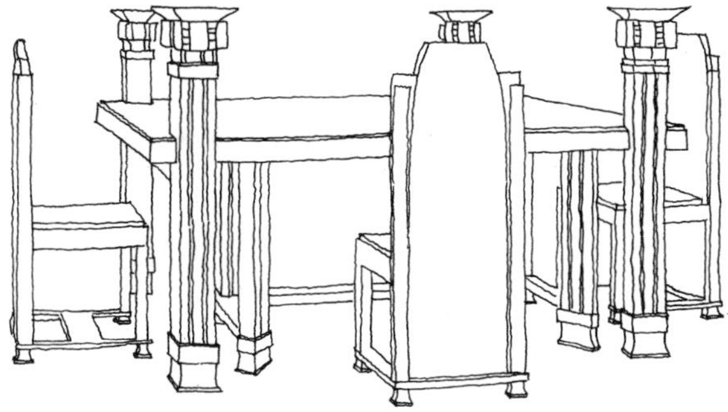

Figure 5.10: In this dining table by Frank Lloyd Wright, not one but all the chairs are tall. Additionally, there are four light fixtures of similar height integrated into the corners of the table. The purpose here is to produce a sense of enclosure around the table to make it feel contained and intimate.

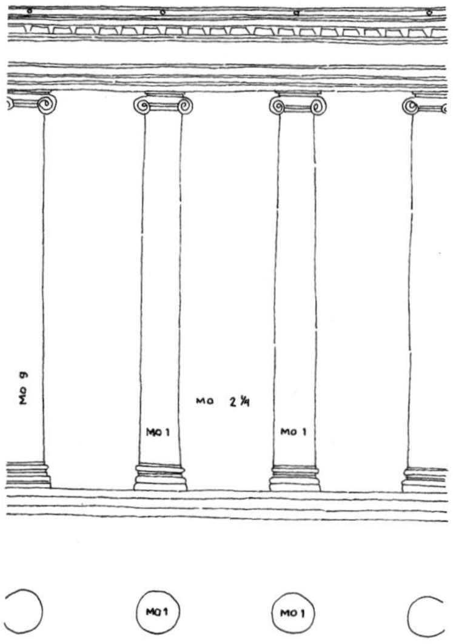

Figure 5.11: During the Renaissance, architects such as Palladio developed rules of correct proportioning for the different classical orders. Palladio's proportioning for Ionic colonnades is shown here. The basic dimension used was the diameter of the column. All other dimensions were developed using this basic dimension as a reference.

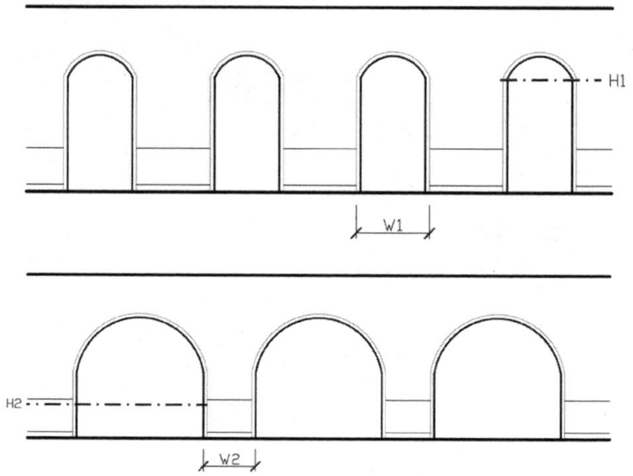

Figure 5.12: The concern for proportion is closely related to scale. Each type of scale has its own set of agreeable proportions. In the two arcades shown here, the types of arches used establish very distinct scales. In this case the height of the arches and the amount of solid wall above them are similar. They seem to work well in both cases. In order for them to work, though, notice how both the cutting point of the arch on the sides and the width of the solid portion of the wall between the arches are different in each case.

palazzos, churches, villas, and so on. Figure 5.11 shows the correct proportions of columns and the spaces between them for the composition of an Ionic colonnade according to Andrea Palladio. Similarly, there were prescribed optimal proportions for the other orders of columns, for room proportions, and so on.

A more pertinent example to interior work today, and also related to the interplay of solids and voids, is the proportions of openings on a solid wall. Figure 5.12 shows two arcades, one with many smaller arches and the other with fewer, larger ones. As you can tell, the issue of scale is also involved here. Notice the different proportions of the arched openings in relation to one another, the spaces in between, and the space above them.

Figure 5.13 shows a similar example. This time we have a wall with punched penetrations. This example involves numbers, scale, and proportion. Notice the progression of adjustments from the elevations shown in Figure 5.13a–c. In Figures 5.13b and 5.13c the heights of the openings seem to work better in relation to their width and the height of the overall wall than in 5.13 a. The widths of the spaces in-between also seem to have a good relation to the size of the openings.

Now examine a freestanding mass in an open space. Depending on the height of the space and the amount of

Figure 5.13: Any two-dimensional surface with multiple features needs to be studied proportionally. This example shows three proportional studies for openings on a wall. The size of the openings, the space between them, and the remaining space above and below are all considered. In these examples, the openings in (a) have too much space between them and the ones in (b) seem a bit oversized. The openings in (c), as well as their placement and spacing, are the most successful of the three.

(a)

(b)

Figure 5.14: The size, shape, and placement of objects in space need to work proportionally. In this example, the effects of the short and wide freestanding mass in (a) and the tall and slender floating mass in (b) are different, the former compressing the horizontal space and the latter compressing the vertical space.

space around the mass, different dimensions of the mass will work better than others. Figure 5.14 shows two variations of this situation. The mass in Figure 5.14a is wide and short, whereas the one in Figure 5.14b is slender and taller. They each fill the space differently. Which one do you like better?

Are there formulas to aid us in achieving pleasant proportions? There are. The golden mean, the Fibonacci Series, and the Modulor are among the proportional systems that have been devised over time and can be helpful to assemble well-proportioned compositions. However,, you don't always need a formula, as you can develop an eye for proportion.

The golden mean is a mathematical system of proportion devised by the Greeks, who applied it not only to buildings but also to sculpture and the design of small objects and details. The basic ratio of the golden mean is that produced when a line is divided into two unequal segments such that the ratio of the smaller segment to the larger one is the same as the ratio of the larger one to the entire line (Figure 5.15). The proportions of the golden mean are universal and can be found in flowers, vegetables, and other examples from nature. They have also been adopted by architects and designers from Palladio to Le Corbusier.

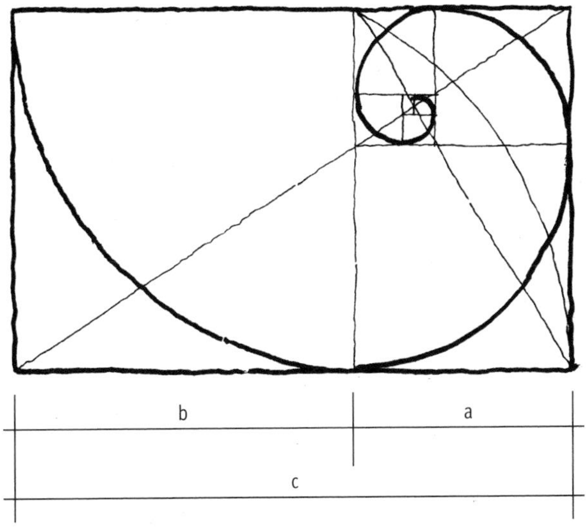

Figure 5.15: This basic drawing shows the proportioning system prescribed by the golden mean. The proportions are such that the ratio of segment a to segment b is the same as that of segment b to the entire length c (a + b).

The Fibonacci Series is named after a famous Italian mathematician of the 13th century, Leonardo Fibonacci. The proportions of the series are very similar to those of the golden mean. The series consists of the addition of consecutive whole numbers in a series such that the sum of any two sequential numbers equals the next number in the sequence. This produces a series of whole numbers as follows: 1, 1, 2, 3, 5, 8, 13, 21, 34, and so on. Similar to the golden mean, with this series, if you have a line of, say, 8 units of length and divide it into two unequal sections of 3 and 5 units, respectively, the ratio of the short segment (3) to the long one (5) is equivalent (approximately) to the one between the long one (5) and the total length (8).

The Modulor was a proportional system devised in the 20th century by Le Corbusier based on the golden mean

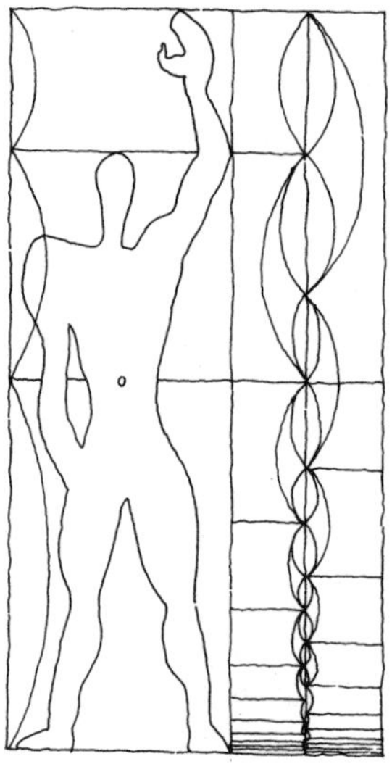

Figure 5.16: Le Corbusier's Le Modulor system was derived from the proportions of the golden mean and the proportions of the human body. It addressed all kinds of proportions, from those of small objects to those used at the town-planning scale.

and the dimensions of the human body (Figure 5.16). It is derived from the division of an average human height into segments of ratios based on the golden mean. He found the derived proportions useful in determining heights of spaces and fixtures and other anthropomorphic relationships.

Although such proportional systems are helpful in providing some basic guidelines to follow, it is wise to avoid the obsessive use of mathematical formulas for two reasons. It will make your design process stiff and mechanical. And it will not always produce satisfactory results. Not even these three well-known proportional systems will work satisfactorily all the time. The golden mean, despite its wisdom, was considered to produce monotony if applied strictly. For that reason, it became necessary to perform intuitive corrections in order to produce more satisfying proportional results. Similarly, some critics believe Le Corbusier's best work was produced when he relied less on mechanical means and more on artistic intuition. In matters of proportion, thus, it is helpful for you to develop a good intuitive sense through continued practice.

In addition to the examples already presented, issues of proportion arise in cases where you have two-dimensional patterns on surfaces. Whether the variety is achieved by different materials or different colors, the same principles apply. You stand back, look at the proposed composition, and start telling yourself: The red strip needs to be wider and moved to the center; the blue squares are too small, and so on. This kind of analysis, though, gets into the issue of balance, our next topic, so we will elaborate there.

Balance

The resolution of both scale and proportion in a project requires the achievement of proper balance. These three factors—scale, proportion, and balance—are closely intertwined. **Balance** in design refers to the visual equilibrium of elements in a composition. It is affected by the size, shape, and placement of the parts of the composition. The goal is to produce an assembly of parts that looks right, a composition that is harmonious. The principle of balance applies to both two- and three-dimensional compositions. Two-dimensional compositions are seen as planes composed of parts, such as in an elevation or patterned floor.

Three-dimensional compositions are perceived differently. Here the element of depth comes into play, so not only do we see things to the left, center, and right, but objects and elements are also in the foreground, middle ground, or background. These form a more complex kind of composition that incorporates, among other things, the changing apparent size and location of objects as one moves about the space.

Symmetrical Compositions

Symmetrical compositions employ equivalent, usually identical, elements mirrored on either side of a central vertical axis. We are all familiar with symmetry. For many centuries, the only acceptable way to compose was using symmetry. Symmetry is pervasive in our world. Not only are humans composed symmetrically but so are many of our creations, like cars and many of the other machines and pieces of equipment we make. There seems to be a natural tendency toward symmetry in design. Many novice designers cannot seem to get away from it. This may be due to the fact that it is easy to use symmetry and it always achieves a good sense of balance.

There is nothing wrong with using symmetry. It is when the designer starts to impose symmetry on every aspect of every design, whether it is called for or not, that the tendency becomes problematic. Symmetrical organizations carry connotations of logic and formality. Combined with the proper materials and details, they can also express elegance and dignity. Ideal applications include formal, traditional, and dignified projects, such as government buildings, churches, and courthouses. On the other hand, symmetrical organizations are static and can be dull. The obvious way in which the elements of the built environment are presented through symmetry provides limited perceptual challenge to the observer and, therefore, has limited interest. Symmetrical compositions, however, offer an instantly perceived equilibrium and a strong figural whole seen against the background of everything else around them. There are several important considerations when composing symmetrical arrangements. Four particularly relevant ones are the location of the focus ahead, the relationship between the central axis and the approach, the level of intricacy of the composition, and the purity of the symmetry.

The focal point of symmetrical compositions is usually along the central axis. The center of a composition is normally differentiated, often emphasized (Figure 5.17). Whether a framed view to the outside, a piece of artwork, or a formal arrival space, central foci tend to make symmetrical compositions particularly powerful. They frequently give the ceremonial feeling of walking straight toward a meaningful destination. Another approach possible is the placement of two strong, symmetrical elements on either side of the center. If nothing is provided at the center, the composition may sometimes seem incomplete, so it is a good practice to have something, even if only a detail, featured at the center (Figure 5.18). The composition goes from having two parts to having three by the addition of something in the middle. In fact, three-part (tripartite) compositions are among the most used and most successful kinds of symmetrical compositions.

In scenarios where the center is equal to the sides its power isn't as strong but can still work (Figure 5.19a). Magnetism will be strongest when there is a dominant center, as shown in Figure 5.19b. The one approach that always tends to look wrong is the placement of a weak element at the center, as shown in Figure 5.19c. Figure 5.20 shows two tripartite symmetrical elevations of a wall that might be found in a corporate conference room. The one in Figure 5.20a features two lateral entrances, whereas the one in Figure 5.20b has a central entrance. They both feature niches with casework and artwork. Notice their different effects and the local symmetries in each of their three sections.

A factor of considerable importance is the correspondence between the central axis of the composition and the approach toward it. In cases where one moves straight on toward a symmetrical composition, the effect is heightened

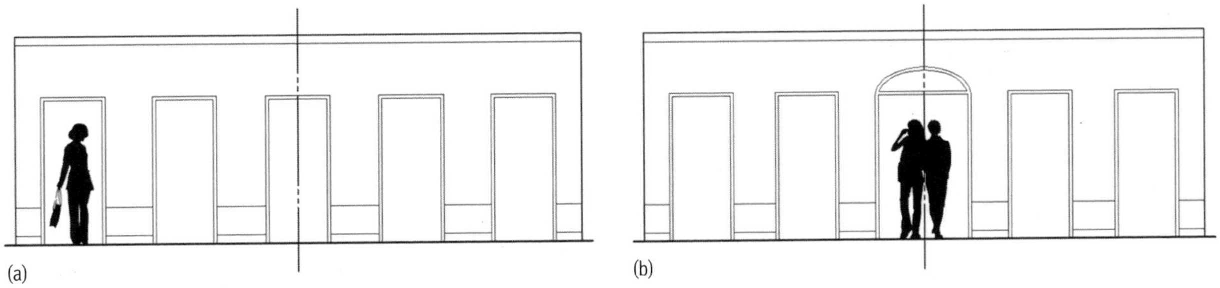

Figure 5.17: Strong symmetrical compositions rely on a strong center and two flanking sides. Of the two elevations shown, elevation (a), although symmetrical, reads more as a series than a static symmetrical composition. Elevation (b) is better anchored by the added emphasis on the central archway.

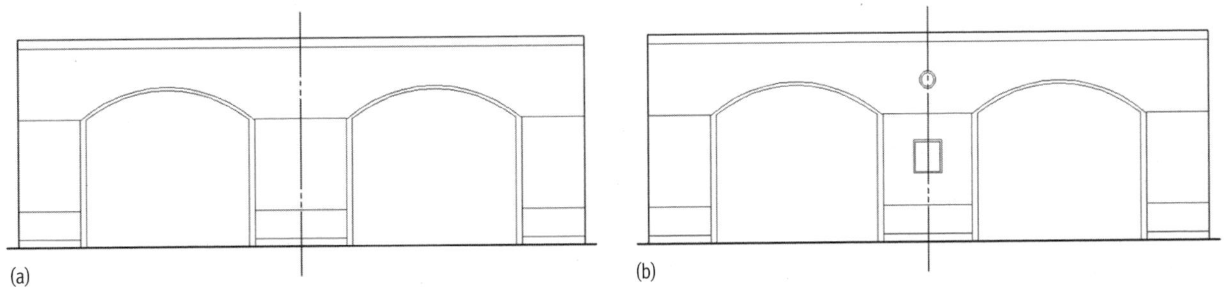

Figure 5.18: Symmetrical compositions with a feature at the center are stronger In this example the flanking sides are intended to be dominant. Although example a works well, the addition of a a small detail at the center seems to complete the elevation better, giving it an enhanced sense of balance and resolution.

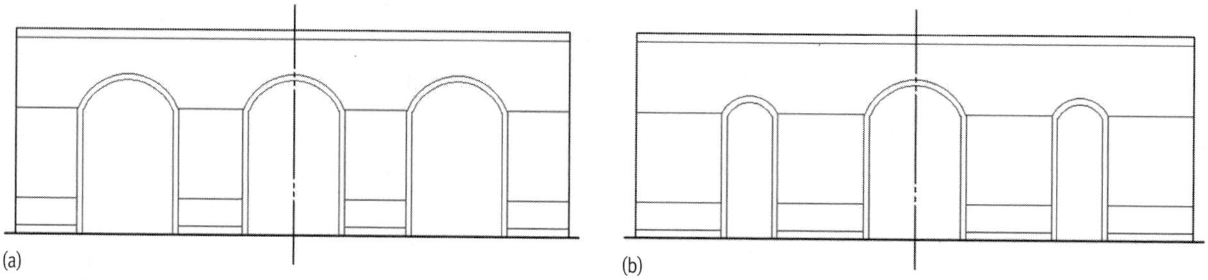

(a)

(b)

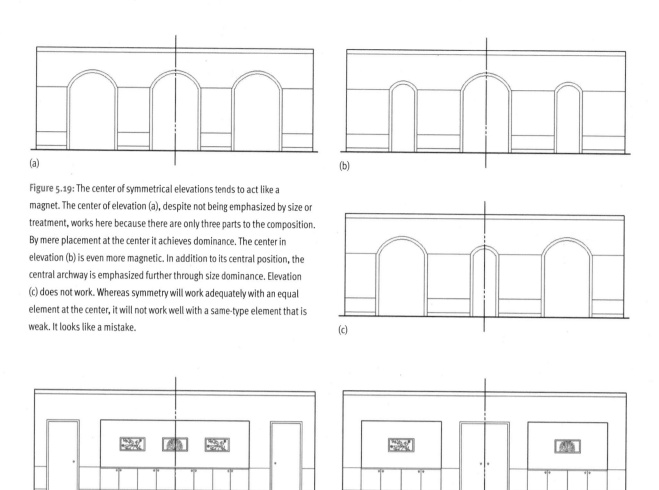

Figure 5.19: The center of symmetrical elevations tends to act like a magnet. The center of elevation (a), despite not being emphasized by size or treatment, works here because there are only three parts to the composition. By mere placement at the center it achieves dominance. The center in elevation (b) is even more magnetic. In addition to its central position, the central archway is emphasized further through size dominance. Elevation (c) does not work. Whereas symmetry will work adequately with an equal element at the center, it will not work well with a same-type element that is weak. It looks like a mistake.

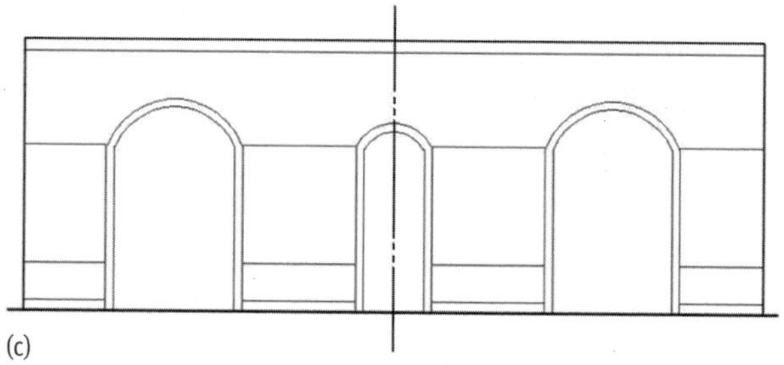

(c)

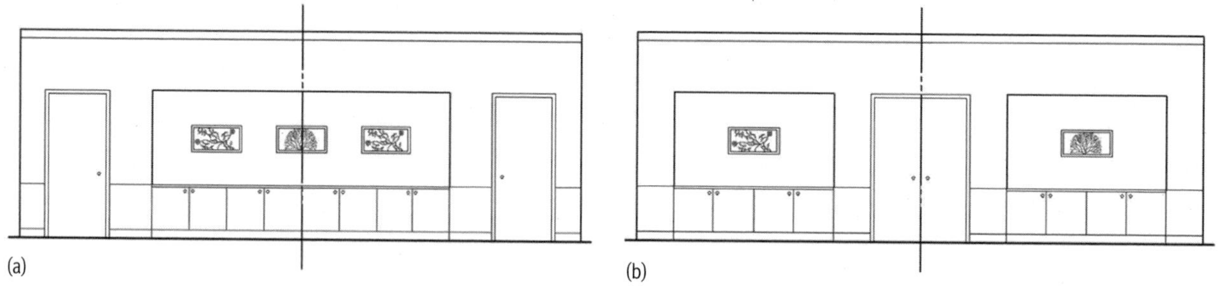

(a)

(b)

Figure 5.20: Both these possible elevations in a corporate conference room work well. Elevation (a) features a dominant central niche with local symmetry and two flanking sides with the entry doors. Elevation (b) features a pair of dominant doors at the center with two smaller niches at the sides.

by having a path, symmetrical itself, centered along the central axis of the composition. This achieves a strong formal, stately, and ceremonial effect (Figure 5.21). A different approach is to have symmetrically arranged paths flanking the central space of the approach, thus creating two lateral approaches toward the end wall (Figure 5.22).

Symmetrical compositions are meant to be seen straight on. When one walks in parallel to the symmetrical composition the view of the composition is oblique, and the compositional effort is wasted, as it will not be seen as intended. In cases where spaces are narrow, as in corridors, it is best to rely on other compositional techniques dealing with sequence, such as the use of rhythm, instead of symmetry.

While simple symmetrical compositions may sometimes lack interest, complex ones can be quite engaging.

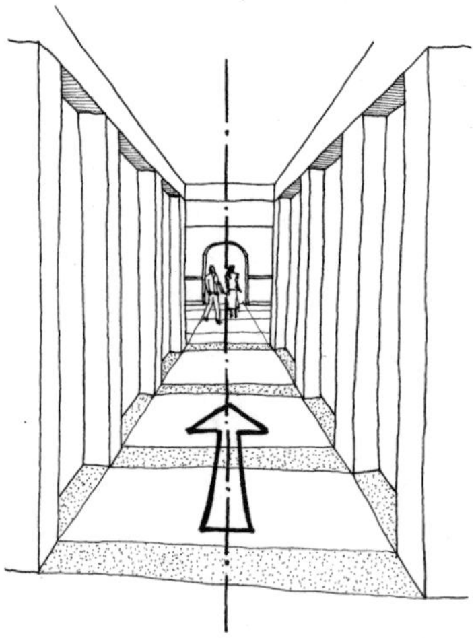

Figure 5.21: Whenever a symmetrical composition, such as a wall, is approached via a central, symmetrical path, the overall effect of the composition is strengthened. This adds formality and a literal sense of walking toward the center.

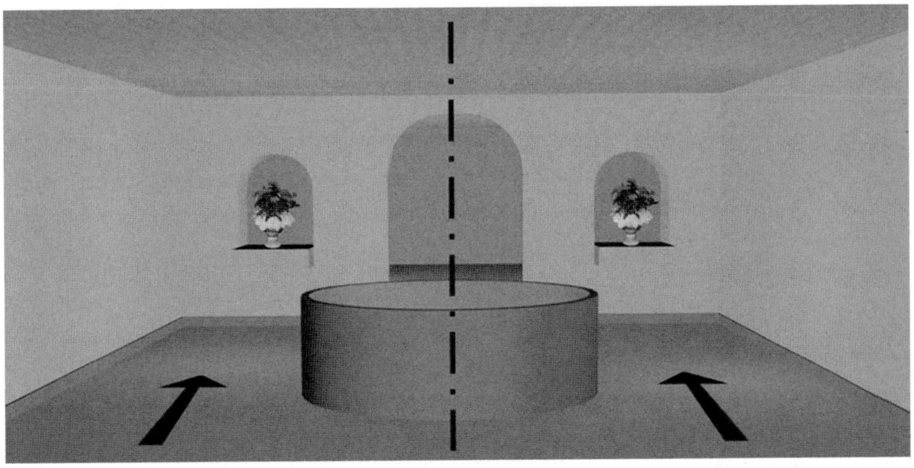

Figure 5.22: Whenever a symmetrical composition, such as the one here, is approached laterally and not centrally, the effect is different. The composition shown, although allowing visual access from the center, forces people to approach the end wall from one of the two sides.

Complex symmetrical compositions that have secondary symmetries and different lateral and vertical relationships provide richness and variety and can be quite stimulating. The elevation composition shown in Figure 5.23 progresses from a simple idea to an elaborate composition. The addition of layers of articulation shown in Figures 5.23b and c make the elevation come to life, endowing it with sufficient intricacy to attract, engage, and delight the eye.

Symmetry does not always have to be perfect. Although most symmetrical compositions tend to be pure with both sides mirroring each other identically, it is possible to have imperfect symmetry by having inequalities between the sides in such a way that symmetry is apparent, but, upon further scrutiny, what is on the right is not exactly what is on the left (Figure 5.24).

Figure 5.23: Although symmetrical compositions tend to be static, they can certainly be stimulating. This example shows the transformation of a simple symmetrical composition into a highly articulated creation. The simple idea of the arched openings in (a) is enriched by the modulation of the arches, and the addition of columns with capitals and pedestals between them (b). The composition is elaborated further in (c), where more detail is added and surfaces are enriched by the addition of relief.

Asymmetrical Compositions

Asymmetrical compositions in Western design are a product of the 20th century. Their use increased with the advent of modern architecture and the free-flowing plans introduced by the likes of Frank Lloyd Wright and Mies van der Rohe. Wright rejected the formality and rigidity of classical architecture and favored more natural and organic approaches to planning. He described the emerging composition attitude as follows:

> Modern architecture rejects the major axis and the minor axis of classical architecture. It rejects all grandomania, every building that would stand in military fashion heels together, eyes front, something on the right hand, and something on

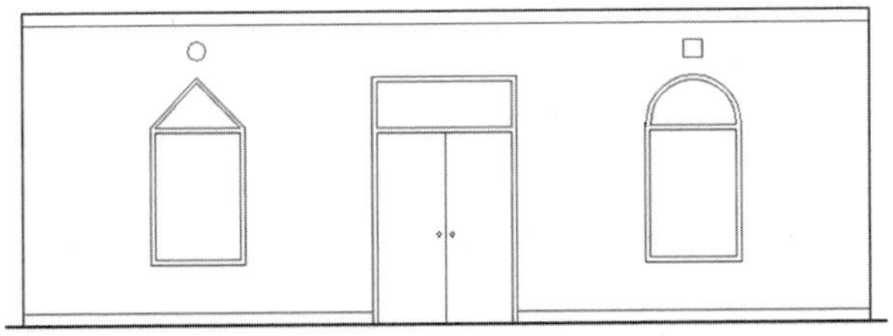

Figure 5.24: Symmetry does not always have to be perfect. The elevation shown has a symmetrical composition that is not exactly the same from side to side. If you take a close look you'll notice that the pediments over the two side windows and the ornamental motifs above them are shaped differently.

> the left hand. Architecture already favors the reflex, the natural easy attitude, the occult symmetry of grace and rhythm affirming the ease, grace, and naturalness of natural life.[5]

Asymmetrical compositions achieve balance through the careful placement of different elements of varying sizes and proportional weights. They avoid the kind of side-to-side repetition employed in symmetrical planning. For instance, a mass on one side may be balanced by a group of carefully placed elements of a different size and shape on the other side. Asymmetrical balance relies more on a painterly eye than on specific rules. It requires greater skill and control by the designer but can produce very satisfying results. Figure 5.25 shows two successful office reception area scenes composed asymmetrically.

(a)

(b)

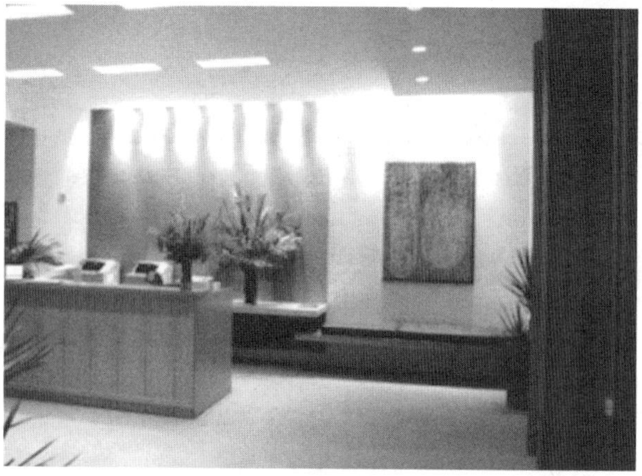

Figure 5.25: Today's design is full of examples of asymmetrical compositions. Two office reception areas are shown here. Both are well balanced. The horizontality of the sofa on one side and the verticality of the display on the other create balance in (a). The central chair in the foreground and the flower arrangement in the background serve to produce some secondary interest and act as a pivot point. In (b), the reception desk on one side is balanced against the prominent painting on the other. The sharp vertical line just to the right of the center of the composition serves as a visual break point on this composition. The flowers, once again, serve as a secondary point of interest.

One of the characteristic effects of asymmetrical compositions is their tendency to be more casual and informal than symmetrical ones. They work best in compositions having no symmetrical components. Figure 5.26 illustrates the difficulty of imposing asymmetry on elevations with strong symmetrical components. The doors in Figures 5.26a and b establish fairly strong symmetrical traits that are hard to counteract without moving them. The results are ambiguous compositions with a mix of symmetry and asymmetry.

Asymmetrical compositions tend to also be more dynamic and engaging than symmetrical ones if executed properly. They work best when there is nothing located at the center or equally spaced on either side. Figure 5.27 shows two elevations equivalent to the two symmetrical ones shown in Figure 5.20. Notice how different these are, much less formal and static. Asymmetrical compositions can still have a sense of formality, as shown in Figure 5.28. Although the path shown has a formal side of uniformly placed rhythmic elements, the opposite side supplies contrast with its planar, nonrhythmic treatment. There is a level of formality produced by the rhythmic composition

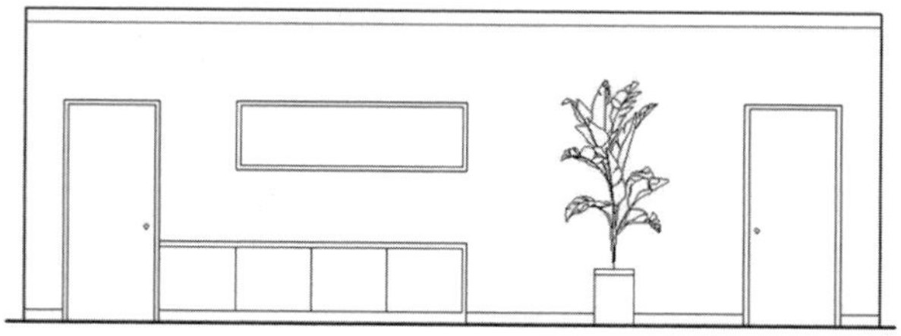

(a)

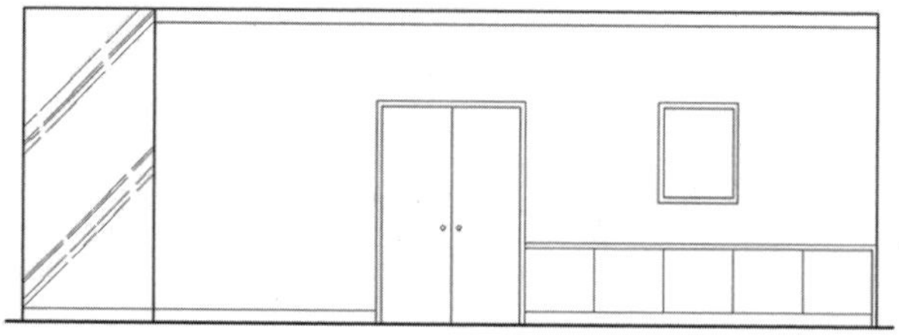

(b)

Figure 5.26: It is difficult to impose asymmetry on arrangements containing strong symmetrical properties. Of the two examples shown with given locations for the doors, elevation (a) is particularly difficult to resolve due to the powerful symmetry imposed by the doors. The resulting elevation is ambiguous and weak. In elevation (b), despite the power of the centrally located pair of doors, the fact that it is just one element makes it easier to incorporate into the asymmetrical composition. Even so, there is something strange about an asymmetrical composition with a principal component perfectly centered.

(a)

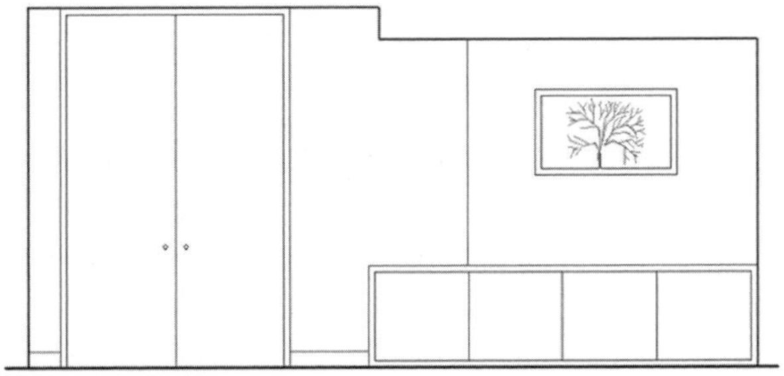

(b)

Figure 5.27: Asymmetrical compositions work best with nothing centered. These two elevations are equivalent to the two shown in Figure 5.20, except they are not symmetrical. Compare the two approaches and notice the different effects produced.

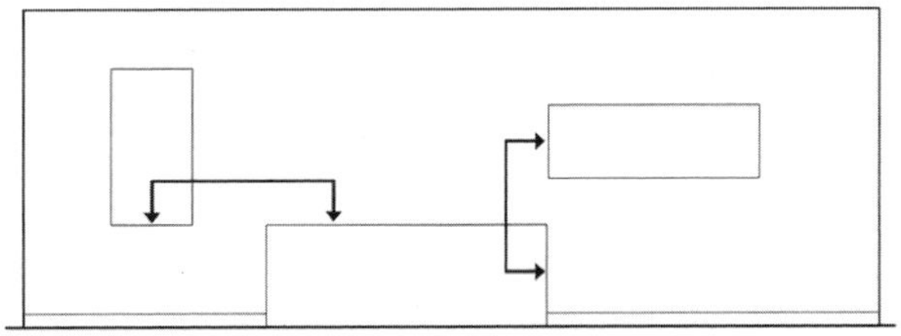

(a)

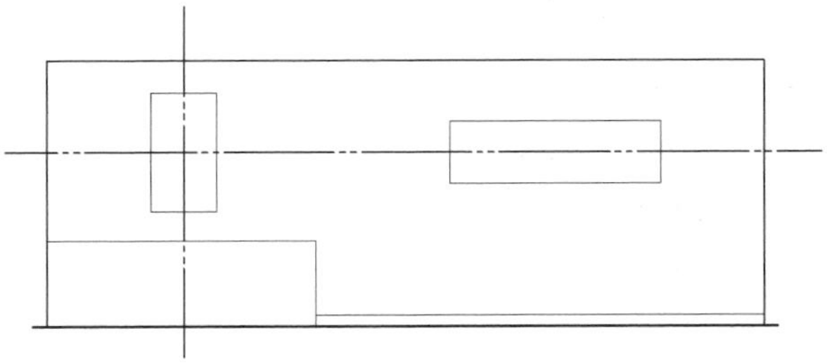

(b)

Figure 5.29: Components of asymmetrical compositions can have strong geometrical relationships. This can be achieved by the use of alignments. These can be edge alignments, as shown in elevation (a), or center line alignments, as shown in (b). These alignments add regularity to the composition.

Figure 5.28: Despite their relative informality, asymmetrical compositions can still be arranged in ways that elicit formality. The asymmetrical path shown here has unequal elements on either side. The presence of a regular colonnade on the left side gives it a sense of decorum and formality, even if a casual one.

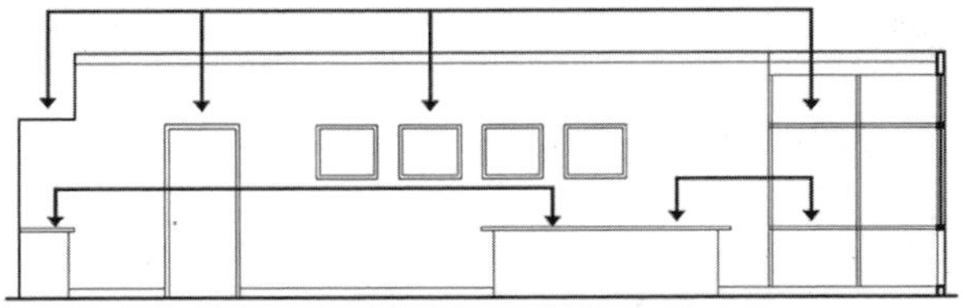

Figure 5.30: A strategy often used to create strong relationships in compositions, either symmetrical or asymmetrical, is the alignment of regulating horizontal lines. These are often derived from existent components in the shell space. In this example, horizontal lines established by an existing window wall are used to establish the heights of the door, the bench, and the artwork. Additionally, the heights of the cabinetry and the underside of the artwork are also coordinated. These relationships help create a consistent unified overall effect.

of the left side, while the contrasting right side counterbalances and softens the rigidity of the overall effect.

Another way of regulating asymmetrical composition is by the alignment of lines in the composition. In Figure 5.29 there is no identical repetition from side to side, although the regularity produced by the alignments helps to give a sense of order. Alignments can be at the edges of elements (Figure 5.29a) or through their center lines (Figure 5.29b). Height alignments are particularly useful devices to achieve balanced compositions. The regularity produced in Figure 5.30 by the consistent alignment of elements in relation to the window wall's horizontal lines gives this elevation a sense of resolved equilibrium.

Asymmetrical compositions can also be totally free compositions having no repeated parts or alignments of any kind. The result of such an approach is increased informality and dynamism. The elevation shown in Figure 5.31 uses this approach and still achieves a sense of equilibrium and harmony.

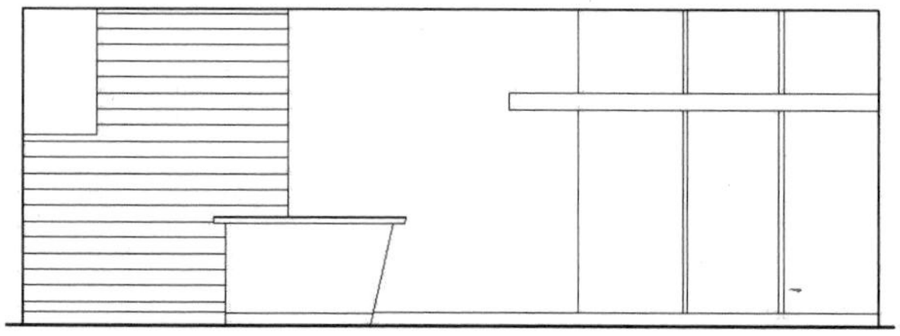

Figure 5.31: Free asymmetrical compositions can work without repeated elements or alignments of any kind. They rely on a painterly eye and, if done properly, can have very satisfying results.

Unifying the Whole

Ultimately, the totality of a project has to come across as a unified whole, conceived by a single mind and displaying a clear and cohesive design plan. No matter how complex a project is, the obligation is there to solve the "whole." As Robert Venturi expressed it:

> An architecture of complexity and accommodation does not forsake the whole. In fact, I have referred to a special obligation toward the whole because the whole is difficult to achieve. And I have emphasized the goal of unity rather than of simplification in an art "whose . . . truth [is] in its totality." It is the difficult unity through inclusion rather than the easy unity of exclusion.[6]

Unity

Unity in design is accomplished by composing elements with goal of achieving one cohesive whole. To achieve unity, all the components of the interior must relate to each other and the overall approach of the project. The result of a unified project is a sense of connectedness, relatedness, and coherence, where the project becomes one and reads as a whole. Consider the following explanation:

> The word "unity" means oneness. Of course, no actual oneness exists, unless you get down to the single cell organism or the atom. . . . When we speak of unity we do not mean this kind of oneness. We are referring to the putting-together of things, the composing of things, the combining of things into a group to which we can then attribute the quality of oneness.[7]

Unity occurs at different levels. Within a project, unity needs to be addressed at the level of individual scenes, such as rooms, and at the level of the entire project. Any given part of a project, when seen individually, should look visually unified in itself. Beyond the individual scene or room, the project as a whole also needs to achieve a quality of oneness. As one moves from space to space, one should get the feeling that all the spaces and parts are components of the same entity.

How the project relates to the building in which it is housed may sometimes be an important consideration. Many times there is no relationship, and, as soon as one enters a space from the building's public corridor, it appears as though one has entered a totally different world. Such is the nature of a great number of interior projects. There are times, however, when, because of the nature of the building or the project, the designer tries to produce some unity between the qualities of the building and those of the project. The attempts can be subtle, as when using regulating height lines originating in the building spaces outside the project or when repeating motifs of the building within the project. The unification can sometimes be stronger, such as a project that adopts the general feel and detailing of the building, as in some historical buildings, or in cases where the building and the interiors are designed concurrently by the same designer.

Two key strategies to achieve unity are similarity and continuity. Any composition, whether contained and static or free and sequential, needs both these qualities. We will first discuss unity in single spaces and later talk about achieving unity from one space to the next so as to unify the entire project. For the study of unity within a single scene, we rely here on some useful concepts articulated previously by Pierre von Meiss.[8]

Unity within a single scene relies on similarity, proximity, common enclosure, consistency of approach, or complementary composition. **Similarity** can be due to the repeated use of elements sharing similar characteristics such as form, size, material, color, and detailing. **Proximity** fosters unity by clustering elements close enough to produce distinct groups that read as unified clusters. **Common enclosure**, whether by surrounding walls, overhead planes, floor platforms, or background datum walls, also serves to unify a scene. **Consistency of approach** is also essential. Whatever the approach taken, it has to be consistent throughout. If it's a scheme relying on high contrast, then look for the use of high contrast

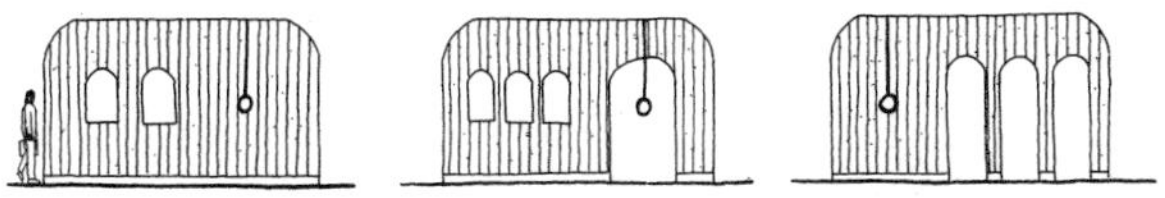

Figure 5.33: Consistency is paramount to achieve a sense of unity. In this example the consistent use of forms, wall finishes, shapes, and fixtures all contribute to unity.

throughout; if it's a scheme emphasizing horizontality, then look for the consistent use of horizontal elements.

To unify the project as a whole, the task takes on new challenges. Now the task becomes to achieve unity from one space to the next, and the next, and so on. The ultimate goal is for the entire project to read as one. For this to happen there has to be a clear concept. As Eugene Raskin expressed it, "Clarity of concept is the inescapable basis of unity."[9] Organizational concepts, as we will see, give the project physical structure and cohesiveness. Although the organizational structure may not be apparent all at once, eventually, as one navigates the project and becomes acquainted with it, the structure is revealed (Figure 5.32).

Experiencing the unity of the overall project is complicated by the fact that you cannot see the various spaces of projects all at once. Most projects, except the very small, are composed of multiple spaces that you experience sequentially as you move through them. In some cases, especially in open, flowing plans, you may be able to see clearly from one space to the next and experience the continuity links the designer has provided. In other cases, where passage from one space to the next does not allow visual connection, you have to rely on memory to tie the spaces together and perceive the unity. Two useful strategies to achieve overall unity are continuity and repetition.

Continuity

Continuity in a project means that there is a continuation of treatments from one space to another, thus linking different parts of the project visually. This can be accomplished through consistency or extension. **Consistency** simply requires treating elements, approaches, and finishes consistently from space to space. An example is the consistent use of forms and wall finishes from one space to the next (Figure 5.33). Another example is the consistent employment of a thematic idea throughout the project. Themes can create strong links between spaces by acting as a thread that weaves through the entire project, thus holding it together. Themes can be abstract constructs, held together by consistency of meaning, such as an ethnic restaurant utilizing symbols of the appropriate culture, or more direct architectural themes relying on consistent form or approach.

Extension refers to the practice of extending elements from one space to another. Examples include the continuation of a pattern from one room to the next (Figure 5.34), the extension of horizontal lines from space to space that provides a common thread throughout the project (Figure 5.35), and the extension of the

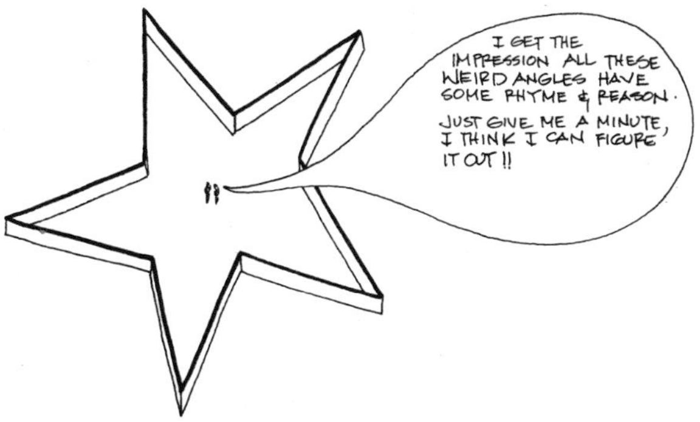

Figure 5.32: The unity of an overall project begins with a cohesive scheme. This oversimplified example illustrates how, if there is some underlying structure, even one not readily apparent initially, it will contribute to a sense of overall unity that sooner or later will be understood.

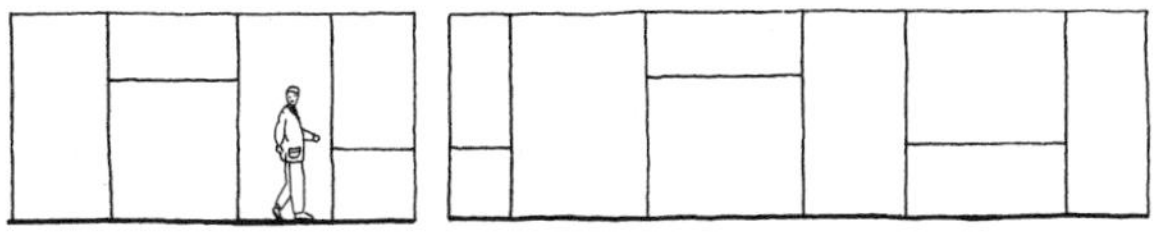

Figure 5.34: The extension of a pattern from one space to another helps to bridge spaces and contribute to a feeling of unity between spaces. There is more than consistency of approach here. The pattern is continued, by extension, from one room to the next.

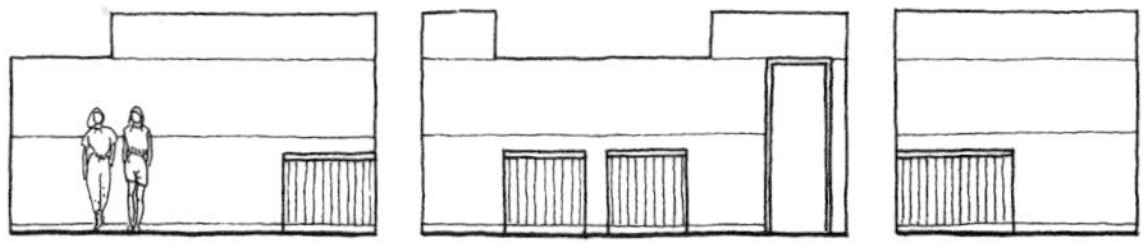

Figure 5.35: Not only can horizontal lines be used to regulate the heights of elements in space, as shown in Figure 5.30, they can also be expressed literally through the use of reveals, moldings, or surface relief. When used, they become an element that can be extended from space to space to help foster a sense of unity.

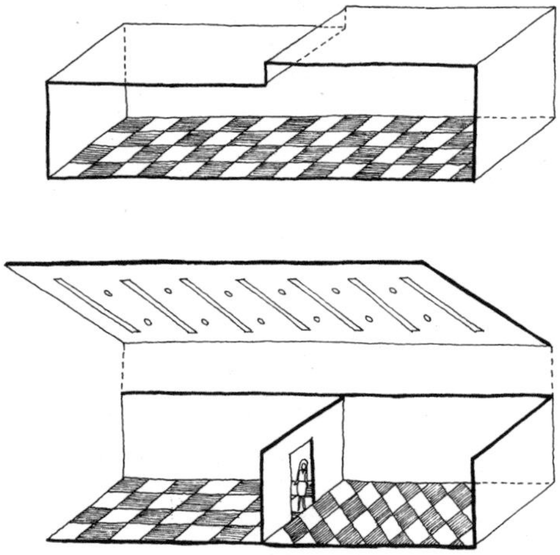

Figure 5.36: The floor plane can contribute much to unity between adjacent spaces. This applies to adjacent spaces seen simultaneously. This example shows a consistent, extended floor pattern unifying two contiguous spaces that are broken up by a change of ceiling height.

floor finish (or ceiling) from one space to the next (Figure 5.36).

A variation of extension is **overlapping**, where a certain element (wall, floor, or ceiling) is extended from the space in which it originates to overlap with the adjacent space, thus creating a strong link. In this case, two spaces share a common area defined by the extended, overlapping element. Figure 5.37 shows an example of an

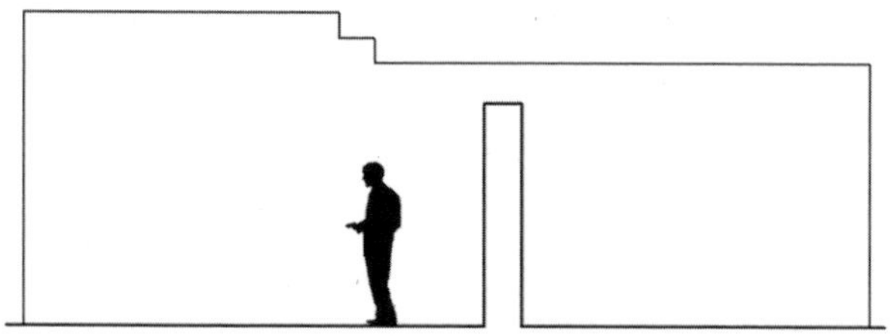

Figure 5.37: Another approach to unity is to link spaces by the use of overlapping elements, such as a ceiling as shown here.

overlapped ceiling that ties two adjacent areas separated by a wall.

Most projects rely on consistent treatments among their spaces for unity. Other than using the same finishes throughout the project, possibilities include consistent shapes, colors, details, scales, patterns, and textures. Consistency does not require identical treatments from space to space, just consistency of approach.

Repetition

Repetition occurs when some element, such as a particular motif, is repeated over and over again. In some cases the recurrence may happen throughout, although in others it will occur only selectively. Repetition is different from extension. With repetition the repeated element appears and reappears from place to place, more like a stamp that gets stamped in one room and then another than a line that extends between spaces. Figure 5.38 shows three rooms unified by the repetition of the anchor-like wall details and the suspended light fixtures. The repeated element may be identical from one place to the next or just similar, as long as the similarity is recognizable. The repetition may also be thematic, where elements tie in thematically and not necessarily in their visual appearance. Thus, in a seafood restaurant, an anchor in one room, a hanging marlin in another room, and a sail in a third room would provide this kind of thematic repetition.

Repeated elements can be details, accessories, motifs, plants, artwork, furnishings, and so on. Special approaches to the use of repetition include gradation and dispersion. With these approaches, equal elements are not repeated in their original form but are transformed as they move from one space to another. **Gradation** involves the gradual transformation of an element or characteristic. To apply gradation to color, for instance, its hue, or

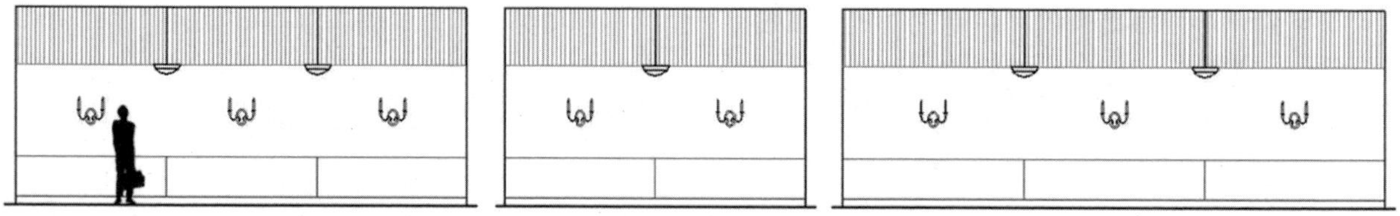

Figure 5.38: Repetition is a powerful unifying strategy. This example shows the repeated use of intermittent decorative wall motifs and suspended lighting fixtures to produce a consistent look among the three spaces shown.

value, would gradually be changed as the color progresses through the space. Another example would be the gradual modification of lighting level.

Dispersion is a special application of gradation where the transformation of an element is less regular. It involves the increase or decrease of density in a planned but somewhat random fashion. It can be especially effective when applied to floor patterns or as a technique of repetition with motifs or materials. To understand the principle of dispersion, try to visualize what would happen if you dropped a large container of marbles on a hard floor. They would bounce around and be dispersed throughout the floor. After the bouncing ceases you would find that a large number of pebbles end up concentrated close to the point of origin, a moderate number end up some distance away, and a few take such bounces that they actually end up quite far from the point of origin. Although the general pattern of this result is predictable, the exact way the pebbles choose to go is not.

You can use this technique to design patterns that vary in regularity and density, creating areas of high concentration of a pattern, followed by areas where the pattern is dispersed, becoming quite faint and infrequent in some places. Although the presence of the pattern is reduced as you move away from the area of high concentration, it never disappears, thus serving as a unifying motif (Figure 5.39).

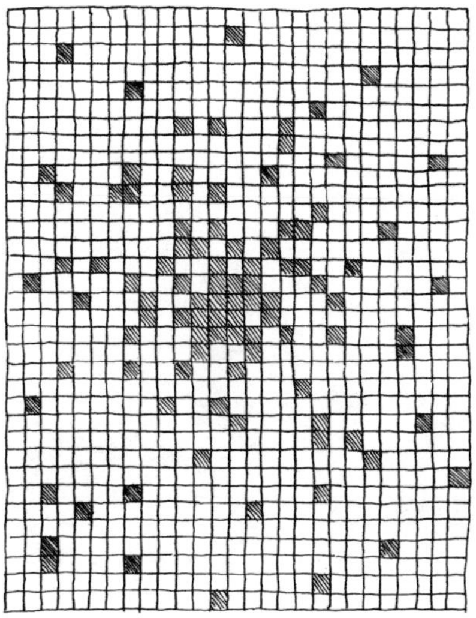

Figure 5.39: This floor pattern illustrates the use of dispersion. The pattern is more concentrated at its center. From there it moves outward in random fashion and becomes less dense to the point where it becomes faint, eventually disappearing.

Similarly, you can use this technique to maintain some continuity of special finishes in a project. You could, for instance, have one or two areas with a high concentration of upgraded finishes and fixtures followed by areas of less concentration of the same finishes. Instead of completely eliminating the use of the special treatments, they are just reduced. Thus, the wood paneling becomes a wood band and, later, a recurring small wood motif (Figure 5.40). Similarly, the marble floor becomes marble borders, and, later, marble thresholds at key junctures (Figure 5.41).

Avoiding Dullness

Unity relies on regularity and repetition; therefore, there is the risk that too much uniformity may produce dullness and monotony. For that reason it is a good practice to seek both unity and interest, order and stimulation, balance and dynamism. Amid the consistency and regularity there has to be variety, contrast, and a sense of hierarchy.

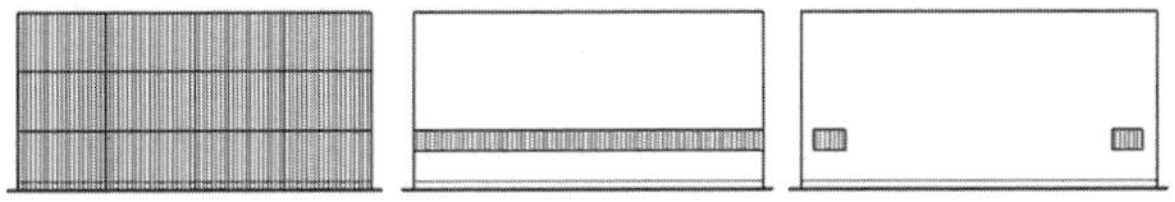

Figure 5.40: This longitudinal section through a space shows the strategy of dispersion used with wall applications, in this case wood. The first space is the most prominent and features wood paneling throughout. As you move into the space the paneling is reduced to a wood band. As you move even further into the space, the wood band becomes a wood medallion that occurs selectively from that point on. The presence of wood, though reduced, never disappears, thus contributing to the sense of unity of the project.

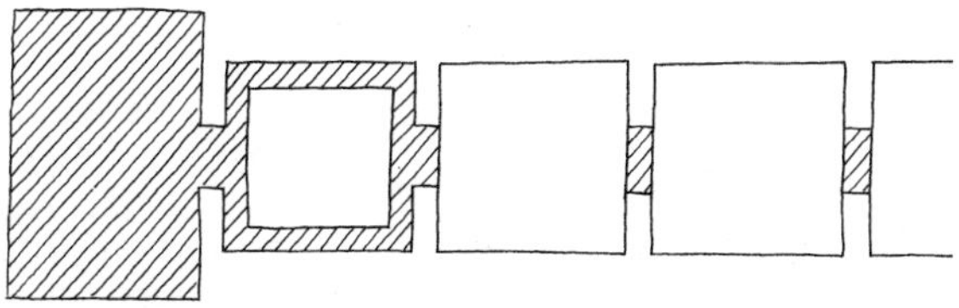

Figure 5.41: In this example the strategy of dispersion is applied to a floor. As in the wood paneling example in Figure 10.49, the first room is a prominent space and features a marble floor throughout. The marble floor gets reduced to marble borders in the next room. Eventually, it is used only at the thresholds between major spaces. Here again, even though the amount of the high-end finish is reduced as one moves farther into the space, it never goes away, thus contributing to the unity of the project.

CAPSULE | Visual Harmony in Figural Composition

The issue of visual harmony is central to the goal of resolution. Not many people have attempted to study the issue of architectural form in depth. One of them is Ralf Weber, who, in *On the Aesthetics of Architecture,* concentrates on the role of form in the experience and judgment of architecture.[1] This valuable book offers many insights about architectural form. Here we summarize some of Weber's contributions to the issue of visual harmony related not to space but to the solid elements in space. These are highly relevant to the art of composing interior environments. We separate this brief summary into the topics of centers, perceptual weight, vertical elements, hierarchy, and figure/ground articulation.

Centers

The perception of order depends, among other things, on the impact of the various perceptual centers in a composition. These can be dominant or subordinate but in all cases act as some kind of visual focus. The dominant visual area of any display is the visual center of gravity, which is determined by the distribution of the principal centers and their perceptual masses. Additionally, areas of high contrast, areas along symmetry axes, areas along the vertical axes of shapes and larger composite patterns, patterns with strong figural characters, concave and enclosed shapes, heterogeneous elements within homogeneous arrangements, and areas of high contrast attract the eye and establish perceptual centers exerting more or less influence (Figure C5.1).

Figure C5.1: Building with clear perceptual center.

Centers are also induced by the contours of a configuration, and it is possible to make some generalizations about the location of fulcrums in simple shapes. The single perceptual center of a square or a circle, for instance, is at the geometric center. Vertically elongated shapes pull the perceptual center upward. Not all shapes, however, enjoy a strong perceptual center. It is hard, for instance, to establish a precise perceptual center in elongated shapes, whether vertical or horizontal, exceeding a ratio of 1:2.

Consciously planning the centers of a composition is important. Their location and interaction play a crucial role in establishing order and determining its dynamic character.

Perceptual Weight

The dynamic character of a pattern is also affected by the perceived heaviness of the various parts of the configuration. Perceptual weight is affected by size, tone, levels of articulation and regularity, location, and direction. Larger, darker, articulated, or regular shapes generally carry more perceptual weight than their opposites. Likewise, shapes that are isolated, placed somewhere in the periphery (instead of in the center or along a major axis) or vertically oriented, assume greater visual weight (Figure C5.2).

Figure C5.2: The treatment and placement of the cylindrical shapes in this building give them perceptual weight.

Vertical Elements

To perceive space, the body favors orthogonal localization. The horizontal and the vertical, thus, provide the framework for stability as well as for the apparent dynamic properties of a composition. The vertical dimension, however, is more significant for figural segregation than the horizontal. Particularly important is the role of the vertical axis of symmetry in the perceived stability of a figure. The highest degree of perceived stability is attained when figures are symmetrical, both horizontally and vertically, and the main direction extends horizontally. The perceptual stability can be increased further by interlocking such a configuration with vertical shapes placed at the axis of vertical symmetry (Figure C5.3). Configurations where the orientation of the shape's main dimension and its axis of symmetry coincide are perceived as dynamic, such as in the case of a vertically symmetrical, tall and slender building, which appears to move upward. This is further reinforced by the natural tendency of the eyes to move upward faster than they move downward.

Figure C5.3: The vertical center on this otherwise horizontal and symmetrical facade gives this building a sense of stability.

Perceptual dynamics in a composition are produced by the interplay between vertical and horizontal elements. Elevations with main centers aligned horizontally appear static. Perceptual stability will increase when the main perceptual center is located above the actual center of balance. Vertical elements stop horizontal visual scanning and help to anchor vision. Horizontal arrangements can be enhanced, for example, by a strong vertical accent at the position of the main focus. It is also useful to utilize vertical elements to demarcate the axes along which the individual centers of a pattern are aligned.

Hierarchy

Hierarchical arrangements that create subordinate groups and sub-groups allow sustained perceptual arousal without overtaxing perceptual capacity. They permit a high absolute complexity while maintaining a moderate level of perceptual complexity. The hierarchical arrangement of perceptual centers in a composition is, thus, generally desirable. Weber points out two crucial factors: The first factor is the need for both a distinct overall fulcrum and distinct centers for each of the subordinate component groups. The second factor is the need for an organization of a subordinate type at the highest levels where small parts form larger patterns, which in turn are grouped to form a larger group, and so on (Figure C5.4).

Figure C5.4: The hierarchical organization of this facade allows a high level of complexity without being overtaxing.

continued

Perceptual hierarchy demands that each of the groups and sub-groups of shapes of a composition should be identifiable as discrete perceptual wholes. A clear compositional center in each group helps in this regard. Ideally, the point of the shape's equilibrium coincides with the perceptual focus (visually strongest) of the configuration. Distinct foci can be created by the use of heterogeneous shapes, contrasting sizes, rhythms or symmetries, and contrasting tones, colors, or textures, among other devices.

When a composition—say, an elevation—is subdivided nonhierarchically into equal parts, and these exceed the maximum number of elements that can be perceived at once (between five and seven), the result is monotonous. This condition can be improved by using a rhythmic alternation of different elements and by the incorporation of foci, such as an overall central vertical symmetrical axis. In a composition of similar elements, a strong focus can also be produced by articulating one of the shapes using tone, texture, or color. Yet, the simplest way of creating a strong overall focus is by using a shape that is either different or scaled differently. The effect of a single heterogeneous element is normally so strong that it can easily center an otherwise homogeneous arrangement, catalyzing an otherwise monotonous appearance.

There are several advantages to organizing the various centers of attraction in a composition hierarchically:

- A subordinate arrangement of parts allows the visual segregation of a distinct fulcrum, whereas a coordinate (nonhierarchical) arrangement results in similar and competing perceptual dominance.
- Hierarchical arrangements permit greater absolute complexity without leading to an equally high degree of perceptual complexity. The organization of parts into groups complies more readily with the demands of wholeness in a complex configuration, thus allowing a more complicated arrangement of shapes to emerge.
- In a hierarchical organization, there is a clear difference between various levels of scale, that is, between the sizes of the individual entities in relation to the whole. Consequently, there can be a greater number of levels without resulting in visual chaos.
- Hierarchical organization allows similar elements to be grouped into larger shapes instead of simply fusing with the overall pattern.
- Hierarchical organizations make it easier to achieve equilibrium of areas of interest when exploring perceptual centers.
- Hierarchical organizations allow a gradual decrease of scales in a composition, thus avoiding abrupt jumps from large scales to minute ones, which often result in low levels of stimulation.
- Compositions that are hierarchical but lack detail and articulation at the smaller subordinate levels also can result in low stimulus. The lack of microstructure leads to poverty of information.

Figure–Ground Articulation

An important factor in the analysis of the perceptual impact of corporeal form is the internal articulation of the spatial boundaries. Two of the most predominant properties of a composition's articulation are its textural appearance and the organization of component elements into figures and ground. The completeness of figure–ground organization largely determines the perceived orderliness of the composition. The distribution of contrast endows the shape with heterogeneous structure.

The parts of an elevation possess different visual dominance, and thus appear to advance or recede, resulting in multiple levels of perceived depth. The effect is due to the perceptual organization of stimulus patterns into figure and ground. Depending on the arrangement, some features will attain perceptual dominance or subordinance. The process of perception involves selecting stimuli and unifying them into perceptual figures that segregate themselves from a surrounding ground. Important to the formation of perceptual units is the function of the contour. Contours function as a boundary for enclosed areas, thus defining figures. The ground appears to continue behind the figure.

Other things being equal, Weber gives the following laws as determinants of figure–ground segregation:

- Orientation: Shapes whose orientation follows the cardinal axes form figures more easily.
- Proximity: Small areas dominate. Larger areas tend to become grounds.
- Closure: Fully closed shapes segregate more easily.
- Articulation: Areas with greater internal articulation will form figures more easily.
- Concavity: The concave side of a boundary will induce shapes more easily than the convex side.
- Brightness and Color: Brighter tones and hard colors segregate into figures more easily.
- Symmetry: The more symmetrical shapes will tend to form figures.

Figure–ground organizations vary. The possibilities can be summarized into five basic categories:

1. Unified ground: Intervening spaces do not form figures. The negative spaces between or surrounding the primary shapes possess no, or only a weak, figural character of their own (Figure C5.5).
2. Unified ground: Intervening spaces form figures. The negative spaces between the principal shapes assume their own figural character.
3. Nonunified ground: Duo-formation of shapes. As in a facade of a curtain-walled building subdivided into endless squares, distinction between figure and ground is impossible, and all shapes assume equal dominance.
4. Nonunified ground: Intervening spaces form figures. Negative spaces form figures in their own right but do not result in duo-formations. The figural character of the negative spaces is weaker than that of the main components.
5. Nonunified ground: Intervening spaces do not form figures. Intervening spaces do not assume a figural character. The negative spaces cannot group themselves, and the overall pattern appears unstable.

Although it is easy to relegate negative spaces to unimportant subordinate status, it is obvious that they impact the overall composition significantly and, therefore, deserve attention. When there is no clear distinction between figure and ground, or when the permeating order of the organization is locally violated, the result is perceptual ambiguity.

Figure C5.5: This facade is an example of a unified ground where the intervening spaces do not form figures.

It is possible for both positive and negative spaces to assume a figural character. Grounds can take on a figural character by reducing it to narrow, regular shapes, as when a group of windows is spaced tightly, producing a pattern of strips between them that takes on the role of figure, thus creating a reversal effect between figure and ground.

1. Weber, R. (1995). *On the aesthetics of architecture.* Aldershot, England: Avebury.

REVIEW

SUMMARY

Interior design requires the proper placement of, and equilibrium between, different components to achieve an agreeable aesthetic effect. Relevant here are architectural issues such as the proper use of scale, the correct handling of proportions, and the proper balancing of project parts to achieve a harmonious state of balance and equilibrium.

A good composition produces a sense of harmony. Three crucial aspects of harmony are the appropriate use of scale, the skillful use of proportion, and the achievement of balanced compositions. Scale can be considered in relation to the size and proportions of human beings, in relation to the particular design application being executed, and in relation to learned expectation of size concerning the elements in a space. Scale can also be measured in relation to the size of the entire project, in the relation of specific contents to the space in which they are housed, and in the relation of certain contents to other contents in the space.

Proportion is concerned with the relationship of elements to the composition they are a part of. Balance is the third requirement for harmony. A composition is said to be balanced if all the components are in perceptual equilibrium. Symmetrical compositions have been used since antiquity. They feature two equal sides, mirrored on either side of a central vertical axis. Asymmetrical compositions are more difficult to balance than symmetrical ones. They can rely on some repetition and alignments to give them coherence or they can be totally free of repetition and alignment.

In addition to harmony, the other essential requirement for proper resolution is unity. Unity occurs at many levels. It is useful to distinguish between unity within a scene and unity within an entire project. Unity within a scene relies on similarity, proximity, enclosure, consistency of approach, and complementary composition. Unity within an entire project requires a strong and cohesive organizational concept to provide a unified structure. Beyond structural unity a project needs to look consistent. This is done through the employment of continuity and repetition. Repetition strategies include consistent repetition, sporadic repetition, gradation, and dispersion.

Harmony and unity rely heavily on similarity and repetition; however, it is important to remember that harmonious and unified projects are not good if they are also dull and boring. It is necessary to provide enough variety to achieve a reasonable level of interest according to the type of project being designed. This calls for a calculated departure from the easy and predictable design tendencies toward regularity.

1. Vitruvius, Marcus P. "The Ten Books on Architecture." Welcome to Dover Publications. Trans. Morris H. Morgan. Ed. Herbert L. Warren. Dover Publications Inc. New York, n.d. Web. 8 Aug. 2014.
2. Ibid.
3. Ibid.
4. Ibid.
5. Wright, F. L. (1988). *In the realm of ideas*. Carbondale, IL: Southern Illinois University Press.
6. Venturi, R. (1977). *Complexity and contradiction in architecture*. New York: Museum of Modern Art.
7. Raskin, E. (1954). *Architecturally speaking*. New York: Reinhold Publishing.
8. Von Meiss, P. (1990). *Elements of architecture*. From form to place. London: Van Nostran Reinhold International.
9. Raskin, 1954, p. 32.

Chapter Questions

1. Related to design, what is the difference between size and scale?
2. As a designer, you need to be able to use scale in two different ways. What are the two ways presented in this chapter?
3. Give an example of scale manipulation related to the human figure (other than the ones presented in this chapter).
4. Name an example of appropriate scale as related to design application.
5. Give an example of scale manipulation related to element type (other than the ones presented in this chapter).
6. Give one example of scale of content in relation to the space in which it is housed.
7. Name an example of scale of an element in relation to other similar elements in the space.
8. State some of the reasons presented in this chapter for the manipulation of scale.
9. Explain how proportion differs from scale.
10. Name the three well-known systems of proportion discussed in this chapter.
11. Do proper scale and proportion ensure good balance? Why or why not?
12. Explain why the focus ahead is important in the composition of symmetrical two-dimensional compositions of vertical surfaces.
13. What is the ideal placement of the approach path toward symmetrically composed elevations?
14. In what ways can complexity and intricacy be added to symmetrical compositions?
15. What would be a feasible way to produce an intentionally imperfect symmetrical elevation?
16. In what kind of instance is a symmetrical composition of elevations not fully perceptible?
17. Describe a way to produce formality in asymmetrical composition.
18. What compositional device would you use to increase regularity in an asymmetrical elevation?
19. Is achieving unity between a project and the building in which it is housed necessary?
20. What strategies can you use to achieve unity within a single scene?
21. In what ways can continuity be utilized to produce unity between different spaces of a project?
22. In what ways can repetition be used to produce unity between different spaces of a project?
23. Give some examples of how you might use the techniques of gradation and dispersion to foster unity in a project.
24. Why is excessive regularity problematic? What can you do about it?

CHAPTER 6
ORDER

INSTRUCTIONAL OBJECTIVES

- Describe different kinds of order related to fit, visual harmony, and orientation.
- Explain three basic factors that facilitate spatial understanding.
- Explain the role of the ten place elements in facilitating project imageability.
- Describe strategies to facilitate the legibility of project parts.
- Describe grouping strategies to facilitate orientation.
- Explain ways to facilitate the understanding of relationships between parts.
- Explain strategies to promote the awareness of motion and sequence.
- Explain strategies to promote the understanding of projects as a whole.
- Describe the limits and possibilities of enclosed corridors related to orientation.
- Show the effects of varying the size, placement, and orientation of single and multiple masses in space.
- Show the effects of different levels of boundary legibility.
- Show the effect of partial-height elements related to disclosure and orientation.

Order must be understood as indispensable to the functioning of any o
whether its function be physical or mental.

—*Rudolf Arnheim,* The Dynamics of Arc

FROM VITRUVIUS IN ANTIQUITY to modern times, writers on the subject of architecture and the environmental design disciplines have spoken about the importance of order in design. Bernard Leupen put it quite simply: "Every design is based on order . . . the need to order is prompted more than anything else by our general desire to arrange the world so as to make it easier to understand."[1]

In this chapter we explore the idea of order and its many dimensions manifested in the design of building interiors with a special focus on spatial order, how to establish it and how to reveal it. Specific design strategies to achieve spatial order will be discussed as well as the importance of the composition of a project's enclosed and open areas.

ORDER IN BUILDINGS

The concept of order is broad and operates at different levels. In the following sections, we start by explaining two basic kinds of order related to built environments.

Kinds of Order

Order in design is manifested in many ways. Architectural and decorative elements have to be balanced in harmonious arrangements (Figure 6.1), and spaces have to be arranged in a way that
have addressed the first kind o
to visual harmony, in the previ
spend any more time on it here.
this chapter to a discussion about t
viding orientation in building interi

Figure 6.1: Visual harmony is achieved when the parts of a composition achieve a sense of perceptual correctness and balance.

Order Related to Orientation

Christian Norberg-Schulz distills the basic act of dwelling into two basic and crucial psychological functions: identification and orientation. Orientation is relevant for our purposes here. It is concerned with "man's need to orientate himself, to know where he is."[2] Romedi Passini has defined spatial orientation as "a person's ability to understand the space around him and to situate himself."[3] We can all relate to this basic human need which, when fulfilled, gives us a sense of security and well-being. Conversely, the effects of disorientation can range from mild apprehension to actual terror, depending on the circumstances.

This chapter focuses on order related to orientation. We will examine the strategies to organize space for strong legibility and the effect of the disposition of open and enclosed spaces on our ability to read the spatial organization.

Levels of Order

The design of environments requires the assembly of multiple parts into a whole that possesses some level of organization. By the mere act of arranging a group of functions or spaces into some logical organization, the designer brings order to potential chaos. The act of building, itself, demands a reasonable use of regularity and, thus, order. Pierre Von Meiss reminds us of this fact: "To build we must use fairly simple geometry. It is first of all a necessity for design and above all for building. . . . Regularity is thus the very essence of building"[4] (Figure 6.2).

The synthesis of programmatic requirements into an orderly arrangement of spaces and the use of regularity, uniformity, and simple geometry in construction, by themselves, have the potential to establish a basic order,

Figure 6.2: The realities of the physical world demand regularity and repetition in construction. Many designs, in fact, emphasize these properties.

the kind produced by the proper assembly of parts; however, a project's sense of order has to go beyond mere regularity and neatness. You should seek to produce meaningful wholes, paying attention not only to the neat organization of parts but also to their assembly into a system based on a clear organizational principle. The relationship to context, internal hierarchy, relationships of spaces, and the way to move around the project have to not only work well together but also respond to the organizational principle adopted.

The ideation stage will be discussed in Chapter 10. It addresses the search for a suitable organizational system for a project. Organizational concepts, we will see, seek a suitable organizational system that endows the project with a sense of hierarchy. Of all the tasks performed during design, early development of the plan based on this organizational concept is key to ensure a strong sense of structure. The plan sets the topological distribution of the project, locating parts and functions according to the organizational principle chosen. Concerns related to its form are also important. First, we look at the way we perceive interior projects in order to gain some insight into the kinds of spatial arrangements and features that facilitate our perception and understanding of a project's organization.

Experiencing Interior Spaces

Interior spaces are never experienced in the same way as the floor plans we draw to represent them. Floor plans allow us to see an entire floor at once and quickly grasp its organization. In real life, walls and distance prevent us from having that kind of instantaneous total disclosure of an entire floor. We usually experience environments one space at a time and form impressions that rely on mental maps we conceive by remembering the spaces we have left behind together with the space that we occupy and the spaces we see ahead. Figure 6.3 shows a sequence of main and secondary spaces, conceptually illustrating the fragmentary and sequential ways we experience most building interiors.

Environmental information and clues are perceived, understood, organized in our minds, and later remembered, helping us compose a collection of individual impressions into a coherent total image. Achieving order requires the creation of spatial arrangements that are well-organized, readable, and memorable.

Factors that Facilitate Understanding and Orientation

From our discussion so far we can state the goal that projects should be designed to facilitate a sense of spatial

Figure 6.3: Most interior projects are experienced in sequences. This drawing shows a series of linked but distinct spaces arranged in a storylike sequence.

understanding for users of varying levels of familiarity. Except in the simplest of spaces, most environments are understood after repeated exposures. At some point, during one of the visits, the environment starts making sense in our minds.

As we move around space, our mental pictures of the environment evolve. Because environments are experienced one space at a time, it is the collection of diverse and fragmented pieces of environmental information gathered from many locations at different times that add up to our total picture of that environment.

Three factors identified by Kevin Lynch as components of environmental images at the city scale give us a useful model to understand environmental images of interior spaces. They are identity, structure, and meaning. Lynch reminds us that although it may be useful to abstract these for analysis, in reality, they are always interrelated.[5]

Identity

Identity is the quality of individuality objects possess that allows us to distinguish them from other objects and recognize them as separate entities. Related to identity is what Lynch called **imageability**, the quality of some physical objects that makes it likely that they'll evoke a strong image in the mind of the observer. Whether due to their shape, color, or arrangement, highly imageable objects are likely to produce "vividly identified, powerfully structured, highly useful mental images of the environment."[6] Projects rich in order have a strong identity both in their parts and as a whole.

Structure

Structure refers to the spatial or pattern relation of the object to the observer and to other objects. It is concerned with the relationships among the different entities and how these are assembled as a unified whole. As discussed earlier, the presence of an organizing principle behind the arrangement will make it easier to comprehend and appreciate. Depending on the project, it may take a while to decipher this organizing principle. After it is discovered, though, one can make logical assessments of the space without having to figure out all the parts. A strong organizing principle, together with a well-orchestrated assembly of parts, will endow the project with greater legibility, allowing users to grasp the structure more easily.

Meaning

Meaning refers to the significance the object has to the observer, whether practical or emotional. While meaning often works somewhat independently of the physical characteristics of environments, it is a crucial variable in the mix of how we perceive environments. Some places are remembered not by the singularity of their form or their placement within a structure but by the significance they have for us. Whether due to the symbolic association, practical function, or degree of familiarity, these places stand out in our mental maps even if lacking in memorable features. As we invest time in projects, they become familiar to us and acquire more significance in our lives. With meaningful places we rely less on mental pictures of spaces having particular features because we see them as places associated with certain functions, people, and events having specific degrees of significance to us.

Of the three factors discussed in this section, identity and structure rely the most on design. Meaning is usually assigned to places for reasons other than their physical attributes. Nevertheless, places that are rich in meaning can be further enhanced by how legible and distinct we make them (identity) and where they are placed within the total organization (structure).

DESIGNING FOR ORDER

So far we have made a strong case for the importance of order and orientation in design. The order afforded by design can help orient us in space by facilitating our understanding of our environment, its place within the larger context, and our position within these environments at any particular time. Now we turn to ways of achieving order in our designs. We will start with the role the place elements play in facilitating order and orientation. Next, we will review ways of facilitating project understanding at various scales. Finally, we will examine the implications of spatial massing and composition.

The Role of the Place Elements in Providing Order

In Chapter 3, we introduced the place elements, a group of environmental entities useful for the creation and understanding of places. Here, we briefly review them again.

Domains are like neighborhoods. In interiors they are the departments in an office or store (Figure 6.4), or the different dining areas in a large restaurant. Their approximate placement and size are important in developing an accurate mental map of the whole. Understanding the boundaries between circulation spaces and these domains, and, in some cases, those between one domain and the next is also important to the formation of accurate mental maps.

Centers become memorable because they are significant. We remember these spaces and sometimes even organize our mental picture of environments around them. Knowing their inherent importance, designers can further emphasize them to evoke a powerful and lasting image that users can use as a point of reference (Figure 6.5).

Arrival spaces give us the first impression of a project and represent the first point of reference from which to construct our mental map of the environment. The nature of the circulation routes that follow from the entrance and how much of the space beyond is visible can also have a significant impact on our ability to understand the total environment (Figure 6.6).

Paths play an important role in our ability to feel oriented. In fact, a strong and clear circulation system may be legible enough to become the structure around which we organize our mental picture of interior environments (Figure 6.7).

Nodes are memorable for a number of reasons. They are places of hightened activity, full of vibrancy, energy, and meaning. They also tend to be physically distinct due to the dynamic qualities of converging paths, expanding space, and so on. Also, due to their strategic placement and often increased size, they are visible from multiple locations and, frequently, they offer opportunities for a wide visual scope. They enhance our sense of order because we tend to remember them vividly (Figure 6.8).

Edges, connectors, and ends help determine the extent of domains and clarify where one area ends and another begins. Their range of legibility varies but can sometimes be strong (Figure 6.9) and enhance our ability to

Figure 6.4: Domains are legible as areas of particular characteristics, uses, and extent. This "neighborhood" in an office setting is a domain. Our mental pictures of some environments feature collections of related domains.

Figure 6.5: This is the principal conference room in an office setting and is one of centers of a facility. Centers are the special destinations. Sometimes they become the highlights among less meaningful domains; other times they are of such importance they become, literally, central features of the organization.

Figure 6.6: Arrival spaces are of great perceptual importance because they function as gateways to the rest of the project. Here, the arrival space of a restaurant reveals glimpses of what lies ahead.

Figure 6.7: We experience projects while walking on their paths, some revealing more than others. Here, a path allows the user to catch glimpses of what lies ahead.

Figure 6.8: Nodes are important points of reference. Whether small or large, like the one pictured here, they are strategically placed and often have distinctive features that make them memorable.

Figure 6.9: This edge between a corridor and the work areas in an office facility provides clear spatial demarcation. It's visual distinctiveness has the added benefit of being memorable.

remember project parts and form good mental pictures of projects.

The main trait of landmarks is distinctiveness and, therefore, they are clearly remembered. Their inclusion in projects and their strategic placement for maximum visibility from multiple locations make them excellent points of reference that can significantly improve our ability to understand and get oriented in interior settings (Figures 6.10 and 6.11).

The insightful use of the place elements can help increase the legibility of interior environments. When they are orchestrated into a cohesive system they produce especially coherent environments. These are further refined to make order and structure clearer and easier to read, but it must be emphasized that it all originates during that all-important stage of concept formulation.

Figure 6.10: Landmarks in interiors are usually prominent features. Sometimes an open connecting space with a sculptural staircase can become one.

Figure 6.11: An oversized design feature, such as the giant circular window shown here can be a memorable landmark.

Promoting Project Understanding

Project understanding takes place at many levels. We distinguish five principal levels for discussion: individual parts, groupings, relationships between parts or groups, sequences, and the project as a whole. We will look at these next and suggest strategies for facilitating project understanding at each of them. These are derived from the work of Von Meiss.[7]

Individual Parts

An individual project part may be a space or a mass. Although not all parts need to be comprehended as individual entities, many do stand out as single features. We offer four design strategies to increase legibility at this level:

Distinctiveness Parts with strong figural qualities read clearly against the background formed by adjacent elements. Ways of achieving distinctiveness usually rely on uniqueness and differentiation from nearby spaces or masses. Also necessary is a clear, uncluttered presentation of the object in question. Figure 6.12 illustrates how a simple offset or slight increase in the level of detail of a wall makes it stand out as a part.

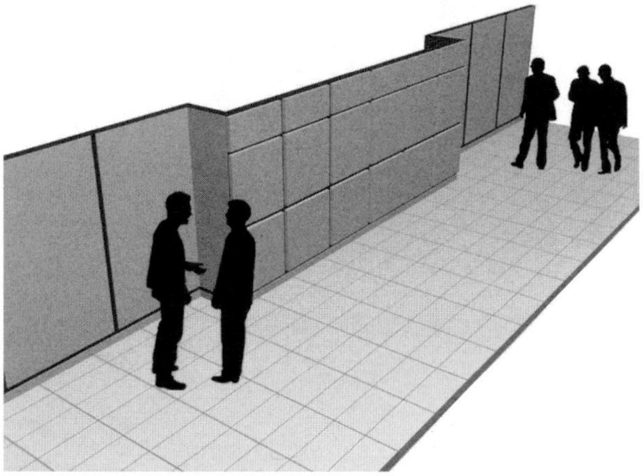

Figure 6.12: The offset and slight increase in detailing are enough to highlight this section of a wall and make it distinctive.

Simple Form Gestalt psychology established that our eyes are drawn to simple shapes first, usually focusing on the simplest one and proceeding to more complex ones only after the initial one has been grasped. Consequently,

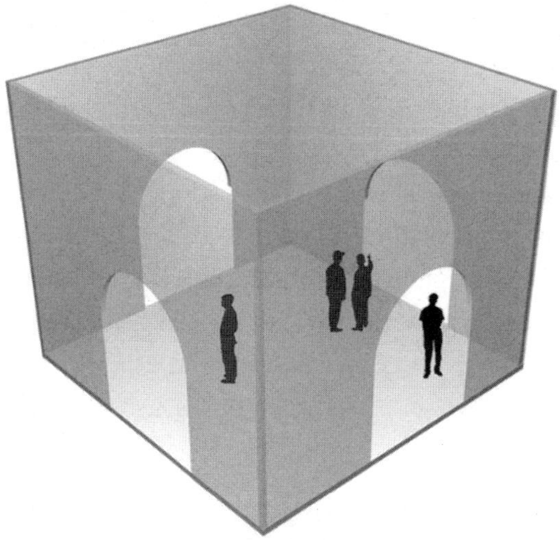

Figure 6.13: Simple form, whether spatial or solid, is easier to remember. Pure shapes, such as this square room, are instantly recognizable.

shapes that are simple, clear, and composed of few parts will be easier to perceive. The principle of simple form applies to both the perception of mass and the perception of space itself. Simple volumes, such as the cube in Figure 6.13, help make spaces distinguishable.

Dominance Dominance is similar to, yet different from, distinctiveness. While in both cases the part in question is differentiated from the rest, in the case of distinctiveness it is merely different, and with dominance it is clearly bold and dominant. Oftentimes, these parts become landmarks around which other parts are organized. Dominance can be established by means of size, intensity, or form. In Figure 6.14, the protruding part is not only different but also clearly the dominant feature of the composition.

Figure 6.15: Contrasts in scale and light are used to differentiate one area from another.

Contrast Contrast is a useful strategy to achieve differentiation among adjacent parts. It helps make entities more readable, especially at the point or edge where parts come together. It requires an abrupt change at the intersection. A common use of contrast is the contrast of scale, as shown in Figure 6.15.

Groupings

Spaces are often clustered together in groups and read more as a group than a collection of parts. Individual parts may or may not be discernible. We present four design strategies useful to achieve legibility of groupings:

Clustering Clustering consists of grouped spaces in tightly configured conglomerations (Figure 6.16). Parts may butt against one another or just come close. In any case, there has to be a high degree of proximity between them. The resulting shape may be simple and regular or irregular,

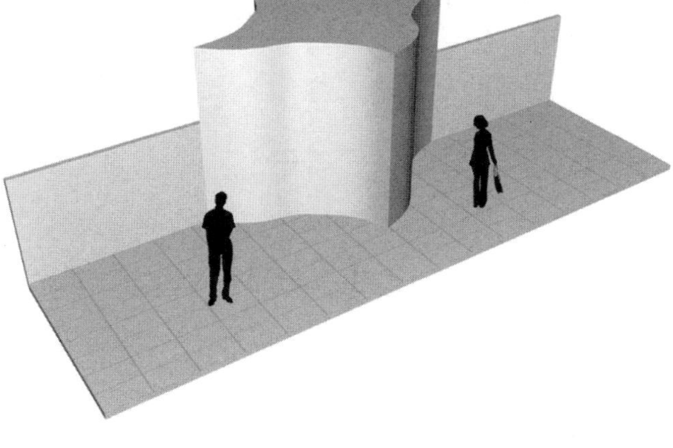

Figure 6.14: Dominance requires accentuated contrast in size, shape, or level of finish. This example features contrasting size, shape, and surface treatment.

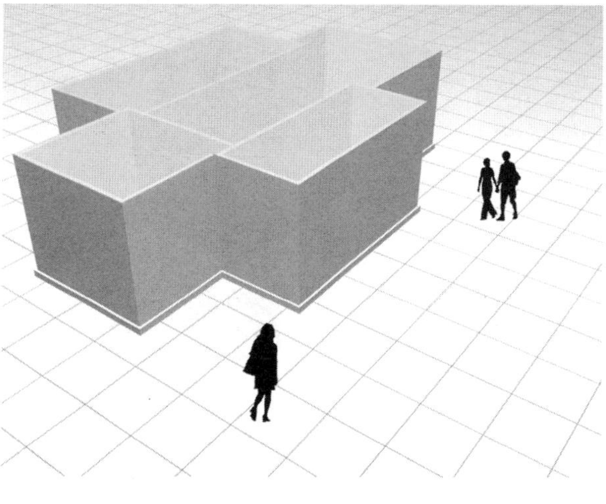

Figure 6.16: Rooms clustered together read as a group, even if their resulting boundary is irregular.

expressing the individual volumes, protrusions, and indentations of the component parts. The key to their legibility is that the cluster read as a single entity bound together.

Common Enclosure In the case of parts sharing a common enclosure, the parts may be grouped tightly, as in a cluster, or loosely. What unifies them and makes them read as a single group is their common boundary, which serves to unify all the parts within it. The tables inside the common container shown in Figure 6.17 are grouped by virtue of being inside the same partial height wall.

Common Orientation In the case of parts sharing a common orientation, closely spaced parts are oriented in the same direction and, consequently, read as a group. In these cases, proximity between elements is as important as the common orientation. Figure 6.18 shows an example of similarly oriented furniture clusters.

Figure 6.17: When objects, furnishings, or even rooms occur together inside a common boundary, they read as a group. This group of tables is held together by its enclosure.

Figure 6.18: Objects sharing the same orientation, such as these neatly arranged groups of chairs, reinforce their sense of group.

Figure 6.19: A datum groups parts, even if disparate, together by acting as a common backdrop. In interiors it is usually a plane below, above, or behind the parts. In this example the tall and continuous horizontal backrest with the slats acts as a datum for the tables occurring along its length.

Datum A datum is a powerful unifying device used to group dissimilar parts through a common field or point of reference. It can be a vertical backdrop against which a number of parts are arranged, a floating ceiling plane grouping several parts underneath, a unique flooring plane or pattern on which a group of parts are arranged (Figure 6.19), or a line at a certain height unifying the parts of an elevation. Key to the success of a datum is correspondence of extent between the datum and the parts it groups. It has to read as if the background wall, the overhead plane, or the distinctive floor had been custom made to house the parts they group.

Relationships Between Adjacent Spaces

The next aspect requiring legibility is the relationship between spaces. Positional relationships between spaces as well as the nature of the connection between adjacent ones can be made easier to perceive and understand. Two design strategies are discussed:

Clear Intersection Clear intersection occurs when joints or seams between spaces are visible and clearly articulated. This usually involves an edge or a connector. Whether they are tall or low, full- or partial-length, separating barriers that reveal the two sides enhance the readability of the relationship between them. Other than walls, clear intersections can be achieved through intermediary spaces, ceiling or floor treatments, furniture arrangements, and so on. Figure 6.20 shows an example of a separation between two areas clearly revealed by the characteristics of the dividing partial height partition.

Visibility Visibility simply refers to the increase of the visible field by means of openness, expanded views,

Figure 6.20: The strategy of clear intersection relies on the disclosure of the point or edge where adjacent areas connect. In this figure, the partial height partition/planter successfully separates the two areas while simultaneously revealing their relationship.

Figure 6.21: The strategy of visibility works by maximizing the extent of what is seen from a particular space. Openness and the minimization of view obstructing elements are key components to make it work.

transparencies, or overlaps, such as in the space shown in Figure 6.21. Open environments are generally much easier to figure out because the relationship between parts is clearly seen.

Sequences

Sequences are concerned with how two or more spaces link together to form a pattern and give users clues about where they are or where they are heading. We discuss two design strategies here that facilitate legibility of sequences.

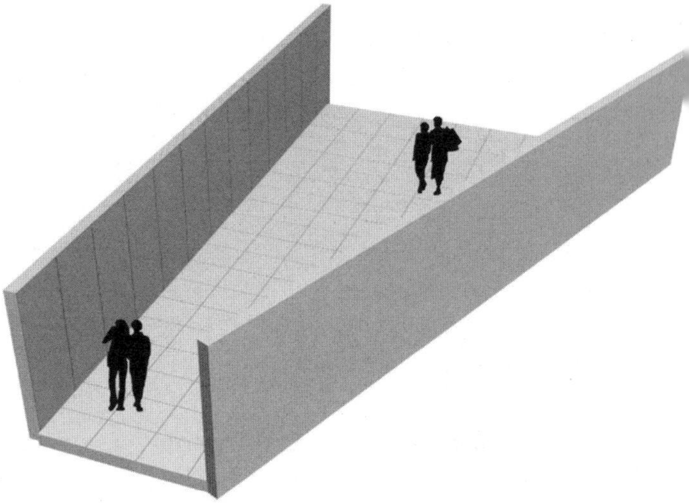

Figure 6.22: This corridor is an example of gradation. The different widths can help visitors remember whether a particular space is near the narrow or wide end of the corridor.

Gradation Gradation is achieved through subtle asymmetries, gradients, and any method of differentiation that successfully makes one side gradually become different from the other. The differences can be subtle, but as the observer notices them, he or she understands the progressive differentiation and can, therefore, distinguish among them, especially between the contrasting ends. The widening effect of the corridor in Figure 6.22 makes it easy to distinguish which end of the corridor you are in.

Contrast We listed contrast as a design strategy for singling out individual parts. Contrast is also highly effective in creating different experiences as one moves along a sequence. Changes of scale or lighting levels help to break down sequences into discrete parts with unique characteristics, thus making the sequence more memorable and legible. Once again, contrast of scale is a commonly used and effective way of making sequences readable and memorable (Figure 6.23).

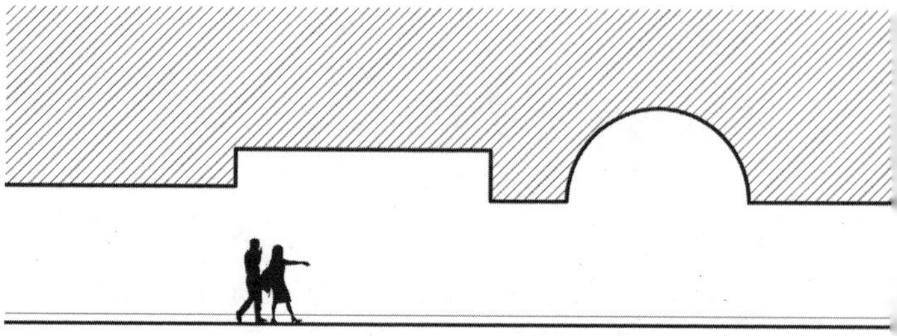

Figure 6.23: A good strategy to make a sequence memorable is the use of contrast. Whether achieved by the alternation of open and closed spaces in plan or by the alternation of low and tall spaces, as shown, the contrasting spaces are marked and remembered.

The Whole

Understanding the whole is the most difficult level of order to grasp, especially in large or complex projects. The problem is that we never see the entire space at once. Sequences may be long and difficult to remember, and we may never actually move through the entire space. Sometimes it is sufficient to understand where you are in relation to where you came in, or where you are in relationship to the exterior. Nevertheless, the better the mental picture of the total environment, the more at ease users will be. We suggest three design strategies to facilitate legibility at the overall project scale:

Repetition As the name implies, this strategy relies on the repetition of design elements or approach. Repetition of elements occurs when perceptible units such as space modules are used repeatedly in some kind of regular pattern. Repetition of approach involves the repetition of sequences or arrangements of multiple parts. In the latter case, the sequence or arrangement acts as a unit, and it is the unit that gets repeated throughout the space. Repetition is helpful because it reinforces patterns and can help us make accurate predictions about spaces we haven't visited based on what we have seen. Yet it must be used with caution, as too much repetition can be disorienting.

Consistency Consistency of approach helps users decipher patterns by reinforcing their assumptions as they attempt to figure things out. It is, similar to repetition described previously, a strategy that also relies on the recurrence of a pattern. Consistency, however, does not require repetition of units. All that is required is continuity of intent. An example of this would be a long wall with a gradated use of color, slowly becoming lighter as one moves on. After a minute, one could assume that the wall color will continue to get lighter ahead. Consistency of approach provides users with consistent clues that they can use to make reasonable generalizations.

Points of Reference As we have stated before, it is seldom possible to see entire projects at once. We form our mental idea of the whole by combining perceptions of the various individual spaces. This usually requires some educated guesswork on our part as we try to figure out relationships between spaces we have not experienced together.

The principle of visibility works by providing certain spaces or vantage points from which multiple spaces can be seen. Examples include multistory spaces and other large spaces that allow us to see many spaces and/or features at once, providing instant information about how spaces relate to one another and relate to their position within the whole. Similarly, it is possible to provide spaces or features that can be seen from multiple parts of a project, thus providing useful markers for orientation. Either one provides a large space from which a lot can be seen or common spaces that can be seen from different vantage points. Spaces providing visual scope also serve as points of reference since they can be seen from various vantage points. Spaces that provide visual scope are large, show a multitude of spaces at once, and thus make spatial relationships readily understood; spaces serving as points of reference, although connected visually to several areas, don't necessarily reveal the relationship between areas (Figure 6.24).

Space Composition and Order

One of the most important attributes in the perception of space is **legibility**, the extent to which space is readable. If there is some unifying organization that successfully ties a project together, and if we are allowed to see enough of the project parts and how they go together, sooner or later we will be able to understand the whole. Two factors affecting legibility are the clarity of individual parts and the relative complexity of the spatial composition. The degree of legibility will vary depending on how we arrange a project's open and enclosed areas. Enclosed spaces are often seen as masses or objects in space. Open areas are often leftover spaces defined by the enclosed spaces. We turn our attention now to different effects derived from their composition.

In projects consisting of mostly enclosed spaces, little information is revealed as we travel through corridors

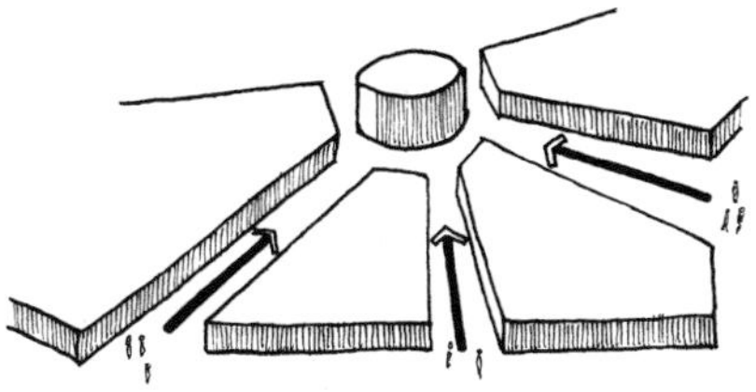

Figure 6.24: With the strategy of points of reference, views from different areas converge on a common space, object, or plane. In this example, the space and object are centrally located, although they are not large.

Figure 6.25: It is hard to find points of reference for orientation in totally enclosed corridors. The examples here show a full loop corridor (a), a straight-run corridor (b), a diagonal corridor (c), and a curved corridor (d). Despite their configurational differences, these corridors share the quality of low imageability.

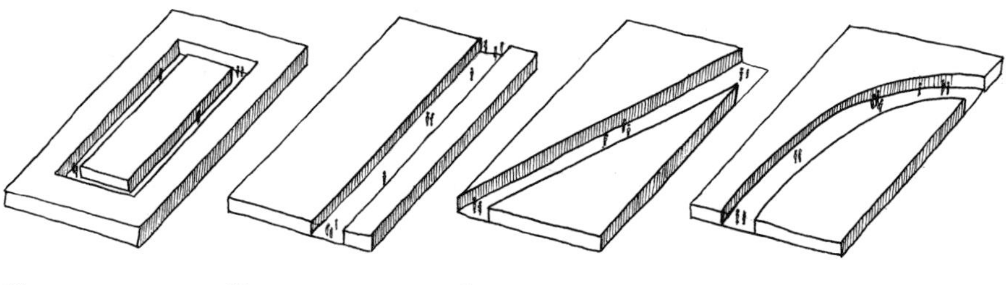

(a) (b) (c) (d)

and we have limited visual access to the enclosed rooms we pass by. It may be impossible in some of these projects to get an idea of the whole. At the very least, however, we should feel oriented in relation to the point of entry, the sequence of the path, and the location of our destination. In open plan projects, we enjoy much greater visual access to a project's parts and features. Because we see more at once, we become better acquainted with the whole and can rely more on accurate real-time impressions and less on our memories.

The following sections look at some examples of how the composition and placement of enclosed spaces affects the resulting spatial patterns and our sense of orientation. Among the variables are the number, size, and arrangement of the open and enclosed areas, the legibility and integrity of the bounding planes, and the use and arrangement of partial-height partitions or of furnishings that obstruct our ability to see beyond.

Enclosed Spaces with Closed Corridors

The spatial experience of projects consisting of enclosed spaces is limited to the experience of enclosed corridors and individual rooms. It is difficult for visitors not familiar with these projects to get a sense of the whole because these projects are partitioned so much. Corridors usually offer no useful clues to help the user know where he or she is. Institutional and office buildings often have these characteristics. Guest room floors in hotels also tend to be this way. Figure 6.25 shows four diagrammatic floor plans as examples. Figure 6.25a shows a circulation loop, a common occurrence in institutional buildings. There is no visual access to rooms on either side of the corridor or to the exterior. The only points of reference serving as orientation cues are the point of entry to the loop, the location of doorways leading to specific rooms, and the signage that identifies the occupants of the suites. Even with those clues, it is easy to lose one's sense of orientation in these corridors. Figure 6.25b–d shows variations of linear arrangements. It is also difficult in these examples to get a real sense of orientation. In Figure 6.25c, users don't even know they are moving diagonally because they have no sense of the configuration of the floor's boundaries. Even when they find out about this relationship they can never experience it directly from the corridor. Only when inside a room or suite can they really see both the diagonal orientation of the front wall and the straight exterior wall. In Figure 6.25d, one experiences walking on a curved corridor, but, once again, from the corridor, one has no sense about how it is oriented to the building's perimeter.

In Figure 6.26a–d the corridor changes direction near the center, therefore establishing a useful point of

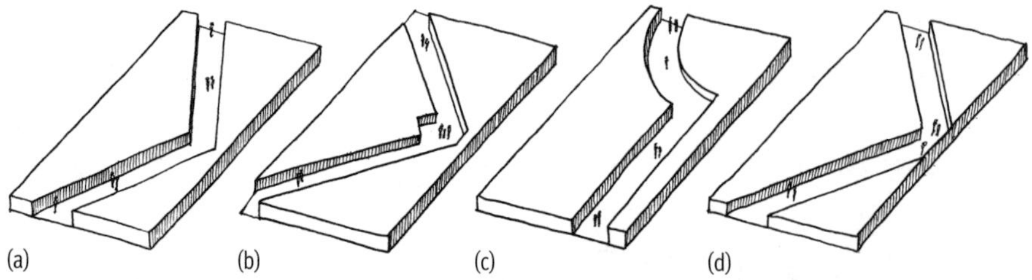

(a) (b) (c) (d)

Figure 6.26: Closed corridors that change directions facilitate orientation by breaking the corridor into segments and providing a specific tangible point of reference at the intersection point. Configuration (a) is a simple example of this. The other three options add features to enhance legibility. Configuration (b) features an expanded intersection point. Configuration (c) features different shapes for the two segments. Configuration (d) brings the intersection point to the exterior perimeter.

reference. Without looking at doors or suite numbers you can conceptualize the corridor into three parts: the first leg, the transition point, and the second leg. In Figure 6.26b the transition point is articulated slightly and given more importance, thus becoming more memorable. In Figure 6.26c each leg of the corridor has a unique configurational character, making it possible to distinguish each leg by its shape: the straight one and the curved one. There is less room for misinterpretation when explaining to someone which leg of the corridor you were on at a given time. Figure 6.26d is similar to Figure 6.26a except the transition point occurs all the way at the perimeter window, thus increasing its impact and offering a welcome sense of orientation in relation to the exterior. In this instance it becomes possible to see where you are in relation to the neighborhood outside.

Open Spaces with One Enclosed Mass

Visual disclosure is ampler in open spaces. This makes them easier to understand. Figure 6.27a–b shows two diagrammatic plans of open spaces with one single freestanding mass of enclosed spaces. In all three, the perimeter wall is left untouched, thus making it possible to grasp the totality of the open space when walking around it. Notice that it is necessary to move around to see the whole space. The location of the floating mass in all three cases is such that the entire space is not visible from a single vantage point. The character of the open areas is different from case to case. The fact that the solid masses in Figure 6.27b are closer to one side improves the legibility of the space, making it possible to distinguish between the narrow sides and the wider sides.

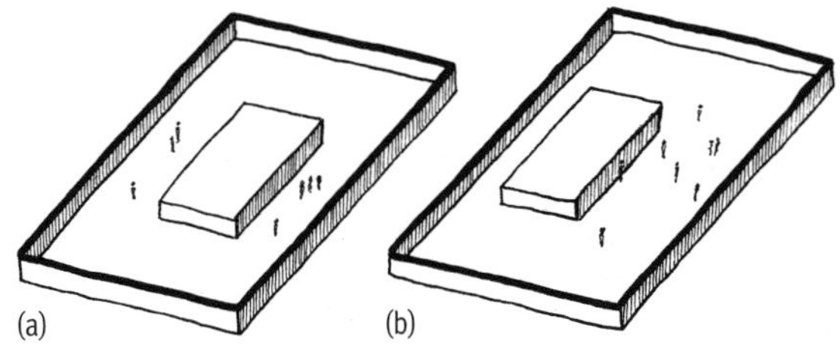

Figure 6.27: The simplest example of a solid element within an open space consists of a freestanding single mass within the space. Here are two examples of this arrangement. In example (a) the mass is centered in space; in example (b) the mass is pushed to one of the sides. The floating mass is readable in both examples, although the spaces around the mass in example (b) are different from one another and are, thus, easier to differentiate.

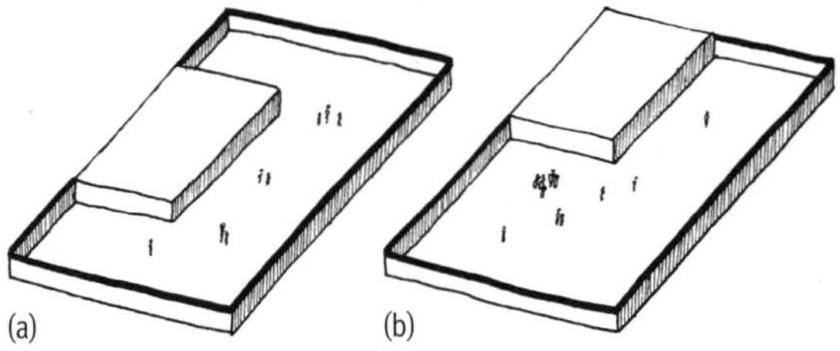

Figure 6.28: In these two examples, a single solid mass is attached to the boundary. Space legibility is simple in both cases. The resulting configuration of the open space varies. In example (a), the resulting open space is U-shaped but has different proportions. In example (b), the resulting open space is a simple L-shaped configuration.

Figure 6.28a–b shows two diagrammatic plans similar to the ones we just saw except, in these, the solid mass is attached to the perimeter. The effects are similar to the previous ones except the attachment to the perimeter wall system breaks its continuity, thus making the extent of the outer boundary somewhat ambiguous. In terms of overall orientation within the open space, the task is actually simplified because the open areas are easier to read with the mass moved away from the center.

Open Projects with Multiple Enclosed Masses

We now turn to examples having not one but multiple solid masses in space. One inevitable result of having more parts is an increase in spatial complexity. Even the simple configurations shown require more investigation than before to get a sense of spatial understanding. Figure 6.29a–b shows two diagrams of plans with two freestanding masses each. The arrangements are similar to the ones in Figure 6.27. The same general observations made there apply here, but now the number of sub-spaces is greater and more walking around is necessary to assess conditions.

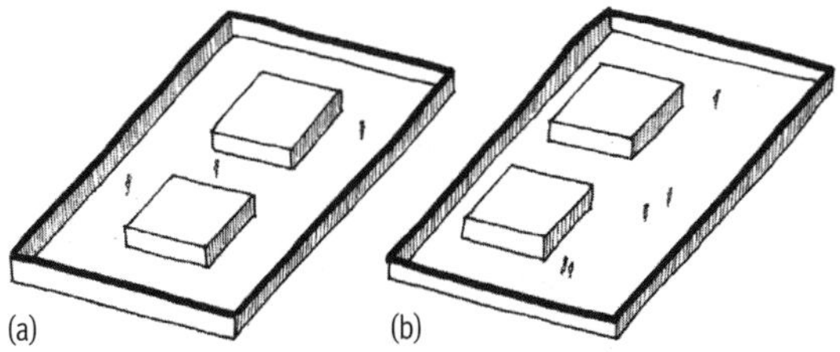

Figure 6.29: These examples feature two freestanding masses each. The masses are centered in both directions in (a), and pushed to one of the long sides in (b). Although similar to the examples in Figure 6.28, these configurations are slightly more complex due to the increased number of parts (one added mass and one added space sandwiched between the two masses).

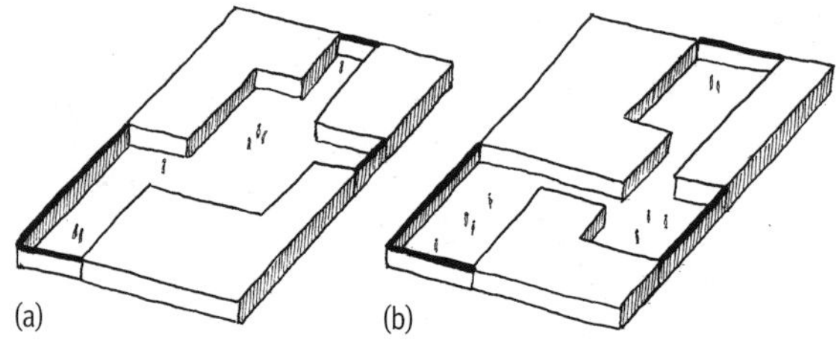

Figure 6.30: These two examples feature masses attached to the perimeter. Both configurations (a) and (b) mix rectangular and L-shaped masses, adding some complexity. In these cases, due to the obscuring of the boundary, the principal clues used for legibility are the resulting configurations of the internal spaces. The examples with the most visual continuity tend to be the clearest.

Spaces with Partial Obscuring of Boundaries

As we saw earlier in this chapter, arrangements in which the perimeter boundary has an exposed, simple, and uninterrupted shape tend to be easier to read than those in which the configuration of the boundary is interrupted by attached masses. We will focus here on a few examples where a substantial portion of the perimeter boundary is claimed by masses of enclosed spaces. Figure 6.30a shows an example with three rectangular masses of different sizes claiming three of the four corners. Notice the irregularity of the remaining network of open spaces.

The central space and the two partial corridors of the configuration in Figure 6.30a make it simpler to understand at once than the configuration shown in Figure 6.30b. Figure 6.30b results in a network of three open spaces with a couple of short corridors joining them. These conceptualizations, of course, are much easier to make when we see the floor plan from above. In real spaces the twists and turns have a disorienting effect, and it takes much longer to figure things out.

Spaces with One Irregular-Shaped Mass

Irregular-shaped masses can enrich or confuse, depending on their legibility and the characteristics of other building components around them. Figure 6.31a–c shows diagrammatic examples of plans having one irregularly shaped mass in the middle. Differences include the regularity of the offsets and the treatment of the different sides.

These examples are oversimplified to make a point. The geometry of the central mass helps to differentiate one side from the others.

Let's turn our attention now to examples where the internal mass is rotated at an angle in relation to the bounding planes. The principles at work are the same as those discussed earlier. Namely, the use of uniform or consistent patterns, and the deliberate differentiation among physical characteristics of the sides, will make it easier for users to understand their environment and feel oriented in it.

Figure 6.32a–c illustrates three examples with a single rotated mass floating in the center. In these examples all sides form unique spatial configurations between the

Figure 6.31: Single but irregular freestanding masses are shown here. Despite the complexity of some of the shapes, the fact that they are single masses assures a reasonable degree of clarity. Because the masses have unequal sides it is easier to differentiate among the different sides.

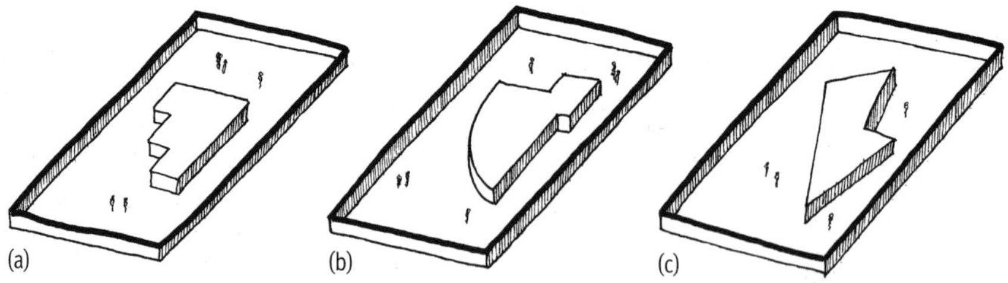

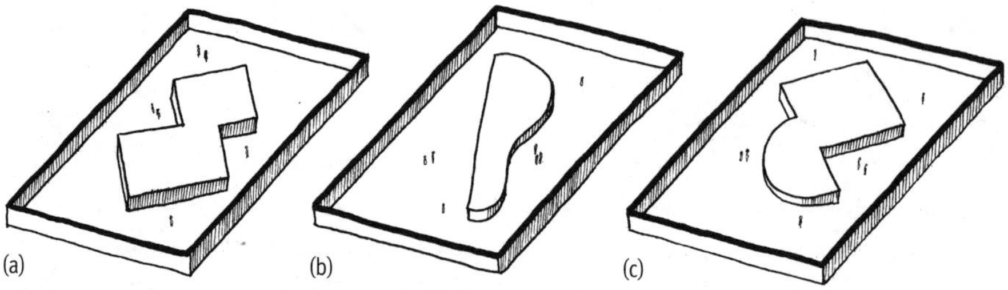

Figure 6.32: These three examples feature single, irregularly shaped, freestanding masses. The spaces created are dynamic and complex. Configuration (a) features an L-shaped mass positioned diagonally. Configuration (b) shows a mass with one straight and one curving side. Configuration (c) features a composite shape composed of a square and a semicircle. Flowing shapes (b) tend to be easier to read as a continuous mass, while masses with offsets require more walking around for verification.

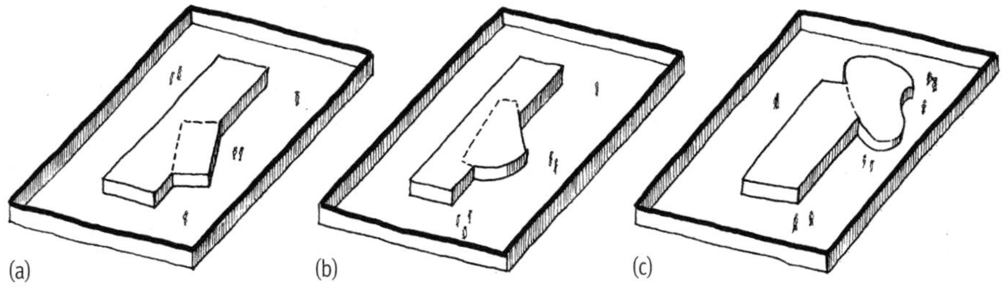

Figure 6.33: The three examples feature simple rectangular masses with asymmetrical superimposed forms protruding from them. Example (a) shows a diagonally oriented rectangle coming off the main straight one. Example (b) shows a fan-shaped mass superimposed over the main rectangle. Example (c) shows a curvilinear mass coming off the corner of the main rectangle. All these protruding masses become distinct, if not dominant, parts that stand out and are remembered.

mass and the perimeter. Every side becomes unique. The object's shape is irregular, however, and its relationship to the container is further complicated by the fact that the two are not parallel. Nevertheless, as soon as the observer realizes that the mass is one continuous uninterrupted object, the mystery is solved and the observer can enjoy the richness of the composition.

Let's now look at one variation of these mass-in-space studies: the regular mass with superimposed accent. Many projects don't have the kinds of curved, offset, or angled masses we have been showing as examples. Instead, they have ordinary simple rectangular masses. Sometimes the superimposition of portions having unique form characteristics helps to improve imageability. For one thing, the mass becomes more memorable. Additionally, better distinction between sides is possible, and the unique part becomes highly legible and thus a serves as a point of reference.

Figure 6.33a–c shows three examples that have similar effects, although using different geometries and compositions. This technique can effectively increase the imageability of otherwise plain and featureless masses in a project and identify important destinations.

The Shape of the Boundary

Interior projects take place inside given compartments in buildings that have particular geometric characteristics. The actual boundary may be readable as such, as in the case of an office building of simple geometry with glass windows around the entire perimeter. At other times it is only partially revealed. The legibility of the boundary is important to our sense of orientation. It will be nearly impossible to get a clear mental picture of the whole if we don't get a reasonable sense of the boundary.

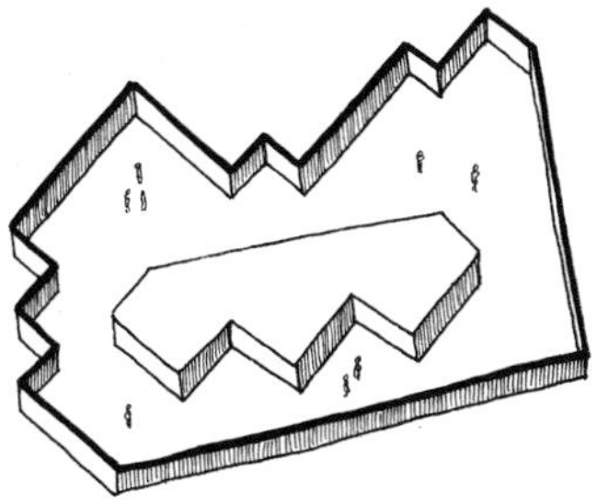

Figure 6.34: This example features an irregularly shaped perimeter configuration. There is one mass, zigzagging on one side and running diagonally on the stepped perimeter side. The variation aides in differentiating one side from the other.

Figure 6.34 shows an example of a building with a complex boundary. The freestanding mass aims to complement the perimeter walls. The resulting spaces between them and the perimeter are varied and irregular due to the complex shapes of the boundary and the floating mass.

Open Spaces with Partial-Height Elements

So far we have focused on full-height boundaries and internal masses. These masses go all the way to the ceiling plane, creating a complete visual separation between one side of the wall and another. A very different effect is achieved when partial height walls are used to separate different areas. Although a separation is achieved between both sides of the partition, the implications for orientation are different. With partial-height walls, even when they are high enough to obstruct the view straight ahead, one can see the ceiling plane continuing above, an important visual cue. Noticing this, one instantly knows that the condition is merely a break within the same container, and not the end of the space, and that both sides of the partial wall are inside the same boundary, an

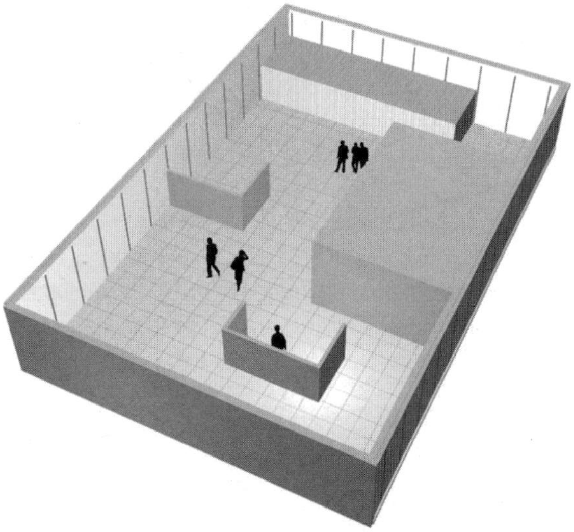

Figure 6.35: This drawing shows the effect of a space with partitions that block the view ahead but do not extend to the ceiling. The user's sense of the whole is disrupted less than it is with full-height partitions, because the continuity of the ceiling plane is visible.

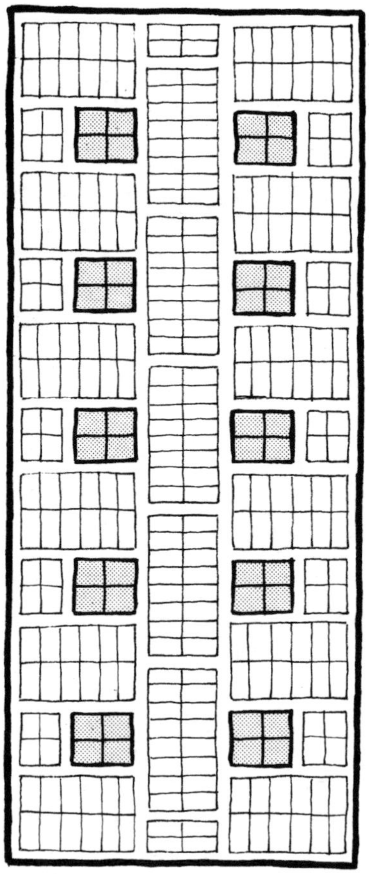

Figure 6.36: Excessive regularity is as disconcerting as disorder. Notice how this floor plan lacks differentiation. It is spatially monotonous and lacks instinctive clues useful for orientation. Users must count modules and workstations to orient themselves.

important orientation clue. Figure 6.35 shows a perspective view illustrating this condition.

In sum, the compositions formed by a project's enclosing boundaries, the masses in it (whether freestanding or attached), and other view-obstructing interior elements establish what we see when we move around a project. Designers need to devote enough time to arrange these elements so they maintain a good degree of order and legibility.

Order and Complexity

It is impossible to separate the issues of order and complexity because they go hand in hand. Order is possible, and necessary, at all levels of environmental complexity. More complex environments require more order; simpler ones can get by with less. This brings up the issue of appropriate levels of order. Does that mean that all projects need to be crystal clear to achieve the desired order?

The answer is no. Total order can result in boring environments. Total order could mean total regularity without differentiation. Imagine a large project laid out with total and unyielding regularity. It would become as disorienting as a project lacking order. As the layout in Figure 6.36 demonstrates, too much order for a given project will result in monotony.

Appropriate levels of order and regularity need to be considered in relation to the project's size, program, and users. Large projects of many interrelated units serving the visiting public, for instance, need more order than smaller projects for familiar users. Some projects may even have two levels of order: a clearer one for strangers who visit, and a more challenging one for those who spend time in them daily.

Even in projects that cater to the visitor, it is often unnecessary to reveal the entire order right away by providing instant clarity and disclosure. In fact, it could be argued that order that requires some effort to discover is more rewarding than order perceived without effort.

Are we saying now, after arguing so strongly for order, that some disorder is actually desirable? Not quite. What we are saying is that complex or discoverable order is sometimes appropriate. The key is that there has to be a system or principle of organization behind the arrangement, and it should be possible, with not too much effort, to figure it out.

CAPSULE | Complexity, Order, and Other Environmental Attributes

People demand a certain degree of clarity in the environment. The optimal degree of order for a given environment varies depending on the people involved and the specific circumstances. It is unrealistic to attempt to understand order without considering factors such as variety and complexity. In fact, a great deal of research has focused on complexity and the degree of preference associated with stimuli of different levels of complexity. Here, we briefly discuss a few basic aspects of this research with a special focus on a framework developed by Rachel and Stephen Kaplan involving complexity and other environmental attributes.

Amos Rapoport has summarized some of the findings of complexity-related research as follows:

- Animals and humans prefer complex patterns in the visual field.
- There is an optimum preference range, and both simple visual fields and chaotically complex visual fields are disliked.
- Complexity can be achieved through ambiguity (meaning multiplicity of meanings and not uncertainty of meanings), through rich and varied environments, and through environments that unfold and reveal themselves gradually.

Daniel Berlyne was one of the pioneers of complexity research. His area of research was animal behavior, with a special emphasis on curiosity and exploratory behavior. When Berlyne started his investigations, the prevailing view about animal motivation emphasized the fact that animals act to satisfy basic needs, such as food and sexual gratification. But, as Ray Crozier explained, Berlyne observed that much behavior was driven by motivations other than the satisfaction of specific needs. He observed that a great deal of behavior was driven by the desire to explore novel situations and events.[1] Based on this insight, Berlyne conducted research and developed theories about exploratory behavior in humans. He suggested that the pleasure derived from works of art could be related to arousal level. He chose to express this in terms of arousal because states of arousal, from sluggishness to high alertness, can be detected and measured objectively.

According to Berlyne, "a work of art is regarded as a stimulus pattern whose collative properties, and possibly other properties as well, give it a positive intrinsic hedonic value."[2] Much of his research focused on his collative variables, named *collative* because they require one to combine the effects produced by them. The variables were ambiguity, complexity, novelty, and surprise. *Hedonic value* is a technical term for pleasure or enjoyment. Berlyne's findings corroborated some existing notions of aesthetics that posited that pleasurable effects are produced when there is a balance between simplicity and complexity, or between order and variety.

In simple terms, Berlyne's findings established that increases in ambiguity, complexity, novelty, and surprise increase one's level of arousal. Thus, scenes of, say, high complexity can be said to have a high arousal potential. He proposed, and his research demonstrated, that hedonic value will increase as the arousal potential of the stimuli (for example, the complexity or novelty of the environment) increases; however, the increase in pleasure will not continue indefinitely. It will reach a peak and then start to decline when stimuli produce uncomfortably high levels of arousal. Figure C6.1 shows the result as an inverted-U curve, known to psychologists as the Wundt curve. What this means is that people prefer moderate over either low or high levels of ambiguity, complexity, novelty, and surprise. They want some stimuli but not too much, with the optimal level varying somewhat from person to person.

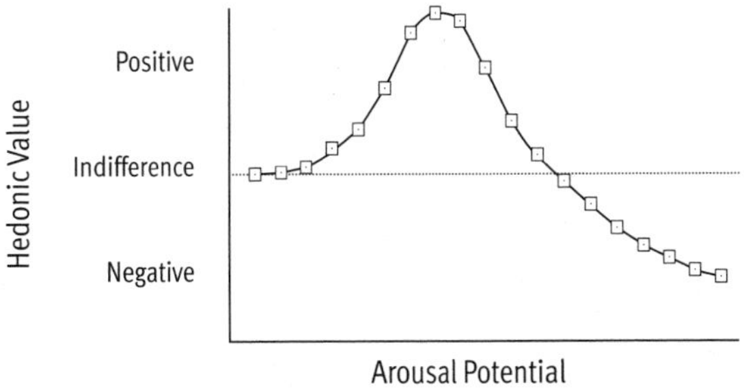

Figure C6.1: Berlyne's inverted-U curve showing the effects of arousal potential on hedonic value.
Source: Copyright ©1994 by Ray Crozier. From *Manufactured Pleasures*, by Ray Crozier, Manchester University Press, Manchester and New York, 1994, p. 63.

In an effort to remove distracting associations with known figures and shapes, Berlyne and his colleagues used randomly generated nonsense images for their experiments, as opposed to images of real art or environments. Another researcher, Joachim Wohlwill, later performed similar studies with works of art and photos of outdoor environments. While the results of his research produced the inverted-U relationship, Stephen Kaplan noted that in the case of the outdoor environment, stimuli were relatively weak and the results failed to reach an acceptable level of significance.[3]

Fueled by, among other things, a conviction that the actual content presented by real environments has an important effect on how much people like them, the Kaplans started conducting research of their own concerning environmental preferences. First, they compared preferences of natural and man-made environments. Natural environments were uniformly preferred over their built-environment counterparts. Due to the high variation in preference from scene to scene and a somewhat inconsistent performance of complexity as a predictor, the Kaplans suspected there had to be other predictors of environmental preference. After some analysis, they came up with three other variables.

They noticed that the most preferred scenes featured either a trail that disappeared around a bend or a brightly lit clearing partially obscured from view by foliage in the foreground. In both types of cases, the scene appeared to promise new information if one moved deeper into it. These characteristics were adopted as a variable and labeled *mystery*. Another variable was devised as a result of the realization that scenes varied in the degree that their elements "hung together." Scenes where the elements did not hang together were difficult to grasp and were generally disliked. They named this variable *coherence*, referring to "the ease with which the information in the scene can be organized into a relatively small number of chunks."[4] The fourth and final predictor in their framework was concerned with the perception that it was possible to predict and remain oriented in space as one wandered deeper into the scene. It was called *legibility*, after Lynch's term with a similar meaning.

What these four variables share is the fact that they all provide information that users can utilize to make sense of the environment. The Kaplans divided the information offered by the variables into two categories: understanding and exploration (Figure C6.2). The degrees of coherence and legibility afforded by the environment assist in its understanding. Coherence can be determined within a single scene. As the Kaplans explained, "A coherent scene is orderly; it is organized into clear areas. People can readily discern the presence of a few distinct regions or areas, and those make it easier to make sense of, or understand, a place."[5] Legibility requires anticipating characteristics of the rest of the space based on a present scene. It requires that some features in the environment be distinct. Featureless environments possess low legibility; however, environments with a strong sense of hierarchy and distinctive features make the reading of their organizing structure easier.

Complexity and mystery, in turn, are related to exploration, although in different ways. The exploration associated with complexity is stationary, visual exploration, as when you visually scan an intricate pattern to explore its contents and relationships. The exploration associated with mystery is more ambulatory. A scene rich in mystery tends to draw you in with the promise of additional information.

It is interesting to note that the Kaplans do not subscribe to the view that too little complexity is boring and too much is overwhelming. They attribute this view to confusion between coherence and complexity

Preference Matrix

	UNDERSTANDING	EXPLORATION
2-D	*Coherence*	*Complexity*
3-D	*Legibility*	*Mystery*

Figure C6.2: Matrix of the Kaplans' model of preference.
Source: From *With People in Mind: Design and Management of Everyday Nature* by Rachel Kaplan, Stephen Kaplan, and Robert L. Ryan. Copyright ©1998 by Island Press. Reprinted by permission of Island Press, Washington, D.C., and Covelo, California. All rights reserved.

and believe that these two variables act together and influence each other. It is possible, for example, to have acceptably high levels of complexity as long as the organization of the parts is coherent. Conversely, a scene with even moderate complexity can overwhelm if its parts are disorganized or lack coherence.

Unlike other areas of research, this is one where research specifically geared to interior environments has been conducted. Separate studies conducted by Suzanne Scott in relation to interior environments confirmed some of the Kaplans' assertions. In an open-ended study aimed at identifying visual attributes related to preferences in interiors, Scott confirmed preferences for environments that are complex, exhibit strong legibility, and possess some degree of mystery.

A separate study by Scott aimed at testing the effectiveness of complexity and mystery as predictors of interior preferences also found positive correlations between these two variables and preference. As stated by Scott, "The strength of the positive correlations observed between complexity and preference and mystery and preference offer rather convincing evidence supporting the contention that people prefer more involving settings."[6] The study also found a fairly strong correlation between mystery and complexity scores and suggests that "these are not independent qualities and that manipulation of physical design characteristics contributing to perception of one may also contribute to perception of the other. For example, subdividing a larger setting to increase its complexity may simultaneously provide screening devices that introduce mystery."[7]

This study also contributed to a better understanding of the physical characteristics that produce complexity in interiors as well as the influence of the exact nature of the view beyond on perceptions of mystery. In addition to confirming that the number and variety of the elements present in a scene are related to perceived complexity, the study also suggests that composition or pattern of elements in a scene as well as its spatial geometry (volumetric shape and internal articulation) are important contributors to environmental complexity. In terms of mystery, the study provided an insight into the fact that the exact content of the view beyond is likely to influence the degree of preference expressed for the scene. In the study, correlations between mystery and preference were greater when the qualities offered by the view beyond were considered preferable, thus pointing out that the content of an upcoming space is at least as important as the evidence that the space lies beyond and can be accessed if one ventures farther into the scene.

The two quoted studies by Scott demonstrate the frequent correlation of research conducted in different fields. In this case, cognitive models of preference, born of studies of natural and urban landscapes, were also found to be useful to explain preferences in interiors. It is important to note, though, that there are slight, sometimes important differences between one discipline and another. Thus, preferences indicated for nonsense random patterns, natural scenes, urban scenes, buildings, and interior spaces, despite their commonalties, will also exhibit nuances specific to the scale and discipline involved.

The application of these findings is not clear-cut and presents some challenges. In an office setting, for instance, it may be desirable to have a relatively low level of complexity so that people can concentrate. Yet, a case can be made for a relatively high level of intricacy in such an environment since people spend so much time in it day after day. Higher levels of complexity can enrich such an environment by making it possible for the regular user to discover new things from time to time, as happens when one reads a good book for a second and third time.

1. Crozier, R. (1994). *Manufactured pleasures: Psychological responses to design*. Manchester, UK: Manchester University Press.
2. Ibid, p. 61.
3. Kaplan, S. (1987). Aesthetics, affect, and cognition: Environmental preference from an evolutionary perspective. *Journal of Environment and Behavior*, 19(1), pp. 3–32.
4. Ibid, p. 10.
5. Kaplan, R., Kaplan, S., & Ryan, R. L. (1998). *With people in mind*. Washington, D.C.: Island Press.
6. Scott, S. (1993). Complexity and mystery as predictors of interior preferences. *Journal of Interior Design*, 19(1), pp. 25–33.
7. Ibid.

CASE STUDY

Plan for a Very Large Interdisciplinary Science Facility That Promotes Diverse Thinking, a Culture of Transparency, and a Hunger for Collaboration

Project: University of Alberta; Centennial Centre for Interdisciplinary Science (580,000 sf)

Location: Alberta, Canada

Design Firm: Flad. Photo credits: KJC Photography and Steve Hall@Hedrich Blessing

"In this building today, researchers and students in all scientific disciplines are working side-by-side. Where once there were walls and buildings separating them, there are now windows shedding light on the inner workings of laboratories, offices, and equipment shops."

Dr. Indira Samarasekera
President and Vice-Chancellor of the University of Alberta

Challenge: How does one design a 580,000-square foot multi-functional, interdisciplinary science facility that combines diverse thinking, visual contact/transparency, improved opportunities for interactions, and the cultivation of ideas?

The University of Alberta's Centennial Centre for Interdisciplinary Science (CCIS) is located in the heart of the University of Alberta (UA) academic campus. The science and educational program areas within the LEED Silver certified facility are integrated throughout eight floors, forming an interdisciplinary center composed of chemical biology and proteomics, integrated earth and landscape management, physics, resource geosciences, planetary dynamics, nanostructures and new materials, instructional facilities, and offices for the faculty of science.

The design team's challenge was to create opportunities for interaction among disciplines that foster thinking beyond conventional boundaries, producing a true social center.

Deliberate emphasis was placed on the strategic location and function of spaces between labs and offices—the integration of teaching spaces, conference and meeting areas, cafes and lounges, and social functions draws adjacent faculty and students to the CCIS as part of a lifestyle rather than a specific programmatic destination.

The design team conceived the idea of a major circulation node for students, creating an integrated circulation system that encompasses the site, ground floor, and interior atria, thus linking five primary zones (Figure CS6.1). An artistic ten-color terrazzo floor spans throughout the first floor and offers key wayfinding solutions and a journey through

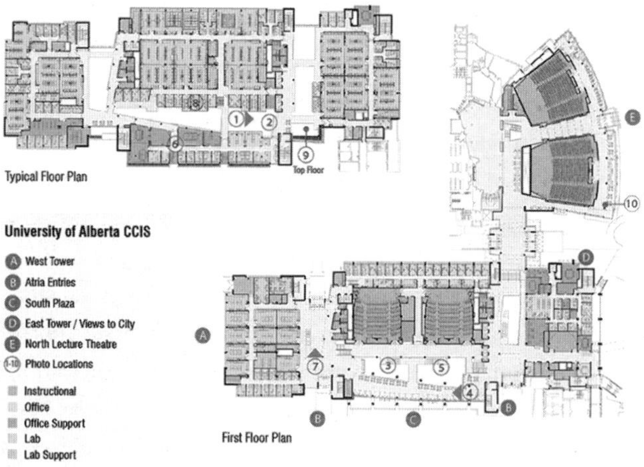

Figure CS6.1: University of Alberta floor plan.

the history of scientific investigation—depicting all of the sciences in the building from plesiosaur to neurons, fractals, and stars. It is the critical unifying element, stitching together the various functions and paths (Figure CS6.2). As a crossroads that serves nearly 4,000 graduate and undergraduate students hourly, wide and visually open interaction stairs and linking bridges are key factors in connecting floors, mezzanines, and lower-level lecture theatres in the CCIS (Figures CS6.3 and CS6.4).

Other major goals of the project were to maximize daylighting and to create a transparent, barrier-free environment. Perimeter offices are fully glazed on the interior side, allowing light from low winter sun angles to penetrate through to interior graduate offices and even into labs 40 to 50 feet inside the building. Transparent materials in the labs and offices in the center atrium (Figure CS6.5) further enhance the spread of natural light deep into the floors while providing a visual connection between work environments.

To allow a measure of privacy for these spaces, a polyester film covers the glass walls, filtering views while preserving opportunities for interaction and light transmission (Figures CS6.6 and CS6.7). These glass walls double as

Figure CS6.2: Main floor showing terrazzo floor pattern.

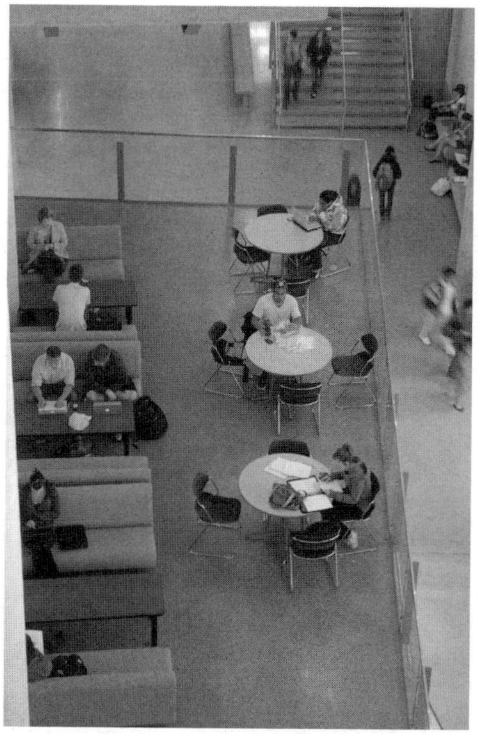

Figure CS6.3: Typical social zones.

Figure CS6.4: Typical informal seating area by the atrium.

Figure CS6.5: Central atrium displaying transparency and light penetration.

Figure CS6.6: Private work areas are fully transparent and enjoy the abundance of natural light.

Figure CS6.7: Transparency and writing surfaces at offices.

functional marker boards and are also found in small, four-person meeting areas located along the south façade that offer views to the Quad and soft, comfortable seating for impromptu discussions (Figure CS6.8).

The selection of interior materials was guided by the desire to achieve interior/exterior continuity. A warm, elegant finish palette of terrazzo, terra cotta–colored brick, architectural-finished concrete, beech wood veneer, glass, and stainless steel defines a foundation for the interior material palette. Offices, conference rooms, and lounges received softer finishes of carpet tile and acoustical walls and ceilings to support the functions of quieter spaces (Figure CS6.9).

Much attention was devoted to the design of lighting solutions for the atria, offices, conference rooms, and labs. As part of the lighting scheme, the design team devised a wayfinding element that uses vertical and horizontal light bars at the concrete elevator cores and serves as a focal point. This feature towers up all eight floors of the east and west atriums.

Many of the atria finishes are light in value to achieve effective reflectance and support their daylighting strategies. Artistic wall-mounted reflectors are located across the top of the center atrium and redirect sunlight from the clerestory, providing much of the illumination needed during daytime hours. The optimal angle for the reflectors was determined using animation modeling of sunlight patterns throughout the year, and their design of multiple mirror-like metals are inspired by—and an abstract reference to—the Northern Lights. To provide lighting from the highest point of the atrium, and meet the criteria of no access to this area, large projector lights and floating circular reflectors provide artificial light when needed.

Figure CS6.8: Typical meeting area along south façade.

Figure CS6.9: View of conference room.

REVIEW

Summary

One of the major contributions a designer makes is endowing the built environment with order. Environmental order manifests itself in different ways: order related to proper fit, order related to visual harmony, and order related to spatial orientation.

Designers should strive to provide more than just neat and functional organization and provide an overall structure based on sound organizing principles. Interior environments are experienced sequentially, one space at a time. Sometimes, what appears clear on paper while looking at a floor plan is hard to figure out as we move about in built space. Three factors that help facilitate the understanding of interiors are identity, structure, and meaning. Environments strong in order have easily identifiable main components, a systematic structure derived from an organizing principle, and meaningful destinations.

The ten place elements introduced in Chapter 3 play important roles in providing environmental legibility and order. Notable are the role of arrival spaces, paths, nodes, and landmarks. To feel oriented inside buildings it is necessary to understand components at various hierarchical levels: parts, groups, relationships between parts, sequences, and, finally, the whole. Many design strategies are available to make these various components stand out clearly so they can be understood and remembered. By making individual parts and groupings recognizable, their points of intersection visible, their sequences memorable, and the structure of the whole comprehensible through the proper provision of environmental information, designers bring order to the projects they design.

A crucial aspect related to legibility and order is the composition of the masses and spaces of a project. Predominantly enclosed projects with closed corridors are the most difficult to understand due to the lack of visual accessibility. Open spaces are easier to decipher. Nevertheless, it is possible to design predominantly open projects of great complexity. The number, size, placement, orientation, and shape of masses and the complexity and level of disclosure of the boundary all combine to produce spaces of different levels of complexity and readability.

Order is possible at all levels of complexity. In general, the more complex a project is, the greater the need for order to help users feel oriented. Optimal levels of order will vary from project to project depending on their scope and users. The level of order established and the level of difficulty involved in understanding it are factors controlled by the designer. If appropriate design choices are made, the level of order achieved will help orient users in space by facilitating their understanding of the environment, its place within the larger context, and their position within these environments at any particular time.

1. Leupen, B. (1997). *Design and analysis.* New York: Van Nostrand Reinhold.
2. Norberg-Schulz, C. (1980). *Genius loci.* New York: Rizzoli International.
3. Passini, R. (1992). *Wayfinding in architecture.* New York: Van Nostrand Reinhold.
4. Von Meiss, P. (1990). *Elements of architecture.* London: Van Nostrand Reinhold International.
5. Lynch, K. (1960). *The image of the city.* Cambridge: MIT Press.
6. Ibid, p. 9.
7. Von Meiss, 1990, pp. 31–52.

Chapter Questions

1. What are the main concerns of order related to orientation?
2. Describe how interior environments are experienced.
3. Name and define the three factors that facilitate understanding and orientation in interiors.
4. How can domains and centers contribute to order?
5. Why are arrival spaces so important for orientation?
6. How can paths be used to supply order?
7. How do nodes and landmarks contribute to order?
8. Name and define four design strategies to facilitate understanding of project parts.
9. Name and define four design strategies to facilitate legibility of groupings.
10. Name and explain two design strategies to clarify the relationships between project parts.
11. Name and describe three design strategies to increase awareness of motion and sequence in interior environments.
12. Name and explain four strategies to help users understand a project as a whole.
13. What effect does attaching masses to the perimeter boundary have on legibility and orientation?
14. Why does it sometimes make sense to design freestanding masses with no equal sides?

Exercises

1. Select an important space, a *center*, of a past or present design project and determine three design strategies to make it more memorable inside and outside.
2. Sketch two ways to make an *arrival space* enhance the user's sense of orientation.
3. Sketch three *paths* with different levels of disclosure to the rest of the project.
4. Design two versions of a vibrant *node* for any project type.
5. Design one memorable *landmark* for an interior project.
6. Make a part (mass or space) of one of your projects stand out by using one or more of the strategies discussed in this chapter.
7. Sketch two ways of using a *datum* to group parts of one of your past or present design projects.
8. Select a prominent space from one of your past or present projects and expand its level of *visibility* toward other interior areas. Sketch the result.
9. Sketch two *sequences* of past or present projects using some of the strategies we discussed to make them legible and useful for orientation.
10. Design one idea using the concept of *points of reference* to facilitate orientation in interior projects.
11. Sketch two ideas to increase the imageability of closed corridors in a compartmentalized project.
12. Sketch two ideas (one formal, one casual) to group all the solids of a past or present project within one (freestanding or attached) mass.
13. Sketch two ideas (one formal, one casual) similar to the ones in Exercise 12, but use two masses, not one.

Chapter 7
Enrichment

Instructional Objectives

- Explain the need for both environmental stimulation and environmental stability.
- Present general principles to enrich interior spaces.
- Show ways to incorporate meaningful events along circulation routes.
- Present strategies to enhance the formal qualities of the path itself.
- Show ways to design the views within and beyond the path.
- Suggest a framework for the enrichment of personal experience while stationary.

My house is practical. I thank you, as I might thank Railway engineers, or the Telephone service. You have not touched my heart.

—*Le Corbusier,* Towards a New Architecture

The introductory quote by Le Corbusier reminds us of the need to address a key, and sometimes forgotten, function of design: to enrich, to touch the human heart. The commitment to find ways to do this is what generally distinguishes a designed solution from an engineered solution. This chapter addresses ways to enrich experience in interior environments.

In Chapter 6 we discussed the role of order in design. Regularity and clarity make interior environments easier to understand, satisfying our inherent need for making sense of the world. However, too much order can be monotonous. We also need variety and interest in our environment. One of the challenges for the designer is achieving an adequate balance between these seemingly conflicting needs. In reality, order and enrichment are highly intertwined and form part of a single puzzle. Expression is also a piece in this puzzle, and it will be covered in the next chapter.

In this chapter we first discuss the role of enrichment in the design of interiors. The rest of the chapter presents ways of making projects and our experiences in them richer. The strategies are broken down into three categories: general enrichment strategies, enrichment while in transit, and enrichment while stationary.

ORDER AND ENRICHMENT

The human mind values predictability and constancy in the environment, but it also seeks novelty and variety. Opinions about how much and what kind of these qualities are optimal can be quite personal. They can vary from project to project and from designer to designer. Furthermore, the potential approaches and combinations used to produce order, novelty, and variety are limitless. It is possible to achieve a desirable balance of these qualities with alternate design solutions.

Let's start by examining how reducing the degree of regularity can enrich a project. Consider an alternative version of the highly regular project presented in the last chapter in Figure 6.36. Suppose you had the same programmatic needs to fulfill but wanted to add some novelty and interest within a similar design vocabulary of rectilinear forms. Just by manipulating the placement of the solid modules, as shown in Figure 7.1, the project acquires enough variety to alleviate its severe sense of repetition. The project is now inherently more interesting and has more differentiation between zones, even though the parts are still highly repetitive.

The typical worker, regardless of location, now has an identifiable sense of place that provides a focus for the area and anchors users in space. If the solid masses viewed from there had some special surface articulation or wall treatment that was pleasant to look at, the experience would be further enhanced. Figure 7.2 shows a similar example with an even stronger sense of definition and containment, especially in the interior zones.

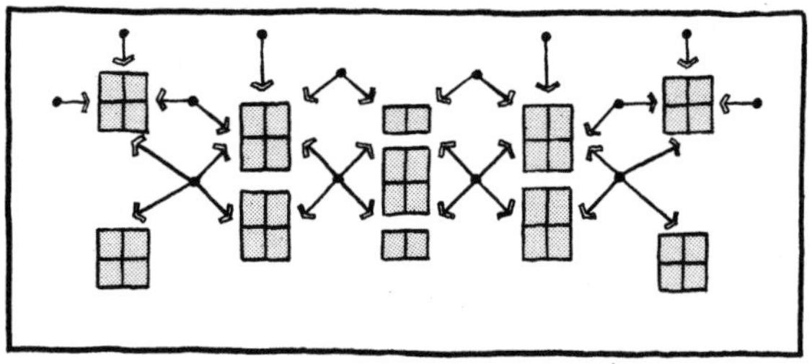

Figure 7.1: Depending on their desk location, workers in this facility have one or more masses close by that act as anchoring devices and internal focal points.

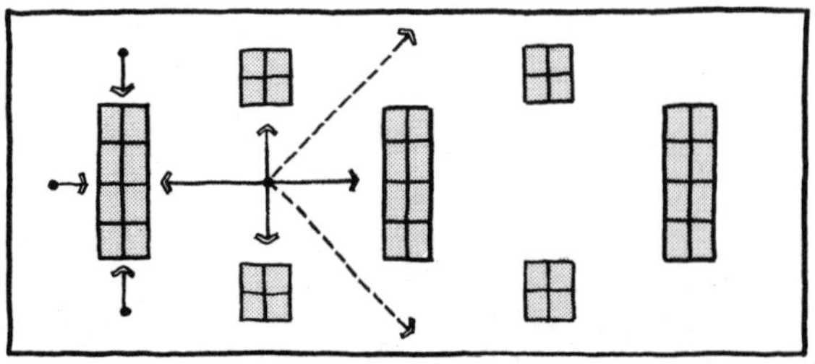

Figure 7.2: This arrangement is similar to the one in Figure 7.1 but provides an even stronger sense of containment and group territory.

Additionally, instead of interior masses being just rooms, they now perform the additional duties of anchoring adjacent open areas and providing beneficial focal points on which to rest the eyes.

Are these kinds of interventions necessary? Not really. Projects can be functional without them. Are they desirable? Of course they are. They enhance the experience of the people using the space. Some designers give more consideration to these matters than others. It is important that you develop your awareness and skills to perform these kinds of manipulations to make your projects more enriching.

A Case for Project Enrichment

The success of most interior projects relies more on function than anything else. As mentioned earlier, the context of the project and the requirements of the program give a project its fundamental form. Response to these alone determines the size and location of the different areas of a project. However, response to function alone will rarely produce the best form. Form has to be dealt with in its own right, respecting the placements and adjacencies dictated by the context and program, but following its own agenda to produce experiential desirable qualities. It takes conscious and intentional effort from you as the designer to provide more than just a functional space.

What we are proposing is that design should be just as concerned with the way things are, the way they are arranged, and the effect these design decisions have on those who experience them. You may think of this dimension as the poetic dimension of projects.

Designers, as part of their craft, have the responsibility to shape the spaces and sequences of buildings. In doing so, they have the power to create experiences that seduce and stimulate.

Achieving qualities and experiences that engage the user and enrich his or her experience requires designers to adopt a separate agenda concerning these issues. These qualities and experiences rarely occur without a conscious desire to produce them. They require the designer's commitment to seek them out and work on them so they occur seamlessly without neglecting or disturbing the other requirements of the project. It may become necessary for you to negotiate between the various requirements and agendas of the project in order to balance them satisfactorily. This will often require compromise. For example, you may occasionally consider moving a room a couple of spaces down from its optimal functional position in order to achieve a more desirable experiential or compositional effect. These types of decisions are sometimes difficult and are not always possible. They need to be considered on a case-by-case basis and require proper insight and input from the users and design team alike.

So, your task is to manipulate parts of the project in order to achieve more evocative effects and meaningful encounters within it. Is this really possible, you may ask, with the kind of strict and limiting programs designers have to work with? It's seldom simple. It often requires an approach where project parts perform double functions. A wall may be the enclosing plane of a room needing privacy and also the canvas for an experientially rich corridor on the other side. The resulting configuration of the wall, therefore, may be a compromise that works for both of these intentions.

Another approach used sometimes is the incorporation of spaces and events not required by the program to enrich the experience of users. The enlargement of an important intersection to create an energetic node and the addition of small niches for people to gather in are examples. Of course, the addition of space to a program is a sensitive matter requiring proper justification in the eyes of the client. It is often impossible to add additional square footage to a project, and whatever amenities are desired have to be planned skillfully within the physical size constraints of the project.

Intentionality

The effect the interior of a building has on its users is produced by a combination of factors, some having nothing to do with the environment itself. In Chapter 2 we explained how the nature of the occasion, the people involved, nearby activities, and other similar factors affect our experience. Even when we consider building aspects only, the resultant effect is produced by an interplay between a number of elements we perceive simultaneously at different levels, many of them subconsciously. The spatial character, the order of spaces, the furnishings, the materials, the colors, the sounds, the lighting, the artwork, the details, and the specific combinations of all act in unison and produce an overall effect on us.

It is impossible to separate form from meaning. Most everything in the environment elicits associations that conjure certain connotations and levels of personal response. Certain aspects of design stimulate more symbolic associations than others. Specific design styles, materials, and graphic representations (artwork and photography, for instance) usually have strong associations with specific attitudes and ways of being. Other aspects are more neutral and harder to label. We tend to experience these as they are, for what they offer or present to us, without much symbolic interference. In this chapter we will focus on formal rather than symbolic aspects of form. Symbolic aspects of design are addressed in the next chapter.

Designers need to consider important questions in order to formulate a personal philosophy regarding the enrichment of projects. Is it right to perform somewhat arbitrary manipulations for the sake of effect? To what extent is well-intentioned artistic license a right or privilege of the designer?

Personal positions related to these questions are likely to vary. Some designers favor straightforwardness over cleverness, some favor simplicity over complexity, some like the realistic and pictorial over the abstract and obscure. Whatever your personal position may be, it is important that you are clear about it and pursue it consistently within each project. Design manipulations for effect may sometimes come across as superficial. It is therefore necessary that all interventions are well thought out and considered carefully before implementation. Many seemingly good ideas are better left undone if they will lose their impact and seem foolish after their novelty wears off.

Stimulation and Stability

Having issued the previously mentioned warnings, we maintain that it is worthwhile to manipulate project forms, spaces, and elements to increase their richness and enhance the users' experience. The rest of this chapter addresses strategies for your consideration. We will start by introducing two opposing human needs that you must understand before embarking on the task of manipulating projects for enrichment. They are stimulation and stability.

Stimulation

We have said that optimal qualities of the visual field lie somewhere between total regularity and total disorder; the exact levels depend on the particular realities of each project and the disposition of the person perceiving the environment. The majority of people have a desire to experience some level of environmental stimulation. An efficient, functional, and orderly environment that does not stimulate will rarely satisfy.

Optimal levels and kinds of stimulation are relative. A nightclub, for instance, demands much more stimulation than a hotel guest room. In the nightclub, the combination of design features, colors, lights, loud music, and interesting people produces a high-load environment. This, we recognize, is appropriate for the project type. The hotel guest room, in contrast, other than being cheerful and welcoming, needs to be a good place to unwind and relax. Therefore, bright blinking lights, extra vivid colors, and loud music are not likely to be appreciated.

Stability

Although some level of stimulation is healthy for all projects, some projects, or parts of projects, benefit from less environmental stimulation. Spaces where repose, peacefulness, and concentration are desirable don't want to be highly stimulating. Hospital rooms, for example, need to be pleasant in a quiet, non-agitating way. Stable places can be evocative and powerful in some ways, but should not be visually loud. Areas of mental activity requiring high concentration, such as private offices in some work facilities, should be conducive to concentration without much distraction. Areas meant for relaxation, such as the hotel guest room mentioned above, usually need to be subdued more than stimulating. Keep in mind, however, that the desire for subtle and subdued qualities doesn't necessarily mean the elimination of all stimulating features.

Part of the challenge of design is determining the appropriate level of stimulation and the means of achieving it. Understanding the effects of these two fundamental, and opposite, needs will help you make judgments about the correct balance for a specific project. In the rest of this chapter we discuss attributes and strategies that help make projects engaging. They can all be handled in ways that provide more or less stimulation and can, therefore, be utilized in both high-load and low-load environments.

Enrichment in Building Interiors

In Chapter 2 we analyzed the basic events of the building experience. Starting from the approach to the building, we described the process of arriving, waiting, proceeding to, and arriving at the target destination within the facility. In Chapter 3, we presented the place elements. Some of these, such as arrival spaces and destination spaces, relate directly to the various rituals of the building experience. By thinking of the basic events of the building experience and the places where they occur, we can gain awareness of opportunities to enrich the experience of users. In the rest of this section, we address a few of the place elements especially apt for enriching design manipulations and point out some instances in which to use them.

The arrival space gives visitors their first impression of a project. Whatever message that is to be communicated to the user begins here. Additionally, this space represents an important transition from the space immediately outside, and between itself and the rest of the facility. Among the design variables available for manipulation in order to provide opportunities for engagement are the overall impact of the space, the level of visual disclosure to other spaces in the facility, and the freedom of movement from the space.

Waiting involves anticipation. It sometimes induces a state of heightened awareness as we anxiously wait for someone to rescue us and take us to our real destination. Other times, the act of waiting supplies a few minutes between tasks during which we can have a chance to unwind. For some, the close proximity to other people can be uncomfortable. Waiting areas offer opportunities to provide engaging graphic or verbal information about the entity housed in the facility (whether a corporation, a healthcare facility, or a restaurant). They are also good places to add elements of visual relief.

The circulation spaces of a project present great opportunities to engage the user with building elements as well as with the rest of the facility. Unfortunately, corridors are often not given the attention they deserve. If properly orchestrated and articulated, the circulation experience can delight, entice, and provide engaging sequences.

Destination spaces, you may recall, are the spaces where we do what we came to do in the facility, be it work, eat, study, socialize, or shop. When we engage in our target activity, the building and its interiors and elements take a secondary, supporting role. The actions in these spaces may focus on paperwork, food, books, people, or merchandise, among many possibilities. Even in these spaces, where the facility, like a good butler, should be unobtrusive except to provide utilitarian assistance when needed, there are opportunities for enrichment. Design manipulations can enhance users' abilities to focus on the task at hand, connect with adjacent surroundings, and find momentary relief in well-conceived and well-placed views and vistas.

GENERAL ENRICHMENT STRATEGIES

In this section, we present a number of enrichment strategies. For convenience, we have grouped them into three categories: general enrichment strategies, enrichment strategies for users while in transit, and enrichment strategies for users while stationary. The first group of strategies can be exercised anywhere within the project, either throughout or in select areas. The second group is specific to circulation areas. The third group is closely associated with areas where we spend time doing something while stationary, such as destination spaces and waiting areas.

Variety

The relatively simple manipulations performed in Figures 7.1 and 7.2 at the beginning of this chapter show the effect of variety in projects. Although the organization of the project in the various schemes remained relatively formal and regular, the modifications provided relief and interest. In projects where parts are not repetitive, there is a natural occurrence of variety. In projects that feature repeated parts, it is up to the designer to provide enough variety to avoid monotony and make the project more challenging perceptually. Sometimes all it takes is a few basic shifts, as seen in the examples. Other times a greater degree of variety and differentiation may be desirable.

Complexity

Environmental complexity has been a well-researched topic in studies of environmental preference (see Capsule C6.1 titled "Complexity, Order, and Other Environmental Attributes"). Research indicates that people tend to prefer higher levels of environmental complexity up to a certain point, beyond which any increase produces discomfort. That critical point varies from individual to individual. Design features to add complexity can be anything from lines on a wall to the heavy articulation of surfaces, ornamental features, or multiple and varied objects in space.

The relationship between complexity and order is also relevant. Environments high in order have been found to tolerate higher levels of complexity than those with less order. Therefore, the number and kind of elements in a space and their specific arrangement go hand in hand and work together. Complex orchestration of parts requiring some mental effort to decipher is stimulating as long as the effort required is not overly taxing.

Environmental complexity occurs at many levels and can be produced a number of ways. The surfaces of enclosing planes and other elements (such as columns) can be articulated in increasingly complex ways. The number and arrangement of masses and objects in space can be manipulated to achieve increasing levels of complexity. Also, the treatment and orientation of project components (floors, walls, furnishings, and so on) can be treated as different layers and arranged in contrasting ways to achieve complexity. We examine them in more detail in the following sections.

Surface Articulation

One way to provide environmental complexity is through the articulation of the enclosing planes. The degree of complexity can be minimal, just enough to provide some interest, or it can be substantial, enough to challenge the senses. One simple way to provide subtle articulation is by **modulation**, the subdivision of any element, such as a surface, into smaller components or modules that, in turn, add up to the whole. Modulation on surfaces is accomplished by the use of regulating lines. Thus, a simple and featureless wall can acquire a sense of texture by the addition of lines produced by either molding strips or reveals.

Figure 7.3a shows a simple wall subdivided by the use of lines. Although the level of complexity achieved is minimal, the modulation of the wall is enough to give it some interest. The lines have to be placed so that a good sense of scale and proportion is achieved. Figure 7.3b shows the wall modulated into an increased number of equal parts. The modules of the wall in Figure 7.3c feature an irregular rhythm, thus resulting in a more varied and complex arrangement incorporating a sense of hierarchy. If the material used is wood or stone, their graining and veining would supply still another level of richness due to their subtle patterning. Figure 7.4 shows an example of the use of surface modulation on the interior walls and floor of an academic building.

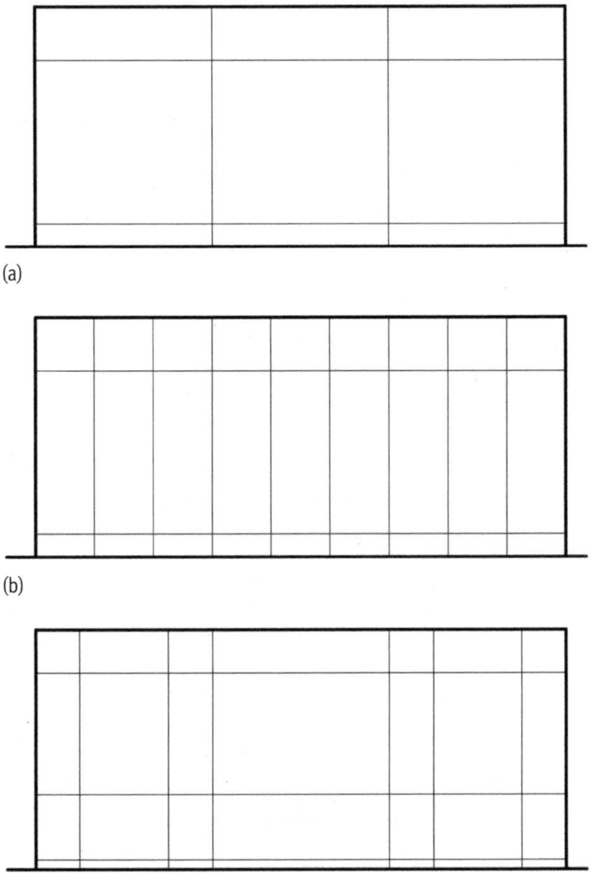

(a)

(b)

(c)

Figure 7.3: The three elevations shown are examples of modulation using lines. The level of intricacy can be minimal (a), moderate and regular (b), or moderate and irregular (c).

Figure 7.4: This corridor in an institutional facility utilizes horizontal, vertical, and turning lines on the walls and ceiling, thus giving some articulation to could otherwise be featureless architectural elements.

Figure 7.5: Pattern, texture, and lines applied to floors and ceilings also increase relative complexity and supply richness. The orderly arrangement of the floor pattern, texture on the stone wall, and ceiling lines contribute subtle richness to this scene.

The example in Figure 7.5 shows additional examples of surface modulation on various surfaces of the same academic building. Here, the modules are smaller in size and larger in number than in the previous wall example. There is some complexity by virtue of the modulation but also additional richness produced by the texture of the floor tiles. The floor tiles are arranged in a somewhat random pattern, and this adds variety to the composition.

Modulation can also be accomplished by **surface relief**. With this technique, alternating parts of a surface advance or recede to create differentiation. The result is similar to the one created by lines, but, in the case of relief, the sense of depth is manipulated to create more pronounced effects. Notice how the composition shown in Figure 7.6

Figure 7.6: Surface relief provides modulation three-dimensionally. In this scene, surface relief and reveal lines contribute to the overall effect.

uses depth to provide a sense of articulation to the wall unattainable with just lines.

Spatial Composition

Complexity can also be attained by the composition of architectural and interior elements in the visual field. Factors that play a part and can be manipulated are the number of parts and their size, shape, and arrangement. While the number of parts is often dictated by the program, such as the number of tables in a restaurant's dining area or the number of display fixtures in a retail store, it is possible to manipulate the amount of architectural articulation around them to increase or decrease the overall level of complexity. Figure 7.7 shows a view of an office facility where curves and an angled ceiling grid are used to add texture and interest to the environment.

Figure 7.7: Spatial complexity adds richness and interest. A sense of complexity is accomplished in this office through the playful interplay between wall, ceiling, and floor elements.

Arrangement is important in manipulating complexity. You can make a simple group of a few components more interesting by using an irregular spatial composition. Conversely, you can control the complexity produced by a collection of many disparate parts by utilizing more regular arrangements. Even projects that have immense inherent density and variety of parts can be controlled by the use of pattern and regularity.

Overlapping Layers

One unique way to increase complexity and interest in the interior environment is to think of different spatial components as layers that can be manipulated independently of each other. You can think of a project as consisting of the following systems: the enclosing boundary, the floor plane, the interior walls, the ceiling plane, the furnishings, the building structure, the miscellaneous objects in space such as suspended elements and fixtures, and details. All these systems overlap with one another to produce the final composition. A perfectly ordered arrangement would have all these systems aligned neatly in parallel or perpendicular relationships to one another. When some of these systems are pulled forward, or recessed, or rotated laterally in relation to the others, an interesting, more complex effect is produced while maintaining a sense of order. Figure 7.8 shows an office

Figure 7.8: In this example, the floors, ceilings, enclosing walls, and furnishings are treated independently and given different orientations to produce a more complex arrangement.

scene with an interesting interplay between the walls, the floor, and the ceiling planes and their respective modulation.

This technique can be used in subtle ways by performing slight rotations (or other kinds of variations) and by the alteration of a few systems. It can also be used in bolder ways by simultaneously rotating several systems so they each have different orientations.

Novelty

Another enriching factor in the environment is novelty. Novel shapes and arrangements attract our attention and engage our minds. Novelty goes beyond mere variety. The novelty can be due to the uniqueness or the unconventionality of the approach taken. As with any of the other variables, the degree of application can vary from subtle to extreme. A space can be slightly unique or highly unusual.

Spatial novelty can be produced by the characteristics of individual masses and elements in space and their shapes, as well as by their combination into specific arrangements having novel effects. In general, regular shapes, usually rectangular, and uniform rectilinear arrangements are considered the norm, the conventional default approach we customarily see. Almost any design deviating from these approaches has the potential for being novel and attracting our attention if done skillfully.

Examples of novelty include unusual shapes of architectural elements such as curvilinear shapes (Figures 7.9 and 7.10), unusual treatment of specific visual elements, such as

Figure 7.9: One of the ways to achieve novelty is by making the shape of space itself unusual and different.

Figure 7.10: Architectural elements with playful shapes are novel and increase the interest of a space, as the overhanging curved soffit does here.

Figure 7.11: The surfaces of elevations can be treated in enriching and novel ways. In this scene, elevations are treated with a rich texture in one case and a full wall mosaic mural in the other, thus enhancing the resulting quality.

Figure 7.12: The nonorthogonal orientation used for the framing members of this storefront window creates a novel effect.

openings and elevations (Figures 7.11 and 7.12), and unusual arrangements in space, such as the effect produced by taking otherwise normal arrangements to an extreme, as in the case of extreme repetition and rhythm (Figure 7.13).

Boldness

Boldness, a specific kind of novelty, requires its own category. It relies on exaggeration to make something stand out in the environment. Often associated with boldness of treatment, such as surface treatment, it can also be expressed spatially. Accomplishable in interiors by exaggerated applications of anything from color to light to texture, when related to space it usually involves the

Figure 7.13: A simple arrangement, if handled with severity, can stand out as different and novel. In these two examples, the severe repetition of building and interior elements stands out and makes a bold statement.

exaggeration of shape or scale, making them much more intense than normal.

Examples of boldness include the exaggeration of a shape to an extreme, the use of very bold color, and the use of imposing form, as shown in Figure 7.14. Boldness of scale involves the exaggeration of size. Whereas large spaces can be associated with grandiosity, large masses are more effective at achieving boldness because of their heaviness and their figural character. They become almost defiant. It helps if they have some degree of verticality and detachment from surrounding walls. Being able to see the entire mass as a freestanding object in space helps to accentuate its massiveness.

Tension and Release

A strategy that is sure to engage the mind and the emotions is the use of deliberate tension in the environment. The goal is to create a situation of temporary tension in order to heighten the user's emotions momentarily. Short-term exposures of appropriate intensities can be enhancing, especially when part of a sequence that eventually provides welcome relief.

Tension can be produced by overtaxing the senses with high levels of the already discussed conditions of complexity, novelty, and boldness. High levels of these conditions can actually be appropriate in high-load environments like nightclubs, some retail applications, and short-term high-load settings, such as some restaurants.

Another strategy to provide enrichment through tension is the use of intentional compression. Tension through compression can be successfully applied in selected points along a route or sequence by the deliberate compression of space to produce a tightening effect. The tightening can be sudden (Figure 7.15a) or gradual (Figure 7.15b). Its duration can be just an instant (Figure 7.15c) or longer (Figure 7.15d). Finally, relief can come suddenly or gradually (Figure 7.15e).

Ambiguity

The use of ambiguity to engage users relies on the presentation of ambiguous visual messages in order to challenge the mind. Instead of a crystal-clear and consistent message, a muddled one is presented. This is a tricky strategy requiring good judgment and skill for success. American architect Robert Venturi argued for the value of ambiguity in design in his classic book, *Complexity and Contradiction in Architecture*. He noted: "An architectural element is perceived as form *and* structure, texture

Figure 7.14: The richly articulated curvilinear room shown here is highly unconventional and somewhat playful, the kind of room one likes to be in.

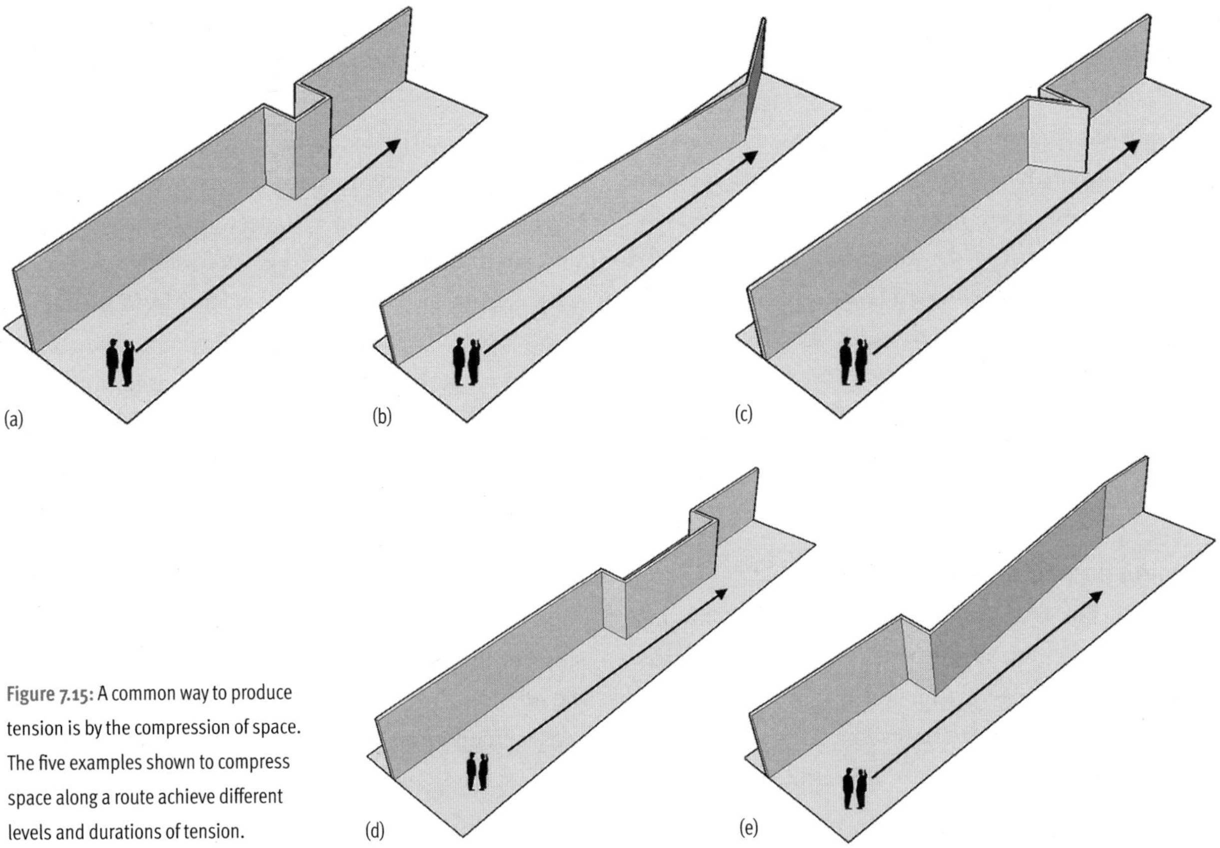

Figure 7.15: A common way to produce tension is by the compression of space. The five examples shown to compress space along a route achieve different levels and durations of tension.

and material. These oscillating relationships, complex and contradictory, are the source of the ambiguity and tension characteristic to the medium of architecture. The conjunction 'or' with a question mark can usually describe ambiguous relationships. Is it a square plan or not? Are they near or far? Big or small?"[1]

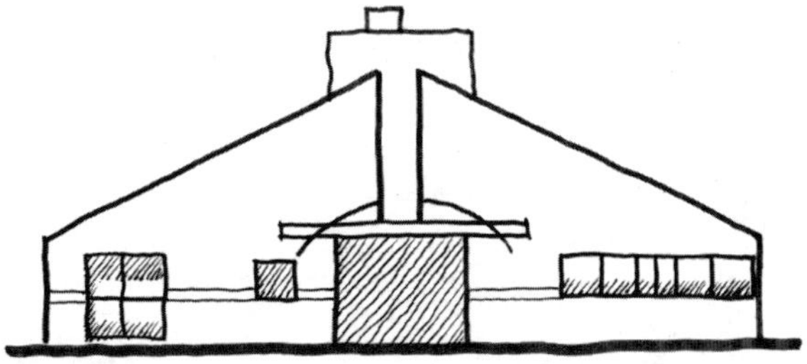

Figure 7.16: Ambiguity can be used playfully, such as in this house elevation by Robert Venturi that appears to be perfectly symmetrical although, upon closer inspection, the elements on one side don't match the other perfectly.

Examples of ambiguity include an almost perfectly symmetrical elevation—with enough inconsistencies to provoke the question: Is it symmetrical or not? (Figure 7.16)—and a corridor utilizing a forced perspective to make it seem longer than it actually is, provoking the question: Is it a short or long corridor? Which way is it directing me? (Figure 7.17).

These instances of ambiguity may or may not be justifiable. In general, they are more justifiable when they are a result of the inherent complexities and contradictions of a project. They can be questionable when they are arbitrary, although there are times when they may serve a worthwhile purpose. There may be some usefulness, for instance, in making a corridor seem longer than it actually is to exaggerate and enhance the sense of transition between two areas of a facility.

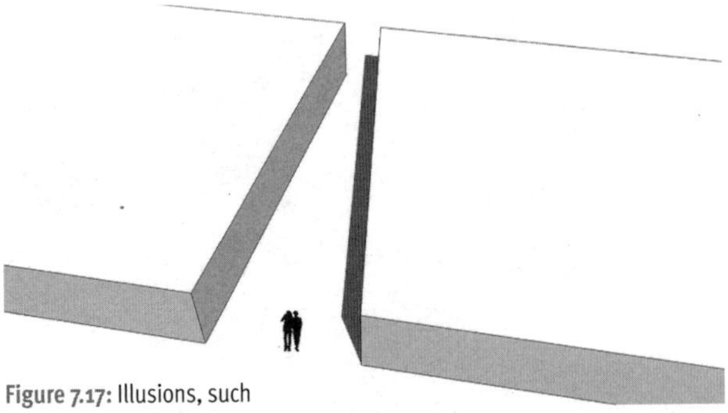

Figure 7.17: Illusions, such as the use of a forced (exaggerated) perspective here, are also ambiguous. The corridor will seem longer than it really is, and a user may wonder why it feels so deep when it really isn't.

Pictorialness

As modern design has evolved, we have grown accustomed to environments that are complex and more abstract than in the past. There is greater tolerance and demand for the less literal and the more cerebral. The pictorialness, symmetry, and straightforwardness of the past are no longer dominant. Nevertheless, well-composed pictorial project parts still continue to engage and delight many of us. Not everything has to be complex, novel, or ambiguous to be enriching. In fact, many people still prefer the straightforward to the overproduced or ambiguous and consider well-composed, pictorial elevations, often formal and symmetrical, a joy to look at. They engage our minds and make us appreciate them. The same is true for the well-composed and balanced detail, be it a column or a railing. Whether simple and serene or more active through articulation, it is still a source of delight (Figure 7.18).

Heightened Activity

One final general strategy for enrichment involves the strategic placement of certain functional areas so they attract people. Examples include spaces whose vitality results from a concentration of human activity and spaces that foster in us a sense of special meaning because some specific affordance has been thoughtfully provided.

A specific example of a vital space whose energy results from a concentration of human activity is a space, such as a node, located strategically in such a way that it is impossible to get around the building without going through it. Because of its centrality, it is likely to have constant traffic and activity. Furthermore, if some strategic function can be located within or adjacent to that area, acting as a magnet, then not only would people pass by, some would stay. This may elicit images of the urban plaza with cafes around it. It is not that different, although the scale and specific functions are likely to vary in interiors. In these cases, the vitality and energy of the people themselves enrich the space and attract others to join in. It has nothing to do with the composition of elements for effect and everything to do with the strategic placement of functions to maximize the impact of human presence.

These kinds of spaces can be most successful in public or semipublic areas not requiring high degrees of privacy or tasks requiring concentration. Applications are possible in restaurants, stores, hotels, some areas of office projects, and within the major circulation routes of most projects (Figure 7.19). In Figure 7.20 the heavy use of a student area endows it with much vitality.

An example of spaces that foster in us a sense of special meaning because of the kind of opportunity they present for a given use is a well-placed, small-scaled space off a main route or major space, where one or two persons can sit to talk, work, or just rest. We are talking, of course, about the small human niche. These spaces are seldom included in the program of requirements supplied to the

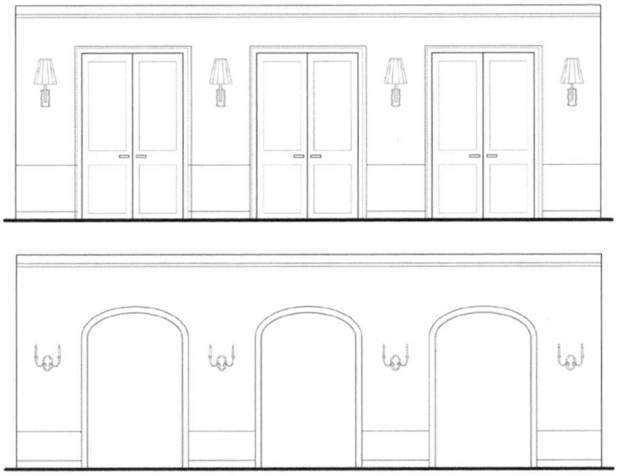

Figure 7.18: Well-composed pictorial spaces and elevations have delighted for centuries and are still appropriate today. Here are two straightforward, formal, symmetrical elevations. There are no fancy maneuvers on these, just good old fashioned elegant composition.

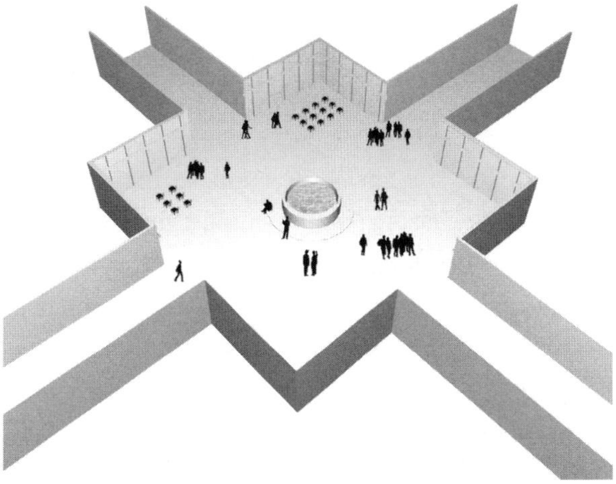

Figure 7.19: Intensifying use to create vital areas of high energy produces enrichment by use. Activity, sounds, and movement themselves become the agents of variety and complexity.

Figure 7.20: This student area in an academic building is usually filled with people. The increased level of activity makes the space one of the most energetic and vital in the entire building.

designer at the onset of a project. They are provided by thoughtful designers who understand the nature of people and their desire for small, intimate spaces in certain settings that provide a comfortable place to step into without losing connection to the greater totality beyond. Figures 7.21 and 7.22 show examples of these kinds of spaces.

Figure 7.21: Off-the-path spaces where users can go and work or socialize while feeling both grounded and connected provide enrichment.

ENRICHMENT WHEN IN TRANSIT

Enriching projects have engaging circulation routes. There are many opportunities to create enrichment along a project's circulation spaces. People are usually between tasks when in transit. During those times they are more receptive to environmental stimulus. It is while moving that we truly experience what has been called the fourth dimension of architecture, seeing the physical environment changing and emerging as we move through space.

In the following sections, we consider the path or corridor as a vehicle for enrichment. We'll look at the effect of sequences, the qualities of their components, and their capacity to engage users.

Sequence

Our perception of space while moving is important because the physicality of movement and the goal-oriented nature of most walking episodes produce

Figure 7.22: This pocket off to the side of a stairway is a perfect example of the thoughtful use of off-the-path yet connected spaces.

a state of alertness that helps us absorb more of the surroundings.

Moving through space offers the potential for exploration, providing variety and distraction. Whether through a trip to the coffee room at the office, a trip to the restroom in a restaurant, or a side trip while shopping, we welcome opportunities to take a break and look around. Sometimes these trips are meant as a break; other times they are necessary. In any case, they provide the benefit of providing an opportunity to explore the environment around us.

Regardless of the degree of urgency and our level of familiarity with the environment, just about every trip we take within a given environment offers an exploratory experience. We can discover the spaces of a new environment as we move through it, and we can also notice qualities and details we hadn't noticed before in familiar territories. Additionally, the unfolding human drama often seen from the path is like an ever-changing theater stage, full of interest and surprises.

Exploration can be actual exploration of unfamiliar territory, but it also refers to the kind of exploration we do when we visually scan, say, a wall with intricate pattern and detail. In the latter case, the brain is engaged in the exploration of a complex composition. Assuming there is some engaging complexity and a well-composed arrangement, we are likely to be not only momentarily entertained but also delighted.

Designing the circulation system of a project requires taking into account the kind of movement its different segments are required to facilitate. Movement in buildings is not always leisurely or recreational. In fact, it is rarely so. Most movement in buildings has a specific purpose and destination. We move with resolve to reach our destinations, often so preoccupied that we barely notice the environment around us. In cases of emergency or extreme rush, we actually run, and anything we encounter on our path is an obstacle. In those cases, the only image we welcome is that of the door or passage leading to our destination.

Environments require efficient movement. Most movement inside projects will have a fair amount of resoluteness. Therefore, while we want to still provide experiences along the way, these should not be so distracting or indirect as to be annoying. Attempts to enhance the experience of users while moving should not slow people down excessively. Emergency egress paths, especially, need to be clear and direct for obvious reasons. But even clear, efficient paths can provide opportunities to slow down and step aside.

A journey to a certain destination may include several sub-goals or intermediate arrival places. When visiting a clinic on an upper floor of a multistory building, for instance, we arrive first at the front door, then in the building lobby, the elevator lobby, the elevator, the elevator lobby of the target floor, the entrance outside the destination clinic, the reception area of the clinic, and, finally, the examination room.

If unfamiliar with the clinic environment, we may, at any given time, not be able to think beyond the next intermediate destination, moving in chunks from one to the next until we arrive at our real target destination. All the transition points become the salient locations that will be mentally recorded and remembered during subsequent visits. Those locations may very well have special design features that, when traveling more leisurely, users will notice and appreciate. After all, transitions force the user to slow down or stop, setting up, potentially, a moment of enough conscious awareness for an aesthetic experience.

Many routes will lack the natural transitions presented in our clinic example. In those cases, it is up to you as a designer to find ways to break up the route and provide meaningful events along the way, especially for long routes.

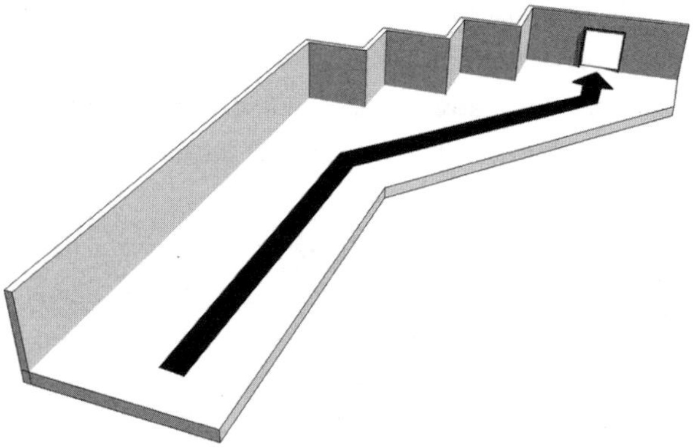

Figure 7.23: Altering the shape of the path can make it dynamic and exciting. The zigzagging effect combined with the diagonal line in this corridor makes the last leg quite stimulating.

Here is where you can put on your movie director hat and plan the route in ways that produce enriching experiences.

Events along the Route

Think of the route's sequence as a story line with plots, subplots, and one or more climaxes. To do this, keep in mind that we tend to move from goal to goal until we reach our destination. It is those goals that often stay in our minds. That's where your planning of the nodes, centers, and landmarks of your project can become a factor, and make a positive contribution, turning ordinary circulation systems into experiences full of events.

A sequence can be made engaging by transitions along the trajectory and by the presence of distinct events along the way. Transitions can be changes in direction or transitions in the physical character of the path. Figure 7.23 shows an example of a route featuring some changes in the path's direction and configuration. Figure 7.24 illustrates how changes in the physical spatial character of the path provide a story line in themselves.

Other potential distinct events include the centers, nodes, landmarks, and even small vestibules along the route. Figure 7.25 shows a fairly linear and potentially uneventful route sequence enhanced by the incorporation of strategically located small vestibules.

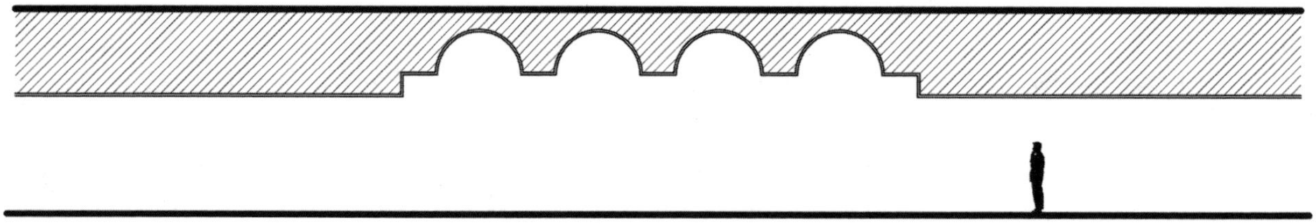

Figure 7.24: Segments of a sequence can be defined in section, as shown here. Different heights and the distinctiveness of the central section makes the experience of moving through this circulation sequence exciting and memorable.

Figure 7.25: The selective expansion of space at strategic intersections along circulation routes is an effective way to add vitality at certain locations. In this example three small vestibules establish distinct, recognizable points along the path that can be activated by humans.

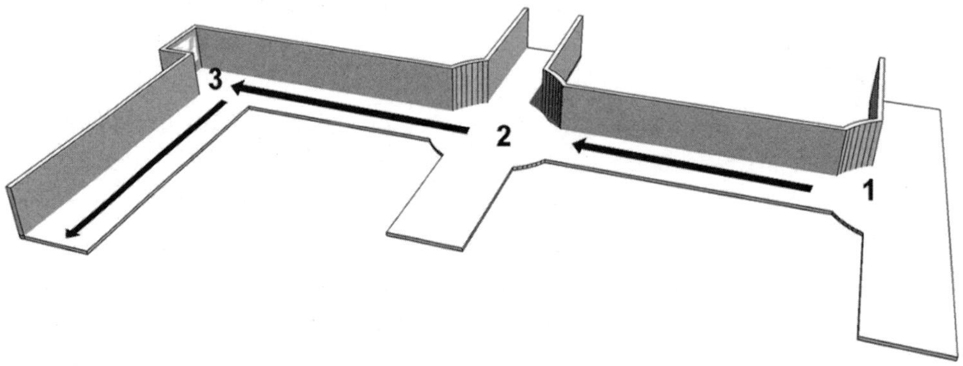

Other possible events along the route are surprises (or rewards). These are often in the form of enriching encounters with meaningful objects, details, and views. These may come as total surprises or be anticipated destinations hinted at prior to reaching them.

Qualities of the Path Itself

In addition to having an engaging sequence, the circulation route can be enriching by virtue of its inherent physical qualities. Despite their typological similarities, paths can have distinctive characters. Let's examine the components of a prototypical path. Most path segments are, basically, similar. They tend to be long, narrow spaces. We normally travel along them in linear fashion. As we move, we see the sides of the path obliquely, from the near parallel relation of our line of vision to them. There may be some view, planned or unplanned, at the end of the corridor that we see straight ahead and some distance away. As we move along we may, depending on the specific situation, see may adjoining spaces beyond the corridor (Figure 7.26).

Our job is to make the path special. After we have a basic path outlined on our preliminary floor plan, we may ask the questions: Are the visible components of the path engaging in and of themselves? Should they be? To what extent? Answers to these questions will inform the direction we take. Aspects that can be controlled and enhanced include the shape of the path and the qualities of its enclosing surfaces.

The Shape of the Path

There are a few variables that give paths different characters. These are length, degree of enclosure, height-to-width proportions, and configuration in both plan and section.

Paths come in different lengths. Many of these are perceptually comfortable, but others get to be too long. Acceptable lengths vary depending on the height-to-width proportion of the path, as well as the degree of lateral enclosure and the articulation of the side walls. In general, enclosed corridors with solid side walls on both sides will seem longer than those connected visually to adjacent spaces, especially if the side walls are flat and plain (Figure 7.27).

One way of keeping long paths within acceptable length limits is to break them up into smaller segments by the

Figure 7.26: A view from a typical corridor is long and narrow, featuring some defining side boundaries, a view straight ahead, and perhaps views of adjacent spaces.

(a)

(b)

Figure 7.27: The level of openness or enclosure of a corridor greatly affects its character and psychological length. Enclosed corridors that are self-contained can get uncomfortably long (a). Corridors with openings provide visual relief to adjacent features and activities and don't seem as long and tedious (b).

addition of intermittent spaces, such as cross-corridors (Figure 7.28), or by offsets in the path or enclosing walls (Figure 7.29).

At a more subtle level, articulations on the side walls and ceilings affect the perceived character of a path. Figure 7.30a and b shows the effect of side wall articulation on two corridors.

Figure 7.28: Intersections and intermittent spaces help relieve the perceived length of corridors by breaking up their linearity.

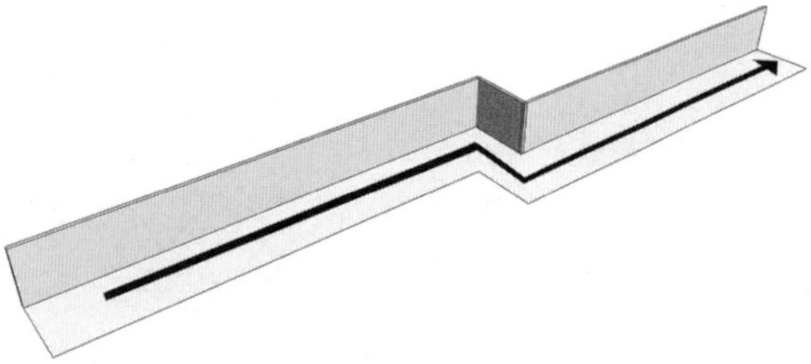

Figure 7.29: A strategy to alleviate long corridors is to offset the path at some point before it starts to seem too long. This breaks the path into sub-segments.

(a)

(b)

Figure 7.30: Modulation on the side walls enriches the formal visual qualities of a corridor by the addition of rhythm, pattern, and texture. Vertical planes or protrusions, whether straight (a) or angled (b), provide relief and add interest.

Although the level of enclosure around a corridor is somewhat dictated by the privacy and enclosure needs of the spaces adjacent to the path, there is some room for manipulation. Thus, paths range from fully enclosed to fully open. They can also be a combination of these pure conditions. To the extent that the program will allow flexibility, it is a good idea for you to design paths that offer variety through contrast. This can be achieved by contrast between the two sides of the path or by contrast between successive segments of the path (Figure 7.31).

Another important contribution of the enclosing planes is their role in determining the relative autonomy of the path. A path with no barrier on one side has the potential of blending with it. It can read as an extension of the adjacent space, or it can read as a distinct path if some differentiation is provided by the ceiling and floor planes. Whether through height changes or through a change of finish, the treatment of the two important horizontal planes can change the feeling the path has in relation to the adjacent spaces. This is one case where the design can result in autonomy, affiliation, or an ambiguous condition where one may question whether it is a corridor or a continuation of the adjacent space. Figure 7.32 shows examples of both a path with little architectural differentiation (Figure 7.32a) and one where the ceiling helps to accentuate the distinction between the path and its adjoining space (Figure 7.32b). The heights of corridors (paths) can also have a significant perceptual effect on our experience going through them as seen in the two similar corridors shown in Figure 7.33.

Despite the predominance of the path with parallel sides, due in part to its inherent economy, there are

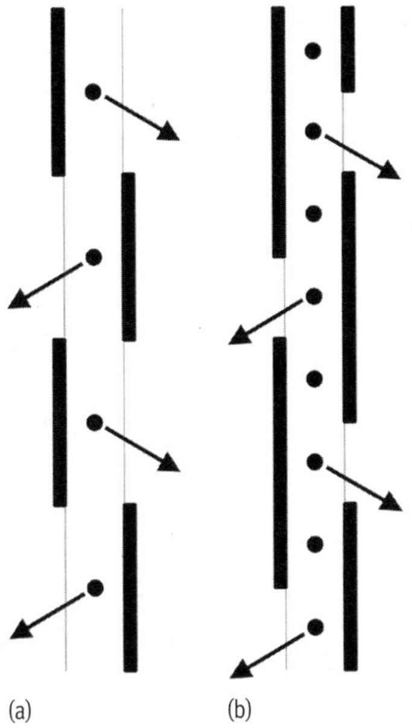

(a) (b)

Figure 7.31: The experience of moving through corridors can be enhanced by the use of variety and contrast. These conceptual examples show a corridor with alternating open and closed sides (a) and a similar corridor with overlapping walls resulting in smaller openings (b).

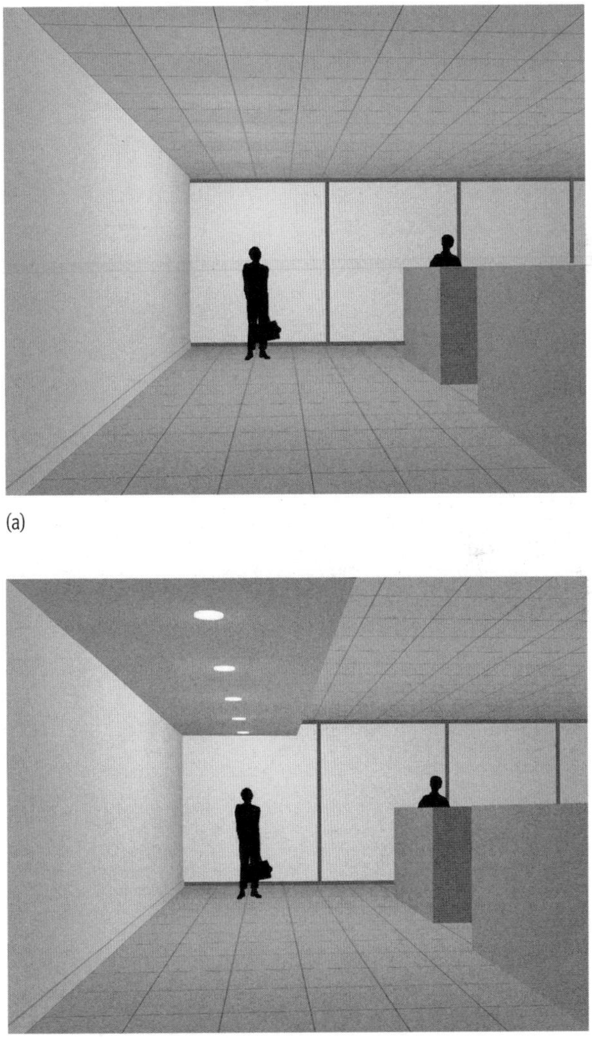

(a)

(b)

Figure 7.32: The ceiling and floor planes are important elements in the determination of perceived autonomy of a path. Example (a) reads as one space where the edge defined by the furniture establishes an aisle. In example (b) the path reads as a distinct, well-defined corridor due to the ceiling treatments.

(a)

(b)

Figure 7.33: Corridors come in different heights. Some are short (a) and some tall (b). Even relatively minor height differences, as shown here, can make significant perceptual differences.

other possible plan configurations. While these normally require more space, they add dynamic qualities and produce path segments of great interest. Figure 7.34 provides one of many possible examples. You may experiment with other similar ones and try to use them where sensual or dynamic qualities are needed.

Similar manipulations are possible in section. Most corridors consist of parallel, plumb side walls and a flat ceiling plane above, but this is by no means the only configuration possible. While some of the possibilities can violate the sense of what is considered normal, some of them will be appropriate at times. Your repertoire of corridor sectional configurations should include a wide range of possibilities, from the articulated to the unconventional. Figure 7.35 shows some examples.

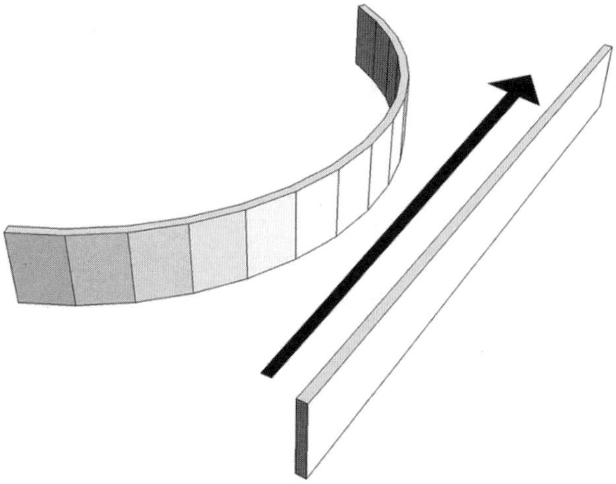

Figure 7.34: Corridors do not have to always consist of parallel walls. There are times when it is possible, and desirable, to make corridors dynamic by the modification of one or both sides. This example curves one side of the corridor to achieve dynamic results.

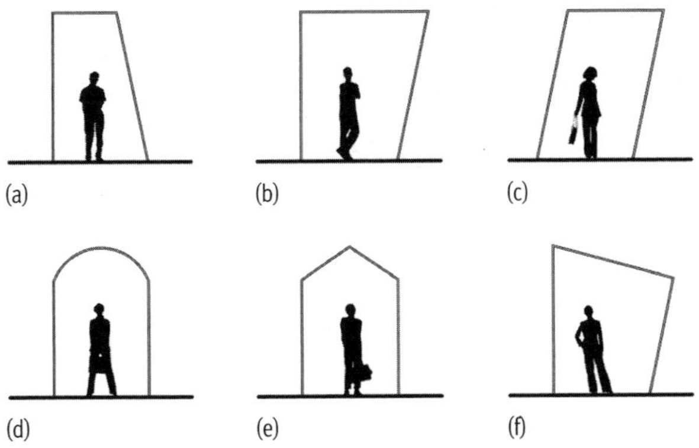

Figure 7.35: Most corridors tend to be boxy in section. There are times when the geometry can be changed for effect by changing one side wall (a and b), changing both side walls (c), changing the shape of the ceiling (d and e), or a combination (f).

Qualities of Enclosing Surfaces

The treatment of enclosing surfaces affects the level of interest of a path and should be carefully considered. Included are the sidewalls or screens, the floor plane, and the ceiling plane. Design variables to consider include modulation, spatial texture, rhythmic sequences, and pattern. Modulation can be used on any of the enclosing planes alone or in combination. A rhythm of vertical elements on one or both of the side walls, a subdivision of the ceiling plane into units through articulation, and the use of pattern via modular flooring materials can all be used to modulate surfaces (Figure 7.36). The subdivision of paths through modulation endows them with a sense of strong rhythm that can be rather attractive if well executed.

The articulation of paths does not need to always result in distinct modules. In some cases a reduced approach will provide a pleasant rhythm without a feeling of strong subdivision. Rhythm along one of the dominant surfaces can be quite engaging and afford the path a nice sense of spatial texture (Figure 7.37).

In addition to the kind of articulation shown in the previous examples, simple elements such as openings on the side walls and cross-corridors form part of the overall path composition and contribute to its sense of variety, rhythm, and texture.

Manipulation of Disclosure

So far, we have talked about the role of events along the path sequence and the inherent qualities of the path in providing experiential richness. A third way paths engage us is by manipulating the kind, degree, and rate of disclosure of spaces and features within and beyond them. Equally important is how the path is perceived when looking into the path while being outside of it.

The View at the End

One of the most noticeable aspects of any path is the view straight ahead. Depending on the arrangement, it may or may not be possible to see the final view at the end of the path from a given point in it. In paths that zigzag or meander, the end is often blocked from view until one arrives at the last leg of the path. In straight paths we see the view at the end. Except for the portion of a side wall

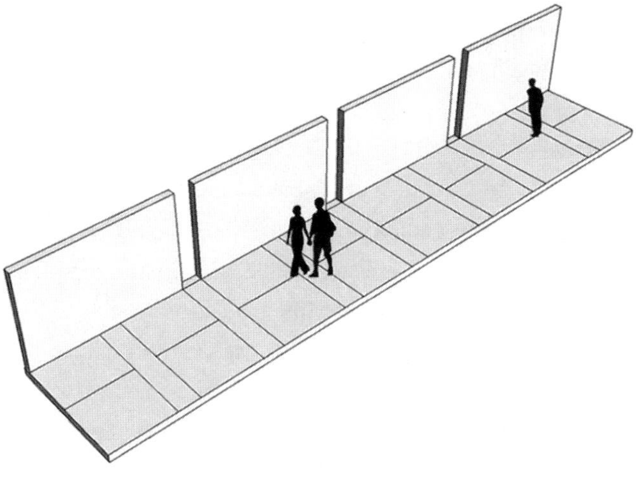

Figure 7.36: Modularity on the side walls and floor can give corridors a nice sense of richness through articulation.

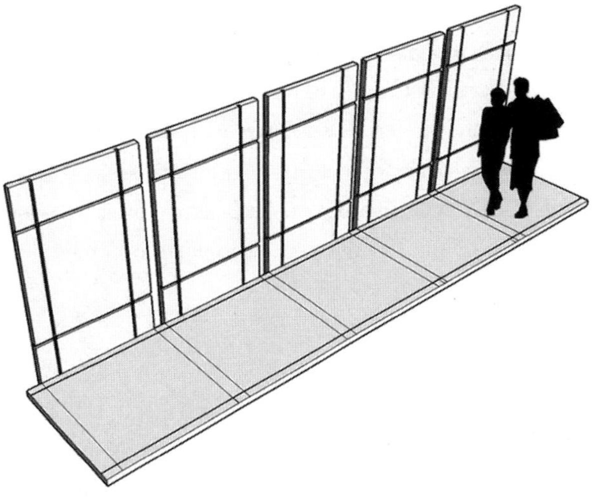

Figure 7.37: When the modules used are smaller and feature additional line work or pattern, the result is a greater sense of spatial texture.

(a) (b) (c)

Figure 7.38: The framed view at the end is an important strategy used in many corridors. Variations include the framed exterior view (a), the framed piece of artwork on the wall (b), and the important room at the end (c).

immediately next to us at any given time in our trajectory along the path, nothing is likely to be as strong as the view at the end, whether we are conscious of it or not. Even if we are still at a distance, we are looking at it head-on. Figure 7.38 shows examples of various end views.

Possible strategies to consider for views at the end include the strategic use of focal points, prospect, and enticement.

Focal Points

The use of focal points can be an effective strategy to enrich users' experience in circulation areas. Focal points usually occur at the end of the view ahead. These views are carefully framed. Possibilities include a view to the exterior or space beyond, a piece of artwork, or some well-placed evocative object, such as a flower vase on a shelf, perhaps set into a well-proportioned niche on the wall.

Prospect

Prospect is the framed view we see at the end or beyond the turn. It serves as somewhat of a focal point, except its composition is not necessarily a framed termination. In the case of prospect, we see what lies beyond, say, a wall of an adjacent mass in the distance. You could think of prospect as a carefully composed partial view of something beyond. Because what is seen beyond has a degree of visual prominence, it requires careful attention to make the resulting view adequate. Unfortunately, the view at the end of many interior corridors is the default result of whatever happens to be beyond, with no effort to control it. Although not every view at the end of a path needs to be treated with special accent pieces, every ending view should be designed to produce agreeable, if not engaging, results. Figure 7.39 shows an example of a prospect view that is not quite a focal point but has been carefully arranged to be pleasing and intriguing.

Enticement

In addition to careful, focal compositions of the views at the end of the path, and sensitively composed views of what lies beyond, it is also possible to design arrangements that lead the moving person in a desired direction. This is usually achieved through the use of arrangements with directional properties, the use of arrangements that disclose what lies ahead only partially, and the use of powerful elements that attract at the ends. Diagonal arrangements and circular configurations favoring one direction

Figure 7.39: Prospect is the view seen beyond the corridor. Consideration needs to be given to the placement of elements seen in order to produce an enticing view.

Figure 7.40: Compositions can be arranged to entice and attract. Curved walls allow partial views beyond that arouse our curiosity and make us want to move forward.

are effective in this regard (Figure 7.40). It is possible to increase the level of attraction of the view at the end by arousing people's sense of curiosity. Circular shapes and compelling distant views (because of their composition, boldness, brightness, and so on) arouse our curiosity and draw us toward them. See the Capsule titled "Complexity, Order, and Other Environmental Attributes" for a discussion of the concept of mystery in environments.

The View Beyond the Path

Lateral views to adjacent spaces also form an important part of the circulation experience. How much is revealed depends on the functional level of connection or separation needed and the intentions of the route designer. The variables of disclosure and access discussed in Chapter 4 come into play here.

The process of placing corridor walls and their points of access into the spaces is somewhat automatic and driven by functional needs. However, there are sometimes opportunities to perform manipulations for effect. Two useful design strategies to create engaging routes are the manipulation of points of visual connection to adjacent areas and the manipulation of the correspondence between visual and physical access.

Points of Visual Connection

Most circulation spaces afford some degree of visual connection to adjacent spaces. Total and continuous visual connection can sometimes be as monotonous as total separation. The optimal level often lies somewhere in the middle. Partial visual connection is gratifying, because it provides relief from the enclosure of the corridor. It is possible to create a playful pattern of "now you see it, now you don't" between the corridor and adjoining spaces to stimulate users' minds and enrich their experience.

Although a balanced mix of visual separation and visual disclosure generally works, it is possible to locate the points of visual connection strategically for effect. If a certain opening between a corridor and an adjacent space coincides with a point along the route where visual relief would be desirable, the overall impact is likely to be greater. If openings between the corridor and adjacent spaces are rhythmic or gradated, the result will have an increased level of playfulness and engagement (Figure 7.41). If the visual connection is framed strategically to reveal a particularly special view of the adjacent space, then the impact is going to be stronger.

In addition to their placement, the degree of physical connection afforded is also an important consideration. Connections range from a narrow glimpse through a small opening to a full view of the adjacent space. It is possible to use uneven rhythms such as the glimpse, glimpse, wide-view sequence shown in Figure 7.42a. You can also do the opposite and have column, column, wall (Figure 7.42b).

The view from the adjacent space back to the path is as important as the view from the path to the adjacent space. The composition of the framed view back toward the path should be given proper consideration and not left up to chance. Figure 7.43 shows three of many possible arrangements. Figure 7.43a and 7.43b create focal points, one terminating the view in a piece of artwork on the wall and the other extending it into the gateway to a corridor centered on the framed view. Figure 7.43c shows a view without a dominant focal point, but one that has been thoughtfully composed to make the framed view rewarding.

Finally, in addition to internal views, views from the corridor to the exterior are enriching when they occur. These can be lateral views at a distance, immediate lateral

Figure 7.41: Openings along side walls of corridors connect us visually to adjacent spaces. Their arrangement can be straightforward and rhythmical (a) or rhythmical in pairs (b), among others.

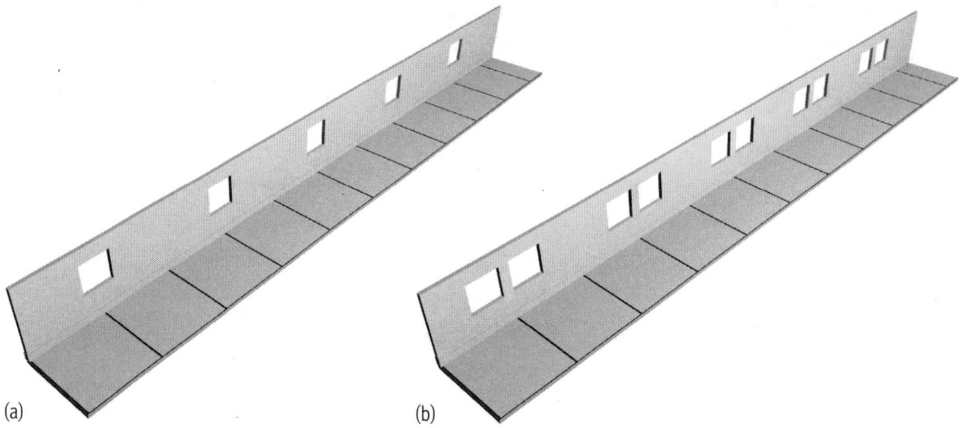

Figure 7.42: It is possible to perform playful orchestrations between open and solid portions of side walls. The play of openings in a mostly solid wall (a) and the play of solids in a mostly open boundary (b) are two examples.

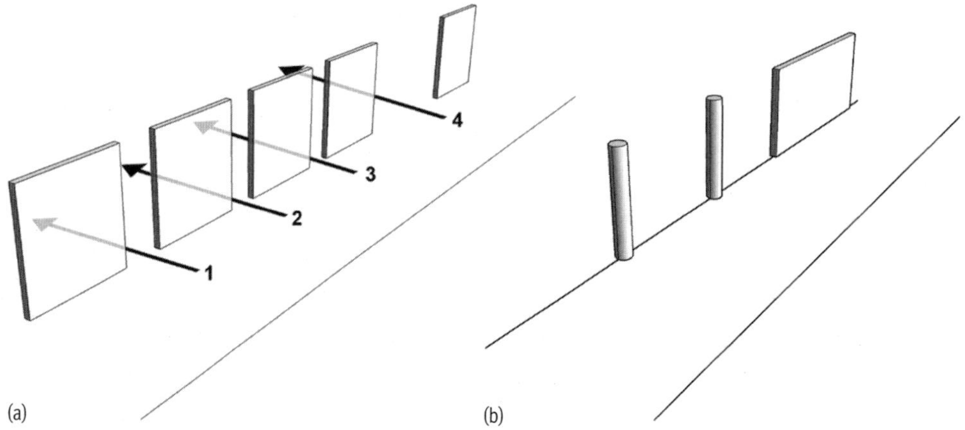

(a)

(b)

(c)

Figure 7.43: The view from adjacent spaces back to the corridor should be planned carefully. Possibilities include the framed view toward a focal piece (a), the aligned view with an intersection (b), and the prospect view of a corridor segment without any focalization (c).

views, or views at the end of the corridor. These views can be panoramic or carefully framed views that look in a particular direction with something beyond as a focal point. Exterior views have the effect of extending the perceived space horizontally. They can provide a great amount of relief, not to mention a sense of connection to the external context. In some cases, circulation routes may even be located along the perimeter of a building to provide external views all along the way.

Correspondence of Visual and Physical Access

The design of visual access in relation to the actual point of entry to an area presents some interesting opportunities to provide enriching experiences. In projects where a clear and efficient path is necessary, either because of a project's particular use or the population for whom it is being designed, correspondence between visual access and physical access will be important and, generally, will be the norm. In those cases it is useful to see a view of the destination before arriving at the entrance.

In cases where more playfulness can be tolerated, it is possible to manipulate the relationship between visual disclosure and physical access to an area in order to create either a sense of anticipation or intentional tension. Figure 7.44 shows an arrangement featuring a view on axis with the circulation of an area, yet requiring the person to go around the corner to enter the space. Figure 7.45

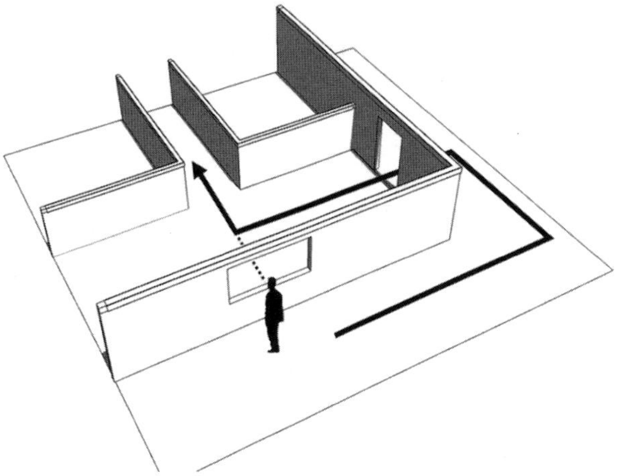

Figure 7.44: Interaction between visual and physical access to a space can be manipulated to increase anticipation. Here, the user sees the internal corridor leading to his destination but has to walk around a corner to enter the space leading to the corridor.

CAPSULE | Safety Versus Opportunity

One of the main themes of human behavior and, consequently, of the design of places for people, is the duality of exposure and withdrawal. British geographer Jay Appleton devised a theory that provides much insight into these fundamental human necessities. Called prospect-refuge theory, it was conceived to help understand human appreciation of the exterior landscape. The theory is a specific application of habitat theory, which Appleton explains as follows:

> All this leads to the proposition that aesthetic satisfaction, experienced in the contemplation of the landscape, stems from the spontaneous perception of landscape features, which in their shapes, colours, spatial arrangements and other visible attributes, act as sign stimuli indicative of environmental conditions favourable to survival . . . "Habitat theory" thus asserts that the relationship between the human observer and the perceived environment is basically the same as the relationship of a creature and its habitat. It asserts further that the satisfaction which we derive from the contemplation of this environment, and which we call "aesthetic," arises from a spontaneous reaction to that environment as a habitat, that is to say as a place which affords the opportunity for achieving our simple biological needs.[1]

Prospect-refuge theory can be generally exemplified by Konrad Lorenz's account of the advantage afforded by the point between enclosure and openness found while taking a walk in the forest. He states:

> Before we break through the last bushes and out of cover on to the free expanse of the meadow . . . we reconnoitre, seeking, before we leave our cover, to gain from it the advantage which it can offer alike to hunter and hunted—namely to see without being seen.[2]

Both the hunter and the hunted need strategies to fulfill their goals and protect their best interests. The hunter's strategy involves putting himself in a position to maximize opportunity. He must approach his prey as close as possible without getting noticed.

The strategy of the hunted involves assuring safety. It requires having a place inaccessible to the pursuer and putting himself in a position to, if needed, reach that place before being prevented by the hunter. To accomplish this, the hunted will have to be in a position where the hunter will not see him or, if visible to the hunter, one that will give him enough time to react and reach safety. In both cases, as Appleton points out, "it is in the creature's interest to ensure that he can see his quarry or predator, as the case may be, without being seen, and the achievement of these conditions becomes a first objective which renders more likely the achievement of the second, to catch or to escape."[3] Obviously, familiarity with the environment would give either hunter or hunted an advantage, as it would potentially increase the number of routes for attack or escape.

According to the theory, environments whose characteristics are perceived to offer the ability to see without being seen tend to be aesthetically more satisfying. During primitive times, more than now, the ability to see and the ability to hide were both necessary for survival. Appleton suggests that humans carry those evolutionary tendencies within them even though they have long evolved from a primitive existence when hunting and protection against hostile tribes were prevalent. He calls the unimpeded opportunity to see *prospect* and the opportunity to hide *refuge*.

One may question the magnitude with which these programmed tendencies really influence our aesthetic judgments and preferences for places. After all, life in most of the civilized world is relatively safe from antagonistic hunters. We also have to acknowledge that in certain types of situations people want to see and to be seen, such as at the type of bar or cafe where people go to socialize. Nevertheless, and excluding the obvious application to settings high in crime or terrorism, prospect-refuge theory still offers wonderful insights into some fundamental traits of human behavior. People's tendencies to approach or avoid a place, after all, depend as much, if not more, on who is present rather than on the issue of environmental load discussed in a previous chapter.

At an even more fundamental level, the issue of prospect and refuge brings us back to the topic of existential space, discussed previously in Capsule 3.2, "A Phenomenological View of Space and Dwelling." There, we described the notion of center at the heart of human dwelling in contrast to the beyond, conceptualized as paths and domains away from the center. Just these three existential space-elements serve to articulate the basic and most fundamental duality of existential space, between the "here" (what is familiar and safe) and the "there" (what lies outside and involves exposure and risk). These correspond to all kinds of dualities frequently found in design, such as open-closed, sheltered-exposed, and private-public.

With prospect-refuge theory we start addressing the important role of the environment in influencing interactions between people by the positioning of places and the visibility between those places. It is important for a person to be not only at his or her safe and familiar center but also in a strategic position to see who is coming and have a chance to react by welcoming or hiding, as well as to know who is outside and have a chance to decide whether to use the front or back door. Likewise, someone on a path approaching a place can strategically scope a scene and make decisions about whether or not to enter and which way to go depending on the potential opportunities or threats presented by it.

Potential application of prospect-refuge thinking is found in many types of settings, some more than others. Public settings where people spend time, such as restaurants, cafes, and clubs, present some of the best opportunities to use prospect-refuge thinking. At a cafe, a preference for prospect is likely to dominate. People will want exposure to see and be seen, although it would be wise to have a few tables in the back for those seeking less exposure. At a restaurant, people may prefer a table that affords some anchoring—in other words, a refuge. Depending on circumstances, they may opt for one visually accessible from the rest of the space (reducing the sense of refuge but increasing prospect) or one tucked away, allowing them to see without being seen, thus providing both prospect and refuge. A good practice is to provide a variety of tables with different degrees of privacy and exposure, so people can choose one that fits their particular needs at the moment.

For a quiet, intimate dining experience, the emphasis is definitely on refuge. In fact, the desire for prospect may be limited. Through careful zoning of areas, positioning of tables, and use of local lighting (e.g., individual candles at tables), it may be possible to create an atmosphere in which each table feels like an oasis, even though it may be just a couple of feet from an adjacent table.

Prospects and refuges occur at different scales. A town on a hill may be a refuge (familiar and secure) from which you may enjoy views of the prospects beyond. Within the town, the house represents another level of refuge, having views from the windows that connect with prospects beyond. Within the house, the personal bedroom represents yet another scale of refuge and the chair tucked away in the corner still another. We can see how the concept of refuge has many similarities to that of center in existential space.

Frank Lloyd Wright was a master of the art of providing a good balance between prospect and refuge. In *The Wright Space*, Grant Hildebrandt applies prospect-refuge theory to analyze Wright's residential designs. In relation to the preferred landscape dispositions of prospect and refuge advocated by Appleton, Hildebrandt writes, "The houses Wright designed after 1902 almost all held an extraordinarily rich array of these analogies, at several hierarchical levels—and did so through a complex and repetitive composition of elements unique to him in his time."[4] The overall structure of Wright's houses was based on a principle involving a strong and protective center from which the house grew outward toward infinity. Many of his houses emanated from a central hearth space that anchored them in space and symbolized the center of centers. While the houses obviously had bounding walls, they provided open

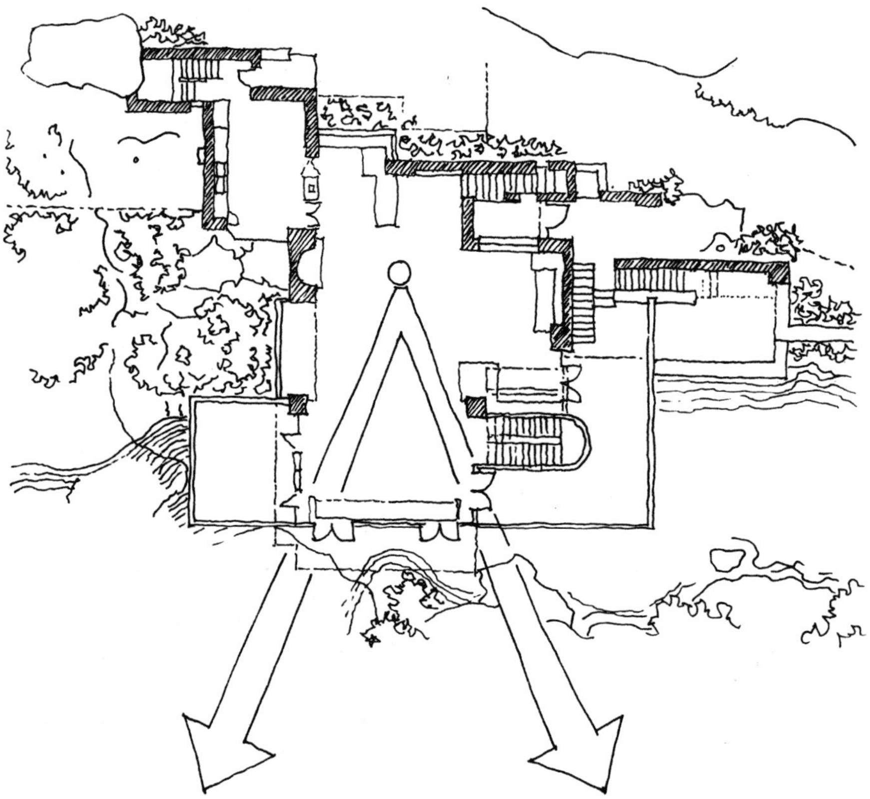

Figure C7.1: Wright's Fallingwater is one of many houses designed by him that exemplify the concepts of prospect (openness, view, opportunity) and refuge (enclosure, protection, safety) in built environments.

vistas that extended the actual perceived space infinitely (Figure C7.1).

The organizational structure was just the beginning. As Hildebrandt pointed out, the occurrences happened at several hierarchical levels, providing opportunity and choice. He explained: "The degree of refuge or of prospect is subject to infinite variety and can be manipulated by the occupant at will simply by moving to the condition he wishes to enjoy at any moment. We move around, we take our pick, we suit our mood. And when our mood changes we know there are other spaces in the house that can suit the new mood too. That Wright was able to provide not only a rich array of these conditions, but also a range of choice with regard to them, is an extraordinarily important legacy of his work."[5]

Suggested Exercise

List a few places you have been that afforded both good prospect and refuge. Discuss them in one or several groups. What were the circumstances? What design features contributed to the perceptions of refuge? To what extent was one able to see without being seen?

1. Appleton, J. (1996). *The experience of landscape.* New York: Wiley.
2. Ibid, p. 52.
3. Ibid, p. 64.
4. Ibid., quoting Grant Hildebrandt, *The Wright Space* (Seattle: University of Washington Press, 1991), 250.
5. Ibid, p. 253.

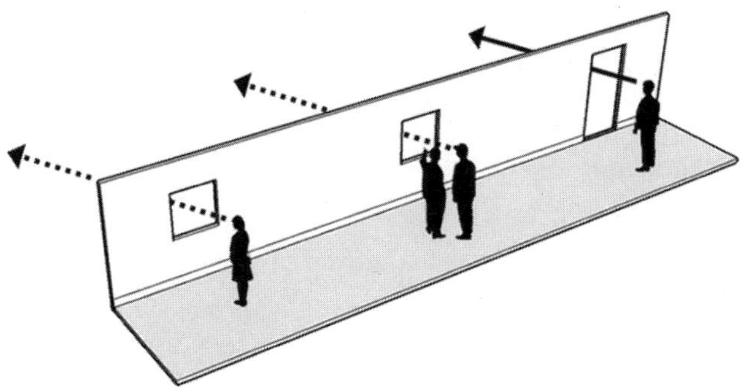

Figure 7.45: A simple way to produce anticipation is to provide visual access a few times before the entry point can be reached.

shows an example where several views of the area are presented to build anticipation before arriving at the eventual entry point.

ENRICHMENT WHILE STATIONARY

Building users spend most of their time stationed in the destination spaces of a facility. The tasks performed in these spaces are dominant and the environment assumes the secondary role of quiet facilitator. Given an adequate amount of space and acceptable ambient conditions, people manage to do what they need to do. Conditions, however, can be taken to higher levels of function and perceptual enrichment.

In general, we would like to suggest that a complete task experience consists of the task at hand in a grounded setting that provides opportunities to connect with nearby surroundings and allows episodes of relief on demand. A way of illustrating this with an everyday example is the experience of food preparation in a residential kitchen. An enriching experience would include a spatially well-defined kitchen with a layout that facilitates the various tasks of food preparation while providing visual access to other parts of the house (to connect with adjacent activities and the comings and goings of family members) and to the outside through a well-placed window (to enjoy the view but also to monitor a young child playing outside). If, in addition to all this, it also had a couple of focal points on which to anchor the view occasionally (one internal and the other external), the kitchen would offer quite a range of enriching features beyond mere functionality.

Facilitating the Task

Facilitating a task requires providing appropriate conditions. Spatially, these include appropriate levels of space, privacy, and connection to related functions. When these basic needs are met, the next level of facilitation occurs at the proxemic scale of the furnishings and objects in the space (the table in the restaurant or conference room, the individual desk at the office, and so on). When it gets to the task itself, the selection, composition, and arrangement of these objects in space becomes dominant. Other relevant factors, such as complementary lighting and pleasant materials and finishes, are also important.

The location, size, and arrangement of the spaces housing these functions will have an impact on the overall experience. An intimate scale may enhance the experience at the restaurant table, a well-proportioned room of comfortable volume will enhance the experience at the conference room table, and a quiet space of adequate size may facilitate the work done at the desk in the office. Additionally, users are more likely to be satisfied if they have a physical connection to the greater whole of which their space is a part, and if opportunities are offered to take occasional brief breaks by focusing momentarily on well-planned views and focal points. We discuss these various types of contributions next.

Grounding

The tasks people perform in buildings involve interactions with things and other people at the material level and data and ideas at the nonmaterial level. In our restaurant example the main focus is on the table, with the plates, glasses, silverware, and, of course, the meal itself taking center stage. If we have company, they are also likely to be a primary focus of the experience. Behind all this is a certain mood that will vary from restaurant to restaurant. The decor and lighting will provide much of that mood. How each table is grounded will affect the individual experience from each table.

Grounding refers to the manner in which a space, or part of a space, is defined in the total environment in ways that make one feel anchored in space, as opposed to drifting in space. People like to feel grounded. An example of this in a restaurant environment is the reassuring experience of being next to a wall rather than feeling like you are floating in the middle of a large room. Our spatial location in relation to vertical elements, corners, and edges of the space come into play. Sitting along a defined edge, next to a column, or in a corner generally offers good grounding experiences (Figure 7.46).

In large rooms, even though the external envelope may provide only four corners and four edges, it is possible to subdivide space internally to create more corners and edges. Compare the two plans shown for a restaurant in Figure 7.47. The one in Figure 7.47a has a large internal zone with floating tables that don't feel grounded. The one in Figure 7.47b shows the same space subdivided to create more edges and corners inside, thus adding opportunities for feeling grounded. Figure 7.48a–c shows views of well-grounded tables in restaurant settings.

Connection

Even if we sometimes appreciate isolation when we need privacy to concentrate and perform certain tasks, we also value the ability to stay connected with our surroundings, not only because of our inherent interest in human activity but to know what's happening around us, who is coming and going, and when we need to be on alert. For that reason, it is desirable to have some degree of connection between areas. That way, people in a restaurant can see other tables and areas beyond, people in an office can see adjacent workers, and people in a hotel lounge can see people in the adjacent lobby. The optimal degree of connection to adjacent areas will vary from project to

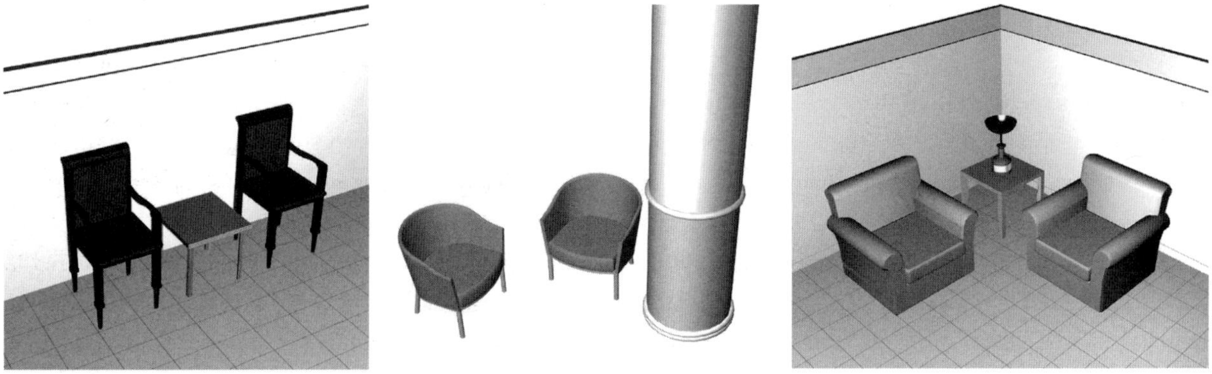

(a) (b) (c)

Figure 7.46: Good grounding can be achieved by proximity against an edge (a), a column (b), or a corner (c).

Figure 7.47: Designers often craft internal edges and corners to create grounded, well-defined spaces. In this example, the floating tables (a) find better grounded locations where edges and corners have been added (b).

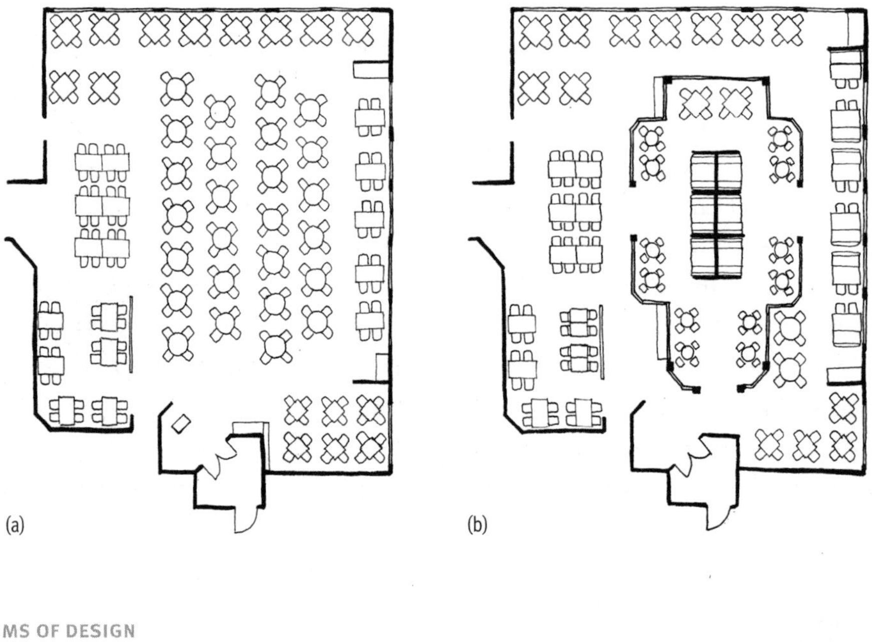

(a) (b)

(a) (b) (c)

Figure 7.48: Accommodations that help us feel grounded in a restaurant include the table against the window wall (a), the booth (b), and the table along a low wall or railing (c).

project, from department to department, and from individual to individual. Even though having some connection is desirable, having too much connection can be a real annoyance to anyone not desiring it.

People love to watch other people. In settings such as cafes, teahouses, and even the theater, the social aspect of seeing and being seen is an integral component of the overall experience. Exchanges of stares can be open and candid or they can be discreet. Sometimes we feel especially at ease when located in strategic spots that allow us to look at people around us without being noticed, such as when we look down from a strategic location higher up (Figure 7.49).

Another type of desirable connection is to the outdoors. In addition to providing relief, visual connections to the outside give people valuable information about the approximate time of day, weather conditions, and other external contextual conditions. Figure 7.50 shows a good example from a cafe setting.

Relief

In addition to providing valuable stimuli and information, the kinds of connections described above also provide relief. The visual openness to the adjacent areas allows for expansion of vision and mind, providing beneficial mental breaks.

Figure 7.49: Visual connection to adjacent spaces provides stimulation and useful information. It is especially satisfying to find protected spaces from which to look out or down into space, like the space from which this photo was taken in a restaurant.

Figure 7.50: Visual connection to the exterior provides interest, information, and relief. This cafe features built-in tables along the front window.

Views to adjacent areas and the exterior allow the eyes and the mind to expand outward and experience relief. Also useful are focal points where views to framed features are provided. With external foci, the strategy consists of framing specific views whether ordinary or ones having special meaning due to their significance, beauty, or other associational qualities. Examples of the latter include framed vistas of important monuments, natural or landscaped features, or areas of special vitality based on their use.

Thoughtful designers provide internal features for people to focus on from their stationary locations. People in places such as waiting areas, office cubicles, and lobbies need spots they can focus their attention on from time to time to give their eyes and minds a rest. Examples include artwork (both flat and sculptural), intricate detailing of architectural and decorative elements, and all types of accessories. Figure 7.51 shows an example of a digital display in an academic building providing an internal focal point.

Figure 7.51: Providing internal relief is a neglected art. This digital display in an academic building provides a pleasant and informative internal focal point, providing relief when one looks in that direction.

CASE STUDY

Creating a State-of-the-Art Learning Facility on the Site of an Old Library (89,000 sf)
Project: iLoft
Location: Elyria, Ohio
Design Firm: Sasaki Associates. Photo credits: Pease Photography

Challenge: How do you transform an old library building into a state-of-the-art learning facility that promotes interaction and improves retention rates?

In 2009, Lorain County Community College in Elyria, Ohio engaged Sasaki Associates to develop prototypical designs for teaching and learning spaces to support a campus-wide effort to examine more efficient and effective ways for students and faculty to interact. The design team was asked to address the way today's students learn through group work, unplanned interactions, and relying on the instructor as a mentor who guides them through the learning process.

The initial thought was to house the new Learning Center in a new building. Sasaki's study revealed how through a sequence of renovations to existing buildings coupled with better classroom scheduling it was not necessary to construct a new building, but in fact a much more dynamic campus plan would be created by renovating existing buildings.

As a result, a 50-year-old, 89,000-square-foot library was transformed into iLoft, a cheerful and dynamic learning center that produced a highly energized learning environment that extends learning beyond the classroom, and fosters collaboration between faculty and students. The design included complete demolition of the existing interior and systems, and the insertion of a second floor into the space. Light and acoustics were carefully considered in material selection to create a bright and serene atmosphere. Figure CS7.1 shows the former library space.

The design concept zones classrooms on the long sides of the building, student and faculty areas at the ends, and a central and focal learning oasis at the center. See the design concept diagram (Figure CS7.2). Classrooms are arranged along flexible bars along the east and west sides of the building. These feature a flexible system of dividing walls that allow for multiple configurations (Figure CS7.3). All chairs

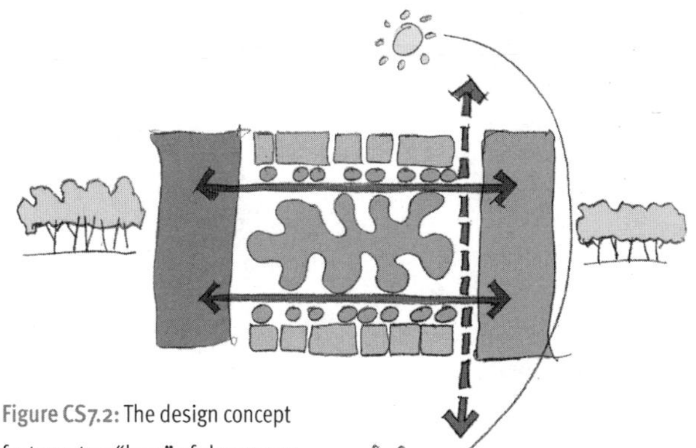

Figure CS7.2: The design concept features two "bars" of classrooms along the long sides of the building, with a faculty center on one end, and a student commons area at the other. At the center sits the heart of the space, an organic, curvilinear, technology rich learning center.

Figure CS7.1–12: The 50 year old library was packed with book stacks and surrounding dark offices but featured nice volumes of space that Sasaki capitalized on.

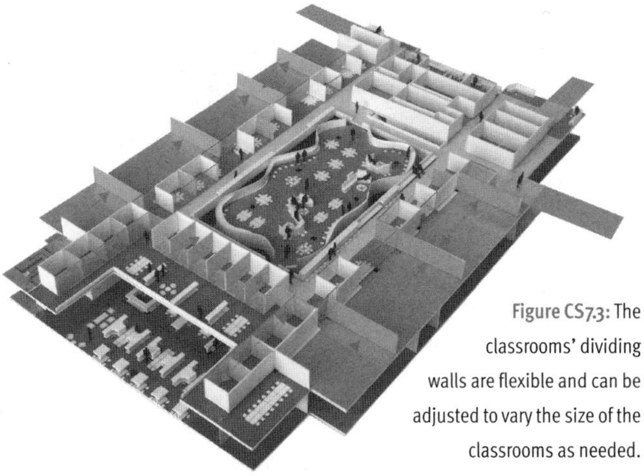

Figure CS7.3: The classrooms' dividing walls are flexible and can be adjusted to vary the size of the classrooms as needed.

continued

and tables are on casters for mobility and the instructor station can be docked in multiple locations allowing for total flexibility. Outside these classrooms are a variety of open and enclosed group study rooms that can be used by either students for informal study or by instructors for breakout discussion groups during class (Figure CS7.4).

At the center of the building is the Learning Oasis—a technology-rich study space that allows students and faculty to collaborate in soft seating areas where they can work on a shared computer monitor while accessing the same software simultaneously (Figure CS7.5).

The centrally located, amoeba-shaped, learning oasis is clad in light beech veneer. The rest of the surfaces are white with accents of cheerful colors. Together, the curves and the coloration result in an uplifting environment that is also serene (Figure CS7.6). Sasaki also paid much attention to acoustics to produce a nice buzz while avoiding an annoying cacophony.

Along the corridors students can work in study counters, linear horizontal planes that occasionally drop down and become benches (Figures CS7.7 and CS7.8). Additionally, organically shaped niches are carved into walls are available for study and conversation (Figure CS7.9). Beneath the Oasis sits the Teacher Education Resource Center. A double-height space on the south end of the building includes the student commons. The faculty is located in a double-height suite at the north side of the building (Figure CS7.10). Other features include the provision of ample writing surfaces along

Figure CS7.4: The many group study rooms are used by students for informal study and breakout discussion groups during class.

Figure CS7.6: The learning oasis floats next to, but independent from the adjacent corridors. The undulating curves contribute to the dynamic qualities of this uplifting environment.

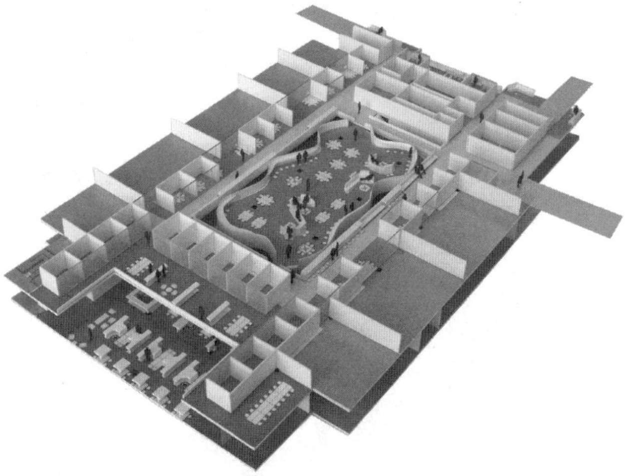

Figure CS7.5: The Learning Oasis is surrounded by the classrooms and group study spaces and is the symbolic heart of the facility.

Figure CS7.7: Linear Corian-clad counters along the corridors provide students with plenty of heads-down study space.

the student work spaces (Figure CS7.11) and a scheme for light penetration that affords brightness and access to views (Figure CS7.12).

This versatile learning center successfully creates a highly energized learning environment that extends learning beyond the classroom, and fosters collaboration. Users say the space is dynamic but feels serene due to its bright but soft lighting, soft coloration, and well-balanced sound levels, all contributing to produce just the right buzz of activity.

Figure CS7.8: The lower benches along the corridors provide students with more relaxed study spaces.

Figure CS7.9: Some of the most popular spots are the organically shaped niches carved into walls.

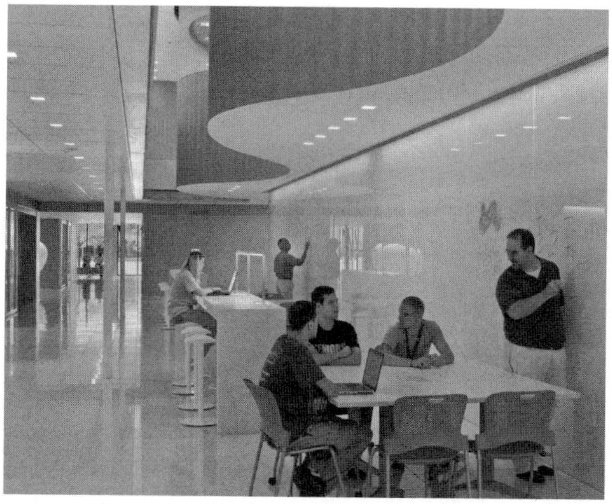

Figure CS7.10: Opaque glass walls outside the central Teacher Education Resource Center on the first floor double as writing surfaces for the adjacent study areas.

Figure CS7.11: The double-height suite at the north side of the building is for faculty use. The light penetrating through the tall window-wall penetrates deep into the space.

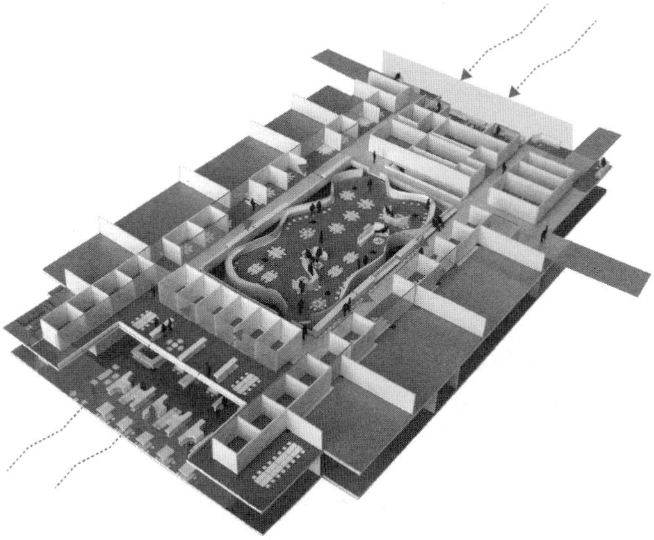

Figure CS7.12: Large exterior glass windows, extensive use of glass walls inside, and skylights combine to allow sky views from almost anywhere inside the building.

CAPSULE | Surface Pattern as Enrichment

Eighteen Alternatives to the Carpet Border

There is a tendency among many designers, especially but not exclusively among novices, to resort to the same solution when attempting to add interest to the floor (usually the carpet) of a room such as a conference room. That solution, the proverbial "carpet border," is usually manifested by a band around the room. It comes from a tendency many people have to always put a frame around things. Our aim here is to give you some alternatives to this common but limiting tendency.

Figure C7.2a–c shows three common variations from the common carpet border: the simple band around the room (Figure C7.2a), the band with accents on the corners (Figure C7.2b), and the band with hexagonlike ends (Figure C7.2c). These are simplistic and not very sophisticated but show a desire to add pattern to an otherwise homogeneous flooring. Our first three alternatives are shown in Figure C7.2d–f. Their aim is still to define a rectangular area centered in the room, but they accomplish it by using different means: defining the desired area by a rectangle with a contrasting color or value (Figure C7.2d), with a field of stripes (Figure C7.2e), or with a field of squares (Figure C7.2f).

Figure C7.2g–i, in turn, provides three variations to the ones just presented. In Figure C7.2g the colors or values are reversed to accentuate the perimeter instead of the rectangle. We recognize this may be considered another case of the proverbial border. Figure C7.2h is similar to Figure C7.2e, except the shape defined by the lines is no longer a rectangle (one side progresses diagonally). In Figure C7.2i, the squares, unlike the regularly spaced ones in Figure C7.2f, are fragmented from a regular and dense center to a dispersed perimeter.

The approach to our design challenge is handled differently in Figure C7.3. The six alternatives shown here are variations on a common theme. These do not attempt to define a rectangular area in the space. The approach here is irregular and asymmetrical. In Figure C7.3a, a wide strip is provided along one of the long ends of the room. Figure C7.3b is similar, but the strip is along one of the short sides. Meanwhile, Figure C7.3c features a combination of the previous two, having strips along one long and one short side with a contrasting intersecting area at the corner. Figure C7.3d–f features more irregular approaches using diagonal (Figure C7.3d) and curvilinear (Figure C7.3e and C7.3f) shapes. Notice the differences between the two curvilinear solutions. The different radii and orientation of the curves produce quite different effects.

Figure C7.3g–i provides three more variations. They become more complex. These add a layer of shapes on

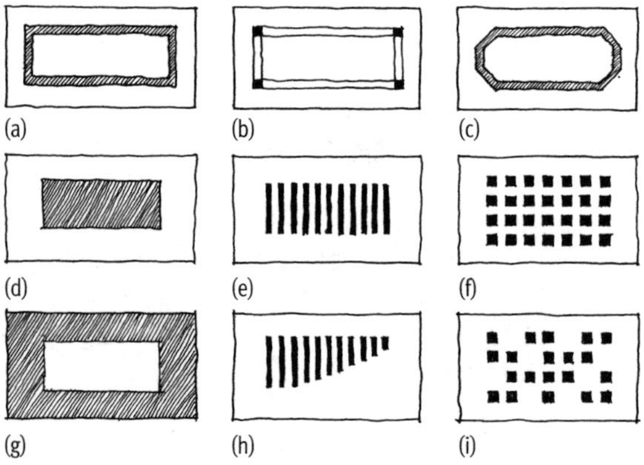

Figure C7.2: Basic carpet borders: rectangular band (a), rectangular band with accent on four corners (b), band with angled ends (c), dark rectangle on light field (d), field of aligned squares (e), aligned grid of squares (f), light rectangle on dark field (g), progressively shorter stripes (h), random squares (i).

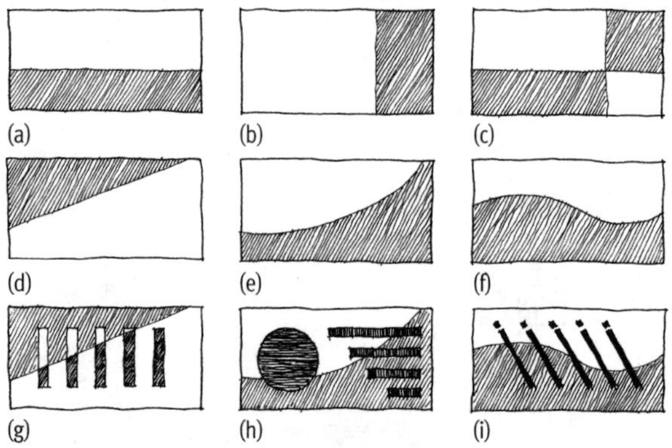

Figure C7.3: Alternatives to borders: wide band along long side (a), wide band along short side (b), combination of a and b (c), corner diagonal field (d), sweeping curve (e), undulating curve (f), corner diagonal with stripes (g), sweeping curve with circle and uneven stripes (h), undulating curve with diagonal stripes and accents (i).

top of the patterns shown in Figure C7.3d–f. The added shapes clearly become figures on a two-toned field. Figure C7.3g adds a series of stripes. The two other solutions add uneven stripes and a large circle (Figure C7.3h), and diagonal stripes and points (Figure C7.3i).

Finally, Figure C7.4 shows an entirely different approach. Here, the conception of the context is expanded. The area to which a pattern is applied is no longer confined by the boundaries of the original space (even if they are walls). The resulting shapes within the room (or space) are a segment of a larger pattern that continues beyond the space. This is a powerful design device useful to unify spaces in projects where it is okay to go beyond the borders. The variations shown are three of the many possible. Figure C7.4a shows what appears to be one end of a rectangle. A segment of a curve is shown in Figure C7.4b. In Figure C7.4c, a diagonally shaped strip starts narrow inside the room and moves out, while getting progressively wider. Notice that in these cases it is not necessary to complete (i.e., close) the shape. By just showing enough of it, the mind can read the shape. These applications work best when it is possible to see the shape continuing from one side to the other. Therefore, in cases where the two sides are separated by a wall, it is a good idea to use glass or have an opening near the point where the inside and outside meet so the effect can be perceived.

Nine Alternatives to the Checkerboard Pattern

When it comes to a modular pattern with tile, nothing is as popular as the checkerboard pattern. While not an unattractive pattern, it has become the default pattern for many designers. Creating patterns with tile is one of the most enjoyable and, potentially, creative design activities possible. It is necessary, however, to move beyond the checkerboard pattern. The possibilities are endless. Here are nine ideas for starters.

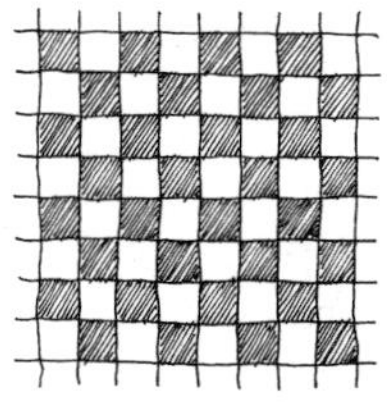

Figure C7.5: The checkerboard pattern.

Figure C7.5 shows the well-known and widely used checkerboard pattern. You are likely to be familiar with it. Contrasting tiles are alternated horizontally and vertically to create a textured field. A popular alternative to the checkerboard pattern is one that places diamonds (or diagonal squares) at the intersections of tiles. These can be placed at every intersection (Figure C7.6a) or at wider intervals (Figure C7.6b). These two patterns, like the checkerboard, normally occur uniformly throughout—that is, the entire area is treated the same.

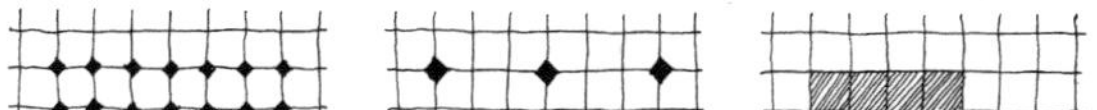

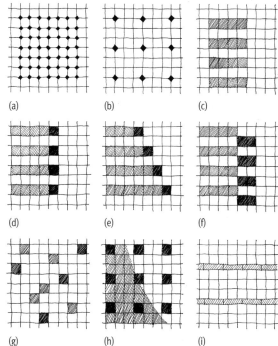

Figure C7.6: Alternatives to the checkerboard pattern: diamond (or inverted square) at each joint (a), diamond (or inverted square) at wider spacing (b), even parallel bands (c), even parallel bands with accents at ends (d), uneven parallel bands with accents at ends (e), even parallel bands with short accent bands at in-between spaces (f), random squares (g), evenly spaced squares over two-toned field with curve (h), bands of contrasting width and finish (i).

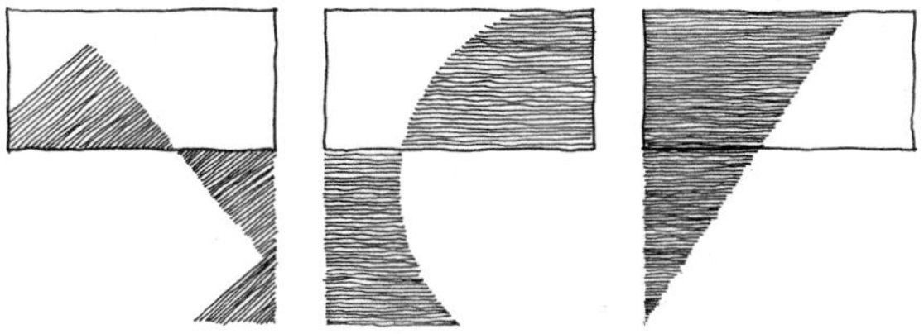

Figure C7.4: Patterns that go beyond the borders: angled rectangle (a), curve (b), diagonal (c).

continued

Patterns created with tiles do not necessarily have to be uniform throughout the entire area. Nor do they have to be of the alternating type (black tile, white tile, black tile). It is possible to create lines with tiles by placing several tiles next to each other on a contrasting field. These can be simple uniform bands, as shown in Figure C7.6c, or they can have accent pieces at the ends, as shown in Figure C7.6d. The next two patterns show variations of this idea. In Figure C7.6e the length of the strips vary, getting uniformly longer to create a diagonal slant. In Figure C7.6f, the accent pieces at the ends are two tiles wide and they are shifted to occur on the in-between strips.

A random pattern is used in Figure C7.6g. In a random pattern, accent tiles are placed as if they had been sprinkled on the floor from above. The density can vary. Accent tiles can have a prominent presence or be sparse. Also, the density does not need to be uniform throughout. This strategy relies on a painterly eye to achieve good results. The pattern in Figure C7.6h shows two things. First, it is possible to spread apart a uniform pattern of squares. When you do that, they read more as figures than the background. The other thing that takes place in that pattern is the division of the background into a light and a dark zone that meet along a curved line.

Finally, Figure C7.6i illustrates the fact that you are not required to keep the same tile module throughout. Although the field probably needs to be composed of uniform pieces for practicality, accent bands can be of a contrasting size. It is even possible to use contrasting finishes of the same color tile (or stone) for subtle differentiation. A layout that uses narrow bands of a roughly textured stone against a smoother field of larger tiles can be quite pleasing. The subtle tone-on-tone effects produced by the variations between the two sizes and finishes can produce a restrained, elegant effect.

One last note: Remember that just because the majority of tile and stone available commercially is 12-inch × 12-inch does not mean that you have to accept this size as a given. This is one example where optimal practical size does not equal the optimal perceptual size. While the 12-inch square module looks fine in some applications (mostly residential), the module looks out of scale in many commercial applications where an 18-inch × 18-inch or 24-inch × 24-inch module would better complement the scale of the space. Similarly, many instances call for the use of smaller modules such as 8-inch × 8-inch, 4-inch × 4-inch, and small mosaic tiles. In some projects it is even possible to have the installer cut tiles to a custom size. You may, for instance, want to use rows of 12-inch × 3-inch strips. In that case, the installer (or factory) would cut 12-inch × 12-inch pieces into four strips to meet your specifications. Cutting tiles requires additional labor and expense and is, obviously, out of the question for low-budget projects. However, it is done frequently on high-end projects.

Six Variations of the Eye-Level Decorative Tile Band

The eye-level decorative tile band has limited applications but is seen frequently in places such as public restrooms and hallways. It usually occurs in places with a field of tile, although it can also be set into a drywall wall as an accent. It is another example of the type of application that gives designers a chance to create meaningful expression, and yet they often resort to simplistic solutions. The application requires some length of uninterrupted wall (Figure C7.7). Although it is normally placed somewhere around eye level, there is no reason it couldn't be treated as a focal feature on the upper section of walls in cases where the wall is seen from a distance.

Figure C7.8 shows three examples of simple patterns. Figure C7.8a, the checkerboard, is well known and needs no elaboration. It is not the most imaginative pattern but it is playful in a simple way and serves to engage the mind. Figure C7.8b and C7.8c have certain similarities.

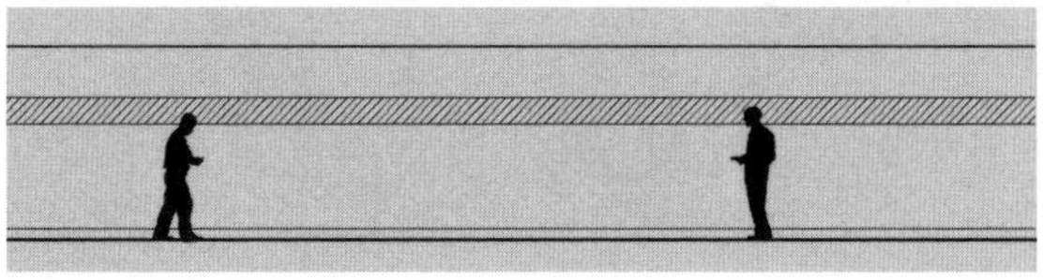

Figure C7.7: Elevation of band on the wall.

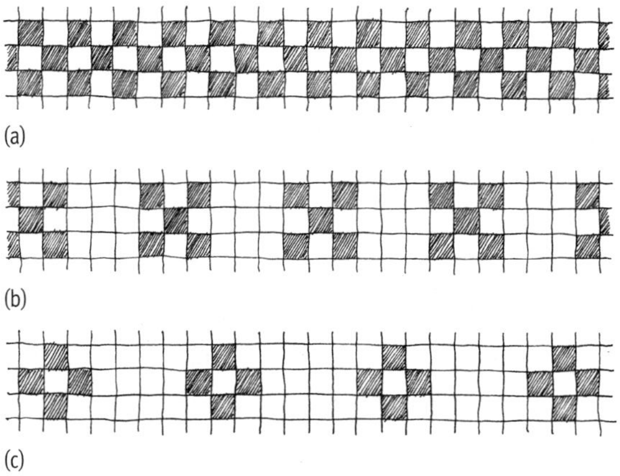

Figure C7.8: Checkerboard band (a), four corners plus center (b), cross pattern (c).

They both use a repeating pattern spaced regularly. The pattern itself fits in a square defined by nine tile spaces (three vertical and three horizontal). Figure C7.8b consists of four corners and a center. Figure C7.8c consists of a top, bottom, left, and right. These patterns, although not very imaginative either, are seen frequently and provide some interest along the band.

We recognize that designers seldom have much time to devote to such tasks as designing tile patterns; however, it is possible to achieve interesting effects with little additional effort. Five reminders shall serve to multiply the patterns you can do quickly:

1. Not all accent pieces have to be of the same color or value.
2. You can combine pieces to create lines.
3. Rhythm intervals can vary.
4. You can combine pieces to create a contrasting background.
5. You can combine the horizontal and the vertical.

Figure C7.9a features a simple pattern featuring a rhythm of aligned short light lines and dark points. It is not complex, yet it displays the ability of the designer to think in more than one modality simultaneously (points and lines). The pattern shown in Figure C7.9b highlights a background band by using a contrasting tone. It also shows an example of a simple irregular interval of accent pieces (alternating single and paired accent pieces). Figure C7.9c features long lines and paired dark accent pieces. In this pattern, vertical bands intersect the horizontal band. The exact location of vertical bands would have to be determined to suit the circumstances of the application. They can occur regularly or at strategic locations. Our example shows them coinciding with the locations of the paired accent pieces.

These are just a few possibilities to get you started. Using the five reminders discussed in this section, it is possible to create many different combinations of background, lines, and points using different lengths, tones, and intervals. Give them a try.

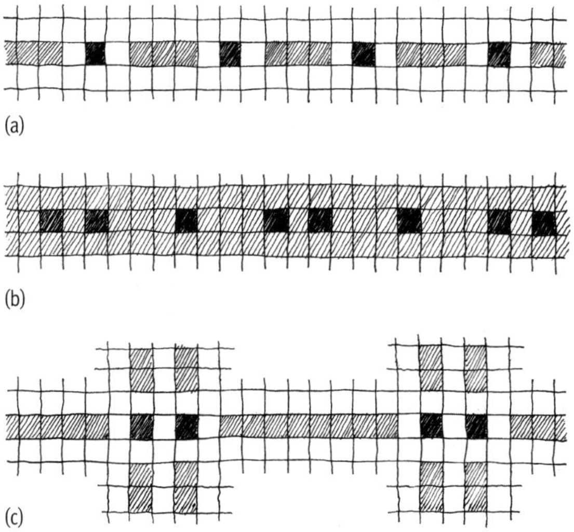

Figure C7.9: Line, square, line (a), contrasting with irregular intervals of single and paired square (b), line, pair of squares, line, plus vertical bands (c).

REVIEW

Summary

Projects need regularity and order to be perceptually clear and satisfying, but they also need to be rich and stimulating. Humans need both stability and stimulation. It is necessary, thus, to achieve a balance between these two seemingly opposing forces. Providing a sense of enrichment in projects requires the commitment of the designer. Enrichment is possible and desirable in any space of a project, particularly in arrival spaces, waiting areas, circulation spaces, and destination spaces.

General enrichment strategies are applicable anywhere in a project. These include the use of variety and complexity. Project complexity can be achieved in many ways through strategies such as the use of surface articulation and complex spatial compositions. Other enrichment strategies include the use of novelty, boldness, and tension.

Two somewhat opposite general enrichment strategies are ambiguity and pictorialness. Ambiguity is produced when an arrangement has more than one possible interpretation. Pictorialness relies on the careful composition, articulation, and framing of harmonious, straightforward spaces and surfaces. Enrichment can also be produced by creating spaces that concentrate human activity in ways that increase the sense of vitality of the space.

Some of the most enriching experiences in interior spaces occur while people move around along the circulation route. Sequences can be like stories, with plots, subplots, and climaxes. The shape of the path itself can be a source of enrichment. The length of the path and its configuration, proportions, and degree of connection all play a major role in the character of the path. Also crucial is the articulation and modulation of the side walls, floor, and ceiling.

The view at the end of a path and the view along a path to adjacent spaces are also important considerations. The size and placement of openings can be orchestrated in stimulating ways. For example, the level of correspondence between visual access and physical access can be manipulated to create a sense of anticipation and tension, followed by relief upon arrival at the destination.

In addition to facilitating the tasks people perform in buildings, designers can provide enriching environments in a project's destinations. Enrichment strategies in these cases include providing proper grounding, connection, and relief.

1. Venturi, R. (1977). *Complexity and contradiction in architecture* (2nd ed.). New York: Museum and Modern Art.

Exercises

1. Think about past or current design projects you have been involved with. What attempts to enrich experience have you tried to use? Has there been a pattern to your use of enrichment strategies?
2. Name three specific design strategies you would use to enrich the following spaces:
   - an arrival space
   - a waiting area
   - a corridor segment
   - a design studio space
3. Draw a plan or axonometric of a highly regular and modular space and perform at least one variation to make it more varied and interesting.
4. Think of one of your projects. Name three ways you could increase its level of complexity.
5. Take a single important elevation from one of your projects. Draw three rich and complex variations of it.
6. Draw one space and one mass using the principle of novelty.
7. Draw a mass and an elevation using the principle of boldness.
8. Draw three corridor segments using compression to create tension followed by relief.
9. Draw one spatial arrangement featuring intentional ambiguity.
10. Take a circulation sequence from a previous project. Modify it as necessary to incorporate some enriching events along it.
11. Take a circulation segment from one of your projects and explore different treatments for the side walls, floor, and ceiling to achieve different effects.
12. Pick one of your projects with several corridors. Add a focal point at the end of one of the corridors.
13. Pick one of your projects with several corridors. Draw an enticing composition at the end of one of the corridors to attract people by making them curious about what lies ahead.
14. Draw a corridor sequence incorporating various views of the destination space prior to getting to it in order to build anticipation.
15. Pick a past or current project. Design an internal focal plane or mass on which to occasionally rest the eyes in order to take a visual break from the task at hand.

Chapter 8
Expression

Instructional Objectives

- Introduce the concept of expression as an integral part of design.
- Explain some of the factors affecting design expression and interpretation.
- Present two different kinds of architectural meanings and how they work.
- Explain how design features can express fundamental aspects of humanity.
- Explain how contextual factors can be expressed in design.
- Discuss ways in which design properties and assemblies can be expressive.
- Discuss the expression of two basic aspects of design related to programmatic necessities.
- Explain how identity is expressed in design.
- Describe the many variables that affect identity.
- Explain how the mode of self-presentation affects the way expression is manifested.
- Explain the roles of the designer's personal style, attitudes, and preferences on expression.

"Architectural expression" is a wide term covering not only the outward manifestation of the inner purpose of the building, i.e. the characteristics of the building programme, but also questions of manners, of the personal equation of the "ego" of both client and architect, and of the claims of materials and structure to be expressed for their own sake, either directly or by implication.

—*Howard Robertson,* Modern Architectural Design

So far we have elaborated on important design tasks, such as establishing order and providing enrichment in design projects. Our next topic, expression, is particularly important because it permeates and colors all of these other aspects of design. In the process of determining which kind of structure, what kind of order, and which enrichment strategies to use for a particular project, the designer has to decide what type of expression the project should have. Structure, order, and enrichment need to be customized into a unified response to the particular realities of the project. The qualities thus embodied will give the project particular meanings appropriate to its unique realities. The project will then attain a presence similar to that of a living organism, with a distinct personality of its own.

Should a given project be a self-conscious, elegant, subtle, and self-disclosing one, perhaps even with a few metaphoric allusions thrown in for the enjoyment of the high-brow connoisseur? Or should it be self-conscious, boldly elegant, even pompous, with straightforwardness and no intellectual games? The possible qualities attainable through design expression and their combinations are countless. The possibilities appropriate for a particular project are narrowed down by the specifics of the project but still leave ample room for interpretation. What are the possibilities, and how does one decide among them?

Gaining competence at the task of determining appropriate expressions for projects and then executing designs that incorporate those expressions successfully is one of the goals of design. Some aspects of expression are straightforward and objective, although much of expression in design is highly personal and subjective. This chapter presents some of the ways design expression can be manifested in your projects. It is difficult to give precise rules about how to incorporate specific expressions in design, much less about which one is appropriate for a particular project, because project details vary widely from case to case—what's appropriate in one case is not in others. We suggest some of the possibilities and, hopefully, provide some insight about the factors to consider when making decisions about project expression.

EXPRESSION IN DESIGN

Every design expresses something, whether intentionally or not. It tells us something about the character (real or desired) of those who use the space, the attitude toward the context in which the project occurs, and the preferences and design tendencies of both the designer and the user group. Designs, like people and their belongings, embody ways of being and acting. Particular expressions are chosen and approved by clients because they help convey, materially, who they are or aspire to be. The interior design of a place often embodies the particular essence of the group using it.

Expression

The particular expression adopted for a project is usually pervasive and, thus, seen throughout the project. Nevertheless, specific expressions can also be localized, occurring only in certain parts of a project. A project or portion of it may express desired emotional qualities (joy or somberness), attitudes of the client (conservatism or innovativeness), specific intentions (a desire for a heightened sense of entry and arrival), and the status of the owner (powerful and successful, or emerging and upcoming). The room in Figure 8.1, for instance, strongly communicates information about the character of its owner.

The particular project being designed and its context, owners, programmatic needs, and designers all contribute to the final expression. The self-image and personal intentions of both the owner and the designer are particularly important, as we will see.

Figure 8.1: The particular characteristics of interior spaces communicate the attitudes and beliefs of the people who own them. The treatments in this room give us clues about the character of its owner.
Source: *Here of All Places*, by Osbert Lancaster (John Murray Ltd., 1958).

Interpretation

Communication in design, in many ways, operates the same way as other types of communication. It involves the sending of a message by the sender and the reception and interpretation of the message by a recipient. The built environment, due to its physicality, is always present in very tangible ways and, therefore, is always up for interpretation. Every aspect of a design is open to interpretation, whether intended or unintended. A design message may even be accidental. An example of an intentional message is a project designed with a formal layout, classic forms, overpowering volumes, and rich materials to convey a sense of dignified power. An example of an unintentional message is the inaccessibility of an important public area of a building (due to careless design or legitimate design constraints) resulting in the perception (erroneous but understandable) that you are intentionally being discouraged from going there. An example of an accidental message is the unplanned effect caused by direct sunlight penetrating a project in some magnificent way at certain times of the day. The designer may be praised for orchestrating such a powerful and inspiring combination of forces when he or she was really not consciously trying to produce it.

Design as a language communicates through **formal properties** and **symbolic content**. Particular arrangements created by the specific forms used constitute the formal properties of the project. The meanings conveyed by these properties, as well as the materials, finishes, furnishings, and accessories used, constitute the symbolic content. Whatever associations are derived from them likely vary from culture to culture, from group to group within a culture, and from person to person within a group. Despite the variety of interpretations, however, there tend to be similarities of interpretation among people from the same group. In general, people from a particular culture or group share certain attitudes, values, and physical vocabularies related to building forms, physical symbols, and so on. This may make it easier to communicate through design with users from a homogeneous group that share similar views.

Another highly influential factor affecting how people interpret the built environment is the background of the person or group doing the interpretation. Given average conditions, people tend to develop visual affinities with certain environments they encounter during their formative years. For example, a typical restaurant in a rural area may be simple and rustic, and one in downtown New York City may be artsy and pretentious. Someone simple and unpretentious may feel more at home entering the restaurant shown in Figure 8.2a while an urbanite may prefer the one in Figure 8.2b.

(a) (b)

Figure 8.2: These two restaurants would carry different appeal for people from different backgrounds based on their relative level of exclusivity.

A person's cultural literacy also has a significant influence on how they interpret the physical environment. We can expect different interpretations from a person with minimal design literacy and a person who makes a living as a designer. A client trained in the arts is more likely, for example, to appreciate nuance and subtlety, abstract gestures, and historical allusions. Someone else may not care much for any of these attributes.

Even among people of similar design literacy levels, interpretations can be quite personal, often colored by the lens through which they look at a design. The historian, the art critic, the designer, and the technical person will all tend to assign greater value to different aspects of a design depending on their particular areas of knowledge and interest. To complicate matters further, it is not uncommon for people from similar backgrounds and areas of knowledge, such as, say, two design critics, to have opposing views about a particular design and to defend their respective points of view passionately.

Furthermore, as design philosophies, fashions, and trends change over time, interpretations and meanings will change too. What is valued today may not be appreciated tomorrow, and vice versa. Expression and interpretation in design are, indeed, very subjective and unstable matters.

Interpretation and Meaning

To understand the dynamics of expressing meaning through design and the way those meanings are perceived and interpreted, it is useful to distinguish between two types of meanings: those that are understood spontaneously and those that are learned through convention. **Spontaneous meaning** can be conveyed through literal iconic signs or through inherent expression. These are understood directly, without training. Iconic signs utilize literal representations of the desired meaning, as when a building for an automobile corporation is shaped like a car.

Inherent expression relies on the spontaneous symbolism associated with the formal qualities of objects or compositions and what these represent. Spontaneous symbolism, Rudolf Arnheim explains, "derives from the expression inherent in perceived objects. To be seen as expressive, the shape of an object must be seen as dynamic. There is nothing expressive, and therefore nothing symbolic, in a set of stairs or a staircase as long as it is seen as a mere geometrical configuration. Only when one perceives the gradual rising of the steps from the ground as a dynamic crescendo does the configuration exhibit an expressive quality, which carries a self-evident symbolism."[1] Arnheim is referring to the symbolic meaning of ascending and the deep connotations it carries (Figure 8.3).

Most associations we make in our efforts to interpret the environment are not spontaneous and natural but learned associations, acquired by convention. **Learned associations** between symbols and meanings can vary widely from one culture to another. The same phenomenon occurs between different groups and sub-groups of the same culture who learn to perceive and give meaning to certain aspects of the physical world (symbols) in particular and consistent ways. Charles Jencks speaks about differences in **visual codes**. People from different

Figure 8.3: Some very basic architectural expressions carry profound existential connotations. Stairs, those utilitarian devices that transport us from one level to another, embody the act of ascending, a powerful symbolic act.

Figure 8.4: Interpretations of design works vary according to the point of view of the person doing the interpreting. The pure volume that provides so much pleasure to the modernist designer can be seen as a lifeless filing cabinet by the general public.

backgrounds, upon looking at the same design, will use different codes (based on learning and culture) for its interpretation. Buildings that incorporate various codes can be seen as having opposing meanings: "the 'harmonious, well-proportioned pure volume' of the modern architect becomes the 'shoe-box' or 'filing cabinet' to the public"[2] (Figure 8.4).

How is a designer to proceed, you may wonder? What kind of expression is best? How concrete do our expressive messages need to be? Opinions vary among designers and critics. Of the two critics mentioned earlier, for example, Arnheim advocates going beyond arbitrary convention, allying design intentions "with features of more basic, spontaneous expression."[3] He adds that "the most powerful symbols derive from the most elementary perceptual sensations because they refer to the basic human experiences on which all others depend."[4] Arnheim warns, "The use of identifiable subject matter (such as, literal, pictorial, iconic signs) as a component of architectural shape may interfere with a building's spontaneous symbolism because of the concessions its dynamics must make to the shape of that subject matter." He notes that "Eero Saarinen's TWA air terminal might soar more purely if it looked less like a bird."[5] Arnheim, thus, prefers elementary symbols that are perceived naturally and are associated with basic human experiences.

Jencks is in favor of iconic signs, which "speak with exactitude and humour about their function. The literalism, however infantile, articulates factual truths . . . and there is a certain pleasure (which doesn't escape children) in perceiving a sequence of them."[6] Unlike Arnheim, he praises the literalism of Saarinen's TWA terminal (Figure 8.5): "The TWA terminal in New York is an icon of a bird, and by extension, of aeroplane flight. . . . Here the imaginative meanings add up in an appropriate and calculated way, pointing towards a common metaphor of flight—the mutual interaction of these meanings produces a multivalent work of architecture."[7] Looking at architectural components as words, and these in turn as signs, Jencks points out the predominance of conventional symbolic signs over natural ones: "Most architectural works are symbolic signs; certainly those that are most potent and pervasive are the ones which are learned and conventional, not 'natural.'"[8] For Jencks, the symbolic sign learned by convention is clearly the dominant one.

Vehicles of Expression

There are many ways to manifest expression. Selecting which ones to use is a matter of personal preference. Beyond personal preferences, the requirements and context of a project will suggest pertinent expressions for the specific project. The best way for you, as the designer, to be prepared is to have an awareness of the possibilities, become familiar with different ways to execute expression, and develop the ability to diagnose a project to discover what particular type of expression is most fitting. Keep in mind that it is desirable to communicate with different groups at different levels on any given project. In fact, projects with multiple meanings acquire multiple

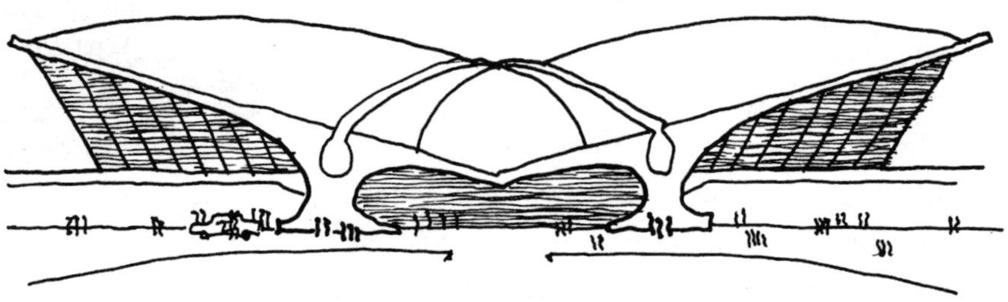

Figure 8.5: The birdlike form of Eero Saarinen's TWA terminal in New York carries meaning beyond its sculptural articulation.

levels of validity and have the power to delight many audiences.

When it comes to architectural expression, the entire spectrum of the physical environment comes into play. Successful designs have a sense of coherence among all their layers and, as a result, communicate clearly. In these cases, all (or most of) the elements reinforce each other to produce a consistent and powerful expression. Vehicles of expression include layout, space, surface, detail, furnishings, and accessories.

Layouts require many decisions about the placement of functions in relation to the context and to one another. They establish who goes where and who is next to, or far from, whom. They communicate messages about status, hierarchy, relationships between different groups, the degree of constraint or freedom throughout the project, and so on. The two simple office plans shown in Figure 8.6 show different attitudes about hierarchy. Figure 8.6a shows a strong hierarchy, with large corner offices, medium-sized perimeter offices, and small interior offices. The plan in Figure 8.6b is much more democratic, with same-sized offices located away from the perimeter and open office areas given exposure to the outside.

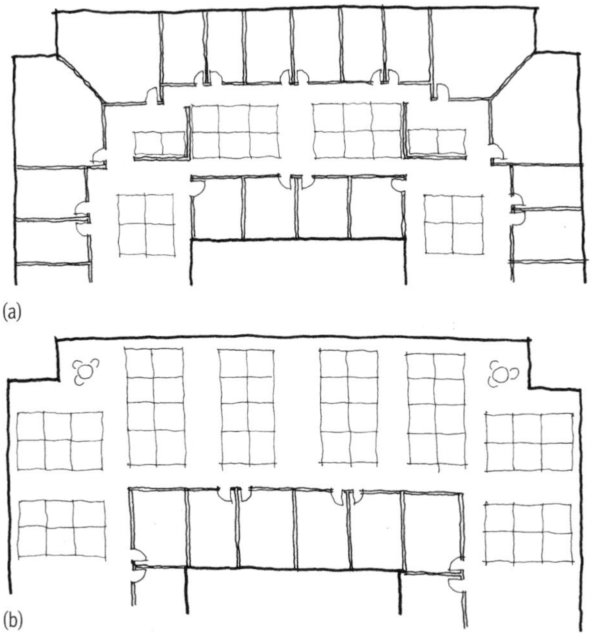

Figure 8.6: The size and placement of functions project attitudes about the hierarchy of an organization. These two plans reflect two different organizations, one (a) more hierarchical than the other (b). Hierarchical levels are embodied in corner offices, other perimeter offices, interior offices, and general workstations.

Space and its articulation communicate stylistic approach, hierarchy level, and degree of conventionality. Surfaces communicate stylistic approaches and preferences. Through the use of composition, pattern, texture, material, and color, designers can create combinations that communicate an infinite number of expressions. Figure 8.7 shows a view of a prominent civic building interior with generous volumes, strong architectural shapes, and well-articulated surfaces. Details can be shaped in many ways and can incorporate materials and colors that convey a myriad of different expressions. Compare, for example, the two railing systems shown in Figure 8.8. Each different expression has its own unique character.

Furnishings, whether chairs, desks, tables, or display cases, can also have variations in shape, materials, colors, and trim, conveying widely different styles and meanings. The many stylistic and material choices make it possible to achieve almost any desired look. Beyond furnishings, accessories also contribute to expression. These include items like desk accessories for work settings and the tablecloths, china, candleholders, and silverware in restaurants. Accessories, like most furnishings, are manufactured products that come as they are, and are generally not changed by the designer. Nevertheless, as with furnishings, there is a wide range of styles available, which makes it possible for designers to specify accessories congruent with the desired expression of the project. The lounge space shown

Figure 8.7: Shapes and surface character contribute much to the architectural expression of this civic building.

Figure 8.8: Particular expressions are manifested through the detailing of architectural features. These railing systems manifest different characters.

Figure 8.9: Furnishings and accessories contribute greatly to the overall expression of a space. These highly functional and decorative interior design elements come in many styles to suit the particular expressions desired by the designer. Notice the influence of the chairs, tables, plants, planters, and decorative railings and light fixtures in this room.

in Figure 8.9 illustrates the important contribution of furnishings and accessories to the character of a space.

TYPES OF EXPRESSION

There are many types of expression, and designers have great latitude in determining what types of expression to emphasize consciously for a given project. These are not just personal whims but represent the designer's responses to the specific qualities of the project and the client. When these intentions are clear, it is up to you as the designer to decide how to best achieve the desired expression. In the following sections, we discuss different types of expression grouped into six classifications: expression of universal human experiences, expression of contextual factors, expression of formal design properties and assemblies, expression of programmatic necessities, expression of identity, and designer's personal expression.

Expression of Universal Human Experiences

Certain expressions found in the built environment operate at a very basic level by revealing to us simple fundamental aspects of our own humanity. Arnheim talks about "the symbolic overtones of practical life"[9] and explains that works of architecture make symbolic statements that convey relevant human qualities and situations. "We speak of 'high' hopes and 'deep' thoughts, and it is only by analogy to such elementary qualities of the perceivable world that we can understand and describe non-physical properties."[10] Thus, elements such as verticality, depth, and the like can be utilized to evoke some of these human associations. Expressions in this category are most effective when the function expressed is asserted strongly for emphasis. Among the possible expressions in this category are the following three dualities.

Ascending/Descending

Ascending is associated with improvement, moving toward better things, even toward the sublime. Heaven is always up, as are the offices of the top-ranking officials of a corporation. The act of ascending, thus, can be a very symbolic act. One climbs a few steps up to get to a special location, such as a king's throne. Descending can carry connotations of moving deeper into the earth, where one can find security and protection, or perhaps

Figure 8.10: The act of ascending carries powerful symbolic connotations that may vary depending on the particular occasion and arrangement.

the intriguing, obscure, and unknown. Figure 8.10 shows a rising staircase inviting users to the rewards above.

Constraint/Freedom

Another aspect with strong symbolic connotations is the relative degree of constraint or freedom allowed by a given space. These are usually related to programmatic requirements, but the way they are treated can carry symbolic connotations. People form perceptions in response to the level of overall space available around them and also the degree to which the space permits them to move about at will.

We have talked before about how the use of contrast can be a powerful tool to heighten the awareness of specific qualities. In this case, moving from a tight space to a generous one can emphasize the sense of freedom the larger space affords, and vice versa. Similarly, progressing from a confining and inflexible system of corridors to an area that offers many travel choices and the freedom to pursue them can surely heighten the sense of freedom given by the latter space.

Admittance/Rejection

As in the previous example, the duality of admittance/rejection is usually dictated by programmatic requirements. Here, too, you can find opportunities to emphasize either the admittance or rejection aspect. Admittance refers to the degree of welcoming offered by a particular arrangement. Admittance presupposes connection and openness between spaces while rejection prevents admittance, either by mere discouragement or by absolute denial.

Rejection usually involves some kind of barrier to prevent passage. The solidity of the wall, the number and character of points of connection between the two sides, and the level of control at those points can send clear messages about how welcome one is to come in. Even more fascinating is the handling of admittance. Admittance has many levels. It can be allowed (reluctantly or indifferently), encouraged (enthusiastically), or demanded (aggressively). The three storefronts shown in Figure 8.11 feature portal-like gateways that highlight the point of entry into the respective stores, thus encouraging

Figure 8.11: The gateway, or portal, is one of the most powerful ways of expressing admittance. These three portals of stores in the same complex are representative of the variety possible within the portal idiom.

admittance. Notice the different expressions of the same basic idea of welcoming.

Expression of Contextual Factors

Often, the contextual forces related to a project not only influence some of the design decisions but actually acquire a dominant form of expression. These forces can be historic, cultural, regional, or related to current norms.

Historic Expression

Many interior projects occur in older buildings or neighborhoods having distinct design features typical of the time when they were built. In many cases the style adopted for a project is congruent with the style of the building. Examples include literal, carefully researched restorations, where every aspect is reproduced as it was originally; renovations, where the basic character of the original style is preserved without getting overly literal; respectful rehabilitations, where new functions going into old buildings respect the character of the original style without feeling an obligation to mimic what was done originally (Figure 8.12); and historical re-creations, where new projects are designed in an older, historical style (Figure 8.13).

In these cases, stylistic approaches from the historical period in question are either incorporated into the project or taken as points of departure for the development of new designs. Depending on the project, these may be applied in pure form or expressed abstractly to retain their original essence.

Figure 8.12: Respectful rehabilitations retain elements that convey the historic expression of a place without subjecting the vocabulary of the new design to the same stylistic constraints.

Figure 8.13: Historical re-creations manifest historical expression on new construction. In these cases, a new environment is inspired by an older design style, as shown in this old-world setting in the lounge of a new hotel.

Cultural Expression

Whenever a project has a strong and specific cultural component based on its location or the nature of its users, the project may need to reflect design expressions from the culture in question. Most cultures have recurring design characteristics one can draw from literally, such as arches and sombreros traditional in Mexican architecture and culture. Even more challenging is when the designer is attempting to interpret aspects of a culture in a nonliteral way, like designing a Mexican restaurant without cacti, sombreros on the wall, or the colors of the Mexican flag.

As in the case of historic expression, **cultural expression** can incorporate the entire spectrum of design elements or just select ones. Figure 8.14 shows ethnic forms used in a Middle Eastern restaurant setting.

Figure 8.14: Forms based on ethnic traditions, such as the pointed and ornate arches in this restaurant, contribute to the expression of culture.

Regional Expression

Regional expression can vary due to regional cultural differences or to regional topographical differences. In the United States, for instance, certain regions possess strong subcultures with unique characteristics and particular visual affinities. One such region is the Southwest, where the strong presence of Mexican and Native American people and culture has created a unique visual style associated with it.

Topography and location also affect the visual character of a region as well as the materials used for construction. The arid topography of the Southwest makes the visual uniqueness of the area even more pronounced. Projects done in this region are likely to reflect this expression and incorporate adobe construction and unique regional shapes, as the exterior and surroundings of the church shown in Figure 8.15 illustrate.

Current Norms and Conventions

Design is also influenced by certain set of cultural norms and conventions prevalent at the time. The German word *zeitgeist* is often used to describe the spirit of the time. Some periods in history have enjoyed consistent and widely accepted rules, while others have been characterized by disagreement and change. Whether you, as a designer, adopt the prevailing design tendencies of your time or take a different view becomes your prerogative.

Figure 8.15: Some regions, such as the Southwest, possess strong regional character due to topography, ethnicity, and other factors. The view shown here is unmistakably typical of the region.

Individual designer positions will be dealt with a little later. For now, it is sufficient to say that some projects, especially during times of stylistic transition and progress, can become conscious efforts to express the new spirit of the time. During the reign of modernism, for instance, the desire was to incorporate the machine aesthetic, using it as a metaphor of the industrial progress of that time. Designs became streamlined and devoid of decoration. Although many designs started looking alike, there were still various ways of interpreting these prevailing tendencies. For instance, Figure 8.16 shows cartoonish versions of two different interpretations of modernism.

(a)

(b)

Figure 8.16: Every period in history has its own prevailing stylistic norms and conventions. Modernism was characterized by a simple austere machine aesthetic (a). Some designers operated within the new conventions but gave them a more organic feel (b).

Source: *Here of All Places*, by Osbert Lancaster (John Murray Ltd., 1958).

Expression of Formal Design Properties and Assemblies

Designers have much control over the treatment of design elements. Shapes, textures, thicknesses, colors, and lighting can be emphasized or deemphasized at will to create particular forms of expression. These design properties are objective and tangible. They can be manipulated as part of a greater design strategy of expression or for their own sake. For example, the texture of a wall could be accentuated to create a rich and evocative surface (Figure 8.17). It can become expressive and possess a strong character without having to symbolize any meaning beyond the desire to be rich and textural. Conversely, you may choose textured surfaces on a project in order to symbolize a cave or fortress.

In addition to manipulating specific design properties for effect, you can also manipulate composite design assemblies. These assemblies, as a whole, produce parts of the design that fulfill and express specific functions. Examples include the functions of support, shelter, and connection. These basic functions can, if deemed appropriate, be emphasized or deemphasized to produce specific effects. A greater number of columns spaced closely together would exaggerate the function of support. Fewer but oversized columns would accomplish the same effect with a different feel (Figure 8.18). A floating ceiling canopy over a space in a high area tends to accentuate the function of shelter (Figure 8.19). Emphasizing a connecting

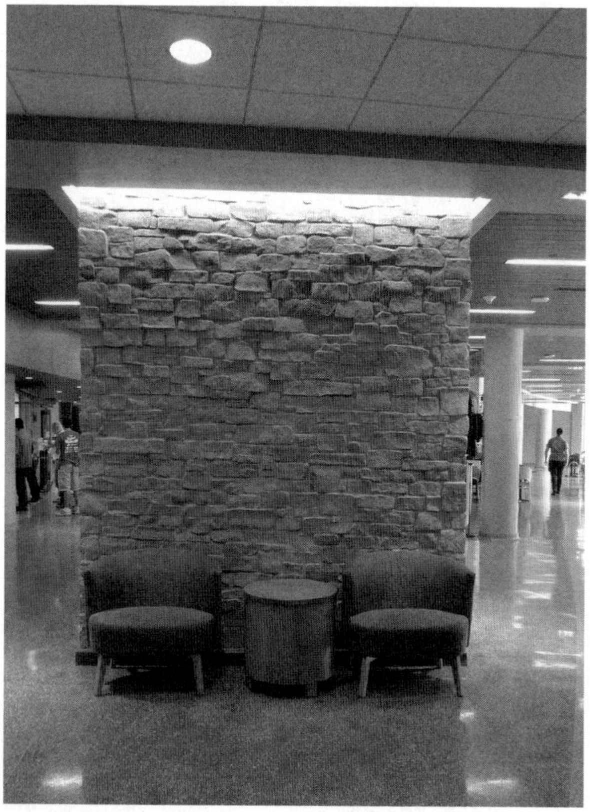

Figure 8.17: Certain physical characteristics of the environment can be accentuated and highlighted for their own sake, like the emphasis on the texture of this wall.

(a)

(b)

Figure 8.18: The function of support can be expressed in many ways. One of them is through the treatment of supporting columns. A normal-looking arcade, for instance, can be transformed through the use of slender columns spaced close together (a) or the use of fewer but heavier columns (b).

Figure 8.19: The floating overhead canopy shown reduces the scale of the defined area below and, thus, gives it a greater sense of shelter.

Figure 8.20: The function of connection can be highlighted by emphasizing the threshold between the parts being connected. Highlighting a connecting path by differentiating the floor material is one way to emphasize connection.

path through the treatment of the floor reinforces the idea of connection between two points (Figure 8.20).

Expression of Programmatic Necessities

The programmatic requirements of a project dictate the basic configuration a project takes. Here we discuss two basic aspects of the programmatic realities of a project that help to shape its basic spatial expression and give it overall character. These are the degree of openness of the spaces and the degree of connection between them.

Openness/Closedness

In Chapter 4 we elaborated on issues of spatial definition, containment, encapsulation, and so on. Choices made regarding layout and spatial definition, largely in response to the program, give spaces distinct characters in terms of their degree of openness, spatial definition, and encapsulation. In the past, there was not much choice. Due to structural limitations, projects were mostly subdivided into compartments bound by load-bearing walls and connected via doors and corridors. Luckily, we have more choices today. A project's degree of openness is one type of expression easily apprehensible on most projects. The openness, or compartmentalization, of a project will quickly tell us information about the level of privacy users require and whether people operate individually or in groups. These visual cues immediately tell us something about the nature of the project and how it is structured and organized. It may be composed of a few large spaces, of one large space and a few small ones, or of many small

Figure 8.21: Openness can be manifested through the freedom produced by generous and/or uncluttered spaces. It is often a function of spatial density as illustrated by these two scenes.

spaces. Openness, of course, can refer to the overall feeling of openness in a space, which is the result of spatial volume, light levels, and density of components, among other factors. Compare, for example, the different degrees of density in the two spaces shown in Figure 8.21.

Connection/Segregation

The way in which different spaces are connected to one another reveals much about the nature of an establishment and the way it operates. Connections between main parts, as well as between sub-parts, tell us about their level of autonomy, as well as about the levels of flow and admittance desired between parts of the project. Are the spaces relatively open to one another or are they encapsulated by full walls on all sides with small punched holes providing restricted access? Both the level of physical access and the degree of visual disclosure between separate areas are involved. This aspect is related to openness/closedness. The two work hand in hand, the first one referring more to the general character of spaces and the second one to the nature of separations between them.

IDENTITY

Perhaps the most exciting and vital design expression of a project is the visual expression of its identity. **Identity** refers to the embodiment, in tangible ways, of the qualities that distinguish a particular person or group. You can think of it as the physical manifestation of the entity's personality. This identity may be real or ideal. A simple example to understand the interaction of real versus ideal identities would be the case of a person shopping for a car. Let's suppose this person is a conservative, middle-class man but thinks he is hip and likes to project an image of wealth. If this person were to select a car that expresses his perceived self-identity, he would most likely select an expensive sports car. If others were to select the car on his behalf, relying on objective perceptions, they would probably select a less expensive, conservative car.

In determining what identity to reflect, there is sometimes a fine line between reality and fiction, between what some entity really is and what it wants others to think it is. As a rule of thumb, designers are more like public relations professionals trying to show their clients in the best possible light than journalists trying to disclose them objectively.

There are many factors that contribute to a group's personality and, therefore, many considerations that have to be made to decide how to externalize identity. The topic of identity and its expression in design is complicated and sensitive.

Projects where the client is a single individual are the simplest, because there is only one identity to reflect; however, most interior projects are designed for more than one person. Designing projects for larger groups becomes more challenging. A designer does not attempt to address every identity involved, but designs for the identity of the group. Large corporations have their own collective identities, and most stores, restaurants, hotels, and nightclubs cater to very specific publics, making the task of design more targeted. Below we address the topics of individual identity and group identity.

Individual Identity: Personality and Self-Image

Much research has been done over the years in the fields of marketing and consumer behavior to understand people and what factors influence their consumption patterns and preferences. These efforts have looked at individual variables such as personality, self-concept, and personal lifestyle. An individual's identity is related to his or her personality, loosely defined as the patterns of thoughts, emotions, and behaviors that characterize the individual. Personality, in turn, comprises those specific combinations of traits that are innate in the individual and are, therefore, consistent and predictable. Raymond Cattell and his team of trait-theory researchers, for instance, developed a group of 16 traits that can be helpful in suggesting corresponding characteristics of the built environment:

Reserved versus outgoing
Serious versus happy-go-lucky
Shy versus uninhibited
Trusting versus suspicious
Practical versus imaginative
Unpretentious versus polished
Conservative versus experimenting
Relaxed versus tense[11]

While personality may address relevant aspects of an individual, it may be difficult for a designer who has just been hired for a project to determine a client's true personality. The information offered by clients is usually based on their self-image, which is their own assessment of who they are. This is also tricky. Research suggests that people have not one but multiple selves. Some of the self-images identified in the consumer behavior literature are:

Actual self-image, or how people actually see themselves.
Ideal self-image, or how people would like to see themselves.
Social self-image, or how people feel others see them.
Ideal social self-image, or how people would like others to see them.

Expected self-image, or how people expect to see themselves at some point in the future. This one tends to fall somewhere between the actual and ideal self-images.[12]

Understanding the existence of multiple selves is important to designers because, among other challenges, designers need to know which of the client's self-images to address.

Associated with the self-image of any individual is a group of products and material objects that support and communicate that image. According to the image congruence hypothesis, individuals actively seek those products and places that correspond to their self-image.[13] The props and settings individuals use to define themselves become extensions of self. Russell Belk describes four levels of extended self: individual, family, community, and group.[14] Included in the family level, for instance, are the individual's residence plus its furnishings and objects. The house is, in fact, one of the most important aspects of self-identity. Personal collections are also important extensions of self, as they represent the person's judgment and taste. A person's close attachment to neighborhood and town at the community level can also be a strong aspect of his self-image. Finally, included at the group level are an individual's attachment to specific social groups, which often comprise consumer subcultures that influence many of the individual's consumer choices.[15]

Ultimately, the self-image of an individual manifests itself outwardly as a particular lifestyle. The person's way of life, money-spending habits, use of time, interests, and opinions are all part of that lifestyle. The concept of lifestyle has proven more useful to marketers than isolated traits and other aspects of personality in their efforts to correlate people and their preferences related to consumption (including the consumption of houses, furnishings, and all the stylistic variables that go with them). Lifestyle is a compounded concept influenced by factors such as demographics, social class, reference groups, cultural environment, and family.[16] Lifestyles have been studied systematically and some generalized segmentation models have been developed, such as VALS and VALS2, developed by the Stanford Research Institute. VALS2, for instance, classifies the American public into eight distinctive segments.[17] Whereas such classifications are useful to marketers, their usefulness to designers is minimal due to the relative broadness of the groups.

Factors Affecting Identity and Its Expression in Interiors

One of the designer's tasks is to make sense of the client's image and seek a corresponding expression through design. This expression is made visible in many different ways through the materials used, the style used for the interior architectural elements, the furnishings selected, and the detailing of the project. Choices made regarding the design of the project will address questions such as: Should it be conservative or innovative? Should it be pompous or down to earth? Should it be classic or modern? What is the most appropriate expression for this client and this particular project?

Among the motives that drive consumers to formulate their self-images and related product constellations, Eric Arnould, Linda Price, and George Zinkhan highlight five that marketers often use in their promotions. These help explain some of the factors that influence the determination of expression in interior projects.[18]

The Achievement Motive is defined as "the drive to experience emotion in connection with evaluated performance," and its followers strive for achievement and recognition. Expressions of achievement include luxurious and expensive environments and other material symbols that convey high status.

High status, in turn, relates to things like having a high rank in an organization, a high social standing, and wealth. Although high rank and social standing are reflected through symbols associated with power (such as getting the corner office), it is wealth that really serves to communicate achievement and having "made it." People of high status usually seek environments that reflect their status. They shop and dine in places where the status expressed by design is consistent with their own. Likewise, people aspiring to high status often commission designs that reflect such a level of success. Conversely, one can have a rich client with few pretensions who prefers to downplay his or her success and communicate a sense of restraint.

Admittance to the prestigious private clubs of the privileged may be reserved for those that meet certain status qualifications, but admittance to prestigious restaurants and stores is more public, and most of us can enter these places as long as we dress and behave appropriately. In fact, many people enjoy going to expensive shops and restaurants for an occasional splurge. Conversely, it is possible to make an economically priced restaurant or store appear classy and exclusive so it will attract both economy-minded and image-conscious high-class patrons.

Exclusivity due to status is expressed through the use of expensive materials, furnishings, accessories, and merchandise. In a store, it is likely to be expressed by expensive merchandise, sophisticated finishes, upscale graphics, and low merchandise density. In a restaurant, low-level intimate lighting, tablecloths, and fancy dinnerware and china are symbols of exclusive establishments (Figure 8.22).

The Power Motive "is defined by the drive to have control or influence over another person, group, or the world at large."[19] Ways to show power include the display of prestige possessions (e.g., fancy cars, expensive watches, and prestigious offices and furnishings), formal and intimidating environments (home or office), and the possession of impressive real estate (such as having the corner office with the best view and greatest square footage). Office layouts, in general, say much about a company's attitude related to power. How those in power decide to position themselves and everybody else becomes an important factor. Are groups mixed or are they arranged by status level? Are the arrangements democratic or hierarchical? Who gets the perimeter offices with windows? Who has the corner offices? Are there certain places accessible only to the powerful few, or is every part of the facility accessible to all? Are some areas fancier than others, or is the level of finish and detail consistent throughout the facility?

Figure 8.22: Projection of status is an important component of group membership. Restaurants range from inexpensive and unpretentious to expensive and exclusive. Low-level lighting, tablecloths and cloth napkins, and fine plates and silverware are usual indications of exclusive, status-conscious restaurants.

The Uniqueness/Novelty Motive is another identity factor that drives consumers. Whereas some people strive to fit in (integration), others prefer to stand out (differentiation). Consumer behavior researchers distinguish between dogmatism and innovativeness. A person who is dogmatic tends to think rigidly and to have an intolerance for new ideas.[20] Innovativeness, in contrast, refers to the tendency to seek novel things and situations. Highly dogmatic people are closed-minded and "more likely to choose established, rather than innovative, product alternatives."[21]

This motive relates to what we could call progressiveness, referring to how conservative or innovative someone is. In general, the younger generation will tend to be more progressive than older generations. Youngsters tend to have a taste for the new, different, and, sometimes, radical. Older adults, on the other hand, generally pay less attention to the latest fads and tend to be, in general, more dogmatic. There is, however, a range of progressiveness within every age group. Every age has innovative people who defy conventions and conservative ones who stick to traditions.

A challenging situation arises when the progressiveness level of the client differs from that of the space visitor. The person who owns the space (e.g., a store or restaurant) may be highly conservative but the prevailing audience that supports the establishment may be creative and innovative. In this case, the owner may choose to cater to the tastes of the patrons. In most cases the owner targets a specific kind of crowd and tailors the level of progressiveness of the facility to cater to that specific market segment. In general, conservative projects rely on proven, conventional, and straightforward forms and compositions. Progressive projects defy convention and utilize novel forms, finishes, and compositions. The storefronts shown in Figure 8.23 portray two levels of progressiveness, with 8.23a being more conservative and 8.23b more progressive.

The Affiliation Motive is defined as "the drive to be with people."[22] Unfortunately, alienation and detachment have been some of the byproducts of societal progress

Figure 8.23: Some environments project innovativeness while others project conservatism. This applies to all building types, regardless of age group, status, or background. The two stores shown convey different degrees of progressiveness.

and development. As a result, people are often driven to seek ways to connect with others, especially with people with whom they share certain affinities. Common backgrounds and interests bring people together. Similarly, environments that are friendly and welcoming may serve to invite strangers to join in and feel at home.

Motivated by affiliation needs, many people identify with, aspire to, or may be associated with membership in specific economic and social groups. Their participation integrates them with and differentiates them from other consumers. Factors involved include class, ethnicity, caste, religion, gender, and age.[23] Retail corporations are particularly conscious of these differences. Through careful market research, they determine specific market segments and develop specific strategies (including design strategies) to cater to very specific clientele. Projecting an image consistent with the characteristics of the group will validate and reinforce the self-concept of the group members and send messages to outsiders in an effort to invite and attract compatible members.

People can also feel bound together as groups based on a common contextual background. Whether due to shared culture, subculture, or geographic location, these commonalities establish bonds and mutual understandings and affinities that find expression in the built environment. One can generalize that people of the same nationality will feel at home in environments reflecting traits from their culture and that people from the coast will enjoy the presence of water.

Other common backgrounds affecting membership are those established by occupation, neighborhood, membership in special interest organizations, and so on.

Related to affiliation needs is the idea of friendliness. Some people and organizations, by innate personality or by calculated intent, project feelings of warmth and friendliness. Others project a sense of coldness, sobriety, and impersonality. In either case, their built environments typically communicate those traits. In some cases, it may be necessary to compensate to make the prevailing tendency more fitting with other organizational goals. For example, an overly friendly client may choose to tone down the friendliness aspects of his built environment in order to project a more professional image.

Friendliness is often expressed by openness, cheerful colors, and a general sense of admittance. Many designers and clients make conscious efforts to produce reception areas that are friendly and inviting, as the one shown for an office in Figure 8.24.

Figure 8.24: Friendly environments are welcoming. Friendliness can be expressed by bright, cheerful environments with comfortable and accessible furniture that invites and comforts.

The Self-Esteem Motive refers to the need to maintain a positive view of the self. It is often expressed as an appeal to "be and express yourself."[24] Individuals with high self-esteem are likely to express themselves confidently through their environments. One way they may express themselves is by showing a sense of pride.

Some people and organizations like to project a sense of pride through the design of their built environment. The level of pride, which can range from mere self-confidence to blatant arrogance, will affect the character their spaces take: assertive, upright, and distinguished or pompous and pretentious. Other people and organizations give less importance to matters of pride, even if they possess self-pride. In these cases, the environment is likely to express a sense of restrained success or even tasteful humbleness. These combinations are likely to produce slightly different design expressions.

Pride can be exhibited through elegant and sophisticated designs that project success or through details and accessories that speak of the success, sophistication, and status of the client. To some, displaying treasured possessions and accomplishments is a way of expressing pride as shown excessively in Figure 8.25.

Figure 8.25: Displaying the sense of pride of owners and users can be accomplished in different ways. One of the ways of expressing pride is through display of treasured possessions, accomplishments, and hunting trophies. Source: *Here of All Places*, by Osbert Lancaster (John Murray Ltd., 1958).

Sophistication and Taste

Clients have a wide range of aesthetic sensibilities. Characteristics of aesthetically discerning clients include the ability to intuitively sense good composition (proportion and balance), to appreciate nuance and subtlety, to understand and appreciate abstraction, and to distinguish and appreciate special artistic content. In general, discerning clients will be more in tune with the sensibilities of the designer and appreciate, sometimes demand, sophisticated design efforts. The not-so-discerning client is likely to prefer more ordinary solutions. Note that good taste is not indicative of preference for a particular style or design approach. In fact, different levels of aesthetic sophistication are possible within any style, from traditional to contemporary. The two spaces shown in Figure 8.26 are examples of tasteful designs using two radically different styles.

Expressions of sophistication sometimes carry a degree of pretentiousness. A barbershop, for instance, usually makes no attempt to look sophisticated. It is quite content being ordinary and straightforward. An exclusive hair salon, on the other hand, often makes a conscious effort to look sophisticated and even pretentious.

Muddy Waters: The Issue of Taste

We know that tastes vary widely and that part of the designer's training aims to cultivate a sense of good taste. Good taste, however, is a very relative thing.

Figure 8.26: Sophisticated expression can occur in any kind of project, regardless of style, as shown in these two scenes from very different projects.

Arnould, Price, and Zinkhan define *taste* as "the making of judgments based on ideas of beauty, order, and arrangement."[25] They explain how "taste is part of the social world and helps consumers find their place in the world."[26] In fact, one of the most important and personal aspects of expression is taste. It acts as a form of cultural capital, giving individuals membership in certain groups and excluding them from others. In many ways, taste defines who we are. People even intentionally adopt certain tastes, with all their accompanying objects and activities, in order to signal membership in a certain group (e.g., museumgoers, wine tasters, and so on).[27]

In an effort to sort different patterns of taste, Herbert Gans identifies five taste cultures. He is careful to avoid making value judgments about them. In fact, he argues that each taste culture is valid and real. Factors that contribute to a person's choice of taste culture include age, class, religion, ethnic and racial background, regional origin, personality factors, and place of origin.[28] Gans posits that the major source of differentiation between taste cultures and publics is socioeconomic level or class, adding that "among the three criteria sociologists use most often to define and describe class position—income, occupation, and education—the most important factor is education . . . not only schooling but also what people learn from the mass media and other sources."[29] As a designer, your task is to recognize a client's taste preferences while acknowledging your own. Then you must come up with the corresponding modes of expression. The five taste cultures are:

High Culture This culture differs from others in "that it is dominated by creators (such as designers)—and critics—and that many of its users accept the standards and perspectives of creators. Users in this culture tend to either look at culture from a creator perspective (thus, embracing the nuances of, in our case, design), or merely be interested in the output from the creators, but not necessarily in their methods. Members of this culture are almost all highly educated people of upper- and upper-middle-class status, employed mainly in academic and professional occupations. . . . The culture's standards for substance . . . almost always place high value on the careful communication of mood and feeling, on introspection rather than action, and on subtlety, so that much of the culture's content can be perceived and understood on several levels. . . . Since the culture serves a small public that prides itself on exclusiveness, its products are not intended for distribution by the mass media. . . . High culture . . . perceives itself as setting aesthetics standards and supplying the proper culture for the entire society."

Upper Middle Culture "This is the taste culture of the vast majority of America's upper-middle class. . . . They do not find high culture satisfying . . . but prefer a culture that is substantive, unconcerned with innovation in form, and uninterested in making issues of method and form a part of culture . . . As a result, upper-middle culture is far less 'literary,' and art and music (and design) are much less abstract than in the case of high culture."

Lower Middle Culture "Numerically the dominant taste culture and public in America, it is comprised of middle- and lower-middle-class people in the lower-status professions. The aesthetics of lower-middle culture emphasize substance: Form must serve to make substance more intelligible or gratifying . . . Lower-middle art continues to be mainly romantic and representational, shunning harsh naturalism as well as abstraction."

Low Culture "This is the culture of the older lower-middle class, but mainly of the skilled and semiskilled factory and service workers. . . . Low-culture publics are still likely to reject 'culture,' and even with some degree of hostility. They find culture not only dull but also effeminate, immoral, and sacrilegious. . . . The aesthetic standards of low culture stress substance, form being totally subservient, and there is no explicit concern with abstract ideas or even with fictional forms of contemporary social problems and issues."

Quasi-Folk Low Culture "This taste culture is a blend of folk culture and of the commercial low culture of the pre–World War II era, which catered to audiences who were just emerging from ethnic or rural folk cultures at the time. It is the taste culture of many poor people . . . many of them rural or of rural origin and nonwhite. Data about quasi-folk low culture are scarce, but it seems to be a simpler version of low culture . . . Because this culture is almost entirely ignored by the mass media, its public probably has retained more elements of folk culture than any other."[30]

Gans makes a few qualifications regarding his taste cultures. First, the descriptions exaggerate the extent to which cultures and publics are cohesive and bounded systems; they are analytic rather than real aggregates. Second, many people regularly choose from more than one culture and, thus, can be classified as being in more than one public. Although most people probably restrict their content choices to one culture or to two adjacent ones, everyone occasionally chooses from a much higher or lower culture. Third, upward straddling sometimes involves explicit status motivations, as when people choose from a higher culture for status-seeking purposes or to encourage cultural mobility on the part of their children. Fourth, high culture has more influence than either the size or the status of its people would suggest. While high-culture standards are explicit and to some extent even codified, the standards of the other taste cultures are rarely discussed and taught and are, thus, implicit, uncodified, and for all practical purposes invisible. Fifth, standards from all taste cultures include criteria for bad content as well as good. People from high culture have more explicit standards, have been trained to make judgments based on those standards, and often have critics supporting their judgments. Other taste cultures lack explicit standards, the training to apply them, or a body of published criticism. The difference between those in high culture and those in the lower cultures is in the amount of aesthetic training, but this does not justify assuming a difference in aesthetic concern.[31]

Self-Presentation

The expressions manifested in a design include not only the basic content being expressed (tradition, glamour, and so on) but also a certain tone or approach. These have to do with the chosen mode of self-presentation. Variables include the levels of conformity, explicitness, and strength used in the process of giving expression to a client's image.

Some research conducted on interpersonal self-processes has focused on self-presentation, or impression management. Self-presentation approaches vary widely. Some people, for instance, are high self-monitors; they are concerned that their behavior is consistent with their conception of what the appropriate, or expected, behavior is in a given situation. They want to fit in and will tend to do what's in and acceptable. Others are low self-monitors; they are more concerned with being themselves and less with whether their behavior matches that of other people. This group makes little effort to conform to trends and other kinds of expectations. In general, high self-monitors are more concerned with image and are self-conscious while low self-monitors give more importance to pragmatic matters.[32] In the following sections, we discuss some variables related to self-presentation and individual preferences.

Load Level

The issues of order, complexity, and environmental load have been introduced already. Projects have a range of possible load levels, depending on the nature of the project and its users. Environments can range from highly stimulating to calming environments. In some cases, such as a nightclub or a relaxation spa, the desired load levels will be self-evident. In other cases, the designer has to probe further to determine the ideal level and make a choice congruent with the realities and goals of the project. The three restaurants shown in Figure 8.27 illustrate how the load level of a setting can range widely.

Abstraction

Not everyone appreciates abstraction, something many designers love to employ. Many people prefer more straightforward and literal compositions that look like something familiar. The more traditional client will demand flowery carpet borders and landscape scenes for their artwork; the more modern one will frown at such choices. Designers need to understand the preferences of their clients in this regard and design accordingly. Figure 8.28 shows two storefronts, one that is more symmetrical and pictorial and another that is more abstract.

Humor

This variable is concerned with the level of seriousness a client wants to project. Although related, humor does not always have to be consistent with friendliness. A warm, friendly enterprise may also have a serious tone whereas a cold, impersonal one may exhibit a slight bit of humor, even if dry. Depending on the desired intentions, the environment can be straightforward and serious or may tolerate humor through the use of unlikely objects, funny artwork, and so on. Sometimes humor is produced by the incorporation of unexpected content, be it through space and form or furnishings and accessories. Figure 8.29a

(a)

(b)

(c)

Figure 8.27: Environments, depending on their use and nature, have a preferred load-level range. The three restaurants shown vary in load level from low (a), to moderate (b), to high (c). As can be seen from these examples, one of the main factors affecting load level is the density of objects and accessories in the space.

shows the clever use of props, in this case stuffed animals, to give a children's clinic a humorous and friendly tone. Figure 8.29b features a retail space with a Volkswagen vehicle in the display area. This unconventional approach contributes to the playful and humorous character of the store.

(a)

(b)

Figure 8.28: Compositions can vary widely in their degree of abstraction. Some can be pictorial and literal (a) and others, more abstract (b).

(a)

(b)

Figure 8.29: Humor has useful applications in the design of some environments. This children's clinic uses stuffed animals to liven things up and reduce the fear of its patients (a). The store incorporates a car with the merchandise to produce a humorous surprise (b).

Formality

Related to both friendliness and humor is formality. Despite the general notion that warm, friendly people have a sense of humor and are more casual, other combinations are entirely possible. It is not uncommon to project warmth and friendliness in a formal environment or to have humor and formality, or seriousness and casualness, coexist harmoniously. A formal environment is produced by straight, symmetrical, rigid, and static arrangements. An informal or casual environment is associated more with asymmetrical, irregular, more organic arrangements. A formal environment is also characterized by uprightness, seriousness, and stiffness, while a casual environment is relaxed and pliable. Compare the levels of formality of the two storefronts shown in Figure 8.30.

(a)

(b)

Figure 8.30: Arrangement, materials, shapes, and content all contribute to formality. The store in (a) is relaxed and casual; the store in (b), serious and formal.

Intensity

Another important variable affecting self-presentation is the intensity used to express a project's character. It is a potency measure and is related to levels of extraversion and intensity. Like the other factors discussed in the previous sections, the type of presentation used will depend on the personality of the client and the requirements of the project. Intensity is related to and affects all the other variables, as every client preference will be colored by the intensity with which those variables are expressed. A client may like to show off success in a big way or may rather keep a low profile despite the success. An extroverted client may desire an office painted with bright, bold colors. On the other hand, a mellow restaurant owner may prefer a mellow kind of expression. A useful way to talk about intensity in design is through the concepts of boldness and subtlety.

High intensity environments are bold. Visually bold environments are intense and extroverted. Expressions of achievement, power, uniqueness, and other preferences are presented forcefully with little restraint. If part of the environment is to be off-limits to certain people, for instance, the barrier will be huge and there will be no confusion about the message. If the company is successful, you may expect to see exuberance. If the client is progressive, innovation will be expressed in no uncertain terms. If the users have a sense of humor, the place will surely make you laugh. If a group has preferences for, say, sensual form and complexity, expect to see unabashed curves and a very intense and complex environment. Of course, the designer is likely to help a bold client tone down a few items to achieve a healthy balance, but, if left untamed, this group would go all out and express all of its bold predispositions forcefully and loudly.

Boldness can be achieved many different ways, including the incorporation of high complexity, bright lighting, accented contrasts, strong colors, bold graphics, and unusual forms and furnishings. The gigantic wristwatch suspended from the ceiling in Figure 8.31 is an example of intentionally using bold props for expression.

Subtlety relies on restraint. Visually subtle environments express themselves in quiet ways. By subtlety, we don't mean lack of expression. In these cases, preferences and predispositions are communicated without

Figure 8.31: Expression can be loud and bold. The gigantic wristwatch suspended from the ceiling of this clock store is a rather bold statement.

Figure 8.32: Opposite to boldness is subtlety, characterized by light-handedness and restraint, as shown in the design of this office environment.

boasting. Success may be expressed without being ostentatious; traditionalism may be shown without getting too literal and stuffy; warmth may be shown without being cloying.

A project may have subtle expression due to the personality of its users, or it may be a conscious choice made to fit the project. Subtlety is often influenced by the designer. Taken to an extreme, subtlety can become minimalism, although subtlety implies intricacy handled delicately rather than simplicity and absence of expression. Subtlety is characterized by slimness, the use of soft colors, soft lighting, low contrast, and overall restraint. Obviously, there is a lot of ground between exaggerated boldness and pure subtlety, and many projects find their comfort zone somewhere in the middle. Notice the restrained character of the office scene shown in Figure 8.32.

Formal Properties

Under the heading of formal properties we group a number of miscellaneous stylistic aspects related to expression. These preferences are usually the concern of designers (creators) because clients, except the most sophisticated, are more concerned with other aspects of design, such as utility and comfort, and rarely get into this level of detail. Nevertheless, choices made about formal properties are often part of the designer's attempt to capture and express the essence of a client's identity.

Figural Character of Spaces, Masses, and Objects

The ways in which space and its elements are shaped and assembled can have different resulting characters. Some compositions flow; others are choppy. Depending on the character of the client and the desired expression, some design arrangements will be more suitable than others. Important factors include the shapes used, the perceptual weight of elements, and the character of the compositions.

The shape of interior space can take many configurations. These are most apparent on the shape of walls, the configurations of lines and patterns on two-dimensional surfaces (walls, ceilings, and floors), and the shape of furnishings and their components. Designers make conscious choices about the character of the shapes in their projects. A certain project may call for straight lines, others diagonal lines, others tight curves, and others smooth, sweeping curves. Curves often carry connotations of flair and sensuality, straight lines of straightforwardness and

(a)

(b)

(c)

Figure 8.33: Client and designers have preferences about shapes and forms. Areas of project often suggest particular geometries. Curvilinear shapes always make an impression. Notice the three applications of curves shown: one showing a round room (a), one a semicircular seating arrangement (b), and the third the powerful contributions of curved elements on the ceiling and the floor (c).

formality. Figure 8.33a–c shows applications of curvilinear shapes on a ceiling, wall, and floor plane.

Perceptual weight is another important formal property. It refers to the light- or heavy-handedness of design elements. Applications may include the size of vertical supports or the proportions of trim, column bases,

(a)

(b)

Figure 8.34: Weight is also an important consideration in the proportions chosen for trim. The two storefronts shown display various degrees of trim heaviness, ranging from very heavy (a) to light (b).

and other elements. Some projects call for a "light" feel, whereas others need a "meatier" look. A good example is the trim used for, say, framing a glass wall. Consider, for instance, the trims of the two storefronts shown in Figure 8.34 and look at their relative weights.

In addition to shapes and weight, the actual design composition plays a significant role in determining the figural character of spaces, masses, and objects. The size, number of parts, and arrangement of subcomponents impacts the final appearance of a given composition. To give a project its proper expression, a designer may ask the following questions: Should a certain composition be broken down into a few large pieces or many smaller pieces? Should parts be assembled seamlessly, or should they read as individual pieces on the same background?

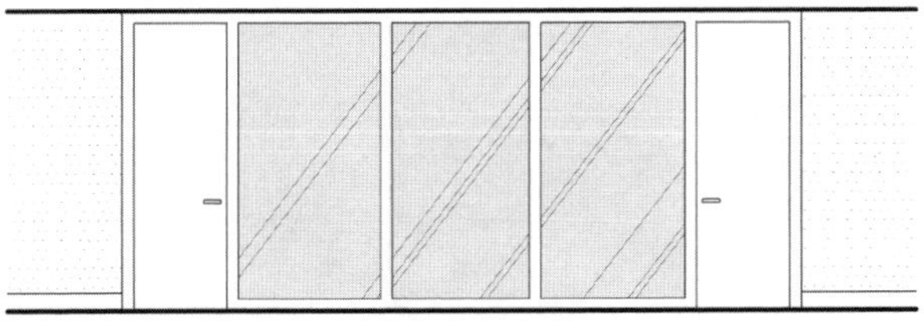

(a)

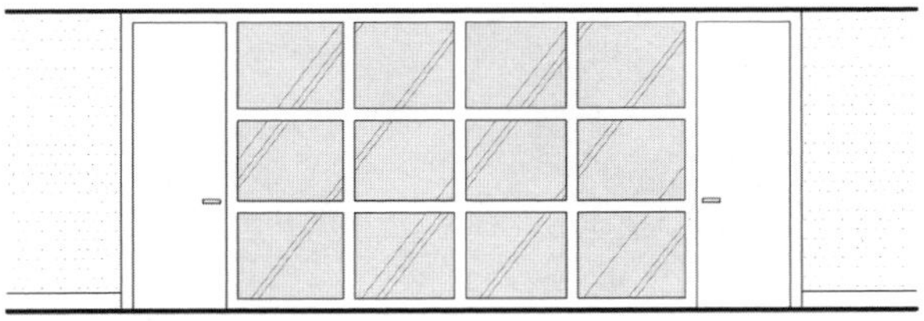

(b)

Figure 8.35: Different compositions convey different expressions. The wall composition in (a) features a few full-height parts and produces a subtle, uncluttered elevation. The composition in (b) features greater modulation and produces a richer, more complex effect.

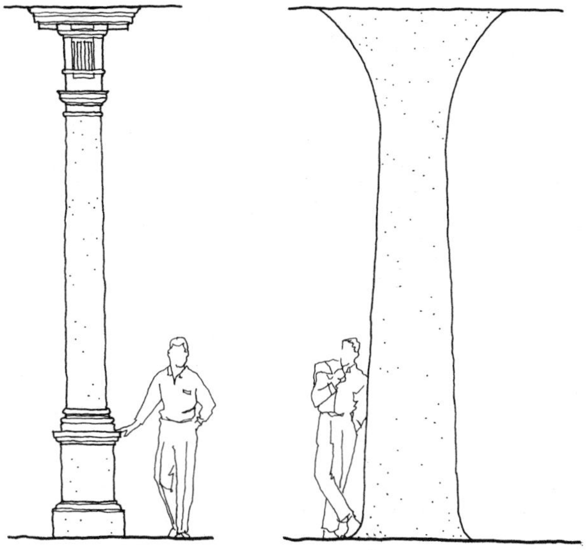

(a) (b)

Figure 8.37: Objects, masses, and planes can look like assemblies achieved by the careful combination of many parts (a). They look like plastic-type objects that are shaped from a single piece (b).

Figure 8.35 shows the composition of two elevations. Figure 8.35a features just a few large pieces, while Figure 8.35b shows the same wall divided into a greater number of smaller pieces. Notice the difference. Now look at Figure 8.36, which shows the same elevation shown in Figure 8.35b fragmented into separate individual sections. Notice the specific look it takes.

Another related composition issue refers to the method of construction used to shape form. Some elements look like they were carved from a single piece; others appear to be composed through the assembly of many pieces arranged into a single composition. Compare the two columns shown in Figure 8.37. The column in Figure 8.37b is made up of one piece that has been shaped. It is pure as it is and consists of only one part. It can be changed only by "carving" it further. The character of the column in Figure 8.37a is quite different. It is clearly composed of parts that have been assembled together in a specific arrangement. Each part contributes to the whole but also reads as a distinct part that can be changed independently.

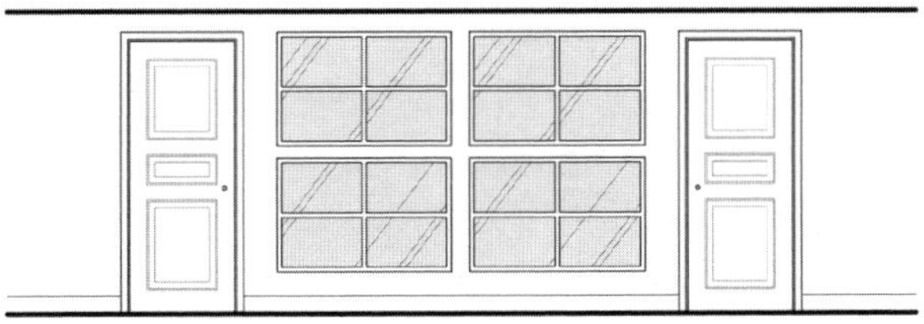

Figure 8.36: Compositions can look like an overall piece that has been subdivided, such as the two elevations shown in Figure 8.35, or they can look like individual parts that have been brought close together to form a group. This elevation is similar to the one in Figure 8.35, but this time it is fragmented into distinct individual parts and has a very different feel.

Material Palette

A highly influential aspect of projects is the choice of the material palette. Materials have an immense impact on the expression of a project. Possibilities and variations are countless. We will focus here on one particular kind of differentiation among material palettes to illustrate the point: the distinction between natural material palettes and manufactured ones. Natural material palettes use wood, stones, and natural textiles and give a more organic, or natural, feel. Manufactured palettes use materials such as metals, plastics, and glass and give a more industrial look. Some designers favor one approach over the other, while some combine the two successfully. Choosing one or the other will produce radically different looks and project very different expressions. These material expressions can be found mostly on walls, frames, doors, trims, and furnishings. Notice

(a) (b)

Figure 8.38: Different materials carry different expressive connotations. Note the different effects produced in the two environments shown by virtue of their materials. Notice the different effects created by the use of wood paneling and granite floors (a), and steel and glass (b).

(a) (b)

Figure 8.39: Ornamentation, although still used, has been substituted by detailing. Ornamentation implies applied decoration, while detailing implies intrinsic form. The approach used carries specific connotations and stylistic inclinations. The modern detailing approach used for the coffee bar design (a) is quite different from the ornamental drinking fountain (b).

the different feel of the two scenes in Figure 8.38 based on their material palette.

Ornamentation

One final important category is the attitude toward ornamentation. Today, many designers see applied decoration as fake and unnecessary; however, many designers and clients enjoy ornamentation, and some projects demand it. Each project and client has a specific character, and many times the use of applied ornamentation will be the most fitting approach for a project.

As an alternative, it is also possible to utilize inherent detailing and carefully selected accessories, artwork, and finishes to give projects the richness once supplied by applied ornamentation, shunning away from applied embellishments. Figure 8.39 shows a carefully detailed contemporary coffee bar and a more ornamental, yet restrained, drinking water fountain in a niche.

GROUP IDENTITY

So far, our discussion of identity has focused on personality traits, self-images, and preferences of individuals, both in general and as clients. It is not difficult to think of groups and organizations that would have some of the same self-images and personalities as those discussed. Now we shift our attention to group or collective identity, referring to the identity of larger enterprises. The development of these identities into expressive environments relies strongly on the design concepts adopted for the projects. Examples include the image that corporations adopt and the identity of establishments that cater to specific publics such as shops and restaurants. In the following sections, we look at corporate, restaurant, and retail identities. A capsule in this chapter takes a specific look at branding.

Corporate Identity

Not only individuals have a sense of self. An organization also has a sense of self, an identity. As Nicholas Ind explains, such identity is unique and "is formed by an organization's history, its beliefs and philosophy, the nature of its technology, its ownership, its people, the personality of its leaders, its ethical and cultural values and its strategies. . . . It is not something cosmetic, but is the core of an organization's existence."[33] During these times of increased diversification and globalization, companies are becoming decentralized and, consequently, losing their sense of cohesion. For these companies, now more than ever, it is essential to find a common identity. Ind explains:

> Corporate communication is the process that translates an identity into an image. This is a vital part of the process because a corporate identity, if it is to have any value, has to be communicated to employees, shareholders and customers alike. Without communication the values and strategies of the organization will not be understood or owned and the company will not have any clear sense of identity.[34]

Although corporate communications cannot turn a poor company into a success, it can "convey a consistent and credible message of what a company is, what it does and how it does it, by trying to control the messages it transmits."[35] Wally Olins states that corporate identity is concerned with four major areas of activity:

1. Products and Services: What you make or sell
2. Environments: Where you make or sell it, the place or physical context
3. Information: How you describe and publicize what you do
4. Behavior: How people within the organization behave to each other and to outsiders[36]

The identity mix of product-based companies is dominated by the product, how it feels, what it looks like, what it costs, how it works, and so on (e.g., Apple and Nike). Some companies, in turn, have identities dominated by environments (e.g., Hilton or Marriott), and it is the places themselves that come to mind and dominate our impressions.

Many identities are communication-led. Often associated with generic products or commodities, these otherwise anonymous and undifferentiated products are brought to life through information techniques, especially advertising. This is how a product like Coca-Cola, "a maroon fizzy liquid of—some would say—no intrinsic interest of merit,"[37] became a global success. Finally, there are service-based organizations that depend on how their people behave for their success (e.g., a police force). In practice, the identity of a company is a mix of all four areas of activity, even if one area dominates.

Olins explains how Vidal Sassoon was an early pioneer of the successful use of identity programs, utilizing all the classic identity tools to exploit a commercial opportunity in the 1960s. The products were the styling of hair and the hair-care products required for hair maintenance; the environments were the open, lively, unisex salons; the information was the cleverly devised publicity, advertising, and public relations used to heavily promote the business; and the behavior was the relaxed, informal, and friendly atmosphere created by the staff working in the salons (Figure 8.40).

Shops and Restaurants

Our main interest as designers is in the environment component of the identity matrix, because it is there that we make our main contribution. In the retail and restaurant markets, the role of the facilities is crucial. The identity of restaurants is closely linked to the restaurant concept, something that is chosen intentionally by the owner and his consultants. Restaurants try to project a total image to appeal to their chosen market, whether defined as families or executives, formal or informal, inexpensive or pricey. Here again, various factors work together to create the total image: location, layout, decor, menu, operational style, the appearance of the staff, the background music, and, of course, the actual food and its presentation. The image produced is most successful when it is vivid, clear, and easily remembered.

A great example of a strong concept with a strong sense of identity is the Hard Rock Cafe. The original, in London, was conceived to offer economical American food

Figure 8.40: Vidal Sassoon was an early pioneer in the use of identity programs. The company's program, which included hair products, lively unisex salons, and friendly staff, still thrives today.

in an energetic environment that celebrated rock music, past and present. The concept caught on and spread to other major cities. Decorations consist of memorabilia from rock stars, from Bowie to Hendrix, from Presley to Madonna. Apparel and memorabilia for sale help to propagate the image.[38]

In restaurants, every detail contributes to the total image and experience: Materials, color, form, space, light, uniforms, napery, glassware, flatware, china, and menu graphics constitute the stage setting and the props. The staff and clientele are the actors. At the Chart House restaurants, servers are dressed in attractive Hawaiian shirts and dresses. Their natural nautical decor, warm woods, and privileged locations next to water complement the total experience.[39]

Retail stores, like restaurants, cater to well-defined markets and rely on strong concepts to convey their identities. Millard Drexler of the Gap explains the importance of an easy-to-recognize identity: "It was critical, not only to our image but to our success, that the customer get an immediate visual sense of what the store stood for. . . . Today, the Gap's philosophy is to have an easy, simple-to-shop, very pointed assortment of clothing with color as an emphasis."[40] Their stores, merchandise, and advertising are clean, simple, and uncluttered.

The Pea in the Pod store in Dallas was conceived to cater to the pregnant woman "who had any sense of style." The philosophy of the store is to provide pregnant women high-quality and stylish clothing in a high-service kind of environment. The stores are designed "to have the sparkle, ease, and light of one's own home . . . an architecture not to interfere with the clothing, but to create a feeling of comfort in an understated way, so that the customers would not even be aware of why they felt comfortable." Also important was the goal of creating "architectural touches that were consistent with our customers' own personal environment and socioeconomic level."[41]

Catering to a specific age group and socioeconomic status is an important consideration in the design of many shops and restaurants. Shops, accordingly, will project an image sensitive to the affinities of the target group. This is especially pronounced when it comes to fashion, where every store will project an image that will attract the intended audience by catering to their age and status. The visual symbols used through the architecture, signage, graphics, and merchandise project an image that caters to a specific group, be it children, teens, young adults, adults, or mature adults. Looking at the two stores shown in Figure 8.41, one gets an immediate sense that the store in Figure 8.41a caters to a younger crowd than the store in Figure 8.41b.

Specific expressions can be manifested through design. In some cases, these expressions cater to the members of a particular group while sending messages to others that the place is not for them; however, many environments are intentionally designed in such a way that everyone can feel at home. Some types of projects, such as clinics and some public buildings, even demand it. If done with sensitivity and skill, these can be attractive, genuine, and successful. If not, they can be as bland as food that tries to cater to all tastes.

(a)

(b)

Figure 8.41: Particular treatments and images can project qualities that are congruent with the affinities of specific age groups. This is particularly evident in the world of retail, where some stores cater to a young crowd (a) and others cater to a more mature crowd (b).

CAPSULE | Branding

Think of big powerful brands and what comes to mind? Coca-Cola, Microsoft, Nike, Apple—just to name a few. Big powerful brands have existed as long as the media that has disseminated their message. Behind them have been the megaworlds of advertising, radio, and television. Why, all of a sudden, would the world of architecture and interior design enter the world of branding? For years, the powerful brands have relied upon clever copywriters, graphic artists, and other ad makers. Why are designers, all of a sudden, claiming some ground in this competitive arena? What do we have to offer? Let's first go back and try to understand how branding became such a powerful phenomenon.

Although the idea of bolstering product names through the media was widely acknowledged as important, the focus of manufacturers was, until recently, on the production of goods. Yet, all that changed in the mid-1980s. As Naomi Klein explains, the immense growth in the wealth and influence of multinational corporations in the recent past has been triggered by "a single, innocuous idea developed by management theorists in the mid-1980s: that successful corporations must primarily produce brands, as opposed to products."[1] As the Nikes and Tommy Hilfigers claimed and proved, the secret was to produce not goods (those could be made cheaply overseas) but images of their brands. There was no need, they reasoned, to have oversized corporations full of employees and things, when the real secret was owning the least, having the fewest employees on the payroll, and producing powerful images.

One company who had success with the newfound secret was The Body Shop. During the recession of the late 1980s and early 1990s, The Body Shop started an aggressive growth campaign in the United States, opening 40 to 50 stores a year. As Klein relates, "It pulled off the expansion without spending a dime on advertising. Who needed billboards and magazine ads when retail stores were three-dimensional advertisements for an ethical and ecological approach to cosmetics? The Body Shop was all brand." Also expanding during this time without spending much in advertising was Starbucks, the coffee chain. Pretty soon Starbucks was everywhere, from the airport terminal to the airplane cabin, to the corporate boardroom, to the strategic downtown corner, "incorporating marketing into every fiber of its corporate concept—from the chain's strategic association with books, blues, and jazz to its Euro-latte lingo." The new companies had transcended the old routine of splashing logos on billboards. "Here were two companies that had fostered powerful identities by making their brand concept into a virus and sending it out into the culture via a variety of channels: cultural sponsorship, political controversy, the consumer experience and brand extensions. Direct advertising, in this context, was viewed as a rather clumsy intrusion into a much more organic approach to image building."[2] Starbucks knew about the importance of establishing emotional ties with customers. As Starbuck's CEO Howard Schulz once expressed, the people who line up for Starbucks aren't just there for the coffee: "It's the romance of the coffee experience, the feeling of warmth and community people get in Starbucks stores."[3]

In the brand builders' vision of success, products are presented "not as commodities, but as concepts: the brand as experience, as lifestyle."[4] Now instead of presenting Brand XYZ as a product, it is presented as "a way of life, an attitude, a set of values, a look, an idea." Consequently, Nike's mission "is not to sell shoes but to *enhance people's lives through sports and fitness* and to *keep the magic of sports alive*." Likewise, IBM is not about selling computers but "*selling business solutions*," Swatch is not about watches, it is about "*the idea of time*,"[5] and McDonald's is not about selling burgers, it is about "*convenience*" and "*fun*."[6]

For a brand to work well it has to speak to its audience in some way, representing a desired lifestyle or a unique service it aspires to experience. More than ubiquity, visibility, and function, brands are now more about "emotionally bonding."[7] Their personalities communicate the brand proposition to their target audiences through design. A brand can be designed to be old-fashioned and traditional, glamorous and romantic, or, in the case of the Virgin brand, "fun, wacky, impulsive, and irreverent."[8] Being responsible for giving form to brand ideas,

continued

designers have to be able to think of a brand as a person and then ask questions, such as: If you were a shop or a restaurant, what kind of shop or restaurant would you be?

Helen Vaid classifies brands into two broad categories: corporate and consumer brands. "Corporate brands usually relate to a company itself . . . but can also be used broadly to describe services offered to other businesses (rather than to consumers). Consumer brands, on the other hand, relate to the physical products or services that the company offers to its (noncorporate) customers."[9] She also classifies brands by industry, as follows:

Service brands deal with not an object but a performance. The impression made by a particular airline during a typical air-travel experience is a good example.

Retail brands offer great opportunities to designers, as they require special environments that offer unique and engaging experiences. "The various aspects of interior design—graphics, layout, display systems, color schemes, fascias, signage, and even sounds and smells—all have to be considered, planned, and created for a given floor space, but still within the boundaries of the overall brand design."

Consumer product brands are the most commonly and heavily branded. Included here are many familiar product brands, such as Wheaties, Pepsi, and Sony.

Industrial product brands deal with products intended for businesses, not consumers.

Commodity brands are used for commodity goods (generic goods such as toothpaste, oatmeal, and bananas). Despite the lack of differentiation between these generic products, their branding campaigns influence our perceptions of their apparent desirability and influence our choice of brands such as Colgate, Quaker, and Chiquita over their competitors.[10]

Now we come back to the earlier question. Why has the world of branding become so important to architects and interior designers? Or, why are architects and interior designers so important to today's branding efforts? After all, as Eleanor Curtis puts it, "Can the interior spaces and hanging rails really inform the customer about the brand?"[11] A common-sense reply is the argument that good design helps clients stand out in an oversaturated, crowded business world. Nancye Green explains: "Today, it is clearer to all marketers that the real threat to dominance in any single market segment is the difficulty of establishing, and then maintaining, relationships with empowered customers in a world of abundant choices, shifting distribution channels, and powerful new retail formats."[12] Today, the need to promote a message of being distinctive in order to stand out is essential for survival. Good, attractive design by itself is often not enough, though. Businesses must go further and establish an emotional bond with their clients by creating strong and engaging brands their clients can buy into.

As Curtis explains, in regards to fashion retail, "Today, in our all-consuming, all-pervading culture, when we purchase a product we are buying into the brand. The building, the logo, the advertising, the fashion model, even the shop assistants, in addition to the clothes and accessories themselves, all tie-up this thing called 'image' or brand. In a sense, buying into this is like buying into a club membership. A customer will identify with a brand that reflects his or her tastes and will gravitate towards those names, reinforcing his or her self-image, just as one becomes a member of a club."[13] She goes on to explain what architecture can add to the overall image the customer has already bought into. One of architecture's contributions, according to Curtis, "is in the all-encompassing nature of the built form: the store is more than just products and may say something about a way of doing, a way of being, or a way to organize. . . . The design of a space can represent our social background, our income, our cultural values, our age, our aspirations."[14] Otto Riewoldt reiterates, "Brands signal our membership of an 'in' group. They are the tools with which we build status. They ensure we belong and give us security. Brands build emotions, promise happiness and provide kicks. This decisive paradigm shift has taken place on the emotional plane of the brand experience."[15]

"Brandscaping," as Riewoldt explains, "the three-dimensional design of brand settings—is all about forging backdrops for experiences with a high entertainment value."[16] While advertisers may get a few seconds on the air or a two-page spread, designers of environments "can formulate and shape narratives, drawing on the dimensions of space and time, to weave together the breadth of elements necessary to build a totally immersive experience."[17] The quality of the brand experience is founded on direct interaction and a very specific kind of encounter. "We are not talking about virtual non-experiences in the no-man's-land of the internet, but about concrete encounters in real locations, where the world of the brand is staged and enacted. Here we can experience the manifestation, the messages and the emotions of the brand in company with the products themselves, in unadulterated, unusual, and unique style. . . . By staging the brand experience in flagship stores, shop designs or entire theme parks, companies communicate the image of the brand and imprint a characteristic atmosphere on the customer consciousness."[18]

Interior design, in fact, has become one of the most powerful tools for creating the brand experience by stimulating emotions, sensory experiences, and, ultimately, sales. "Sensory experiences are instant, potent and capable of influencing buying decisions in both the long and short term," states Vaid. In place of traditional retail, now there's "the 'art of shopping,' which is less about purchasing and more about creating all-embracing experiences of a brand."[19] Extreme examples include the shrinelike Niketown stores and Disney, one of the first to create a microcosmos reflecting a brand.

Julian E. Markham, author of *The Future of Shopping*, believes design innovation is key in today's rapidly changing and competitive marketplace. Today, Markham writes, "it's no longer enough to do it well, you also need to do it new. . . . A new age of innovation is in progress. The key words are 'surprise,' 'delight,' and 'surpass.' . . . Architecture and spatial design have become major elements in retail presentation. Their place in the overall scene and promotion of the retailer, the merchandise and the message is a delicate balance of complementary aesthetics, seduction, and comfort."[20]

Sociologist Gerhard Schulze explains the way some of these "experience settings" act as "backdrops to happiness, providing a brief experience, a short sensation of happiness," where the customer becomes a character in the play. The most important thing becomes to engage the customer, "not to sell the product but to generate a fascination with the brand: to get the customer to identify with the world of the brand, creating a brand awareness and providing it with a deep-set emotional anchor."[21]

Riewoldt believes the balance between familiarity and surprise is also critical. "As actors, customers must encounter familiar aspects and be able to find their way around by recognizing landmarks or layouts, but at the same time there must be exciting new elements for them to experience. In brandscaping, architecture and interior design are the stage that provides a setting for ever changing scenes. As the immediate environment of the brand experience, salesrooms and shopping centers themselves take on brand character. Down to the finest detail of interior design, they are geared to transmit a message that translates design into emotional impact."[22]

Branding has indeed become an important topic in the lives of many architects and interior designers. Green puts it in perspective: "This kind of brand-building is the topic du jour, and what is specially compelling is that we are now critical members of the brand-building team. Today, we have the chance to bring to the table more than design expertise. We can be true partners in giving life to brands and in building relationships with customers through deeply engaging experiences. We have a tremendous opportunity: our domain is extraordinarily rich and uniquely powerful."[23]

As a critical member of the branding team it is the designer's responsibility to learn how the interior design medium can create the kinds of sensory experiences required to consummate the emotional bonding so critical to the branding experience. It is also important to understand the interplay between the interior design medium and other messages conveyed by other media. As Riewoldt stresses, "The design of the retail environment must merge with the brand image down to the finest details. Expressiveness, the purposeful use of characteristic forms, and calculated elements of surprise combine to make an integral whole."[24]

Green concludes, "We are not simply designing stores and restaurants and shopping malls . . . we're impacting the total relationship between brand and customer. We are creating the *experience* of the brand."[25]

continued

Exercise

Next, we present paired photographs of well-known brands from different retail niches. Discuss in class your perceptions of these brands, addressing the following:

1. How would you describe the *brand idea* in a short statement?
2. How would you describe the *brand experience* in a short statement?
3. How is one brand different from the one it is paired with?
4. Invent a third brand in each of these market segments. What is the idea? What is the brand experience like? What kind of physical environment would best support the brand?

(a)

(b)

(c)

(d)

(e)

(f)

1. Klein, N. (2000). *No logo*. New York: Picador.
2. Ibid, p. 20.
3. Ibid.
4. Ibid, p. 21.
5. Ibid, p. 23.
6. Vaid, H. (2003). *Branding*. New York: Watson Guptill.
7. Ibid, p. 8.
8. Ibid, p. 36.
9. Ibid, p. 30.
10. Ibid, pp. 30–33.
11. Curtis, E. (2004). *Fashion retail*. West Sussex, UK: Wiley.
12. Green, N. (1998, May). Creating the brand experience. *Interiors Magazine*, Vol CLVII(5), p. 241.
13. Curtis, 2004, p. 14.
14. Ibid, pp. 14–15.
15. Riewoldt, O. (Ed.). (2002). *Brandscaping: Worlds of experience in retail buildings*. Boston: Birkhauser.
16. Ibid, p. 7.
17. Green, N. (1998, May). Creating the brand experience. *Interiors Magazine*, Vol CLVII(5), p. 241.
18. Riewoldt, 2002, p. 8.
19. Vaid, 2003, p. 82.
20. Markham, J. E. (2000). E-tail and the increased importance of retail innovation. In H. Castle (Ed.), *Fashion and architecture* (pp. 25–26). London: Wiley-Academy.
21. Riewoldt, 2002, p. 10.
22. Ibid, p. 11.
23. Green, N. (1998, May). Creating the brand experience. *Interiors Magazine*, Vol CLVII(5), p. 241.
24. Riewoldt, 2002, p. 79.
25. Green, N. (1998, May). Creating the brand experience. *Interiors Magazine*, Vol CLVII(5), p. 241.

Designer's Personal Expression

Every project's expression, however indicative of the realities of the program, context, and client's identity, is also an expression of the attitudes and beliefs of its designer. All the kinds of expression discussed up to this point, after all, get filtered through your own judgment and you ultimately decide what gets expressed and how strongly. Additionally, as the designer you carry a responsibility to the profession, and your decisions are made within the context of a set of current norms in design. Both timeless principles and current trends affect the design climate in which designers operate. There are also personal tendencies and beliefs held dear by individual designers. All these affect the ultimate expression of a project.

Next, we look at three major factors that affect the kind of expression designers choose for a project: the designer's personal style, attitude about current design norms, and use of symbolic expression.

The Designer's Personal Style

All designers have particular design tendencies and a certain design range within which they like to operate. For some the range is broad, encompassing diverse ways of designing, whereas for others it is quite narrow. Many designers develop distinct styles that become their signature style. People who share affinities with that style will seek them out to be their designers. Some designers operate within strict modernistic principles of simplicity and austerity, while others are more flamboyant and decorative.

Designers, like clients, have specific preferences and predispositions. They will, consciously or not, try to influence the project to arrive at an expression within their own range of preferences. The final expression the project takes is usually a combination of the expressions agreeable to both client and designer. When clients seek designers whose style is compatible with their own tendencies, the bargaining process becomes a much smoother one. Many clients either don't feel comfortable making or don't have time to make choices about expression and look to their designers to take charge and get the job done.

Other than style, per se, designers can endow projects with particular expressions based on their personal attitudes about composition, materials, and construction approach. They can also express their own convictions about materials and their use. Some will prefer natural materials, whereas others will choose man-made ones.

Some will strive for a highly crafted look and others for a very artsy look.

When it comes to craftsmanship, some designers believe that it is important to reveal the way design elements are put together for all to see and understand. American architect Louis Kahn, for example, was known for designs that revealed the structure of a building in its many details. This approach carries with it the additional burden of having to resolve every detail clearly so they can be displayed, understood, and appreciated. Many designs express exquisite detailing and craftsmanship. These attest to the great skill of the designer who conceived and worked out the details and, in many cases, to the skill of the individuals who built them.

Another important aspect of design for which designers develop personal convictions is the issue of honesty of expression. This involves questions, as Robertson said, "of architectural 'deceit' or 'honesty,' and of the borderline between legitimate make-believe and trickery."[42]

The Designer's Attitude about Current Design Norms

All design occurs within a given artistic climate of the time. At any time, certain tendencies and trends will be in vogue, and designers often feel compelled to go with the flow and design of the current trends. This is not always the case. The design profession, not unlike music and the other arts, has its share of rebels who enjoy going against the tide, either for the sake of noncompliance or because they genuinely disagree with the trend. Instead of adopting the current style, they ignore it or even mock it.

Although it is essential that you recognize the current design trends at any one time, you are not obligated to abide by them. If you dislike a current design trend, cultivate whatever you believe is the correct approach; just do it with care and skill.

The Designer's Use of Symbolic Expression

Many architectural and interior designers like to go beyond the basic expressions of a project. They do so through the use of often sophisticated symbolism, metaphoric expressions, and similar devices. All these are legitimate in design but must be used with skill, restraint, and caution because often these clever design expressions go unnoticed by most people. If the level of symbolism or abstraction is too high, most people will fail to make the desired associations between symbol and meaning. Nevertheless, these techniques can be useful and meaningful in projects whose users or public share common meanings and symbols. In these cases, allusions to common symbols, historic events, or important people can be understood and appreciated by all the insiders familiar with them. Possible gestures include the placement of a given function of particular symbolic importance in the center of the project, or the orientation of the main circulation spine of a project on axis with the original location of the company three blocks away.

Another way designers try to endow projects with meaning is by responding and giving expression to the essence of the product or service associated with a given entity. The expressive characters of the two storefronts in Figure 8.42 fit the nature of the merchandise sold in

(a)

(b)

Figure 8.42: Sometimes the shapes, proportions, and materials used can reinforce the character of the products associated with a place. Compare the heavier approach of the fur store (a) to the lighter feel of the lingerie store (b). Both approaches seem to fit with the character of their merchandise.

them. The graphics, geometry, and massing of the fur store are appropriately heavy while the same elements in the lingerie store are much lighter and delicate. Figure 8.43 shows an example of a straightforward shoe display in a corporate environment celebrating the product associated with the company. In Figure 8.44 the designer expresses the essence of the company's name and products by emulating the fluidness of water through the forms used. Finally, Figure 8.45 is an example of the use of humorous expression by the integration of one of the main characters associated with Warner Bros., in this case Daffy Duck.

Figure 8.43: The functions or products associated with a given enterprise can be manifested in many ways. One effective approach is the use of straightforward displays that feature the function or product in question.

Figure 8.44: Forms and materials can be expressive of the products and functions associated with a given enterprise. This example shows the clever use of fluid forms and glass to capture the feel of water, the name and theme of the store.

Figure 8.45: Props are often effective in reinforcing the products and functions associated with a given entity. In this example, the forms, logos, and signs of the store are reinforced by the presence of a well-known Warner Bros. character.

Any long-lasting intellectual or artistic pursuit requires an ideology, a framework of principles and ideas that explains and justifies our actions and gives them direction. An artist today needs a personal ideology in order to accomplish original work. We build our ideology using pieces we gather throughout our lives from parents, teachers, books, friends, other artists, and most important, from our own thoughts and experiences.[1]

Designers usually start their careers with a vague and loose ideological framework consisting largely of borrowed ideas. That is fine. As they gain experience, though, they start to develop more precise personal beliefs that they express in their designs. As Cesar Pelli points out, "In order to do significant work, however, we need to reinterpret and modify shared ideas and make them part of a personal body of thoughts. The more we develop our individual position, the more we move away from that of our peers."[2]

In this piece, we expose you to beliefs expressed by four influential design thinkers. They are excerpted from proclamations committed to writing by them at particular points in time. To become a great designer, you will need clarity and consistency of approach. This requires having, at any one time, a set of personal convictions that helps you decide, for each project, which is the right path to take from among all the design approaches possible for that project. The intent of this piece is as much to present four different ways of thinking about design approaches as it is to encourage you to initiate your own personal ideology.

Venturi on Complexity and Contradiction

In 1966, the Museum of Modern Art published Robert Venturi's *Complexity and Contradiction in Architecture,* a highly influential manifesto that critiqued the shortcomings of modern architecture. In it, Venturi attacks the reductive tendencies of modern architecture and the pure, but boring, designs it produced. He thought architecture had to get up to par with science, poetry, and visual art and acknowledge complexity and contradiction.

"I like complexity and contradiction in architecture," Venturi's manifesto begins. "I do not like the incoherence or arbitrariness of incompetent architecture nor the precious intricacies of picturesqueness or expressionism. Instead, I speak of complex and contradictory architecture based on the richness and ambiguity of modern experience, including experience which is inherent in art."[3] He points out not only the inherent complexity of life but also the increasing complexity of buildings and their programs. How could anyone try to simplify, he wonders, that which is inherently complex?

"The doctrine of 'less is more' bemoans complexity and justifies exclusion for expressive purposes."[4] Here Venturi condemns the practice of selectivity in determining which problems to solve. One can be selective in how one approaches problems but shouldn't select which problems to approach. Isn't one supposed to tackle them all? "Mies's exquisite pavilions have indeed had valuable implications for architecture, but is not their selectiveness of content and language their limitation as well as their strength? . . . Such forced simplicity is oversimplification. . . . Where simplicity cannot work, simpleness results. Blatant simplification means bland architecture. Less is a bore."[5] This doesn't mean that one cannot strive for simplicity. But, according to Venturi, "aesthetic simplicity . . . derives from inner complexity,"[6] and he goes on to demonstrate how the Doric temple achieves apparent simplicity through real complexity. He is obviously referring to resolved complexity.

Venturi also favors contradiction in his aim for vitality as well as validity. He explains: "I like elements which are hybrid rather than 'pure,' compromising rather than 'clean,' distorted rather than 'straightforward,' ambiguous rather than articulated, perverse as well as 'impersonal,' boring as well as 'interesting,' conventional rather than 'designed,' accommodating rather than excluding, redundant rather than simple, vestigial as well as innovating, inconsistent and equivocal rather than direct and clear. I am for messy vitality over obvious unity."[7] He strives to produce an architecture that "evokes many levels of meaning and combinations of focus: its space and its elements become readable and workable in several ways at once."[8]

Contradictory levels of meaning involve paradoxical contrast, and the level of ambiguity varies. Something can be closed, yet open. Venturi prefers "both-and" to "either-or" and the finer distinctions it permits. He also advocates the "double-functioning" element, which performs multiple functions related to use and structure, as opposed to "both-and," which emphasizes double meaning.

"An architecture of complexity and contradiction," he stresses, "does not mean picturesqueness or willfull expressionism. If I am against purity, I am also against picturesqueness. False complexity currently counters false simplicity."[9] Complexity must arise out of the program and the structure of the whole and not from just the desire to be expressive. In the end, he assures, "an architecture of complexity and contradiction has a special obligation towards the whole: its truth must be in its totality or its implications of totality. It must embody the difficult unity of inclusion rather than the easy unity of exclusion. More is not less."[10]

Graves on Figurative Architecture

Michael Graves, another critic of modernism, rejects the lack of character of modernism. His humanistic architecture is representational and suggestive, relying on articulation, color, and historical references. He distinguishes between building (the practical aspects of architecture) and architecture (the symbolic representation of culture and its myths).

"The poetic form of architecture," he explains, "is responsive to issues external to the building, and incorporates the three-dimensional expression of the myths and rituals of society. Poetic forms in architecture are sensitive to the figurative, associative, and anthropomorphic attitudes of a culture."[11] Graves strongly believes in architecture's duty to register society's patterns of ritual and condemns the nonfigural abstract geometries of the modern movement.

While acknowledging the practical physical side of architecture, he reminds us "that the components of architecture have not only derived from pragmatic necessity but also evolved from symbolic sources." A defender of the integrity of an element's anthropomorphic and figurative meanings, Graves expresses dismay at modern architecture's audacity to transform the window from an element that helps "us make sense not only of the landscape beyond but also of our own position relative to the geometry of the window and to the building as a whole"[12] to disorienting window walls. He advocates the use of thematic and figural aspects of design. Associations can be made with natural phenomena (ground as floor), and anthropomorphic allusions (column as man).

Figurative architecture assumes "that the thematic character of a work is grounded in nature and is simultaneously read in a totemic or anthropomorphic manner."[13] Thus, a wall, similar to the window that helps us understand our size and presence in the room, fulfills both pragmatic and symbolic functions. Its tripartite division (wainscot, body, soffit), while not intended to imitate man, helps to stabilize the wall relative to the room, an important secondary function.

Modern architecture lost its sense for figural void, the form of space. Amorphic, continuous space, such as in Mies's Barcelona Pavilion (once again) "dissolves any reference to our understanding of figural void or space." Such space is "oblivious to bodily or totemic reference, and we therefore always find ourselves unable to feel centered in such a space. This lack of figural reference ultimately contributes to a feeling of alienation in buildings based on such singular propositions." It is crucial, Graves concludes, "that we reestablish the thematic associations invented by our culture in order to fully allow the culture of architecture to represent the mythic and ritual aspirations of society."[14]

Porphyrios on Classical Architecture

Another critic of modernism, Demetri Porphyrios also attacks the scenographic and eclectic tendencies of postmodernists and instead advocates authentic classicism. "The aim of modern eclecticism," he points out, "has been to look at historical styles merely as communicative devices, as labels and clothing. Style itself was seen as having no natural relationship to the tectonics of building." He criticizes "the pluralism that sprung out of an age of conciliatory culture, widespread visiting of the

continued

beliefs of all countries and all ages, accepting everything without fixing any part, since truth is everywhere in bits and nowhere in its entirety."[15]

Although modernism showed, and not concealed, the elements used to construct a work of art, "postmodernist works show themselves for the contrivance they are, but in doing so they also state that everything else in life is a contrivance and that simply there is no escape from this. Hence the self-referential circularity of the postmodern quotation and the extreme fascination with parody and metalinguistic commentary."[16]

Porphyrios believes the metalinguistic attempts of the high-tech branch of postmodernism resulted in buildings that are "only make-believe simulations of high-tech imagery."[17] Meanwhile, the postmodern classicists rely on parody. "They favour playful distortion, citation, deliberate anachronism, diminution, oxymoron, and so on. Ultimately, this is yet another make-believe cardboard architecture."[18] The third group of postmodernists criticized by Porphyrios are the deconstructionists who "loudly reject such ideas as order, intelligibility, and tradition. Architecture is supposed to become an experience of failure and crisis. And if crisis is not there, well then, it must be created."[19] Although these three versions of postmodernism are different, they all share a similar scenographic view of architecture.

His view is that of a classicist. Classicists, he explains, "adopt the theory of imitation. Art, it is argued, imitates the real world by turning selected significant aspects of it into mythical representations. . . . Similarly, a Classicist would argue architecture is the imitative celebration of construction and shelter qualified by the myths and ideas of a given culture."[20] Contrary to the mute realism of modernism, "what makes classical architecture possible is the dialogic relationship it establishes between the craft of building and the art of architecture. Our imagination traverses this dialogic space between, say, a pergola and a colonnade, and establishes hierarchies, levels of propriety, and communicable systems of evaluation."[21]

Wheras many designers tend to value what is new and different, Porphyrios suggests that the contribution of an architect "lies in what he/she chooses to borrow."[22] He sums up his view: "Architecture has nothing to do with 'novelty-mania' and intellectual sophistries. Architecture has nothing to do with transgression, boredom, or parody. It has nothing to do with parasitic life, excremental culture or the cynical fascination with the bad luck of others. Architecture has to do with decisions that concern the good, the decent, the proper . . . Surely, what constitutes a proper life varies from one historical period to another. But it is our responsibility to define it anew all the time."[23]

An Architecture of Reality

The final view presented is by Michael Benedikt. He, like Porphyrios, condemns postmodernism's insistence on communicating superficially through architecture. Instead of the return to classicism, though, Benedikt advocates an architecture that relies on "the real" for effect. He speaks of moments when reality produces an "unreasoned joy" due to the "simple correspondence of appearance and reality" and "the evident rightness of things as they are." During those moments "the world becomes singularly meaningful, yet without being 'symbolical.' Objects and colors do not point to other realms; signs say what they have to and fall silent. Conventional associations fall away. . . . We are not conscious of reference, allusion, or instruction."[24]

Benedikt calls those privileged moments "direct aesthetic experiences of the real" and suggests that "in our media-saturated times it falls to architecture to have the direct aesthetic experience of the real at the center of its concerns."[25] He questions the view that for something to be meaningful it has to "say" something, that reality has to be "read like a book or deciphered like a code for its messages."[26]

He compares the allusion, reference, and symbolism in postmodern architecture to "the much-discussed process in postmodern literature where the . . . dizzying self-reflection on and in the literary act are typical"[27] and poses the question of whether a building's meaning should be "fabricated with building-parts by the architect . . . by any process analogous to the way writers construct worlds and meanings with words in literary fiction." Of course not, he says. "We count on buildings to form the stable matrix of our lives, to protect us, to stand up to us, to give us addresses, and not to be made of mirrors."[28]

"Real architecture is architecture especially ready—so to speak—for its direct esthetic experience, an architecture that does not disappoint us by turning out in the light of that experience to be little more than a vehicle contrived to bear meanings. . . . Real architecture is, then, architecture in which the quality of realness is paramount. And here, with realness, is how the idea of reality can best enter the realm of architectural discourse. Like 'proportion' or 'scale,' like any number of qualities ascribable to architecture good and bad, 'realness' becomes an attribute of buildings that can be pointed out and discussed, can be found lacking here, present in greater degree there . . . and so on: in short, realness becomes an observable quality amenable to some level of conceptual formulation."[29]

Benedikt concludes: "While it may be argued that ironic poses and movie-set history, allegories and recondite allusions, reflect most accurately and properly our information- and entertainment-oriented culture, they can also be seen as a defeat: a sliding of architecture into the world of television. For it can be argued equally well that an architecture that stands against, or in contrast to, the culture-wide trend to ephemeralization and relativism—as a kind of last bastion of dumb reality and foil to it all—constitutes the more appropriate, timely, and potentially esthetic response."[30]

These four views are personal, sincere, and different. They represent the thinking of these designers at a certain point in time. Whether we agree with them or not, they affirm a position, an ideology, a strong belief. A personal ideology gives direction to our work. In developing a personal set of core beliefs, and in facing the many design decisions that require judgment and reflection, it is good to bear in mind two questions proposed by Cesar Pelli: The first one—Is it correct?—seeks to find out whether the solution satisfies external expectations. The second question—Is it right?—seeks to find out if the solution is helping or harming people and surroundings. As Pelli explains, it is relatively easy to find out what are the correct options. These are constantly being defined for us. "But we have to seek the 'right' direction for ourselves, using our own internal compass."[31]

1. Pelli, C. (1999). Observations for young architects. New York: The Monacelli Press.
2. Ibid, p. 196.
3. Venturi, R. (1977). Complexity and contradiction in architecture. New York: The Museum of Modern Art.
4. Ibid, p. 17.
5. Ibid.
6. Ibid.
7. Ibid, p. 16.
8. Ibid.
9. Ibid, p. 18.
10. Ibid, p. 16.
11. [AU: Author needs to supply more info here. The same book title is used for two different authors in this list, but it seems more like they wrote articles or chapters within this book, since there is an editor listed as well.]
12. Ibid, p. 87.
13. Ibid, p. 88.
14. Ibid, pp. 89–90.
15. Nesbitt Kate, *Theorizing a New Agenda for Architecture*, Princeton Architectural Press: New York, 1996. p. 86.
16. Ibid, p. 93.
17. Ibid, p. 94.
18. Ibid.
19. Ibid.
20. Ibid, p. 95.
21. Ibid.
22. Ibid, p. 96.
23. Ibid.
24. Benedikt, M. (1988). For an architecture of reality. New York: Lumen Press.
25. Ibid, p. 4.
26. Ibid, p. 8.
27. Ibid, p. 12.
28. Ibid, p. 14.
29. Ibid, p. 30.
30. Ibid, p. 64.
31. Pelli, 1999, p. 194.

CASE STUDY

Transforming an Outdated Corporate Culture Based on Silos into a Collaborative Environment While Leveraging The Client's Multiple Brands

Project: Yum! Restaurants International's Latin American Headquarters (18,000 sf)

Location: Fort Lauderdale, Florida

Design Firm: ASD Inc. Photo credits: 414 Foto

Challenge: How do you transform a corporate culture consisting of encapsulated silos into an open, collaborative environment that promotes synergy among the client's multiple brands?

ASD's solution was to develop a design steeped in their brand(s), push the boundaries of visual transparency, and adopt a new furniture standard to create an open plan environment with a low horizon.

When Yum! Restaurant International recently relocated their Latin America headquarters to Fort Lauderdale, Florida, ASD/sky design was charged with designing an environment that integrated Yum! and its brands in a way that would reinforce their core message to visitors and franchisees. The design team responded with a highly transparent and open environment that promotes collaboration and a sense of well-being. The space is non-hierarchical, featuring offices around the core only and no enclosed spaces around the perimeter other than a few shared huddle spaces and the main conference room. See Figure CS8.1 for the floor plan.

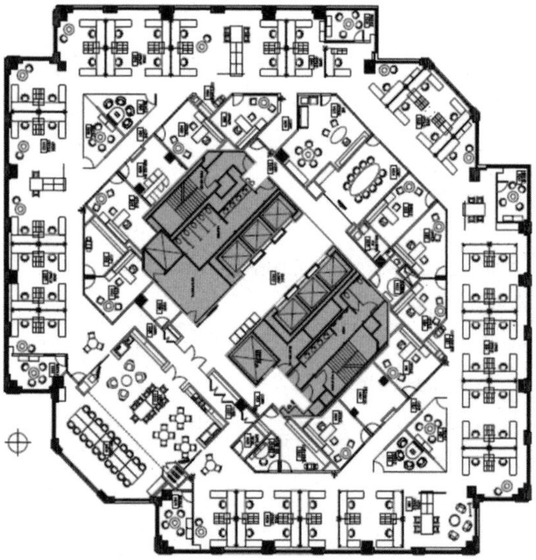

Figure CS8.1: Yum! floor plan

Upon arriving in the elevator lobby one is greeted with the vibrant Yum! logo as well as graphics depicting employees and logos of sub-brands such as Taco Bell, KFC, and Pizza Hut (Figure CS8.2). Graphics also play an important role when inside the office space, where applied graphics on glass panels permeate the environment with messages steeped in the firm's brands and core values (Figures CS8.3 and CS8.4).

Figure CS8.2: The elevator lobby features the vibrant Yum! logo as well as photos of employees and brand imagery from their clients

Figure CS8.3: Graphics applied to glass with messages of the firm's core values

The heart and soul of the new design centers on the Town Hall, an area that includes the main conference hub as well as ancillary spaces to greet visitors, share ideas in a relaxed, collegial atmosphere, and share meals with colleagues and clients (Figure CS8.5).

Figure CS8.4: Informal stand-up meeting area

Figure CS8.5: The town hall features ancillary spaces to greet visitors, share ideas, and have meals with colleagues and clients

REVIEW

SUMMARY

Designed environments embody the qualities of the people and organizations that inhabit them. Previously discussed design aspects such as order and enrichment are treated in particular ways to give the project its unique personality. These expressions communicate messages whose meanings vary widely from culture to culture, from group to group within a culture, and from person to person within a group. These meanings are based on associations, some spontaneous and others learned by convention.

Designers can give expression to all aspects of design. They control most of the elements that go into a project, such as layout, space, surface, detail, furnishings, and accessories. There are also other expression-contributing factors that are beyond the control of designers, such as the people who use the space and their attire, language, and so on.

Expression works at many levels, and there are many types of design expression. Among them are expression of universal human experiences, expression of contextual factors, expression of formal design properties and assemblies, and expression of programmatic necessities.

The expression of identity is one of the most important and challenging. Identity is like the personality of a project and is determined by the client's character and preferences. Factors such as the client's self-image (and the motives informing that image), her taste, and her preferred ways of self-presentation all act together to determine the expressed identity.

Designers' own personal attitudes, convictions, and preferences are also expressed in projects. Three factors that affect the kind of designer expression manifested are the designer's own personal style, his or her attitude toward current design norms, and the designer's use of symbolic communication.

1. Arnheim, R. (1977). *The dynamics of architectural form.* Berkeley: University of California Press.
2. Jencks, Ch. (1984). *The language of post-modern architecture.* New York: Rizzoli.
3. Arnheim, 1977, p. 208.
4. Ibid, p. 209.
5. Ibid, p. 211.
6. Jencks, 1984, p. 46.
7. Ibid, p. 46.
8. Ibid, p. 4.
9. Arnheim, 1977, p. 209.
10. Ibid, p. 208.
11. Mowen, J. (1990). *Consumer behavior* (2nd ed.). New York: McMillan.
12. Schiffman, L. G., & Kanuk, L. L. (1997). *Consumer behavior* (4th ed.). New Jersey: Prentice Hall.
13. Mowen, 1990, p. 195.
14. Belk, R. (1998). Possessions and the extended self. *Journal of Consumer Research* 15, 139–168.
15. Solomon, M. R. (1999). *Consumer behavior: Buying, having and being* (4th ed.). New York: Prentice Hall.
16. Arnould, E., Price, L., & Zinkhan, G. (2003). *Consumers* (2nd ed.). Boston: McGraw-Hill. p. 437.
17. Schiffman & Kanuk, 1997, p. 70.
18. Arnould, Price, & Zinkhan, 2003, pp. 272–275.
19. Ibid, p. 273.
20. Mowen, 1990, p. 183.
21. Schiffman & Kanuk, 1997, p. 127.
22. Arnould, Price, & Zinkhan, 2003 p. 274.
23. Ibid, p. 476.
24. Ibid, p. 275.
25. Ibid, p. 324.
26. Ibid, p. 325.
27. Ibid.
28. Gans, H. J. (1974). *Popular culture and high culture: An analysis and evaluation of taste.* New York: Basic Books.
29. Ibid, p. 70.
30. Ibid, pp. 75-94.
31. Ibid, p. 118.
32. Arnould, Price, & Zinkhan, 2003, p. 414.
33. Ind, N. (1992). *The corporate image: Strategies for effective identity programmes* (Rev. ed.). London: Kegan Page.
34. Ibid, p. 24.
35. Ibid, p. 25.
36. Olins, W. (1990). *Corporate identity.* Cambridge, MA: Harvard Business School Press.
37. Ibid, p. 33.
38. Lundberg, D. E., & Walker, J. R. (1993). *The restaurant: From concept to operation* (2nd ed.). New York: Wiley.
39. Ibid, p. 27.
40. Barr, V., & Broudy, C. E. (1990). *Designing to sell: A complete guide to retail planning and design* (2nd ed.). New York: McGraw-Hill.
41. Ibid, p. 178.
42. Robertson, H. (1932). *Modern architectural design.* Westminster: The Architectural Press.

Chapter Questions

1. Which two types of meaning were introduced in this chapter? How are they different?
2. Within the spectrum of the physical environment and its parts, which components can the designer affect and use to give expression?
3. Which three dualities did this chapter introduce as expressions of universal human experiences?
4. What are four types of contextual factors affecting expression?
5. Which two dualities did this chapter present as basic determinants of the project's programmatic necessities?
6. Could you explain the concept of identity as presented in this chapter?
7. What five motives that influence consumers and their product constellations were presented in this chapter?
8. Name and explain five of the eight variables presented in this chapter under self-presentation.
9. What are the differences between high self-monitors and low self-monitors related to self-presentation?
10. Which aspects of designers' personal expressions were presented in this chapter?
11. Name two examples of spontaneous associations.
12. Name two examples of associations learned by convention.
13. Name one example of constraint/freedom as it relates to the expression of universal human experiences.
14. Name one example of admittance/rejection as it relates to the expression of universal human experiences.
15. Name a situation that would be appropriate for the manifestation of historic expression.
16. Name a situation that would be appropriate for the manifestation of cultural and regional expression.
17. Discuss with your classmates the dominant design norms and conventions of our times. What are they and how are they changing?
18. Discuss what kinds of environments would be appropriate for individuals or groups driven by the following motives. Be as specific as possible.
    a) the achievement motive
    b) the power motive
    c) the uniqueness/novelty motive
    d) the affiliation motive
    e) the self-esteem motive
19. Which characteristics would your design for a social club have for the following target audiences, based on Gans's taste cultures? Identify a prototypical building in your city or region that would fit each of the three cultures
    a) a high-culture audience
    b) an upper-middle culture
    c) a lower-middle culture
20. Describe your idea of an environment at each end of the range (from high to low) of the following modes of self-presentation:
    a) load level
    b) abstraction
    c) ambiguity
    d) humor
    e) formality
    f) intensity
21. Describe your current design tendencies in relation to the following formal properties of design. What do you tend to favor?
    a) shapes
    b) weight
    c) composition
    d) material palette
    e) ornamentation
22. Vidal Sassoon was mentioned as an early example of a company with a strong identity program, integrating its products, services, graphics, physical environment, and advertising into a cohesive total identity message. Name three companies in your community (large or small) that similarly combine these elements into a successful identity message.
23. What are your current design tendencies? Which others would you like to develop?
24. How would you use symbolism in a retail application?
25. How would you use symbolism in a restaurant application?

CHAPTER 9 UNDERSTANDING

INSTRUCTIONAL OBJECTIVES

- Explain how a project occurs within a given historic, cultural, and geographic context.
- Explain the contextual impact of the surroundings on interior projects.
- Explain the contextual impact of the building in which the project occurs.
- Present the concept of types and show its relevance to interior projects.
- Present the roles played by a project's internal players.
- Present examples of external context analysis.
- Present examples of internal context analysis.
- Present an approach that seeks to understand a project's most basic realities.
- Present approaches that seek to distinguish among projects of the same type.
- Present a format to acquire specific detailed information about important project spaces.
- Present a format to collect detailed information about relationships between project spaces' aspects.
- Present ways of expressing the driving forces of projects.

My own approach is to try to first understand the characteristics of the project. Before I try to conceive a formal answer I, with my partners and members of the team, become familiar with the site and its physical and cultural environment, the specific functions and purpose of the building, and relevant historical precedents. We have long meetings with users and clients to try to learn as clearly as possible the particulars of their hopes and needs.

—*Cesar Pelli,* Observations for Young Architects

Before a designer can begin to design a project, it is necessary to collect pertinent information about the project and its needs. This information is collected during the programming (data collection) phase through conversations, surveys, group sessions, and observations. Successful design solutions rely on accurate and complete information. Only when a project is based on accurate and well-understood information can we know for certain that the stages that follow (ideation, development, and resolution) will be addressing the right design problems. Otherwise, no matter how thoughtful and skillful the design efforts, the project could easily provide good solutions to the wrong set of problems. The process of shaping interior space starts with the understanding gained during this important stage.

Understanding requires a considerable amount of analysis. During this stage all the project's evident realities, both inherent and contextual, are considered. The following aspects of the project need to be understood properly in order to produce a responsive design.

Context

- general context
- surroundings
- building in which the project will take place

Internal Players

- client
- users

The Project Itself

- type of project being designed
- project's parts and their functions
- relationship among the various parts
- relationship of the parts to the whole

The analysis stage, particularly for large or complex projects, can be overwhelming. While collecting data and starting to think about project needs and strategies, it is important to remember that design needs to fulfill, first and foremost, the project's functional purpose. Order, enrichment, and expression complement and enhance function but they are never a substitute for it. Cesar Pelli makes this point eloquently when he states: "The artistic purposes of the architect need to somehow combine with the many purposes and functions of clients and users. Skillful architects manage to achieve their personal artistic goals while respecting the goals and needs of those for whom the building is being designed. This balance is simple to propose and difficult to achieve."[1]

Although the user's specific functions shape a project from the inside out, physical context shapes a project from the outside in. Responses to this collection of internal and external forces determine the arrangement of project parts and are, therefore, a critical aspect of the process of shaping interior space. This chapter will focus on the task of gaining proper understanding about both the project's functional purpose and its contextual circumstances.

CONTEXT

A project is part of many contexts. It takes place at a certain time in history (historical context), within a certain culture (cultural context), and in a specific location (regional and local contexts). Each context comes with its own set of realities within which designers need to operate.

General Context

Designers are usually familiar with the contextual realities within their geographic area of operation, such as stylistic tendencies related to particular cultures and time periods. The situation is different, however, any time the designer steps into a different culture, region, or neighborhood. In these cases the realities change from our own, thus requiring different design responses.

Designing in a historic district, a foreign culture, or within a neighborhood having a particularly strong stylistic character are all instances requiring proper understanding and response by the designer. When confronted with these unfamiliar circumstances, we need to carefully study and understand what they suggest and then respond accordingly.

Surroundings

A project's immediate physical context provides a tangible context. For convenience, we can divide surroundings into two categories of different scales: the neighborhood and the specific site. Neighborhood characteristics usually have a greater impact on the designs of new buildings than on interior spaces. They can, however, be relevant to interiors when they have dominant tendencies, as in the case of an old historic neighborhood. It is, however, the project's immediate site that provides the most significant information requiring a design response.

The immediate site can significantly influence the placement of a project's parts on the floor plan. The immediate surroundings provide opportunities to take advantage of or undesirable conditions to avoid. Thoughtful consideration and response to these amenities and problems enhance a project's harmonious and complementary coexistence with its setting.

In architectural projects, architects consider the site's location, orientation, and configuration in order to make proper decisions about where the building should be placed on the site, as well as how it should be oriented.

In contrast, most interior design projects occur in buildings that either already exist or, if new, are designed by others. The designer is therefore confined by the given boundaries and geometry of a predetermined building and must work within its constraints, taking advantage of its strengths and downplaying its weaknesses. The building itself now becomes another layer of the context since it is the container within which the interior design will take place.

In response the interior designer locates interior rooms and spaces according to what the exterior has to offer responding to such factors as the neighborhood, existing natural features, circulation around the site, access points to the building, and environmental issues.

Immediate Neighborhood

The immediate neighborhood consists of those surroundings close enough to the project building to have an effect on it. Depending on the project, this may be anywhere in extent from a segment of a street to an area of several blocks. The main things to look for are the surrounding buildings (size, character, proximity) and patterns of use. Figure 9.1 shows a diagram of an office building with observations about significant aspects of the immediate neighborhood that will need to be considered during design.

Natural Features

Three natural features require analysis: single natural elements, such as significant trees and other plants; external regions of particular character, such as woods, lakes, and clearings; and topographic characteristics of the site, such as slopes, peaks, and valleys. Some natural site features, like a lake, may provide visual relief. Others, like a group of trees, may provide shade to cool the building or a visual buffer that provides privacy.

Charles Moore wrote about the importance of outlook, a concept related to the relationship of interior spaces and the exterior "in which something outside the room attracts

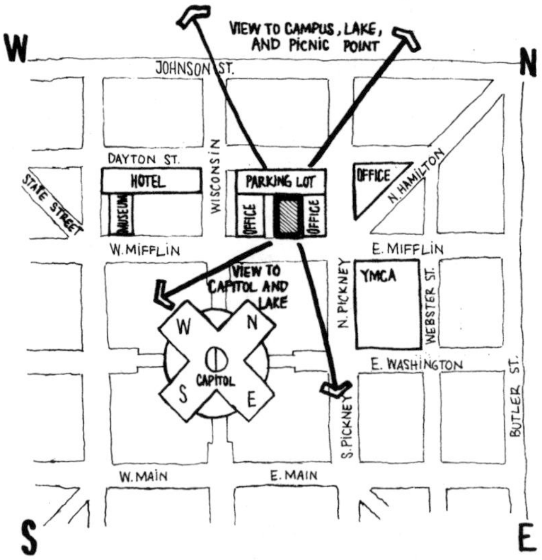

Figure 9.1: External features, mainly the characteristics of neighboring buildings and their users, can inform design decisions. In this example, a prominent civic building across from the building site becomes a significant presence that demands a design response. The selection of which areas will have access to views of this building becomes an important design consideration.

the attention of the inhabitant without requiring him to give up those advantages enclosure brings. Outlook occurs through openings, generally windows, and is, in effect, another kind of focus."[2] Such instances of favorable outlook usually demand a design response; thus, a certain room may be located on the side that faces the desirable feature. "The distinguishing characteristic of rooms enfronting the outside," adds Moore, "is that they are arranged in relation to something beyond themselves, and the chief advantage of this arrangement is that it allows the rooms to have an outlook over whatever they face and share its qualities. By the same token, it is only useful if there is something worth facing: either something already there; or something made and shared."[3]

Figure 9.2 shows a diagram identifying significant natural elements around an academic building.

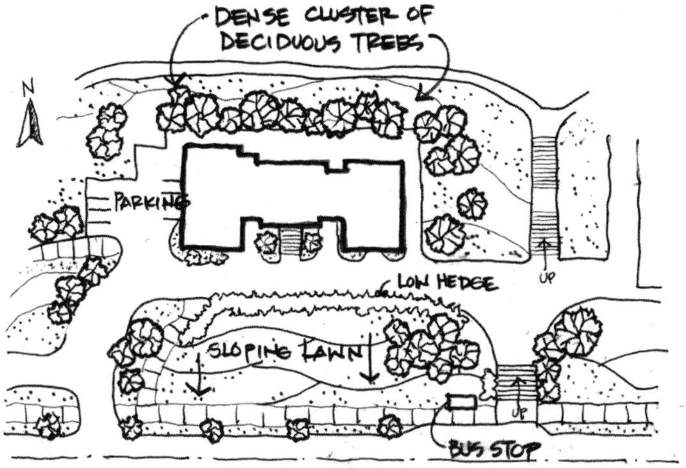

Figure 9.2: This diagram shows a survey of natural features outside the project site for an academic building. The most significant natural feature in this example is the trees on the north, behind the building, which provide pleasant, filtered views from the rooms located on that side of the building. The lawn in front of the building slopes away from the building, resulting in expansive views, even from the lower floors.

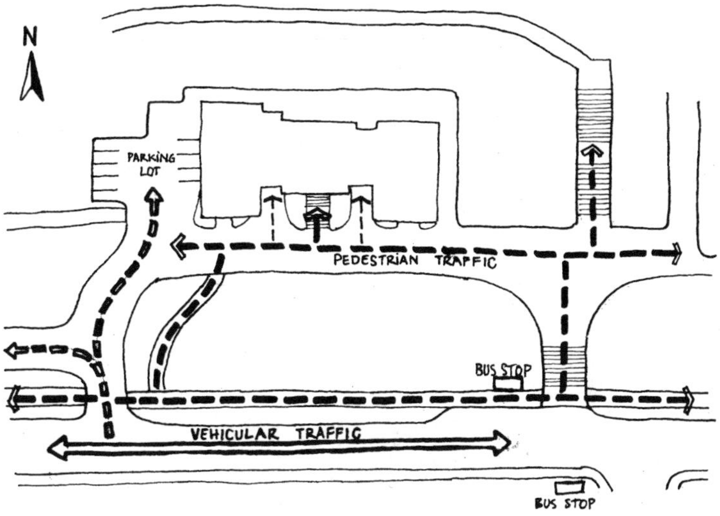

Figure 9.3: This kind of diagram shows the analysis of circulation and access points to the building, showing both vehicular and pedestrian circulation and giving the designer useful information for design.

Circulation and Access

The analysis of circulation patterns and building access (both vehicular and pedestrian) provides useful information about patterns of movement adjacent to the building. It provides information about how people get to the subject building (by car, bus, bike, or on foot), and from which side they approach it. Additionally, information about general patterns of movement outside helps determine what parts of the building people walk by the most, providing insights about where to place internal functions that need more or less visibility and exposure. Figure 9.3 shows the circulation and access diagram for the school building previously introduced. It identifies, among other patterns, two important parallel arteries, one intended primarily for pedestrian circulation (adjacent to and parallel to the building's long dimension), and one farther down dedicated to vehicular traffic.

Environmental Features

Environmental features include factors such as general climate characteristics as well as the relationships to the sun path, prevailing winds, and sources of external sounds (including noise) and smells (including offensive ones). These factors are often influential in the zoning of interior functions. Exposure in relation to the sun path determines which spaces will get the morning sun (and the resulting light, heat, or glare it provides) and which will get sun in the afternoon.

As early as the first century BC, the Roman architect Vitruvius wrote about the virtues of giving proper exposure to the different rooms in buildings according to climatic considerations:

> Winter dining rooms and bathrooms should have a south-western exposure, for the reason that they need the evening light, and also because the setting sun, facing them in all its splendor but with abated heat, lends a gentler warmth to that quarter in the evening. Bedrooms and libraries ought to have an eastern exposure, because their purposes require the morning light, and also because books in such libraries will not decay. In libraries with southern exposures the books are ruined by worms and dampness, because damp winds come up, which breed and nourish worms, and destroy the books with mould, by spreading their damp breath over them.[4]

Although much has changed since Vitruvius's days, such as the advent of sophisticated heating and air conditioning systems, designers still consider a room's placement in relation to the outside seeking to enhance everything from functional needs to energy conservation.

Awareness of the source of winds, sounds, and smells is also important, and rooms should be placed appropriately in relation to them. Figure 9.4 shows an environmental feature diagram for a restaurant contending with sights, sounds, and smells.

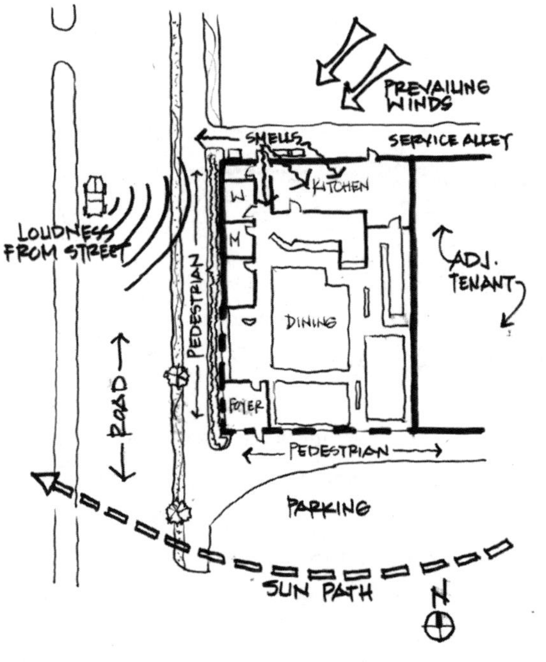

Figure 9.4: Conducting an analysis of environmental factors, such as this one for a restaurant site, helps to identify sources of light, glare, noises, winds, and smells.

Building

Beyond its surroundings, the building that houses an interior project presents a context of its own. It has its own geometry, circulation, modularity, column placement, core-to-perimeter distance, and, in some cases, unique configurations or characteristics. Depending on the project to be accommodated and the building's features, these may be seen as assets or liabilities. Significant aspects of a building's context include the interior context, the circulation patterns, and the features of the actual project space, the site.

Interior Context

The analysis of **interior context** considers the space to be occupied in relation to the rest of the building. The pertinent factors include the location of the space within the overall building, the neighbors within the building, the location of building systems and features, the adjacent building's activities, and the surrounding sounds and smells. Is the space in a corner, in the middle, on the perimeter, by the entrance? Is it on the sunny or the shaded side? Who are the neighbors in adjacent suites? What do they do? Do they generate noise or offensive odors? Performing this kind of analysis will provide useful insights to help you make appropriate design decisions. Figure 9.5 shows a diagram analyzing the interior context of a site in a regional shopping center. This tenant is located near the food court, meaning employees and customers will have to contend with distracting noise and tempting smells throughout the day. It also means the store will be seen by a great number of people.

Circulation

Analyzing circulation patterns provides insights about movement systems within the building, points of access to and egress from the space or suite, and egress from the floor or building. Circulation patterns are crucial for any business that relies on proper exposure, such as restaurants and retail stores. Locating such businesses in strategic areas of high exposure is paramount to their success. Points of access are important both for the ease of the

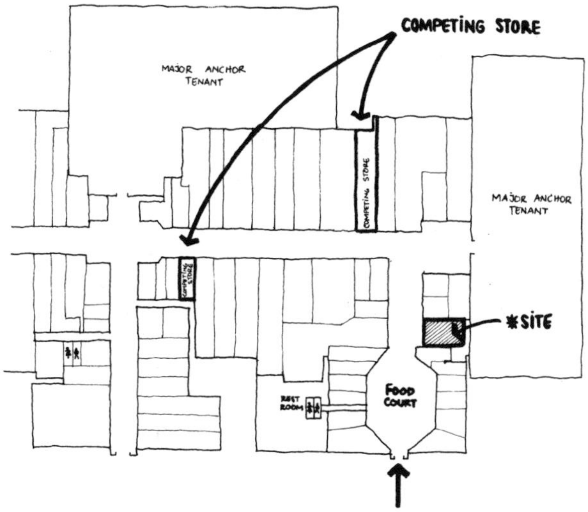

Figure 9.5: The interiors of large, multiuse buildings act as homogeneous neighborhoods. These, like exterior neighborhoods, feature miscellaneous functions and neighbors that can have an impact on your project. In this example of a store site inside a shopping center, the analysis reveals two nearby stores with similar merchandise (competition) and the location of a food court near the site (good exposure).

visitor and the convenience of the locals. Appropriate egress patterns are necessary to ensure safe exiting during emergencies. All these factors will affect the choice of location within a building and design strategies after a location has been chosen. Figure 9.6 shows a circulation analysis diagram for the store near the food court mentioned earlier.

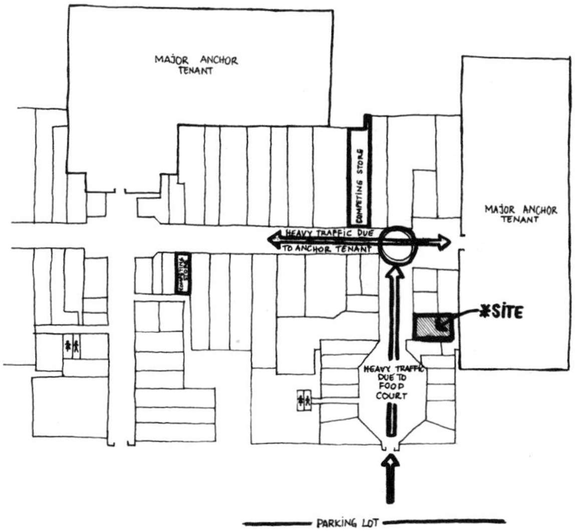

Figure 9.6: Similar to an external circulation analysis, this internal version identifies patterns of movement inside. In our example, the proximity to the food court and a major anchor tenant is likely to ensure substantial pedestrian traffic nearby.

Features of the Space

Here the concern is with the project space itself. Whether the client is occupying the entire building, an entire floor, or a portion of a floor, the aspects needing attention are the same. Among them are the size of the floor area to be occupied; the space's shape and overall geometry; significant features, such as the size, location, and spacing of columns; the characteristics of the perimeter wall; window spacing; light penetration and exposure to outside views; and the location of miscellaneous building components, such as mechanical equipment, ducts, and sprinkler systems.

Figure 9.7 shows a space feature diagram for a floor of an office building. It shows some of the internal aspects of the site that will impact the design of the space, such as column locations and sizes, perimeter window

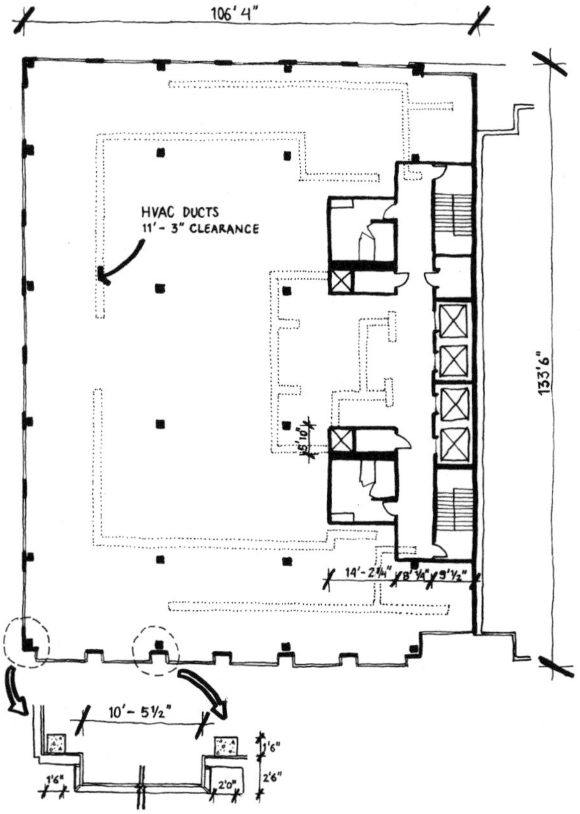

Figure 9.7: This diagram focuses on the internal space features of a floor in an office building. Existing conditions are surveyed and notes made of key dimensions and locations of significant elements such as overhead ductwork.

characteristics, and clearance heights to existing mechanical ductwork overhead.

The size and geometry of buildings vary greatly. Figure 9.8 shows three of the many configurations possible in office buildings with central service cores. Figure 9.8a features a rectangular floor plate with a two-part building core. The configuration provides usable space in the very center of the building as well as space around the two core masses. Articulations on either end of the building, behind the cores, provide special spaces for potentially special functions. The designer will have to work around rows of interior columns on either side of the core when rooms or furniture workstations are laid out in those areas. Figure 9.8b also consists of a rectangular floor plate. The linear core occupies most of the center spine and is pushed toward one side of the building, opening up space on the opposite end. The zigzagging at the four corners produces eight corner locations instead of four, a welcome feature for any organization requiring many corner offices for its executives. Figure 9.8c is another predominantly rectangular plan with a central core. Like the previous example, its core is also off-center resulting in one tight, and one generous, end. Its most distinctive feature is the curving wall on one end. This feature can present planning challenges. It may be a blessing or a curse, depending on the requirements of the project to be accommodated.

We will now examine the effect of different plan configurations with varying shapes, exposures, and points of entry. Figure 9.9 shows four basic shapes for a retail store: the narrow rectangle, the normal rectangle, the square, and the L-shape. A basic diagram is shown for each of the shapes for two scenarios: one with access on the narrow side (Figure 9.9a_1–d_1) and one with access on the wide side

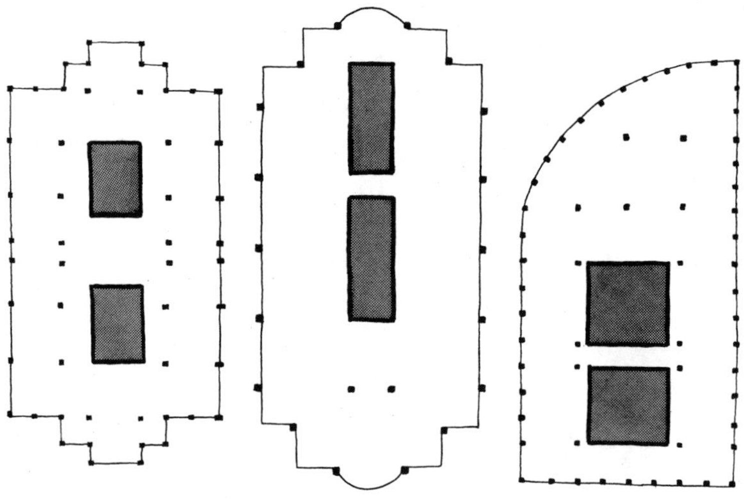

Figure 9.8: Building configurations vary significantly. A task during the understanding stage is to analyze the configuration of the floor plate and determine what it presents as opportunities and challenges. The unique configurations and geometric features of these three office buildings may or may not be suited to house a particular prospective tenant, depending on the particular needs of that tenant.

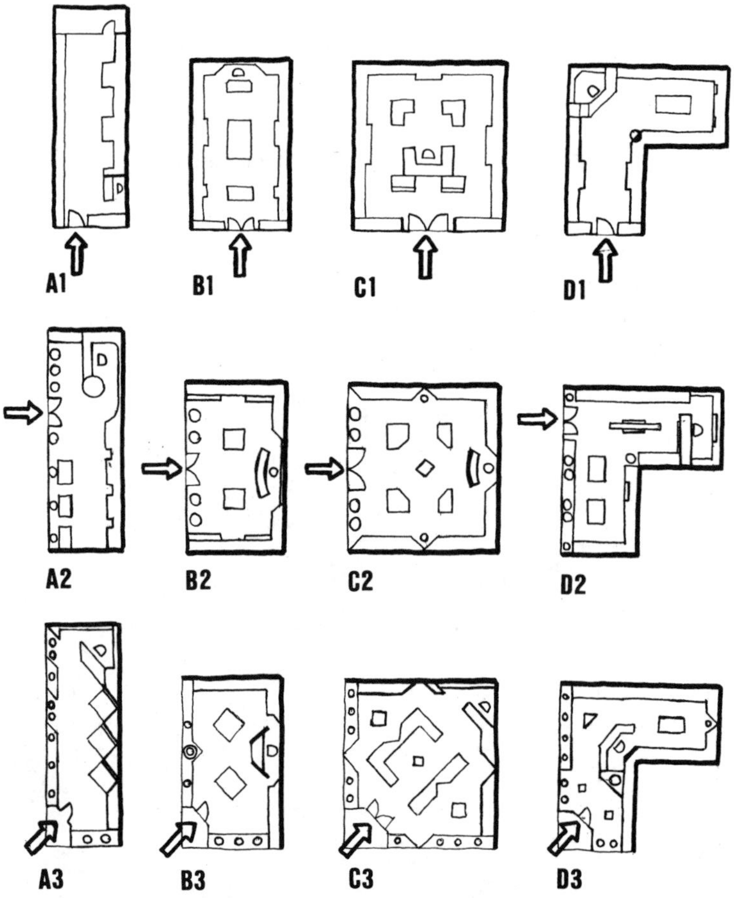

Figure 9.9: In addition to geometry, factors such as which side is front and which one has the entrance will have an effect on design. Notice the different configurations these hypothetical stores assume as the location and number of exposed sides and the entrance location change.

(Figure 9.9a_2–d_2). Additional diagrams show the effect of visual exposure (glass) on a second side plus corner entrances (Figure 9.9a_3–d_3). Notice the way the schemes change depending on configuration, orientation, point of access, and the number of sides visually exposed to the outside.

Let's return to office buildings and examine two floor plates and their interior contexts (Figure 9.10). The service cores of these two buildings occur along one end and not at the center of the building as is more customary. Figure 9.10a offers a large usable central area. The service core elements occur along one of the long sides, thus providing freedom in the center but also potential challenges when planning for multiple tenants on one floor. Additionally, one side provides pleasant views. The eight large freestanding interior columns in the space will require careful planning around them.

Figure 9.10b shows the floor plate of another office building. It features a narrow rectangular floor area with elevators on one of its short ends and minimal core elements elsewhere. Distinctive features of this building include a high perimeter-to-area ratio and a short distance from the perimeter to the center. Additionally, it features two areas of special architectural articulation: one bay window on the wall near the entry side and an outward-expanding, curved area on the far end.

Understanding what the building and its surroundings have to offer is an essential part of the analysis task. Good analysis and understanding will increase the likelihood that project parts are placed in the most appropriate locations and that the configurations used are complementary to the building's geometry.

The following are design considerations to keep in mind:

- Orient spaces in response to what's outside, seeking or avoiding outside features as appropriate.
- Take advantage of the building's geometry.
- Plan your modules carefully if the building has many interior columns. Use a module that works with the column spacing.
- Carefully plan modules along the exterior perimeter to work with the existing module of window mullions and solid elements.
- When planning tall spaces, consider limitations posed by existing elements overhead.
- Decide which characteristics of the building you want to adopt, feature, ignore, downplay, or hide.

INTERNAL PLAYERS

The internal players who most affect decisions of a project are the client and the users. By client, we refer to the owner or the designated representative in charge of the project. By users, we mean the actual people who will spend time in it, either residents or visitors. Often, the client is also one of the users of the space, such as when the president of a company is the project's client in addition to being one of its users.

Clients

The client is the person controlling the project on the owner's side. This is often the owner, although sometimes a designated representative is in charge of managing the project. In any case, the client is the person or group of persons who makes important decisions about the project. Clients tend to be practical people and are

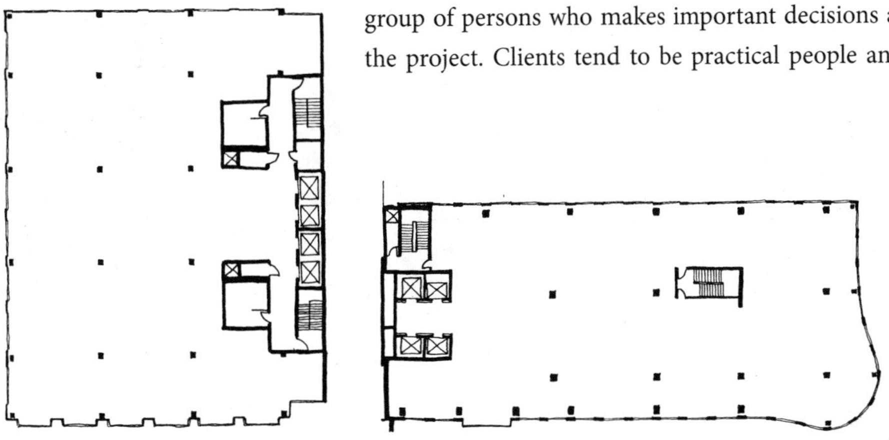

(a) (b)

Figure 9.10: These two floor plates of office buildings reveal some information about their size and geometry. It is not until we have the details of the surrounding context, as described in the text, that some of the real opportunities can be understood.

responsible for the feasibility of the project. As such, they are always deeply concerned about issues of function, cost, and schedule. Clients have a tremendous influence on the projects they control. They decide how money will be spent and approve or reject design proposals from the designer as they see fit.

The client's influence can be either beneficial or detrimental to the project, depending on the client. "A good client," says Cesar Pelli, "used to mean the supportive patron, one who would approve all proposals and agreed on whatever direction the architect wanted to give the design. Such patrons are now very rare. Good clients are needed more than ever, but today that means people who care about the building and the art; are involved through the whole design process; are explicit in their needs and goals, likes and dislikes; and make clear and timely decisions. We can learn much from our clients and depend on them to keep us on track as we move toward the most appropriate, functional, and exciting buildings for their needs."[5]

Users

If clients set the tone for projects, users shape their content. Buildings and their interiors are for users. As we saw in Chapter 2, the outlook of users varies depending on their role within the building or project. In a restaurant, for instance, the roles of the maître d', the chef, the bartender, the food servers, and the cashier are different, and this influences their individual opinions about the needs of the project. The view of a patron who comes in to dine is, likewise, different from those of the group above. The patron's opinion will be colored by impressions gained while entering, waiting for a table, proceeding to the table, ordering, consuming the food, visiting the restrooms, and paying the bill. The staff members' experience will be influenced by how much the facilities, as well as other factors, ease the execution of their roles. For the cook this will mean a functional kitchen, an adequate supply of ingredients, and a competent help staff. For the food servers it will mean a manageable workload, comfortable traffic paths between tables and kitchen, and functional waitstations.

In Chapter 2 we mentioned the difference between locals (those people who work in a facility) and visitors (those people who visit the facility but don't spend much time there). Clovis Heimsath makes a similar and useful distinction by dividing user roles into served and service roles.[6] The restaurant example from earlier serves to illustrate this point. All the players in the first group, such as cooks, food servers, and busboys, perform the role of service. The patrons are the ones served. Another useful distinction is the one between "front-of-the-house" and "back-of-the-house" functions. Front-of-the-house functions are public ones, such as those performed in the dining area of a restaurant or in the main hall of a theater. These functions tend to be performed in the more image-conscious areas of a facility, areas where a facility's main purpose takes place, be it eating, shopping, or watching a movie. Back-of-the-house functions are support functions, usually highly utilitarian in nature. Some workers never leave the back of the house whereas others operate strictly up front. Still others, like food servers in a restaurant, go back and forth between these two worlds. Hotels, restaurants, hospitals, and theaters are service-oriented institutions involving massive behind-the-scenes activities that support the experiences of those being served in the front of the house. Figures 9.11a and b show individuals performing service roles in an eating establishment.

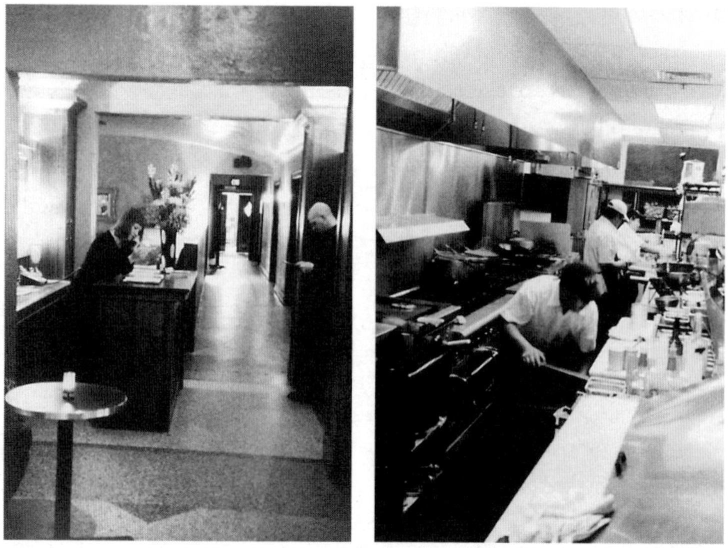

(a) (b)

Figure 9.11: The people shown here are performing service roles in restaurant settings. (a) shows the hostess in a front-of-the-house service role. (b) shows cooks performing back-of-the-house functions.

Finally, it is useful to understand nuances from the various user groups. Users of interior spaces not only perform the usual functions associated with their roles, but they often perform them in distinct, sometimes unique, ways. In some cases, workers of a company may have a specific style because of their collective personality, a certain tone set by the owner, particular company traditions, or some other reason. This accounts for differences among groups performing similar roles in different establishments. This sense of unique tone and attitude becomes a consideration that influences the expression given to the project. The food servers at a formal, exclusive restaurant are likely to have a different collective personality than a group of servers at, for instance, a school cafeteria, although both groups perform a similar role.

THE PROJECT ITSELF

The project itself is the central concern of all predesign and design activities. In this section we examine five key aspects of projects: the project type, the project's essential purpose, the parts of a project, their relationships to each other, and their relationship to the whole.

Project Type

Most projects are a specific application of a **project type** that has been done before; whether a retail store, a restaurant, a theater, a clinic, or an office, projects share commonalities with similar projects of the same type done previously. Therefore, it is usually unnecessary to invent ways of solving old design problems, as long as the existing solutions work. Studying these old solutions can teach invaluable lessons and provide insights. The practice of analyzing prototypical solutions to common project types, with all their variations, is a good habit to acquire.

Whenever you find yourself working on a type of project new to you it is helpful to spend some time studying past projects of the same type (called precedent studies). This can be done by reading the literature available on this type of project. Information is widely available in reference books as well as in specialized books and magazines. Better still are the insights gained by actually visiting similar projects and spending time observing and using them.

Projects of a common type share a basic purpose, a number of core elements essential to their function, and some recurring issues that always have to be addressed. Following is a cursory analysis of a few common project types. The intent is to give you a basic idea of the kind of information useful in understanding a certain type of project. The information given is, therefore, representative and does not attempt to present a full analysis of all the types. Detailed information about different project types is readily available in reference books for architectural and interior standards. When carrying out a project it will often be necessary for you to consult these guides to get more detailed information.

A Retail Store

Essential Purpose

A retail store brings consumers and merchandise together.

Means of Achieving Purpose

The goal is to bring the consumer in and entice him or her to buy. Presenting merchandise at every turn will increase the chances of the customer buying.

Dominant Features

The most important physical presence in a store is the merchandise. Everything else is secondary. Merchandise rules.

Basic Components

Storefront display, merchandise, fixtures, cashier, provisions for trying on merchandise, such as shoes or clothing. Also, merchandise stock in the back.

continued

A Retail Store, *continued*

Common Issues

Stores require proper merchandise display with appropriate customer service and surveillance. The staff, sometimes limited, needs one or more strategic central locations from which to oversee all the public areas of the store to monitor customers.

Crucial Aspects

The way merchandise is displayed (the fixtures, lighting, and so on), how the design moves the consumer around the store and presents the merchandise, and how the staff can monitor customers, both to assist them and to prevent theft, are all crucial elements of a design strategy for a retail store.

Particularities of the Experience

Retail stores can offer simplicity and clarity in applications where the customer wants predictability and efficiency (such as in a grocery store). At the other extreme, they can offer complexity and ambiguity to disorient and entice. In most cases, the shopping experience is performed in transit. Whether in a grocery store or a fashion boutique, the customer is on foot moving from aisle to aisle or from rack to rack. Sales staffs spend their day attending to customers, arranging merchandise, and conducting transactions at the cashier desk. They are usually on their feet all day long.

Opportunities

Retail stores offer opportunities to use design strategies related to order, enrichment, and expression. Depending on the type of store, greater or lesser levels of order may be appropriate. The experience of customers can be enhanced by providing creative circulation patterns as well as creative merchandise placement and display. Strategies can be explored to help bring merchandise and customer together. There are also opportunities to enhance the experience of those who work in stores by increasing the comfort of their stations and providing visual relief in overly busy environments.

Prototype

Retail stores come in all shapes, sizes, and styles. There are many variations on the theme, depending on the industry, the intended audience, and the level of service offered. Figure 9.12 shows a prototypical diagram for a simple generic store.

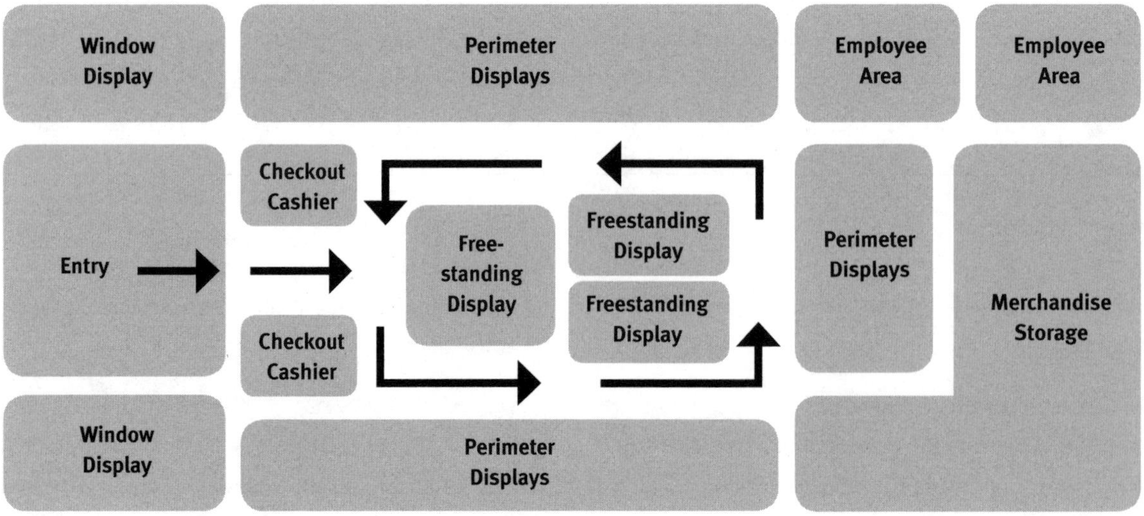

Figure 9.12: The following basic elements are included in this prototypical diagram of a store: window display, entry, checkout/cashier, perimeter displays, freestanding displays, employee areas, and merchandise storage.

An Office

Essential Purpose

People come together in offices to perform work related to their line of business; the work is part of the process of performing some service (medical, legal, design, and so on). The nature of the work is typically administrative and involves the production and communication of information through documents transmitted by manual and electronic means.

Means of Achieving Purpose

Typical tasks include talking on the phone, reading and producing letters or documents, and staging meetings and presentations.

Dominant Features

People, furnishings, and equipment dominate the visual field in office settings.

Basic Components

The workplace consists of private offices, large open areas shared by many workers, conference rooms, and miscellaneous support areas for arriving, waiting, copying, storage, and so on.

Common Issues

The amount of floor area occupied, the ratio of open to enclosed areas, and the amount of flexibility desired are some of the common issues encountered.

Critical Aspects

Space efficiency, the interface with technology, and the accommodation of changing needs are some of the critical aspects.

Particularities of the Experience

Most activities are performed at a workstation, a desk, or a conference table. There is a marked increase in the use of computers. Workers do most of their work while sitting, except when in transit between areas or when standing and presenting. Work is performed individually as well as in teams. Depending on the type of office, a number of visitors (clients or customers) will stop by every day.

Opportunities

Office environments can easily be boring because of the constant repetition of elements and tasks and the need for economy. There are many opportunities for designers to manipulate the sense of order to achieve an appropriate level for the office's size and level of complexity. Design interventions provide enrichment and can be explored for both circulation and stationary areas to add interest and variety for workers. Given the wide variety of corporate personalities, it is also possible to manipulate expressive components to seek a proper fit between the company and its environment.

Prototype

It is somewhat difficult to describe a generic office without discussing **subtypes** since offices vary significantly from subtype to subtype. Even among generic offices there are major differences between the open office plan and the closed plan. For the purposes of generating a workable prototypical plan we will use a combination of open and closed areas (Figure 9.13).

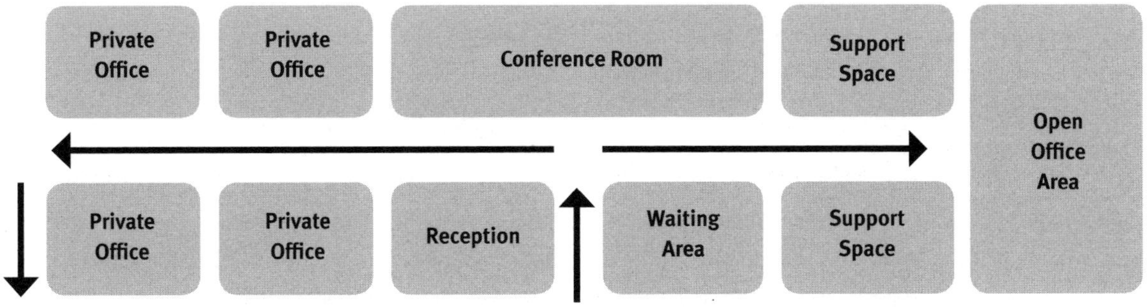

Figure 9.13: The following elements are included in this prototypical diagram of a small office: reception, waiting area, conference room, support spaces, private offices, and an open office area.

CAPSULE | Considerations for Office Design

Resolving an office design project requires a good understanding of the many units in the office, their roles, and their relationships with one another. The first step of any office design solution is to carefully place all elements for optimal function. The second step is to organize these into a coherent system of open and enclosed areas. Below, we present some useful considerations for the organization of open and enclosed areas and a conceptual model for space planning based on the kind of work people do.

Office design projects normally take place within the shell of an office building in a business district (usually downtown) or an office park. Typical floors consist of a core (usually somewhere near the center of the floor) containing elevators, exit stairs, mechanical and electrical rooms, and restrooms, with open space around it that is leased to businesses.

Solids and Voids

One of the most important design tasks for office projects is the previously mentioned disposition of solids (enclosed spaces) and voids (open spaces). Private offices, conference rooms, storage rooms, coffee rooms, and copy/supplies rooms are enclosed spaces. We will consider the first two "people rooms" and the others "service rooms." Additionally, there are open spaces. These include corridors and common open areas with systems furniture.

Offices vary widely. Some offices (e.g., law firms) are very hierarchical and consist mostly of enclosed private offices. Other offices (e.g., a customer service center) consist of mainly open space with systems furniture. Next, we consider various generic office design scenarios within a hypothetical office building shell and point out some important planning considerations.

Figure C9.1 shows four different schemes within the same building shell. Figure C9.1a and C9.1b are for offices requiring many private offices along the perimeter, such as in the case of a law firm. There are three main things we want to point out. First, if at all possible, leave certain areas open to the exterior to allow natural light into and views out from the space. You don't need a lot of them; just a few well-placed ones will do the trick. Second, don't use window space for service rooms. Put those inside and try to integrate them with the core. The core is a solid mass that is already there. In cases like these, it often makes sense to grow the core by continuing its shape outward (as shown at the ends) or by creating a carefully conceived protrusion (as shown along one side in Figure C9.1b). Third, articulate long walls. Where you have long stretches of walls, as in these examples, they will appear flat and monotonous unless you articulate the plane to provide variety. The guidelines given in these two examples are not exact prescriptions for how to do it, just reminders to do something to articulate these long planes.

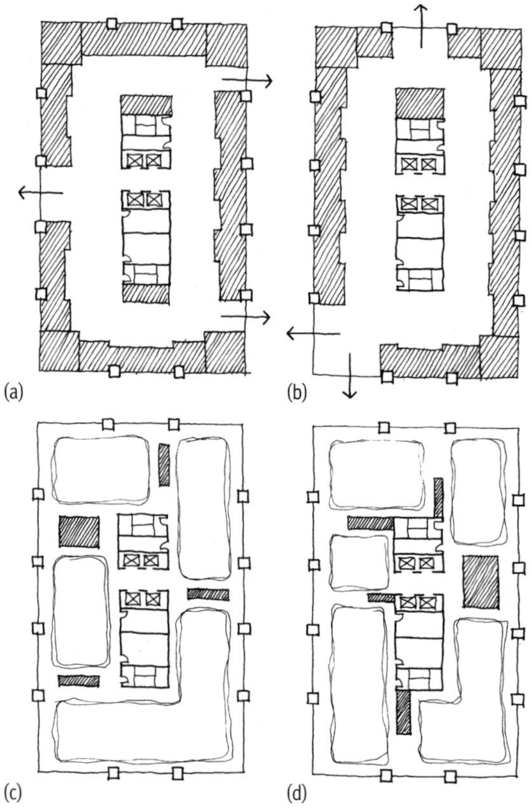

Figure C9.1: Depending on the project type enclosed rooms may occur along the perimeter or floating inside. Other elements such as walls are used to separate adjacent spaces.

Figure C9.1c and C9.1d show two schemes for a very different kind of project: the mostly open project.

This type of project may require a few enclosed offices but usually has some requirements for the usual service rooms (or spaces). The problem with the mostly open plan is its tendency to have too much openness, making it perceptually uncomfortable, disorienting, and potentially monotonous. A useful strategy is to use the few required rooms or service areas to subdivide the floor into more manageable neighborhoods. Figure C9.1c shows free-floating elements. It features a floating room and a few narrow service walls. These don't need to be full height, but should be tall enough to achieve separation between the areas. They may incorporate files, work counters, coffee areas, copy areas, and so on. Figure C9.1d shows a similar approach, but, in this case, many of the elements are attached to the core at strategic locations. Notice how in these two schemes, the floor is divided into four or five areas of more comfortable sizes and proportions than if the entire floor was left open.

Now we will consider cases that feature a balanced mix of open and enclosed areas. We start with two cases requiring a few people rooms along the perimeter. In other words, there are just a few of those rooms, but they have to be on the perimeter, by the windows. In these cases, a useful strategy is to group the offices and put them all on one or more sides, so that the other sides can remain fully open (Figure C9.2). The idea is to let the open areas have significant uninterrupted exposure to natural light and views. Notice that service areas are still incorporated as attachments to the core. As seen in Figure C9.2a and C9.2b, their size, proportion, and location produce different leftover open spaces.

Figure C9.2c and C9.2d show two schemes with balanced open and enclosed areas where the enclosed spaces don't have to be on the perimeter. The scheme in Figure C9.2c incorporates all the rooms (people and service) into the core. It is possible, as shown, to extend fin walls beyond the main shape if one desires to give an open area a better spatial definition. Finally, Figure C9.2d shows a scheme featuring two floating blocks consisting of back-to-back (although they could just as well be single) rows of offices. Their strategic placement in this case also utilizes these masses as space dividers. The service areas in this scheme are attached to the ends of the core, and there is a floating dividing wall that may incorporate some utilitarian function.

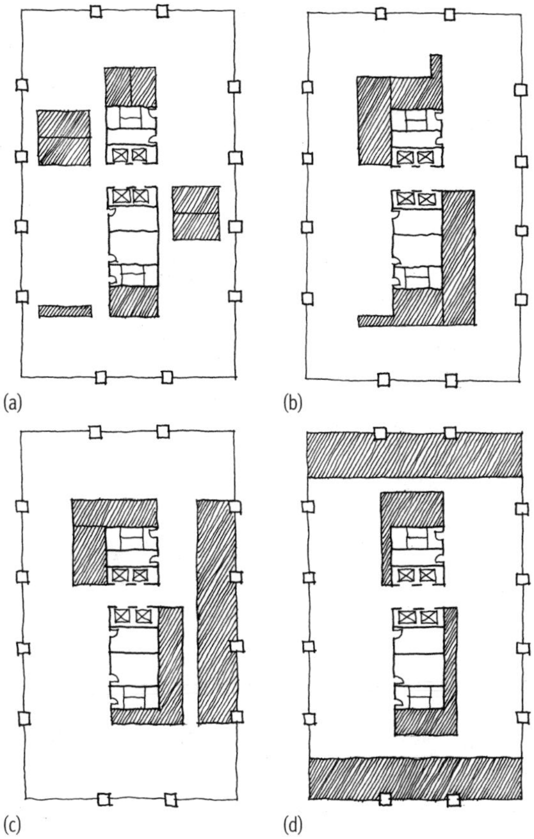

Figure C9.2: Many projects feature rooms attached to the building cores. Examples of these in combination with floating and perimeter rooms are shown.

Work Processes and Space Planning

Most office projects have some open areas that utilize systems furniture. In fact, many projects almost exclusively consist of open planning. Open space planning does not consist of generic rows of equal cubicles stretching over vast open areas in buildings, although we have seen examples like that. Open space planning has become quite sophisticated, with strategies and customizations to cater to every conceivable working process. Steelcase, the giant systems furniture manufacturer, provides us with a useful model for thinking about work processes and devising appropriate corresponding design solutions.

The model considers the work a person or group performs in terms of two variables: interaction and autonomy. Somebody's work may require much interaction with others or it may be solitary, individual work.

continued

Work Process Examples

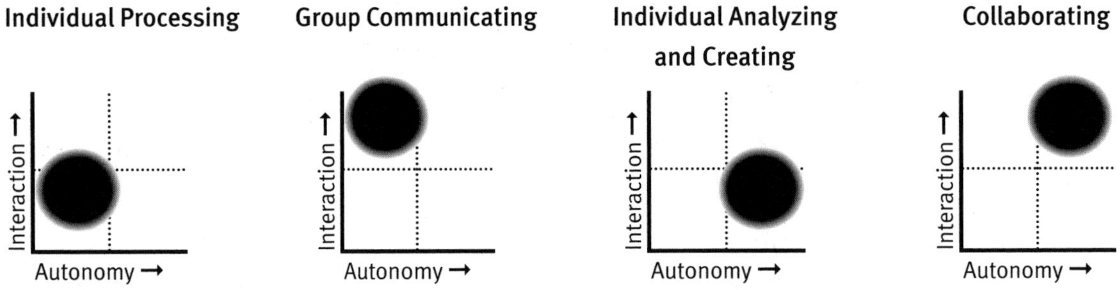

Figure C9.3: Four basic work styles can be identified based on levels of interaction and autonomy. Used with permission of Steelcase.

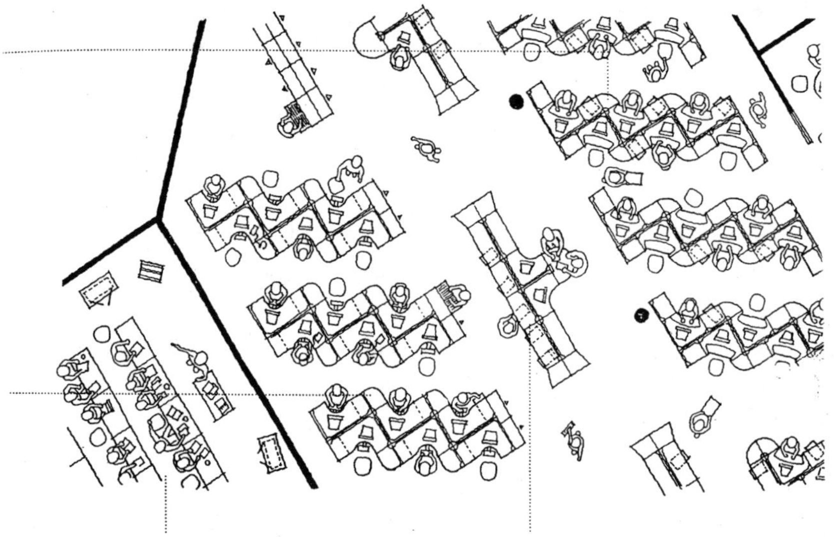

Figure C9.4: Hypothetical layout for individual processing work process. Used with permission of Steelcase.

It may also range from the autonomy the worker has over such things as to how, when, and where the work is done. Putting the two variables together along vertical and horizontal axes we can see the four possible combinations (Figure C9.3). These define four different types of work approaches requiring different design responses. A designation has been given to each of the four work processes. They are described below.

Individual Processing (Low Interaction, Low Autonomy)

This type of work involves pragmatic, repetitive tasks like inputting data, preparing reports, filing, and doing repetitive telephone tasks. It's individual, steady, and repetitive work. Required individual work spaces are usually compact, with some but not much privacy. The overall space density is usually high. Telemarketing and customer service centers are good examples of this work process. Figure C9.4 shows a generic example of an office area planned using this type of approach.

Group Communicating (High Interaction, Low Autonomy)

This type of work process, unlike the one above, requires the sharing, transferring, and/or exchange of information. Although the key word is sharing, workers and groups still require a certain amount of privacy. Also, workers are not sharing the entire time. Their work could be described as individual work with frequent exchanges. In these cases, it is crucial to understand

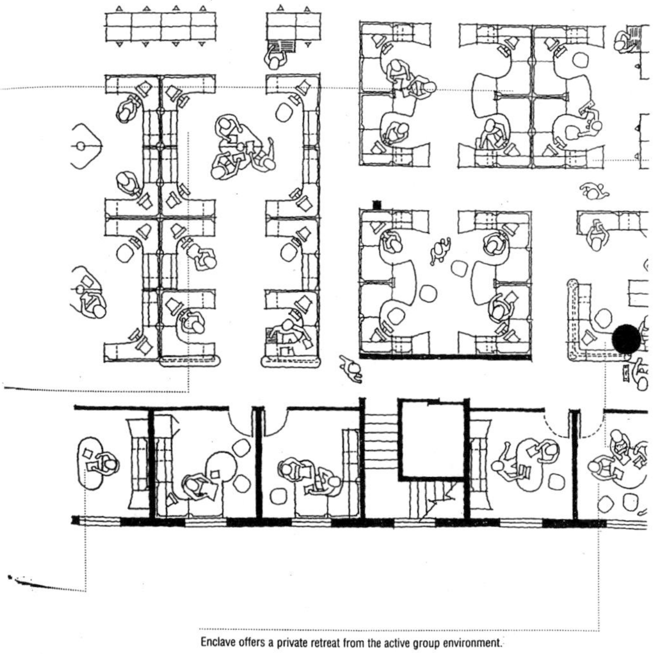
Enclave offers a private retreat from the active group environment.

Figure C9.5: Hypothetical layout for group communicating work process. Used with permission of Steelcase.

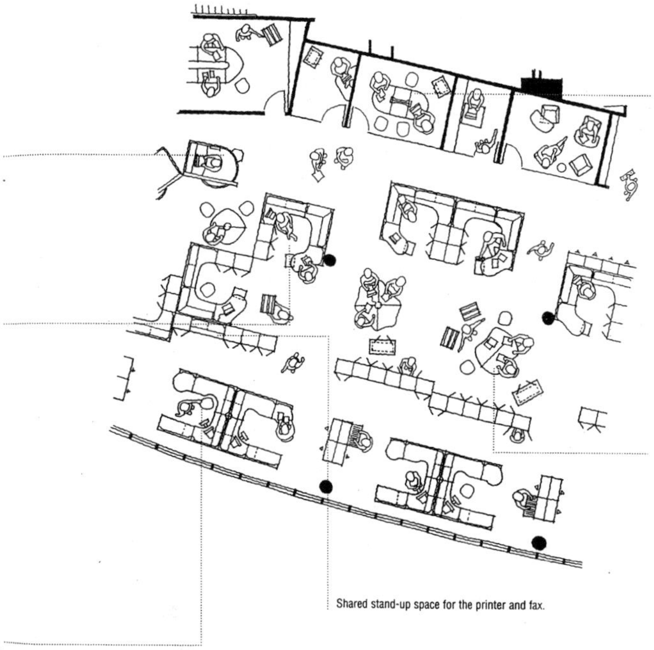
Shared stand-up space for the printer and fax.

Figure C9.6: Hypothetical layout for collaborating work process. Used with permission of Steelcase.

the extent of the physical sharing in order to optimize the balance between openness and enclosure. Figure C9.5 shows an open area planned to facilitate interactions among groups of four and between one group and adjacent ones.

Individual Analyzing and Creating (Low Interaction, High Autonomy)

This type of work is individual and intense. It's strategic, cerebral, and focused and requires an environment that facilitates concentration (i.e., privacy). It normally implies a private office, although it is possible to create conditions favorable for this kind of work with systems furniture by using tall privacy panels and locations away from the main flow.

Collaborating (High Interaction, High Autonomy)

This type of work also requires cerebral analysis and creative thinking, except a good amount of it is done with others. You could think of it as group problem solving. Not all the work is done in groups, though. Consequently, this type of work requires both individual privacy and one or more spaces to come together. Figure C9.6 shows a team area that features both individual workstations and a prominent central space where one or more groups can come together.

These distinctions between different work processes give us important insights into what we can use to better design individual open areas. These open areas often accommodate varied and complex work requirements and become small microcosms in themselves. Using the proper type of individual workstation, team clusters, and relationship between teams or clusters are all imperative to enhance the productivity of the office.

A Restaurant

Essential Purpose

The basic purpose of a restaurant is to provide the patron with a meal. The experience of dining out, however, can satisfy more than the need for food. Other potential benefits include the convenience of not having to prepare the meal, the quality of the meal (sensual gratification), the quality of the service (pampering), and the quality of the overall experience (entertainment, shared activity, and so on).

Means of Achieving Purpose

A meal selected by the patron is prepared on the premises and served at a table or counter.

Dominant Features

Tables and chairs dominate a restaurant. There is often a bar as well. Amount and type of decorations vary from case to case.

Basic Components

Despite the differences, there are common factors in restaurants. They feature front- and back-of-the-house activities. The most important components are the kitchen and dining areas. Other components include bars, an entry foyer with a waiting area, a cashier station, and restrooms.

Common Issues

Issues include decisions about the kind of restaurant, and thus, the kind of experience to provide. What's the menu? What's the atmosphere like? Important decisions need to be made about the levels of privacy, sound, and light to be offered. Other issues involve the subdivision of space and traffic patterns.

Critical Aspects

Restaurants are tricky businesses and often fail. Many of the critical aspects for success (such as location, target population, number of tables, menu choice, and quality of food and service) are outside the control of the designer. Providing an appealing, comfortable, and efficient backdrop to the show performed by the cast of employees is the contribution of the designer.

Particularities of the Experience

For the patron, the majority of the experience takes place while sitting at a table. The patron's focus can be directed at the table and its contents, toward accompanying guests, or toward views away from the table,

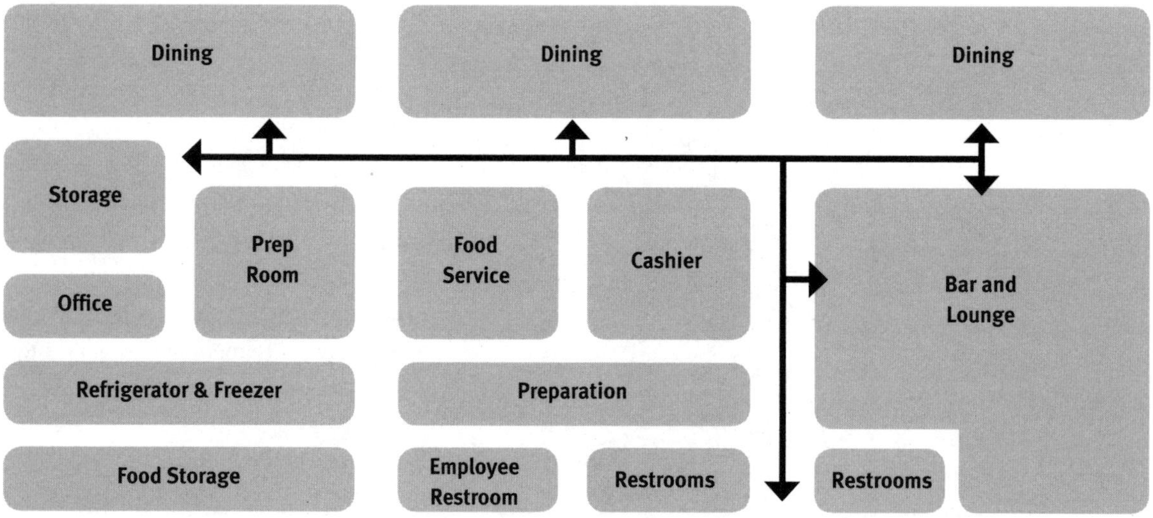

Figure 9.14: Prototypical diagram of a restaurant. Notice how the functions are divided by the circulation into front-of-the-house functions (top and right) and back-of-the-house functions (bottom left quadrant).

either within the restaurant or outside it. For the staff, the experience varies widely depending on their role as kitchen staff, waitstaff, bar staff, or management staff.

Opportunities

Spatially, the biggest opportunities in restaurant design are those involving the subdivision of space and the placement of tables to create desired levels of privacy as well as connection. Additionally, there are above-average decorative opportunities given the thematic character of many restaurants.

Prototype

The experience in a restaurant can vary depending on whether one is there to get a quick, inexpensive, practical meal or to experience an unforgettable meal in a luxurious setting while being pampered by the waitstaff. As with retail stores, there are many variations depending on the type of food served, the location, the clientele, and so on. Figure 9.14 shows a prototypical diagram for a generic restaurant. Refer also to the capsule titled "The Art of Table Layout in Restaurants."

CAPSULE | The Art of Table Layout in Restaurants

Two realities operate simultaneously in restaurants: the back-of-the-house reality and the front-of-the-house reality. On the one hand, restaurants are like factories, requiring the assembly of products from raw materials that come in periodically. The creations are made on demand and on the spot, requiring great organization and efficiency. On the other hand, there is the front-of-the-house experience. Above all, this experience should be pleasant. Although it is clear that the highlight of the experience is the meal itself, all the surrounding factors help to shape the total experience. Sights, sounds, and smells are some of the important environmental contributors. Themes and styles transport patrons to a temporary reality with a very special mood and character.

Designers have little control over such aspects as the quality of the food or how courteous and expedient the service is in a restaurant. They do, however, enjoy great influence over the ambiance of the place. Thoughtful composition, sensitive and well-conceived lighting, and appropriate detailing are some of the ingredients for success. As we have stated before, success requires both good ideas and good execution. You should plan to devote much time to these matters. It is not these that we want to highlight here. Instead, we address a more mundane but very important aspect of restaurant design: seating. The goal is to help you with this often time-consuming task so that you can produce a layout quickly and move on to more intricate tasks of the design, such as developing the theme and mood through detailing, color, lighting, and so on.

We begin by considering the two types of possible spaces in which you have to do your layout: the narrow space and the wide space. The first one implies a linear type of arrangement and has several possible layouts, depending on the actual width of the space. The second one presents more options and requires some preliminary decision making. With narrow spaces you can pretty much go at it and start your layout; however, with wide spaces having a central zone you have to decide what you are going to do with the center. Figure C9.7 shows your three basic choices. You may put

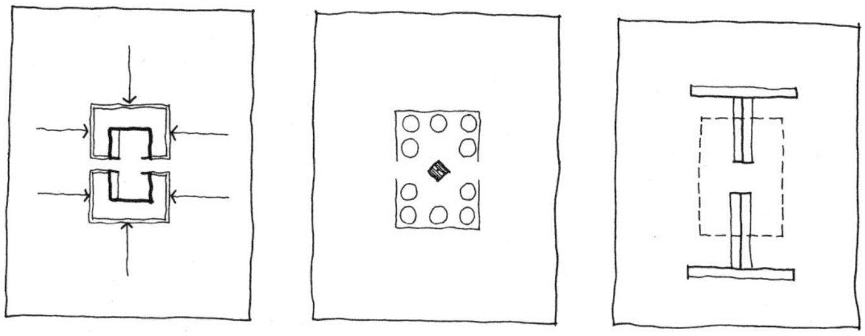

Figure C9.7: The center of deep plans presents the designer with different options. The designer may choose to emphasize or deemphasize the sense of center. The area may be compact or elongated, centered (as shown) or off-axis.

continued

something other than seating in the middle, such as a mass with waiter stations and/or decorative or focal elements (e.g., planters, fountains, and so on), as shown in Figure C9.7a. Your second choice is to have a central seating area, in turn surrounded by narrower, perimeter areas (Figure C9.7b). Your third choice is to eliminate the center through the addition of one or more dividing elements (e.g., linear partial-height walls, planters, and so on). The solution shown in Figure C9.7c, an example of this approach, divides the room into four zones, one per side.

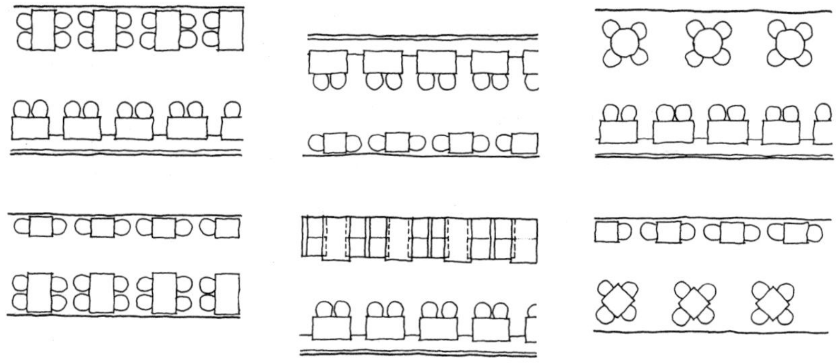

Figure C9.8: Linear layouts with parallel walls.

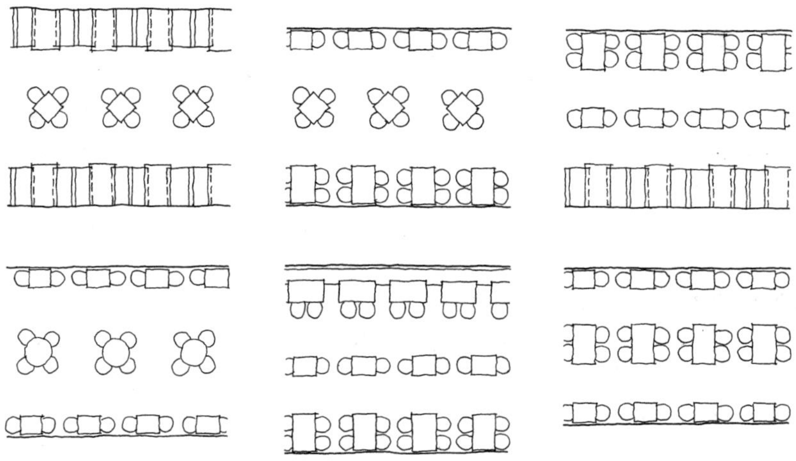

Figure C9.9: Linear layouts with central seating rows.

Before we begin looking at layout ideas, let's take a moment to reflect on the limited number of seating zones and table types. There are only two types of seating zones: perimeter and open. Perimeter seating is against a wall or some other boundary. Open seating, as the name implies, is in the open. Table types for perimeter seating include the booth, the two- or four-person against-the-wall table, and the two- or four-person against-the-wall table/banquette combination. You can also, of course, use one of the open-seating table arrangements along the perimeter. Open-seating table arrangements include the round table for four or more, the angled (usually 45 degrees) square table for four, the nonangled square table for two or four, and the nonangled rectangular table for four (seating on long sides). Those are pretty much the possibilities. There are, however, many possible ways of combining perimeter and open seating. The layout you choose depends on the proportions given by the space (or created intentionally by you through subdivision), the mix of tables desired for the restaurant, and your own preferences.

We give our layout ideas here, starting with narrow arrangements. Figure C9.8 shows six layouts consisting of two parallel perimeter walls (no central zone). The layouts in Figure C9.9 feature a center row between two parallel perimeters. Figure C9.10 shows layouts with a central zone of two rows. In Figure C9.11, a partial-height, dividing island is used along the center, thus subdividing the overall space into two narrow spaces. The environment still reads as one room, because the center divider is low. The island reads as an object in the middle.

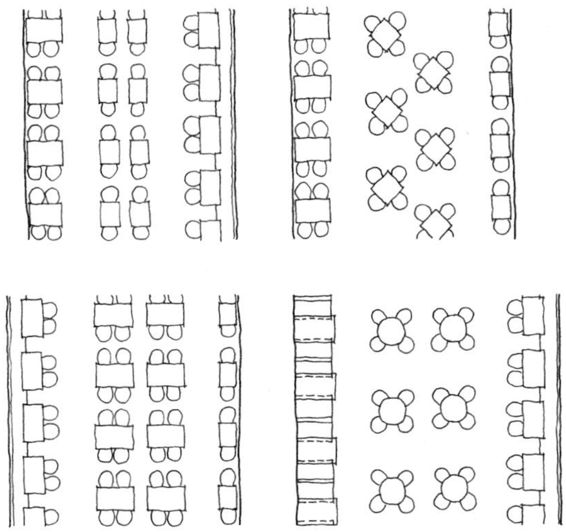

Figure C9.10: Linear layouts with wider central zones.

Figure C9.12a features a perimeter on the left and a zone on the right. Notice that it is no longer one or two rows of tables in the open but a larger area that reads as a zone. The layout in Figure C9.12b is slightly different. From left to right, it reads as a perimeter/single row/zone arrangement. Finally, Figure C9.13 shows how a large central zone can be subdivided into smaller regions. Whenever possible, avoid very large, undivided zones with a sea of tables. Sitting at one of the center tables is not a very pleasant experience. One feels lost in the middle. In a restaurant it is reassuring to feel anchored against, or at least close to, a wall column or some other element with anchoring properties.

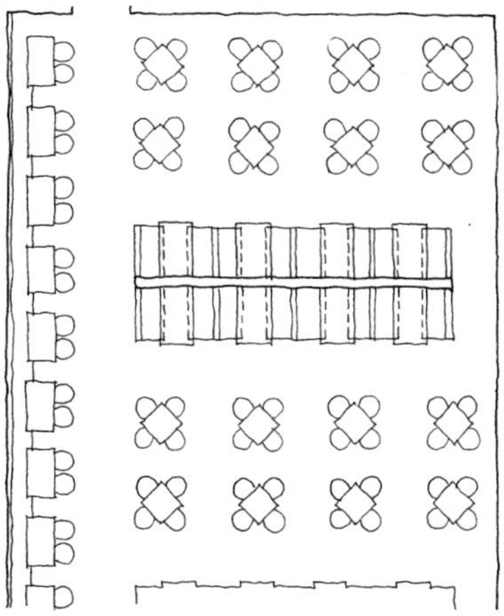

Figure C9.11: Rectangular room with seating island as space divider.

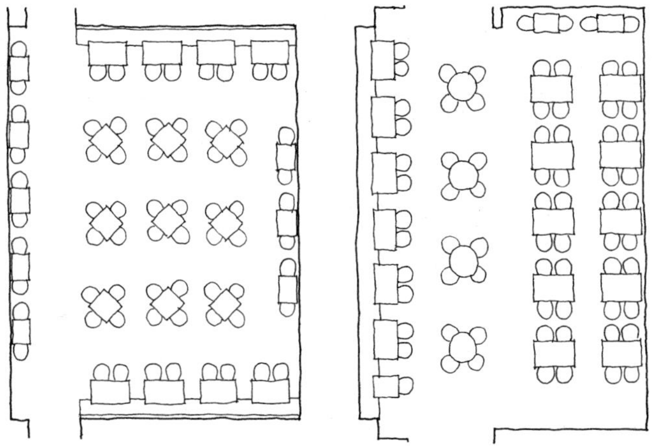

Figure C9.12: Layout with perimeter rows and central zones.

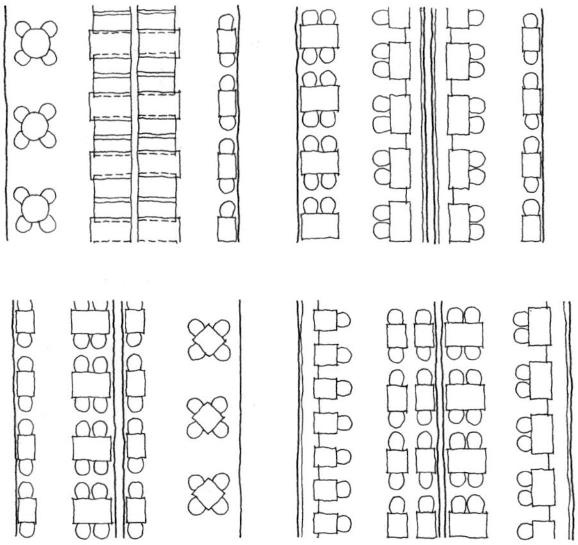

Figure C9.13: Rooms subdivided into two linear zones through central linear seating

A Library

Essential Purpose

A library is a building where recorded knowledge is stored and made available to the public. The public sometimes looks at the materials in the library; however, materials are often borrowed and taken home for limited periods of time at the end of which they must be returned. A strict control of materials leaving the facility is necessary in order to avoid theft.

Means of Achieving Purpose

Knowledge finds its way to users through various media. Information is stored in books and other media such as audio, video, and CD-ROMs. Computer usage is becoming widely prevalent and is already transforming the way we store and distribute knowledge.

Dominant Features

Dominant elements in public areas are book stacks to store books, carrels and tables for people to use, and computers to perform searches.

Basic Components

These include a prominently situated control desk, staff areas, search areas with computers, and public areas with stacks and tables. In public community libraries, there is often a division between the adult and children's sections. Specialized areas include a section for periodicals and one for audiovisual materials.

Common Issues

A challenging issue with libraries is distributing zones in order to achieve a good balance between stacks and reading areas as well as between quiet and loud areas.

Critical Aspects

The back-of-the-house activities in libraries are essential for their proper functioning. Adequate facilities to receive, catalog, and distribute books are imperative. Environmental and sunlight controls to protect books and a proper control point near the exit to monitor people leaving the facility are also important.

Particularities of the Experience

For the library user, activities include searching for materials (first at a computer and then physically searching for the material in the aisles), reading or

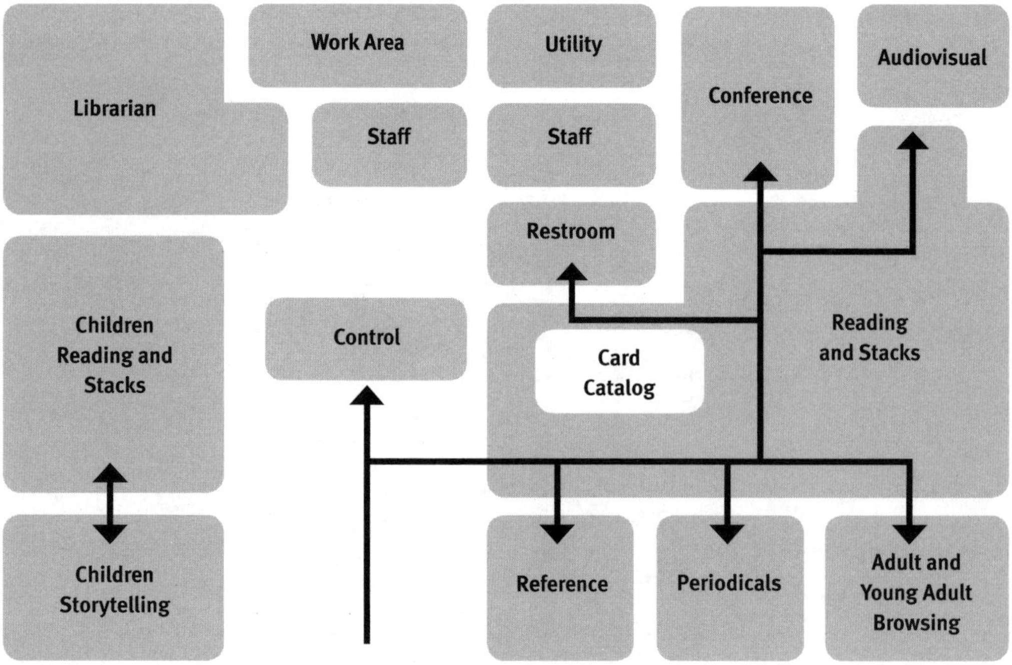

Figure 9.15: Prototypical diagram for a small community library.

studying the materials within the library, and checking out materials. A library scene involves a combination of transitory patrons looking for materials, settled ones enjoying the materials found, and others returning books or checking out new ones.

Opportunities

Libraries require orientation and clarity. For that reason, order is paramount in libraries. Subtle design gestures to enhance experience are adequate as long as they don't dominate and distract the user. The same is true of attempts to provide expression.

Prototype

Figure 9.15 shows a prototypical diagram for a community library.

A Theater

Essential Purpose

The theater brings audience and actors together. The actors dramatize aspects of reality and present them in focused, heightened ways that help the audience experience them much more intensely than in real life.

Means of Achieving Purpose

The theater achieves its purpose via live performances of theatrical productions.

Dominant Features

Theaters are examples of functions dominated by a central principal space. Although there are a series of spaces (often prominent) leading to them, and many crucial spaces behind them, there is little doubt that the combination of stage and auditorium represent the heart of any theater facility.

Basic Components

Like restaurants, theaters have front-of-the-house and back-of-the-house functions. The back-of-the-house functions can be quite extensive, housing dressing rooms, rehearsal rooms, costume storage rooms, workshops, and the stage itself. Front-of-the-house functions are public and include entry foyers, lobbies, and the auditorium itself.

Common Issues

The proper design of back-of-the-house spaces is always a challenge in theater design. Although not public and prominent, these need to facilitate smooth back-of-the-house operations if productions are going to be successful. Also important are all aspects of crowd management and control, including means of egress in case of emergency.

Critical Aspects

Because of the nature of live performances, all aspects of production (back-of-the-house activities) need to be coordinated and executed flawlessly. There are no second chances. Although the execution of the production relies heavily on the skill and preparation of the actors and the production staff, a well-functioning back-of-the-house facility is essential to make them work as smoothly as possible.

Particularities of the Experience

Preshow and intermission are times when the activities of the crowds become a show in itself. Theaters are prominent public places in which to see and be seen. Once in the hall, the spatial volume of the auditorium is often impressive, but when the lights are dimmed, everything vanishes except the production itself. Theater audiences experience the production while seated. There may be several thousand pairs of eyes focusing on exactly the same thing on stage at once.

Opportunities

Theater design, because of its complexity, is often done by specialists. There are opportunities to make the public spaces outside the auditorium a stage of sorts, where the drama and excitement of the patrons become the event, enhancing the theatricality of the whole experience. There are also opportunities to build anticipation

continued

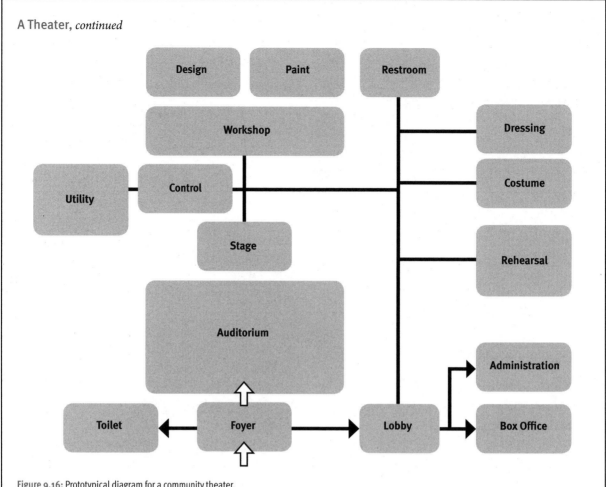

A Theater, *continued*

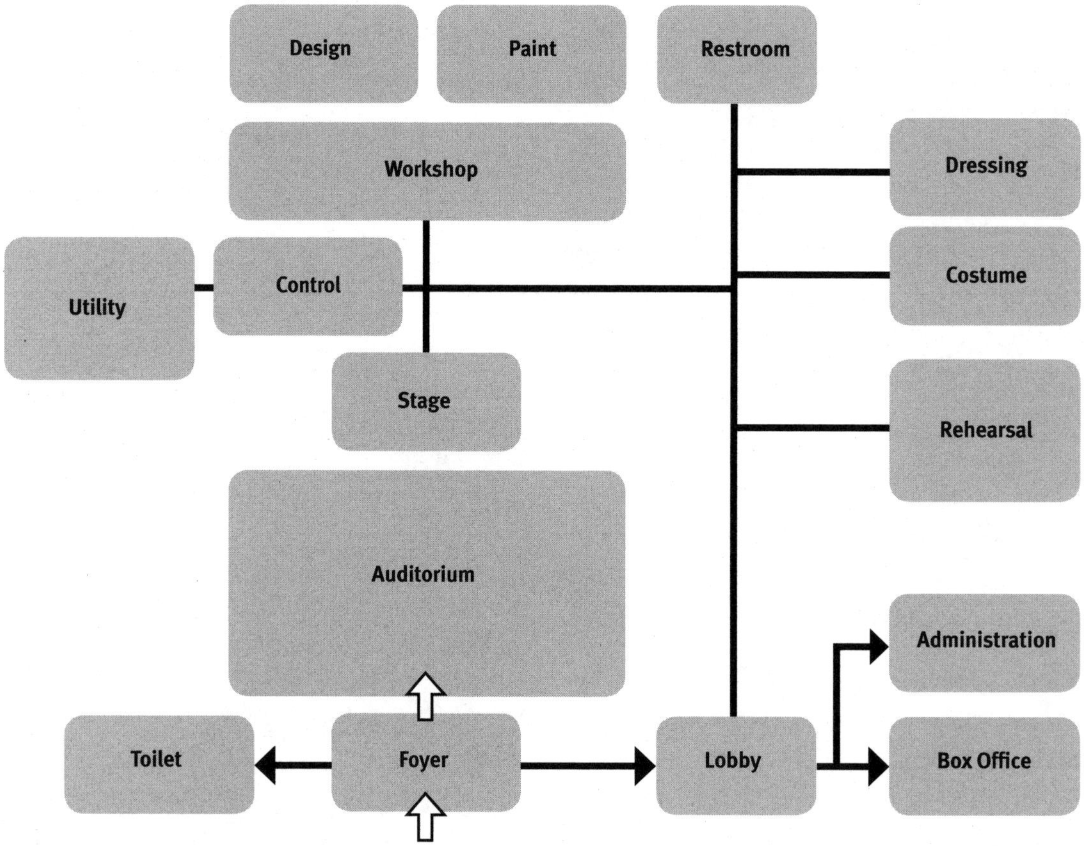

Figure 9.16: Prototypical diagram for a community theater.

through the progression of spaces leading to the main hall. In the main hall, there is always the challenge of making the immense space rich and dignified when the lights are on and giving patrons something worthwhile to look at while they wait for the show to start.

Prototype

Figure 9.16 shows a prototypical diagram for a community theater.

As these simple descriptions show, there are always some essential functions intrinsic to a particular project type. Before one embarks on the design of an unknown type of project it is necessary to study and understand its type and its basic characteristics. Having this knowledge will provide a solid foundation from which to start the design process.

Types occur at various levels of specificity and detail. In addition to belonging to a basic type such as "store" or "office," projects are usually a subtype of a general type, such as "shoe store" and "interior design office." Consequently, even though the spirit of retail is similar from store to store, the requirements for, say, a shoe store and a candy store are very different. Even within the same subspecialty there are variations. A shoe store that sells exclusive, high-end Italian footwear, for instance, is likely to be organized differently than a budget family oriented shoe store. It is necessary to consider the particularities of a project: its specific niche, approach, or philosophy. A handful of factors define the varieties within types. These include product or service offered, target customer profile, particular style or kind of product or service, level of quality, type of service or delivery, image or theme projected, and, in some instances like restaurants, type of experience promoted. Let's apply these to retail stores and restaurants as examples. Consider, first, the two stores profiled as follows:

STORE A	STORE B
Product: Fashion	Product: Fashion
Store Format: Small Boutique	Store Format: Large Warehouse
Customer: Young Females	Customer: Entire Family
Style: Chic and Trendy	Style: Traditional
Quality and Price: Moderate	Quality and Price: Low
Service: Full-Service	Service: Self-Service
Image: Irreverent, Urban	Image: Rugged, Country

Clearly, the two profiles shown for these stores suggest different design strategies, the urban boutique needing to be small, articulated, and to have some flair; the country warehouse needing to be large and rustic.

Let's now consider two restaurants:

RESTAURANT A	RESTAURANT B
Product: American Food	Product: Italian Food
Store Format: Stand-Alone Restaurant	Store Format: Leased Space Downtown
Customer: Families	Customer: Young Professionals
Style: Steakhouse	Style: Trattoria
Quality and Price: Moderate	Quality and Price: Moderate
Service: Table Service	Service: Table Service
Image: American Prairie	Image: Urban Casual

Here again, the different profiles of the two restaurants are likely to result in two spatially and visually different restaurants. Despite their differences, they will both have the basic components of all restaurants, such as a waiting area, perhaps a bar, one or more dining areas, and all of the back-of-the-house spaces, such as a kitchen and a storage area.

Sometimes different subtypes require substantially different arrangements. Let's compare three different jewelry stores. The three small stores in Figure 9.17 all share the basic components of a jewelry store: window displays up front, display cases inside, an area to complete transactions, and several back-of-the-house rooms. Yet they are different from one another in their spatial organization. What at first may appear to be differences in the designers' interpretations of a jewelry store are actually insightful responses to three slightly different approaches to selling jewelry.

The store in Figure 9.17a has a linear arrangement leading to a transaction counter centered in the back. The arrangement is simple and straightforward. Customers stand in front of the display cases at either side, move from front to back, and are assisted as needed by someone standing behind the counter. Sales take place at the counter, and the transaction is completed at the counter in the back. The jewelry store in Figure 9.17b is also housed in a long and narrow space. In this case, however, the linearity of the space is deemphasized. Instead, a somewhat static space is created in the center of the store as defined by four wall protrusions and the furniture arrangement. Here the customer is encouraged not only to stand in front of a particular display case but to sit down in one of the provided chairs, where they are assisted by a salesperson sitting opposite the display case. The center space reinforces the invitation to get comfortable and stay for a while. Unlike the first case, the sale occurs, and is also completed, at the display cases.

The approach to the customer/salesperson interaction in the store shown in Figure 9.17c is similar to the one in Figure 9.17b. They sit across from one another at one of the display cases. The difference here is that the store consists

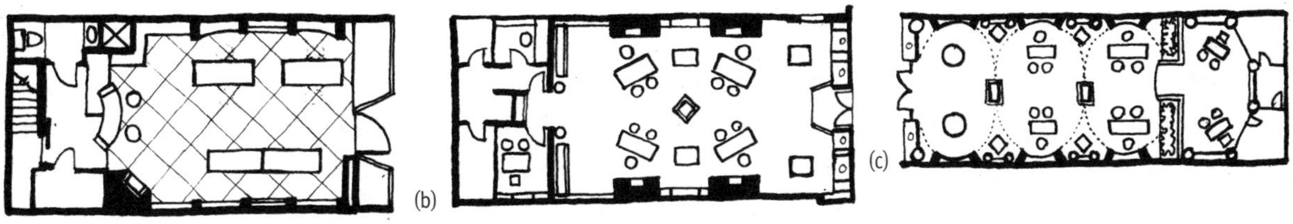

(a) (b) (c)

Figure 9.17: Three variations of the jewelry store. The way of conducting business transactions varies from one example to another. Store (a) is the most informal. Store (b) is a bit more formal. Store (c) is the most formal and ceremonial.

of not one main space but a progression of four spaces culminating in a formal and climactic closing area at the end. The sales transaction takes place and is completed ceremonially in a raised circular space that features two small desks; there are no transaction counters. This approach is much more formal than those of the first two stores.

Projects, then, despite forming part of a type, are specific applications of that type. Their particularities need to be known and understood. It is these particularities that give projects the nuances that make them different and, in many cases, special. They have important implications for the use, subdivision, and expression of space.

The Project's Parts and Their Functions

Few tasks are as important during the understanding stage than accounting for all the required functions, understanding how they work, and determining what kind of space and layout they require. Some functions occur only once, others repeat themselves; some are large and some small; some are really important and others not so important. Yet, they all have to be included and worked into some kind of cohesive system.

Despite a designer's familiarity with the parts of a given project type, it is only by working with a project's client and users that a list of complete requirements can be generated. The goal is to account for all functions and to learn the particular application for the given project. The type and number of spaces need to be identified and desired qualities described. Figure 9.18 shows a typical summary of spaces for two departments in an office project.

Beyond accounting for all spaces, however, it is also useful to set specific criteria for at least the principal spaces. Figure 9.19 shows a list of requirements for the entry area of a college building. It gives specific information about function, relationships, qualities, and so on. Sometimes brief descriptions of spaces are written and included in the program. Figure 9.20 shows an example for the college building. This programmatic information goes beyond the space names, quantities, and sizes usually given in the summary. Having this kind of detailed qualitative information will fuel the search for thoughtful and detailed design solutions.

Finding out how a client wants to treat a given part of a project is important. You may have your own ideas about how to design a particular project area; yet, unless you understand the client's intentions and the particular realities of the project, you may be off target. Let's take two entry sequences to two office projects to illustrate this point.

Figure 9.21 shows entry sequences to two office suites in the same building. The reception area for the office in Figure 9.21a occurs within the elevator lobby itself. The modest reception space is appropriate for the client's modest intention. From it one proceeds through a formal corridor that leads to an internal conference room straight ahead and to the rest of the office on either side.

The client for the office in Figure 9.21b wants a grand reception area. The elevator lobby space is not suitable to become a tall and grand space. Consequently, the lobby is used as an arrival space only. From there, a short formal corridor leads to the center of the suite where a grand two-story space serves as the reception area. It, in turn, serves as a gateway to the rest of the office, completing the entry sequence.

Collecting detailed project information during programming can be an arduous task. Few clients will have it available and ready to use. The existing facilities of the client may not be a good or complete representation of what is desired for the new facility. It often takes a multitude of meetings, needs surveys, field observations, and several checkpoints to compile an acceptable list of project parts and their requirements.

Projects may consist of a series of unique and discrete parts in some sort of arrangement. They may also consist of typical parts that repeat. In these latter cases, it is the aggregate created by the addition of many typical units that determines the overall layout of the project. An example of this would be an office project composed of the repetition of typical neighborhoods. Such is the case in the office project shown in Figure 9.22. The typical module of the office consists of a U-shaped arrangement of offices with workstations for secretarial staff inside the space created by the configuration. Here again, the module repeats itself. It is subject to some modifications at the ends and near the center, where two office spaces are combined to create a conference room. In both these cases we see how modules, or neighborhoods, are assembled from the repetition of basic units and these, once determined, are themselves repeated, giving the plan its configuration.

Space Summaries by Department

Management

Position	Office (sf.)	W. S. (sf.)	Quantity	Total (sf.)
President	300		1	300
Executive Vice President	225		1	225
Comptroller	175		1	175
Account Assistant		64	2	128
Collections Person		64	1	64
Human Resources Director	175		1	175
Research Director	175		1	175
Secretary (for Pres., VP, HR/RD)		74	3	222
TOTAL			11	1464

Advertising / Public Relations Account Management

Position	Office (sf.)	W. S. (sf.)	Quantity	Total (sf.)
Advertising Account Executive		150	4	600
PR Account Executive		150	1	150
Advertising Account Supervisor		64	4	256
PR Account Supervisor		64	2	128
Advertising Secretary		56	2	112
PR Secretary		56	1	56
TOTAL			14	1302

Figure 9.18: The quantitative data of programming documents includes space summaries showing allocations of required spaces and square footages for every part of the project.

Room	Entry
Function *Occupancy* *Activities* *Time*	• General building entry. • Common lobby area connects to major public rooms. • Residential entry of common lobby allows the residences to be secured, but use the main building circulation. • Open all hours—provide security at residential entry.
Space *Area* *Height* *Configuration*	• 180-square-foot general building entry. • 900-square-foot common lobby. • 120-square-foot residential entry. • Spaces should be tall and feel generous. • Establish clear patterns of circulation—plan for the first-time visitor.
Relationships *To other rooms* *To outside* *To grade*	• The building entry and common lobby should be clearly visible to the campus and be open and welcoming—provide some outdoor cover at entry. • The residential entry should provide a convenient connection to campus but draw the residents through some of the common circulation to promote interaction.
Light and Air *Natural light* *Electric light* *Outlook or "inlook"* *Natural ventilation* *Mechanical ventilation*	• Provide generous windows—emphasize openness and views in and out. • Do not overlight circulation with artificial light.
Special Elements *Focus* *Edges* *Machines and service*	• Restrooms should be conveniently located relative to common lobby. • Provide places to sit and wait in visible spots near both entries, including some protected outdoor areas. • Provide niches, walls, and other elements for information and display.
Materials and Details *Character* *Floor* *Wall* *Ceiling*	• Hard, durable floor surfaces with area carpets in areas of heavy traffic. • Natural wood trim. • Plaster walls and ceiling.

Figure 9.19: Design criteria for the entry space of a project include function, relationships, materials, and so on. Courtesy of Gary Moye.

INTERNATIONAL COLLEGE NARRATIVE DESCRIPTION OF SPACES

1. Common Space	
1.1 Entry Lobby	Entry place and the orientation area for the International College.
General Building Entry	should be visible and welcoming to the university community. Connect to:
Common Lobby	which provides orientation and public circulation to the principal program realms of the college. The character of the circulation should encourage interaction through appropriate openness and visibility to public college activities.
Residential Entry	provides a secure entry to the residences in a convenient location off the common lobby. Residents will have a security pass to enter the residences.
1.2 Events Room	A flexible and divisible gathering space for formal catered dinners, receptions, and speakers and for college or university social occasions such as international coffee hour, potlucks, and dances.
Catering Room	adjacent to the events room provides a staging location for serving formal dinners and receptions.
Storage	for tables, chairs, portable stage, and dance floor.
Restrooms *Men* *Women*	in a convenient, discreet location near the event room.
1.3 Exhibit Display Area	Located along an articulated edge of common lobby circulation, or in a separate but visible room. Locked glass cases provide a secure place to display unsupervised exhibits.

Figure 9.20: Short verbal descriptions are used to capture and communicate the essence of each area. Courtesy of Gary Moye.

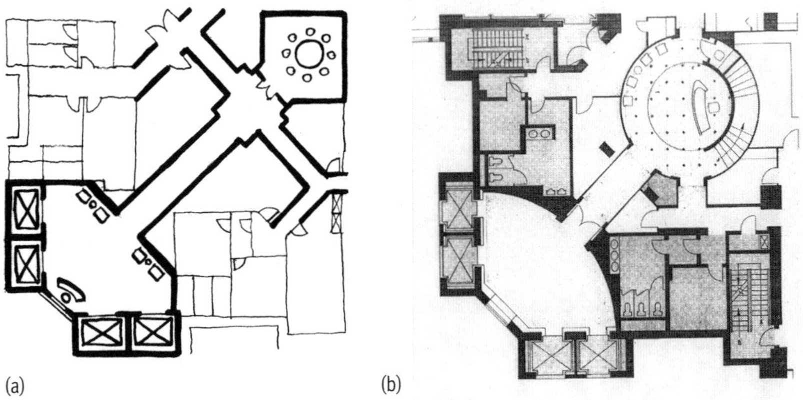

(a) (b)

Figure 9.21: Entry sequences to two office spaces in the same building. Sequence (a) utilizes the elevator lobby space for the office's modest reception area, whereas sequence (b) brings the reception area inside into a grand two-story lobby space at the heart of the office.

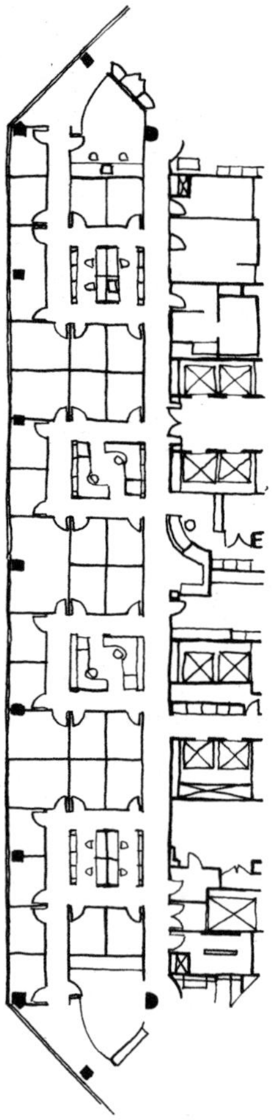

Figure 9.22: This office is composed by the aggregation of repeated modules that combine enclosed offices and open areas in between them.

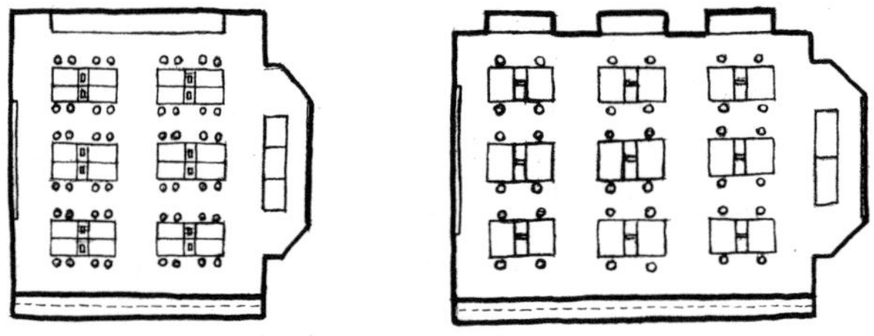

(a) (b)

Figure 9.23: Two typical modules of teaching laboratories to be used (and repeated) in the planning of a science academic facility.

Determining optimal configurations for specific repetitive units is often done early in the process. These are then tested as additive configurations in order to determine their functionality. Figures 9.23a and b show layouts for two teaching labs in a science building. The layouts explore different arrangements and dimensions for the rooms. When optimized, the arrangements become critical for the development of the floor plan where they occur as they get multiplied many times over.

Other times, a highly specialized part, occurring just once, is important enough to merit the designer's detailed attention during the early stages of a project. Such is the case of the kitchen in a restaurant (Figure 9.24). The kitchen is the hidden heart of a restaurant operation. It needs to be conceived appropriately from the beginning, as it represents a large area of the total restaurant

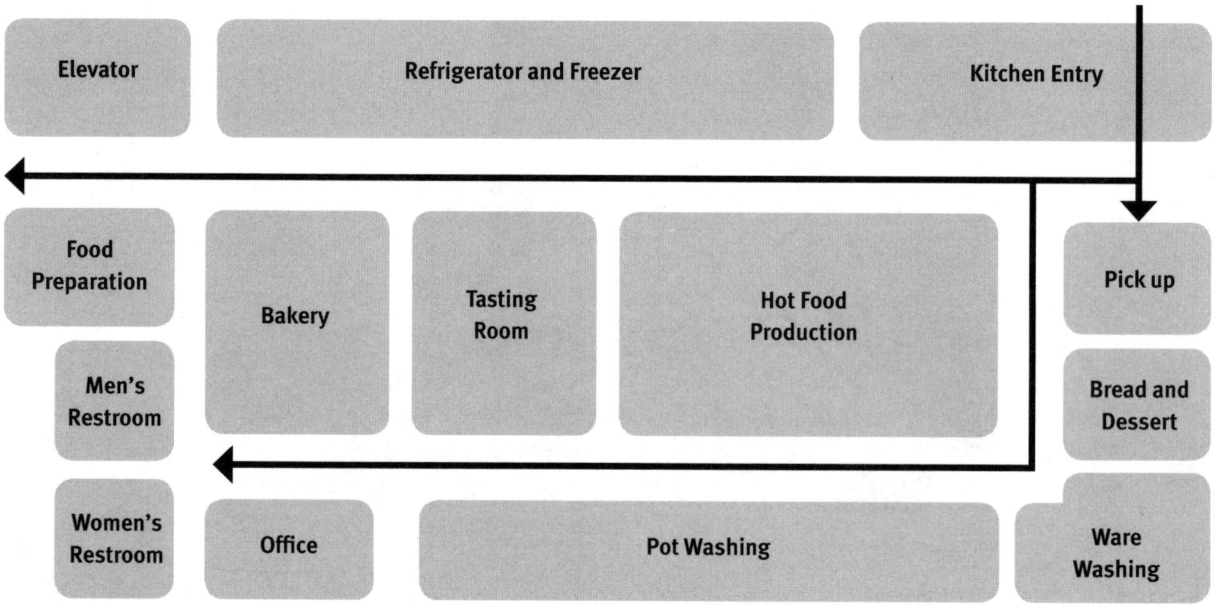

Figure 9.24: A single space worth understanding early is a restaurant kitchen; optimal relationships among its various parts facilitate a smooth and productive operation.

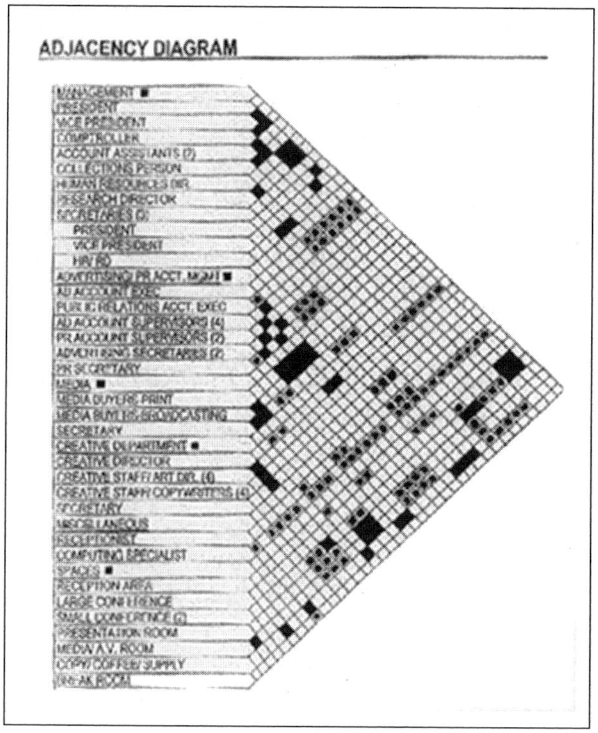

(a)

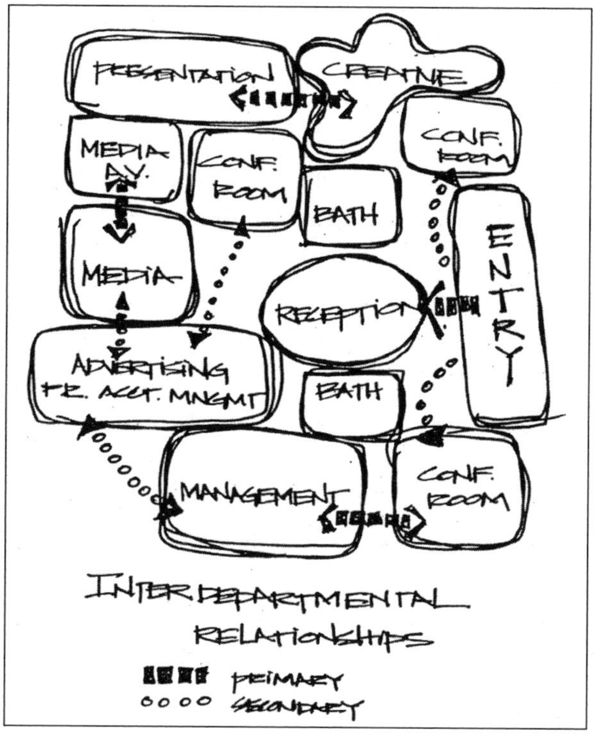

(b)

Figure 9.25: Matrix (a) and bubble (b and c) diagrams for an advertising agency project. Notice how much easier it is to intuitively grasp relationships in the bubble diagrams.

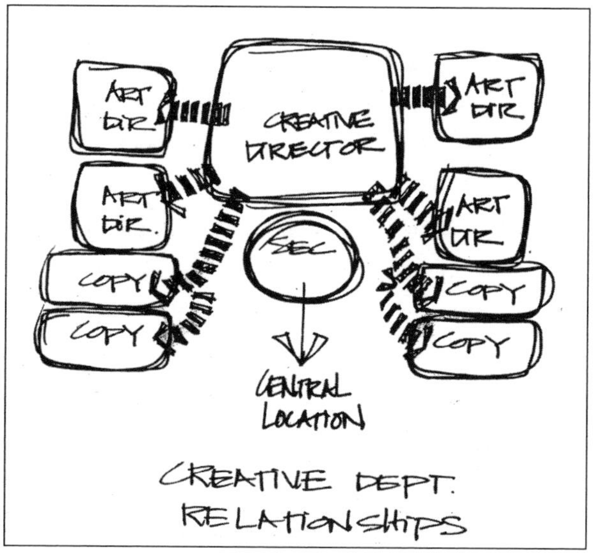

(c)

footprint. Preliminary studies will provide important information related to its final size and shape.

Relationship among the Various Parts

The next thing to understand about project parts is how they relate to one another. Project parts need to be accommodated in the project site in such a way that they fit and work together, sort of like a puzzle. To assemble the project's puzzle, it is necessary to combine parts into groups. These groups, in turn, are assembled as a project. In this section we will focus on parts and groups.

One of the basic tasks needed to determine how to structure the parts of a project is to analyze desired adjacencies between the different units and functions. This is done by determining which other units a particular project space needs to be in close proximity to, and which ones it should maintain some distance from. You can think in terms of three basic relationships between parts: need for proximity, need for separation, or, in some cases, indifference. You probably are familiar with this practice and have some experience using the adjacency matrices and diagrams normally used to illustrate adjacency information graphically. These graphic tools can be useful and convenient and are used widely. Figure 9.25 shows examples of matrix and bubble adjacency diagrams.

These tools, if used incorrectly, especially in large and complex projects, can also burden and confuse. The potential danger with the use of adjacency matrices, for instance, is one of unnecessary fragmentation. It is common practice, especially among young designers, to indiscriminately list every single space given in the program on both axes of an adjacency matrix and start indicating desired relationships between spaces. This is problematic for two reasons. First, it creates an unnecessary degree of complexity in projects other than really simple ones. Second, it tends to promote a myopic view of the project, encouraging the analysis of fragmented parts only in terms of how any two parts relate to each other. While the mutual relationship of many spaces to each other is important, there are many cases of two given spaces having no relationship whatsoever.

The unit used for the analysis of adjacencies does not need to be the individual space. Although this will work well for small projects, it will be unsuitable for large ones. The advertising agency example of Figure 9.25 shows how the use of the matrix can become cumbersome. Adjacencies of large projects are best done hierarchically. Early on, your goal is to understand the project in terms of its groupings. This approach will accelerate your understanding of the project and save you valuable time. The size of the beginning unit will depend on the size and complexity of the project. The initial search for the relationship between parts should be for these groupings. The first question asked should not be about the relationship between any two parts. Instead, the questions should be what are the basic groups in this project? And then, what are their parts?

A hospital, a project of considerable complexity, should serve to illustrate the points made earlier. If you were to list all the components of a hospital on the two axes of an adjacency matrix and get information from hospital experts about ideal adjacencies, two things would happen. It would take a very long time to make sense of all the information, and you would find out that many pairs of spaces or functions have no relationship. It would be difficult to arrange many spaces in relationship to everything else due to ambiguous data. Approaching the search hierarchically would help you make sense of the project. Several levels of hierarchy are necessary for such a complex building type.

Let's start with the basic components of a general hospital. Data at this general level would produce a diagram, as shown in Figure 9.26, that seems manageable. Every one of the components shown, however, has a complex internal organization of its own. Let's take the outpatient unit next to the emergency area to illustrate this. Figure 9.27 shows its relationship to the other units of the hospital. Figure 9.28 shows a diagram of the components within the outpatient unit and their relationships. If we focus on the specialty clinics, a new set of relationships at another hierarchical level is revealed (Figure 9.29). Similarly, if we go back to Figure 9.28 and focus on the examination treatment center, we see it is subdivided into various clusters, as shown in Figure 9.30, which, in turn, are assembled of

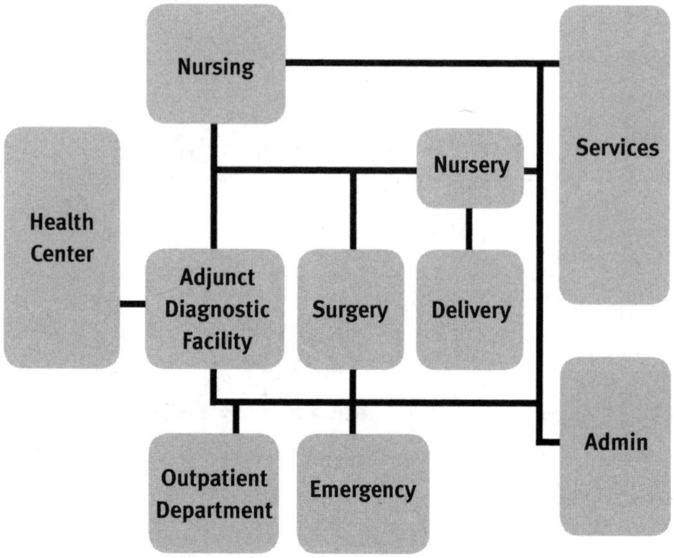

Figure 9.26: Main components of a hospital.

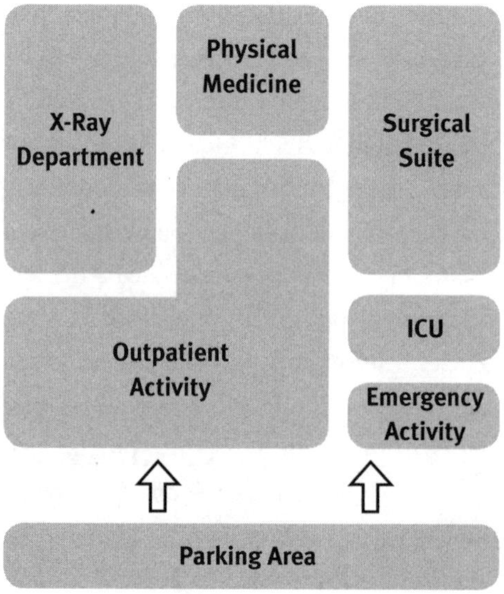

Figure 9.27: Outpatient Unit in relation to adjacent departments.

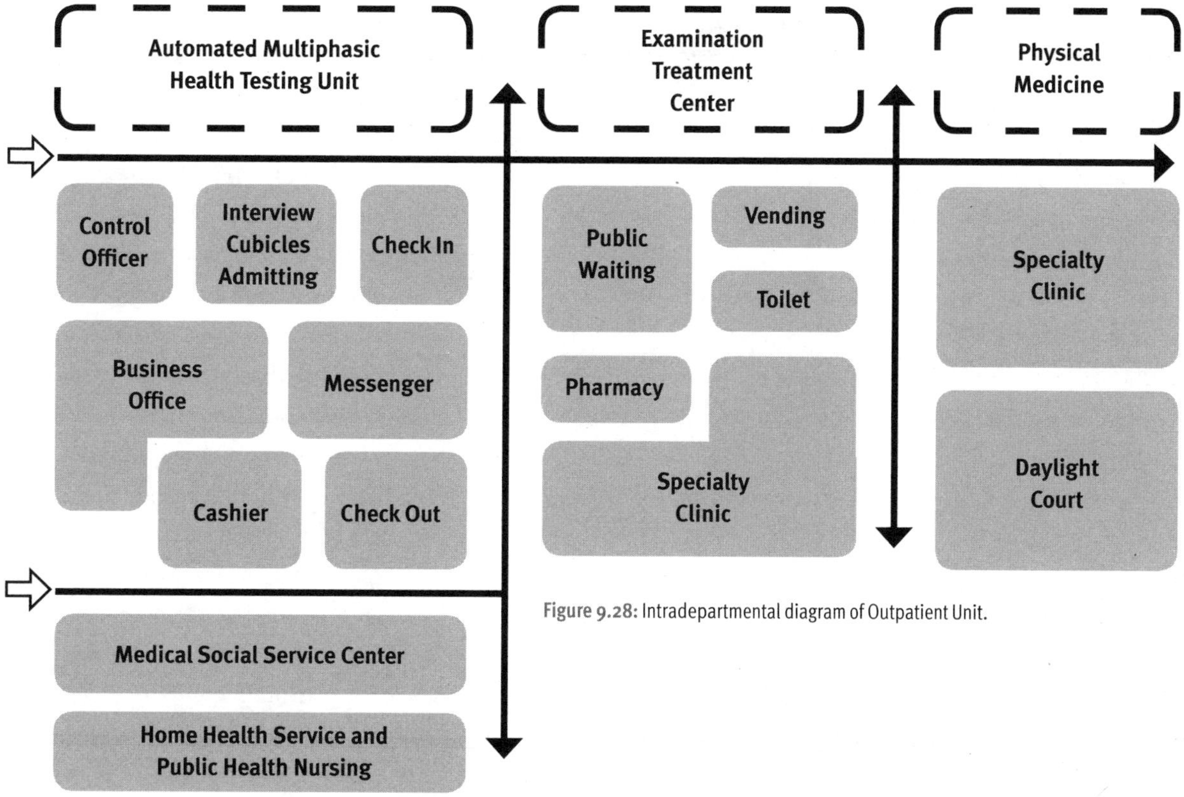

Figure 9.28: Intradepartmental diagram of Outpatient Unit.

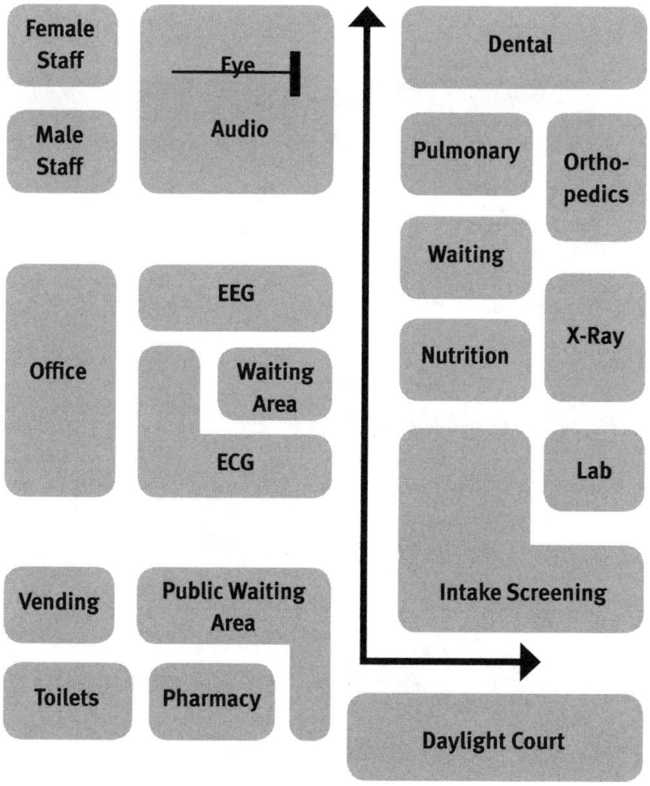

Figure 9.29: Components and relationships within Specialty Clinics area in the Outpatient Unit.

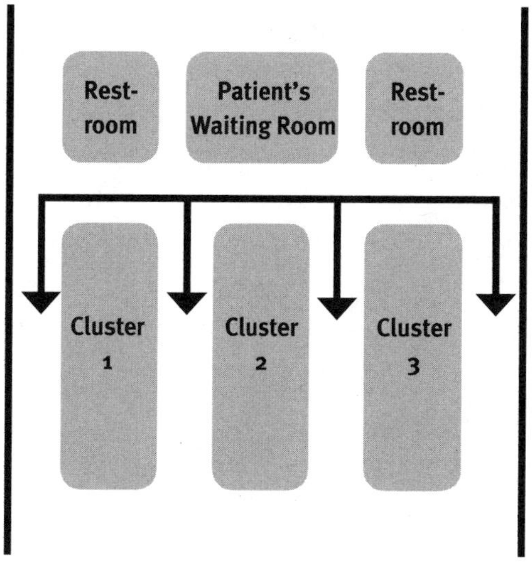

Figure 9.30: Outpatient Unit's Examination Treatment Center components and relationships.

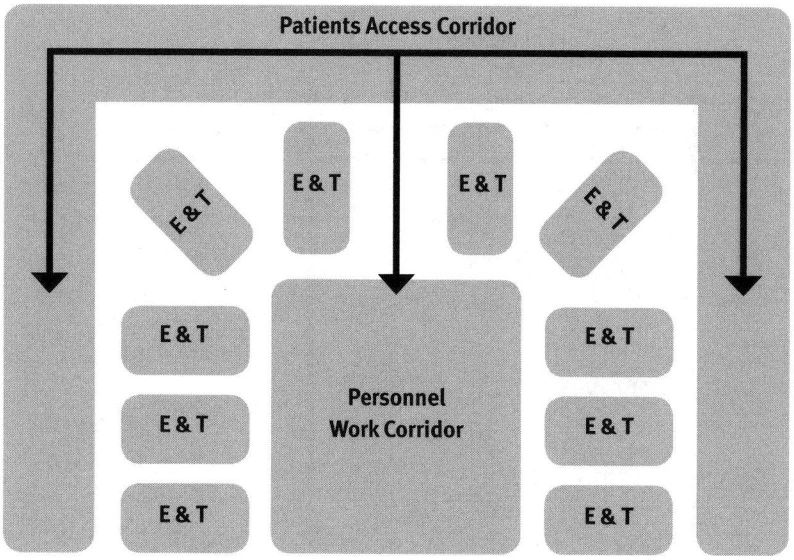

Figure 9.31: Examination Treatment Center clusters' components and relationships.

the components shown in Figure 9.31. Investigating relationships between components of this outpatient unit is necessary and relevant, but seeking relationships between the detailed components of this unit and those of, say, the administration of the hospital, would not be. Taking small parts out of context (without regard to their departments) and trying to understand their relationship would be highly unproductive and confusing.

At the appropriate level in the hierarchy, determining desired adjacencies between pairs of spaces is both necessary and useful. Here again, matrices and bubble diagrams can be both helpful and limiting. They are helpful because they give us a general idea of desired adjacency between any two spaces. They are limiting because they lack detail and nuance and, therefore, fail to tell the full story.

Most adjacency matrices and diagrams distinguish the various levels of adjacency desirability among spaces, such as high priority, medium priority, and low priority. While this is helpful, it will seldom give us enough information to introduce specificity and nuance in our designs. A more complete and helpful approach would be one expressing desirable relationships between spaces utilizing three kinds of data: the level of proximity desired, the importance of achieving that level of proximity, and, for adjacent spaces, the nature of the desired connection/separation between the two spaces.

In addition to proximity, determining a desire for distance is also important. Figure 9.32 lists possible relationships between units. These relationships range from a desire for close proximity to a desire for great distance. Figure 9.32 also incorporates a way to express the degree of importance of the request as well as a means of indicating the degree of connection between adjacent spaces.

Issues other than the functional adjacency needs between project parts are also helpful to determine how to group the various parts. These issues arise because of common characteristics or needs of spaces otherwise functionally unrelated. They include grouping according to privacy needs (public vs. private), degree of acoustic quality (loud vs. quiet), degree of accessibility (accessible vs. remote), need of exposure to exterior (internal vs. external), and enclosure extent (open vs. enclosed). These criteria will frequently bring together spaces to form groups.

Adjacency Options

- ☐ Interlocked
- ☐ Adjoining
- ☐ Across the hall
- ☐ A couple of rooms away
- ☐ Down the hall
- ☐ On the same side of the floor
- ☐ On the same floor
- ☐ Don't care
- ☐ Not next to
- ☐ Not close to
- ☐ Far away
- ☐ Totally open, no barrier
- ☐ Open to allow flow but some physical separation
- ☐ Barrier with door between the two spaces
- ☐ Barrier with no direct point of entry

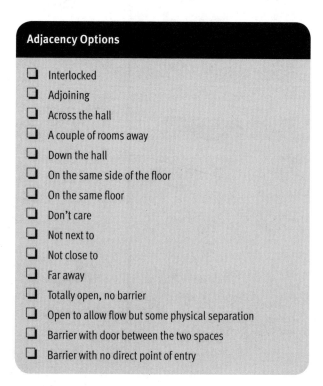

Figure 9.32: Adjacency Options form.

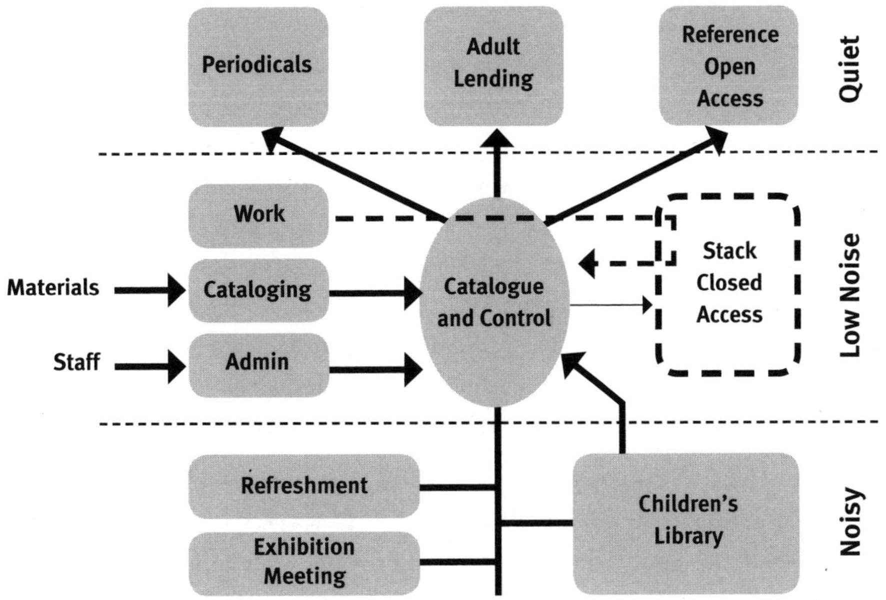

Figure 9.33: Acoustical zoning diagram for a library.

Figure 9.33, for instance, shows a diagram of a library organized by acoustical zones.

A Project's Driving Forces

Projects, we know, are much more than a series of rooms and spaces serving utilitarian functions. They embody and enable the performance of human rituals having specific nuances and meanings. To start making sense of the kinds of issues that may not come up in the quantitative analysis of a project, it is necessary to get a sense of the main qualitative aspects of the project. Most projects have a handful of main issues that stand out above the others. It is vital to understand these as early as possible in the process and to externalize them in some way. A very useful model is the one employed by the office of architect Gary Moye. His approach consists of identifying early the main guidelines or themes of a project and developing preliminary goals and strategies related to those driving themes.

The example that follows grew out of a series of workshops with user groups for a project to design an International College at a major university. The objective of the workshops was to facilitate the emergence of common themes to guide the project. As explained in the document from the architect, "the guidelines offer a synopsis of the themes which were developed by the group, within a structure which will serve the programming, site selection, and design phases of the project." The guidelines are developed as patterns, "design statements that describe and analyze project-related issues and suggest ways in which those issues might be resolved. The design guidelines articulate shared values which will guide the development of the project. As the project progresses the concepts and characteristics will test the validity of future decisions and the diagrams and strategies, which now hint at the means to fulfill the International College ideals, will become more precise and literal."[7]

Figure 9.34 explains the format used to present the guidelines. In Figure 9.35, the seven guidelines that emerged from the workshops are given a one-word title and explained very briefly. Specific characteristics and strategies originating from the discussions are then presented for each of the seven guidelines. Figures 9.36, 9.37, and 9.38 show examples of the way the guidelines were developed and presented in the program. Figure 9.36 addresses the guideline "community," Figure 9.37 addresses the guideline "oasis," and Figure 9.38 addresses the guideline "place."

Another useful approach, developed by Donna Duerk, consists of the identification of issues, goals, and

Design Guidelines

The design guidelines for the University of Oregon International College grew out of a series of workshops where a group representing the users of the college discussed the nature and provisions of a residential college. Some of the concepts described below were established at the beginning of the workshops through individual interviews; others grew out of the group workshop discussions. The characteristics and strategies listed under each concept were assembled from the discussions and evolved and were reviewed by the group over time. Since the intent of the workshops was not to force the project into a predetermined framework but to allow common themes to emerge, the development of the guidelines was parallel to but not the focus of the workshops. For the full record of the workshop sessions refer to the workshop appendix.

The guidelines offer a synopsis of the themes that were developed by the group, within a structure that will serve the programming, site selection, and design phases of the project. They are intended to carry out the principle of "patterns" described in the University's Long Range Campus Development Plan. Patterns are design statements that describe and analyze project-related issues and suggest ways in which those issues might be resolved. The design guidelines articulate shared values that will guide the development of the project. As the project progresses, the concepts and characteristics will test the validity of future decisions and the diagrams and strategies, which now hint at the means to fulfill the International College ideals, will become more precise and more literal.

Design Guideline Organization

The guidelines are organized to follow this general format:

Concept

General principle, which applies to the academic, social, and residential mission of the International College

Characteristic		Strategy
Attributes that support the general principle.	Diagram	Means identified to achieve the desired attributes.

Figure 9.34: Design guidelines format description. Courtesy of Gary Moye.

performance requirements.[8] Figure 9.39 shows an example of a student's adaptation of Duerk's approach for the design of a hypothetical advertising agency. Other formats may work as well. The important point is to identify the main issues or guidelines early and to envision ways to address them.

Synergy: Efficiency and Impact

Good projects achieve efficiencies that go beyond the additive result of their individual components. Three strategies that help achieve this are creating spaces that serve more than one function or can be shared; creating meaningful use of space between the programmed spaces; and creating spaces that add up to more than the sum of their parts in ways other than function.

Spaces that can be shared include conference and workrooms shared by departments in office settings and classrooms shared by different units in schools. Spaces that serve more than one function can include theater lobbies, community rooms in offices and civic facilities, and the

Summary of Concepts

Community
The college supports a residential learning community that integrates domestic and international students in an intensive and challenging experience at the university.

Center
The college is a focal point of "things international" on campus, is a symbol of internationalization, and contains some services and facilities unique to the International College.

Culture
The college fosters artistic and cultural expression.

Threshold
The college expresses a sense of openness to the University and is a "door" to the globe.

Oasis
The college cultivates interdisciplinary academic, cultural, and social experiences unavailable in existing departments. It is a setting where all faculty and all students can do special things.

Fit
The college serves and enhances the university, complements existing international programs, and respects the university's established development guidelines.

Place
The college is a positive physical environment that attracts residents, faculty, and visitors.

Figure 9.35: Summary of concepts for a college building project. Courtesy of Gary Moye.

well-known cafetorium (cafeteria/auditorium combination) in some school settings. Sharing like this results in economies for all the groups involved.

Meaningful in-between spaces can sometimes be added to projects to enhance the experience of their users. This is often the case in large projects where pockets along the circulation and off main public areas provide spaces for users to congregate, rest, or stop for a moment to reflect or perform a secondary activity.

The principle of spaces adding up to more than the sum of their parts was eloquently expressed by Charles Moore while talking about house design: "A good house will have resonances that extend beyond a set of discrete elements. The principle is that, in the assembly of parts, one plus one must equal more than two. . . . To make one plus one equal more than two you must, in doing any one thing you think important (making rooms, putting them together, or fitting them to the land), do something else that you think important as well (make spaces to live in, establish a meaningful pattern inside, or claim other realms outside)."[9] The way to give special qualities to otherwise plain and utilitarian spaces and functions requires purpose and resolve beyond the mere assembly of parts in functional ways.

Community

The college supports a residential learning community that integrates domestic and international students in an intensive and challenging experience at the university.

Identity

The residents belong to an identifiable and independent spatial unit within the college.

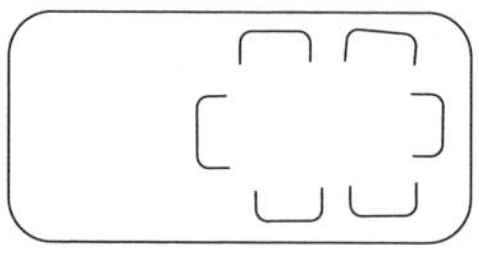

- Residences "read" as residences
- Internal focus
- Residents have a backyard

Integration

The college fosters the integration of academic, social, and residential life.

- Located near other residences
- Convenient and informal relationship between living and learning spaces

Interaction

Spatial variety, physical connections, and visibility within the college promote interaction at many scales.

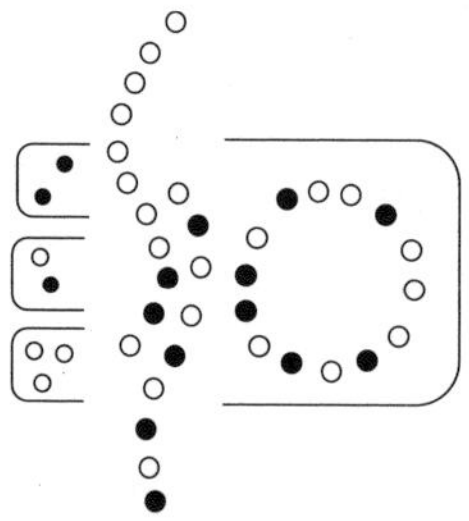

- The structure of the living environment promotes "mentoring"
- Living, dining, and bathing occur in shared spaces to promote interaction
- Windows and visibility "advertise" gathering
- Tangential circulation allows gatherings to coexist with passersby

Retention

The nature of the interaction at the college retains the interest of upper-level ICOL students and draws in students, faculty, and visitors from the university.

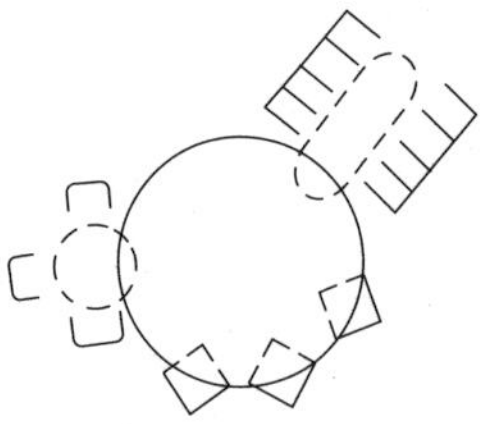

- Accessibility to different things in a cluster or on a level
- Study and work space for ICOL students who live elsewhere
- Variety of accommodations attracts returning students

Security

A clear, securable separation exists between the residential spaces and the facilities open to the university community.

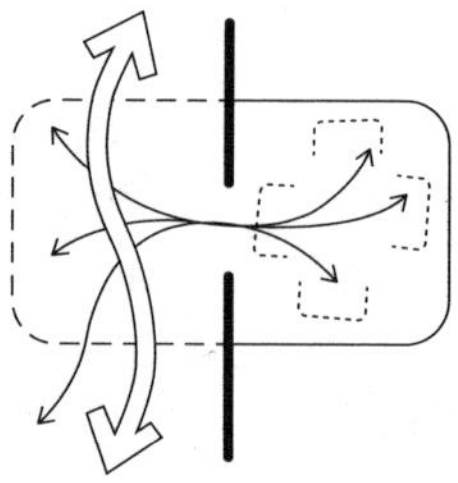

- Transition or zone between living and learning spaces
- Visitor access only to university-related spaces/Resident access to the whole place

Figure 9.36: The goal "community" broken down into more specific strategies. Courtesy of Gary Moye.

Oasis

The college cultivates interdisciplinary academic, cultural, and social experiences unavailable in existing departments. It is a setting where all faculty and all students can do special things.

Enrichment

Cultural and educational events and "happenings" are visible and conveniently accessible to college residents and to the university.

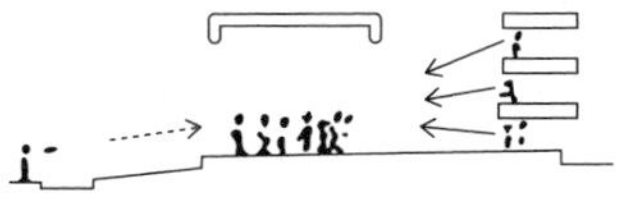

Public gathering areas in accessible and visible locations to the residents and university community.

Places for firesides, slide shows, films, music, and receptions

Exchange

Interaction between students and faculty is personal, frequent, and informal. The college is a good place to spend spare time together.

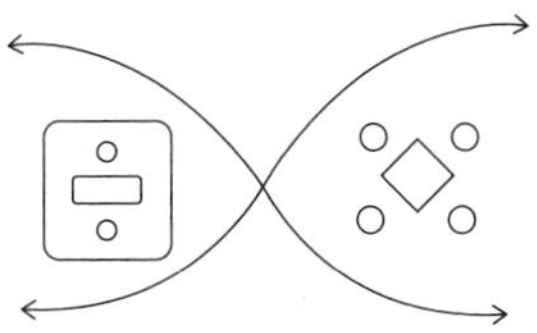

Department hearth for impromptu meetings

Catered dinners

Visitors stay as guests

Nearby social spaces for games and relaxation

Faculty firesides

Visibility of faculty and administrators

Innovation

Learning occurs outside the classroom and in different parts of the college. Students and faculty have individual and group access to information and communication technology.

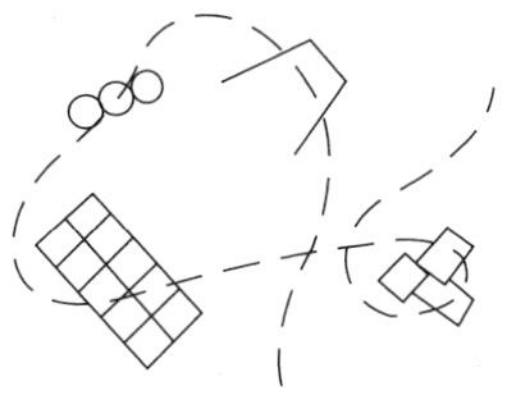

Formal and informal places for classes to meet

Computer resource center near classrooms

Language lab

Study areas and computer access in the residences

Inventiveness

The college has "flex space," which can be programmed for different users and different activities.

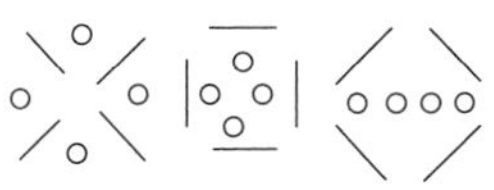

"Spec office" with an anchor tenant

Exhibit space open for different uses.

Lecture hall and classrooms can be configured for a variety of uses

Figure 9.37: The goal "oasis" broken down into more specific strategies. Courtesy of Gary Moye.

Place

The college is a positive physical environment that attracts residents, faculty, and visitors.

Coherence

The organization and definition of spaces promote a natural comprehensibility in the building.

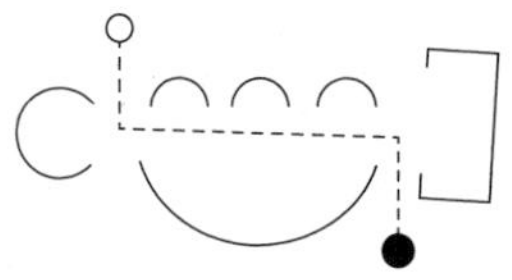

Clear, positive rooms and circulation patterns

Integration of service and served

Hierarchy of spaces and activities

Variation

The spatial variety in the college supports different activities and different needs.

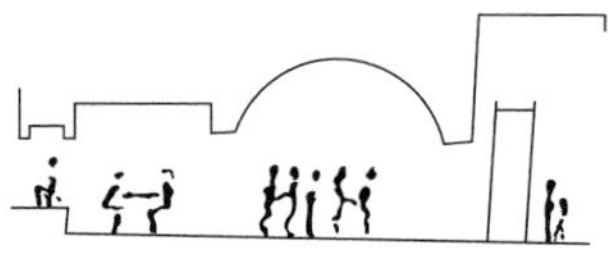

Different types of places to do things together

Places to be noisy, quiet, alone

Openness

Views and connections inside and outside give the college a sense of openness and informality.

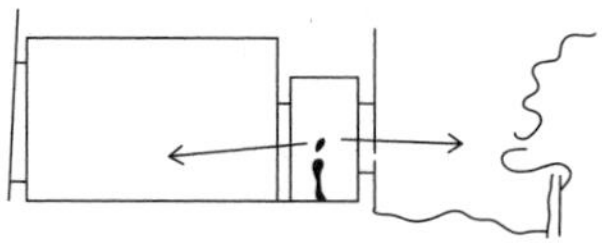

Tangential circulation

Generous windows

Interior windows

Light

The atmosphere of the building is bright.

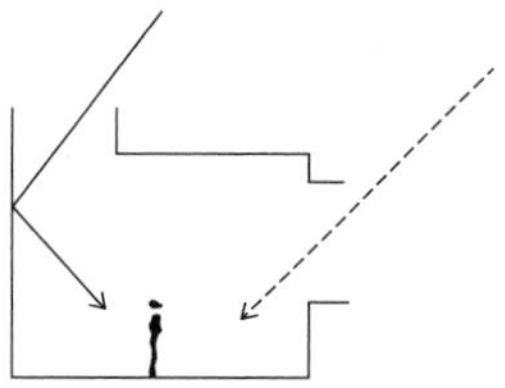

Natural light in every room

Balanced lighting systems

Reflective surfaces

Comfort

The rooms in the college are inviting and pleasant to inhabit.

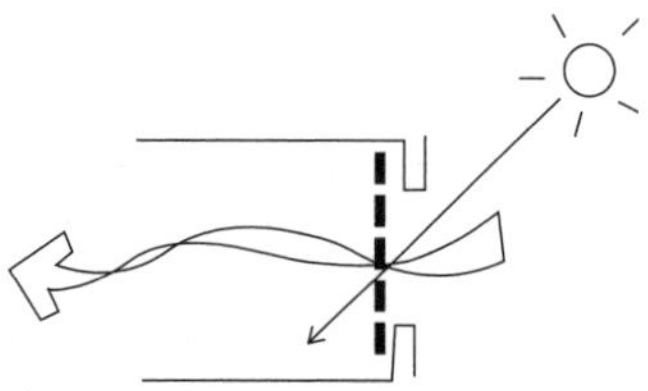

South-facing orientation

Materials that are pleasant to touch

Adequate ventilation and control

Longevity

The fabric of the building is durable, maintainable, and can adapt to different uses and tastes.

Figure 9.38: The goal "place" broken down into more specific strategies. Courtesy of Gary Moye.

Goal Statements and Performance Requirements	
Issue 1:	**Levels of Interaction**
Goal	the environment should provide an energizing environment that supports teamwork while also having areas where individuals can achieve their desired level of privacy
PR1:	the office should provide a diverse selection of work areas
PR2:	teamwork areas should be integrated within departments
Strategy:	use of spanner tables and pass-through areas at workstations facilitates interaction while overhead cabinets, panels, and orientation provide privacy; use of flexible small convergence room encourages reconfiguration
Issue 2:	**Image/Ambiance**
Goal	the environment should achieve a balance between bold creativity and professional conservatism
PR1:	the office should be visually stimulating in order to foster creative thinking
PR2:	important client areas and upper management spaces should portray a reserved professionalism
PR3:	the balance should be achieved through visual separation or a careful transformation
Strategy:	use of a '50s/retro/techy style to portray the nature of the agency; use of traditional full-height walls in private offices and client-centered areas blended with varying ceiling heights (from open to above to islands of suspended acoustical ceiling); use of rough, cold materials balanced by more polished, warmer finishes
Issue 3:	**Hierarchy**
Goal	the environment should express the relatively flat organizational structure of the agency, distinguishing top management from the remainder of employees
PR1:	orient employees so they can take maximum advantage of exterior views
PR2:	upper management should have private offices while most employees have workstations
Strategy:	use of clearly distinguished departments and workstation areas that can accommodate various positions; use of minimal full-height and partial-height walls

Figure 9.39: Example of a format consisting of the identification of project issues, goals, and performance requirements, followed by a responsive design strategy.

CAPSULE | Affordances

You may wonder, with good reason, to what extent the built environment can influence human behavior. This is a difficult question, but we can provide an acceptable answer with the help of James J. Gibson's concept of affordances.[1] This term is derived from "to afford" but does not exist as such in the dictionary. As conceived by Gibson, it refers to the way the particular configuration or arrangement of an object or setting makes it suitable for some overt activity. The horizontality of a concrete slab on the ground together with the natural law of gravity afford the possibility of walking on it with ease. The covered shelter at the park affords a good refuge when it rains. One does not necessarily have to run toward the shelter when it starts to pour outside, but the potential for refuge is there for those who desire it.

A good amount of what designers do is to create environmental opportunities and constraints. As seen from the examples above, the presence and arrangement of certain features encourage and facilitate certain actions and behaviors. Similarly, the absence or specific arrangement of certain features eliminate or discourage certain actions or behaviors. If the slab mentioned above was on a very steep incline instead of being flat, walking on it would be difficult for most people. Incidentally, the neighborhood's young and daring skateboarders would probably be delighted with the possibilities created by the inclined arrangement. At the park, if the shelter was not provided, one would not have the potential for refuge against the rain. Cover from the rain would be impossible, not because of imposed difficulty, but because of the omission of a sheltering structure.

Designers have great control over the provision or omission of features. They also enjoy considerable control over the specific arrangements of a project's parts and pieces. By manipulating these variables, they encourage certain behaviors and discourage others in response to the needs of the project. The environments they design, with all their inherent affordances, represent an environment full of potential; however, just because certain affordances are provided does not necessarily mean that they will be used, or even noticed. Perception of the possibilities offered by the environment varies depending on the straightforwardness of the affordance as well as the needs and motivations of the people using it. Motivations are particularly significant in determining whether and how a presented affordance is interpreted. As a result, sometimes the same condition is interpreted differently by different people. The half-open window in the house kitchen, for example, affords exposure to fresh air for the occupant, but it also affords a potential burglar an opportunity to get into the house.

Affordances occur at various levels of explicitness and sophistication. Many affordances are direct and obviously related to the requirements of the program, such as the provision of a desk, a chair, and four solid walls for someone who works in an office and needs privacy. Others are less tangible but work in subtle ways to influence behavior, such as the act of progressively widening a corridor to encourage movement in a particular direction. Still others serve secondary and even nonprogrammed desirable activities. These are often the most rewarding ones and the ones responsible for creating great environments. Just by being conscious of human nature and tendencies, the thoughtful designer can add meaningful gestures to a project. A place to rest somewhere in the middle of an excessively long path is likely to be used and appreciated by many users. It would be good to have it whether the program asked for it or not.

Other affordances can allow secondary activities in certain places, or even the transformation of those places in order to perform double duty. The introduction of comfortable lounge seating in many bookstores has transformed them from places to browse, buy, and leave to places where lingering in comfort is strongly encouraged. Likewise, providing a strategically placed pivoting or otherwise moving panel can, on demand, transform two moderately sized rooms into a large one suitable to host the periodic all-staff meeting or annual open-house party in an office setting. Windowsills of such construction, height, and depth as to permit sitting may help increase the seating capacity in the new "great room" during those special occasions.

Therefore, it is through the ability of built environments to invite certain activities and discourage others that they often exert their strongest influence on behavior. The concept of affordance is a useful one. You may start thinking of different ways of arranging or detailing parts of projects in order to add humanizing gestures, support secondary activities, and create areas that serve double duty. You may also want to look at your designs and see how they can discourage undesirable or inappropriate behaviors. You may also check for unintentional invitations or denials. The concept of affordance implies that there are many different degrees of a space's permissiveness related to any specific behavior. At one extreme, you can create conditions that not only allow but actually mandate a certain behavior, such as when entering a corridor with turnstiles that will not let you go back, thus imposing one particular type of action, forward movement. At the other extreme, you can deny access to an area from a given side by having a solid wall between the two areas. In between these extremes, affordances can exhibit different intermediate degrees of invitation or denial, such as strong invitation, subtle encouragement, possibility without encouragement, possibility with some difficulty (discouragement), or very difficult possibility (strong discouragement). As the designer, you are the permission granter. Think hard and choose wisely.

1. Gibson, J. J. (1979). *An ecological approach to visual perception*. Boston: Houghton Mifflin.

CAPSULE | Corporate Culture

Rob Goffee and Gareth Jones have developed an interesting model of organizational culture based on a pair of variables related to how human beings interact in organizations. The two variables are sociability and solidarity. The authors describe sociability as "a measure of friendliness among members of a community. . . . The level of sociability at a company is often the first thing a new hire notices. . . . When a coworker has a birthday, it gets celebrated. When a coworker lands in the hospital, he or she gets visited. . . . High sociability promotes high morale, creativity, and collaboration. On the negative side, close friendships among members of an organization may promote tolerance for poor performance and an environment in which "the best compromise gets applied to problems, not the best solution."[1]

Solidaristic relationships, the authors explain, "are based on common tasks, mutual interests, and clearly understood shared goals that benefit all the involved parties, whether they personally like each other or not."[2] The no-nonsense emphasis on the work to be done means that groups high in solidarity are industrious and productive. The organization is likely to have very clear goals and procedures that must be strictly followed. On the negative side, high-solidarity organizations can be heartless and even brutal at times, showing little regard for workers who don't conform to their goals and procedures.

Combinations of high or low levels of sociability and solidarity yield four possible cultures, which the authors call **networked** (high sociability, low solidarity), **mercenary** (high solidarity, low sociability), **fragmented** (low in both), and **communal** (high in both). These four tendencies, in turn, can be classified as either positive or negative, depending on how well the approach responds to the competitive environment at a particular time.

The four types of cultures have an effect on not only physical space but also patterns of communication, use of time, and sense of identity. In terms of physical space, a networked organization may have an open-door policy and more personal displays in workers' offices and cubicles; a networked organization may enjoy an above-average amount of social spaces such as break rooms and lounges. Mercenary organizations may exhibit arrangements that are highly functional and help to get the work done. Space allocations are likely to be related to achievement, and one may see more merit ribbons and awards hanging on the walls than family pictures.

In communal organizations space is shared both formally and informally, there are few barriers between departments, and the office-by-rank mentality is nonexistent. There are likely to be places for socialization, personal displays, and corporate symbols around the office, all coexisting harmoniously. The fragmented organization, by contrast, is likely to be characterized by closed doors that promote individual work and discourage socialization. There may be a conspicuous lack of both personal and corporate displays around the office.

continued

CAPSULE | Corporate Culture, *continued*

Understanding the corporate culture of a client is critical because it may give the designer important clues as to the proper way to dispose of space, allocate square footages, and devise appropriate connections or separations between departments.[3]

Mission Statements

Another important piece of information that often helps designers understand a company is the company's mission statement, the document used to express the essential goals and shared values of the company. Although these can be, as Wally Olins puts it, "the corporate version of the old Boy Scout oath, which demanded, as I recall, that thirteen-year-olds should be clean in body and mind," reflecting "the wish rather than the reality,"[4] most companies have a mission statement, and they are often included in the programming document prepared by the designer during this stage. Most mission statements are like a declaration of all the predictable and generic things that shareholders and the public expect to hear (quality, profit, integrity, and so on), but they can give the designer good clues about the personality of the company. A few examples should help illustrate their nature and how they can give us important clues about the company.

Autodesk, the software company, has the following vision and mission statements:

> Vision: To create software tools that transform ideas into reality.
>
> Mission: To create quality software solutions and support services that foster innovation, creativity, and productivity for customers and partners around the world.[5]

While the vision statement is broad and vague, the mission statement gives clues about the company's commitment to innovation and its global nature. These are traits that could be used or alluded to in the actual design for the company's facilities.

Some companies extend their missions beyond quality and profits and integrate a broader societal component. For instance, Ben & Jerry's Homemade Inc., the premium ice-cream makers from Vermont, declare their social mission as follows:

> To operate the company in a way that actively recognizes the central role that business plays in the structure of society by initiating innovative ways to improve the qua lity of life of a broad community: local, national, and international.[6]

Their statement speaks to a commitment to seek ways to enhance the lives of those around them. For Ben & Jerry's, mission goes beyond quality and profits—although they make sure to include quality and profits in other sections of their mission statement document.

The mission statement for Coca-Cola, the soft drink giant, in addition to mentioning value, quality, service, leadership, and so forth, adds some useful clues for designers when it declares: "We refresh the world."[7] One can easily start imagining ways to create an environment that conveys the idea of refreshment.

Southwest Airlines Co., the low-fare, high-customer-satisfaction airline, uses a statement that conveys a sense of the quality of the human interactions they seek to have with both customers and employees: "The mission of Southwest Airlines is dedication to the highest quality of Customer Service, delivered with a sense of warmth, friendliness, individual pride, and company spirit."[8] One can sense the warm and friendly qualities that could be expected from their facilities.

In order to service clients properly in a competitive marketplace, designers need an intimate knowledge of the companies they serve. A company's personality, culture, and mission become important aspects to be understood.

1. Goffee, R., & Jones, G. (1998). *The character of a corporation: How your company's culture can make or break your company*. New York: Harper Collins.
2. Ibid, p. 28.
3. Ibid, pp. 21–43.
4. Olins, W. (1990). *Corporate identity*. Cambridge, MA: Harvard Business School Press.
5. Abrahams, J. (1999). *The mission statement book*. Berkeley: Ten Speed Press.
6. Ibid, p. 96.
7. Ibid, p. 132.
8. Ibid, p. 394.

CASE STUDY

Ingenious Strategy to Connect Existing Dormitory Buildings Yields a Strong Sense of Place and Dynamic Spaces for Students.

Project: Ohio State University Student Housing (611,000 s.f.)

Location: Columbus, Ohio

Design Firm: Sasaki Associates. Photo credits: Pease Photography

Challenge: How can one transform two pairs of outdated 1950's campus dormitories into a thriving and unified complex with a strong sense of place and dynamic social and study spaces?

When a new policy was established at Ohio State University (OSU) to house all freshman and sophomores on campus, a need arose to look for opportunities to increase the university's housing capacity. Important goals were to enhance the image of the campus residential neighborhood and to create a state-of-the-art 24/7 living-learning environment for the residents.

A study conducted by Sasaki Associates as part of a comprehensive master plan identified three areas of opportunity for housing development aimed at enhancing the image of residential campus and fostering a strong sense of place. The South High-Rise District area was selected for redevelopment. The existing 1950s-era dormitories in the district needed significant mechanical system upgrades in order to comply with current codes and offer the required levels of thermal comfort. Additionally, the existing dorms were dated and lacked program spaces for student life—an important goal of the OSU Residential Life group(Figure CS9.1).

Figure CS9.1: Example of existing conditions

The complete project involved renovations of and additions to two pairs of towers, resulting in two new residential halls. The project included the creation of new drop-off courtyards, streetscape definition, passive green space, exterior lighting, outdoor furniture, and signage.

The solution devised by Sasaki featured innovative connecting structures that linked pairs of existing 11-story residential towers (Figure CS9.2). These new bridging structures provided spaces for new entry lobbies, as well as social and study spaces for students, additional rooms, and newly defined courtyards. By adopting an energy-efficient envelope design, the design team was able to use expansive glazing to wash the new lobbies and lounges with natural light, thus enhancing the quality of these social spaces and increasing the visual connectivity between areas. (Figure CS9.3). The design team was also able to anchor the additions to the existing infrastructure of bathrooms, stairs, and elevators, thus

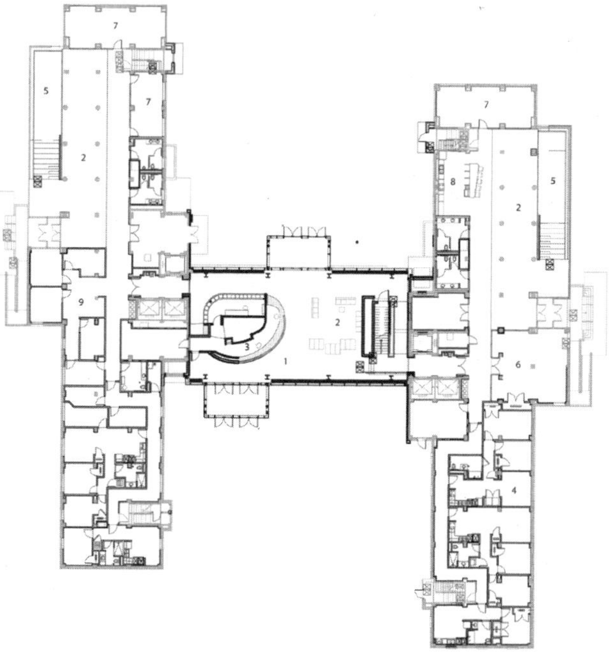

Figure CS9.2: Floor plan showing the new connecting structure between the two residential towers.

continued

Figure CS9.3: The multistory main lobby is washed with natural light and features a memorable reception desk/mezzanine structure (a landmark) and multiple seating zones.

achieving economies that allowed for the further improvement of open spaces and landscapes.

The newly created entry courtyards established a new front door to the lobby, allowing for a comfortable drop-off zone, temporary parking, space for daily deliveries, and an area for queuing during move-in and move-out days. On the other side of the lobby, a lawn dedicated to informal recreation established a "back garden" for the students (Figure CS9.4).

The connector areas provide seamless accessibility between towers while creating unique social spaces. On the second floor a bridge connects the existing wings and provides access to a new mezzanine lounge (Figure CS9.5). The lounge, called "the nest," provides a formidable and exciting stage for student social interactions (Figure CS9.6). Upper floor lounges with gentle ramps create additional social nodes while providing accessible connections.

New networks of space dedicated to student life are strategically located throughout the building. In the existing wings, new openings on the ground floor slab connect to the lower levels, bringing in natural light and vitality. As a result, otherwise undesirable basement spaces were transformed into active student zones populated by laundry rooms, game areas, study rooms, and hangout space (Figure CS9.7).

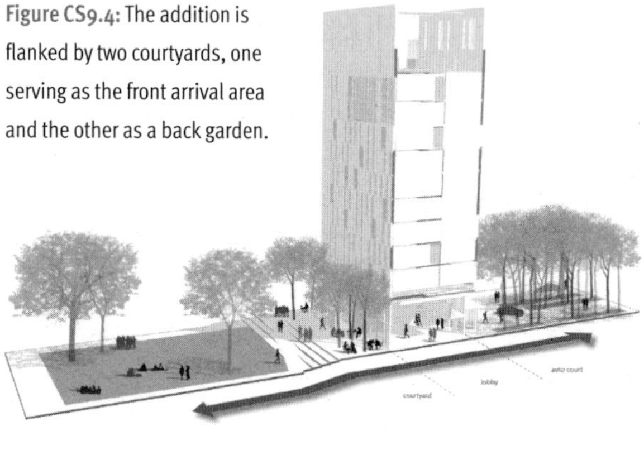

Figure CS9.4: The addition is flanked by two courtyards, one serving as the front arrival area and the other as a back garden.

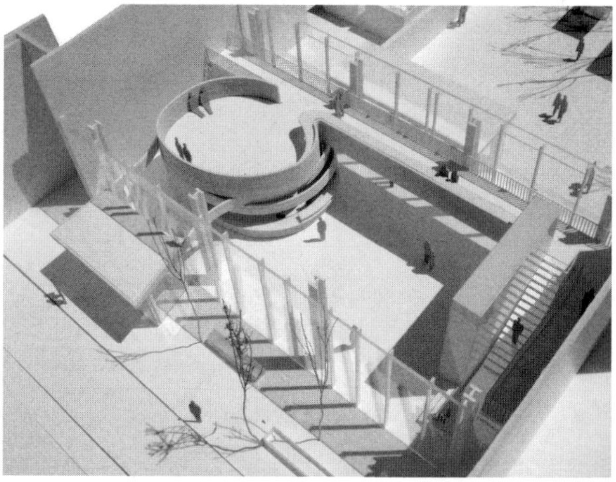

Figure CS 9.5: View of the sculptural reception mezzanine structure and the second floor bridge that connects the existing wings and provides access to the gathering nest area.

Figure CS 9.6: View of the nest

In the upper floors, new activity nodes were created where old and new spaces meet, unifying the communities. At the 10th floor, a double-height sky lounge and mezzanine allows for larger gatherings with breathtaking views toward the campus and downtown (Figure CS9.8).

The South High Rises project revitalized the two pairs of older buildings into a dynamic destination area, enhancing the image of the neighborhood and creating a state-of-the-art living-learning environment that provides memorable, student-focused accommodations for 4,500 residents. The new design gives the district a revitalized look and a distinct sense of place while adding student capacity and many dynamic social and study spaces for the students.

Figure CS 9.7: Openings on the ground floor such as the one shown bring in natural light and create a sense of vitality. Basement areas were transformed and given new life with desirable destinations and hangout spaces.

Figure CS 9.8: The double-height sky lounge and mezzanine on the 10th floor provides a space for gatherings with breathtaking views.

REVIEW

Summary

Designers need to understand the specific realities of the projects they design. The basic understanding of a project is acquired during the programming phase. In general, designers need to get a good understanding of the realities of the context, the internal players, and those of the project itself.

All projects occur within, and are influenced by, specific historic, cultural, and geographic contexts. Additionally, and varying from project to project, are the contextual realities of both the immediate surroundings of a project and the building in which it occurs.

The immediate neighborhood provides an important context with specific adjacent buildings, important long-standing patterns, and so on. The site and nearby surroundings provide specific natural features, circulation patterns, and points of access to the building. Environmental features such as the sun path, climate, sounds, sights, and smells are also crucial considerations.

The building in which the project takes place also offers an important context at an even more immediate scale. Particular aspects to be analyzed include the other tenants in the building and the public circulation inside the building. Additionally, it is necessary to analyze the physical features of the space designated for the project. A thorough understanding of the space's size, geometry, internal components, perimeter conditions, views to the outside, and so on always provides essential information.

Another important aspect requiring proper understanding is the nature of the project's internal players, usually the client and the users. The users are those people for whom the building is intended. The building must, by all accounts, work for them and their own particular circumstances.

Perhaps the most important aspect requiring understanding is the project itself. All projects are instances of project types that have been designed and built before. Therefore, there is a substantial body of knowledge about most building types, as well as built examples. Every type also has different applications, or subtypes. Even among different subtypes there are specific variations, like those among different kinds of clothing stores.

The specific requirements of the project must also be understood. Each part and its role in the overall scheme needs to be identified and understood. Additionally, the relationships among parts, their hierarchy, and the project's driving forces need to be analyzed and understood.

1. Pelli, C. (1999). *Observations for young architects.* New York: Monacelli Press.
2. Moore, C., Allen, G., & Lyndon, D. (1974). *The place of houses.* New York: Holt, Rinehart & Winston.
3. Ibid, p. 173.
4. Vitruvius. (1974). *The ten books of architecture* (M. H. Morgan, Trans.). New York: Dover Publications.
5. Pelli, 1999, p. 181.
6. Heinsath, C. (1977). *Behavioral architecture: Toward an accountable design process.* New York: McGraw-Hill.
7. Moye, G. (1994). *Facilities program: International College, University of Oregon.* Private document. p. 3.
8. Duerk, D. (1993). *Architectural programming: Information management for design.* New York: Wiley.
9. Moore, Allen, & Lyndon, 1974, pp. 147–148.

Chapter Questions

1. Name and describe the four contextual aspects discussed under surroundings.
2. Name and describe the three contextual inside-the-building aspects discussed.
3. Explain the difference between clients and users.
4. Think of as many subtypes as you can for different kinds of retail stores, restaurants, and offices.
5. Name the various adjacency categories mentioned in this chapter.
6. What factors other than adjacencies can assist in grouping project parts?

Exercises

1. Analyze the building that houses your design department. Use diagrams to illustrate significant factors for the building's interior and the building's surroundings.
2. Analyze the building that serves as context to the project you are currently working on in your design studio. Use diagrams to illustrate significant exterior and interior factors of the building.
3. Perform a typological profile study similar to the ones shown in this chapter for a church, your school building, a movie theater, and a ski club.
4. Produce a series of detailed bubble adjacency diagrams for your current project. Proceed hierarchically. First do one diagram of the main project parts, and then proceed to do one for each major department or section.
5. Formulate a series of concepts, characteristics, and strategies for your current project using the two formats shown in the section of this chapter titled "A Project's Driving Forces." See Figures 9.34 through 9.38.

CHAPTER 10
IDEATION

INSTRUCTIONAL OBJECTIVES

- Explain the meaning and function of concepts in design.
- Explain the difference between character and organizational concepts.
- Identify the stages of concept development.
- Present an approach to spatial organization using the place elements.
- Explain how to select a design idea from a project's dominant issues.
- Suggest ways of formulating concept ideas.
- Explain how to draw parti and functional concept diagrams.
- Explain how to prepare graphically strong concept diagrams.
- Explain how to write concept statements.

Just as the success of any design will be limited by the wisdom of the concept it follows, the wisdom of any concept is limited by the vision and knowledge of the designer who conceives it.

—*Stanley Abercrombie,* A Philosophy of Interior Design

In chapter 9 we looked at some of the variables that make each project unique, such as the users, context, and program. We also explained the importance of making sense of large amounts of information and reviewed some of the graphic tools designers use to account for project requirements and their relationships. At the conclusion of the analysis stage, you should have a good understanding of the client's nature, the project's parts, how these relate, and the context (physical, cultural, and historical) in which the project will take place. In some cases, you may even have preliminary notions of a potential design approaches.

The phase that follows, **ideation**, is a critical and challenging one. After all the project entities have been accounted for and the relationships between parts have been understood and diagrammed many times over, designers have to come up with a suitable approach for the project. For some designers this is a paralyzing moment in the design process; for others it is the most exciting moment in the design process. You can compare what happens during this stage with the first broad strokes on a painter's canvas. These first strokes communicate the artist's intentions and commit the painting to a certain approach, one that will be refined and added to as the work progresses. This chapter is about the process of moving from an understanding of the project and its requirements to the production of insightful concepts that respond to its unique circumstances. We discuss the design concept, with a presentation of both character and organizational concepts. As you will see, the decisions made during this early design stage become the foundations upon which the rest of the design is built. It is essential, then, that they are sound and fitting.

SEARCHING FOR PROPER FIT

Designers are often hired to provide solutions to projects with complex and sometimes conflicting requirements. A company may want to reduce the amount of leased space while increasing morale and productivity; a store may want to emphasize certain merchandise without a decrease in sales of the deemphasized merchandise; a restaurant may want to increase seating capacity while preserving a sense of intimacy. Good solutions to these types of problems require imagination and insight on the one hand, balance and compromise on the other.

The proper fit refers to the appropriate correspondence between a set of requirements and the design solution that addresses them. It is concerned with issues of comfort, style, and occasion.

The ideation stage is responsible for establishing the design's basic fit in relation to the project's needs. During this stage of design the most basic overall decisions concerning project parts and places, as well as their placement, shape, and orientation, are made. The process of assembling places and functions, as you will see, involves much more than transposing adjacency diagrams to a given floor plate, placing dividing walls between functions, and then selecting elegant finishes. This rarely produces a satisfying design. A successful design requires the organization of all required functions within a coherent conceptual and physical structure that will make users' experiences orderly and engaging. This is accomplished with an insightful and fitting overall basic strategy, also known as the **design concept**. The concept produced during this stage is eventually developed, refined, and articulated to achieve the final design.

THE CONCEPT

A successful design possesses a structure that is uniquely derived from the requirements of the project and a character that reflects the nature and personality of the users. These attributes give the project a real sense of cohesion and identity. Yet the design concept remains one of the most misunderstood topics among interior design students. Part of the blame for this can be attributed to the myriad of existing definitions for "the concept" as well as the mystical connotations implied by some of them. Furthermore, no clear explanation of the process of generating concepts exists.

What Is a Design Concept?

American Heritage Dictionary defines *concept* as "a general idea or understanding, especially one derived from specific instances or occurrences."[1] Based on this definition, a concept in interior design could be said to be a general strategy or approach for the solution of a design problem having specific circumstances. A design concept aims to conceive a response to solve a design problem in a very particular way. Projects, however, are made up of not one but many problems of different scope and level of importance, and the solution to each of these problems requires the use of appropriate strategies. Each one of these ideas or strategies is a concept. There can, in fact, be dozens of concepts for a single project.

To work with concepts, then, you have to be able to understand their hierarchy. There are big concepts and little ones. It's the big concepts that we are most concerned with here, although the smaller ones are important to resolve design issues at more detailed levels. The smaller concepts are subordinate to the big ones in such a way that, in the end, the finished product is one cohesive whole.

Every design project requires a main concept at the overall project scale. This **main concept** addresses the main design problems of the project and provides a dominant structure or framework that all other design ideas adhere to. Whereas the distinction between major and minor concepts and the need for one big concept may seem plausible enough, there are still some nuances that need to be understood in order to grasp how to use concepts.

A major misconception about design concepts in design is the belief that they consist of one single big idea. While some main concepts may consist of a single idea, most consist of a handful of ideas that, together, constitute a single, or at least consistent, approach. Students are often paralyzed by the difficulty of having to synthesize an entire project into one idea when they are legitimately trying to respond to dozens of important issues. A concept consisting of a single idea is unrealistic in most cases. Thinking in terms of a series of ideas pointing to one dominant approach is a more realistic proposition.

Another misleading notion is the suggestion that concept ideas arise out of spontaneous flashes of inspiration. Again, this is far from the truth; neither students nor practitioners should sit and wait for such flashes to strike. The generation of concept ideas involves a great deal of systematic left-brain thinking and analysis. Although it is true that ideas may arise spontaneously after a thorough analysis of the design problem and a period of incubation, there are no guarantees that this will happen. The best advice is to approach the process systematically and rely more on rational, insightful thinking than on flashes of inspiration.

To further confuse the novice, main concepts can be expressed in many different ways depending on the criteria used. Concepts can be philosophical (less is more, equal amounts of space for all, and so on), thematic (a western bar), functional (a two-wing configuration separating two distinct groups), artistic (a balanced composition of bold colors), mood related (a place that induces tranquility), or stylistic (a space that projects an outlook toward the future while remaining rooted in past tradition). Does the designer adopt one of each? Of course not. How can a designer arrive at a dominant concept then?

You may begin to realize the challenge of working with and selecting "the concept among concepts." Is there a best approach? Although there is no simple answer to this question, we can say that all projects have salient aspects that become important design drivers. These may be external, such as contextual forces, or internal, driven by function, desired image, client history and personality, or brand characteristics. Many projects have more than one such driving factor, and it is up to the design team to decide which factor or factors will drive the overall design response. The design response will, of course, translate into how the project's floor plan is organized (most visibly at first through diagrams and loosely drawn floor plans), what architectural forms and elements are adopted (most visibly at first through loosely drawn elevations and three-dimensional sketches), what detailing approach is used (most visibly at first through loose sketches), what materials are chosen (most visible at first through samples or rendered sketches), and what furnishings, accessories, and other appurtenances are incorporated.

In some cases, a particular way of performing the functions that occur in the project will drive the design. One example of this is the way the Swedish furniture company IKEA has chosen to display and sell their products. Their approach is quite different from the approach taken by conventional furniture retailers. At IKEA, the customer selects products from showroom areas on the upper floors, writes down the product information (name and number) on a note pad provided, and, ultimately, picks up the "boxed" products from the rows and rows of shelves on the warehouse like ground floor. One then proceeds, with oversized shopping carts full of boxes, to the check-out areas, pays, and finally loads up the goods in the convenient loading areas just outside. To address this unique way of selling furniture, the entire facility is designed to facilitate the flow from one stage to the next.

Sometimes the main concept is driven by style, image, or theme. These tend to occur in highly creative environments such as restaurants, stores, clubs, and hotels. The intentionally minimalist showrooms designed by Claudio Silvestrin for Giorgio Armani are examples of these high-image kinds of projects.

At other times, a series of more pragmatic organizational concerns, such as relationships between departments and clear circulation systems, determines the main concept idea. Design concepts can only be determined on a case-by-case basis when the particularities of a project are known. They are externalized through verbal statements, concept diagrams, and concept sketches.

Design Concept Statements

Written statements are most often used to convey character (image) concepts. They come in many varieties. Upon examination of the many kinds of concept statements ordinarily written by students and practitioners alike, one notices a broad range of approaches with different degrees of clarity. Some designers repeat, sometimes in great detail, the needs and wants of the client; others write detailed play-by-play accounts of the experience, starting with the moment one enters the space; some talk about their intentions to create a productive office or a stimulating restaurant. The list goes on and on. The problem is that many written concept statements never get to the point.

The point of design concept statements is to tell the audience, as efficiently as possible, about the designer's approach to solve the design problem. Your statement may be as brief as "to create an intimate candlelit environment comprised of multiple zones" or "to place all the important public functions along the perimeter of the space to take advantage of the magnificent views." The main thing is that the design concept statement needs to address what you will do (or have already done) to solve the design problem.

As straightforward as this may appear, many young designers struggle with written concept statements. Let's examine four of the most common problems.

Problem 1: Statements that regurgitate the project goals from the program.
For example, someone may repeat "the concept is to create a new office facility for a client that wants to consolidate units" directly from the information given in the program. This information is not a design concept but part of the design problem definition.

Problem 2: Statements that state the obvious.
For example, "the concept is to create a productive and functional office environment" or "the concept is to design a restaurant that will attract customers." It is obvious that offices need to be productive and restaurants need to attract customers. Those things go without saying. A design concept statement has to go beyond that.

Problem 3: Statements that use many adjectives without really saying much.
For example, "the concept is to design a grand and magnificent space that will be a source of delightful inspiration to all." This may be an adequate beginning but is still too vague; plus, there are many ways of producing grand and magnificent spaces and no hint is given here about the specific approach to be taken.

Problem 4: Statements that are lengthy descriptions of every single feature of the project.
There is no need to describe every feature of the project in the concept statement; the statement should include only the main aspects that are driving the design.

What then makes a good concept statement? Although there are many approaches to the verbal externalization of concept statements, the best concept statements share the following three attributes:

- Design concept statements speak more about the design solution than the design problem.
- Design concept statements are selective.
- Design concept statements are economical.

Let's examine these one at a time.

Design concept statements speak about the design solution.

The first attribute requires that the concept state something about the design solution and not the design problem. These are two closely related but different elements that together help to give the project definition. The design problem, however, precedes the design strategy to be used. Consider the following statement: "The concept was to create a luxury residence for discerning, affluent empty-nesters and semiretired executives seeking a California coastal lifestyle." Is this a design concept? To test a concept to determine whether it is a design concept, simply ask yourself the following question: Does this statement tell me anything about the approach to the design solution? In the previous example, the answer is no. Although the statement tells us a great deal about what kind of residence the project will be, it defines the problem without stating the solution. Nevertheless, having a clear project definition is an important step that needs to take place before the design concepts are generated. Clients have to define, with some level of specificity, what type of project it will be, who is it for, whether it will be formal or casual, and so forth.

Consider now the following statement for a restaurant: The idea is to deliver "excellent food and service at a reasonable cost in a casual but intriguing environment," attracting "a wide range of customers—from formally dressed theater-goers to casually dressed diners."[2] Here again, the statement is helping to define the kind of restaurant it will be but, so far, is not saying much about the designer's idea of how to accomplish this. The statement is part of the design problem statement, which speaks to the owner's goals and vision.

If the preceding statements are about design problem definition, the design concept has to be a response to these kinds of statements. So, the designer studies the situation, and after some consideration decides on a design approach to take. After all, many design solutions could reasonably produce the luxury residence and the casual and intriguing restaurant prescribed above. Let's examine a design concept statement written by a student to address an office project: "The concept behind my design . . . is openness and visual stimulation. All spaces are designed to pull you from one to the next smoothly. The angular rooms and shapes are intended to create an energetic feel in the workplace." Notice that the statement is talking about the designer's response to the design problem. Notice, too, that the statement mentions both the student's intentions (openness, stimulation, creating an energetic feel) and some specific ideas about how to achieve these (spaces that pull you, angular rooms and shapes). Now, consider another student's design concept statement for the same project: "The goal of this design is to create an innovative and dynamic environment that is attractive to Identity Consortium's image-conscious clients and employees. This is achieved through an open and flowing configuration of space and the use of modern classic pieces paired with an exposed and slightly industrial contemporary setting." Once again, notice the presence of both design intentions and more specific strategies for accomplishing them.

Although the designer's initial design concept statement might be somewhat vague and broad, as the design progresses the means for achieving it become progressively more defined. Consider the following example, a Levi's Dockers Shop by Bergmeyer Associates, Inc. One can imagine how the designer (perhaps with help from the owner) may have come up with the main idea and how over time the more specific strategies (and other discarded ones) may have evolved.

What? (design idea): Design a store that "recalls soothing images of days on holiday."
How? (design strategy): Use "a nautical theme and vacation vignettes."
But how? (more specific design strategies): "Merchandise backdrops of wicker furniture and sailing, plus V-grooved panels stenciled with the Dockers logo, cherry soffits, and backlit art glass and props."[3]

Design concept statements are selective.

The second attribute of good design concept statements is selectivity. One cannot possibly hope to address every single issue of the project in the design concept. The process requires the designer to assess the design problem and exercise proper judgment in selecting the concept's driving forces. When we examine the design concept statement for an office project stated earlier ("The concept behind my design . . . is openness and visual stimulation. All spaces are designed to pull you from one to the next smoothly. The angular rooms and shapes are intended to create an energetic feel in the workplace."), we notice that the designer chose to focus on just two factors: openness and visual stimulation. Surely there were many other important factors of that project but, for this designer, openness and visual stimulation drove the main design direction. Here is another example: "The main concept behind my design is energy. By using an organic plan and strong color I hope to energize people and draw them through the entire space." A single idea—energy—was selected to lead the design approach.

Design concept statements are economical.

The third attribute of good design concept statements is economy. Consider the following succinct concept statement for a Los Angeles restaurant "featuring space-age dining for the jet set": "Use high-tech lighting and a lunar-look interior to invoke a futuristic fantasy that reflects the building's flying saucer architecture."[4] Beyond selectivity, this statement also exercises a great deal of economy by packing a lot of information into a rather brief statement. Even when one has more to say, it is possible to slim down the concept statement through selectivity and proper editing. In the concept statement for the Identity Consortium office project introduced earlier, the designer's main goal and three strategies to achieve it are packed into a 48-word statement. That's economical.

Design Concept Drivers

In the process of conceiving a design concept for a project, the designer will look at the realities of the project and decide how to express the main concept. This will depend on many factors, including the project type, inherent challenges of the site, the twist given to the project, personal intuition, and so on. Design concepts will range from the pragmatic to the symbolic and emotional. Next are some examples showing a variety of concepts driven by different aspects of the project.

The first example is driven by existing physical constraints on the project site. An Italian restaurant in Philadelphia occupied a space that was left over following the construction of a mezzanine office space. As a result, the ceiling over most of the restaurant was low, presenting a difficult design challenge. The design concept involved finding an inventive solution to this problem. The designer's response? "Create a vaulted ceiling in the high space along the window dining section to achieve volume. Use floating abstract planes in the low-ceilinged areas to provide relief and achieve an attractive sculptural effect."[5]

Design concepts for restaurants are often determined by some sort of theme related to the kind of food served and its place of origin. If the theme is Italian, designers try to make patrons feel like they are in Italy; if the theme is French, attempts are made to recreate the feel of a French bistro or sidewalk cafe. Consider the following examples for two different restaurants:

RESTAURANT 1:
Food Concept: American Southwest
Designer's Idea: Convey the feeling of a stage set using abstractions of plateau landscapes and buildings as architectural elements.
Design Strategies: Utilize architecturally sculptured plaster walls painted with colors and textures found in the desert Southwest. Use simple, spare furnishings and halogen spotlighting to further enhance the stage-set character. [6]

RESTAURANT 2:
Food Concept: Caribbean seafood with a large market selection of fish and seafood.
Designer's Idea: Recreate a Caribbean great house with the influence of British colonial design elements.
Design Strategies: Use gentle arches to separate dining areas and highlight the seemingly domestic scale of architectural detailing. Use lattice, cove lighting, and tropical murals to further add to the feeling of endless tropical expanse.[7]

Design concepts for highly thematic kinds of projects such as restaurants, shops, and clubs usually allow the designer a great deal of room for creative and personal inspiration. Barbara Lazaroff explains the approach she took when confronted with the task of designing an Asian-French restaurant:

> I began to sketch the yin and yang logo, and the "energy waves" I added, along with the emotional ideas of balance and flow, were the inspiration for many of the forms at Chinois . . . I wanted to create a relaxed, yet exotic environment. I refer to my design as "my five-year-old fantasy of what China would look like"; it doesn't look like this, but who cares—all the better.[8]

Other ways of approaching design concept statements include the use of statements that try to paint a picture of the experience you can expect in, say, a restaurant, and statements that evoke a certain spirit, be it of a past era or a certain attribute, such as elegance, austerity, or intimacy. The next three concepts are examples of these approaches. The first one, from a student, tries to evoke the warm, energetic, and pampering characteristics of a restaurant.

Patio

> Patio blends Japanese and Spanish architecture and flavors into an exciting experience that will warm you from the inside out. Cozy up in a booth to the glow of a candle or enjoy the energy of the kitchen as chefs prepare meals before your eyes. If you need some relaxation after a hard day in the office, sit down and enjoy appetizers in a lounge bed. Take off your shoes to feel the fresh cool grass against your toes in our indoor courtyard.

This concept statement uses enticing sensory images to communicate the experience of being at the restaurant. The final examples are concept statements for two perfumeries—the first, for Lancôme in Paris, is by Jacqueline and Henri Boiffils; and the second, for The Garden Perfumery in London, is by McColl Architects.

Lancôme

Design Problem Definition: Create a combined shop/institute of beauty imbued in an atmosphere of aseptic luxury and elegance.

Design Concept: Create an establishment characterized by stripped-down structural austerity through the use of symmetrical forms, the strategic disposition of products, exhibited as if they were valuable jewelry or museum pieces.[9]

The Garden Perfumery

Design Problem Definition: Create a perfumery that reflects a combination of romanticism and a certain sophistication. Attract, through the design, passersby in this central and exclusive area of London.

Design Concept: Evoke the spirit of The Garden Perfumery's products through the products themselves. Display them in a diaphanous way, converting them into the principal decorative element, to which all other design decisions are subordinate.[10]

Organizational Concepts

Earlier, we made the distinction between character concepts, those that inform the image and identity of the project, and organizational concepts, those that inform the organization and layout of a project. Character concepts give a project its image; organizational concepts help organize the project's parts. As we saw in the previous section, character concepts are usually formulated and expressed verbally. Organizational concepts can be described verbally but are most often externalized as diagrams.

A good organizational concept does several important things. First and foremost, it establishes a responsive scheme. Additionally, it provides a strong initial foundation for order, enrichment, and expression. We will examine each of these separately.

Establishing a Responsive and Coherent Scheme

The **scheme** you develop from your concept must be an appropriate response to the project type, its particular programmatic requirements, and the context in which it occurs. The fundamental organizational issues of a project are resolved at this stage. The following examples show both successful and unsuccessful early schemes in response to type, program, and context.

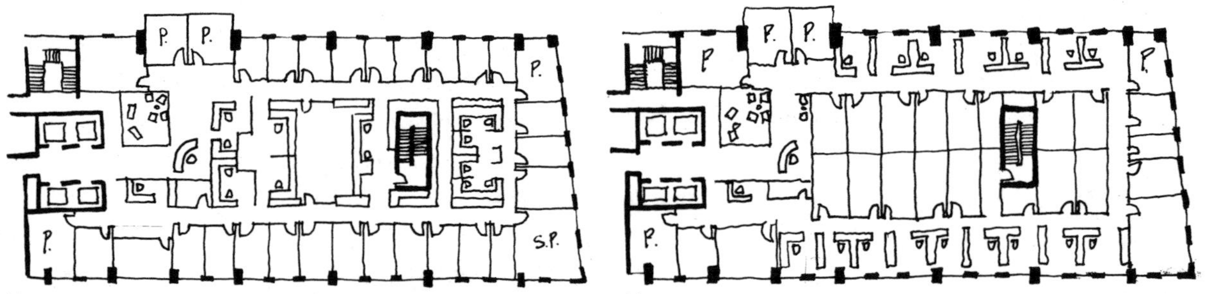

Figure 10.1: Scheme (a) is a better response than (b) to a given programmatic requirement to arrange private offices along the exterior perimeter of the building.

Figure 10.1, for instance, shows two designs for a law firm. The user has clearly stated the need that partner and attorney offices be located on the perimeter, by a window. Furthermore, the stipulation has been made that partner offices be located at corners. The scheme in Figure 10.1a is more responsive to these particular programmatic requirements.

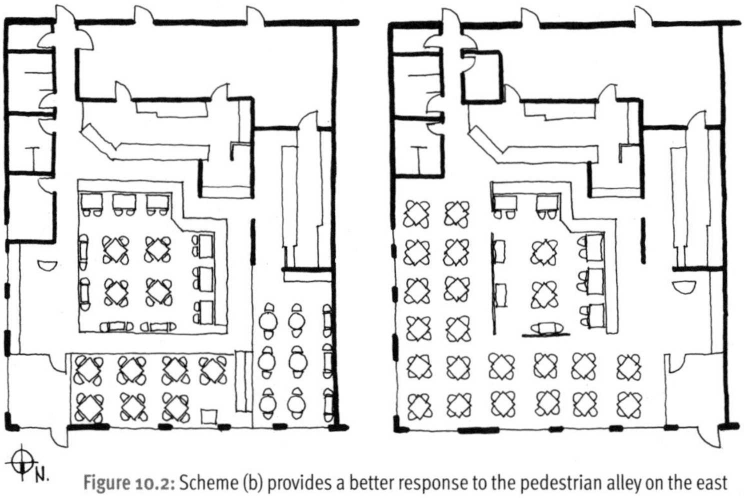

Figure 10.2: Scheme (b) provides a better response to the pedestrian alley on the east and the lively street on the north and turns its back to the service alley on the west.

Figure 10.2 shows two schemes for a casual restaurant in a northern climate. The restaurant faces a pleasant pedestrian alley on the east side, a lively street with shops on the north side, and a service alley on the west. Both schemes shown are workable; however, scheme Figure 10.2b takes better advantage of the desirable exposure to the northern street and the pedestrian alley and, thus, is a better response to the particular contextual realities of the site. These examples, however simple and obvious, help to illustrate the common-sense notion that crucial project requirements require proper design responses.

It is helpful to think of the project as a puzzle of reduced but essential pieces that must be arranged with insight and precision. This has to happen first, before you get bogged down with the many little problems at the micro level. Those get resolved as the design is developed. After a process of give and take, the scheme and all the project parts get resolved.

A good organizational concept also helps to produce a coherent scheme. Organizational concepts forçe the designer to make explicit decisions about an organizational structure based on the particularities of the project. Try to think about the project in terms of a few essential components. This requires some abstraction. Thinking in terms of the place elements introduced in Chapter 3 becomes extremely helpful. For instance, you may be able to abstract a complex project into four distinct domains and two centers of approximately equal importance connected by a direct circulation system. For the purposes of the scheme, the project is reduced to six main components and a circulation loop. This makes it simple and focused. The aim is not to ignore all the detailed pieces of the project but to collapse them into fewer groups, at least for now.

Next, it is necessary to arrange these parts in response to the realities of the project. The main concerns are placement of parts, circulation, and configuration. Issues such as public versus private; the shape, size, and proportions of the site; and the hierarchical importance of the parts play a major part. Figure 10.3a–c shows three possible schemes for the hypothetical four domains/two centers scenario just described. We could easily think of a few additional configurations. The reduction of parts makes the exploration of scenarios easier and faster.

In addition to the tendency to try to solve everything at once, the tendency to literally transpose adjacency bubble diagrams into a given site and make that "the scheme" can be problematic. This is where many projects lose their sense of coherence, becoming an agglomeration of parts rather than a unified structure. The literal transposition of a bubble diagram into the site rarely produces such a structure. Figure 10.4 illustrates how the adjacency diagram for a small sales office can be manipulated and given different form to fit the circumstances. Figure 10.4a shows the diagram, Figure 10.4b shows a literal translation, and Figures 10.4c, 10.4d, and 10.4e show three different schemes based on the diagram. Some configurations

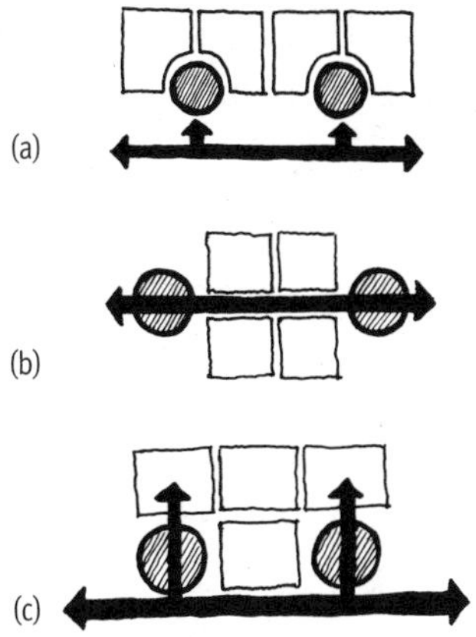

Figure 10.3: After distilling the fundamental parts of a project, you must decide how to arrange them as a system. There are many possible schemes composed of four districts and two centers. Three are shown here.

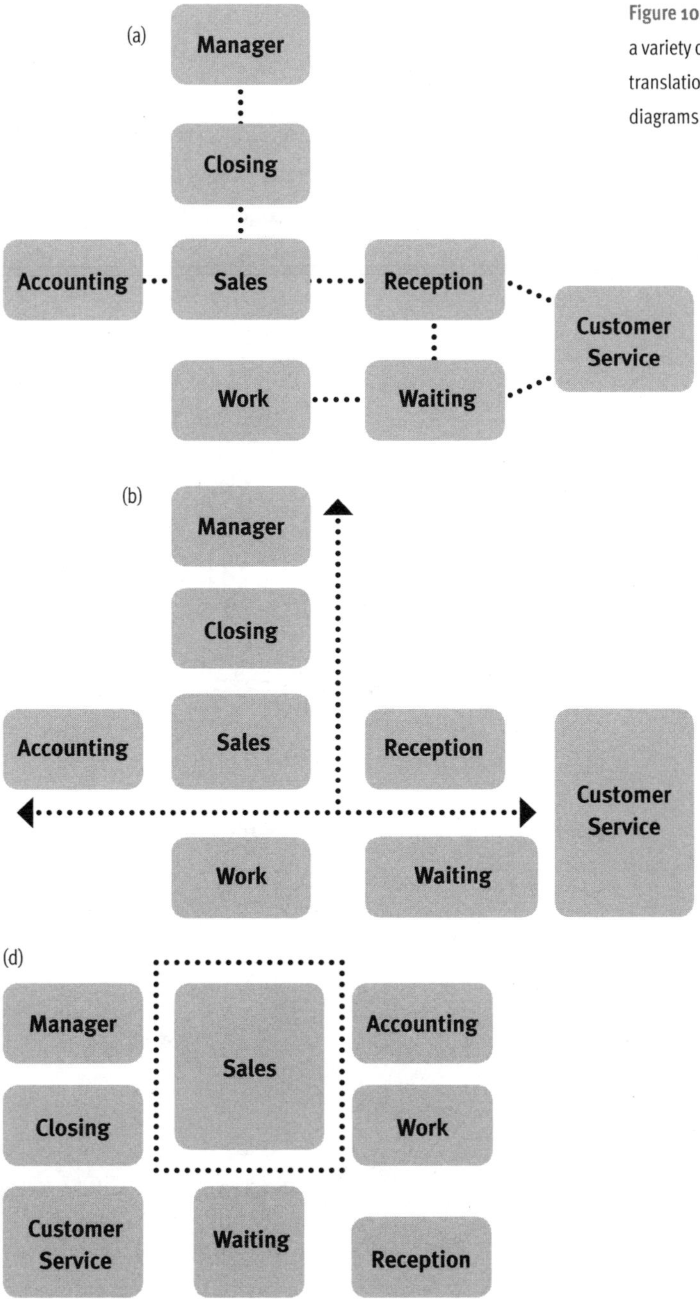

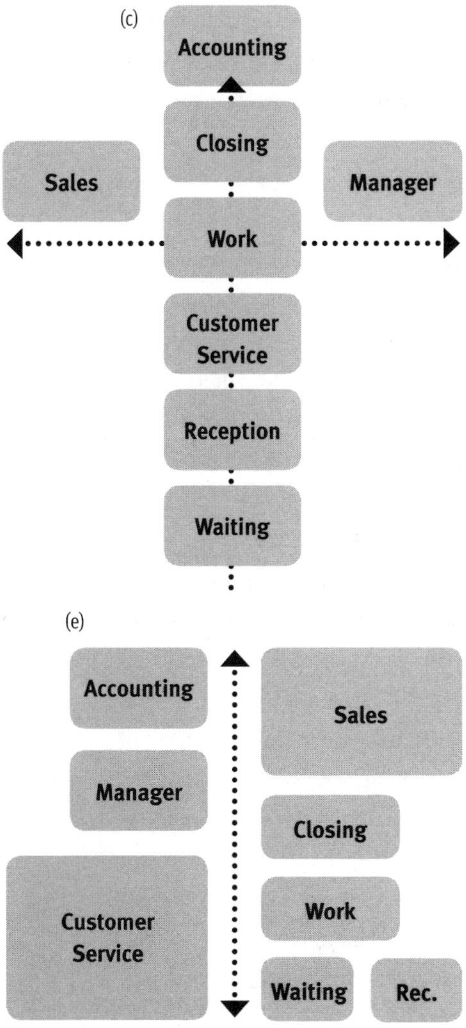

Figure 10.4: It is possible to convert any set of adjacency requirements into a variety of organizations. The scheme for a project should not be a literal translation of the adjacency diagram. The designer must convert adjacency diagrams into a responsive structure.

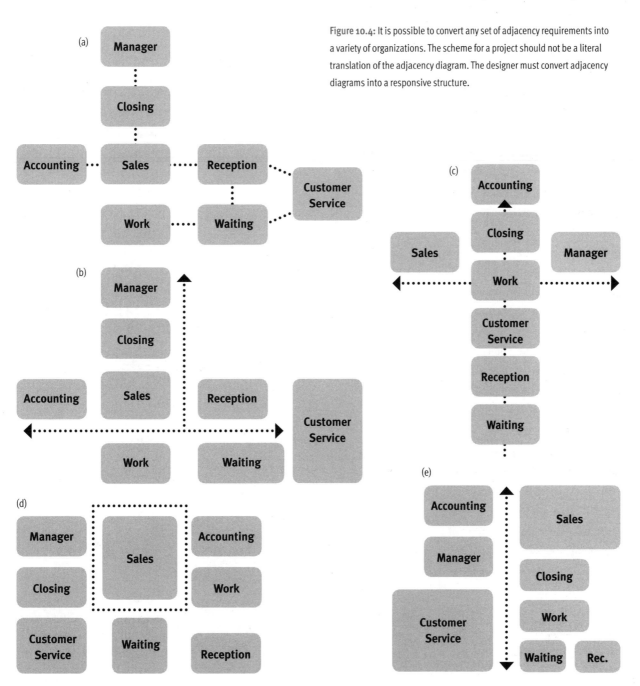

will address the project's circumstances better than others, and it is up to the designer to select the most responsive configuration.

Establishing Order, Enrichment, and Expression

One of the virtues of a scheme based on a sound structure is the order it automatically produces. Order implies proper arrangement, something that is determined during the development of the organizational concept. As we will see later, this order also needs to be made legible, a design concern that needs to be addressed throughout the entire design process.

Simple arrangements tend to work best. While one may fear that a simple scheme will be dull and uninteresting, even the simplest schemes can be given enough perceptual interest through other means. Even if the project is inherently complex, it can be arranged in an orderly fashion and be clear and legible.

Similar to order, enrichment can be initiated during the ideation stage. An astute designer thinks simultaneously about form and detail while generating organizational concepts. Refer to the simple manipulation for enrichment illustrated in Figure 10.5a and b. Notice how the form of the basic scheme can be manipulated to produce a configuration that provides a richer experience. While many such form manipulations occur later in the design process, they can be, and often are, introduced at this stage.

Some aspects of expression have to do with form and geometry, two aspects of design introduced at this stage of organizational concept development. Different arrangements, for instance, carry different connotations about levels of openness, formality, and progressiveness, whereas different sizes and geometries imply different levels of power and influence. Additionally, bold form, often introduced at this stage, can certainly be a very powerful expressive component of the design.

Not only do the size and proportions of rooms and spaces have expressive qualities, manipulations of the enclosing planes can also be rich in expression. Articulation of a scheme often starts during the concept generation stage. **Articulation** refers to the modification of planes or volumes by their skillful modulation into clearly expressed sub-parts to facilitate legibility, add interest, and afford order a greater degree of complexity. Some spatial articulation can occur during the ideation stage, while surface articulation usually occurs later in the process. Figure 10.6 shows three levels of surface articulation for a wall plane.

Inflection means deviation from a given course, as when a straight scheme becomes angular or curved. This type of manipulation, like articulation, often starts during the generation of the organizational concept. It is important to distinguish between articulation and inflection.

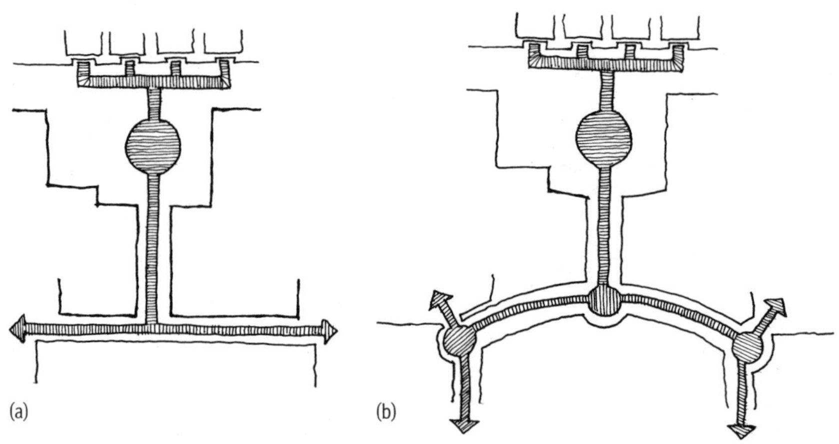

Figure 10.5: Drawing (a) shows the basic idea and drawing (b) the developed one. The curved forms and nodal points added in (b) provide a richer experience.

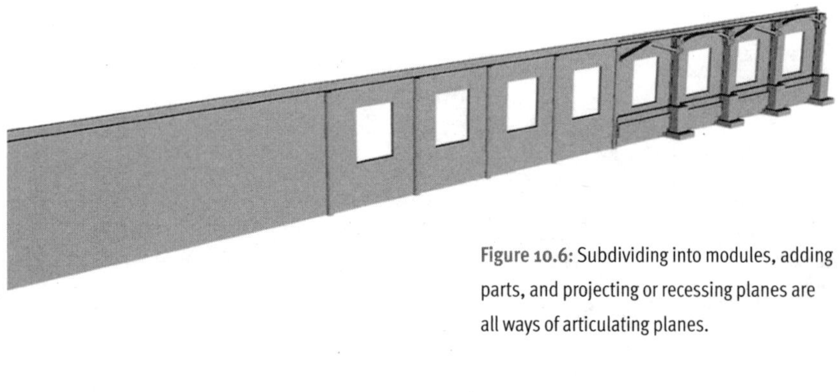

Figure 10.6: Subdividing into modules, adding parts, and projecting or recessing planes are all ways of articulating planes.

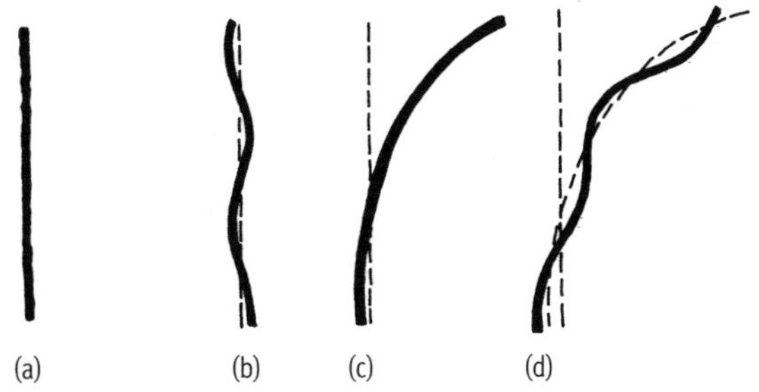

Figure 10.7: Scheme (b) articulates the straight wall, (c) inflects it, and (d) does both.

Figure 10.7 shows three diagrammatic transformations of a straight wall into curved walls. In Figure 10.7b, the course of the wall stays the same and an undulating curvature is added for flair and interest. This is an example of articulation. In Figure 10.7c, the wall is no longer a straight wall. It is now curving to the right. This is an example of inflection. Figure 10.7d combines the previous two examples to produce a wall that is both articulated and inflected from its original state. Figure 10.8 shows various straight and crossing path schemes transformed with angular and circular inflections.

Considerations in Determining a System of Organization

There are four important aspects to consider when coming up with the organizational concept for a project: placement, circulation, massing, and geometry.

Placement

One of the main challenges to be addressed with the organizational concept is determining where to place

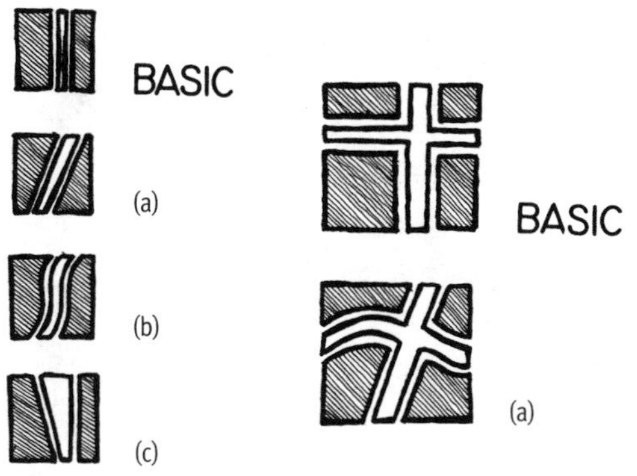

Figure 10.8: A basic plan arrangement can be transformed by using inflection and articulation. In these examples, straight paths and walls are transformed into angled and curving ones.

the different rooms and spaces that need to be accommodated. Factors include the function of each space, the relative prominence of each space, and the relationship among the spaces.

Rooms require proper placement based on their purpose and the functions performed in them: Public areas generally want to be in the front, private areas need to be tucked away, and shared areas should be centrally located. Some spaces may be prominent due to their symbolic importance (a grand dining room) or their functional importance (the sample room in a design firm). Both rooms need special placement consideration; however, the grand dining room could be placed at one end of the building with, perhaps, a grand corridor leading up to it and the sample room needs to be centralized in relation to the design studios.

In terms of hierarchy, you may have one project in which all spaces have approximately equal importance or prominence and, at the other extreme, another project in which a single space is dominant. The hierarchical combinations are virtually limitless (e.g., a project with three major and five minor spaces and a project with one dominant, two intermediate, and five minor spaces). The specific requirements of projects will suggest specific arrangements in most cases. The diagrams in Figure 10.9a–d illustrate these examples.

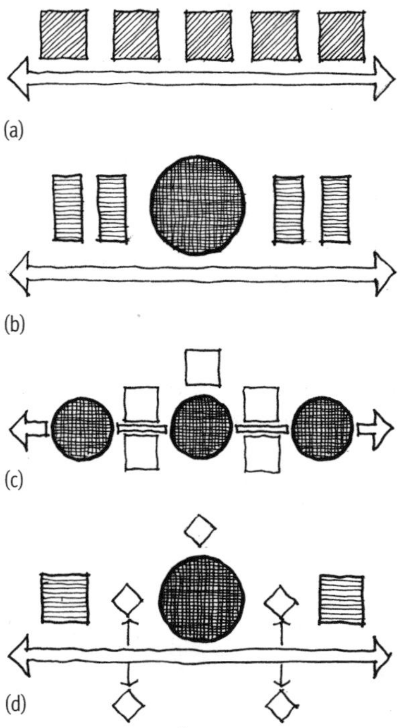

Figure 10.9: Spaces and functions in projects have different levels of importance or dominance. Some projects have no dominant space (a), while some have one or more centers (b–d).

Figure 10.10: This basic concept diagram (a) and developed floor plan (b) for an academic building project feature a dense layout of enclosed rooms and one distinct area of prominent shape and location.

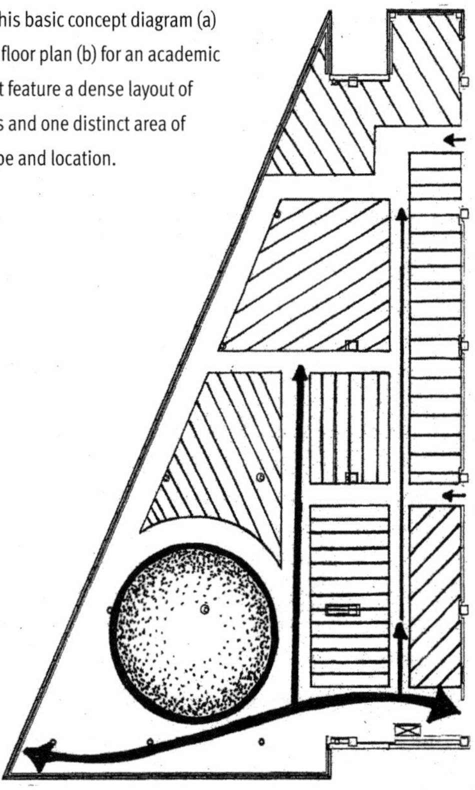

(a)

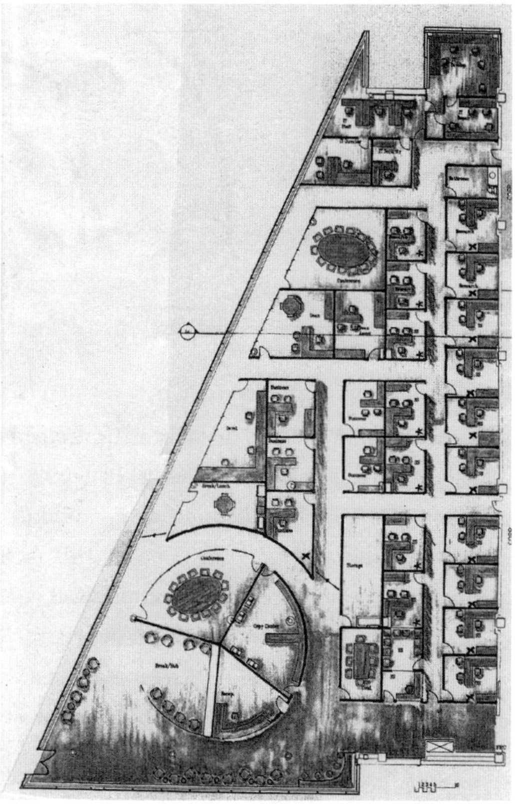

(b)

Figure 10.10a shows a concept diagram for an administrative suite in an academic building where the main shared public spaces get a prominent location and a unique shape. The resulting floor plan is shown in Figure 10.10b.

The way spaces relate to one another will also determine their organization as a system. Relationships determine issues of proximity. Some spaces may belong together and form a cluster. Other spaces may need to be as far apart as possible. Relationships also determine issues of centrality. Some spaces, like the sample room discussed earlier, need to be accessible to other spaces and, therefore, need to be centralized. In Figure 10.11, a scheme for the aforementioned academic building is based on the designer's interpretation of the project as a collection of autonomous suites. The designer, thus, treated them as independent units, adjacent to one another but not connected.

In terms of placement, the designer decides who gets the "sweet spots" and who gets the less desirable pockets, who gets the peace and quiet and who gets the noise, who gets the morning sunlight, who gets the afternoon sunlight, and who gets no exposure to the sun at all. Who gets the window? Who gets the nice view? Who gets the exposure up front? These and other similar questions need to be addressed in the process of placing the spaces

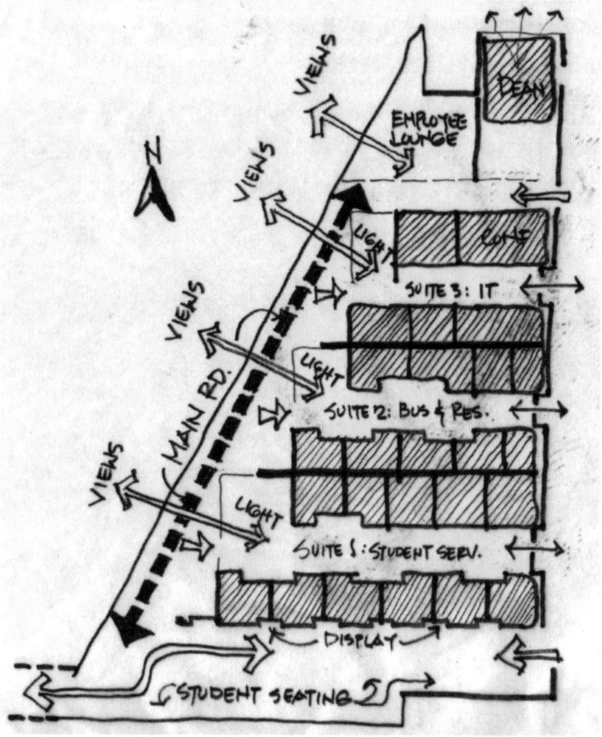

Figure 10.11: This diagram shows a radically different idea for the same project shown in Figure 10.10. Here the area is subdivided into private suites to give departments the autonomy they desire and to enhance department recognition. Moving the main circulation to the perimeter makes better use of the magnificent views beyond the long, tall glass wall.

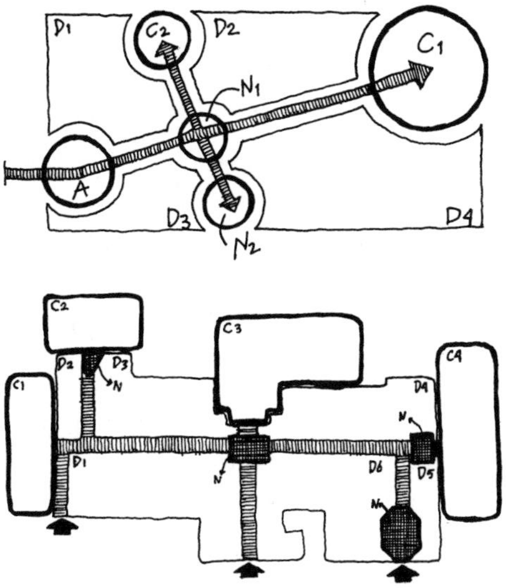

(a)

(b)

Figure 10.12: These concept diagrams are depicted in terms of our five basic place components: arrival space (A), paths, centers (C), domains (D), and nodes (N).

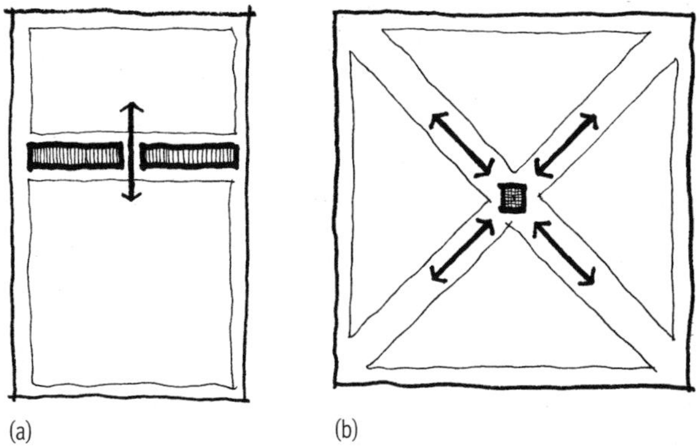

(a) (b)

Figure 10.13: Diagram (a) shows a project with a strong edge separating two sections. Diagram (b) shows a project with a central landmark as generative force.

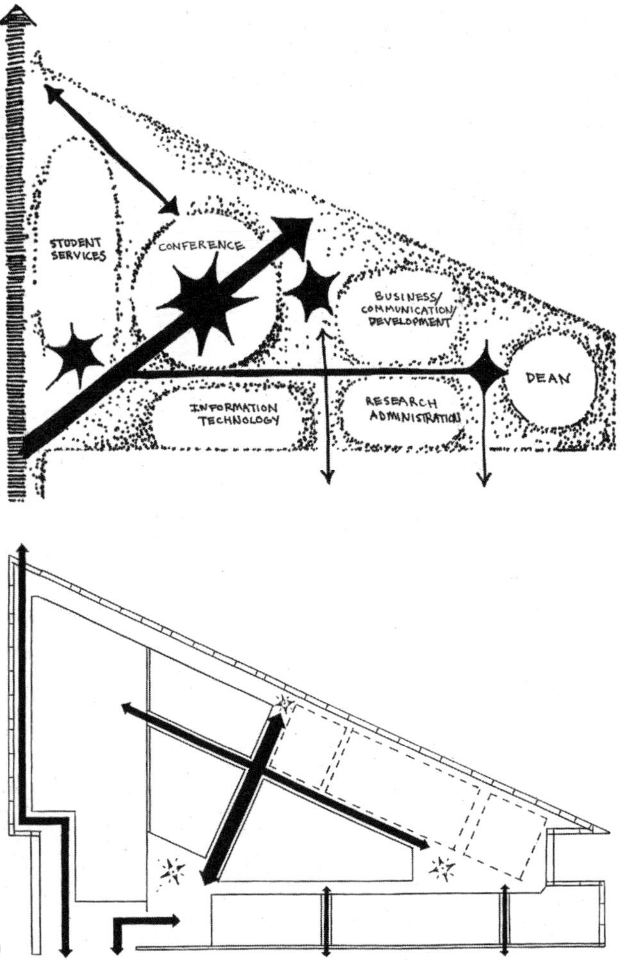

(a)

(b)

Figure 10.14: These two concepts feature strong diagonal circulation within different configurations.

of a project. Although project types usually suggest a certain type of organization, there is always room for variation. Does the bar in a restaurant always need to be close the entrance? Do private offices always need to be on the perimeter? Obviously, the answer is no.

You may also find it useful to think of a project in terms of the place elements introduced in Chapter 3 in order to arrange its parts. Arrival places, paths, nodes, domains, and centers are especially useful for the overall organization of space in interior projects. You may think of certain destination places as important centers, or you may treat some intersections as special nodes. Figure 10.12 shows diagrams for a hypothetical retail store and a shopping center, both reduced to these five elements.

The other place elements can also become important elements in the early organization of a project. Figure 10.13a shows a conceptual diagram for a project in which a strong separating element (edge) is a crucial part of the concept. Figure 10.13b shows the diagram for a project in which a landmark is central to the concept scheme.

Circulation

In Chapter 4 we discussed the important role of movement in the shaping of space. Quite simply, you cannot generate an organizational concept without committing to a circulation system to link your spaces. Whether movement will be free or constrained, dignified or casual, grand or minimal, it needs to be reflected in the organizational concept. One of the main aspects an organizational concept must clearly show is the main circulation pattern being proposed. Consider the circulation pattern shown in Figure 10.14a and b, and compare it to the circulation patterns shown in Figures 10.10 and 10.11 for the same project; the three very different circulation approaches greatly affect the resulting schemes.

Massing

The best organizational concept diagrams address the massing of the overall project. Specifically, they address the relationship between enclosed areas (solids) and open spaces (voids). One of the difficulties young designers have is in clearly visualizing three-dimensionally what they are creating with their schemes. Common problems are the creation of masses having awkward configurations and plans that are excessively fragmented.

The goals are to create masses with good configurations and to create well-shaped and comfortably scaled open areas. Specific strategies include grouping enclosed rooms together, attaching to existing walls or masses instead of starting new ones, and carefully watching the integrity of the shapes of both the solid masses and the open areas. Figure 10.15 a and b shows a scheme in which the enclosed rooms of an office suite (shown hatched) have been carefully grouped, resulting in masses

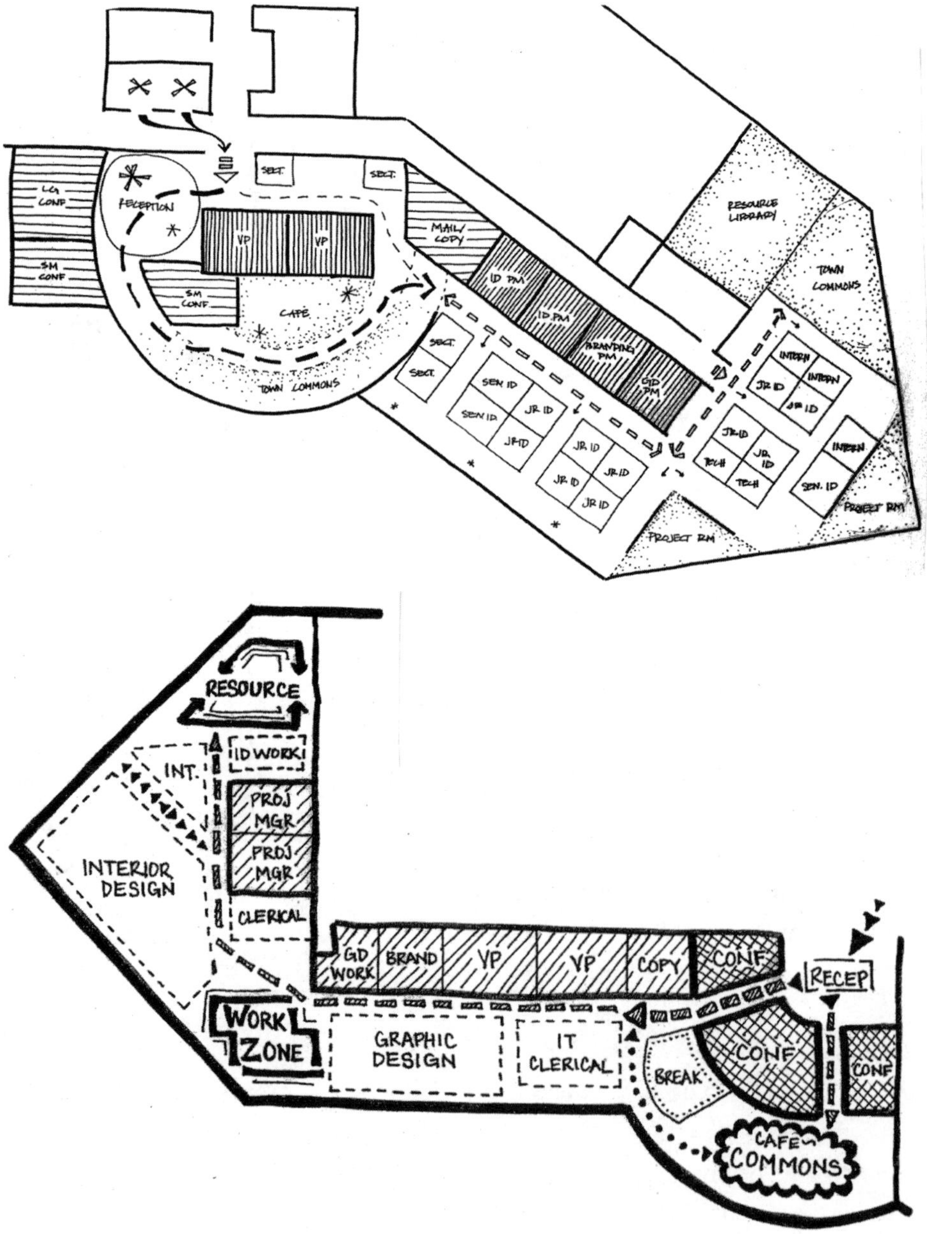

Figure 10.15: These two concept diagrams for an office suite successfully group the enclosed areas and pull them away from the window to create comfortable open areas adjacent to the perimeter light and views.

of good shape and comfortable open areas. Generally speaking, it is a good practice to have less rather than more masses in space and simple rather than complex configurations.

Geometry

Another aspect that should be visible from the organizational concept diagrams is the intended geometry for the project. Is it straight? Angular? Circular? Many projects are straight; many others have interesting geometries, some using angles, some using curved surfaces, some using combinations. Whatever the intentions, they should start being visible in the diagrams produced during the ideation phase. Figure 10.16 shows two diagrams for the same project, each with its own unique organization and geometry. Notice the impact the geometry has.

Stages of Concept Generation

The process of generating concepts varies from designer to designer; however, the process of concept generation should encompass a handful of important steps. In the next few paragraphs, we explain these steps and recommend a sequence that will help you become comfortable with this important design stage.

As we said earlier, at the heart of a concept is an idea or series of ideas that establishes the basic design approach

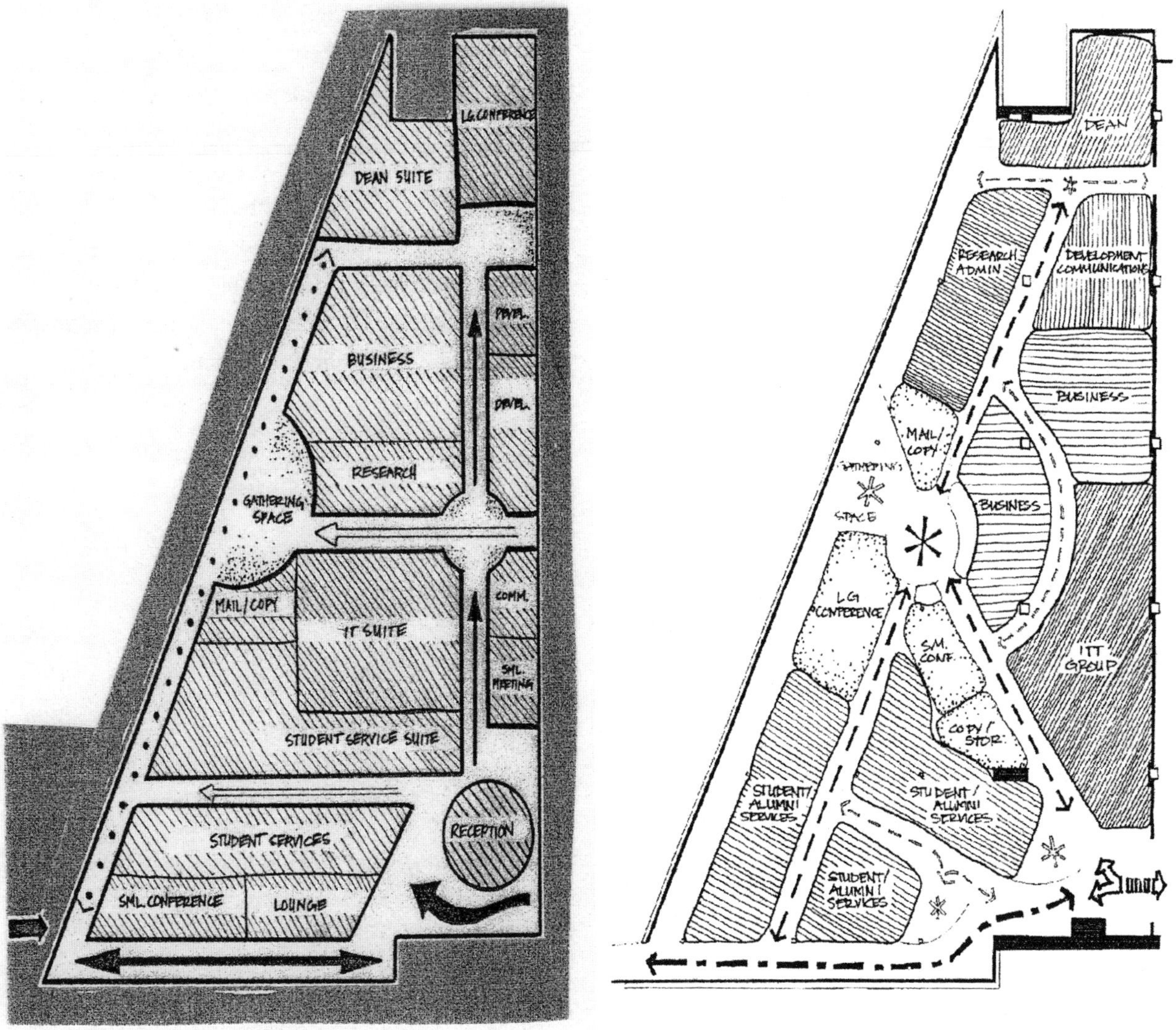

Figure 10.16: Notice these two schemes for the academic building introduced in Figure 10.10. Although both schemes aim to bring users to a central node, the resulting experience is very different by virtue of their respective geometric compositions.

for the project. There can be sub-approaches that complement the main approach, but a strong concept has to have one identifiable main approach. The formulation of this approach (or structure, in the case of organizational concepts) is the main goal of the concept generation process. There are, however, other tasks that must occur before and after this formulation. We recommend the following stages of concept development:

1. Understand the project.
2. Identify salient issues.
3. Conceive workable approaches.
4. Externalize the approaches.
5. Evaluate the approaches.
6. Consolidate ideas and choose a direction.

A good concept relies on the proper understanding of the project and identification of its *salient issues.* After you have identified these salient issues, you are ready to use logic and intuition to formulate potential design approaches. These approaches are then externalized through drawings and verbal statements. When externalized, you can evaluate them, consolidate ideas if necessary, and, ultimately, choose the most appropriate direction.

Understanding the Project

In Chapter 9 we discussed the factors that make up a project's reality: the nature of a project's user population, the realities of its context, and the requirements of the program. Chapter 9 also reviewed some of the tools used by designers to consolidate and make sense of information. The understanding of this information is essential to the development of appropriate concepts and must precede the concept generation stage. Additionally, an understanding of the project as an example of a particular type as well as a unique manifestation of that type is also useful for the generation of concepts. The level of understanding achieved during the early stages of a project represents just the initial level of the project's understanding. You will never have the luxury of full understanding at the onset, but you will hopefully understand the requirements and existing realities enough to move forward. The more you get immersed in the project, the greater the level of insight and understanding becomes, resulting in design refinements as you go.

Identifying Salient Issues

At this stage, it is not enough to understand the project's users, context, type, and program. To truly understand the essence of a project, the designer needs to exercise his or her judgment in order to identify its *salient issues.* These vary from project to project, and sometimes they are more obvious than others. A particular program requirement, a crucial functional relationship between project parts, a gifted (or problematic) site exposure, a particular feature of the building or site, and a desire for a particular historical or symbolic gesture are all examples of salient issues.

Some projects are loaded with salient issues, whereas in others the designer may struggle to identify a handful. Salient issues can be self-evident (as in the case of a project within a historical district) or explicitly requested by the user (as in the case of a particular relationship between two departments or units). Some important issues are the product of reflection and insight (as when the designer realizes that a particular unit is more, or less, important than was previously thought). They can even be the product of an accidental discovery (such as the way the sun's rays penetrate one side of the building in the late afternoon). Completing statements like the ones listed below can help you identify salient issues for a project.

- This project is all about . . .
- Truly significant aspects of the site include . . .
- Unique aspects of this project include . . .
- The functional requirements obviously point to an organizational pattern that . . .
- A few adjectives that fit this project are . . .

When you have identified some salient issues you must choose which ones are the most relevant and can help inform the project's design concept. When it comes down to generating ideas for concepts, designers have to rely on their ability to think not only analytically but creatively, and to make selections from among competing ideas. When the salient issues are identified, you must scrutinize them closely and pinpoint ways in which they may influence decisions about organization, form, and aesthetics. Figure 10.17 shows the salient issues for a hypothetical project. One can start to speculate how each of them may inform the project's organization.

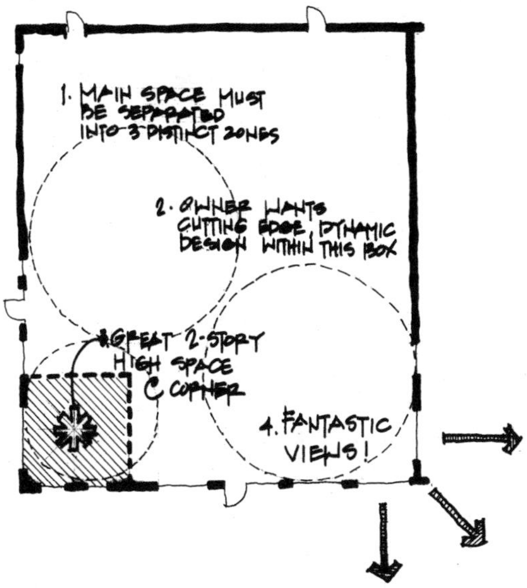

Figure 10.17: The four considerations listed are important issues to address; each has the potential to become the dominant aspect of the concept.

Conceiving Workable Approaches

The next task is going from a short list of salient issues to concept ideas. There is a myth that concepts have to be unique and different. This is not so. Although concepts are often unique and different, they are frequently straightforward and ordinary. There are times, in fact, when the most extraordinary thinking results in ordinary, but fitting, design approaches. While insight and creativity play a role in the generation of concepts, rational, systematic thinking is just as important.

A period of reflective, critical thinking follows the generation of salient issues. This is usually done with pencil in hand, as many ideas are sketched loosely in diagram form along the way. The goal is to generate ideas for the main approach, ideas that respond to an important essence of the particular design problem. Some designers believe there is a period of incubation during which the subconscious digests information, eventually leading to inspiration and insight. This inspiration and insight, again, does not necessarily lead to innovation and far-out ideas but to a focused, appropriate response. The ideas are the result of insight, not divine inspiration. You could call it informed and fitting inspiration.

The ideas generated in response to salient issues may come up as a logical, sequential development or may pop up either while sketching or even unexpectedly, while doing something else. Ideas usually arise as thoughts, mental pictures, or diagrams or drawings while you sketch. It is important to capture ideas when they arise, even before judging them. We recommend that students initially generate and record more than one (approximately three) design concept approaches. As a rule of thumb, if it pops up in your brain, record it. This brings us to the next step, formalizing the approach through externalization.

Externalizing the Approaches

The two ways to externalize concept approaches are visual and verbal. Visual approaches include diagrams and sketches; verbal approaches can be short statements, such as the ones shown earlier in this chapter, or longer descriptive scenarios. Let's take a closer look at each of these approaches.

Short statements can be effective for recording ideas, even when dealing with organizational ideas. A good short statement should include a description of a physical arrangement or relationship and the effect it produces. For example, the following two statements serve to concisely articulate a specific design intention: "a binuclear arrangement that splits control" or "a long evocative wall that provides a strong linear and unified backdrop to activity." Statements don't need to be long, provided they express the basic approach clearly.

Scenarios are longer descriptions that describe a sequence of events and their effect. Scenarios get more specific and detailed. Although scenarios are better suited as tools to articulate experiential intentions later during the development phase, they can be used to describe complex relationships or projects whose functions have a sequential nature. They are also helpful, given their highly descriptive nature, to integrate organizational and character concepts. The following scenario integrates the organizational and character concepts for a hypothetical restaurant/bar:

The project consists of a series of aligned chambers, each transversed by a cross-axis leading to related zones at either end, except the last one, which includes an additional termination point straight ahead. One enters into a small chamber that serves as a welcoming area. To either side are waiting areas, each one having its own unique character. Moving forward, one enters the second chamber. To the right is a bar area, to the left a comfortable lounge. Next is the third chamber, which leads to two dining areas, one on either side. The one on the left is more private and formal. Still ahead are two more chambers. The next one incorporates a bar within it and leads to two different lounge areas. These are more part of the club than the restaurant. Finally, the last chamber, which also serves as a control point to the club. Straight ahead is a dancing area with a band stage at the very end. To the left is a bar and informal seating area (more for standing and hanging out). To the right is a more comfortable seating area.

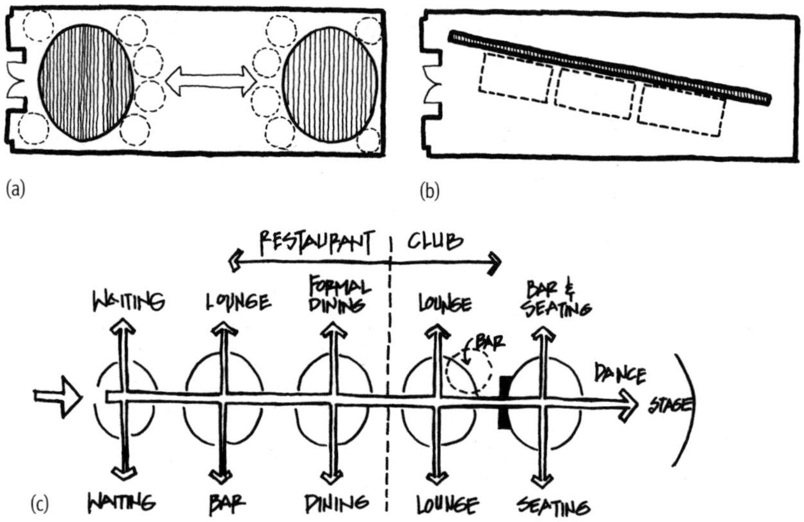

Figure 10.18: Graphic diagrams convey ideas differently than verbal descriptions. The overall organization is grasped almost instantaneously.

Scenarios are tools to describe qualitative attributes of projects. It would be easy to take the previous scenario to the next level of detail. Notice how the added qualifiers and details paint a more vivid picture of the scene:

The project consists of a series of aligned cylindrical chambers. They are each distinct in their finishes, progressing from the subtle to the bold, and are transversed by a cross-axis expressed by straight paths from side to side, which lead to related zones. . . . One enters into the first chamber, the smallest and the only one immediately adjacent to the exterior. During the day it is bathed in natural daylight that reflects off the light-colored fabric on the walls and the polished stainless steel trim. This chamber serves as a welcoming area, incorporating a free-form cherry wood and green marble maître d' station. To either side are waiting areas. The one on the right is neutral, formal, and elegant; the one on the left is casual and a bit more colorful, the wood becoming reddish. As one moves forward, one enters the second chamber after passing a low, dark, and compressed transitional space.

Whereas these scenarios are good tools for developing and externalizing, keep in mind that the eventual concept statement written for the project should be brief, as emphasized earlier.

Diagrams, as we have seen, are great devices for recording organizational concepts. Proper evaluation of organizational concept ideas cannot occur without some form of plan diagram that gives preliminary architectural form to the idea. Figure 10.18a–c, for instance, shows diagrams of the three concepts described earlier by short statements and scenarios.

Also useful in addition to plan diagrams are three-dimensional sketches. When it is necessary to address qualitative issues or visualize three-dimensional form, it is useful to turn to **conceptual sketches** instead of diagrams. The three-dimensional sketches in Figure 10.19 for the long wall scheme and the first chamber of the restaurant/bar are more effective than the plan diagrams in conveying a loose idea of the spatial qualities of these spaces. Conceptual sketches make it easier to visualize ideas and make their subsequent evaluation easier.

Evaluating the Various Approaches

The evaluation of concept ideas is one of many instances of evaluation during the design process. Each stage of design requires at least one formal evaluation. During the ideation stage, both the quality of the approaches generated (the soundness of the ideas) and their design interpretation (their actual interpretations on paper) should be scrutinized, however vague and abstract they are at this point. As you evaluate, you should ask yourself the following questions: Is this approach appropriate and fitting given the realities of the project? Is it likely to

Figure 10.19: Three-dimensional concept sketches force designers to illustrate, and others to see, a more literal translation of design ideas.

facilitate meeting the project goals? In the following, we evaluate the three examples given earlier.

1. Binuclear Scheme
   - Does it make sense to divide the project into two nuclei, as proposed?
   - Is the proposed way of doing this (in Figure 10.18a) appropriate?
   - Could the idea of separation, if deemed appropriate, be interpreted differently?
2. Long Evocative Wall Scheme
   - Is the idea of the long wall appropriate?
   - Does it address one of the main project issues?
   - Could it be executed successfully?
   - Are there other approaches to achieve the desired simplicity and unity?
3. Multichamber Scheme
   - How much does the chamber idea contribute to the desire to subdivide the project into zones?
   - Is it really necessary to subdivide the project?
   - How would these spaces be perceived?
   - Is the resulting fragmentation detrimental?
   - Are there other ways of implementing such a scheme?

Raising these types of questions helps to discard or modify problematic ideas and retain only the best. These are not the questions you want to be asking late during design. These are fundamental form-generating issues, and after you buy into them you want to commit to them for the duration of the project.

Given the sequential nature of the design process, it is important to resolve issues appropriate to any given stage prior to moving on. The next stage will have its own group of challenges requiring attention. It would be wasteful to start second-guessing and changing concept ideas late during the design, when layers of additional decisions have been made based on the earlier ones.

Consolidating Ideas and Choosing a Direction

Having evaluated the merits of a concept or group of concepts and identified the merits and drawbacks of each, you are in a position to choose the best idea or, possibly, combine aspects of various schemes in order to generate a new hybrid concept. The goal is to select a winning concept for further development. In some cases, time and other resources permitting, you may carry more than one concept forward for further exploration.

DIAGRAMS

Although language, both spoken and written, is the vehicle to describe character concepts, graphic diagrams are the vehicles to externalize, visualize, and communicate organizational concepts. These are usually in the form of sketchy, diagrammatic floor plan views, although three-dimensional drawings are also possible. There are many types of diagrams. Two particularly useful and straightforward types are presented here: parti diagrams and functional diagrams.

Parti Diagrams

The *parti diagram* represents the scheme at its most basic. It expresses the essence of the solution without getting into any kind of detail. To capture only the basic essence, it distills the approach to its most basic components, nothing less and nothing more. If the approach is rigid, formal, and symmetrical, it captures that symmetry and formalism. If the approach is curvilinear and divides the project into two nuclei, it captures that flair and division. The parti diagram is not concerned with details about specific areas; that's the realm of the functional diagram.

A good parti idea helps to establish a sound organization on which to develop the rest of the project. It helps to communicate the single most dominating idea. Figure 10.20 shows two parti diagrams for the same office project suggesting two different approaches. The diagram in Figure 10.20a consists of two movement axes (the principal originating at the entry point) intersecting at 90 degrees at a central, important space. From that space, the axes continue toward three special end destinations. The leftover spaces define four zones or domains within which the project's functions will be organized. The diagram in Figure 10.20b shows a simple loop around a central rectangular mass with a special destination at one of the far corners. Three leftover zones are defined, two long and narrow ones along the main sides and one at the far end of the building.

Functional Diagrams

Functional diagrams are an outgrowth of the parti diagram and include more detail. They show the massing of the project (enclosed versus open areas), the organization (linear, radial, looped, and so forth), the main circulation system, and the specific placement of prominent destinations. They are typically shown diagrammatically but close to scale. Whereas the parti diagram establishes the basic approach to the solution, the functional diagram starts testing its workability. It starts looking more like a floor plan, although an abstract one. In the process of doing one or more of these you start realizing that some ideas may work better than others. In cases where a good concept idea proves unworkable you must revise or abandon it. Figure 10.21a and b shows the parti and functional diagram for an office project.

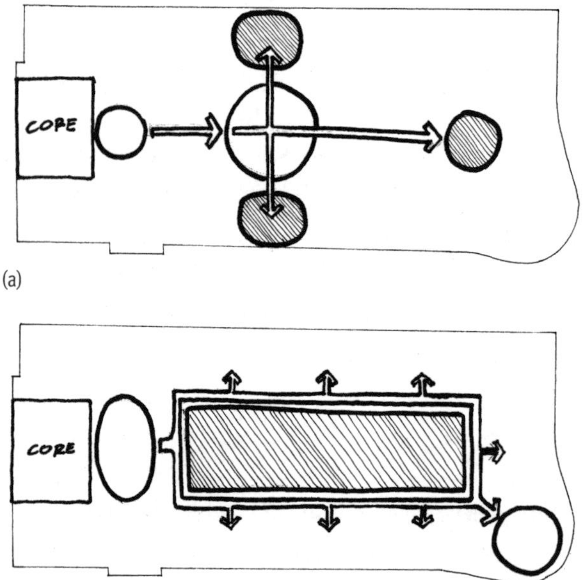

(a)

(b)

Figure 10.20: Two parti diagrams show the basic essence of the scheme: arrival point, movement system, basic arrangement, basic geometry, and special destinations.

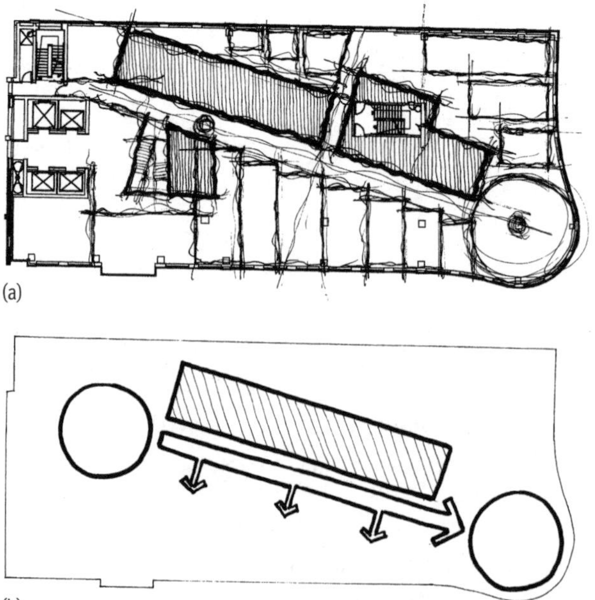

(a)

(b)

Figure 10.21: Functional diagram (a) and parti (b) for an office project. Notice the difference in the amount of information and detail between them.

It is likely that you have already used block plans in your design process. Functional diagrams are similar to block plans, yet they differ in two important ways. With block plans there is the dangerous tendency to lay out a bunch of rectangular shapes on the plan to see if and how they fit. They typically lack imagination. Functional plans, in contrast, are based on powerful (we hope) organizational structures that give projects cohesiveness and personality. They include additional information, such as massing, and they also define a specific geometry for the project. Relationships from the bubble diagrams are respected but do not dictate the scheme.

The second difference is their scope. The purpose of block diagrams is to solve the puzzle of space distribution. The design problem is seen as the need to fit and distribute spaces in the site. Functional diagrams go beyond this requirement and make conscious efforts to create meaningful places at different scales and provide a stimulating experience. A good functional diagram, for instance, not only identifies separations between parts but makes initial decisions about the character of such separations. Additionally, early ideas about the experiential character of circulation, the manipulation of daylight and views, and the location of focal points and planes are explored in the functional diagram.

Like block plans, functional diagrams are also responsible for making all the requirements fit and for respecting the desired adjacencies. In fact, the determination of locations for the different functions and their sizes, configuration, subdivision, and relationships all need to be addressed and resolved in the functional diagram. Remember that all this is done within the context of creating a strong sense of place and a stimulating experience. Notice the difference between the block diagram in Figure 10.22b and the functional diagram in Figure 10.22a.

Despite the relative accuracy needed for functional diagrams, they should be loose enough to facilitate speed in generating them. Two important requirements toward this end are to draw them freehand and to use bubbles and other abstract representations of space and spatial features. Keeping the process loose and quick allows the designer to explore different alternatives during the ideation stage of design, plus it encourages spontaneity. Having multiple schemes enriches the process of exploration. If you draw the contents to scale and with acceptable precision, you will have specific reliable criteria to judge against while you make informed evaluations and selections.

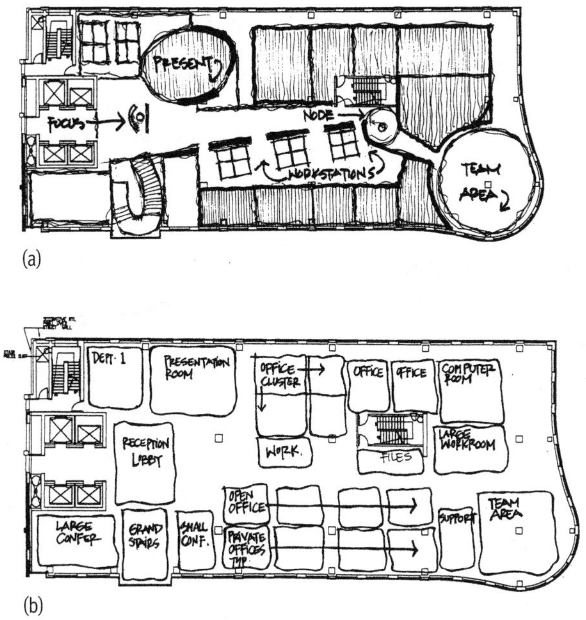

Figure 10.22: The differences between a (b) block and a functional (a) diagram for a project can be considerable. The block diagram may help sort out spaces, but the functional diagram incorporates more design thinking, displaying a specific design approach and incorporating focal points, important nodes, and so on.

Graphics for Diagrams

Diagrams help us communicate with ourselves and others. They help us capture ideas when they arise and record them for later use. Concept diagrams and sketches that arise while we generate ideas can be quite personal and loose. There is no need to be too careful when sketching these for your own use. In fact, looseness and spontaneity are to be encouraged during the creative process. There will be plenty of opportunity to develop them later. Figure 10.23 shows examples of some of these kinds of loose concept sketches.

When diagrams go from private to public they require an increased level of clarity and resolution. In this section, we address the qualities that public diagrams must possess and the graphic techniques to produce them.

Requirements

A good public diagram, whether a parti or functional diagram, possesses three basic virtues: clarity of content, clarity of intention, and economy of means. *Clarity of*

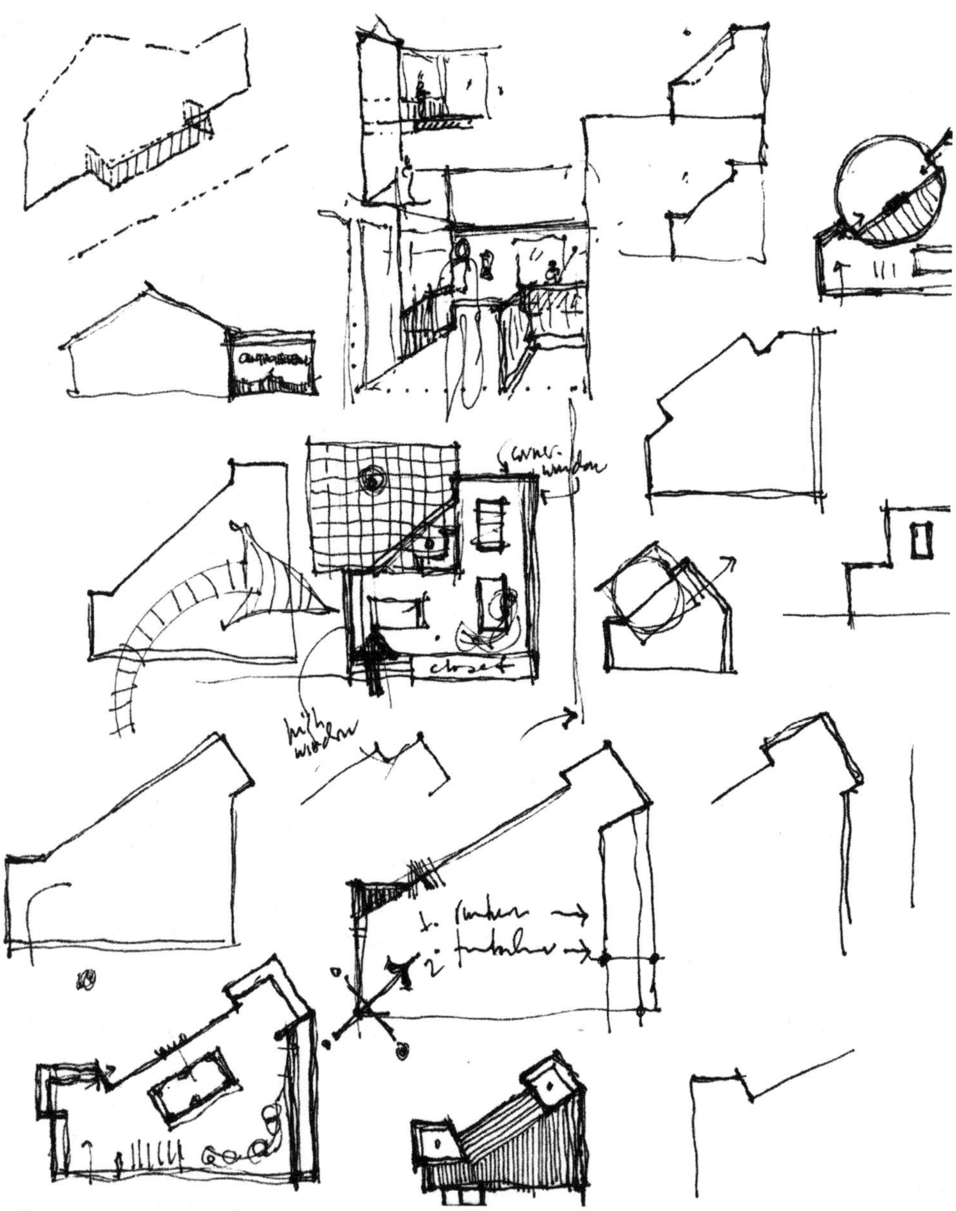

Figure 10.23: Personal concept sketches are usually very quick and loose.

content means that all the pertinent pieces for that diagram need to be shown and delineated clearly. *Clarity of intention* means that the design intent needs to be clear enough so others can understand it. *Economy of means* ensures that information is kept simple. For both parti and functional diagrams the designer decides what will be included and excluded. For parti diagrams, the designer must show the essence of the approach with the fewest possible elements. For functional diagrams, the designer must present a more thorough and inclusive idea without including too much detail.

Of particular importance for clarity of intention is differentiation through hierarchy. Accordingly, the graphics you use in your diagrams must be hierarchical. The types of symbols you use, the weight you give them, and how you use tone and texture are crucial if you want to produce clear, readable, good-looking diagrams. Figure 10.24 shows three levels of graphic resolution. Figure 10.24a is clean and shows the basic distribution of functions. Even though all the parts are there, the diagram lacks differentiation. Figure 10.24b incorporates a hierarchy of line weights and different arrow types. In 10.24c tone, texture, and special symbols have been added to represent areas of special importance. It contains more layers of information than the the other two and an increased sense of hierarchy.

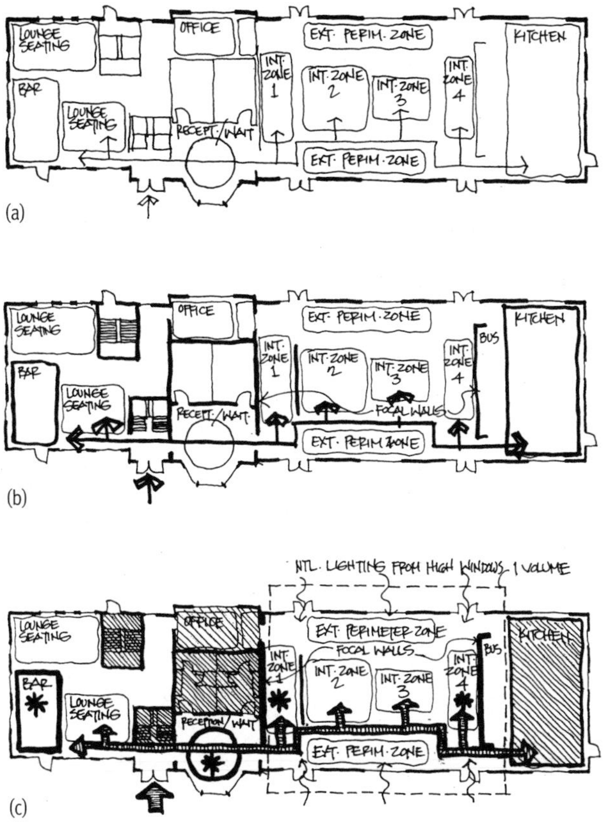

Figure 10.24: Three levels of diagram graphic resolution.

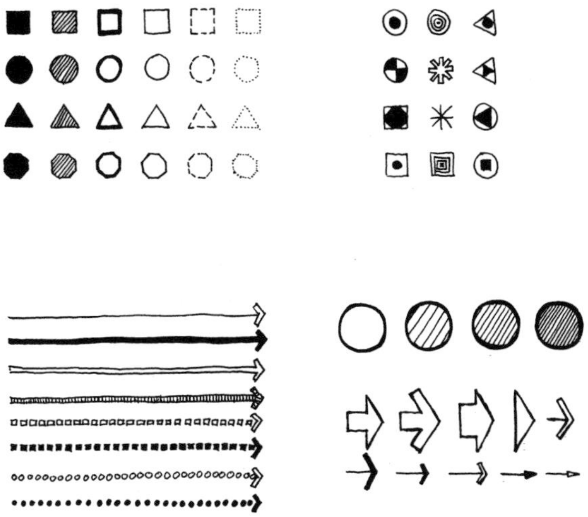

Figure 10.25: The graphic vocabulary for diagramming includes graphic symbols to differentiate bubbles for hierarchy, different lines and arrow styles to indicate movement systems, and special symbols to convey special locations.

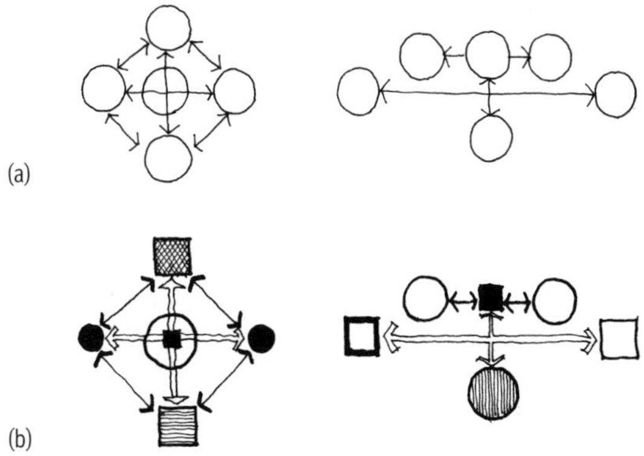

Figure 10.26: These simple diagrams show the enhanced readability of diagrams achieved when you use simple graphic devices, such as varied line weights and textures inside the shapes.

Diagram Grammar

You only need to use a few symbols and a handful of simple graphic techniques to produce clear and strong diagrams. Only three types of basic symbols are necessary to produce concept diagrams: bubbles to define areas, lines with arrows to indicate circulation, and special symbols to represent special spots or events. Next, you need ways to differentiate among same type symbols to convey hierarchy. This is accomplished by varying the size of the symbol, the line weight of its outline, and/or the texture/color you use inside the symbol. Figure 10.25 shows some of the various symbols and their variations. That's your vocabulary. It's that simple. The secret lies in practicing and becoming competent at executing these drawing techniques. Figure 10.26 shows two very simple abstract diagrams in a basic and enhanced form.

Diagram Development

Depending on your habits and personality, you might be the type who likes to work with only one idea at a time—staying with it, modifying it, and transforming it until it is resolved. Conversely, you may prefer to generate multiple ideas with variations and narrow them down through successive evaluations and selections until you have arrived at the winning solution. The second approach is the one we recommend to novice designers. Seasoned designers may have success with the focused approach, but the rest of us will have a greater chance of arriving at an optimal solution by exploring multiple ideas. The only caveat here is for those who might be inclined to exaggerate and explore too many ideas, and for those who get stuck with several ideas and cannot decide on one and move forward. If you have such tendencies, be aware of it and put some limits on your horizontal thinking.

Figure 10.27 shows, in diagram form, a hypothetical path to a winning solution using the multiple idea approach.

The Next Task of Design

The tangible outcome of the ideation stage is a solid design direction for the project. It will consist of two concepts, one to capture the desired image, theme, or character, and the other to determine the project's physical organization.

The next task is development. There is usually some overlap between tasks, and, before the end of ideation, you may have already taken some steps toward development. During the development stage you elaborate and refine your design ideas and intentions.

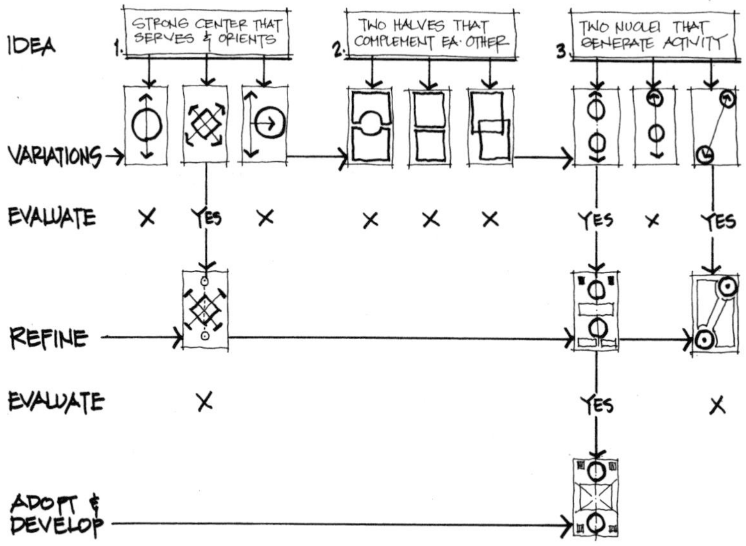

Figure 10.27: Hypothetical path of concept development and selection.

CAPSULE | Different Approaches to Libraries by Two Masters

One of the remarkable aspects of design is that, despite the constraints imposed by the requirements of a project, there is ample opportunity for personal interpretation. A good way to illustrate this is to compare library designs by two late, famous architects: Louis Kahn and Alvar Aalto. Kahn's library at the Phillips Exeter Academy and Aalto's at Mount Angel Abbey are projects whose forms, although derived based on similar understandings of the needs of a library, differ substantially.

Exeter Library was conceived both as a place to celebrate knowledge (through books) and a place for community (students coming together). Kahn saw a library "as a place where the librarian can lay out books . . . and the reader should be able to take the book and go to the light." He felt that reading should occur individually by a window, in a private carrel. In response to this his design solution consisted of two concentric square doughnuts, the outer one being the place to read by the light, away from the books. The inner doughnut was the place to store books away from the harmful effect of direct sunlight. The hole in the middle was a great central space, a multistory atrium from which one can enter and see books all around through large circular openings. In this fashion the invitation to books takes place, and one can grab a book and go to the light to read (Figure C10.1). The central hall is the heart of the building as

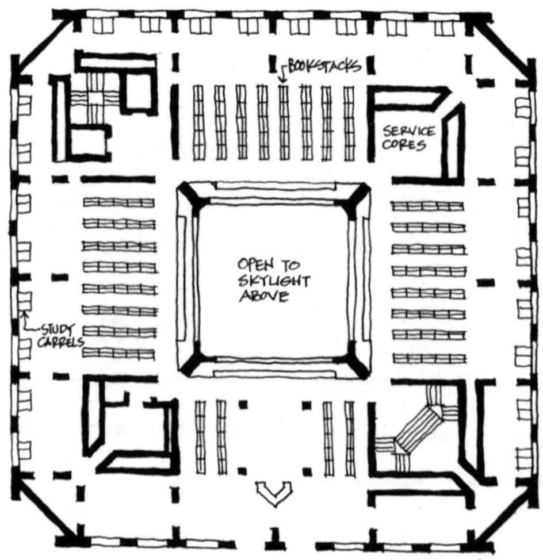

Figure C10.1: Main floor plan at Exeter Library

community, both symbolically and functionally, for it is there that you run into and interact with others.

The design for Mount Angel Abbey Library, like that of Exeter, was developed in part based on the relationship between a person and a book in light. At Mount Angel Abbey we also find carrels and reading rooms around the perimeter, by the light. The book stacks are toward the center, between the readers and the central area, similar to Kahn's approach at Exeter. That is, however, where the planning similarities between these projects end. Concentric square doughnuts defined Exeter's form, but Mount Angel Abbey's form is fan-shaped, as is the case with other Aalto libraries. Although his fascination with this shape is seen in many of his other buildings, the use of the fan shape is especially appropriate in his libraries. One of the basic functional requirements of library buildings is the need for a control point from which the librarian assists and monitors patrons. Aalto gave great importance to such points, placing them at the narrow end of his fan-shaped buildings, the rest of the library expanding outward from it (Figures C10.2 and C10.3). The book stacks are arranged radially from the desk such that the librarian has visual control over the entire library space.

Although there is no monumental lobby space at Mount Angel, Aalto provided a space to serve as the heart of the library and, like at Exeter, one from which

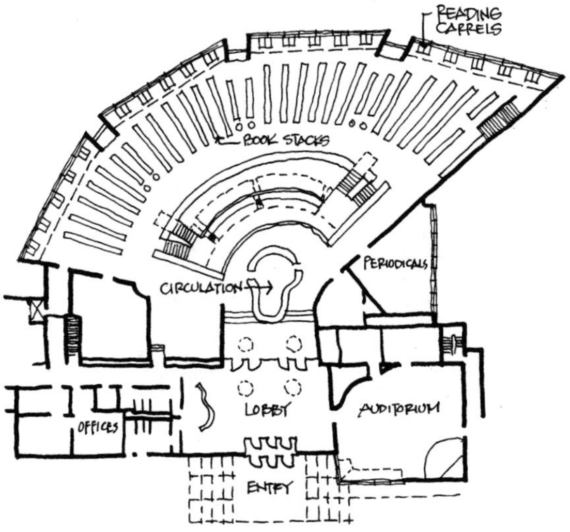

Figure C10.2: Main Floor plan at Mount Angel Abbey's library

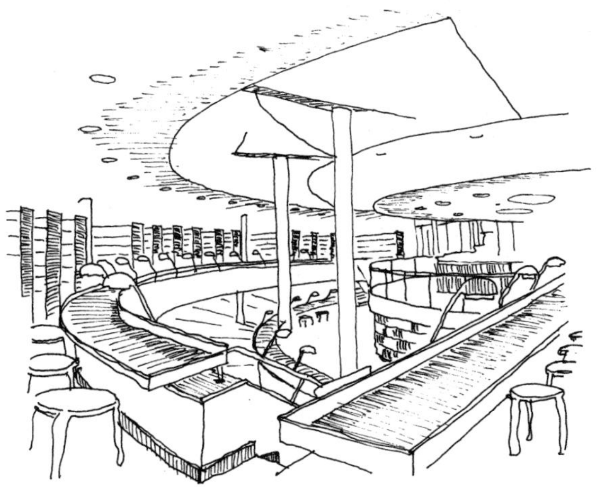

Figure C10.3: Perspective view at Mount Angel Abbey

the library and the books are seen and the invitation to books occurs. This is the mezzanine between the control desk and the rest of the library. It is enhanced with dramatic lighting, making it an important focal area. This circular area features counters and chairs and is itself an interior place for reading. Although it is not at the perimeter, like Kahn's reading areas were required to be, the abundance of natural light it receives makes it consistent with the idea of reading by the light (Figure C10.4).

These two libraries, designed by two of the greatest architects of the modern era, are both exceptionally good libraries. While the basic type requirements for a library were well understood by both architects, they had enough differences of emphasis and interpretation to produce two radically different designs.

Figure C10.4: Perimeter study carrel at Exeter

CAPSULE | The Quick Concept Diagram

Presented here is a quick approach to organizational concept generation. It consists of five steps:

1. Establish basic distribution of spaces
2. Establish main circulation
3. Articulate general solids, voids, and screens
4. Articulate and/or inflect the scheme
5. Test the idea

The first step consists of laying down on paper, more or less to scale, the basic spaces of the project. By *basic* we mean the principal areas. To do this, you have to generalize. If there is a requirement for a cluster of offices, for example, you use only one shape for the entire group. By grouping related functions together, you should be able to reduce the entire project into just a few components. Figure C10.5a shows the requirements for a hypothetical project expressed in terms of five areas placed within the project's site. For our purposes we will keep the example generic. Let's assume that the areas have been placed after carefully considering adjacency and exposure requirements.

The next step (often developed in conjunction with the first step) is to clearly establish the main circulation. Every project has a main axis, loop, or network for moving around. Your task is to decide where this main circulation goes and to reflect it in your concept diagram (Figure C10.5b).

The next step is to consider the project three-dimensionally. Up to now, we have been thinking about our hypothetical project in terms of five general areas. Now we start defining open and closed areas. Some of the areas are likely to be open, others are likely to consist of enclosed spaces, and still others may be a combination of open and closed. Furthermore, the relationships between the circulation path and open areas and between adjoining open areas may be open, closed, or somewhere between.

Figure C10.5c shows the areas of our hypothetical project articulated into closed rooms (shaded), open areas, and screening devices between areas. This is when you start to orchestrate the project massing by making these decisions and reflecting them on your study diagrams. Work loosely on tracing paper, and don't be afraid to change or discard ideas. Crumpling a sheet of tracing paper with a bad solution into a ball and tossing it away can be as pleasurable as keeping a good one.

After you have the basics of a solution established (which you think will actually work when tested), you may perform some basic articulations and/or you may inflect the scheme by turning it, curving it, and so on. Keep in mind that not all projects need to be turned or curved. Figure C10.6a shows our basic scheme with some form articulation added; Figure C10.6b shows it inflected through a diagonal maneuver. Don't get too detailed. Before you do so, you want to test your idea and see whether it is going to work. Up till now you have been using approximations and working loosely, and now is the time to draw the idea up at a larger scale,

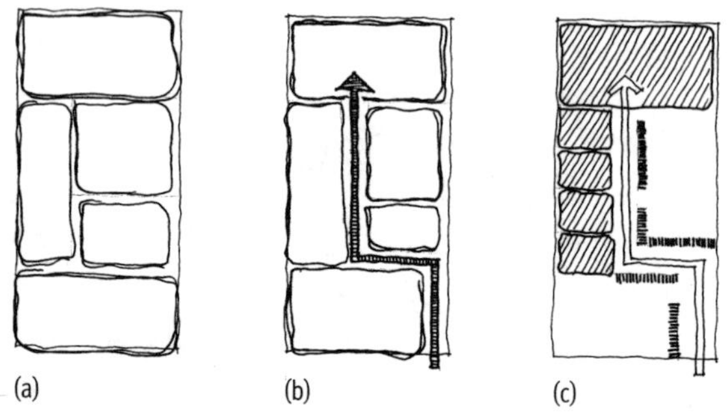

Figure C10.5: The three basic steps for "quick" organizational concept generation: Disposition of major spaces (a); introduction of main circulation (b); preliminary definition of solids, voids, and screens (c).

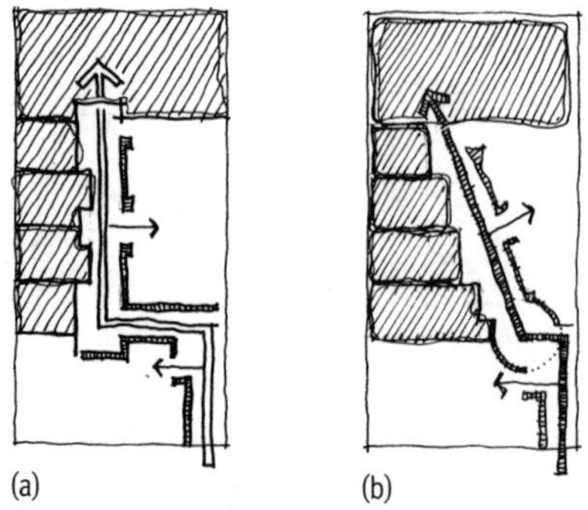

Figure C10.6: Articulation and inflection: You can establish some preliminary articulation early on (a), and/or inflection, if appropriate (b).

to draw furniture and other contents (quickly but accurately), and to see whether it really works. If you are lucky, it will work nicely, and all the pieces will fit efficiently and harmoniously. In most cases, though, you will find that you have to manipulate the geometry to make things work. In some cases, you will find that the idea requires so much modification that it loses its integrity. In those cases it is best to abandon the idea and pursue a new scheme.

Figure C10.7 shows six schemes for a hypothetical store project illustrating different ways of inflecting the forms. The space has been conceived as two longitudinal spaces connected side-to-side at various points. One of the long sides is a little wider and incorporates the cashier's station. Figure C10.7a shows the scheme in basic form with some definition starting to emerge at the transition zone. In C10.7b the side walls and the transition zone show a more refined articulation. Figure C10.7c is similar, but in it, an uneven spacing of the center columnlike elements is explored. It results in a wider cross-opening at the center. Figure C10.7d explores a diagonal arrangement of the same basic idea, and Figures C10.7e and C10.7f explore curvilinear solutions. Notice that the idea is basically the same. Despite the wide variations of geometry, the concept scheme remains two elongated spaces with multiple connections between them.

You can see that the same basic idea can be varied through articulation and inflection. Deciding which scheme is the best for the project requires testing them to see which one works best and which one best reflects the personality of the project.

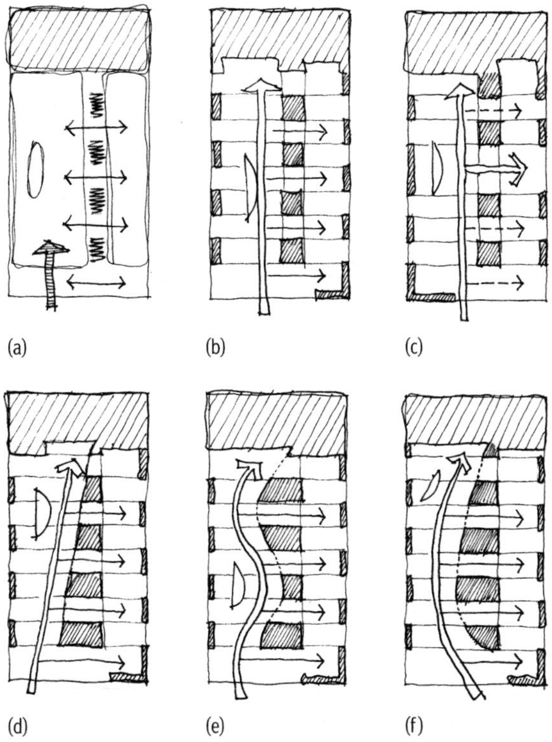

Figure C10.7: The same scheme (a) can be articulated and/or inflected many different ways. Articulation can establish a regular (b) or hierarchical (c) distribution. Inflection can be diagonal (d), undulating (e), or sweeping (f). There are many other possibilities in addition to these.

CAPSULE | Twenty Retail Store Partis

Store design offers some of the best opportunities for creativity and expression in the design field. The main goal of stores is to present merchandise in a way that promotes sales. Crucial design aspects are the effective display of merchandise, the use of interior design to reinforce a particular image or identity, and the effective movement of people through the store.

It is possible to produce, even for a small store space, a wide variety of expressions just by varying the placement and orientation of fixtures and other space elements. In the following, we present 20 different parti diagrams for a small retail store. The goal is not to give you specific models to copy but to present examples of the basic typological possibilities for you to study in order to develop the kind of thinking that will help you come up with powerful organizational ideas for your store projects.

Keep in mind that generating a strong scheme is only the first step in designing a store, and there are many important design features at smaller scales, such as the materials used, the way they are detailed, the fixtures used, and their exact placement. Nevertheless, a strong scheme is crucial to the design of any store. Without one, no matter how beautiful the materials, the detailing, and everything else, the design is not likely to work well as a whole.

Figure C10.8 shows the first eight diagrams. Organizations with central, linear circulation are featured in Figure C10.8a–d. The circulation in Figure C10.8a and C10.8b is determined by the available central space left by the placement of displays and fixtures. Figure C10.8a is asymmetrical, and the circulation spine is just left of center. Figure C10.8b is perfectly symmetrical and is strongly defined by the regularly placed fixtures on either side. Figure C10.8c and C10.8d are also central schemes. The central spine on these is defined not by leftover central space but by some architectural device, such as the floor material and/or the shape of the ceiling above. The shapes of these spines are the main components of these two schemes. Everything else is organized around this dominant central organizational element. Notice that other than the linear aspect of circulation these two schemes expand to create nodes, a central circular one in Figure C10.8c and two square (rotated) ones in Figure C10.8d.

The two schemes shown in Figure C10.8e and C10.8f feature looser, less formal central spaces. In Figure C10.8e, circulation is not straight and axial like the ones before, but is offset around the center of the store and moves to the right side, from which it continues toward a focal end at the rear of the store. Movement in Figure C10.8f is diagonal from front to back with objects and displays also placed diagonally on either side of, and helping to define, the circulation spine. Figure C10.8g and C10.8h feature not the circulation but displays along the central axis. Circulation occurs on either side, along the space defined between the linear central displays and the wall displays. They are very similar except that in Figure C10.8g the central fixtures are dominant, while

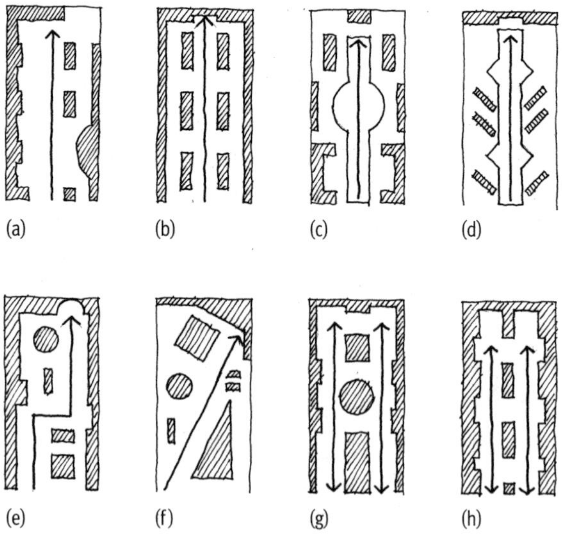

Figure C10.8 a–h: Eight store partis: linear asymmetrical (a); linear symmetrical (b); linear, strongly defined, and symmetrical with dominant center (c); linear, strongly defined, and symmetrical with two nodes (d); two-segment offset (e); diagonal (f); prominently occupied central axis (g); occupied central axis (h).

in Figure C10.8h they complement the sides rather than imposing dominance.

Eight more schemes are shown in Figure C10.9. The schemes in Figure C10.9a–c are hybrids. Figure C10.9a proceeds from a central display with circulation to either side, to central circulation, and then back to a central display with circulation around it. Meanwhile, Figure C10.9b is a combination of linear asymmetrical movement along the left side and a diagonally oriented central area. Figure C10.9c combines symmetrical diagonal movement in the front and back with linear two-sided circulation in the central zone. The next two diagrams feature diagonal bounce schemes. These force you to move diagonally from featured area to featured area. Figure C10.9d is organized around a main central element and features many pockets strategically placed along the side walls. Figure C10.9e is organized around a series of focal points along both the center and the two side walls.

The next three schemes are examples of compartmentalized space. In these, the store is subdivided into explicit compartments, almost like rooms. Figure C10.9f is a simple two-compartment scheme with circulation along one side. The schemes in Figure C10.9g and C10.9h are both symmetrical and axial with circulation occurring down the middle. Figure C10.9g features two circular compartments with a transition passage at the center of the store. Figure C10.9h is a three-compartment arrangement featuring a small central compartment.

The geometry of schemes, of course, can be inflected. Schemes can be curved, angled, or otherwise inflected as long as the move is compatible with the identity of the store. The four diagrams shown in Figure C.10.10 are examples of inflected schemes. Figure C10.10a is angled on one side and straight on the other. Figure C10.10b features both angles and free-floating shapes prominently. The schemes in Figure C10.10c and C10.10d are curvilinear. Figure C10.10c features an undulating compound curve around a central dominant circular shape. Figure C10.10d features a sweeping curve along one side and a smaller opposite curvilinear element anchored on the side wall.

The approaches presented in this Capsule (central linear circulation, central linear displays, loosely organized centers, hybrids, diagonal schemes, compartmentalized schemes, and inflected schemes) are not all the possible approaches, but they cover a fair amount of them. The actual interpretation, articulation, and execution of each approach, however, is subject to infinite variation. That's part of the beauty of design. Not only do you have many approaches to choose from to solve a design problem but you can customize each of them to suit the specific needs of a project.

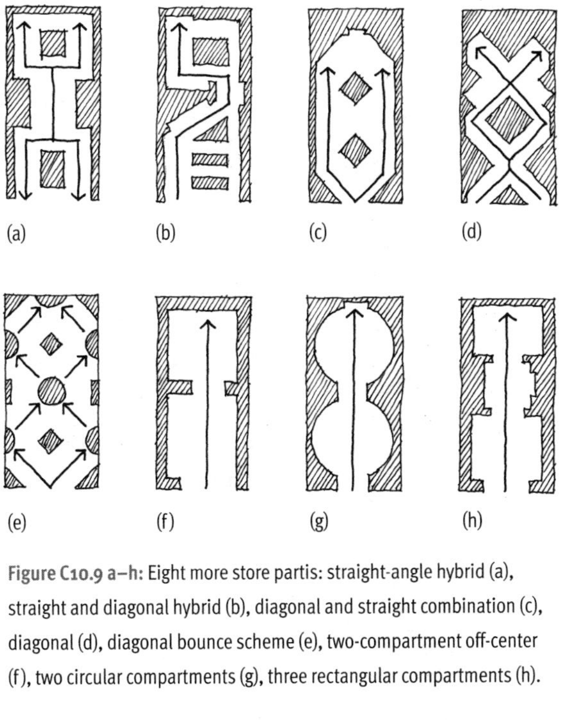

Figure C10.9 a–h: Eight more store partis: straight-angle hybrid (a), straight and diagonal hybrid (b), diagonal and straight combination (c), diagonal (d), diagonal bounce scheme (e), two-compartment off-center (f), two circular compartments (g), three rectangular compartments (h).

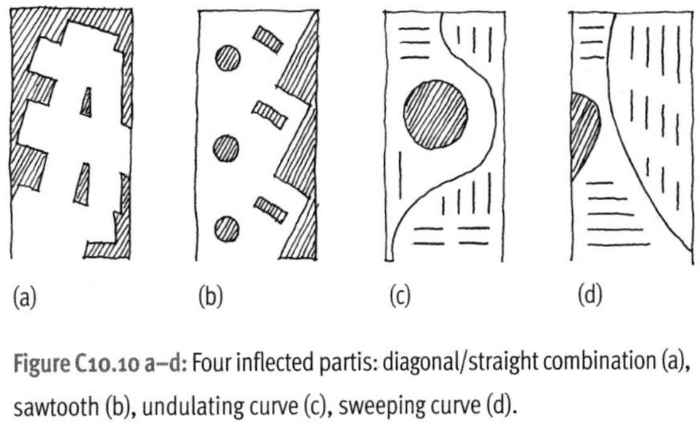

Figure C10.10 a–d: Four inflected partis: diagonal/straight combination (a), sawtooth (b), undulating curve (c), sweeping curve (d).

CASE STUDY

Designing a State-of-the-Art Facility for an Innovative Advertising Agency with an Eye Toward Brainstorming, Collaboration, and Creativity

Project: OLSON, Minneapolis, MN (125,000 sf)

Design Firm: Gensler. Photo credits: Peter Sieger

Challenge: How does one design an office environment for a client that demands innovation and a climate conducive to brainstorming, collaboration, and creativity, for them and for their clients and other people they work with?

A decade ago, OLSON was one of the few companies to foresee the decline of traditional mass marketing and the rise of the social engagement revolution. They built a "post-advertising" agency, one that creates genuine marketing movements more than clever ad campaigns. Their sole purpose is to build and activate communities for leading brands. OLSON is innovative in its strategic thinking, its work, and its client service. Gensler's design solution for OLSON's headquarters is a catalyst for innovation and creates a workspace that strengthens connections to each other, clients, and the community.

Connecting to the community starts outside of the building by standing on a designated red dot and looking up. The ceilings of each elevator lobby are painted with a portion of OLSON's logo; when standing outside the building on the red dot, the text aligns to express the logo. This non-intrusive solution creates connections to the community while adhering to the historical guidelines on building signage (Figure CS10.1).

Figure CS10.1: The Olson name seen from outside.

The building was originally an assembly plant for Ford Motor Company. The plant built Model A and Model T cars and used vertical assembly techniques. The design team embraced the historic openings, structure, and exterior brick walls along with new materials that would complement the existing building shell. Zinc, steel, reclaimed wood, and felt are untreated and these assemblies are intentionally expressed, strengthening the concept of connections.

The design supports innovation by creating spaces that connect people. The stair is the center of the agency and connects all levels of the space. Its four-story felt-and-mirror wall creates a series of unimagined views of the agency as you travel on the stair. Digital displays, cultural artifacts, string art installations, and lounge spaces unfold around the stair creating areas to gather and connect (Figures CS10.2 and 10.3).

Figure CS10.2: View of the central stairs.

Figure CS10.3: Informal work areas around the central stairs.

Figure CS10.4: Meeting room.

Innovation is supported by spaces that are designed for activities, not headcounts and benchmarks. The enclosed spaces are programmed to support connections to clients and teams. Dedicated brand rooms for client and agency working sessions are absent of technology. These spaces foster innovation through dialogue, pin ups, and brainstorming. Client pitch rooms are diverse with formal and relaxed postures, and gathering spaces are flexible and allow for movement (Figures CS10.4 through CS10.6).

The work areas are designed for availability. Change and reconfiguration is constant at OLSON. The open office workstations move easily with a small kit of parts, while the private offices, made of demountable partitions, also support flexibility.

Floors are approximately 30,000 square feet, and each one has a different color story as a mechanism to drive place making and identity. They also have custom graphics that relate to the color story but are connected to key cities across the world (Minneapolis, Sydney, London, and Rio; Figure CS10.7).

The plan is divided horizontally into three components, emphasizing socialization, collaboration, and work, respectively. Places to socialize include living spaces and kitchen spaces with bar areas. Places to collaborate include client spaces that connect with each other. Places to work are places to focus, "heads-down spaces" with open and closed workspaces, team areas, and phone rooms. See the concept diagram in Figure CS10.8.

OLSON's new home honors co-creation and choice, while creating spaces that are dense with opportunities to share ideas.

Figure CS10.5: Informal meeting room.

Figure CS10.6: Client pitch room.

continued

CASE STUDY, *continued*

Figure CS10.7: Graphics for floor number.

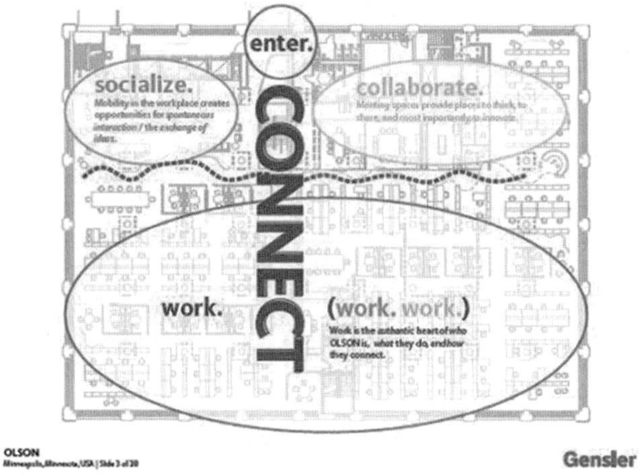

Figure CS10.8: Work zone diagram.

REVIEW

Summary

The two principal tasks during the ideation stage are to establish the project's character concept, concerned with the image or personality of the project, and its organizational concept, concerned with the arrangement of parts. During this stage the project's many realities and needs are synthesized into specific design approaches to be developed further.

To begin exploring concepts, it is necessary to have a sound overall understanding of both the project's general requirements and its salient issues. Concepts are almost always derived in response to one or more of these salient issues and are externalized as short statements, descriptive scenarios, diagrams, and sketches. When recorded, they can be evaluated, making it easier to select specific ideas for further development.

Character concept statements should not repeat the design problem. Instead, they should say something about the solution to the problem. Character concept statements should also be selective and brief. Organizational concepts provide the structure used to shape a project's spaces and their relationships. They establish an organization that is responsive to the project's realities and, at the same time, provide coherence and order.

For purposes of establishing the scheme of a project, it is useful to think in terms of the organizational systems introduced in Chapter 4 as well as the place elements introduced in Chapter 3: arrival space, centers, domains, nodes, and paths. Thinking in these terms helps to reduce the number of project parts to the most essential and to establish a sense of hierarchy in the project.

In terms of character, the outcome of this stage is a verbal statement describing the designer's intentions and strategies related to image and personality. In terms of spatial issues, the required outcome is an organizational concept that establishes a sound organizational structure. It should contain the basic design structure on which future decisions will be based. Two important kinds of diagrams used to depict organizational concepts are the parti diagram and the functional diagram. The parti diagram conveys the structure of the project in its most minimal and essential way. The functional diagram adds more detail and, in general, establishes locations for the project's destinations and a coherent circulation system to get to them.

1. Concept. (1987). In *Random house college dictionary* (AU: xx ed.).
2. Morris Mount, C. (1995). *Restaurant style.* Glen Cove, NY: Showcase Edition.
3. Grattaroti, R. (1994). *Great store design.* Rockport, MA: Rockport.
4. Cohen, Edie. (1997). "L.A. boogie-woogie." *Interior Design.* March: pp. 104–109.
5. Morris Mount, 1995, p. 140.
6. Ibid, p. 45.
7. Ibid, p. 86.
8. Dorf, M. E. (1992). *Restaurants that work: Case studies of the best in the country.* New York: Whitney.
9. Cerver, F. A. (1996). *Commercial space: Shop windows, cosmetics.* Sussex: Rotovision.
10. Ibid, pp. 91–92.

Chapter Questions

1. You have seen that there are many kinds of concepts and that it is often confusing to know what someone is referring to when they talk about the project's concept. Explain, in your own words, what "the concept" of a project means to you.
2. Refer back to the concept for a design project you have done in school. How was it expressed (short statement, scenario, diagram, sketch)? How many ideas were involved? Was it predominantly an organizational concept or a character concept?
3. In your opinion, what kind of project understanding is most crucial to develop good concepts?
4. Have you done concept diagrams before? Were they more like the parti diagrams or the functional diagrams described in this chapter? Explain.
5. Explain the main differences between a block plan and a functional diagram.
6. How do you ensure, during the ideation stage, that every required function is accounted for?
7. Explain two ways you could perform a manipulation for enrichment during the ideation stage.
8. Explain two ways you could perform a manipulation for expression during the ideation stage.
9. Think of examples of centers, nodes, landmarks, and edges for a house, a store, a restaurant, and a dance club.
10. What are the main characteristics of a good written concept statement?

Exercises

1. Identify the salient issues for the design project you are currently working on. Is there a dominant one?
2. Based on the responses to Exercise 1, list five potential concepts (organizational and character) for your design project.
3. Choose three other design projects you have worked on in school, and write two potential concept statements for each. These can represent a different approach from the one you took originally. Emphasize a different aspect of the project for each of the two concepts.
4. Select one organizational concept for your current design project and develop three variations.
5. Working with a partner, each find the final space plan for a project you have done previously. Trade plans so each of you has the other's space plan. Now put a layer of trace paper over the plan and try to diagram the basic parti of your partner's scheme. Discuss with each other.
6. For the design project of your choice, produce the following: a short concept statement; a concept scenario; a quick, loose concept diagram; and a sketch for a particular space or area.
7. For the three projects in Exercise 3, select one concept and draw both a parti diagram and a functional diagram.

Chapter 11
Development

Instructional Objectives

- Explain the process of design synthesis.
- Explain the process of moving from organizational concepts to developed space plans.
- Explain the process of developing vertical surfaces and details through elevation drawings.
- Explain the process of developing the three-dimensional envelope of spaces.
- Explain the important role of the ceiling plane in three-dimensional development.
- Explain the importance of details and a process for developing them.
- Explain the tasks of selecting materials and finishes.
- Explain the task of selecting furniture, fixtures, and equipment.
- Explain the important role played by artwork, accessories, and exhibits.
- Explain the effects of people and goods in the interior mix.

In any worthwhile activity we see what we do with two different sets of eyes. In the midst of doing we give all of ourselves to our labors in constructive sympathy. We are one with our work. A moment later, we look again at what we have done and judge it as if from outside ourselves, with as critical and detached manner as we can muster. We redesign again and again, trying to satisfy our inner demands, though in architecture time is limited and we can rarely please ourselves fully.

—*Cesar Pelli,* Observations for Young Architects

Understanding the needs of a project and arriving at a good concept are important individual milestones of design projects and, if done well, give a project a strong sense of definition and direction. However, there is much design work that needs to follow. Diagrams need to evolve into floor plans, and these, in turn, have to be refined through successive iterations. Additionally, the shapes and volumes of spaces have to be determined, surfaces have to be composed, and layers of furnishings and other objects added. These, too, go through a series of iterations, getting more and more refined with each successive iteration. During the development process parts need to be adjusted, relationships fine-tuned, and details given final form. Additionally, the designer needs to step back, look at the entire project as a whole, and make necessary adjustments to ensure proper cohesiveness.

This chapter is about the process of developing and eventually completing designs. We will first discuss the idea of design synthesis and then move through the various tasks of design development, from arriving at a floor plan to the final development of details and the inclusion of furnishings and other final layers of design.

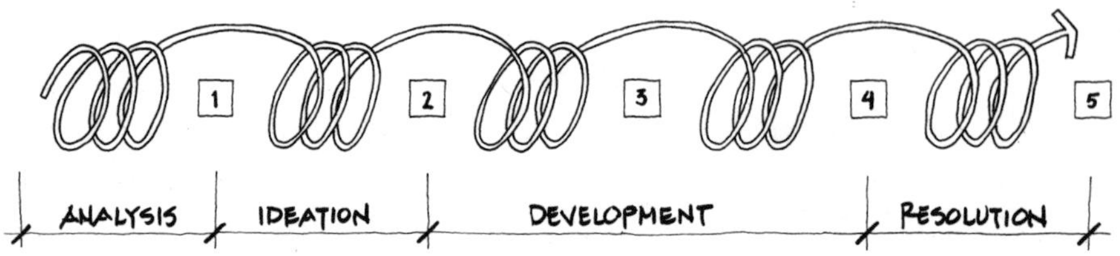

Figure 11.1: Within each stage, the design process should incorporate complete cycles that achieve synthesis to a level appropriate to the stage. Every stage should produce a tangible outcome derived from the understanding of the project at that stage, culminating in the thorough and complete project solution at the end of the resolution phase.

DESIGN SYNTHESIS

The evolution of designs seldom occurs in linear fashion. Except for the smallest and simplest of projects, it is uncommon to arrive at an optimal solution from a single attempt, refine it in linear fashion, and then send it to the contractor to build. Most projects require an ongoing cyclical process of commitment and testing followed by evaluation and adjustment. With every cycle of response and feedback, the designer commits to some aspects of the solution, modifies some, and discards others. With every step the design reaches a higher level of resolution. Figure 11.1 shows a diagram of the process. It is like a spiraling helix, moving cyclically from one stage to the next and incorporating successful ideas as they are developed and additional insights gained during previous stages.

As you move along the process, it is necessary to test design ideas based on your current understanding of the design problem at that point. These ideas, as William Kleinsasser explains, act "like rehearsals before a game, serve as hypotheses or probes out there . . . they will preview the whole and generate better proposals."[1] Each such cycle should include a design scheme developed to a level appropriate to the stage of the project and devote some time to analyze and evaluate the scheme in order to assess its merits and get a greater understanding of the project. These cyclical evaluations need to generally address three things: the appropriateness of the overall design approach being taken, the way particular aspects of the approach are working, and the way the design problem definition is evolving.

DEVELOPMENT OF THE PLAN

During the early, conceptual part of the design process, as we saw in Chapter 10, the majority of the effort goes into developing an organizational structure that will give the project a clear direction. Alternatives have to be closely scrutinized and run through one of the review cycles. After an organizational concept has been determined appropriate, it is tested to see if it truly works with the detailed requirements of the program, the geometry of the space, and other specific requirements of the project. When you choose a concept and determine that it will work, the attention can shift to more detailed aspects of the design solution, all the while ensuring that the integrity of this organizational structure is maintained as the design goes through modifications. As the design evolves it is important to examine periodically the current understanding of the problem for accuracy and breadth, because it will tend to shift and come into clearer focus as one gets more information. This invariably leads to a better understanding of the project and its potential solutions.

Therefore, the problem definition stage is itself cyclical. What starts with a rudimentary understanding of a complex design problem during programming is redefined into sub-issues or components, which in turn produce more detail and a better understanding of components and relationships. While addressing these, new sub-issues continue to surface. The more you keep working on the design solution, the more layers of information and nuance rise to the surface, changing and refining your definition of the problem and the way you think about the project.

From Concepts to Floor Plans

Development starts with the floor plan. Floor plans go through a number of revisions, starting with the first attempt to translate the organizational concept idea into a floor plan and culminating in the final plan that responds to the many pragmatic and experiential issues of the project.

The level of definition of a design concept might vary from designer to designer and from project to project. If the conceptual phase was successful you are likely to have a cohesive scheme that features a good distribution of spaces, an efficient circulation scheme, and an appropriate disposition of enclosed areas (solids) and open areas (voids). You may have addressed not only organizational needs but also other desirable qualities related to the personality of the organization and its outward manifestation. Additionally you would have addressed and responded to contextual factors such as site location, exposure to the sun path, and exposure to views and other external features. If you worked through the conceptual phase with some sense of scale, the spatial allocations are likely to be reasonably accurate. At this point you might have one concept idea or more to test further.

At this stage you need to solve the puzzle aspect of the space plan. Precision is required so you must do the work to scale. The following is a list of some of the issues you are trying to resolve:

- Making all spaces and functions fit in as you had hoped.
- Adjusting the sizes and shapes of spaces to accommodate furnishings and achieve pleasing proportions.
- Evolving the representational language of your drawings from the general shapes of the concept diagram to walls, doors, windows, built-ins, and furnishings.
- Testing furniture layouts for the various rooms and spaces and making adjustments as necessary.

In terms of sequence we suggest that you start with your most important defining elements such as enclosing walls, defining edges, and so forth. Plug in the furniture, and adjust enclosing edges as necessary to make everything fit. As you try to define spaces within the project, remember the role of flooring changes and overhead ceiling elements and start thinking three dimensionally. Which spaces are autonomous, and which ones blend with the adjacent spaces? Which spaces are tall and airy, and which ones are low and cozy? Make notes on your paper as you make decisions. Finally picture yourself in the various spaces you are proposing. Are they pleasant and comfortable? Are they conducive to the activities that will take place in them?

Figure 11.2 shows the development of a student's floor plan for an office project from conception through design development. Figure 11.2a shows the initial organizational concept diagram. Figure 11.2b and Figure 11.2c show the plan at two intermediary stages. Figure 11.2d shows the final solution with the plan fully resolved. After spending time with the design idea, the student was convinced that the challenging geometry being attempted would work. It took, however, many adjustments and some compromises to make it all work in the end.

When the organizational concept has been successfully translated into a floor plan, you can focus on fitting all the requirements of the program more exactly, eliminating wasted space, and, in general, adjusting the plan with greater precision. Even after you have accommodated all the requirements, there are often troublesome parts that require ongoing efforts to resolve. Especially tricky are those areas that seem to have a domino effect such that, upon fixing one area, you manage to ruin the previously successful adjacent area. Figure 11.3 shows three variations developed by a student in the process of resolving one area of the floor plan for an office project.

The Editing Process

The early stages of plan generation need to be fluid. Evaluating and advancing ideas during this stage of development needs to go through what could be labeled an *editing stage*. Even though the term is not conventionally used in design, we find that students understand the task better when it is called editing. Just as we edit writing projects to make the language clearer and precise, we also edit designs for greater clarity and precision.

The thinking part of the editing process for interior design should not happen on the computer. The process of creating and changing drawings using computer programs such as AutoCAD is too rigid to facilitate the necessary fluidity and speed required. Work on trace paper; it is important that you do so. If you have generated some work on the computer, print the current iteration and put a sheet of trace paper over it. Then do your thinking on trace paper using either a pencil or pen.

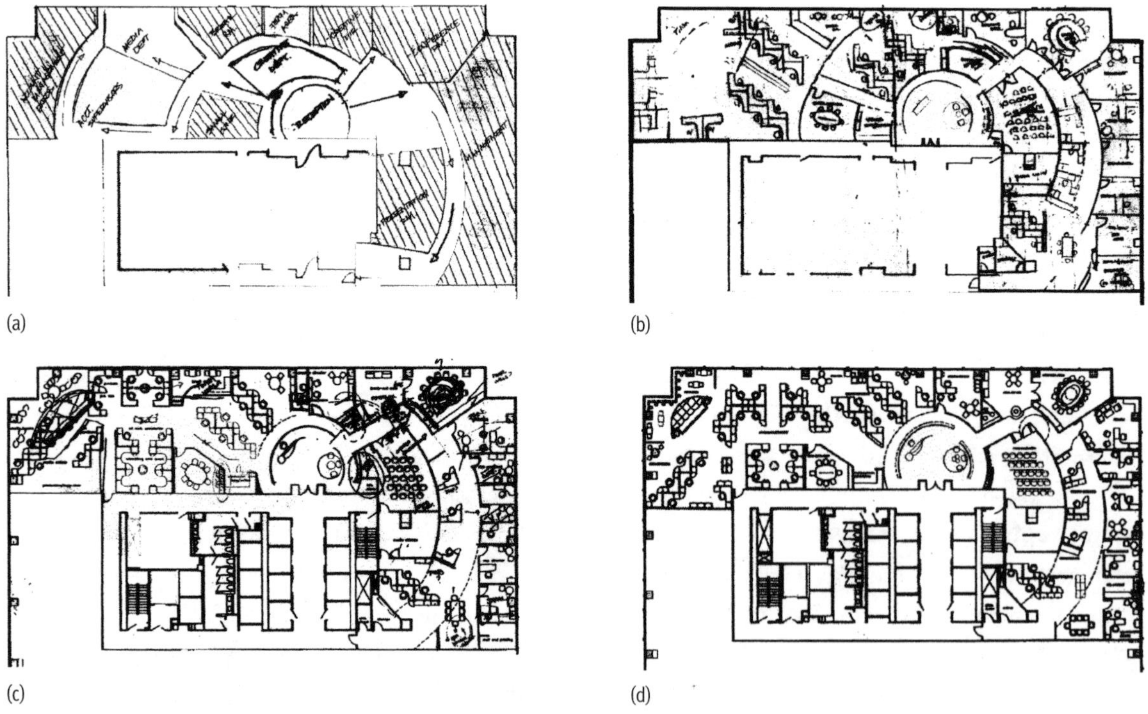

(a) (b) (c) (d)

Figure 11.2: This series of floor plans for an office project shows different stages of resolution, starting with the original organizational concept. This plan was particularly challenging to solve because of the geometry imposed by the concept. It was deemed workable, and the designer succeeded in planning it out. The organizational diagram (a), an early transposition of the program's specific requirements to the plan (b), a developed but not totally refined plan (c), and the final version of the plan (d) are shown.

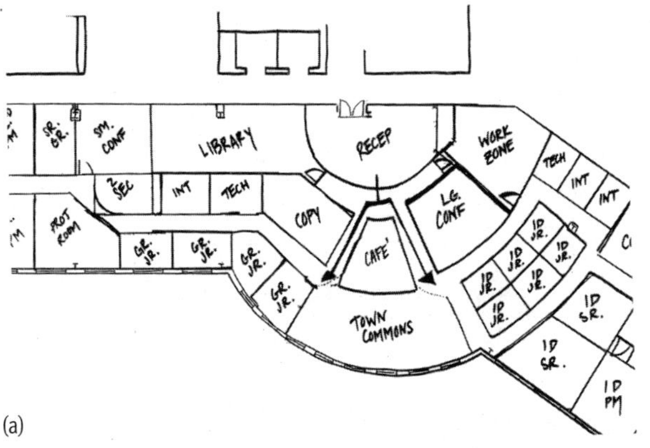

(a)

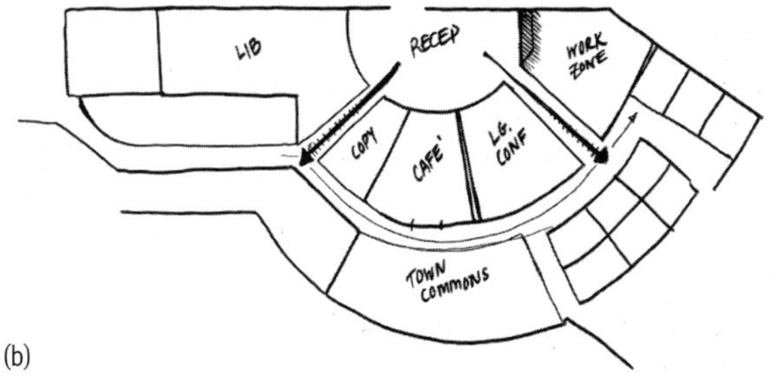

(b)

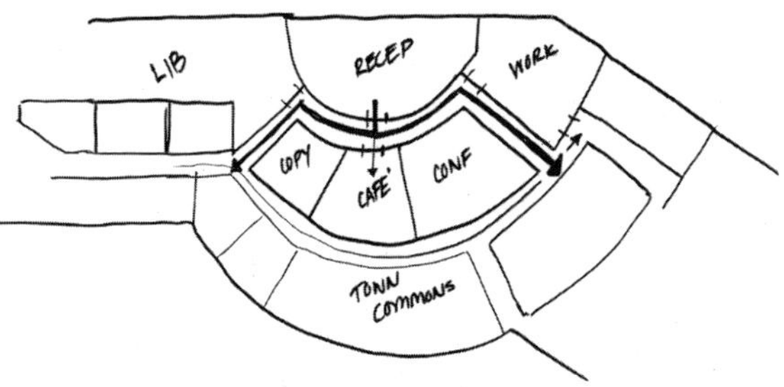

(c)

Figure 11.3: Shown are three of the many studies drawn by one student trying to resolve the area around the main reception area of an office project. One of the main issues was resolving the circulation to the town commons and the rest of the space.

As you attempt to define your floor plan try one or more ideas quickly and loosely but using a scale. Listen to your inner critical voice. You may also listen to the imaginary voices of designers you trust and instructors. What would these voices be telling you? "Good job here, adjust this, move that, turn these." If the layer of trace gets messy just add a new layer over it and continue working. If you ruin one idea, rip the piece of trace into pieces, throw it away, and add a brand new one. Such is the beauty of trace paper. After you start landing on an idea you like, you can go back to your computer to try it out there. Your best thinking will have happened already, and the stiffness of the computer won't slow you down or stifle your creativity (Figure 11.4).

After you arrive at a workable space plan your task becomes to refine it. Utilizing feedback from others as

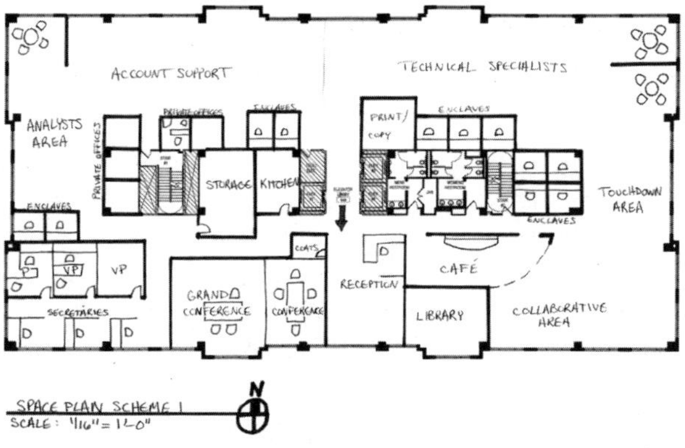

(a)

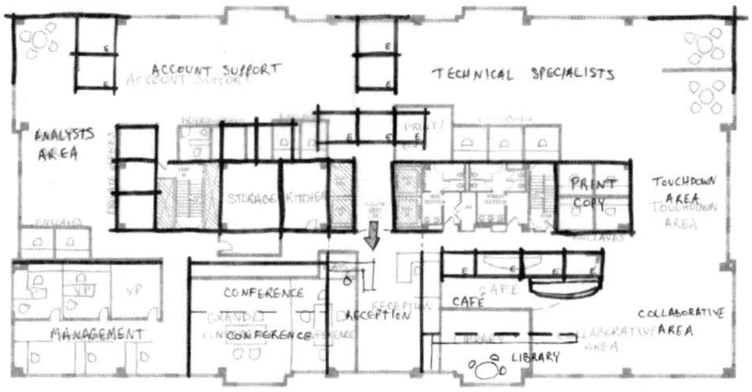

(b)

Figure 11.4: The early plan in (a) was edited several times by the student before arriving at the final version. An overlay with some of the changes made during early editing are shown in (b).

well as your own inner voice, you can engage in a process of gradual improvement. At this point it may be a matter of reducing a little wasted space here, widening a corridor there, and playing with walls to accommodate built-ins and perform form articulations. Figure 11.5 shows an example of editing at a more advanced stage. This time

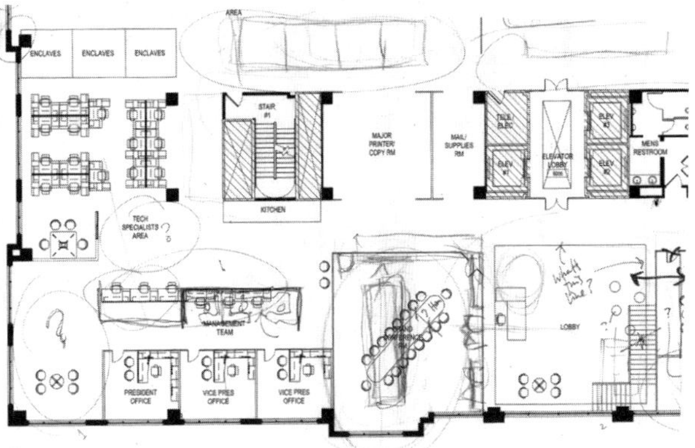

Figure 11.5: Even after one starts producing digital versions of the space plan, it is best to do the edit by hand either on trace paper or directly on the print as shown here.

Figure 11.6: Sometimes floor plans contain minor floor elevation changes as those shown here for two different restaurants. The different levels as well as the steps and ramps need to be shown on the space plan.

the student had printed out her computer generated plan and was performing the edits with pencil directly on the drawing sheet.

Flooring and Ceiling Changes

At some point during the process of space planning you can start addressing the floor and the ceiling as space defining elements or as general form enhancing elements. As you gain experience you can think of these and your space planning simultaneously. The floor and ceiling planes are, after all, important shapers of space.

Floor changes are either floor elevation or floor material changes. Floor material changes are more common because floor elevation changes require steps and ramps for access and these consume a good amount of space. Nevertheless, where enough space is available, floor elevation changes are sometimes used in some projects. The elevated floor platforms shown in Figure 11.6 for two restaurants are examples. Flooring material changes at the same level are generally more feasible. These include changes from hard surfaces such as stone to soft surfaces such as carpet, changes from high end surfaces such as slate tiles to more utilitarian surfaces such as vinyl flooring, and subtle material changes to subtly delineate different floor zones (Figure 11.7). Although flooring changes can be powerful ways to delineate zones and circulation routes, caution must be exercised to not use them so rigidly so as to stifle future re-planning efforts in a given environment, say, one year after move-in.

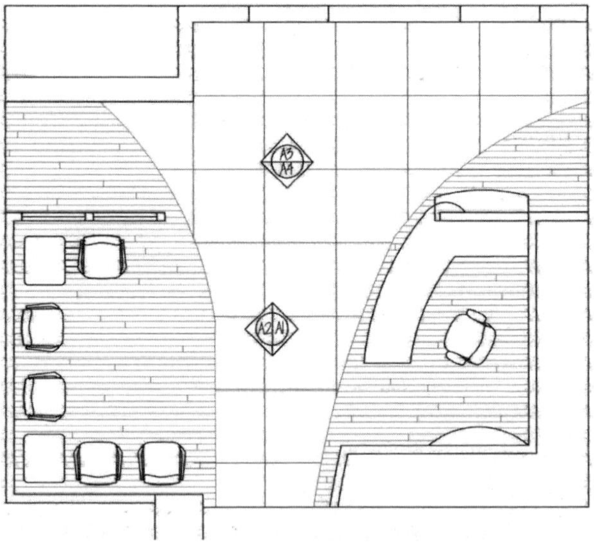

Figure 11.7: Very often designers utilize flooring changes on their plans that do not involve elevation changes. In these cases, the change is achieved by a change of materials as shown on this plan for a reception area.

Ceiling articulation is an important component of your efforts to shape the interior spatial envelope. Although the ceiling is examined in detail during the reflected ceiling plan development stage, some of the early ceiling articulation ideas can happen during early space planning. There are times when you are planning a certain open area in the middle of a space, and you know that you will want to manipulate the ceiling plane above to help give that area stronger spatial definition.

Ceiling height changes and other articulations are quite versatile. Ceiling shapes can be dynamic elements suggesting lines of movement, they can define zones, they can complete forms, and they can act as counterpoints to adjacent forms. They can be autonomous or attached. They can go upwards or downwards. Any time you get an idea for a ceiling change during space planning go ahead and make a note of it. If it's a prominent feature go ahead and delineate it (with dashed lines) on your floor plan. It is a common convention to use dashed lines to indicate major overhead openings and elements. Figure 11.8 reflects an example of a ceiling element shown on the floor plan using dashed lines and a three-dimensional view of the desired effect.

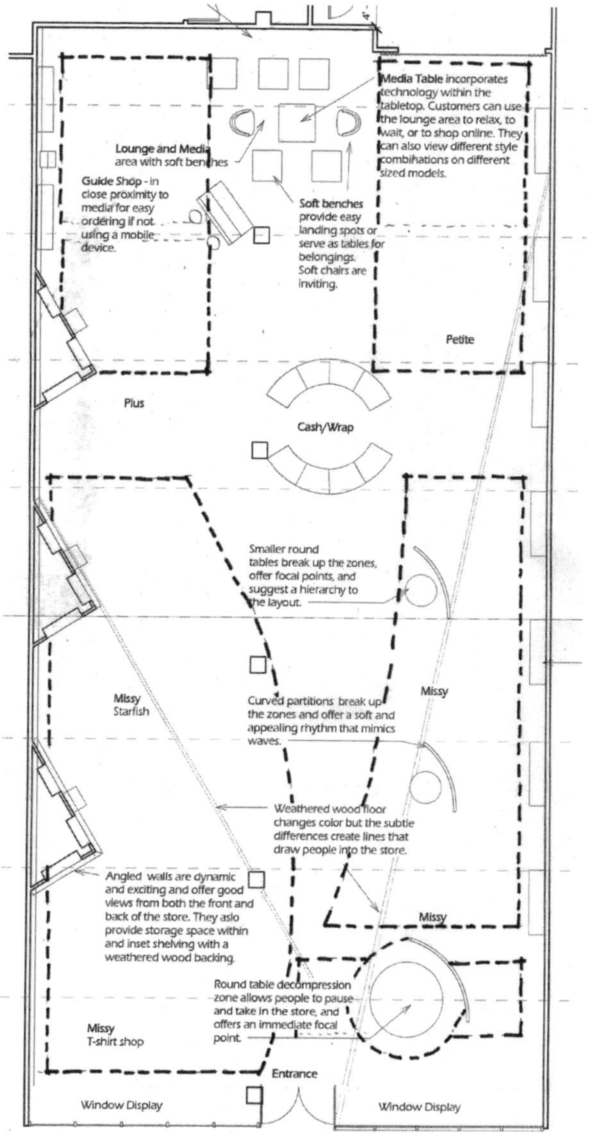

(a)

Figure 11.8: Although ceiling changes are normally shown on the reflected ceiling plan, it is common to show significant items occurring overhead on the floor plan. The convention is to show these items using dashed lines as shown in (a). Here they are shown heavier than they would normally be to illustrate the point. The plan also shows lines representing flooring changes on the floor plane. The perspective (b) shows the effect of the overhead elements on the scene.

(b)

Services and Technology

One final aspect of plan development is the coordination of functions and the services that feed them, such as power, data, and plumbing locations. When planning interior projects you often have to plan the placement of furniture where there are existing power and data sources, such as in a building with floor power and data located on floor trenches in specific locations. Other times you can locate the furniture where you want it and then bring the necessary power and data to it. Even though at some point during design development you will produce a power and communications plan indicating the locations of electrical, telephone, and data outlets in your project as shown in the example in Figure 11.9, you want to make sure early on that you have made good decisions concerning functions and furnishings and their relative location to services such as electrical power and data.

Similarly, break rooms and other spaces needing a supply of water for sinks, coffee makers, or other equipment needing water are best located near existing plumbing in the building. That way new plumbing runs are minimized, and your client benefits from cost savings.

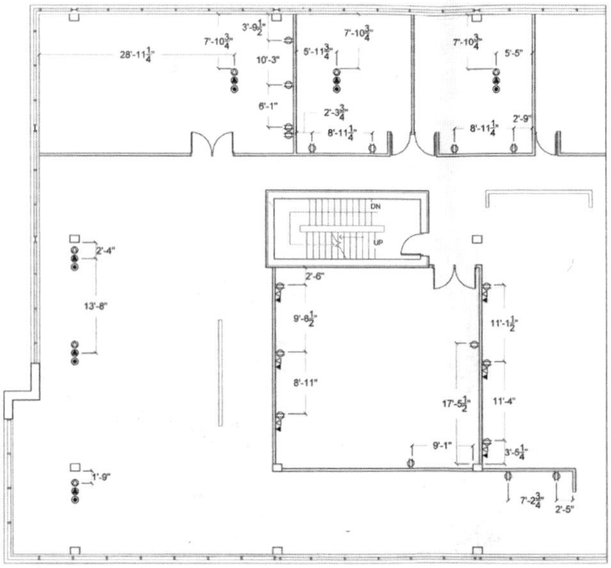

Figure 11.9: The location of power and data has to be closely coordinated with the locations of functions in the space. In existing spaces with existing services the functions respond to existing conditions. In new build-outs the functions are placed in their optimal locations and the services are then located where needed for proper functionality.

REFINEMENT BEYOND THE PLAN

Producing a workable floor plan is important but is just the beginning. In addition to the plan, elevations, the three-dimensional volumes, and design details will also need to be developed. Their resolution occurs in hierarchical fashion, working from the general to the specific. After general decisions are made about details like position, size, and shape, higher levels of detail can be addressed, such as materials to be used, subdivision or parts, and ways of connecting them.

Vertical Surfaces: The Walls

Vertical surface development includes such tasks as establishing the composition of elevations. This requires locating openings, determining finishes, adding details, and articulating the planes. Just as space planning is both challenging and rewarding by virtue of its puzzle-solving nature, the development of elevations is challenging and rewarding by virtue of the need to achieve evocative compositions that enhance both function and experience and the satisfaction of doing it well.

When we refer to vertical surfaces we are talking mostly about the walls and partitions in space, both permanent and moveable. These are the elements that give real presence to a place. Their development often starts early as you work on the plan. In fact, it is a good idea to be sketching elevation ideas on paper as you work on the plan. Figure 11.10 shows examples of two early floor plans for a store where the designer was also beginning to plan (very loosely) the elevations of the perimeter walls. Early elevation diagrams can be quite sketchy like the ones in the example referred to earlier in this chapter. You are the only one who sees these first sketchy attempts. Early elevations to be presented more publicly can also be loose although they have to be drawn with some precision and care. These can be purely architectural or more animated in nature. Figure 11.11 shows examples of early loose elevations. Elevations typically show the composition, materials, and subdivision of wall planes and omit furnishings and other objects in the foreground. These foreground elements can be shown if they are major pieces and relate to the wall behind them

(a)

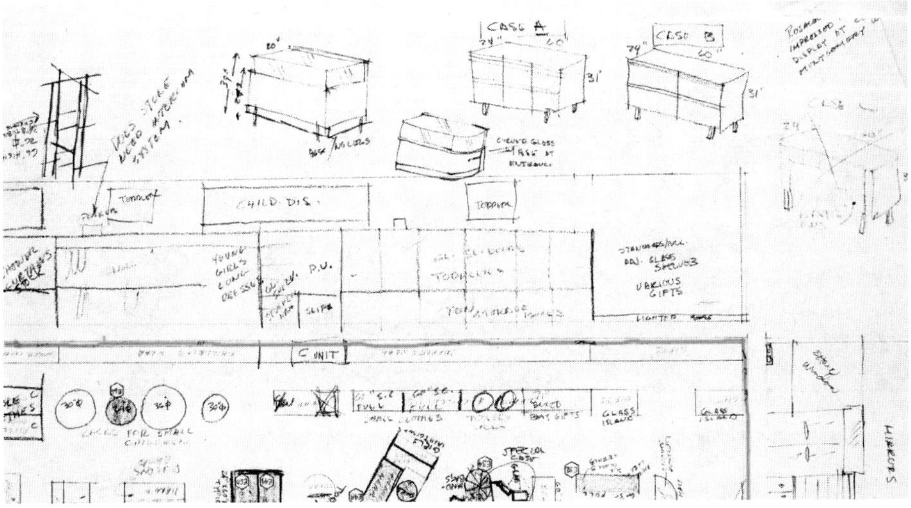

(b)

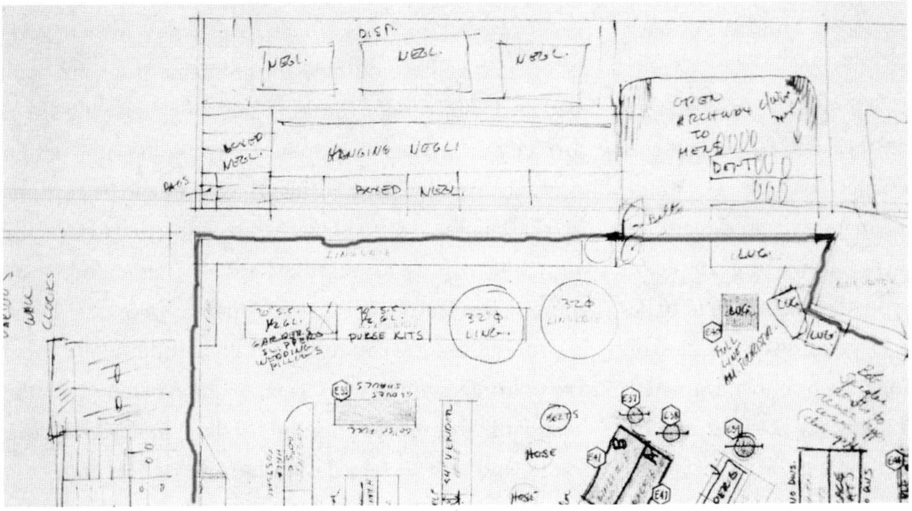

Figure 11.10: Figures (a) and (b) show early loose plans for a store. Drawn loosely above them are rough elevations of the displays on the perimeter wall. In sketch (a) the designer was even thinking ahead about some of the fixtures being considered for the store.

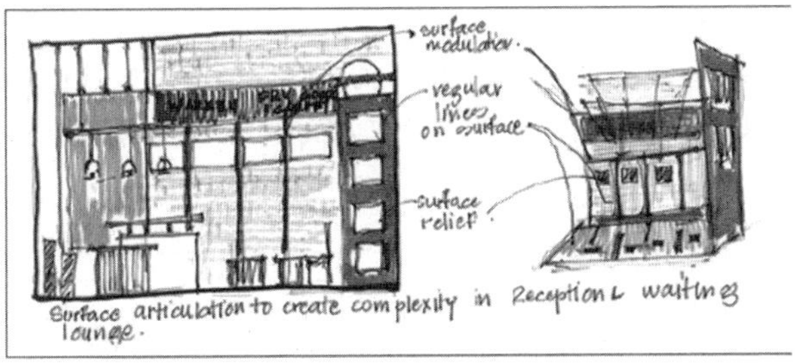

(a)

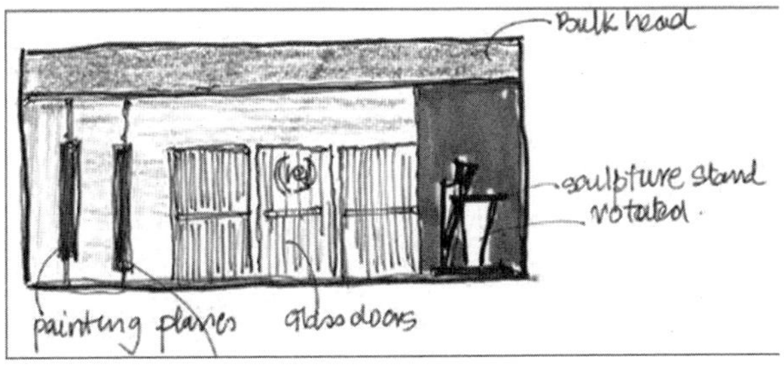

(c)

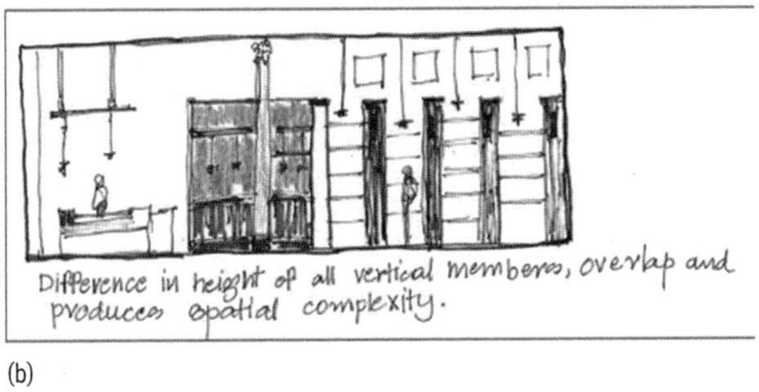

(b)

Figure 11.11: These loosely drawn elevations, although sketchy, do a good job of capturing many detailed features of the design. Courtesy of Tina Patel.

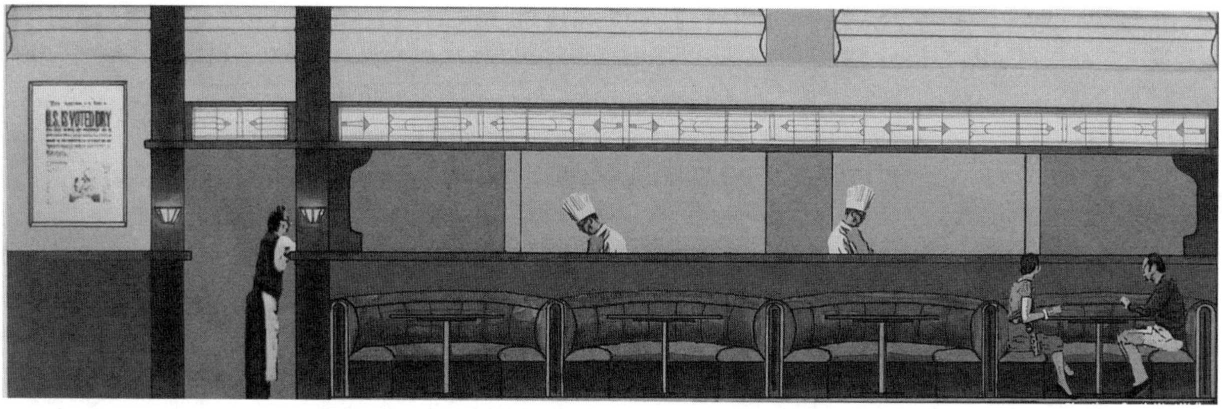

Figure 11.12: In this animated elevation we are given a sense of foreground (booths) and background (cooks in the open kitchen).

(Figure 11.12), but, more often they are omitted or shown lightly with dashed lines to show the relationship between foreground and background.

Elevations, like floor plans, will go through an editing process. Don't pretend that they will be perfect the first time because this seldom happens. Only a back and forth effort of iterations and changes will produce fully resolved compositions. Figure 11.13 shows an example of marked-up elevations pointing out details that need to be corrected or developed further. Depending on the kind of presentation, your final elevations can be either animated elevations showing people and items like merchandise or more formal architectural elevations showing architectural features only. Figure 11.14 shows examples of animated and purely architectural elevations.

Drawing accurate and convincing elevations requires a commitment to learn how things really are. They are never the single line simplifications drawn by many novice students. Materials have qualities and thicknesses. Walls have ins and outs. There are different ways materials come together and how those intersections are handled. A lot of design thinking goes into drawing them correctly. Designers need to become familiar how design elements "usually" are and, also, how they can be customized and handled differently. For instance, there is usually one standard way to treat, say, a door frame, and it is a good idea to learn what that is. A trip to your local home improvement store can help with this. Additionally, there are unlimited other ways (many quite better than the "standard" from a design point of view) to design a door frame, and that's when design becomes a fun endeavor. What are these other ways? How many lines will you need to draw to represent the chosen frame?

In addition to their inherent functionality, the elements seen on an elevation have a major presence in the visual field. Their proper composition requires much attention.

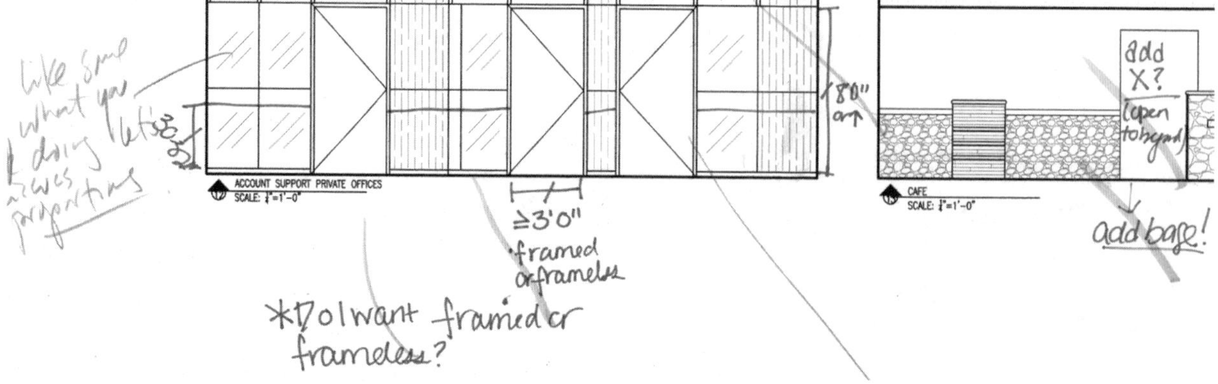

Figure 11.13: Like floor plans, elevations go through a series of iterations (edits) before everything is resolved. Shown here are markups on a printed elevation identifying questions and things to change.

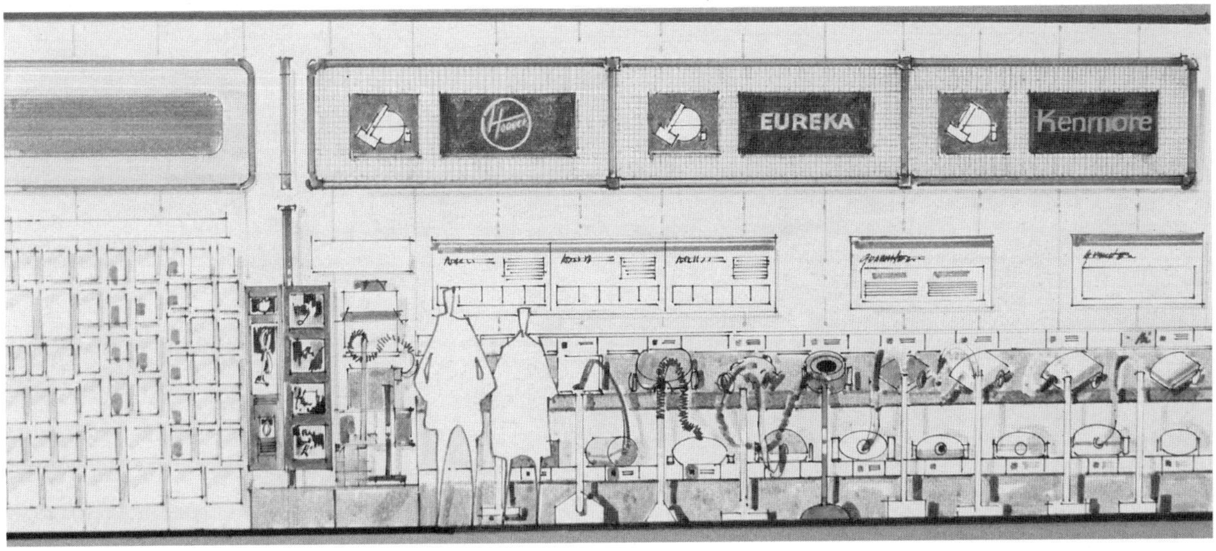

(a)

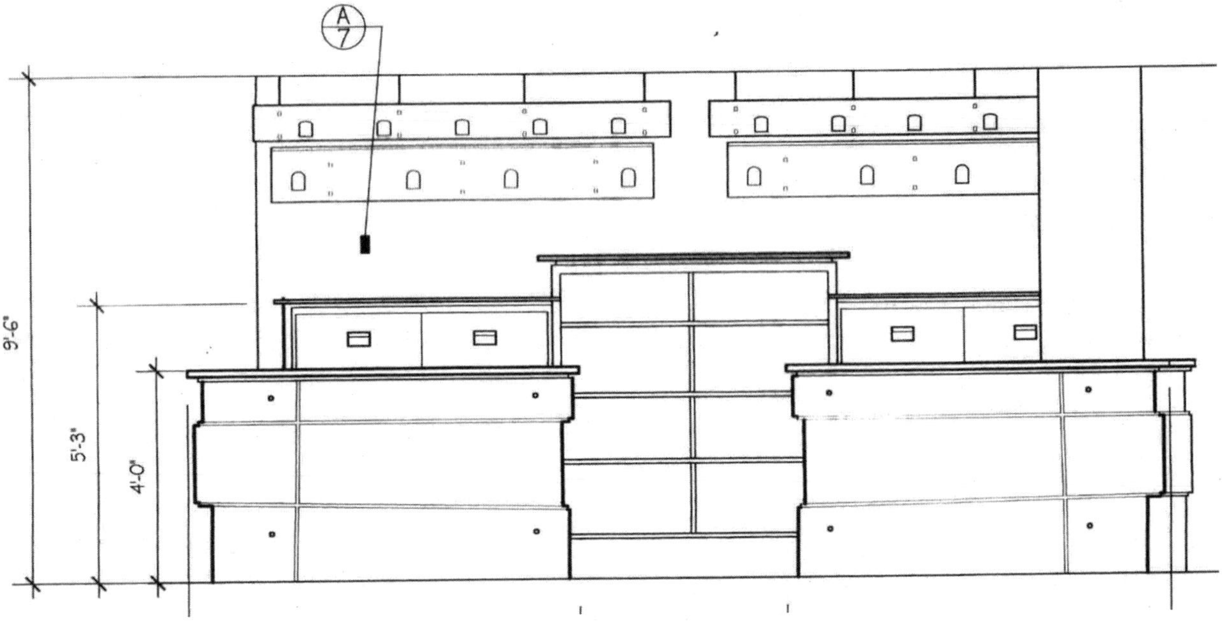

(b)

Figure 11.14: Two hard-lined presentation elevations are shown. Elevation (a) is an animated elevation for a store showing merchandise and scale figures. Elevation (b) only shows architectural elements (both foreground and background elements are shown).

Reviewing some of the basic elements and principles of design can come in handy when developing elevations. You'll find that thinking in terms of points, lines, and planes will come in handy. The concepts of repetition, rhythm, and focal points will also be relevant, as will be the notions of hierarchy and emphasis. The concepts of scale and modulation will be essential. A major aspect of what interior designers do is to subdivide and modulate, breaking big chunks into smaller parts of appropriate scales. And they do this in interesting ways that stimulate and use pleasing proportions that delight (Figure 11.15).

Despite the necessary regularity and functionality of the elevations, they can even borrow much from the same principles that you might use for the composition of a painting. On top of everything, of course, is the practical aspect of design so the drawer here and the shelves there are all where they need to be and at the proper heights, and of the proper depth, and so on. Finally, it goes without

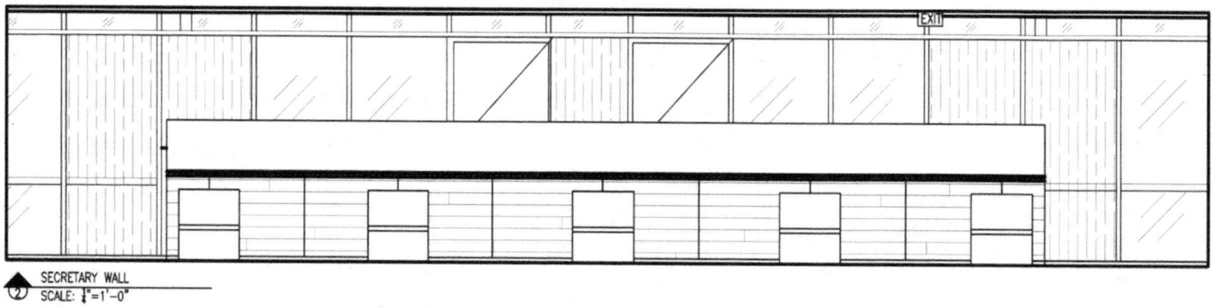

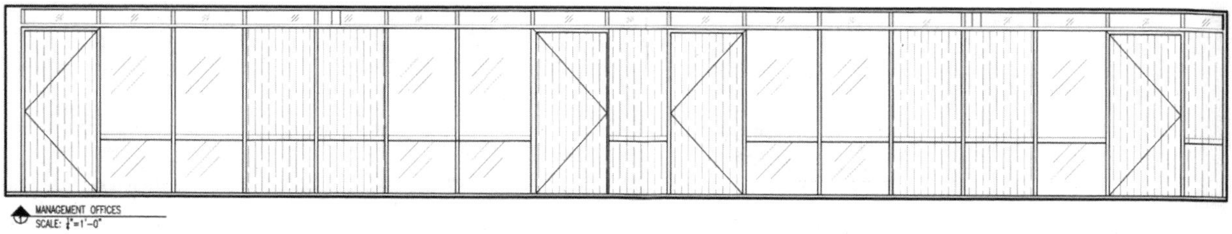

Figure 11.15: Designers break up the environment into smaller chunks that have an agreeable sense of scale. Shown here are two elevations that, although fairly ordinary, do a good job of using lines to compartmentalize the visual array into modules with a sense of human scale.

saying that what one looks at when facing an elevation are real materials and finishes so good material and color selection is a must. Designing elevations is, indeed, one of the most rewarding aspects of interior design.

The Spatial Envelope: Depth, Breadth, and Height

Floor plans and elevations, of course, are not enough. Living environments want to be much more than spaces subdivided and bound by pleasing walls. Evocative interior environments have the added drama that comes from the successful orchestration of volumetric spatial envelopes, each having unique spatial properties of its own. The expansion of space here, its contraction there, successive spaces seen in rich layered sequence, and other such experiential attributes make environments come to life. Here we are concerned with variables such as the depth of space, its lateral breadth, and its vertical rise.

Whether we think of the ordered and rhythmic succession of character-rich rooms from classical designs or the unrestricted spatial flow of more modern ones, spatial disposition is one of the things that interior designers deal with. For every space created, the question becomes: What is this spatial envelope like? Is it tall toward the center and lower along two sides? Does it have a cozy niche for conversation? What are these spaces really like? Also, how is this space visually connected to what's in front? How does it relate to lateral spaces to its sides? How are all those volumes orchestrated? Figures 11.16a–c shows some examples of the interconnection of adjacent spaces with different volumetric properties.

The Ceiling Plane

Of special importance, obviously, is the ceiling plane for it is the ceiling height that most affects the perception of space. Not only is the height of each ceiling portion of importance but also equally important is its shape. The ceiling plane, indeed, can be a splendid expressive entity. To acquire some competency in the design of ceilings (and the resulting volumetric character) it is useful to develop familiarity with the various ceiling types. The following is a list of some common ceiling types. The list is rich with many choices to select from. Figure 11.17 illustrates some of the options.

- The no ceiling option (open to above)
- The dropped tile ceiling
- The dropped hard (usually drywall) ceiling
- The soffit
- The floating plane (of various types)
- The coved ceiling
- The coffered ceiling
- The dome
- The vault
- The wave

(a) (b) (c)

Figure 11.16: As the interior design profession has become more architectural, designers are often engaged in the intricacies of shaping and sculpting complex three-dimensional space, as shown in these examples.

(a) (b) (c) (d)

(e) (f) (g) (h)

Figure 11.17: The ceiling plane is very important in the design of good three-dimensional environments. There are many options of materials, shapes, and strategies. Shown here are a flat wood panel ceiling (a); a lowered section of ceiling utilizing modular metal tiles (b); a two-step soffit (one angular, the other curved) utilizing drywall and wood paneling (c); a curved dropped ceiling with wood planks and painted drywall (d); a tall rhythmic wood plank ceiling (e); a multi-level dropped ceiling done in drywall (f); a floating drywall plane (g); and a tall gable-shaped drywall ceiling (h).

In addition to the volumetric geometry of spaces, it is useful to occasionally reinforce verticality by incorporating elements with a vertical orientation. These often become important focal points and provide relief from the horizontality that predominates in most interior spaces. The columns, the fireplace, and other elements with vertical expression are examples as shown in Figure 11.18.

As important as the spatial qualities is the lighting quality in the spaces, because our perception of spaces is affected by how dim or bright they are. For instance, a dim large room does not seem as spacious as the same room in bright light. This can be compounded by the use of light or dark finishes and lighting in the space as seen in Figure 11.19. Lighting can also serve to unify or break up space. Intermittent pools of light in rhythm will have the effect of subdivision. Uniform light with no shadows will tend to unify and make the space come across as one. Lighting fixtures also make a strong compositional contribution to the ceiling plane, revealing hierarchies of lighting groups that become points and lines and fields on the ceiling plane. All these considerations, of course, are in addition to the necessary duty of illuminating the environment so that users can adequately see and enjoy it. The possibilities are wide open, ranging from the mundane and conventional to the unconventional and adventurous. Figure 11.20 shows some of the options.

For lighting, as with ceilings, it is useful to develop some literacy of the choices available. The following are some common ones.

- The recessed fluorescent fixture (commonly 2-feet × 2-feet or 2-feet × 4-feet)
- The recessed can light or downlight (of many kinds) centered along one line
- The recessed can light or downlight (of many kinds) arranged in grid fashion
- The closely spaced row or field of can lights (downlights) over an object or area
- The row of recessed wallwashers
- The suspended can light (downlight)
- The linear wallwasher
- The linear cove or perimeter fixture
- The linear recessed light fixture
- The linear suspended architectural fixture (direct, indirect, or combination)
- The wall sconce
- The decorative pendant
- The wall mounted up-light fixture

(a) (b) (c)

Figure 11.18: Most elements in interior environments tend to be low and horizontally oriented. The presence of a few significant vertical elements provides good contrast and a welcomed relief, as shown in these examples.

(a)

(b)

(a)

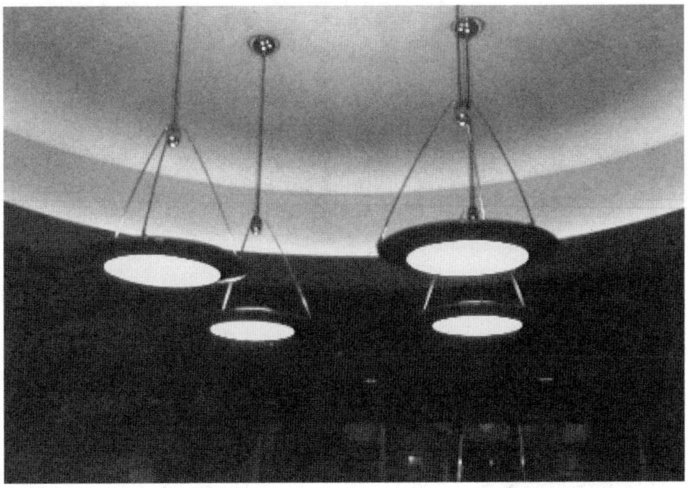

(b)

(c)

Figure 11.19: Color value (lightness, darkness) alone can make a dramatic difference in the overall feel of an interior environment. Compare the difference between the light-colored environment shown in (a) with the much darker environment shown in (b).

Figure 11.20: The design of lighting patterns on the ceiling requires that we revisit the basics of two-dimensional composition. Possibilities vary widely, depending on whether we use many small point sources (a), a group of a few large point sources (b), or rows of linear sources (c).

Useful drawings to study individual space volumes as well as volumetric relationships among adjacent spaces are the architectural section and the perspective. The architectural section drawing, particularly, can be extremely helpful when trying to determine ceiling configurations involving height changes as shown in Figure 11.21. The perspective gives us a more realistic representation of what an arrangement will look like. Figure 11.22 shows examples of loose exploratory perspectives while more developed ones are shown in Figure 11.23. Another type of drawing that can help you visualize three-dimensional massing is the axonometric or aerial perspective. Figure 11.24 shows two examples.

The reflected ceiling plan, ultimately, lays out the design of the ceiling planes and the lighting layout. Producing one can be a frightening experience for the novice

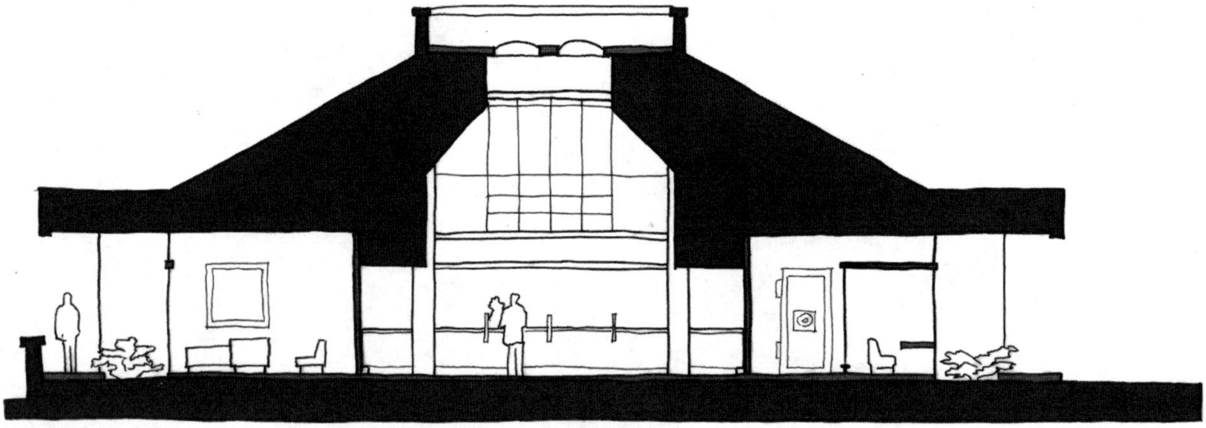

Figure 11.21: There is no better drawing than the architectural section to study (and share with others) the relationships of adjacent spaces with different ceiling heights and shapes.

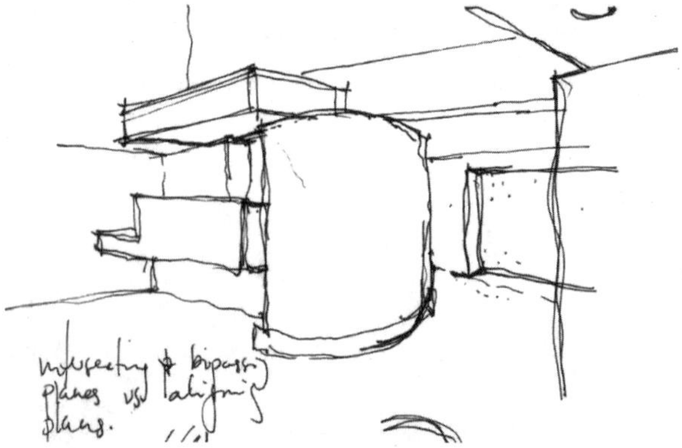

(a)

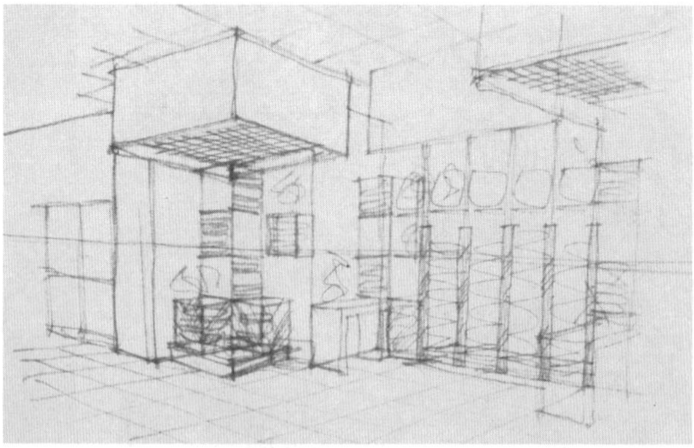

(b)

Figure 11.22: At some point three-dimensional explorations rely on the perspective sketch to study form and make design decisions concerning the spatial envelope and three-dimensional form in general. Three examples are shown.

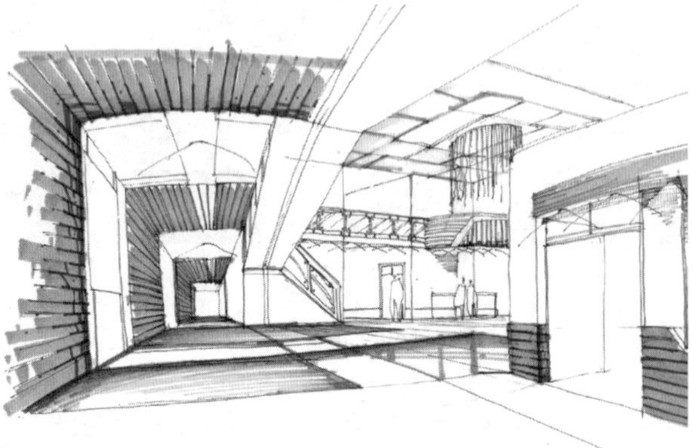

(c)

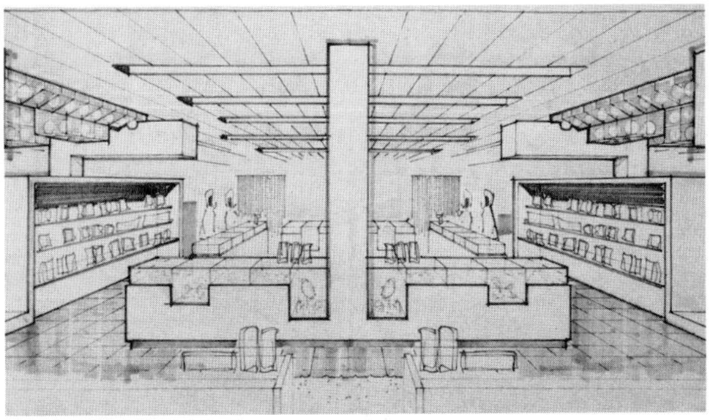

(a)

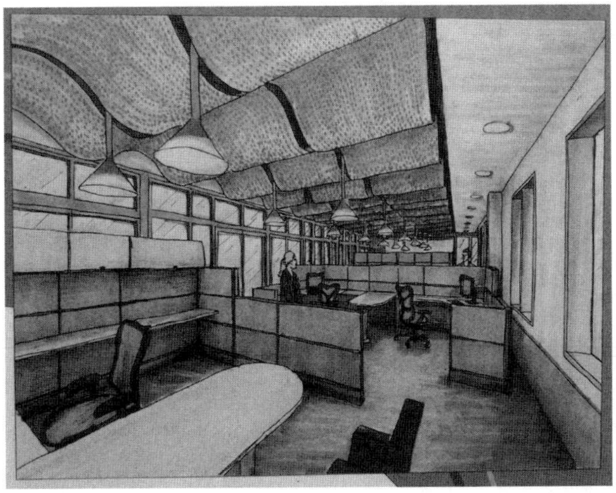

(b)

(c)

Figure 11.23: Perspectives eventually become more accurate and detailed. Styles vary widely. Shown here are three of the many possibilities.

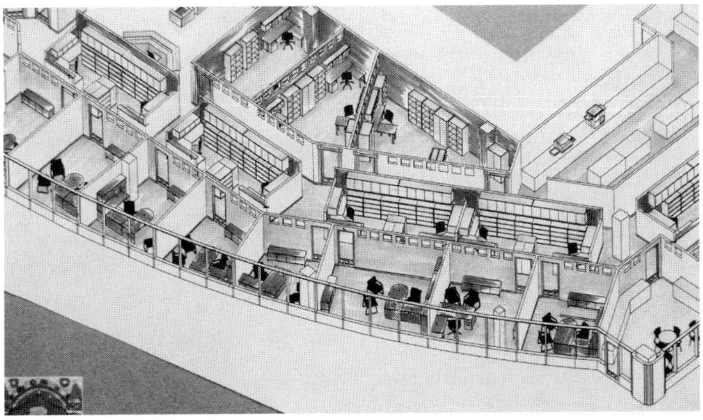

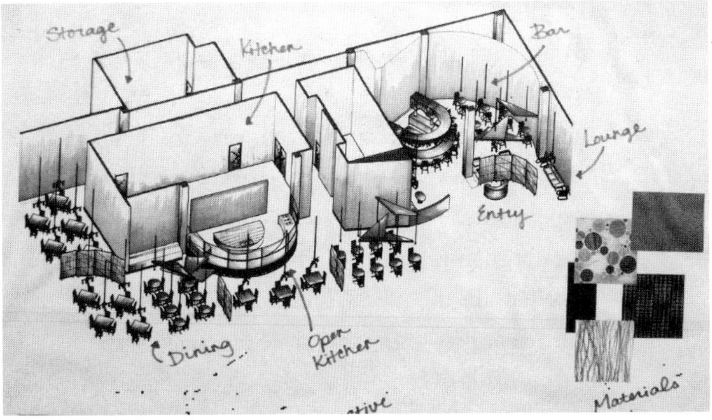

Figure 11.24: Aerial views and axonometric type drawings capture some of the three-dimensional aspects of designs of design really well as shown in these two examples. Two important things they don't show, however, are the ceiling planes and how the space is experienced from inside. Perspective drawings drawn with an eye-level horizon are necessary for that.

designer. A useful technique is to develop an overlay over the space plan indicating ceiling zones as illustrated in Figure 11.25. This way you can identify important areas where special treatments are appropriate, utilitarian areas with more conventional requirements, edges deserving

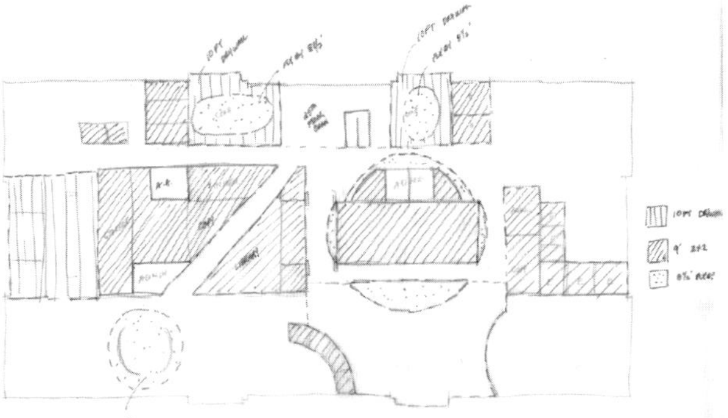

Figure 11.25: Shown here is a quick and loose study of the ceiling planes by a student. Working on an overlay over the floor plan, the student was able to make some basic initial decisions about ceiling heights and materials before proceeding to develop the full reflected ceiling plan.

some kind of ceiling articulation, and the main field areas comprising the majority of the space. This diagrammatic exercise can be then followed by a more thorough effort to fully develop the entire reflected ceiling plan in detail.

Figure 11.26 shows two reflected ceiling plans, illustrating the great latitude of articulation possible. Figure 11.27 shows the development for a custom-designed pendant light fixture in a restaurant, showing the development from the original conceptual ideas to the resolved details drawn with more precision.

Details

If the space plan provides answers to questions such as "What is provided and where is it located?" and elevations and sections provide answers to the questions, "What are the forms and the basic parts?" then, what else is needed? So far so good, but in design there is the extra burden of answering the question what exactly is *it*? What are the pieces, and how do they go together? This phase gets to the true scale of interiors, the scale of objects made of certain well-chosen materials and assembled in very specific ways.

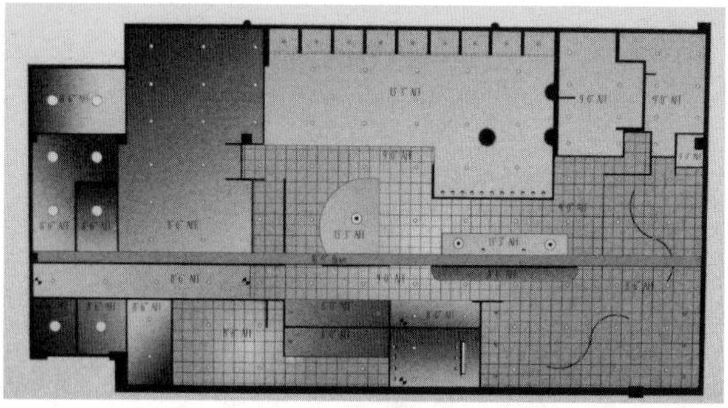

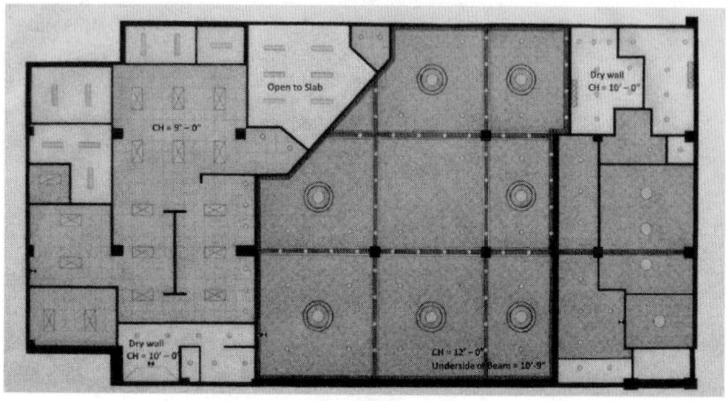

Figure 11.26: Ultimately, the reflected ceiling plan illustrates the ceiling and lighting design, showing ceiling materials and heights for the various sections of the plan, as well as the lighting layout. Two examples for a restaurant are shown.

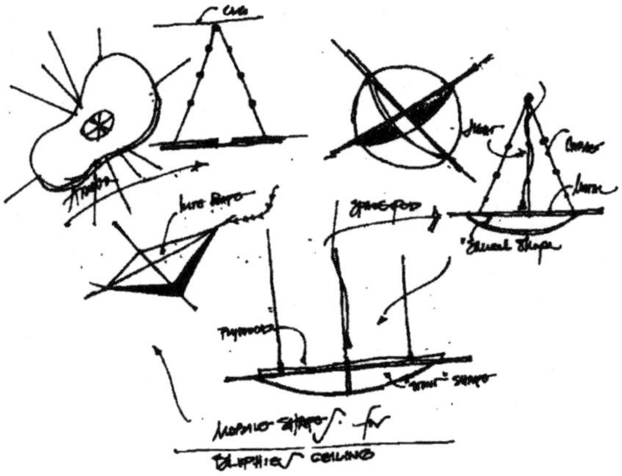

(a)

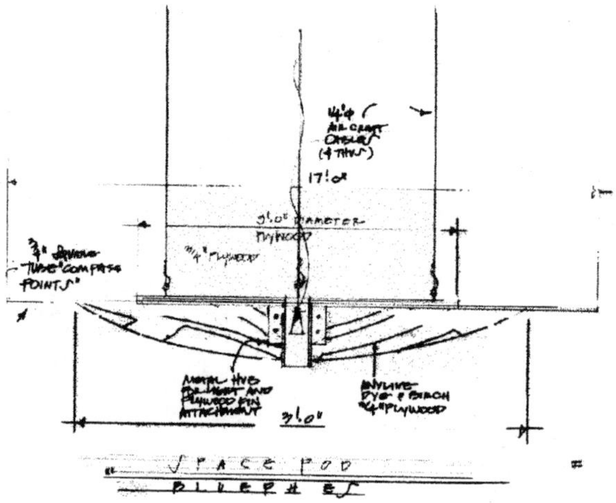

(b)

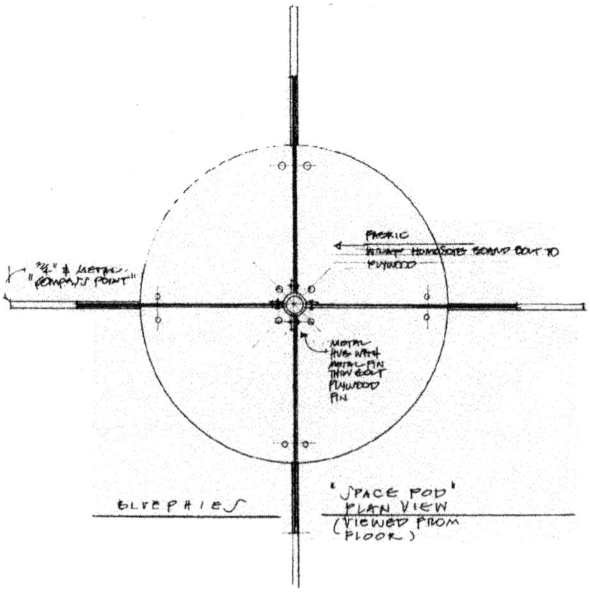

(c)

Figure 11.27: Original details are resolved in stages. The sequence shown for a pendant light fixture started with loose conceptual ideas (a) and was transformed into full construction drawings (b and c).

Details continue what was started with the elevations in terms of showing things as they really are, but this time you zoom in and get even more specific. Here you start to address built-ins, free-standing elements, ceiling elements, and so on. During this phase you move from being a planner to being a creator. It starts with early details studies where you zoom in and start looking closely at the piece you are designing. Figures 11.28 show some examples of these detail explorations. Notice the level of nuance and intricacy.

A column is not the standard column anymore, and a fixture is not the standard fixture. It is you, the designer, who determines exactly what they will be like. Look at the column shown in Figure 11.29. In this case, a design student decided that she was going to make a feature out of the column and make it useful and evocative. By doing so, she developed it into not just a column but into a special object. In doing so she had to figure out how the piece was going to work both functionally and technically in order to achieve the desired effect.

Take a look at the three views shown in Figure 11.30. They show how a corner of an interior wall is detailed, a detail of how the floor, horizontal base, and vertical light fixture come together, and a detail of the layers of a reception desk. Figure 11.31a–c show other detail studies. Detail generation does not come easily to most novice designers and that is normal. It requires knowledge of materials, different stylistic approaches of detailing, and technical knowledge about how things are connected and assembled together. A good way to get started is to concentrate mostly on the look or effect you are seeking and look for help for the technical aspects of how it might be assembled. It also requires some commitment to actively look at both widely available reference standards that show

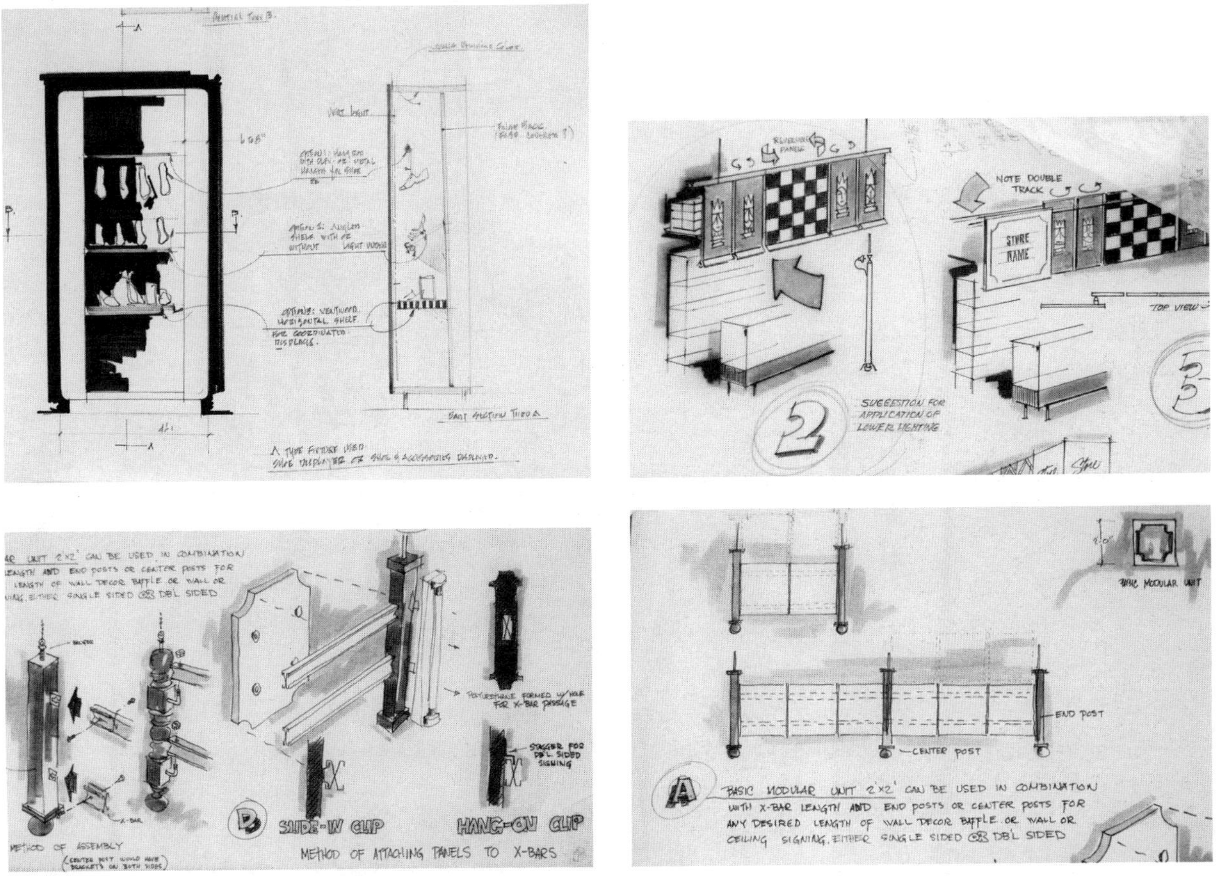

Figure 11.28: Total interior design requires engaging with the detailed aspects of things as exciting environments are seldom made of plain walls, doors, and a few stylish furnishings. Designers look at things closely and make important decisions about exactly how something will be built to achieve the desired effect. These examples give an idea of the level of detail required and some of the types of drawings used to explore ideas.

(a)

Figure 11.29: Here is an example of a custom column designed by a student for a restaurant incorporating a circular countertop and concealed lighting. Although the student might not have solved all the technical details fully, she did a very good job communicating her design intent as shown through the perspective view (a) and the section cut (b).

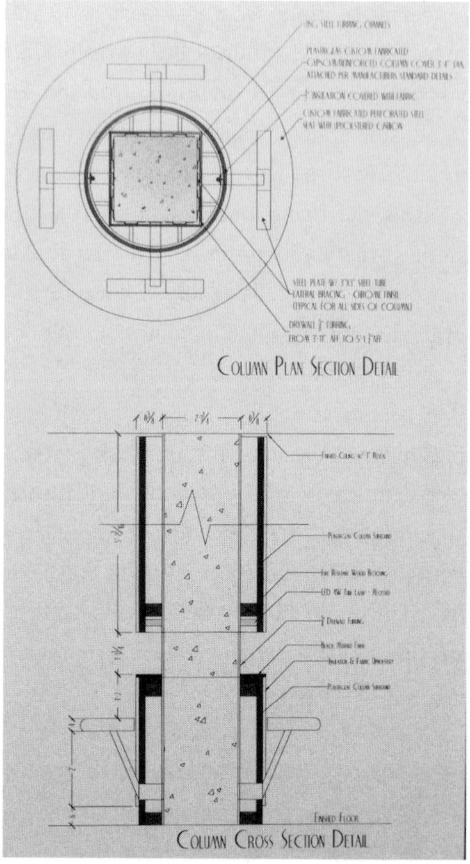

(b)

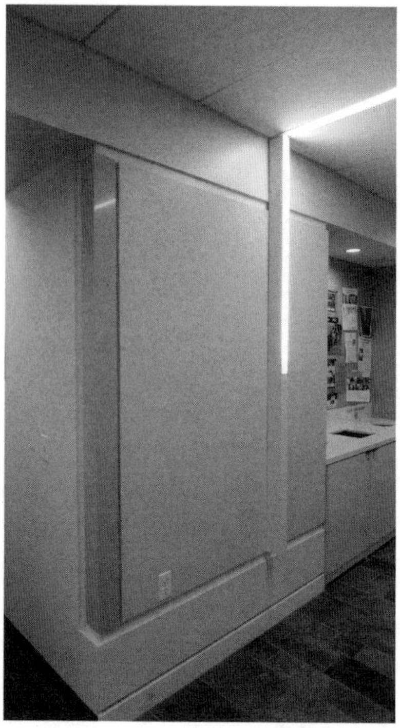

(a)

(b)

(c)

Figure 11.30: These views show the important role of details to give texture and interest to our designs. Shown are a segment of a wall with horizontal reveals, a custom designed corner guard element, and a custom designed linear light fixture (a). A frontal view shows the relationship of the baseboard, the flooring, and the custom fixture (b). A detailed view of a multilayered reception desk elsewhere in the facility is shown in (c).

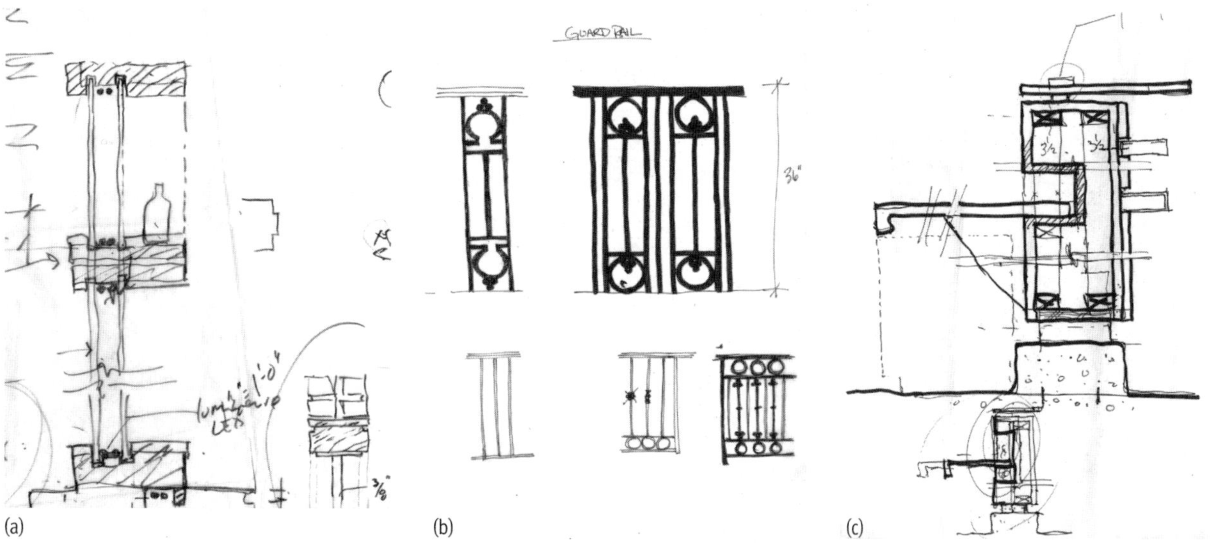

Figure 11.31: These loose sketches show some early studies of design elements for a project.

examples of details, photographs of similar pieces, and best yet, real live examples of similar pieces.

Let's say you are going to detail a custom conference table for the main boardroom of a corporate office. You have some familiarity with tables and know that most large tables for these settings tend to be somewhat rectangular. You also know that it will require some support underneath. Although the old trick of buying a door slab and supporting it with sawhorses may have worked for your own personal studio, it won't do the trick here. You have to dig deeper, because you want a beautiful and impressive table that incorporates technology and makes a statement. At a minimum you need to do the following:

- Study the dimensions of tables. How large a table do you need to accommodate the required, say, 20 people around it? Will it be a single run or something like a U-shape? What is the optimal height? Do the chairs have arms and, if so, how high are they?
- Study options for table shapes. Look at examples.
- Study options for table materials. Woods? Which woods? Stone inset?
- Study ways of combining wood veneers for aesthetic purposes.
- Study ways of detailing the edge of tables. Square, round, reveal, no-reveal?
- Study ways of integrating technology to be able to connect computers and other devices.
- Study ways of supporting tables. Legs? Drums? Slabs? What material?

As you can tell, even the design of a simple and familiar piece like a table entails quite a bit of homework. It is different from buying one, although in that case you would still want to consider the same criteria in order to select the most appropriate choice. The sketches in Figure 11.32 show examples of some of the considerations just mentioned for the detailing of a conference table.

Detailing is design at its best. It is through the creation (or consumption) of well-detailed pieces that you as a designer make a strong statement, even stronger than the red paint on the wall (anyone can do that).

Selections: Materials and the Finish Palette

So far we have talked about the generation of design concepts that provide a design direction, floor plans that locate spaces and determine the way one moves in the project, elevations that tell the story of what is seen on the vertical surfaces of a project, and sections and three-dimensional drawings that explore the spatial envelope. More recently we talked about details and how they determine how pieces of the project are put together in ways that are functional and also convey a certain desired stylistic character. Implied is the fact that certain materials and finishes have been selected to go on those floors, walls, and details. Now we stop to briefly address materials and finishes, because even though they don't shape the space by themselves, the many surfaces that do shape the space are treated with them. For all enclosing surfaces a choice is made about what material will show on its

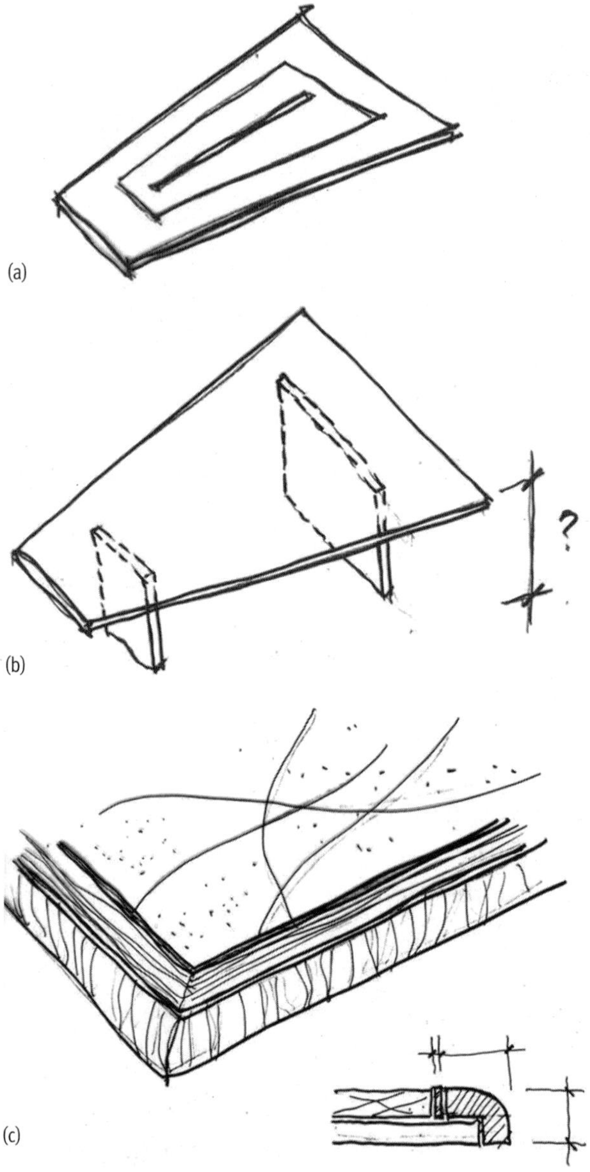

Figure 11.32: The detailing of something as simple as a conference table requires many decisions. Among them are decisions about the configuration of the top, the materials to be used and how to combine them, and how to support the table (a). As one zooms in, there are additional details to solve such as the detailed condition at the edge of the table, as shown in (b).

surface. Even bare, unfinished surfaces, like unfinished exposed concrete, have a finish; in this case the grayish exposed concrete.

Spaces have a spatial character and also a material character, based on the material/finish palette selected. The finish palette helps to convey whether the project is an elegant, high-end project with materials such as marble, glossy wood paneling, and thick, rich carpeting or a high-techy kind of space with stainless steel paneling, vibrant accent colors, and gray tiled flooring.

Every material, every surface, and every exposed part of furniture and equipment will have a finish, and it is up to you, the designer, to determine what these will be as there are always choices. The finishes used on the floors and walls provide a significant portion of the colors, textures, and patterns in the space. In addition to their visual qualities, finishes also help differentiate areas that are soft from those that have harder surfaces. Figure 11.33 shows examples of various flooring surfaces in public spaces with different visual and haptic characteristics.

Beyond the selection of appropriate finishes for individual pieces and areas, it is the designer's responsibility to ensure that the resulting effect of all those surfaces throughout the project add up to a pleasant and cohesive material composition. Materials used for finishes include paint, fabric, carpet, wood, stone, synthetic materials, metals, and so on. There are countless variations within each category. It is part of every designer's responsibility to become familiar with available choices and acquire a sense of what goes well together.

Selections: Furniture, Fixtures, and Equipment

The stage is finally set once the floor plan is done, the spatial envelope determined, and the surfaces and details worked out and finished with appropriate materials. In other words, the container is finished and ready to receive the contents, the moveable pieces that are so vital to the making of interior places. These include the furnishings, the equipment, the fixtures, and the accessories. They also include things like signage, artwork, and plantings.

If arriving at a destination happens when we step into a given room, then settling in occurs when we take possession of that unique element that will serve as our personal home during the activity, be it the podium, the chair, the sofa, or the bed. Figure 11.34 shows the destination pieces of furniture for an office receptionist and some of the visitors to the facility. If we think of interiors as places for people, then the ultimate arrival place has to be the furniture. It is there that we find that very personal space when we gather. Furniture also includes those other important pieces where we gather to do our work or share a meal (the table) and the ones that help us gather and store our possessions (the credenza, the chest of drawers, and the bookcase). Figure 11.35 shows a storage cabinet in a

(a) (b) (c)

Figure 11.33: The detailed consideration of colors, patterns, and textures requires careful consideration. For instance, deciding the exact visual and tactile qualities for flooring finishes can be a complex endeavor. These examples illustrate the point. The size of the repeating units, the density of repeat, and the contrast of the colors, values, and shapes used all make important contributions to the final effect. The floor in (a) features a dense pattern of small pieces in four different values, producing a rich and busy effect. The floor in (b) features larger units grouped in ways that create sub-patterns. Blank spaces between them and less value variation produce a less-busy effect than the one in (a). Floor (c), despite the repetition of the stripes, does not contain identical repeating units. Every stripe is different, and the overall size of each unit is much larger than those in the other two examples.

Figure 11.34: Taking real possession of a space doesn't occur until we arrive at that piece of furniture that will ultimately anchor us in place. In this view, for instance, we can see how the receptionist has found her spot and settled in. One can also imagine the visitors arriving eventually and populating the available chairs.

Figure 11.35: In addition to serving as objects to gather humans in space, furnishings (and built-ins) also help to gather our possessions. Shown here is a built-in piece of furniture that performs a storage function in a preschool facility.

preschool facility. With furniture, it gets personal. It goes without saying that place is never complete, and place-making cannot occur without the furnishings.

Furniture combines convenience, comfort, and style to address the personal aspects of dwelling. It is one of those areas of design where engineering and design come together to address things like anthropometric correctness, structural appropriateness, and stylistic expression. It's no small wonder that a piece so simple and elementary as a chair would find thousands different modes of expression. Add the variable of finishes such as upholstery choices and it becomes a staggering number of possibilities. As a similar example, Figure 11.36 shows two radically different designs for something as simple as a bench. The possibilities are endless, fueled by our creative imaginations. You may think of this as either a headache or a sweet thing, depending on how you look at it.

Challenges for the designer, beyond the obvious need to select furnishings that provide the necessary requirements for their intended use, include others such as knowing how to combine pieces of furniture within a space (what goes well with what), how to create good perceptual groupings of furniture, and even how to select furniture to support different work styles.

Groups of furnishings also have to work well as perceptual groups. Criteria comes from the functional programmatic requirements, where specific instructions are given, sometimes rigidly (tables for four), and sometimes loosely (seating groups for people to gather and socialize). Other considerations have to do with proper orchestration of groups for optimal density, spacing, and overall composition. Figure 11.37 shows an example of groups of furnishings within the same space. In settings such as workplaces, furniture groups are often arranged as neighborhoods that support specific modes of doing work. The furniture arrangements shown in Figure 11.38 were developed by a student in response to the diverse styles of workers within a single office.

Figure 11.36: We may consider the chair to be the ultimate piece of furniture. The fact that something so simple has so many different manifestations attests to the important function of detailed design. While the engineer or scientist can tell us that we need some sort of plank with four legs and possibly arms and a backrest, it is up to a designer to consider the many possible manifestations of such as simple requirement. The same is true for a bench. Consider the stylistic differences of the two examples shown.

Figure 11.37: Furnishings have a strong presence in the visual field, and their careful arrangement is important to achieve a harmonious result. The rhythmic arrangement of furniture groups in this scene shows an example of a careful, in this case formal, arrangement that produces a pleasing result.

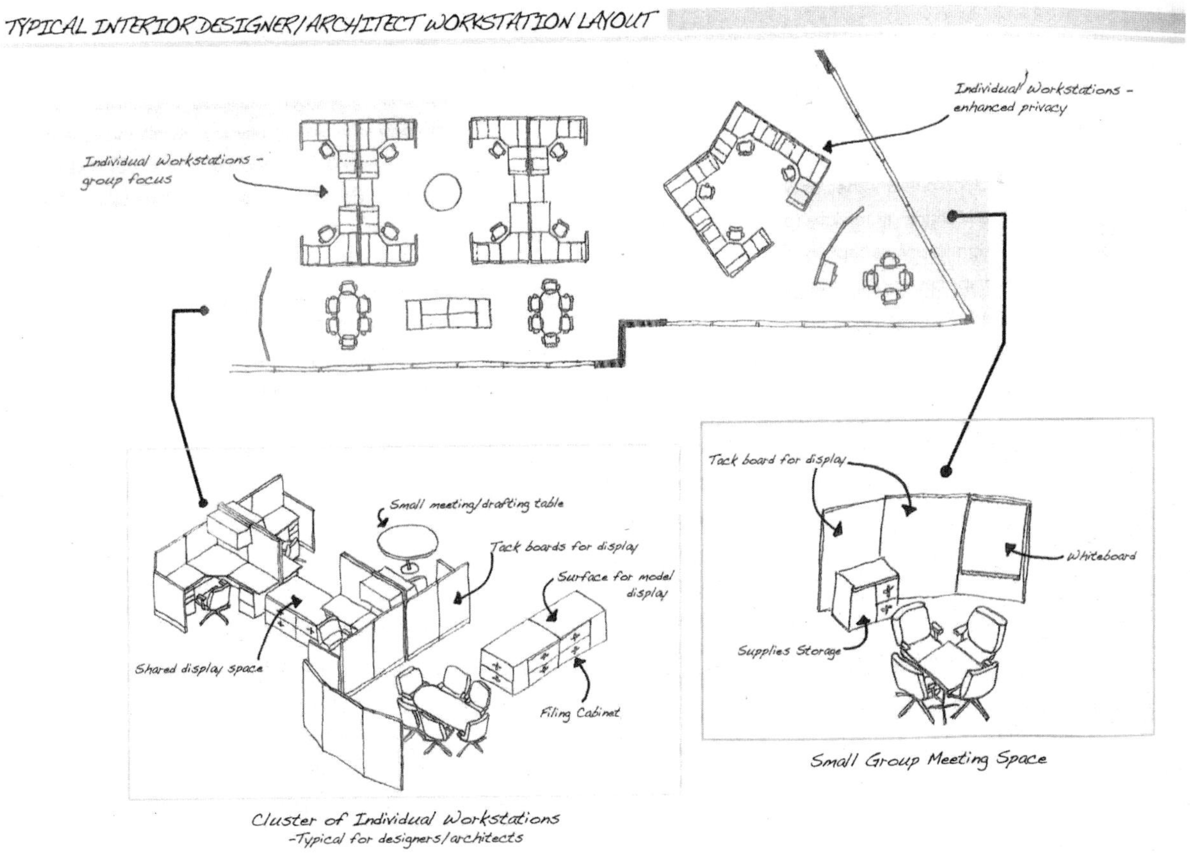

Figure 11.38: Furniture plays an important role in terms of how, exactly, users perform their roles. A good example is how the type and arrangements of office furniture pieces facilitate or hinder a group's ability to perform. Shown here is a study of furniture by a student for a particular type of worker group in an office facility.

Figure 11.39: In some settings, such as retail stores, fixtures have a commanding presence. The display cabinet shown here, for instance, is one of the important elements of this store, commanding a major visual presence and playing a major role in how successfully the items displayed come across to potential buyers.

Figure 11.40: Sometimes equipment can be as prominent as the furnishings themselves (or even more so) as illustrated in this view of a classroom full of play equipment in a preschool setting.

The proximate scale of the piece of furniture, the chair, the desk, the file drawer pulls, and the pencil drawer with the hardware that makes it glide in and out smoothly is the scale of the world in which we dwell and the things we use. That is the stuff of life and in terms of design it is the specific domain of those who make the pieces and the designers who specify them.

Beyond furniture there are fixtures and pieces of equipment. While in an office setting the majority of contents will be pieces of furniture (tables, chairs, desks, and so on); in a store the majority of the contents determined by the designer are display fixtures (Figure 11.39). In a setting like the preschool shown in Figure 11.40, there is a combination of furnishings (tables and chairs) and play equipment.

Additional Layers: Artwork, Accessories, and Exhibits.

There is one final layer of interior design that contributes much to the setting's character and personality. Included here are objects that help direct, identify, humanize, and honor. It is the layer of signage, artwork, plants, exhibits, and accessories. Often neglected in projects assigned in school, this is the layer that often endows a project with its greatest sense of humanity and connectedness. This is a layer of design that is planned by the design team, not to be confused with the personal items that users might bring in with them for their personal spaces, for designers have no control over those.

Signage helps to direct users to their destinations and to identify each place so they know when they have arrived. It also helps to convey other important information such as rules, hours of operation, and so on. Included are both major and secondary signs. These are meant to be seen so they often occupy a prominent position in the visual spectrum. They are functional pieces that also need to tie in with the overall character of the space. Many examples of aesthetically striking signs, both standard and custom-designed, exist. Figure 11.41 shows various signs at the entrance to a reading room in an academic facility.

Related to signage are other types of graphics that are meant to convey branding images which strengthen the branding messages of the user. These could be logos, pictures, and any kind of reference to some aspect of the company or its brand. Examples include logos in the workplace as shown in Figure 11.42.

Plants and artwork humanize environments and contribute much to their character. Some environments require more than others. A retail store may have no plants or artwork (other than their own branding graphics), but a hotel lobby is likely to have both in an effort to provide a soothing and welcoming environment for guests (Figure 11.43). Many corporate clients actually own original artwork collections that they exhibit proudly.

Figure 11.41: Signage plays a key role in many project types. Shown here is a destination in an educational building with signs that convey the name of the room, the room number, hours of operation, and some of the rules.

Figure 11.42: Each day we see more and more use of graphics in environments used, not as informational signage, but as branding elements. This scene shows a powerful use of graphics to reinforce the brand of a well-known corporation.

Figure 11.43: Artwork and plants add the finishing humanizing touches to many interior environments. It is essential to note the humanizing role these additions have in the design of total environments, such as this hotel lobby.

Figure 11.44: Designers often play a role in the selection of detailed accessories for their projects. These include everything from coat racks and waste baskets to things as detailed as tableware, as shown in this scene.

Figure 11.45: Sometimes the final layer of projects include the design of elements such as donor exhibits. Shown here are two views for a donor exhibit in an educational facility where the designer repurposed the backs of chairs that came out of a meaningful historic classroom and used them as a major component of the exhibit.

Accessories add a rich layer of smaller utilitarian objects to projects. These tend to be important components of the overall rituals occurring in these places, such as tableware in restaurants as shown in Figure 11.44. Other examples include desk accessories in offices, coat racks and umbrella holders in public places, wall clocks in schools, and waste receptacles everywhere. To the extent that you, the designer, are in charge of these selections, they are more likely to harmonize with the rest of the environment. Needless to say, becoming familiar with well-performing, aesthetically pleasing options is essential. There is indeed a lot to learn about.

Finally, one last example in this category is the design of exhibits that honor specifics like the company's history, the employee of the month, or the main donors of a project. These are often creative and well integrated into projects. They do not need to be an afterthought. If planned in advance and integrated correctly they can become main destination points as well as stimulating visual foci. Figure 11.45 shows an example in an academic building of a custom-designed donor exhibit that uses the chair backs from one of the historic classrooms of the institution.

PROTAGONISTS OF PLACE

Designers do not control the goods and the people supported by their designs; they react and respond to them. In the process of daily life, humans perform rituals involving other humans and goods. It is the role of design to support and enhance these rituals in order to make them more comfortable and meaningful than they otherwise would be.

The goods of retail stores are the merchandise sold in them. The goods in restaurants are the food items sold in them. The goods in factories are the products fabricated in them. The goods in offices are the pieces of information produced and communicated in them. These goods and the processes behind them (selling, fabricating, communicating) are at the heart of each entity designers provide services to. Understanding, facilitating, and expressing those essences are part of the design task. The goods themselves have a physical presence and often become prominent parts of the visual environment. The nature, size, and packaging of merchandise in a store, for example, can actually dominate the visual field in a store. Figure 11.46 shows the goods in a gift shop and a delicatessen sandwich shop. They have their own visual presence, and their arrangement requires careful planning and response.

The people who use the spaces we design are also a crucial part of both the drama that unfolds in these places and the look and character of the place. They are the "performers," and they come equipped with general scripts according to the roles they will perform. While the nature of the scripts is generally known, its specifics are unpredictable. Nevertheless, enough is known about the basic behaviors typically associated with a place to design a responsive solution. The designer of the scene shown in Figure 11.47 had to be familiar with both the basic needs of people in public spaces and the particular needs of the users in this group to design a successful environment for them.

Scripts are similar to sports events where the players, the arena, and the spectators come together, knowing there is going to be a game but not knowing what the specific outcome will be. The designer does not have much control over the people, their attire, or the scripts to be played but responds to them with the goals of facilitating, enriching, and inspiring. People and goods are really the protagonists of the play; the interior environment is just the stage and the props but still crucial for a successful play.

Figure 11.46: Most interior places feature physical goods that are exhibited, exchanged, or consumed in them. In a deli, the meats and other consumables become prominent features in the visual field.

Figure 11.47: Ultimately, the architecture, furnishings, objects, and people come together in place as humans engage in their daily rituals. Although designers do not control people's behaviors, they surely have some influence over the physical settings in which these rituals take place. Designing places that are functional, ordered, rich, and congruous with the collective character of the client/user can certainly have a positive effect, even if subliminal, on the daily experience of all those who inhabit them.

ACHIEVING COMPETENCE

Your goal as a designer should be to become the best you can be and to truly make a difference in people's lives through the environments you design. There are many levels of competence. It is possible to be a good space planner with a good sense of color and produce clear, efficient, and colorful projects for the enjoyment of all. That alone would make you a fairly competent designer.

What we have been advocating throughout this book goes beyond that. When you try to transcend the limitations of efficient projects with nice finishes and attempt to provide more, then you get into a whole different level of design. It is possible to contribute more to the experiential qualities of projects through thoughtful attention to details in planning and execution. A proper and fitting response to the basic design problem starts the process. If, in addition to a good functional and efficient plan, you can also foster an appropriate sense of order, provide enriching experiences, capture the essence of the organization in the project's expression, and balance and unify the elements used with neither lack nor excess, you will be designing at a very high level.

Although so much of interior design is concerned with high style and sophistication, it is also important to know how to produce goodness and wholeness for all projects, regardless of their budget and level of sophistication. Poetic dwelling is possible at any budget, even if it takes greater effort in some cases than others. Not every project is intended to appear in a glossy design magazine. Even those not destined to be fashion statements can be special. To move and inspire its users, a project's quality must be apprehended spontaneously, without intellectual effort; a few simple, unpretentious elements, well placed and arranged, a nice and engaging flow, a detail here and there, a glimpse, a surprise, and voilà—you have touched people's hearts.

CAPSULE | Color, Image, and Lifestyle

The subject of color has been studied extensively by artists and scholars alike and enjoys a fairly abundant amount of literature. Color, as we all understand intuitively, is an extremely important qualifier of built environments. It is, in fact, an ever-present component of any visual experience. Colors carry connotations and are associated with particular attitudes and moods. When it comes to design, especially interior design, color is one of the major determinants of identity. Determining which colors are appropriate for a specific project is, largely, a search for colors appropriate for the particular identity of a client or project.

The work of Shigenobu Kobayashi and the Nippon Color & Design Research Institute (NCD) in Japan is particularly significant among the great body of literature about color. The extensive work of Kobayashi and the institute links color with its perceived connotations related to identity and personal style and presents it all in a highly usable framework. Their focus is on application, and this makes their work useful to interior designers, who are constantly faced with questions such as: What color should I use to convey an image both delicate and fashionable? Or an image that is bright and casual?

"Ours is an age of increasing sensitivity to color," says Kobayashi. "But what meanings are conveyed by the colors that surround us in everyday life? If we could grasp their real meanings, perhaps we would be able to use them more effectively. The first step toward a more effective use of color is to systematize and classify colors through key words that express their meanings and through images that express the differences between them."[1] This is not too difficult to do for single colors but becomes tricky when colors are used in combination. Kobayashi and his colleagues therefore sought to classify not only single colors but also color combinations in a systematic way and to link them to their associated meanings. They devised the Color Image Scale, a database for the systematic classification of color combinations.

The scale uses 130 basic colors, from which more than 1,000 three-color combinations were assembled. Additionally, colors were matched with a collection of 180 adjectives covering the entire array of people's perceptions of their connotations and moods. From this information, profiles were prepared for each of the 130 colors and particular color combinations using each color, presenting the images connoted by each one of the single colors and each combination.

The 130 colors cover the entire color spectrum: 120 chromatic colors and 10 tones of gray. Chromatic colors are divided into 10 hues (red, yellow-red, yellow, green-yellow, green, blue-green, blue, purple-blue, purple, and red-purple), and each hue is, in turn, subdivided into 12 tones, grouped into the general categories of vivid tones, bright tones, subdued tones, and dark tones.

Colors and their combinations are positioned within a three-dimensional image scale consisting of three interrelated axes: the warm-cool axis, the hard-soft axis, and the clear-gray axis (Figure C11.1). Not only are certain hues (e.g., red) considered warm and others (e.g., blue), cool, but within each hue there is a range from warmest to coolest. The second axis, soft-hard, contains elements of shared human experience related to the relative sense of weight, brightness, and tactility of colors. It is fundamentally linked to weight. In terms of color, this is manifested by the general paleness or deepness of the color. The third axis, clear-gray, is concerned with the amount of gray in a hue or tone.

A key word image scale was developed based on the adjectives people associated with each color and color combination. Descriptors were placed on the three-dimensional scale corresponding with the position of the colors associated with them. Figure C11.2 shows a two-dimensional representation of the key word scale. As Kobayashi explains, "Broadly speaking the key words in the warm-soft area of the scale have an intimate feeling and convey a casual image, while those in the warm-hard section have a dynamic character. The key words in the cool-soft section have a clear feeling and suggest a good sense of color, while those in the cool-hard section convey an image of reliability and formality."[2] This is, of course, an oversimplification, as there are dozens of descriptors in each of the four quadrants. To make the scale easier to understand, similar key words were grouped under more general headings using categories from fashion, such as casual, elegant, and chic. A graphic representation of the scale with just these general image categories is shown in Figure C11.3. It defines the regions occupied by each of the 16 categories.

Three-Dimensional Image Scale

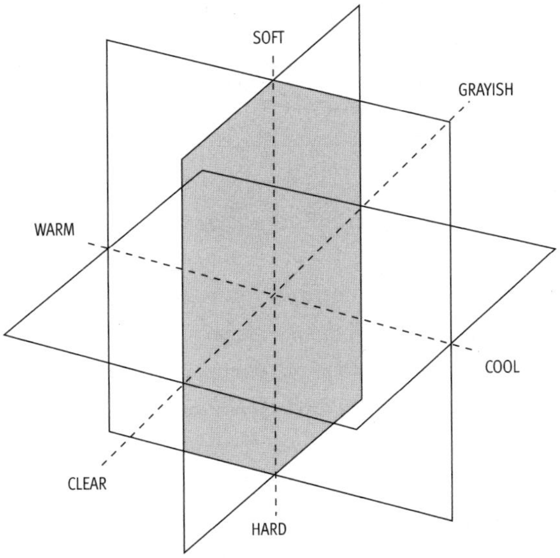

Figure C11.1: Three-dimensional image scale

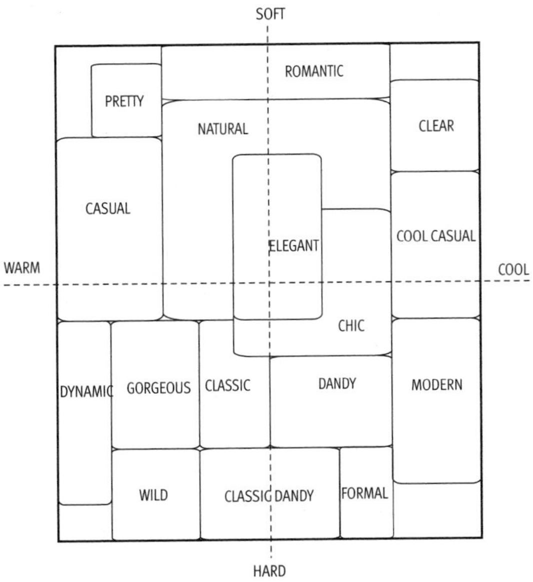

Figure C11.2: Two-dimensional matrix of the key word scale

The next thing Kobayashi and his associates did to facilitate the practical use of their system was to define eight basic lifestyles associated with particular preferences of colors and adjectives. He explains, "Through the interplay of word and color images in the image scales, we can detect a general pattern in the differences between people's sensitivities. From the differences in individual patterns, we can get a feeling for different kinds of lifestyles. So, in practical terms, when you are creating a new product you can make use of the connections between words, colors, and objects."[3] The eight basic lifestyles are derived from the dominant image categories. The lifestyles are casual, modern, romantic, natural, elegant, chic, classic, and dandy. They are briefly described as follows.

continued

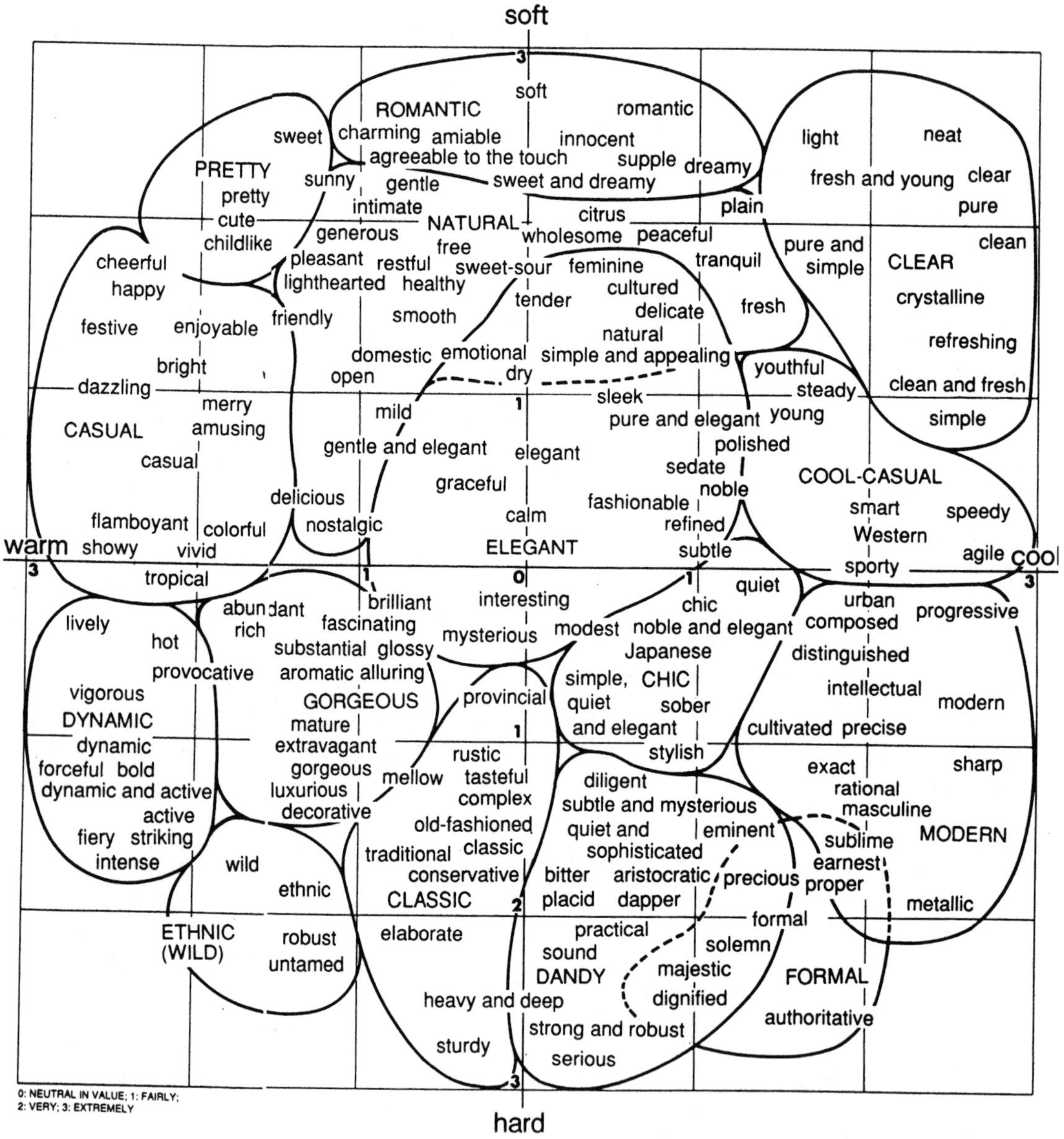

Figure C11.3: Graphic representation of the scale with general image categories and the regions occupied by the 16 categories

Casual Lifestyle (key words: youthful, flamboyant, merry, enjoyable, vivid) This lifestyle is cheerful and easygoing and has an open and happy image. Preference is for vivid and clear colors, with strong and bright tones. People associated with this style are young, such as college students and people in their early 20s.

Modern Lifestyle (key words: urban, rational, sharp, progressive, metallic) The feeling of this group is cool and urbane, with a clear-cut, functional, sharp image. Neutral colors and sharp contrasts are favored. A key color is black. Vivid colors are sometimes used as an accent to create a bold effect. People associated with this lifestyle are young city dwellers who are particular about function and design.

Romantic Lifestyle (key words: soft, sweet, innocent, dreamy, charming) This style is characterized by a feeling of delicacy and sweetness. It is popular with young women. The predominant color qualities are softness, sweetness, and dreaminess. The main color combinations are light pastel tones and white. The colors used are clear.

Natural Lifestyle (key words: natural, tranquil, intimate, simple and appealing, generous) This lifestyle enjoys a natural, warm, simple appearance, with a heartwarming image. Rich, natural materials are preferred; artificial ones are disliked. The main colors are shades of beige, ivory, and yellow-green. People who aim for a cheerful, relaxed, and comfortable feeling belong in this group.

Elegant Lifestyle (key words: refined, graceful, delicate, fashionable, feminine) This group displays a taste for subtlety, a nonchalant style, and a sense of balance and charm. Refinement, tenderness, and calm further describe the image of this group. Grayish colors predominate and color combinations used are subtle gradations. Belonging in this group are women with a sense of gentleness, delicacy, and overall quality.

Chic Lifestyle (key words: sober, modest, simple, quiet and elegant, subtle) This group is characterized by a preference for the sober, calm, quiet, and sophisticated. They enjoy atmospheres that are quiet and polished, with an air of simple elegance. Urban, intelligent, sophisticated adults belong in this group, which has a cooler image than that of the elegant type. Sober, grayish colors predominate, with combinations displaying subtle differences of tones and grayish colors being preferred.

Classic Lifestyle (key words: traditional, classic, mature, tasteful, heavy and deep) An image of authenticity is at the heart of this type. Preferences are toward the elaborate, decorative, and formal. Preferred colors are hard and grayish, with brown, black, olive green, burgundy, and gold used widely. Belonging in this group are older, conservative people who aspire to tradition and authenticity.

Dandy Lifestyle (key words: placid, quiet, sophisticated, sound, dignified, strong, robust) This lifestyle is characterized by a self-possessed tone, stability, masculinity, and quiet sophistication. This type is simpler and cooler in feel than the classic. Preferences are toward hard colors such as brown, navy blue, or dark gray, used in combination with calm, grayish colors. Belonging in this group are adults, predominantly masculine, and with an inclination toward hard and neat atmospheres.

These insightful, research-derived lifestyle categories are the closest thing we have seen to a typology of tastes. Their potential for providing designers with useful insights about people and their taste preferences are enormous. As Kobayashi puts it when referring to his system: "I believe that this classification of colors based on images is the key to understanding the way in which color combinations are perceived, and that this system opens a path to the future, when sensitivity to color will continue to grow."[4] We couldn't agree more.

The information presented here summarizes discussion in the books *Color Image Scale* and *Colorist*, both by Kobayashi. These two books, as well as his *Book of Colors*, are highly recommended.

1. Kobayashi, S. (1990). *Color image scale*. New York: Kodansha International.
2. Ibid, p. 12.
3. Ibid, p. 17.
4. Ibid, p. 2.

CASE STUDY

Developing a Design for a Digital Marketing Firm Using the Concept of Overlap to Achieve Innovation, Customer Service, and Employee Wellness

Project: Outsell, Minneapolis, MN (18,500 sf)

Design Firm: Gensler. Photo credits: Jasper Sanidad

Challenge: How does one develop a design for an innovative digital marketing company whose management believes in the magic of the "overlap," employee wellness, and has a mantra of "eye on the brand, eye on the employee, eye on the customer"?

Outsell is a digital marketing software company, whose analytic software leverages data from real-time online interactions with consumers and then applies predictive algorithms to optimize consumer engagement and sales results. The company's products enable completely customized campaigns based on a customer's online behavior, overlapping technology, and creative expertise. The concept of overlap is central to Outsell's brand: They're analytical *and* creative; they have forward momentum *and* a commitment to values; their products are technologically advanced *and* simple. At the beginning of the project, Outsell's CEO challenged the design team to give them an office unlike any he had ever seen before, full of opportunities for collaboration and spaces to connect to clients and teams, along with areas to promote wellness.

In designing Outsell's new Minneapolis headquarters, Gensler capitalized on the concept of overlap. Spaces where people overlap (meeting areas, café, shared support spaces, and so on) are located along the main circulation path and become significant nodes in the space. Circulation happens through spaces, not around them, encouraging interaction, engagement, and accelerated serendipity.

Zones through the space are further choreographed to reflect Outsell's mantra mentioned earlier of "eye on the brand, eye on the employee, eye on the customer." For example, the large scale, changeable brand wall in the reception area can be customized with Outsell's logo, visitors' brands, or messages important to employees. In just a few minutes, the blocks in the wall can be reconfigured to reflect a completely customized message (Figure CS11.1).

Outsell's dynamic culture encourages camaraderie, so the new space has to not just support gathering but celebrate it. The main gathering space, a large café, is located directly adjacent to the main entry, and is separated from the reception area by a metal drapery, making are visible from the reception (Figure CS11.2). And when the entire staff gathers, the metal drapery is opened, turning the café and reception into one big gathering space. The simple presence of the metal drapery maximizes flexibility and tells an important story about the company, all at once. Beyond the

Figure CS11.1: The large scale, changeable brand wall in the reception area can be easily customized to com pose individualized messages for clients or employees and thus reflect the company's "eye on the brand, eye on the employee, eye on the customer" motto.

Figure CS11.2: The main gathering space is separated from the reception area by a metal drapery which can be opened, to create a large gathering space for staff gatherings.

metal curtain, the Castiglioni Taraxacum pendant becomes the focus of the café, drawing users to gather at the solid walnut tables with Hans Wegner Wishbone chairs below. The clean, black granite-topped cabinetry keeps the open feel and takes advantage of the spectacular views.

The conferencing at Outsell all takes place in the overlap. Each room is specifically designed for the different meeting styles and functions that may take place in them and are strategically placed for ultimate convenience. There are several kinds of technology-based conference rooms. They vary in size, shape, and seating type, but their common thread is how hard they work. From integrated computers and connectivity to walls covered in writable surface, these rooms are meant to get the job done (Figures CS11.3 and CS11.4).

There are several open media lounges for teams to meet, as well. Two of them utilize Steelcase's MediaScape technology and furniture that offer high level technology collaboration at the comfort of a sofa. Signature light fixtures, one a Nelson saucer pendant and one a collection of Herzog & Demeuron pipe suspension lights, help to define these semi-open meeting areas (Figure CS11.5).

Figure CS11.3: Informal conference room.

Figure CS11.4: Formal conference room.

Figure CS11.5: Semi-open meeting area.

The conference room used for pitching to clients is a truly state-of-the-art meeting space. The custom conference table from Nucraft is the workhorse of the room, providing sleek wire management and personal microphones. The table is surrounded by Eames Soft Pad conference chairs. The statement piece in this room is the Torroja Cross chandelier by David Weeks.

One of the most unique meeting spaces is a technology-free room. Located with some of the best views, this room is meant to be a complete getaway. With three signature Saarinen Womb chairs in the classic red Knoll Boucle and a coordinating Saarinen occasional table, this space is about taking a step back and collaborating the old-fashioned way.

Work areas at Outsell support both focused and collaborative work. A simple kit of parts from the c:scape system from Steelcase allows for this, again maximizing flexibility and supporting the different work styles of different functional groups. The standard product screens were replaced with custom writable and magnetic glass partitions to allow for impromptu collaboration or brainstorming right at someone's desk. To further exemplify Outsell's commitment to their employees, Steelcase Walkstations have been placed throughout the workspace. These treadmill workstations allow for a productive getaway and to work-out both the body and mind (Figure CS11.6). Several of the walls throughout the workspace, most along circulation paths, are covered with whiteboard paint and serve as convenient and casual meeting places for teams (Figure CS11.7).

continued

CASE STUDY, *continued*

Figure CS11.6: Steelcase treadmill Walkstations allow employees to exercise both the body and mind.

Figure CS11.7: Many of the walls throughout the workspace feature whiteboard paint and serve as convenient and casual meeting places.

REVIEW

Summary

Successful design requires a cyclical design process involving successive, ever-more-refined solutions to the design problem. The ultimate goal in the end is total resolution of the project or full synthesis.

Development starts with the floor plan, which must evolve from the original organizational concept to a fully functional composition. In addition to making the concept work, the floor plan needs to be developed so that it is efficient and functional at all levels. This entails a series of iterations that undergo a continuous editing process. Next, a designer needs to pay attention to the vertical surfaces of the project and develop functional and well-composed elevations that carefully orchestrate all the parts and materials. At the same time the spatial envelope of the space is studied and ideas are externalized through ever-changing drawings such as architectural sections and perspectives. During this stage the designer pays careful attention to the all-important ceiling, making decisions about tall and short areas, materials to be used, and how to light the spaces.

Working from the general to the specific, the designer eventually arrives at the scale of the detail and has the task of deciding how materials will come together, how parts will be attached or adhered, and what finishes will be utilized to achieve the desired effect for everything from the wall paneling to the two floors coming together, and even the pencil drawer on the reception desk. This, too, requires careful study and multiple iterations before the final solution is clear. Making selections from unlimited possibilities follow, and many decisions have to be made concerning materials, furnishings, fixtures, and equipment. This is followed by yet another layer of decision making, this time involving artwork, accessories, signage, plants, donor exhibits, and so on.

Finally, the stage is set and ready for the things and people who will use the space. Merchandise arrives at the store and food and tableware at the restaurant, followed by the sales associate and the customer, the cook, the bartender, and the patron. The show can now begin.

1. Kleinsasser, W. (1995). Synthesis 9: A comprehensive theory base for architecture.

Chapter Exercises

1. Find the space plan for a project you have completed. It is best if you find one that you feel was somewhat rushed and could be better. Put a layer of trace paper over it and edit it, improving the areas that need development. Work loosely, drawing freehand. Do this once or twice until everything falls in place and works in the best possible way.
2. Using the project from Exercise 1 above, select an area of your choice to develop further. This should be a prominent area with some complexity and potential for detail. Using a copy machine enlarge the area 200% so it's twice the original size. Now play with form, pushing and pulling and articulating planes and corners, using glass here and thick walls there, and so on. Come up with two or three different alternatives.
3. Take the elevations from a previous project and try to refine them. Also, explore alternatives. To do this put a layer of trace paper over the elevations and work freehand over the originals, exploring both improvements and alternatives. Develop three variations.
4. Using a past or current project that encompasses multiple spaces coming together, draw a cross section or a longitudinal section to explore ceiling heights in the various spaces. Vary the ceiling heights and forms. Have some fun but be ready to justify your manipulations when asked by your peers or instructor.
5. Find a past project for which you drew one of more perspectives. Again, put a layer of trace paper over the perspectives and play with the volumes and the surfaces. Work free hand. Explore different ideas. Develop three variations.
6. Select an element from a past or current project. This can be an architectural element (wall, ceiling, floor, door, window, and so on) or a combination of two or more elements. It can also be a built-in, a custom piece of furniture, or a fixture. Now try to figure it out in detail. What are the materials? What are the parts and pieces, and how do they come together? How do things open? Do they swing, slide, rotate? Draw an enlarged plan, two enlarged elevations, and axonometric and a cross section of the piece.
7. Go online and search for two companies that produce architectural accessories and two companies that produce architectural signage. Select three items from each company that you really like and one that you dislike. Discuss in class.
8. At the risk of someone accusing designers of being too controlling, let's attempt to totally brand an environment, either a real one or one from a book or magazine. In addition to the existing nice architecture, furnishings, and perhaps, some accessories, what else can be *designed* for a total designed look? How about the box of tissues on the table with that awful flowery pattern with wrong colors? What can be done to it? How about those pens and pencils and notebooks? Can they be branded and customized? How about the coffee mug? You get the idea. Have some fun.

INDEX

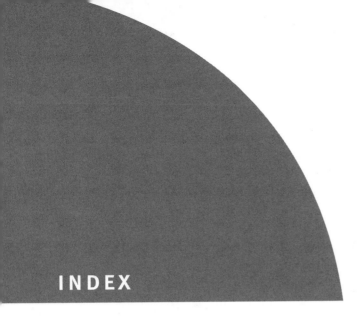

C

D

E

F

G

H

I

J

K

L

M

N

O

P

Q

R

S

T

U

V

W

Y

Z